JERRY SCHUUR – 1995

Introduction	1
Travel	5
Practical A–Z	13
Roman Topics	29
History	49
Roman Art and Architecture	67
The Walks	81
Peripheral Attractions	325
Food and Drink	335
Where to Stay	353
Entertainment and Nightlife	367
Shopping	375
Sports, Activities, Children	385
Living and Working in Rome	391
Day Trips from Rome	397
Glossary, Langua	434
Index, Highlight:	450

D1512018

Cadogan Books Ltd
Letts House, Parkgate Road, London SW11 4NQ

The Globe Pequot Press
6 Business Park Road, PO Box 833, Old Saybrook,
Connecticut 06475–0833

Copyright © Dana Facaros & Michael Pauls 1989,
November 1993

Updated by Ros Belford 1993
Illustrations © Horatio Monteverde 1993

Book design by Animage
Cover design by Ralph King
Cover illustration by Caroline Smith
Maps © Cadogan Guides, drawn by Thames Cartographic Ltd
Macintosh: Book Production Services

Editing: Rachel Fielding, Dominique Shead
Proof Reading: The Davies family, Louisa McDonald
Index by Dorothy Groves; revised by Peter Casterton
Managing Editor: Vicki Ingle
Series Editor: Rachel Fielding

First edition 1989

This fully revised and updated edition,
published November 1993

A catalogue record for this book
is available from the British Library
ISBN 0–947754–482

Library of Congress Cataloging-in-Publication Data
Facaros, Dana
    Rome/ Dana Facaros & Michael Pauls;
    illustrations by Horatio Monteverde -- 2nd ed.
    p. cm. -- (Cadogan guides)
    ISBN 1–56440–131–6
    1. Rome (Italy)--Guidebooks. I. Pauls, Michael,
    II. Title. III. Series.
    D0804.F24 1992
    914.5'63204929--dc20   92-28246 CIP

Typeset in Weidemann and produced on Apple Macintosh.
Printed and bound in Great Britain by Staples Printers (Rochester) Ltd

About the Updater

Ros Belford has spent much time
over the last few years living in
Italy writing and researching for a
number of travel guide series. She is
the founder of the Virago Woman's
Guide series, and author of travel
guides to Rome, Italy and Greece.

About the Authors

Dana Facaros and Michael Pauls spent a year commuting to Rome from a small village in Umbria. They suffered nearly every indignity that Rome can offer—from picked pockets, a grope in the sacristan and nearly being squashed by an ambulance, to indigestion from slices of pizza that really belonged in the Archaeology museum. In spite of it all, they are fond of the city, although they now live a safe distance away in France.

Acknowledgements

We would like to heartily thank Bruce Johnston for his hospitality and sharing his Roman secrets; Michael Davidson, Brian Walsh, Clare Pedrick, Anne and Santino Chianelli, Paul Serrao, and Phyllis Bailey, and Louisa and Jonathon Hynd for their many insights, anec-dotes, moral support, and patience in listening to us eternally talk about Rome. Also, warm thanks to Paula and Piers Fletcher, the first fearless pioneers to walk these walks, and to Anna and Tito and everyone else in Rosciano for more kindness than tongue can tell.

Acknowledgements for Updated Edition

Thanks to Sam Cole for extra research beyond the call of duty; to Bruce Johnston (again) for answering questions on everything from peanut butter to prostitution; to Bettie Petith for abstaining for weeks from CNN so I could sleep; to Jen Zaid for being an exhilarating flat-mate; and to Rupert Small for helping me research bars, explore Termini at dawn and for finding Dinosaur Jr for Jen. Thanks as well to Flaminia Allvin, Barbara Baxter, Marco and Suzy Chelo, Daniela and Francesco and to Angela, Nick, Spartac, Alessandro, Didier, Steve and Venom, Tim Jepson, Sr. Casertano of EPT, Dott. Vattuone at the Vatican, Eugenio Magnani at the Italian Tourist Office in London, and Citalia. Finally many thanks to all readers of the first edition who wrote in with helpful suggestions including: Prof. Luigi Ferraris, W. J. Haswell, Mary Ottara, P. Michael, P.B. Madden, A.D. Matthews and Drs. G. and J. Yudkin.

Please help us to keep this guide up to date

We have done our best to ensure that the information in this guide is correct at the time of going to press. But city life is constantly changing: standards and prices in hotels and restaurants fluctuate; bars and night-clubs come and go. We would be delighted to receive any comments concerning existing entries or omissions, as well as suggestions for new features to include. All contributors will be acknowledged in the next edition and will receive a copy of a Cadogan Guide of their choice.

Contents

Introduction   1-4

Travel   5-12

Arriving in Rome   6   By Metropolitana   10
By Air   6   By Bicycle   10
By Train   7   By Scooter   11
Customs Formalities   8   By Carriage   11
Getting Around Rome   8   By Car   11
By Bus   8   Disabled Travellers   12
By Taxi   9

Practical A-Z   13-28

Calendar of Events   14   Post Offices and Faxing   24
Climate and When To Go   16   Religious Affairs & Vatican Info 24
Consulates   17   Strikes   26
Crime   18   Students & Senior Citizens   26
Medical Emergencies   20   Studying in Rome   26
Money   21   Telephones   27
Museums   23   Toilets   27
Official Holidays   23   Tourist Information   28
Packing   23

Roman Topics   29-48

Cats   30   Plaques   37
Dome-a-Roma   30   Roman Carnival   38
Holy Rome   31   Seven Preposterous Buildings   39
Illusion and Delusion   33   Sub-Roma   40
Know Your Rocks   34   Words   41
Mother of Harlots   35   The Worst Pope   42
Pasquinade   36   A Day in Ancient Rome   43

History   49-66

The Legends   50   Rome's Middle Age   58
Guesses behind the Myths   51   The New Rome   61
Rome Conquers Italy   54   The End of Papal Rule   62
From Republic to Empire   56   Rome in the '90s   64

Roman Art and Architecture 67-80

The Etruscans	68	The End of the Renaissance	75
The Romans Lean Building	68	The Art of the Counter-	
Sculpture, Painting, Mosaics	70	Reformation	75
Early Christian & Medieval Art	71	The Age of Baroque	77
The Renaissance in Rome	73	The Last of Roman Art	79

The Walks and Piazza Venezia 81-4

The Walks 85-324

I: Capitoline Hill and Tiber Banks 85
Santa Maria d'Aracoeli–Campidoglio–Capitoline Museums–Santa Maria in Cosmedin–Temples of Vesta and Fortuna Virilis–Piazza di Campitelli–Portico of Octavia–Tiber Island

II: Forum, Palatine and Colosseum 105
Trajan's Column–The Imperial Fora–Mamertine Prison–Roman Forum–Palatine Hill–Colosseum–Santa Francesca Romana

III: San Clemente and the Caelian Hill 135
San Clemente and Mithraeum–Santi Quattro Coronati–Santa Maria in Domnica–Villa Celimontana–Santi Giovanni e Paolo–Baths of Caracalla

IV: Pantheon and Piazza Navona 147
Santa Maria Sopra Minerva–Pantheon–Piazza di Sant'Eustachio–Sant'Ivo–Sant'Agostino–Via dell'Orso–Santa Maria della Pace–Piazza Navona

V: Corso V. Emanuele–Campo de' Fiori 163
Gesù Church–Largo Argentina Temples–Sant'Andrea della Valle–Chiesa Nuova–Via Giulia–Palazzo Farnese–Spada Gallery–Campo de' Fiori

VI: Around the Corso 177
Galleria Colonna–Galleria Doria Pamphili–Sant'Ignazio–Temple of Hadrian–Piazza Colonna–Trevi Fountain

VII: Spanish Steps—Piazza del Popolo 191
Piazza di Spagna–Keats–Shelley Memorial House–Trinità dei Monti–Villa Medici–S.Andrea delle Fratte–S. Lorenzo in Lucina–Mausoleum of Augustus–Ara Pacis–S. Maria del Popolo

VIII: The Villa Borghese 205
The Pincio Gardens–Galleria Nazionale d'Arte Moderna–Villa Giulia/Etruscan
Museum–Zoo–Galleria Borghese

IX: Quirinale, Via Veneto, Diocletian 215
Palazzo Quirinale–Sant'Andrea–San Carlino–Palazzo Barberini–Via Vittorio
Veneto–Baths of Diocletian–Termini Station

X: Ancient Churches/Big Basillicas 227
San Pietro in Vincoli–Santa Prassede–Santa Maria Maggiore–Museo Nazionale
Orientale–San Giovanni in Laterano–Santa Croce–Museum of Instruments–San
Lorenzo fuori le Mura

XI: The Aventine to San Paolo 245
Circus Maximus–Santa Sabina–Santa Prisca–San Saba–Pyramid–Protestant
Cemetery–Monte Testaccio–San Paolo fuori le Mura

XII: Via Appia Antica 257
San Giovanni a Porta Latina–Museo delle Mura–Catacombs of St Calixtus–
Mausoleum of Fosse Ardeatine–Catacombs of St Domitilla–Catacombs of
St Sebastiano–Circus of Maxentius–Tomb of Cecilia Metella–Via Appia Antica

XIII: Trastevere 271
Santa Cecilia–San Francesco a Ripa–Santa Maria in Trastevere–Folklore
Museum–Palazzo Corsini–Villa Farnesina–Janiculum Hill–Bramante's Tempietto

XIV: Vatican City and the Borgo 285
St Peter's–Vatican City and Gardens–Via della Conciliazione–Castel S. Angelo–
Museum of Dead Souls

XV: The Vatican Museums 309
The Museums–Rafael Stanze–Borgia Apartment–Sistine Chapel

Peripheral Attractions 325-36

Monte Mario	326	The Viminale & Via Nazionale	331
Foro Italico	326	Città Universitaria	331
Parioli and Villa Ada	327	Cinecittà	332
Via Nomentana	328	EUR	333
Sant'Agnese fuori le Mura	329	Villa Doria Pamphili	335

Food and Drink   337-52

Eating Out	338	Prices	340
Food	339	Restaurants	342
Wine	340		

Where to Stay   353-66

Hotels	355	Campsites	365
Students	363	Residential Hotels	365
Religious Institutions	364		

Entertainment and Nightlife   367-74

Finding Out What's On	368	Ex-Pat Pubs	371
Classical Music, Theatre, Opera		Clubs and Discos	372
and Ballet	369	Live Music	373
Film	370	Towards Dawn	374
Cafés and Bars	371	Sex	374

Shopping   375-84

Shopping Hours	377	Jewellery	382
Sizes	377	Music	383
Weights and Measures	378	Paper, Crafts, Stationery	383
Antiques	378	Second-hand and	
Books	379	Alternative Clothes	383
Children	380	Shoes and Gloves	383
Department Stores	380	Leather Accessories	383
Designer Fashions	381	Unusual and Off-Beat	384
Food	381	Wines/Spirits/Oils	384
For the Home	382		

Sports/Activites/Children   385-90

Boating	386	Riding	388
Bowling	387	Swimming	388
Football	387	Tennis	389
Golf	387	Children's Rome	389
Racing	388		

Living and Working in Rome   391-6

Registration and Residency	392	Finding a School	394
Finding a Flat	392	Useful Addresses	394
Finding a Job	394		

Day Trips from Rome   397-433

Ostia Antica	398	Tivoli	417
Etruscan Towns	407	The Aniene Valley & Subiaco	420
North to Lake Bracciano	410	Zagarolo and Palestrina	422
The Monster Park of Bomarzo	412	Castelli Romani	425
Viterbo	413	Pontine Marshes to Anzio	432
Lake Vico and Caprarola	416		

Glossary   434

Language   438

Further Reading   448

Index and Highlights   450

Maps

Rome Walks :   Inside Front Cover
                   and With Each Walk

Central Rome 300 AD	52-3
Ostia Antica	402-3

Site Plans:

Roman Forum	114-5
Palatine	124-5
Baths of Diocletian	225
S. Maria Maggiore	234
St John Lateran	239
St Peter's	294
Vatican Museums	308

Introduction

The ancestor of the book in your hand, the 12th-century *Mirabilia Urbis Romae*, was perhaps the first real travel guide of the modern era. Its English author described a city that was the wonder of the world, built by a race of men that seemed superhuman to the Middle Agers. To account for its marvels, the *Mirabilia* is full of legends and fairytales; the truth, had its author known it, would often have been even stranger. Rome is one city where the improbable is not only a regular occurrence, but is constantly retasted in historical burps—the Renaissance papacy's attempt to recapture the ancient magic, or Cola di Rienzo's, or Mussolini's. Or the Treaty of Rome, creating the European Economic Community. Nothing is new under the sun, but especially under the *sole romano*.

Two thousand years ago Rome the Predator brought the first unity and peace to Europe, while evolving into a new urban life form: the Eternal Parasite. It bullied, battled and excommunicated itself into this unique position, and with smug complacency the city still lives off the pennies of the faithful, the travellers' cheques of tourists, and the grudging *lire* of disgusted Italian taxpayers. In its overfed and overripe state, the Eternal Parasite distorts all that it touches, distorts into staggering proportions. Yet its kitsch-colossal architecture, its enormous appetites, its modern maelstroms of traffic, crime and misbegotten redevelopment throw into focus its rare moments of nobility and beauty; Michelangelo's *Pietà* becomes all the more poignant for its setting in The World's Biggest Church.

Why go to Rome? Not for the exciting nightlife and contemporary culture, surely—as European capitals go, you'd do as well in Oslo or Bonn. Go to see the Pantheon, to snap Aunt Dolly's picture in front of the Colosseum, to visit the bones of the saints; go for a glass of Frascati and a plate of *saltimbocca alla romana*. But besides all the usual reasons, let us add another: go to Rome to understand the excesses that the western world must outgrow for its own survival, an inheritance of imperial brutality and exploitation, religious megalomania, and endless, insatiable greed. It is all on exhibit; in Rome the past lies

1

about higgledy-piggledy at every turn to create an intriguing spontaneous cubism of time and space, layer upon layer, where ancient temples jostle medieval brothels next to your neighbourhood grocer. James Joyce said that Rome was like a man who made a living by putting his grandmother's corpse on display. But what an amazing corpse it is—though goodness knows, it's high time for an autopsy. This book will sharpen your scalpel.

Some facts to get you started

You'll find Rome at 41.53 degrees latitude (about the same as Madrid, New York, and Beijing) and 12.29 degrees longitude. It has an officially registered population of 2,800,000, and an estimated real population of 3,700,000. The lowest point, at 13 m above sea level, is the square in front of the Pantheon; the highest, at 120 m, is Monte Mario. In between are not seven, but 20 hills of varying height.

Rome is the capital of two sovereign states, Italy and the Vatican, and one sovereign order, the Knights of Malta. It is among the most densely populated cities anywhere, but within its extensive boundaries it grows more agricultural products than any local government unit in Europe. Psychiatrists, and neurotics, are extremely rare, even though the most recent studies make Rome the noisiest city on the continent, averaging some 20 decibels louder than the EC standards say is good for your health. In the city of the popes, only 3 per cent of the population goes to mass—perhaps the lowest number in Christendom. Of the great capitals of Europe, it has the most rats and the fewest cockroaches. Rome's birthday is 21 April, and at the time of writing it is officially 2,742 years old.

Seeing Rome

But vital statistics aside, do you know how to look at a city like Rome—how to make sense, find a pattern in the millions of messages your eyes are sending you as you walk the streets of a strange town? There is an art to it, a bit aesthetic, a bit analytical, something like looking at a painting and something like seeing a leaf or a snowflake under the microscope. Of course, reading the history and looking at the street plans are essential for getting to know this many-layered city. When you get there, a good place to start might be ancient Rome—the wonderful, room-sized scale model of it in the Museum of Roman Civilisation, or, if you can't make it out to EUR, the big picture map inside the main Post Office on Piazza San Silvestro. Pay special attention to that masterpiece of ancient urban design, Trajan's Forum.

From looking at any good map, you can begin to see the classical city hiding underneath the modern one—how most of the straight streets in the Campus Martius, like Via delle Botteghe Oscure, Via dei Cestari or Via dei Coronari, have survived intact from ancient times, while the winding lanes around them betray their medieval origins. Oddities on the map give away every sort of old secret:

how the block east of Campo de' Fiori follows the curves of Pompey's theatre, how the course of Domitian's stadium is preserved in Piazza Navona, or how the huge semicircle of Piazza della Repubblica follows the line of the exedra, or exercise yard, of Diocletian's Baths.

In the Campus Martius, where most of the population lived after the 500s, you can explore one of Italy's most complete medieval cities: no cathedral, no centre, but a lesson in the subtle aesthetic of medieval planning, something not at all as careless as it first appears. Here the basic unit is not the street, but the piazza— over a hundred of them between the Corso and the river; the streets serve only to connect them. It's an interesting contrast with modern cities—the difference between *getting* somewhere and *being* somewhere, and the essential background for Rome's *dolce vita* of the good old days. Medieval cities do not give you any obelisks to help you find your way around. They make your eyes and your brain work harder; only spend enough time walking around this old quarter, and you'll begin to get the point. A simple exercise: almost every streetcorner in old Rome has one view worth a picture—the busy engravers of 18th-century prints never exhausted the subject. Just randomly, stop yourself now and then, and look around to find it. Look up, if traffic permits; roofs, towers and domes offer many surprises, along with the clues that helped the old Roman find his way around.

The rest is easy. A new Rome balanced between the Renaissance and the Baroque, with long straight boulevards punctuated by obelisks, appeared around the fringes, an innovation in urban design that has influenced the work of all planners since. Some elements of the Roman street scene:

Water and fountains. Romans are like the Arabs in their love for flowing water. When the city tried to put taps on the hundreds of street corner fountains, people either prised them off or jammed them open. (The water, incidentally, is very good. Some of these little amenities have holes just above the spout; cover the spout and they make perfect drinking fountains.) The big ones are of course one of the attractions of Rome—no other city has such a beautiful collection.

The Tiber. The planners who laid out the Tiber embankments in the 1880s thought they were copying the river-front ensemble of Paris; instead all they did was divorce the city from what had been its watery main street. Old photos and prints show just how much was lost in the interests of flood control (a good dam upstream would have done the job for less money). There are still four and a half ancient bridges to recall ancient engineering skills. Also copying Paris, and generally unsuccessfully, are the Belle Epoque boulevards, such as Viale Trastevere and Via Vittorio Veneto.

Obelisks. Occultists for centuries have had fun with these, and with the Romans obsession with carting them home. Rome has more big ones now than Egypt.

Obelisks seem to have been a tribute to the sun god Ra; the little pyramid on top, originally gilded, represents the sun's rays. Later, some were funeral monuments, while others proclaimed the victories of the Pharaohs. There's no evidence the Romans liked them for any other reason than their size and novelty. With their peculiar religious inscriptions, readable to a very few, they provide an exotic touch at the ends of Rome's boulevards.

Rioni. On the older streets of Rome, you will see small travertine plaques with odd symbols: a pine cone, a griffin, a standing column. Pope Benedict IV had these put up, sometime in the 1750s, to mark the boundaries of the *rioni*, the wards into which Rome has been divided since a decree of Augustus. After the fall of the Empire they survived as political bodies, and offered their people some degree of protection even in the worst of times. Today, with the toadstool growth of the city, there are many more *rioni*, but the ones you will see, bounded by Benedict's plaques, are the originals:

I   *Monti*: its symbol, three stylized hills; includes all the western fringes, almost everything east of the Capitol.

II   *Trevi*: three horizontal swords; Trevi fountain, most of the Quirinale.

III *Colonna*: a column; everything between Piazza Colonna and Via Veneto.

IV   *Campo Marzo*: a crescent moon; the upper Corso and Pincio.

V   *Ponte*: a bridge; western tip of old Campus Martius, opposite Castel Sant'Angelo.

VI   *Parione*: a griffin; Piazza Navona.

VII *Regola*: (means 'fine sand', like Via Arenula); a stag; south of Campo de' Fiori

VIII *Sant'Eustachio*: Jesus between a stag's horns; between Pantheon and Piazza Navona.

IX   *Pigna*: a pine cone (from the giant bronze one, now at the Vatican); from Pantheon to Piazza Venezia.

X   *Campitelli*: a dragon's head; a corruption of 'Capitolium', the Capitol.

XI   *Sant'Angelo*: St. Michael, carrying balances and standing on the devil; the Ghetto, and a few streets to the north.

XII *Ripa*: a wheel; Aventine, southern Caelian, and originally part of Trastevere.

XIII *Trastevere*: a lion's head; Trastevere and the Janiculum.

XIV *Borgo*: a crouching lion with a paw on a stylized hill; everything around the Vatican.

Arriving in Rome   6
By Air   6
By Train   7
Customs Formalities   8

Travel

Getting Around Rome   8
By Bus   8
By Taxi   9
By Metropolitana   10
By Bicycle   10
By Scooter   11
By Carriage   11
By Car   11
Disabled Travellers   12

By Air

It's a little confusing; the big international airport **Leonardo da Vinci** will often be referred to as **Fiumicino**. Officially the first name (℡ 65 951) means the part of this sprawling complex that handles international flights, and Fiumicino is the domestic terminal (most Romans don't know this either). For the 1990 World Cup a train line linking Fiumicino to Ostiense station (and nearby Piramide metro station) was constructed. Trains run approximately every 20 minutes (every 30 minutes in the early afternoon) between 5.40 am and midnight. You're unlikely to arrive after midnight, but if you do, and can't afford a taxi, you could be in for a long wait: there are only occasional buses to the centre after 2.15 am.

When you get to the railway platform at Fiumicino, you might be lucky enough to find the ticket office open. If it's not, you'll have to confront the automatic ticket machines, which have a tendency to reject all but the crispest bank notes. (Spitting on a note and then ironing it against your leg sometimes works.) Tickets currently cost L6000, and the machines, once they've condescended to accept your money, do give change.

Once you arrive at Ostiense, 25 minutes away, there's a longish trek along corridors, flyovers and moving pavements to the Piramide metro station: painless if you can find a luggage trolley, painful if you can't. Metros on Line B only run until 9.30 pm during the week and until 11.30 pm on Saturdays and Sundays, so check your watch before hauling your luggage across to Piramide. If you are too late for a metro, buses 57 and 95 run to Piazza Venezia from Piazzale Partigiani (directly outside Ostiense station). After about 9 pm, taxis tend to be scarce—you've more chance of finding one at Piazzale Ostiense, a five–minute walk from Piramide. At every stage in this wearing journey, **always keep your luggage in sight**. People have been known to lose everything before they even leave the airport.

Ciampino Airport, on Via Appia Nuova (℡ 794 941) is the base for most charters, and takes some international flights. There's an ACOTRAL bus (℡ 591 5551) leaving every thirty minutes between 6.30 am and 9.30 pm from the airport to the **Anagnina** Metro station on Line A. Allow at least an hour to get to the airport from the centre (16 km). **Car hire** branches in both airports generally stay open until 11 pm.

Airline offices in Rome

Aer Lingus: Via Barberini 3, ℡ 481 9940

Air France: Via Veneto 93, ℡ 488 5563, booking ℡ 4718

Air India: Via Barberini 50, © 473 941

Air New Zealand: Via Bissolati 54, © 488 0761 or 486 793

Alitalia: Via Bissolati 13, © 65642 (international booking) 65641 (domestic booking); © 65643 (flight enquiries)

American Airlines: Via XX Settembre 4, © 487 1634

British Airways: Via Bissolati 54, © 479 991

Canadian Airlines: Via Barberini 3, © 482 0961 or 482 0962

Delta Airlines: Via Bissolati 46, © 4773

Kenya Airways: Via Due Macelli 47, © 679 0437

KLM: Via Bissolati 76, © 479 921

Olympic Airways: Via Barberini 1/G, © 473 801 or 474 2201

Philippine Airlines: Via S. Nicola da Tolentino 12, © 483486

Qantas: Via Bissolati 35, © 486 451 or 488 5006

SAS: Via Bissolati 88, © 474 5947

Swiss Air: Via Bissolati 4, © 847 0511

TWA: Via Barberini 67, © 47 211 or 47 241

Zambia Airways: Via Bissolati 76, © 482 6340

By Train

Almost all arrive and depart from **Termini Station** (Piazza dei Cinquecento, info © 4775), chaotic, but modern and efficiently run. The rail information booth is usually terribly crowded, but you can try to find times and destinations on one of the clever, multilingual computer screens installed in the lobby. Keep an eye out for predatory gypsies. There is a taxi stand right in front, car hire booths, buses to most points in Rome from Piazza dei Cinquecento, and two underground stations in its belly. The left luggage (L1500 per piece for 24 hours) is along the first track, on the far left of the station. There are two international telephone offices, one in the lobby and one downstairs, a post office, several bars (the food is terrible; the bar downstairs is less nerve wracking), an *Albergo Diurno* (a day hotel with toilets (L1000!), showers, beds (for men only)), pharmacy, currency exchange, etc. The most important of Rome's other stations are: **Tiburtina** on the eastern edge of town, **Ostiense** (Metro: Piramide) where you catch trains to Fiumicino, and **Trastevere**, where Fiumicino trains also stop. Some north-south trains only stop at Tiburtina (and occasionally Trastevere) so make sure you look carefully at the timetables. There is also a private railway, the **Roma Nord**, with trains to Viterbo from the Piazza Flaminia.

A passport, or a British Visitor's Card will get you into Italy. Nationals of the UK, Ireland, USA, Canada, Australia, and New Zealand do not need visas for stays of up to seven months. If you plan to stay longer, to work or study, you will need to get a *permesso di soggiorno* when you arrive. (see 'Living in Rome', p.392).

In accordance with Italian law, you must register with the police within eight days of your arrival. If you check into a hotel, hostel or campsite this is done automatically. If you come to grief about your status, you can at least get someone to explain it to you in English by calling the Rome Police Office, © 4686, ext. 2858.

The rules of the European Single Market mean that you can lug massive quantities of booze and cigarettes from one member country to another without trouble from customs **as long as you have paid duty on it**. The legal ceilings are: 800 cigarettes, 90 litres of wine, 110 litres of beer, 20 litres of spirits less than 22° proof, and 10 litres of spirits over 22° proof. As for duty free goods, quotas remain as they were before the Single Market was introduced: 200 cigarettes **or** 50 cigars; 1 litre of over 22° proof alcohol **or** 2 litres of under 22° **or** 2 litres of wine.

Pets must be accompanied by a bilingual Certificate of Health from your local Veterinary Inspector. You can take the same items listed above home with you without any trouble—except of course your British pet. To export an antique or work of art, you'll have to apply to the Export Department of the Ministry of Education and pay a tax on the value of the work.

There is no limit to how much money you can bring into Italy, although legally you may not transport more than L20,000,000 in Italian banknotes; they rarely check. The high rate of petty crime in Rome and Italian dislike of credit cards make travellers' cheques or Eurocheques the most secure way of financing your stay in Rome.

Getting Around Rome

Ask Romans on the street for directions and they start to choke. Try instead at a kiosk, or in a shop or bar when they aren't busy, and you'll get friendly, and reliable, advice.

By Bus

Rome's big orange ATAC buses and trams are not as vicious as the name implies. They are the best way to get around, though the complexity of the route system intimidates most visitors, and until you're reasonably familiar with the city, the destinations listed on the signs can seem meaningless (do ask other people at the stop; they won't choke too much). If you're staying in the city for any time it's well worth spending L6,000 on the *Roma Metro-Bus* route map, which contains a comprehensive list of all routes, as well as a directory of streets listing the buses which run along them. All the news-stands at Termini sell it. Most routes run quite frequently, and of course are often crowded. Tickets should be purchased before boarding (at news-stands and tobacconists) and 'obliterated' (validated) in the machines in the back. Spot inspections catch cheaters who have to pay a hefty fine. Purchased separately, tickets are L800 and are valid for 90 minutes (during which time you can hop on and off as many buses as you want). If you reckon you'll use more than two buses or metros a day, it's worth investing in a 7 day tourist ticket valid for all the lines, (L10 000), available from the **ATAC information booths** in front of Termini Station or on Piazza Risorgimento near St. Peter's. Alternatively try a one day pass, called the 'Big', for L2800, available from information kiosks and tobacconists, or a monthly pass, valid from the 1st of each month (L22 000 for all the lines). For more information, ✆ 46 951 or 469 544 44.

There are three lines of particular interest to visitors. The **Circuito Turistico ATAC** (bus 110, special ticket L6000) leaves daily from Piazza dei Cinquecento in front of the station at 3.30 pm (in winter at 2.30 pm, sometimes on Saturdays and Sundays only) for a three hour tour of all the principal sights of the city. Rickety little **tram 30** makes a fun ride when your feet are sore and everything is closed; it circles the city centre, passing many sights along the way. Catch it in Piazza del Risorgimento, near the Vatican, or by St John Lateran, the Colosseum, Porta San Paolo, Viale Trastevere, or by the zoo or Villa Giulia in the Villa Borghese. **Electric minibus 119** tours the medieval lanes between Piazza del Popolo and the Pantheon, a relaxing introduction to Rome's neighbourhoods.

By Taxi

Yellow taxis cruise the main thoroughfares of Rome, and have stands in the major piazzas; or you can call a radio taxi (✆ 3570, or 3875, or 4994, or 4517). The meter starts at L6400. There are supplementary charges: L3000 between the hours of 10 pm and 7 am; Sunday and holidays L1500; L1000 per piece of baggage. Taxis to and from the airports cost around L70,000. Drivers tend to be honest and helpful—the circuitous routes they take are usually as a result of the city's one-way system.

By Bus to Other Towns in Latium

These are run by ACOTRAL, gradually changing its name to COIRAL (information office Via Ostiense 131L, ✆ 591 5551/2/3/4). In Day Trips from Rome you'll find the departure point listed for each trip. All bus stations are close to ⓜ stations. To telephone ahead for times:

Rebibbia (for Tivoli) © 406 7849

EUR Fermi (by ⓜ for Nettuno, Anzio and the southern Lazio coast) © 592 0402

Saxa Rubra (for Viterbo etc) © 332 8333

Anagnina (for the Roman Castelli) © 722 2153 (and Palestrina) © 722 2470

Lepanto (for Lake Bracciano and around) © 386 196 (and Cervéteri, Civitavecchia etc.) © 324 4724

By Metropolitana

Rome's underground, run by ACOTRAL, is efficient, overcrowded at rush hour, though the seats on the end of the cars are a good place to read modern *pasquinades*. Largely designed to shuttle commuters in from the suburbs, it's not as useful for getting around the centre as you might suppose–though it's well worth using for swift hops between, say Piazza di Spagna and the Colosseum, which would take ages on a bus. Tickets have been L700 for years, but may shortly rise to L1000. Not every station sells them; get them beforehand at tobacco shops, kiosks, etc.

Metropolitana A runs from Ottaviano (near the Vatican museums), to Flaminio (Piazza del Popolo), Spagna (Piazza di Spagna), Barberini (Piazza Barberini), Repubblica, Termini Station, Vittorio Emanuele (near S. Maria Maggiore), Manzoni, S. Giovanni (the Lateran), then out into anonymous tumbolia: Re di Roma, Ponte Lungo, Furio Camillo, Colli Albani, Arco Travertino, Porta Furba, N. Quadrato, L. Sestio, G. Agricola, Subaugusta, Cinecittà, and Anagnina.

Metropolitana B: Rebibbia, Ponte Mammolo, S.M del Soccorso, Pietralata, Monti Tiburtina, Quintilliani, Stazione di Tiburtina, Piazza Bologna, Policlinico, Castro Pretorio, Termini Station, Via Cavour, Colosseo, Circo Massimo (near the Aventine), Piramide (Piazza Porta S. Paolo), Garbatella, S. Paolo (St Paul's Outside the Walls), Magliana, EUR Marconi, EUR Fermi, and Laurentina.

By Bicycle

Be careful cycling among the crazies on Rome's streets—you'll note that few Romans ever risk it. Via Appia Antica (Walk XII) is an especially good route to pedal, or if you're more energetic, cycle to Veii or along the Tiber to Ostia Antica. Firms that hire bikes (bring your passport; usually around L5000 an hour) are:

Collalti: Via del Pellegrino 82, off Campo de' Fiori, © 6880 1084

I Bike Rome: Parcheggio di Villa Borghese (underground car park with entrance off Viale delle Magnolie) © 3225240

Bicimania: Piazza Sonnino (summer only)

In summer you can rent bicycles on Largo dei Lombardi and in the Pincio Gardens.

Scooter Hire: Rome is not the place to learn how to ride a scooter, but if you've done it before, it's your chance to see Rome the way the Romans do, with a real buzz. You must be over 21, have a driver's licence, and present your passport.

Scooters for Rent: Via della Purificazione 66, © 465 485 (also bicycles)

St Peter Rent: Via Porta Castello 43,tel 687 4909

Scoot-a-long: Via Cavour 302, © 678 0206

The famous *carrozze* of Rome have gone the way of gondolas and are now used only by tourists. Carriage stands are at Piazza di Spagna, St Peter's Square, Piazza Navona, Via Veneto, Piazza Venezia, and by the Colosseum. Negotiate times and rates before you begin: prices can be as high as L150,000 an hour.

In Goethe's day, traffic flowed on the left—though ambassadors and the Young Pretender had the right to drive on either side of the street! Getting around by car today is nearly as crazy, but not nearly as much fun. Frustration, rude drivers, double and triple parking, thefts and break-ins, and having your car towed away are common features of motoring in Rome. Much of the old centre is closed to unauthorized traffic, and ought to be avoided altogether (you should be walking anyway in this compact area). This includes the 'Trident' south of Piazza del Popolo and nearly all the Campus Martius outside the main boulevards, around the Pantheon, Piazza Navona, Campo de' Fiori and the Tiber. In this area even main streets like the Corso may be arbitrarily closed.

There are almost no guarded parking lots in Rome—the largest and most convenient is the one under the Pincio, near Piazza del Popolo. Parking in the centro storico is for residents only, so if you park on a street here and return to find your car is missing phone or drop by at the Vigili Urbano at Via delle Conciliazione 4, © 67 691 and ask for the Uffizio Rimozione to see if it's been towed away before you go to the police. If it's been picked up in the centre, it will probably have been taken to the Villagio Olimpio, though it's actually more likely that you'll be clamped. If so, the number you need to phone will have been left on the car. It will cost you L140,000 to have your car released. If you have a breakdown, call the ACI (Italian Auto Club) © 116 and they will have your car towed to the nearest garage. (From 1 Aug–31 Dec '95 they will offer free breakdown assistance to all cars with foreign plates, whether or not members of the AA or RAC.) If you have an accident, call the police (© 113). Petrol is expensive; lead-free is widely available. The ACI has information on road conditions, routes, petrol stations, and addresses of garages that repair foreign cars.

Automobile Club di Roma, Via C. Colombo 261, ✆ 514971 or Via Marsala 18 ✆ 4959352 or 44981 or (for road information) 4477.

Car Hire

All the major car hire firms in Rome have booths in Termini Station and at Fiumicino and Ciampino airports. Their main offices are—

Avis:	Piazza Esquilino 1, ✆ 470 1216 and
	Via Sardegna 38/a, ✆ 470 1228
Budget	Rent-a-Car: Via Sistina 24/B, ✆ 488 1905
Europcar:	Via Lombardia 7, ✆ 482 4381 and
	Via del Fiume Giallo, ✆ 674 4018
Hertz:	Via Veneto 156, ✆ 321 6831
Maggiore:	Via Po 8, ✆ 854 8698

Disabled Travellers

Rome isn't very progressive in providing for anyone with limited mobility; in comparison Vatican City stands out, with its considerate ramps and lifts. There are tour operators who specialize in holidays for the disabled: for information about these, along with holiday guides for the disabled containing details of handicapped facilities in major hotel chains and at airports etc. write to Radar, 25 Mortimer St, London W1M 8AB, ✆ 071 637 5400. Once you're in Rome, it's well worth buying a copy of the snappily titled *Guida di Roma: accessibilità, e barriere architectoniche, turismo, cultura, tempo libero* published by Gengami and on sale at good bookshops and some news-stands. It has information on the accessibility (or otherwise) of hotels, restaurants, cafés, public transport, museums and churches. Anyone in a wheelchair could have problems even in upper bracket hotels, as many are housed in historic *palazzi*, with flights of steps (without ramps) leading up to entrances and even the lifts.

The streets and sights of Rome present the most difficulty; propelling yourself along the uneven, cobbled alleys is, to say the least, tiring, though you could have fun playing dodgems with the Vespas. Few churches or museums are without steps. The following sights present few problems: the Forum, the Pantheon, the Lateran, S. Sabina, S. Prassede, Caracalla's Baths, the Modern Art Museum, and the zoo. A bit more difficult (there are a few steps, or a narrow lift, according to the Rome Tourist Office) are the Colosseum, S. Lorenzo fuori le Mura, the Museo Nazionale Romano, the Villa Giulia, and the Museo Nazionale d'Arte Orientale.

Practical A-Z

Calendar of Events	14
Climate and When To Go	16
Consulates	17
Crime	18
Medical Emergencies	20
Money	21
Museums	23
Offical Holidays	23
Packing	23
Post Offices and Faxing	24
Religious Affairs and Vatican Info	24
Strikes	26
Students and Senior Citizens	26
Studying in Rome	26
Telephones	27
Toilets	27
Tourist Information	28

In the 19th century, Rome's traditional Holy Week customs had lapsed through inertia. 'Holy Father,' someone asked. 'Should we not restore the solemn rites of the past?' 'Why not?' replied Pius IX. 'It will amuse the English.' Unfortunately Rome's once excellent summer calendar of concerts, cinema, and dance, etc. lapsed into similar inertia when the Communists lost the municipal government to the Christian Democrats.

January

1   Candlelit procession in catacombs of S. Priscilla

6   Last day of toy fair in Piazza Navona; traditionally the night of the 5th is the noisiest in Rome

21   *Festa di Sant'Agnese*, with shearing of lambs for the wool of the bishop's palliums at S. Agnese fuori le Mura

February

Rome, once famous for its mad carnival, now celebrates at private parties, where everyone spends a small fortune to pose in elegant costumes.

March

9   *Festa di Santa Francesca Romana*, with blessing of cars in Piazzale del Colosseo

19   *Festa di San Giuseppe*, in the Trionfale neighbourhood. Bars serve *frittelle* (fried pastries, often with cream inside) along with the usual *cornetti*; market and bright lights near the church

April

There are so many Holy Week events that the Tourist Office publishes a booklet in English listing them all. On Good Friday evening the Pope leads the Procession of the Cross at the Colosseum, surrounded by candlelight. On Easter Sunday the Pope gives his traditional blessing from the balcony in St Peter's Square. On Easter Monday the whole city evacuates for the traditional first picnic in the *campagna*.

14–16   *Sagra del Carciofo Romanesco* (Festival of Roman artichokes) in Ladispoli, with artichoke floats, folk dancing, and fireworks.

21   Rome's Birthday, celebrated with a civic do on the Capitoline Hill; your one chance to get in the Palazzo Senatorio in Piazza del Campidoglio (come at noon). Also prizes for the best Latin poem and fireworks.

In late April and May, masses of pink azaleas decorate the Spanish Steps. The

International Horse Show in Villa Borghese's Piazza di Siena takes place in the last week of April, with jumping events etc.

May

Throughout the month, the outdoor art exhibition in Via Margutta; also, for two weeks from mid-May, an antique fair in Via dei Coronari, carpeted and torch-lit.

May and June, city rose garden show on Via di Valle Murcia, on the Aventine

June

In mid-June *Estate Romana*—a festival of classical music, film, jazz and rock—begins.

Corpus Domini flowers in various designs carpet the main street of Genzano in the Castelli Romani

23–24   *Festa di San Giovanni*, at St John Lateran. Usual Italian market, and lots of snails and *porchetta* to eat

29   *Festa di San Pietro*, major religious celebration in St Peter's

Throughout June, Strawberry Festival at Nemi, in the Castelli Romani

July

Estate Romana continues.

July and August, opera on Karnak scale in the Baths of Caracalla.

Last two weeks, the *Festa de Noiantri* (of 'We Others'), in Trastevere. Once Rome's most authentic, popular festival, with food, wine, and dancing, the city is trying to poison it with the usual commercial rubbish.

August

Estate Romana continues until the end of the month with treats such as open air films, for the few Romans left in the city.

5   *Festa della Madonna della Neve* at S. Maria Maggiore, with a release of white flowers to symbolize the miraculous snow.

15   *Ferragosto*. Only tourists left in Rome; everything closed.

23   Anniversary of the Great Fire under Nero. Not celebrated.

September

Another art exhibition in Via Margutta, and a crafts fair on Via dell 'Orso.

3   *Santa Rosa*, featuring the *macchina di S. Rosa*, in Viterbo.

        Sagra dell'Uva, in Basilica of Maxentius in Forum, features mountains of grapes

October

1st Sunday Wine festival, when the vintage flows through the fountains in Marino, in the Castelli Romani. Mid–month for two weeks — another antiques fair on Via dei Coronari.

November

1   All Soul's Day, when everyone goes to the cemetery and lights candles for the dead

December

8   *Festa della Madonna Immacolata*, in Piazza di Spagna, when firemen place wreath on head of the column's statue

First week

Piazza Navona toy fair begins; lots of bright lights and a chance to buy sweets or handmade Christmas crib figures. Bagpipe players from the Abruzzi play their strange wailing melodies. Elaborate *Presepi*, or cribs, appear in most churches and in front of St Peter's. The jewel-encrusted Holy Bambino in S. Maria d'Aracoeli is relocated to a crèche scene to receive the homage of Rome's children in little speeches and poems.

22   *Cottio del Pesce*, feast of fish cooked in vats at the Mercati Generali in Via Ostiense, distributed to passers-by

24   Midnight mass at S. Maria Maggiore

25   The Pope's 'Urbi et Orbi' blessing from St Peter's balcony at noon

31   The Pope visits the church of the Gesù for the feast of S. Silvestro and a singing of the ancient Te Deum. The Mayor of Rome presents a silver chalice (arrive by 5 pm to get a good view). Meanwhile, Romans wolf down sausages and lentils for good luck; also stuffed pig's foot (*zampone*) and drink a *spumante* toast, set off a few sparklers, hurl old furniture out of the window (watch out if you're in the street and don't leave your car anywhere near human habitation) then go to bed.

Climate and When to Go

Under blue skies Rome can be radiant, each building aglow in a different shade of ochre, yellow, and red. In the rain the colours seem to be washed away to a uniform grey. The chart of average temperature and rainfall will give you an idea what to expect and what to pack.

	average temp in °C	rainfall in mm		average temp in °C	rainfall in mm
Jan	7.4	74	July	25.7	6
Feb	8.0	87	Aug	25.5	23
Mar	11.5	79	Sept	22.4	66
Apr	14.4	62	Oct	17.7	123
May	18.4	57	Nov	13.4	121
June	22.9	38	Dec	8.9	92

In short, Roman weather rarely meets Mediterranean expectations. It can go down to freezing in the winter, and in July or August hit 37 (98°F), enough to deflate even the most ardent visitor.

It rains as much as in London, if not more, and at times Roman rain reaches monsoon proportions, transforming hills into waterfalls and gutters into rivers.

Spring, despite the threat of showers, is the prettiest time to go, when the flowering trees are in bloom, tubs of azaleas are stacked on the Spanish Steps, and the Roman Campagna is full of wild flowers. It is also the most crowded time of year, as people pour into the city for its Holy Week and Easter rituals. Spring is also the traditional season of Italian school trips, so the main sights tend to be constantly crowded by the bus loads. If you come in the spring, pack your sense of humour. Summer can be stifling hot and the Forum becomes a barbeque pit. The Romans themselves traditionally abandon the city in August, and many restaurants and shops close down. Recently, however, an increasing number are staying behind, willing to put up with the heat for the luxury of traffic-free streets. If you come in the summer, always start your day as early as possible, and consider taking a siesta after lunch, during the hottest hours, so you can take in nighttime activities like the opera in the Baths of Caracalla. Autumn brings both perfect days, cool and dry, or day after day of rain; sights are rarely very crowded, and there's the advantage of wine festivals in the Castelli Romani. The worst thing about winter is the shortness of the days, but it is probably the best time to go to see more Romans and fewer foreigners, and have the museums and churches to yourself.

Consulates

Australia: Via Alessandria 215, © 832 721

Canada: Via Zara 30, © 841 5341

Great Britain: Via XX Settembre 80/A, © 482 5441

Ireland: Largo del Nazzareno 3, © 678 2541

New Zealand: Via Zara 28, ℭ 440 2928
USA: Via Veneto 121/a, ℭ 46 741[

Crime

*Every stone [of Rome] has tasted blood, every house has
had its tragedy, every shrub and tree, and blade of grass
and wildflower has sucked life from death, and blossoms
on a grave.*

– F. Marion Crawford

The Romans will get you if you aren't careful. They have been exploiting visitors,
and each other, for 2700 years. It was worse under the Cæsars, when no one felt
safe on the streets after dark without an armed guard, but it's bad enough now.
We cannot provide accurate statistics (they are available but utterly unreliable)
but you are as likely to be had in Rome as any city in Europe. The latest policing
strategy is to take any children caught thieving into custody, and to charge their
parents when they come to collect them. Whether or not this will be efficient
remains to be seen. Some specialities:

Gypsies. Cultural stereotypes are evil, as we all know, but when you see gypsies
in Rome, jam a hand in your crucial pocket and be ready to kick or bash anyone
that comes close. Rome, unlike other cities, has a hard core of gypsies who live
entirely by crime. In the papers, you'll read about them every day; a favourite
trick is staging fake auto accidents, then intimidating insurance agents to pay fake
damages. Usually they prey on tourists; cowards that they are, they put their children out to do the hard work. The children move in swarms, carrying pieces of
cardboard. When they sight their prey, some of the kids shove the cardboard
under the victim's nose, pretending to ask for alms. The smaller ones, meanwhile,
duck under the cardboard and pick your pockets. Favourite haunts for this game
are Via del Tritone, Via Veneto, anywhere around the Colosseum, Via dei Fori
Imperiali, Largo Argentina. Gypsy children are never shy about putting their
hands in your pockets to see what they can find. You might like to thrash them,
but their Fagins, with knives and chains, are ready to intervene if you do. You can
resist if there is a crowd of ordinary citizens about. All Romans (especially the
honest gypsies) hate the thieving ones like the plague.

Magic Fingers appear in any crowd (Wednesdays and Sundays around St Peter's
Square, for instance) and especially on crowded buses, like the legendary 64.
Picking pockets is one of the less polished Italian arts, though especially prevalent
in Rome. Vigilant men can often intercept a probing hand in the pocket. But what
do you do with it? Bend the fingers back as far as they'll go, and more, until they

break—if you can do it. For alert ladies, a good old-fashioned hatpin will provide guaranteed entertainment. *Ecco; ho trovato una mano nella mia tasca!*—Behold, I have found a hand in my pocket! This can be a provocative statement on Roman buses. Women may find magic fingers in other places where they don't belong— the infamous *mano morta*. If you can identify the culprit, grinding your heel into his foot or elbowing him sharply in the stomach isn't out of the question.

Car Thefts. Don't leave anything of value in a car, even out of sight in the boot. Areas like Campo de' Fiori are worked by gangs who keep an eye on incoming traffic and tourists. If you've been taking photos in the area or have been walking around in an expensive leather jacket, and you go back to dump them in the car, the news will spread.

Gigolos. Any young English-speaking lady who isn't on her guard will eventually find a special someone in Rome. The question is, how to get rid of the damn rotter? If you've the nerve, look him up and down, spit in the gutter and watch his ego shrivel. If you haven't, tell him to leave you in peace ('lasciami in pace'). Hurling abuse at them is not recommended, as swearing with a foreign accent is considered rather sexy. Whenever you meet an interesting male, keep your hand on your wallet at all times.

Bag strippers. Most are junkies working for well-organized gangs; they come on motor scooters, rip off the straps of your purse with a knife, and are gone in a second. Trying to stop them is dangerous. Of course, you shouldn't keep anything valuable in your purse in Rome. You may want to leave your gold earrings and necklaces at home; city hospitals annually treat hundreds of cases of torn ear lobes and bruised necks.

Muggers. This is more a suburban problem; drug addicts cannot afford central Rome rents. Cinecittà and Centocelle have the worst reputations, though central areas are catching up. Moonlight strolls around the ruins are not a good idea; any place with few people about is a prime hunting ground. So are the Termini Station area and parts of Trastevere.

The free **Emergency Number** is 113. Once you've been robbed, however, the only thing to do is register (*denunciare*) the fact with the police at the Questura Centrale, Via S. Vitale 15, © 4686. Don't expect them to chase down the thieves, though if your purse or wallet is stolen, chances are good that someone will turn it in (minus your valuables, but often with your ID intact). But you will have the statement you need for your insurance company. If you lose something in the city or on a bus try your luck at the **Municipal Lost Property Office** at Via Bettoni 1, © 581 6040. There are good **suitcase repair shops**: Sansone, at Via Quirinale 4 and Pascucci, Via di Pallacorda 11.

Medical Emergencies, Insurance, Doctors and Pharmacies

For an ambulance, ✆ 113 or the Red Cross, ✆ 5100.

Public hospitals with 24 hour first aid and medical services are:

Fatebenefratelli: Isola Tiberina (Tiber Island), ✆ 68 371

Policlinico: Viale Policlinico, ✆ 492 341 (for emergencies)

Rome American Hospital: Via Longoni 69, ✆ 22551

San Camillo: Circ. Gianicolense 87, ✆ 58 701

Sant'Eugenio: Piazzale dell'Umanesimo (EUR), ✆ 59 041

San Filippo: Via Martinotti 20, ✆ 33 061

San Giacomo: Via Canova 29, ✆ 67 261

Santo Spirito: Lungotevere in Sassia 1 (near the Vatican) ✆ 650 901

If you want a private doctor or hospital where English is sure to be spoken, try Salvator Mundi International Hospital, Viale delle Mura Gianicolensi 66/67, ✆ 586 041. For a list of English speaking doctors phone the British Embassy, ✆ 482 5651. For dental emergencies, call the Dental Hospital G. Eastman, Viale Regina Elena 287, ✆ 445485/491949. With an E111 a 'ticket' for a consultation cost L15,000. The Istituto Materno Regina Elena Ostetrico, Viale Angelico 28, ✆ 372 4085 is a reliable maternity hospital.

National medical coverage in the UK and Canada covers their citizens while travelling (in Britain, pick up form E111 from the Department of Health and Social Security before you leave). This entitles you to the same medical benefits as Italian citizens, which, in an effort to decrease the country's astonishingly high national deficit, are being severely cut back. Italians have to buy a 'ticket' for all services. At the time of writing a 'ticket' for a prescription cost L3000 plus 50 per cent of the actual price of the medicine up to a maximum of L70,000. If you are ill, either take your E111 to the foreigners' office (*stanza estero*) of the local state health centre (USL) where they will give you a temporary resident's form and a list of doctors. Alternatively, go to the casualty (*pronto soccorso*) unit of a hospital. If you want to avoid all this maddening bureaucracy, take out private insurance, something other nationals have to do anyway. It's worth looking for a policy which covers not only health, but stolen or lost baggage, cancelled or missed flights.

Pharmacies

For minor complaints, or if you know exactly what medicine you need, you can often skip the doctors and go straight to the pharmacy, though without a prescription you'll have to pay the full price for the remedy. Pharmacies stay open after hours on a rotating basis, you can find a list of them in the window of every pharmacy, and in 'La Repubblica' and 'Il Messagero' or by ringing 1921 for a recorded listing. The following are always open all night:

Internazionale: Piazza Barberini 49, ✆ 482 5456

Piram: Via Nazionale 228, ✆ 488 0754

Tre Madonne: Via Bertolini 5 (Parioli), ✆ 807 3423

Cola di Rienzo: Via Cola di Rienzo 213, ✆ 324 3130

Brienza: Piazza Risorgimento 44, ✆ 372 2157

Spinedi: Via Arenula 73, ✆ 654 3278

Money

The currency is the lira, and for the newcomer all the 0s can be confusing. Watch that some unscrupulous Roman doesn't try to take advantage of you: the post office at Termini Station, for instance, is notoriously bad about giving foreigners correct change. (Every Italian, without exception, gives you change for your purchase in the traditional Italian way, pausing a moment before handing over the largest note, in the hope that you'll walk away and forget it). There are convenient exchanges at the airports and Termini, and at most banks. **Banking hours** vary from bank to bank, but as a rule they open between 8 and 9 am, close around 1.30 pm, and open again for an hour mid-afternoon.

Head Offices of banks in Rome are:

Banca d'America e d'Italia: Largo del Tritone 161, ✆ 61 781

Banca d'Italia: Via Nazionale 91, ✆ 46721

Banca Commerciale Italiana: Via del Corso 226, ✆ 67121

Banca Nazionale del Lavoro: Via Veneto 119, ✆ 47 021

Banca di Roma: Via del Corso 307, ✆ 67001

Banco di Santo Spirito: Largo Fochetto 16, ✆ 51721

Credito Italiano: Piazzale della Industria 46, ✆ 54631

Manufactures Hanover Trust: Viale Liegi, ✆ 841 6495

Central branches of the major banks are:

Credito Italiano: Piazza Navona 46;

Piazza di Spagna 20;

Largo Arenula 14

Banca di Roma:	Corso Vittorio Emanuele 251;
	Largo Arenula 32;
	Via della Conciliazione 50;
	Piazza di Spagna 59
Banco di Santo Spirito:	Piazza Parlamento 18;
	Via di Banco di Santo
	Spirito 31;
	Corso Vittorio Emanuele 50-52
BNL:	Via del Corso 473;
	Largo Arenula 28;
	Piazza Venezia 6

Exchange bureaux

If you need to change money outside normal banking hours, go to Termini Station where the Banco Nazionale delle Comunicazione is open Mon–Sat 8.30 am–7.30 pm. If you have Thomas Cook travellers' cheques it's well worth going to one of the company's two offices in Rome to save yourself the L5,000 commission charged by most banks and bureaux. If you have foreign banknotes there are an increasing number of automatic exchange machines around the city but be careful to read the instructions first, or you could end up with schillings or sheckels instead of lire.

Thomas Cook, Piazza Barberini 21D (© 482 8082) open Mon–Sat 8 am–6 pm; and Via delle Conciliazione 23, open Mon–Sat 8 am–6 pm and Sun 8 am–5 pm. Otherwise try one of the following.

Cambio Roma: Via F. Crispi 15, © 678 1076

Eurocambio: Via F. Crispi 92, © 488 0135

Frama: Corso Vittorio Emanuele 106, © 6830 8406 and Via Torino 21/b, © 474 6870

Incafin Italiana: Via Massimo D'Azeglio 3, © 474 3116

Italviaggi: Via della Stamperia 72, 679 5820

Società Rosati: Via Nazionale 186, © 488 5498

Nearly every hotel of three stars or more will accept American Express, Visa, Euro or Diner's Club cards. Below three stars they usually don't. Restaurants and shops along Rome's main tourist trails nearly always accept them, while places frequented mainly by Italians (who rarely use credit cards) rarely do (despite the fact they often plaster their windows with credit card stickers).

Credit Card Offices

American Express: Piazza di Spagna 38, © 67641. Lost/stolen cards © 67864046

Bank Americard (VISA and Access/Mastercard): Via del Tritone 169, © 67 181. Lost/stolen cards © 1678 21001

Diner's Club: Piazza Cavour 25, © 35 755. Lost/stolen cards © 1678 64 064

Museums

The Museidon Card is a museum pass, valid 2–7 days, which allows you to visit 13 museums and sites. You can buy one at tourist offices, museums and some hotels.

Romans are notoriously fickle about keeping opening hours, even when strikes or restoration schemes aren't causing the usual mayhem. The authorities are trying to standardize and extend them, but this is a gradual process and at the time of writing only a few admission times have been changed.

The shameful neglect of the state museums and the Forum may soon be a thing of the past, thanks to legislation allowing them to keep a percentage of the receipts rather than give every penny to the wanton national government.

Official Holidays

Shops, banks, offices, and schools in Rome are closed on the following days: 1 January, 6 January, Easter Monday, 25 April (Liberation Day), 1 May (Labour Day), 29 June (St Peter's Day), 15 August (Assumption of the BVM), 1 November (All Saints'), 8 December (Immaculate Conception of the BVM), Christmas, 26 December (Santo Stefano).

Packing

The voltage in Rome is 220 ac, and outlets take two round prongs; pick up an adapter before you go as they are hard to find in the city. Romans like to dress up, slaves to fashion rather than formality; shorts, tee shirts, halter tops, leisure suits, and funny hats incite Roman disdain (but who cares, after all? And they'd probably kill for your favourite Hawaiian sport shirt). Comfortable shoes are absolutely essential when pounding the pavements. Outside mid-summer bring rain gear or an umbrella. If you plan to attend a papal audience, bring the proper clothes (see Vatican info, p. 24). If you're a light sleeper, ear plugs may help you survive creaky hotel floors and traffic noise. Be warned that film and books in English cost twice as much as at home. Opera glasses or binoculars and a small torch may come in handy in gloomy churches or hotels.

The Italian postal system is the worst in Europe, and if you're only spending a week or two in Rome, you'll almost certainly be home before your letters and postcards, unless you pay an extra L3000 to send them *espresso* at a tobacconist or at the post office, or mail them at the Vatican post office. Stamps may be purchased at post offices or at tobacconists' shops (at the sign of the T). If you don't know where you'll be in Rome you can have post sent General Delivery (*Fermo Posta)* to the Central Post Office (*Posta Centrale*) in Piazza San Silvestro, 00186, open Mon–Fri 8 am–9 pm, Sat 8–12 (© 6771). You can send a telegram from any post office or by ringing 679 5530 (24 hour line). For other postal information, dial 160.

Not surprisingly, there are more fax machines per head in Italy than in any other European country. Even some one-star hotels have them, and virtually all hotels which have a fax will send and receive messages for guests. Alternatively use Esperia Fides, Via di San Pantaleo 63-5, © 6541634, fax 654 2973.

Posting parcels home can be a big bore; Italian postal regulations are sometimes so complex that even postal employees are confused. Your best bet is to show up with your box, and ask where to find the nearest *cartolibreria* that wraps parcels, or send it by a private company: DHL International, Via Labicana 78B and Via Portonaccio 21C, both © 794 191, or UPS/Alimondo, Via della Magliana 329, © 550 3371.

Religious Affairs and Vatican Info

Rome—it is said—has 901 churches and is 99% Catholic, even if only 3% of the Romans regularly attend mass. Since the 3rd century, the Jews have tenuously hung on to second place; followed now perhaps by the Anglicans.The most recent newcomers are the Muslims, who have a wacky new mosque by Villa Ada, designed by post-modern architect, Paolo Portoghesi.

Although the four Patriarchal basilicas (St Peter's, St Paul's Outside the Walls, St Maria Maggiore, St John Lateran) are open all day, **every other church closes in the afternoon** (usually 12–4 or 5). As a rule, don't enter if a service is in progress at the high altar; otherwise be discreet and walk around the chapel in use. If the sacristan opens a chapel or crypt for you, give him a small tip. Coin-operated light machines illuminate the most important works; often a pair of opera glasses or binoculars comes in handy to see a lofty mosaic or fresco.

When globe-trotting John Paul II is in Rome, general **papal audiences** are held on Wednesdays at 11 am in the auditorium; in July and August the audiences are usually held in Castel Gandolfo. To attend in either place, write ahead for tickets from the Prefettura della Casa Pontificia, 00120, Città del Vaticano, with not more than one month's or less than two days' notice. Include name, nationality, proposed date, and your address in Rome. For details or any other information in **Vatican City**, ℂ 6982. At the same time you may want to reserve a place on the English tour of the Necropolis under St Peter's (p.301); write to the Uffizio degli Scavi, with possible dates and the number of your party—and confirm it on your arrival in Rome. **Confession in English** is heard at the Patriarchal basilicas as well as at S. Ignazio, S. Sabina, S. Anselmo, S. Clemente, S. Maria sopra Minerva, and at the Gesù. **Mass** may be heard **in English** at:

> **San Clemente (Irish):** Via di S. Giovanni Laterno 45–47, ℂ 731 5723 (10 am on the 3rd Sunday of the month)
>
> **Sant'Isidoro:** Via degli Artisti 41, ℂ 488 5359
>
> **San Silvestro (English):** Piazza San Silvestro, ℂ 679 7775
>
> **Santa Susanna (American):** Via XX Settembre 14, ℂ 482 7510 (Santa Susanna is currently in the throes of a major restoration. As these unearthed some Roman relics, work is likely to continue for years. In the meantime, services are held every Sunday at 10.30 am at Sant'Agnese in Agone on Piazza Navona)
>
> **San Patrizio (Irish):** Via Boncompagni 31, ℂ 488 5716
>
> **San Tommaso di Canterbury (English):** Via di Monserrato 45, ℂ 686 5808
>
> **Santi Martiri Canadesi (Canadian):** Via G. B. De Rossi ℂ 8552115
>
> Other religions in Rome include—
>
> **Adventist:** Lungotevere Michelangelo 7, ℂ 321 1207
>
> **Anglican:** All Saints, Via del Babuino 153/B, ℂ 679 4357
>
> **Baptist/Waldensian:** Via della Lungaretta 124, ℂ 581 3888
>
> **Episcopalian:** St Paul's Within the Walls, Via Napoli 58, ℂ 488 3339
>
> **Islamic Centre:** Via Bertolini 22, ℂ 808 2167
>
> **Jewish:** Lungotevere dei Cenci 9, ℂ 686 4648
>
> **Methodist:** Ponte Sant'Angelo, Piazza Banco S. Spirito 3, ℂ 656 8314
>
> **Mormon:** Gesù Cristo dei Santi: Via Cimone 103, ℂ 898 394
>
> **Presbyterian:** St Andrew's of Scotland, Via XX Settembre 7, ℂ 482 7627
>
> **International Evangelists:** Via Chiovenda 57, ℂ 721 6400

Russian Orthodox: Via Palestro 69, ✆ 445 0729

Salvation Army: Via Marrucini 40, ✆ 446 2614

Strikes

Official strikes are usually listed in newspapers, but lightning strikes are pretty common—so don't be surprised to turn up at a bus stop, metro or railway station to discover there is no public transport.

Students and Senior Citizens

British citizens under 18 and over 60 with ID have free entrance to Rome's state museums (Museo Nazionale Romano, Villa Giulia, Museum of Oriental Art, Castel Sant'Angelo, Palazzo Barberini's Galleria Nazionale d'Arte Antica, and the Museo d'Arte Moderna). Anyone under 26 can get (modest) fare reductions through the Transalpino booth in Termini Station or one of the organizations listed below. Senior Citizens with a British Railcard are also entitled to a small discount on the return fare to Rome, though they have to pay the full fare for any subsequent travel within Italy.

Students with international ID cards have several cheap housing options (see Where to Stay) and can get some travel discounts by becoming members (L30,000) of the Centro Turistico Studentesco e Giovanile (CTS), Via Genova 16, ✆ 46791 and Corso Vittorio Emanuele 297, ✆ 467 9271 or calling in at the Associazione Turismo Giovanile (ATG), Corso Vittorio Emanuele 108, ✆ 6830 7177, another travel agency specializing in youth and budget fares. **Enjoy Rome**, Via Varese 39, ✆ 445 1843 is also very helpful to young travellers (see p. 28).

Studying in Rome

The EPT's booklet *Young Rome* has lists of universities, institutes, libraries, and workshops in the city that may be of interest for an extended stay. The Dante Alighieri Institute, Piazza Firenze 27, specializes in Italian culture and literature for foreigners. Musicians may want to inquire about courses in the Italian Music International Studies Centre, Conservatorio di S. Cecilia, Via dei Greci 18. The University of Rome's Faculty of Architecture has courses in art restoration for foreigners, from January–June or alternatively there's the Scuola Re Staura, Viale Porta, Ardeating 108, ✆ 5757185. There are scores of language schools, but Italiaidea, Piazza della Cancelleria 85, 00186 Roma, (✆ 68307620) gets good reports.

In Rome (telephone prefix 06), telephone numbers can be anywhere between 4 and 8 digits long, so even if it looks strange it probably isn't a misprint. To make things even more confusing, telephone numbers in the city are in the process of changing. Some (those beginning with 488 and 6880 for example) have already changed, and others are due to do so before the end of 1993. Some new numbers are listed in the telephone directory, others are not. For around two months after a number has changed there will be a message, in Italian and then English, telling you what the new number is. After two months, there will be a message in Italian which simply states that the number is unobtainable, and that you should check the directory or phone directory enquiries (© 12, known as SIP Dodici). If you're lucky there may be an English speaking operator at SIP.

As a whole the city is well supplied with telephones, along the sidewalks (usually on busy street corners), in bars (usually bang next to Euro-pop belching loud-speakers), and in most other public places. Nearly all take phone cards and many take coins, though occasionally in bars you'll need to purchase tokens (*gettoni*). Local calls rarely eat up more than L200, though once you call long distance, the phone becomes a real hog. Don't even try it for international calls: use the metered phones in the post offices (the SIP offices in Piazza San Silvestro and Termini Station, or from your hotel (though beware the surcharges). To save yourself wasting time looking for a coin operated phone, buy a phone card (L5000 or L10,000) from a tobacconist. To reverse charges, dial 172 followed by the country code which will connect you with the appropriate operator, (e.g. 1720044) for Britain. The telephone prefix for Britain is 0044, for the US and Canada 001; for Australia 0061. For information (in English) on international calls, on calling with your credit card or to get an on-line translation into Italian and vice versa (L3000 a minute) dial 170.

Toilets

Emperor Vespasian permitted fullers to place jars in public places to collect the urine they needed for their trade, in return for a small tax. When his son complained that the tax was beneath the imperial dignity, Vespasian held a gold coin to his nose. 'What, does it stink?' he asked. Even today the crumbling urinals you find along the sidewalks of Rome are called *vespasiani*, though they haven't been cleaned since the fall of the Roman Empire.

The sad fact is that the visitor in ancient Rome had a much easier time finding a loo in the city—convenient, marble-seated, flushing *forica*, or latrines, could be found wherever you went, for a penny. Nowadays you have to seek them out in bars, where the byword is grotty and paper a surprising luxury (technically you don't have to buy anything to use the facilities, though if the bar staff are in a bad mood they will claim the toilet is out of order until you buy a drink); loos tend to be slightly cleaner in restaurants, museums, St Peter's Square, and the smarter cafés; but the rare public lavatories are the best, tended lovingly by their attendents. There are public loos on Piazza S Silvestro, Piazza del Colosseo, Via Zanardelli, and by the 64 bus terminus near St Peter's.

Tourist Information

The Central Rome Tourist Office (EPT di Roma) is near the Baths of Diocletian at Via Parigi 5, 00185, © 488 3748 or 488 1851 (open Mon–Sat 8.15 am–7.15 pm). They will reserve you a hotel room free of charge and have plenty of things in English to hand out, including a booklet called *Here's Rome*, with lots of out of date practical information; also the sprightly *Rome for Youth* and a monthly list of events called the *Carnet*, with colourful stories and sidelights about the city. For more personal service go to Enjoy Rome, Via Varese 39, © 445 1843, which has a number of free services for tourists. They'll find you a room in a convent, hostel or hotel which they have inspected for cleanliness, safety etc, advise you on where to eat, drink, shop and boogie, and have up to date practical and cultural information. They also have an emergency help-line, currently operating from 9 am–10 pm.

There are also EPT branch offices in Termini Station, © 487 1270 (open daily 8.15 am–7.15 pm) near track 6 (inside the track area), and at Fiumicino Airport, © 6501 0255 (open Mon–Sat 8.15 am–7 pm) and on the A1 at Frascati Est and Salaria Ovest.

Rome's ACI (Italian Touring Club) has a 24 hour phone line with English-speaking operators to answer not only questions about automobiles but any travel problem that may come up: © 4477 or, for advice on itineraries, the foreign tourists office, © 499 8389.

Cats   30
Dome-a-Roma   30
Holy Rome   31
Illusion and Delusion   33
Know your Rocks   34
Mother of Harlots   35
Pasquinade   36

Roman Topics

Plaques   37
Roman Carnival   38
Seven Preposterous Buildings 39
Sub-Roma   40
Words   41
The Worst Pope   42
A Day in Ancient Rome   43

Cats

Perhaps every country gets the cats it deserves.

– H. V. Morton

The far left-wing parties in Venice once circulated petitions to have their town declared the 'World Capital of Stray Cats'. No Roman, feline or human, has spoken up to defend their own city's right to the title, confirmed by centuries of tradition—a sad reflection on the political lassitude of modern Rome. Well, forget Rome—what about Tàranto, on the Ionian Sea, where the first cats to discover Europe stepped ashore, some 2500 years ago, carried on a Greek merchant ship from their Egyptian home? And what of Naples, with its precarious food chain involving some 30 rats per inhabitant, and in some areas a cat for each rat?

The oldest cat in Rome is the once-pampered stone pussy that sits looking over the city from a cornice on the Via della Gatta, just off the Corso—she used to be part of Emperor Domitian's Temple of Isis. Ever since, millions of cats have found a home in this city. When humans abandoned the Forum and the rest of the ancient centre, the cats made it their own; hordes of them still occupy Trajan's Market, the Imperial Fora and whatever city land hasn't yet been covered with unsightly blocks of flats. Wherever there are colonies of strays, some kind lady comes to feed them the classic Italian cat meal of leftover pasta and boiled celery.

Not every Roman is so solicitous of their welfare. Small circuses have been known to pay children L1000 per cat or dog, to feed them to the lions and tigers. Take time to consider the Roman cat; commonly splotched in white and gray, or black, in most un-aesthetic patterns, he has a dirty face, and doesn't care who notices it. He is an artful thief, and his morals are beneath reproach. Try and talk to him, in English or Italian, and he will show you pure aristocratic disdain. Say 'kitty kitty kitty' or '*mici mici mici*', but he won't even acknowledge your presence until you show him a slice of prosciutto. He's the little pussy heir of the Cæsars, fleas and all.

Dome-a-Roma

Encrusted layers of history can weigh like gravity on the eyeball, and even long-time residents of Rome never look up to the rooflines of their city. But how can you look up, without being ground to pulp by the boiling traffic around you? The less courageous can at least do it indoors. Here is a little quiz, six fine domes seen from below, chosen from among the 901 churches of Rome—not only to encourage you to raise your gaze, but to appreciate the geometrical pastry cooks who designed them. Answers on the last page of the index.

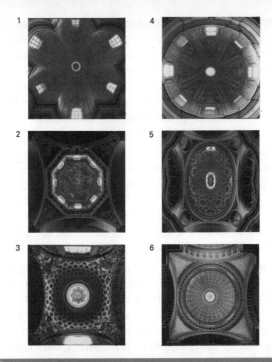

Holy Rome

It was no mere historical accident that made Rome the world centre of Christianity. From its earliest days, the city showed a remarkable instinct for piety and ritual. Romans were terribly haunted by every sort of unseen power, and went to extremes to try and placate them and guess their intentions. The senatorial elite made this their monopoly, with a complex ritual calendar kept secret from the plebeians. All Rome's various priesthoods belonged to them, as did the privilege of taking auguries; determining what actions the state should undertake by reading the flight of birds, and the livers of sacrificial victims, was a Roman passion for centuries. Beyond these, there were the Sibylline Books, bought by Tarquinius Superbus from the Sibyls at Cumae (near Naples), that guided the city's destiny up to Imperial times.

Roman religion had its quirky side. An absolute terror of lightning—the voice of Jove—obsessed even a man like Augustus, who always wore a sealskin vest which he believed would magically avert it. If all the old legends are true, more famous Romans died from Jove's bolts than from battle and old age. Every kind of boundary was charged with sacred taboos. Crossing water was so important that

Rome's highest priest, the *Pontifex* (bridge-maker) *Maximus*, had charge of it. And one of the oldest Latin inscriptions reveals that plowing over a property boundary was a crime requiring human sacrifice. Offering captives, and fellow citizens to the gods was very common—as with the 30 poor souls tossed off the Sulpician bridge each Ides of May, later substituted by straw dolls. Later Roman writers never admit the practice, inventing odd myths to account for the rituals that hint at it—a fascinating case of a community unconsciously repressing past indiscretions, then forgetting them.

One unique religious invention did much to help Rome's rise to power—the *exoratio*, a solemn ritual performed before a siege or battle, whereby the enemy's gods were invited (always successfully, it seems) over to the side of the Romans, who promised bigger temples and better sacrifices. As they conquered the Mediterranean, they acquired the habit of vacuuming up every idol, cult image, and sacred object they found, sending it back to the Temple of Capitoline Jupiter. One wonders what became of them all.

Even though the native Etruscan and Latin gods shared attributes and characters with those of the Greeks, the aesthetic, anthropomorphic Greek approach to religion never really took hold—the Pantheon was part of a failed attempt to import it. By Augustus' time, Romans loved to buy up Greek statues of the gods, but they had become a bit too jaded to take the old religion seriously. Cults from all over found a place in Rome—Isis and Osiris, Mithras, Judaism, and Christianity, Atargatis, Manichaenism, among many others. On the Vatican, very near where St Peter's is now, stood the cult centre of the Phrygian goddess Cybele; from here her bizarre worship, with its self-castrating priests, was disseminated throughout Europe.

State religion was another matter. Besides the cults of deified emperors—never given much respect by the Romans themselves—there was the strange abstraction of the 'Goddess Roma', whose image may still be seen up on the Capitol today (try to imagine tugging at your forelock before the Goddess Birmingham or Divine Baltimore!). Following a strong philosophical trend towards monotheism, Aurelian concocted the 'Cult of the Invincible Sun' as the Empire's official religion—though many, especially the Jews and Christians, found this thinly-disguised worship of the State utterly diabolical. When the Christians took power, they were faced with the daunting task of sorting out this jumble of faith and fakery, bending it for their own purposes. Since they could not easily suppress pagan festivals, they merely took them over; every church holiday has a pagan ancestor (All Souls' Day, for one obscure example, was associated early on with the church of St Mary of the Martyrs—the Pantheon; it replaced a similar

Egyptian festival, celebrated on the same day, a block away at the Temple of Isis).

Isis' priests also contributed the tonsure, that ever-popular monkish hair-do. Their holy processions, if reproduced today, would attract little attention in any Italian town, unless someone noticed that the idol on the cart wasn't quite the Virgin Mary. Roman temples featured familiar items like incense, candles, and holy water stoups; our common marriage ceremony closely reproduces the pagan Roman rite—but brides in those days wore red instead of white. And of course there is the *pontiff* himself—no longer a bridge-builder, but a metaphorical bridge of sorts, spanning a continuous religious tradition almost 3,000 years old.

Illusion and Disillusion

Does Rome make films, or have films made Rome? A question like this might seem more appropriate for Hollywood, perhaps. But the cinema was the first genuinely new thing to happen in Rome in a millennium or two, a rare chance for this fossilized town to actually create something of its own. Although the Italian film industry was born in Turin, it soon relocated to Rome, for obvious reasons—better light, plenty of idle folks for extras, and ready-made sets for 'Colossals' like the 1914 version of *Quo Vadis?*. Before long Rome became the new Italian land of dreams. The perspectives of Baroque ceilings where hosts of heaven seem to dangle or soar overhead are child's play next to the illusionism of film. Cinema could make even Fascism look good to millions.

What has traditionally set Roman Catholicism apart from other religions is its need to make the spiritual as visible and literal as possible, through miracles, art, the pomp and rituals of the Church. Even outright fakes have had their place, as long as they 'increase the faith'. Add to this the national urge to create a *bella figura* and you have very fertile ground for cinema. When the bubble of illusion burst in 1943, Cinecittà was sacked and pillaged by a Roman mob; there followed a few years of remarkable Neo-realist films like *Rome, Open City, Bicycle Thieves, Mamma Roma*. Nowadays they seem like an aberration, and are almost never shown in Rome.

'Cinecittà is not my home; I just live there.' So says Federico Fellini, modern Rome's most famous resident (the Pope after all, lives in Vatican City, and no one can remember who the Prime Minister is this week). Fellini's art has never been to recreate everyday life, but to use it as a springboard to create a more lively, rococo alternative. In his specifically Roman films, *La Dolce Vita, Roma*, and *Interview* he holds a funhouse mirror up to reality. The Romans, one would have thought, would jump at the bait. But you're more likely to see a Fellini film in Milton Keynes than in Rome.

The casual observer begins to suspect the Romans find both the Neo-realists and Fellini too painful—not because they portray the real Rome but because they don't (no other directors show the least interest in doing so, either). Seeking the Felliniesque today in Rome is not an easy task: other Italians say they are spoiled, vulgar and rude (S.P.Q.R., they say, stands for 'Sono porchi questi romani', or, these Romans are pigs), but if they are, it is only in relation to the exquisite politeness of other Italians. They do have a wonderfully sarcastic sense of humour. One of the funniest things you can do in Rome is follow a pair of nuns and watch how every Roman male they pass superstitiously touches his testicles. But where Fellini's view of his fellow citizens rings truest is in their jaded *nomifregismo*, or I-don't-give-a-damnism. When the Allies drove in to liberate Rome, the *nomifregisti* couldn't be bothered to step out of their bars to see. They haunt every Fellini movie, those overdressed people who take up space, staring blankly at the camera.

Know Your Rocks

All joking aside in this topic—this is serious business. Rome spent twenty centuries rifling the quarries of the world for the finest building stone. If you want to tell one from the another (and anyone in the ancient world with an eye for art or architecture thought it very important) here is a brief directory:

Tufa—a cheap volcanic rock, sometimes with a yellow tint; early Rome's most common paving and building material because it is abundant and easy to cut (Servian Wall, Republican temples in Largo Argentina). Today Italians mostly use it for making hay barns.

Travertine—the real Roman stone. St Peter's, the Colosseum, and nearly everything else is made of it. If you drive out to Tivoli you will see the big quarries along Via Tiburtina, in use for millennia. Its various grades range from almost white to pitted grey; you'll notice it suffers quite a bit from the traffic smoke.

Peperino—an ashen grey volcanic stone from the Alban Hills, common, like tufa, in the oldest ruins.

Carrara marble—Michelangelo's favourite for sculpture—he spent months alone up in the Tuscan hills above Carrara, searching out the best veins. Also used in ancient monuments (Trajan's Column, Arch of Titus; the ancients knew it as marble from Luni, after the port in the region).

Pentelic marble—from Attica in Greece (Temple of Hercules Victor in Piazza Bocca della Verità—the oldest marble building left in Rome).

Rarer stones, used mostly for columns and interiors:

Cipollino—'onion' marble, luminous with a glassy green tint (columns of the Temple of Antoninus and Faustina in the Forum).

Granite—usually grey granite from Egypt, as in the columns of the Pantheon, or the Temple of Saturn in the Forum. Most of Rome's obelisks are made of pink granite from Aswan.

Giallo Antico—a beautiful yellow marble from Tunisia, used in some of the interior columns of the Pantheon and the Basilica Jovis in the Domus Flavia on the Palatine.

Verde Antico—marbled with shades of green ranging from the lightest tint to almost black, from Thessaly (pillars in St John Lateran).

Rosso Antico—red marble from the Peloponnese.

Porphyry—one of the hardest and most expensive of all, heavily grained in red, black, and violet; it comes from the isthmus of Suez (columns before Basilica of Maxentius, in the Arch of Constantine, and in some of the best sarcophagi).

Serpentine—similar to porphyry, but intensely green in colour, from Sparta.

Mother of Harlots

Reading most historical accounts of the early Empire and the *pax Romana*—especially if written by an Italian—you would get the impression that Rome was doing the Mediterranean world a favour by conquering and looting it. For a dissenting opinion on the real nature of Rome, there's no one better than St John the Divine. In 95 AD, John escaped the Emperor Domitian's persecution of Christians by fleeing from Ephesus to the island of Patmos. Living in a cave there, he had the memorable visions that resulted in the Book of Revelations, the Apocalypse; an indispensable aid to fire-eating preachers ever since, with an infinity of do-it-yourself interpretations, the Apocalypse, in its time, was intended and widely understood (at least on the earthly level) as a prophecy of the fall of Rome:

… Fallen, fallen is Babylon the great, she who made all nations drink the wine of her impure passion.

(14.8)

Besides the persecuted Christians, John spoke for all the captive nations of the Empire, for the victims of the insatiable Roman tax collector, for the millions of slaves, for serious men who hated the abomination of Emperor-worship, for the great cities like Carthage and Corinth that Rome had wiped from the face of the earth. In Revelations 17, John develops the unforgettable image of the Harlot:

... arrayed in purple and scarlet, and bedecked with gold and jewels and pearls,
holding in her hand a golden cup full of abominations and the impurities of her
fornication; and on her forehead was written a name of mystery: 'Babylon the
great, mother of harlots and of earth's abominations.' And I saw the woman,
drunk with the blood of the saints and the blood of the martyrs of Jesus.

(17. 4–6)

An angel explains to John that the seven-headed beast the Harlot rides represents seven hills, and the surrounding waters the 'peoples and multitudes and nations and tongues' over which she has dominion. Like most prophets, John has an easier time with present realities than with the future. Fallen Babylon was laid waste, 'a dwelling place of demons, a haunt of every foul spirit,' but not nearly as soon as he would have liked. The 'new heaven and a new earth' (21.1) appeared in the fullness of time. For the holy city, the New Jerusalem, we're still waiting.

But history usually turns out less dramatic, more willing to compromise than the words of prophets. Anyone who knows Rome well will sense that the old harlot is still with us—even God couldn't kill her. She's reformed somewhat; no longer a bloodthirsty parasite, or a pious and holy parasite, but still, as any taxpayer from Turin or Milan will tell you, a parasite.

Pasquinade

As you cross over the Ponte Garibaldi, have a look at the monument to Giacchino Belli, the top-hatted Roman dialect poet who stands in his piazza welcoming you to Trastevere. On the back of the pedestal you'll see a relief with a group of old-time Romans, gathered excitedly around a queer broken statue. What makes this shapeless marble lump different from the other ten thousand in Rome is that it is a talking statue. His name is Pasquino, and you can see him today behind Palazzo Braschi, just a block west of Piazza Navona.

Political graffiti, and particularly the habit of making statues talk by hanging placards on them, has been a Roman speciality since ancient times. During the siege of 545 AD, friends of King Totila set up such placards by night to chastise the Romans for their treachery towards the Goths. In the Renaissance it was big business; Pasquino could hold running dialogues with Rome's other 'talking' statues—'Marforio', an old marble river god who now resides in the courtyard of the Capitoline Museum, and 'Madama Lucrezia', a cult figure of Isis moved in front of San Marco. One of their favourite subjects, understandably, was the insane acquisitiveness of the popes and cardinals—Pasquino once appeared with a tin cup, begging 'alms for the completion of the Palazzo Farnese,' and when the

Barberini pope, Urban VIII, robbed the Pantheon of its bronze ceilings, Pasquino remarked 'What the Barbarians didn't do, the Barberini did.' One irritated pope was ready to toss the statue in the Tiber, but thoughtfully refrained when a subtle counsellor warned him that it would 'infect the very frogs, who would croak pasquinades day and night'.

Plaques

Pasquino and his friends may not be talking much now, but you will still find plenty of interesting reading on the streets of Rome. There are enough marble and travertine plaques in Rome to pave all of Liechtenstein. Many commemorate hopelessly obscure former residents or long-ago civic courtesies—like the one facing the Pantheon, thanking the City of Buenos Aires for supplying the piazza with a beautiful and quiet wooden pavement from the virgin Argentine forests (it's under the asphalt today). Others proclaim a building's owner exempt from the pope's taxes, or offer passers-by a few Latin couplets from Horace or Virgil appropriate to the place.

Dozens of plaques record the high water mark of great floods; seeing them, you'll be amazed Rome wasn't washed away entirely. On the Portico d'Ottavia, Rome's old fishmarket, besides papal ordinances forbidding gambling, you'll see one with a marked line; any fish that was longer than the line had to be offered to the city officials before it was sold. The longest, sometimes running to over two hundred words, are nothing more than 'no litter' signs; with all the pomp and Mandarin abstraction of papal Rome, they usually begin something like 'By Order of the Illustrissimo and Reverendissimo Monsignor President of the Street ...' On Via della Luce,in Trastevere, some wag once did a modern version in the same style; in Roman dialect it rambles on: '. . .who throws garbage is a cuckold and the son of a whore, and if he insists, stubborn as a mule, he's likely to get his head broken . . .'.

Many of the best ones are religious—special deals on indulgences, like the one from 1797 near Trajan's Market on Via Buccina, offering 100 days off Purgatory in exchange for a litany of the Blessed Virgin Mary in front of the street corner shrine. On Via Pettinari, just before the Ponte Sisto, you can test your piety with a tiny plaque erected only in 1922. According to its author, if you say a sincere Hail Mary on this spot, you can look up at the skies and experience an epiphany:

'Se tu dirai di cuore Ave Maria,

In cielo tu vedrai la faccia mia.

In a sense the Carnival mirrors the history of Rome itself—only in reverse. When Rome was full of pomp and power, Carnival evoked the Golden Age of Saturn, a time without arms or empires. Under the popes, it became a bawdy free-for-all. And in today's secular, sophisticated city, where anything would be tolerated, nothing happens.

Under the Cæsars, in an age when nothing succeeded like excess, one Carnival just wasn't enough. At proper Carnival time, there was *Lupercalia*, a pastoral feast in honour of the old Latin shephard god Lupercus; Roman men raced through the streets, naked except for goat skins, whipping the crowds with leather thongs for fertility and good luck (as in the first act of Shakespeare's *Julius Caesar*). A more direct ancestor was the Saturnalia, around Christmas time, a week of utter licence, with a mock kingship, gift-giving, continuous parties, and a symbolic inversion of society—the slaves ruled each household, waited upon at table by their masters. The ancient origins of Saturnalia had a darker side: celebrations among the legionaries on the frontiers involved human sacrifices as late as the 4th century AD. Yet a third Carnival came at the spring equinox, the *Hilaria*, a Festival of Joy where no office or dignity was above the general buffoonery. Crowds of maskers thronged the streets all night, though the festival ended abruptly the following day with a solemn procession in honour of Cybele and Attis.

Carnival during the Middle Ages isn't very well documented, but we can guess there were plenty of casualties, and everybody had a good time. In the Renaissance, in a city finally overawed by the clerical and noble elites, the affair seems to have suffered some sanitization; opulent, self-glorifying pageants dominated the festivities, provided by the leading families. But decadence will out, and during the papal twilight the Romans reclaimed their Carnival once more. By the 18th century, it was the most irresistibly *folklorique* attraction in Italy, a must for all Grand Tourists from the north. The best account of it may be read in Goethe's *Italian Journey*: the famous riderless horse races, the masques, and the clowning, all performed with a democratic abandon that proved fascinating to Europe on the eve of the Romantic Era. The races down the Corso from Piazza del Popolo to Piazza Venezia were typically Roman, with sharp barbs fixed to the horses' private parts to make them go faster, and inevitable accidents involving the trampling of spectators. Another kind of race featured elderly Jews, kidnapped from the Ghetto and forced at swordpoint to stuff themselves with cakes before they ran.

Carnival's downfall began with the revolutions of 1849. When Pius IX returned to power, he suspended it for a time to punish the Romans. Since 1879, and the modernization of Rome, the festival has been on a long downhill slide. Nowadays you'll see only children in costumes. Adults still have them (stylish and ridiculously expensive, of course), but they only wear them to private gatherings and to the nightclubs, where there are big New Year's Eve-style parties. Gags like hand-buzzers and exploding cigarettes seem to be popular.

Seven Preposterous Buildings

No city, no place on earth, has ever had such a chronic, incurable edifice complex. As early as the time of King Tarquin, with his matchless sewers and opulent temples, the pattern of Rome's building madness was set. Along the way have come some of the genuine triumphs of European architecture and design: Trajan's Forum, the Pantheon, the Colosseum, the aqueducts, the baths, the early Christian basilicas, Michelangelo's dome at St Peter's, Bernini's colonnades, the stage-set piazzas and fountains of the unchained Baroque. But when Rome makes a mistake, it does so in a big way, and usually it is the desire to impress, the urge to monumentality that leads Roman architects astray. This mercifully brief inventory, included only for connoisseurs of kitsch and gigantism, takes in some of the most ridiculous buildings in our part of the galaxy.

1. **Nero's Golden House**. Not content with the huge palaces on the Palatine Hill, Nero took advantage of the great fire of 64 AD to expropriate nearly a quarter of central Rome for his private pleasure garden. The greatest artists of the day were kept working day and night to fill its endless walls and pavilions, all in the shadow of a 120 ft gilt statue of Nero. His embarrassed successors had most of the place torn down by 104 or so.

2. **St Peter's**. Nearly a dozen architects, and as many wilful popes, combined to turn what was supposed to be the crowning masterpiece of the Renaissance into an awkward mishmash of conflicting ambitions and idiosyncracies. Renaissance popes often get too much credit for taste; St Peter's is a convincing lesson that even the most enlightened of them were interested only in size and that the decoration be larded on thickly.

Most of the real horrors, though, are modern:

3. **Ministry of Justice**. An architect named Guglielmo Caldarini gets credit for the sprawling hippopotamus of the riverbank (completed 1910). Larger than the Colosseum, and probably more expensive, 'Why not?' demanded Caldarini and the clique of politicians behind him. 'It's as solid as its neighbour, Castel Sant'Angelo, and lots prettier, too.' By the 1970s, it was about to collapse, and had to be completely rebuilt.

4. **National Gallery of Modern Art**: Another monster of united Italy, designed by Cesare Bazzani in 1911. Originally called the 'Palace of the Fine Arts', the ironies of this flaccid pile as a home for modern art are profound.

5. **Altar of the Nation**: Unfortunately its vast dungeons of military museums, the only place in Rome from where you *can't* see this sugar monster, are nearly always closed. Intended as a monument to victory, it is so huge that the Romans couldn't finish it before it became irrevocably associated with defeat. Offers to send it piecemeal to Padua have so far been met with polite disdain.

6. **Marble Stadium and Foro Mussolini**: The dictator's modest tribute to himself, originally planned to have a colossal semi-nude statue of Mussolini himself; has to be seen to be believed.

7. **Corviale**: The showpiece of Rome's public housing effort in the 1970s, out in the suburbs near Via Magliana. Corviale is a kilometre-long block of prefab concrete, home to some 7000 people, all of whom dearly wish they were elsewhere. It may have to be demolished soon, if it doesn't fall down by itself.

But after a trip to Rome, you may want to argue with these choices; everyone has their own favourites.

Sub-Roma

Compared to the transit systems of other European capitals, Rome's Metropolitana seems a paltry affair: only two lines, both of which studiously avoid going near any place you want to visit. But consider the problems of building an underground in Rome, where some buildings rest on four levels of earlier foundations, with all the world's archaeologists looking over your shoulder waiting for something interesting to turn up, something that can stop the work for years (in one memorable scene in Fellini's *Roma*, beautiful frescoes are discovered in one such underground foray, though on contact with the air they crumble away before your eyes).

Underground Rome, in fact, may be as interesting as what lies on the surface. Some of it can be visited: the street of ancient pagan tombs under, of all places, the crypt of St Peter's, or the sanctuary of Mithras below San Clemente. Beyond these, no one has ever attempted to catalogue the hundreds of chambers, cellars, monuments, and tombs the Romans have under their houses. Below these run underground streams, like the one under the Quirinale that once flowed through Catullus' famous gardens, or the lake beneath Palazzo Colonna. Julius Cæsar built a network of tunnels under the Forum, linked to the Cloaca Maxima, surely the world's most famous sewer, built by the Tarquins and still in use today. This was overshadowed by a later tunnel, built for horse-drawn wagons to transport firewood from the Campus Martius docks all the way to the Baths of Caracalla. The strangest part of this sub-Roma may be the Capitoline itself, a veritable Great Pyramid of ancient chambers and tunnels and half-excavated, half-forgotten temples.

Not surprisingly, this secret city below has evolved some new life forms fitted to its peculiar environment. We hear of a poor soul trying to excavate a basement for a new pizzeria in Trastevere, and unearthing battalions of monster flatworms, giant albino water scorpions (supposedly harmless however disgusting) and plenty of specimens of Rome's true totem animal, the mighty, cat-eating Royal Pantagana rat. The authorities aren't sure whether Rome has ten rats per person, like any normal city, or thirty, like Naples.

Words

In Rome's case, historical revisionism is all too easy. Like the archaeologists, delving courageously to find the bottom level of its endless tunnels and catacombs, historians have yet to plumb the lowest depths of the ancient city's gluttonous turpitude. Achievements once credited to Rome in the arts and sciences always turn out to have been the work of someone else, and Rome's original civic virtue and later piety have been exposed too many times, and too convincingly, to be cynical frauds. Romans didn't invent concrete, or plumbing, or even gladiators—is there any one thing the Great Pretender has really contributed to our culture?

When you stand in the Forum, consider all the words that had their birth in the bit of land you see around you. *Forum* itself, of course, along with *committee, rostrum, republic, census, plebeian, plebiscite, civic, suffrage, censor, forensics, magistrate, classes, dictator* and even *pontificate*. From the Capitoline Hill in front of you, we get *capitol, mint, money* and *asylum*, and to your left, the Palatine would later contribute *prince* and *palace*. A Latin scholar could probably find a few dozen more of these without too much effort. It is a reminder of just how much we owe to the Romans for our institutions and public life today. They may have failed badly in their visions of the Republic and of the rule of law, but their centuries of anguished constitutional history prove how hard they tried. To us, their ideals have been more important than their failures. For better or worse, all the figures on our political stage—the statesmen, legislators and philosophers, along with the tyrants, the crooks and the lawyers— all went to school in Rome.

The Worst Pope

It would be no easy job to decide which popes made the greatest contributions to religion and culture. The best of them, no doubt, are written up in heaven in St Peter's book; just for fun we have tried to find the worst for ours. This too has its difficulties; out of the myriads of scoundrels, drunkards, thieves, children, idiots, poison artists, political tools, gluttons and perverts who have decorated St Peter's throne over two millennia, we have found some prime candidates, based on a bare minimum of scholarship and a good dose of spleen. We cannot agree with the obvious choice: Alexander VI, the notorious Borgia pope. Though a reasonably effective looter of Church money, a sex-crazed hedonist, and possibly a closet pagan, his greatest sins seem to have been first, not spreading the grease widely enough, and second, not having been born an Italian. The constant vilification he received from his contemporaries convinces us he wasn't such a bad fellow after all, and didn't poison nearly as many people as he is given credit for.

Sifting through the evidence, here are some of the top contenders for the prize: **Benedict IX** (1033–46), heir of Marozia, the third pope in succession to come from the family of the Counts of Tusculum. Elected at the age of ten, this 'Nero of the papacy' took to rapine and homicide at an early age. Twice he was deposed, and once put the papacy up for auction in order to marry an unwilling sweetheart. **Boniface VIII** (1294–1303), the most arrogant and unlovable of popes, who wrecked the powerful medieval papacy with his impostures. He got his job by tricking his predecessor, the saintly but not too clever hermit Celestine V, into abdicating. During a council at the Castel Nuovo in Naples, Boniface whispered through a hidden tube into the pope's cell, pretending to be the voice of God commanding him to quit. **John XII** (955–63). Another of the house of Tusculum, and another teenager, best known for the harem he maintained at the Vatican. **Leo X**, the Medici pope (1513–22). 'Let us enjoy the papacy, since God has given it to us,' said Leo. In fact it wasn't God, but Leo's father Lorenzo de' Medici, whose money purchased the office. Enjoy it he did—and almost bankrupted it, while his attempts to make up the deficit by selling indulgences and bishoprics were an immediate cause of the Reformation. **Stephen VII** (896–7), an agent of the Dukes of Spoleto who was so rotten, he exhumed the corpse of his predecessor, Pope Formosus, and put it on trial (see p. 238).

No one could dispute the credentials of **Paul IV** (1555–9), one nasty piece of work. Giovanni Carafa was the real father of the Inquisition, and his reign of terror in his native Naples caused a revolution there. As pope, he presided over the height of the Counter-Reformation, burning more books and more Christians than any other pope, all the while milking the Church to enrich his family. Paul's hobby was persecuting Jews, and one of the proudest acts of his reign was the creation of the Roman Ghetto.

But there is a sentimental favourite. Not as vicious as many, and living in a quiet and decorous age, he nevertheless could claim the award for his pure grasping, grubby mediocrity—**Innocent X** (1644–55).

Felix I didn't have a very happy papacy, and Urban VI was really a country boy from Campania, but it is this Innocent who can claim the honour of the most misnamed pope. A tremendous grafter, Innocent devoted his undistinguished papacy entirely to the enrichment of his vile family, the Pamphili. A fair judge of art, he oversaw the development of Piazza Navona (meant to increase property values around his new family palace) and installed all the metal fig leaves and dresses on the Vatican's nude statues.

Innocent met a memorable end—dragging out his last hours while his relatives looted everything around him, even his clothes. Finally there was nothing left but the brass candlestick on his night table—until a servant came back and stole that too. No one could be found to pay for a funeral, and for a while the body lay in a tool shed in the Vatican crypt, in a plain coffin so small that the pope's feet stuck out the end. Francis Marion Crawford, who tells the tale (in *Ave Roma Immortalis*), remarks that eventually the corpse was taken to Sant'Agnese in Piazza Navona, where, 'in the changing course of human and domestic events, it ultimately got an expensive monument in the worst possible taste'.

A Day in Ancient Rome

It's almost dawn; time to wake. Marcus Q. Publicus falls out of his little iron bed, head reeling from the rubber chicken and foul Vatican Hill wine his patron served him last night (the patron dined rather better, on stuffed peacock and vintage Falernian). He splashes water across his face, pulls on an old tunic and cloak, and throws back the wooden shutters onto the balcony. It's still raining; no need to water the geraniums this week either. Going down the steps, he passes on the second floor the *aquarius*, the water carrier, struggling under two big amphorae slung from a yoke. 'Can we have an extra bucket so that the wife can wash the floors?' Marcus asks. The *aquarius* spits over the balustrade, grumbles something in Gaelic, and continues on his way.

On the first floor, Marcus tiptoes past the prime tenant's flat. Cæsar's return from Dacia was quite a party, but with all that money flowing into town, everybody's rent seems to be going up; Marcus doesn't want to hear about it. In the lobby, a drunk has crashed out over the mosaic of Venus and Adonis. Marcus asks himself, as he does nearly every morning, 'Why, oh why do I live in the *Subura*?'

It's just light as he hits the street, but most of his neighbours are already at work. The wine and oil shops are folding up their wooden grates, cookshops stoke up their ovens and tinkers bang on pots; the four *cauponae* (bars) on the street are open for business, as are the ladies they keep upstairs. Under the awning of one of the shops, a schoolmaster prepares to assault his sleepy charges with the day's first conjugation. The awning across the street shelters Ajax, a Greek barber—a real butcher, but cheap. As he whets his dull iron blade, he starts in about the coming *munera* at the Colosseum, and inquires discreetly whether Marcus wants a piece of the action.

His thoughts, however, are elsewhere. Like most everyone else in Rome, he is wondering: 'What am I going to do with myself today?'

> It's the Calends of April, in the 11th year of the illustrious reign of Emperor Trajan. Marcus, an average Roman, lives on the third floor of a quite respectable five-storey insula, with balconies and a decorative brick and stucco patterned façade, just off the bustling thoroughfare called the Argiletum (roughly following the course of today's lower Via Cavour). It was only a few streets from the Forum, cheap for a new building, and had the greatest luxury any flat could boast—a bog that drains into the sewers. Julius Cæsar used to live right around the corner, they said. Unfortunately, when Cæsar was courting the plebeians he didn't mind living in the city's toughest neighbourhood. It's gotten worse since Trajan started clearing the worst of the Subura slums to make room for his brilliant Forum; all the bad news has been moving farther up the Argiletum.
>
> It was Marcus' patron, Q. Denarius Totens, who sold him on the flat: when the old insula collapsed, he was part of the syndicate that bought up the land cheap and built a new one. Big cracks are starting to appear in the outside walls, but Marcus is stuck with it. With fortune seekers pouring into the city from Londinium, Baalbek, and every town in between, he would be hard pressed to find anywhere else at the price. Marcus, being an average Roman after all, is between jobs. He gets up at dawn by habit and skips breakfast. Not having a suit pending in the courts, or any public shows to attend, he doesn't need to worry about his troublesome toga (if it weren't for the law, no one would wear them, since they take over an hour to drape correctly, and cost a fortune to clean. On a day like this, it would have become hopelessly filthy before he walked ten blocks.)

It's still drizzling as Marcus putters down the bustling Argiletum, cloak over head, drawn aimlessly towards the Fora. At the end of the street, he ducks under the colonnades of the Forum of Cæsar, and finds his way (as he usually does) into the brand new forica the Emperor has just built into the complex. A home toilet is fine, but marble fittings, hot water and heated seats, all for just one *ass*—that's the way to start the day. But of all the luck, there on the next stool is his neighbour Theodore, the Pious.

Since Marcus moved to the Subura, Theodore (who makes his living scalping Circus tickets, liquidating jewellery lost in the gaming rooms of the neighbourhood *cauponae*, recruiting toughs to assist court bailiffs, and brokering the occasional cock fight) has seemed to follow every new cult in Rome for at least a month—every one save that of the Christians, who even in this enlightened day are still of interest to the police. For a long time it was Mithras (Theodore is a veteran of the legions), and he was bending ears with astrological mumbo-jumbo, and the recreative powers of an initiatory bath in bull's blood. Then he became inspired by Hadad and Atargatis, whoever they might be. And now it's the Phrygian Mountain Mother. The Subura is full of devotees of Cybele; poor folks think she'll help them win at dice. Their spooky processions wind through the city, with flutes and cymbals, ending somewhere out on the Via Tiburtina with a drugged frenzy and some priests castrating themselves (all fake!). 'In the East', Theodore drones, 'they feel the Mysteries of Life ...' But the *forica*, praise the gods, is one place where some careful timing can help one escape from a bore.

Well, Marcus does indeed have a case coming up, but not today. And it isn't even in the Fora, but some basilica he's never heard of, on the Esquiline near the Market of Livia (today Piazza Vittorio Emanuele, but still a market). He does not care to discuss this one with his friends. People do get showered with the contents of chamber-pots, and the law is straightforward. And it was his best cloak, and he does have a witness (promised 25 per cent). If he's lucky, Marcus will break even.

Yesterday Marcus picked up his dole ticket at the Portico of Minucius, next to Pompey's Theatre. His patron Denarius has promised him a nice position with the port authority, where he could accept little bribes of foreign dainties and catch up on his sleep, but Cæsar hasn't been granting Denarius audiences lately. So Marcus has nothing to do. Nor are there any games or races to watch. There are about 160–185 public holidays in the year, but today isn't one of them. And the baths won't be open for an hour or two.

The rain is finally letting up, and Marcus purchases a bag of lupins to chew on from an old woman sheltering under the colonnades along the side of the Basilica Amelia, where the Argiletum meets the Forum amidst the stalls of the booksellers. Perfumed lawyers and magistrates, many followed by straggling bands of slaves and suppliants, swish through the portico of the great Basilica, while crowds of idlers gamble and gossip on the steps—some just like to watch cases; others are hoping some citizen with an important case is willing to pay for the service of a few professional applauders.

Especially after a spring rain, the Forum makes a grand sight, with glistening marble and bronze statues on every side; throngs of people jam the narrow square, while political celebrities and billionaires pass by ostentatiously on litters, rocking gently up to the Palatium. The roofs and columns of Cæsar's palace rise above the mists to the south, a constant reminder that in spite of everything, living in the capital of the world has its advantages. As Marcus turns out of the Forum into Vicus Iugarius, a well-placed elbow in his face sends him flying against a column of the Basilica Julia. The slave who dealt it looks as though he would as soon kill as look at him. Marcus looks away as if nothing happened and continues on, less from fear of the slave, than of the anonymous man in the curtained litter behind him.

Forget it; Marcus ambles quietly up the Vicus Iugarius, that pretty street, around the south slope of the Capitol, under the shining gold roof of Jupiter Greatest and Best, and into the even thicker crowds of the Forum Holitorium. Though still following his usual morning routine, Marcus remembers something he was supposed to do: that's right, Boadicea, his blond and buxom British wife, wanted a big fish tonight with the few extra denarii he picked up at Denarius' dinner. Many of the classier stands of the Forum Holitorium, the ones selling *garum* (gourmet fish-gut sauce from Spain), nightingales' tongues, Colchester oysters (down from Britain in 24 hours) and such have moved to Trajan's new market, but the Forum Holitarium is still the biggest and busiest in the world. After some careful perusal of the stands between the Theatre of Marcellus and the Porticus of Octavia, Marcus accepts a huge chunk of swordfish, fresh from the Straits of Messina; for such a purchase, the fishmonger is happy to send a boy off to his flat to deliver it, along with the pickled eggs, asparagus, and onions he bought from the crotchety old hag behind the Temple of Apollo.

Now comes the best part of the day, a ramble through the Campus Martius, across Octavia's Portico to admire the famous Greek sculptures under the colonnades, through the Saepta Julia, where the jewellers and the art and antique dealers display their treasures (the little Greek bronze, the only treasure of Marcus' household, came from here), and finally a walk through the lovely grove around Agrippa's Lagoon, continuing down the Euripus, the shady, man-made canal full of goldfish that runs into the Tiber. But it's already the fifth hour of the morning (about 11 am), and the bell is ringing for the opening of the baths—or at least their courtyards. For an hour, until the main buildings open, Marcus can amuse himself throwing the ball around the *palaestra*, and eating a modest *prandium* of bread, cheese, and a bit of tripe.

> While waiting for a job, Marcus has been dependant on the system of clientage, the grease that oiled ancient Rome, and though now much reduced, still the prime evil that prevents Italy from having a responsible public life today. Everybody in Rome, save only the emperor, had a patron upon whom he depended for favours and advancement—a new toga and a few pounds of silverware each year at the Saturnalia (the ancestor of Christmas), and money gifts every now and then to see the clients through. In return, a good deal of blatant obsequiousness was required, along with aid in whatever shady business the patron was undertaking at the moment. Having enjoyed the patron's largesse at dinner, Marcus was not required to pay his usual morning visit.
>
> One of the greatest mysteries of Rome is just what the women did all day. The great ladies led a full life, collecting divorces and trying out the newest cosmetics from the east, but the rest seem hardly to have left their homes except for the baths, dinner parties, and public shows. The men did all the shopping. After the sweating, bustling market, packed between some of Rome's most elegant temples and theatres, the Campus Martius provided a remarkable contrast, the garden spot of Rome, almost a square mile of stately quadrangles and parks, the promenade of the wealthy—but an amenity open to any Roman with time on his hands.
>
> Marcus will lounge, gab, and soak in the Baths of Nero, until about 6 pm. The baths are still Rome's largest, though dwarfed by Trajan's new complex on the Mons Oppius; these are due to open in a month or so, and they will be a revolution in Roman leisure. Nero's makes a good prototype for the monster baths of Trajan, Caracalla, and Diocletian, with exercise yards, libraries, exhibition rooms, and snack bars. Men and women used them together (until Hadrian's time); the actual bath usually meant some sitting and sweating in the sudatoria; a splash of hot water in the caldarium, scraped off with an instrument known as the strigil; cooling off in the tepidarium, and finally the frigidarium, a quick plunge in a cold bath.

Marcus makes his way down Via Lata, where the shops are boarding up and locking their fronts, and through the nearly empty Imperial fora. On his own street, Marcus is hailed in from the cookshop; dinner is ready. He carries it up the stairs, and the day closes with a nice little surprise—the relatives Boadicea invited over decided they couldn't make it; they're afraid of staying out after dark. The Subura may not be so bad after all. The oil lamps burn on through a long pleasant repast, and after Marcus' last visit to his flat's modern luxury it's time for bed. A little wax for the ears to keep out the continual rumble of carts in the street below, and another day in the Caput Mundi reaches its end.

Without fireplaces, or any kind of ventilation, it can't be surprising that even the poorer Romans left the cooking to someone else. The flats were small and sparsely furnished, and all Romans—at least the men—spent as little time as possible in them. Besides the bed, a few chests and tables, this flat has a fine wooden triclinium with cushions for dining. Ancient Romans were as obsessed as their modern counterparts with digestion, though their superstitions on the subject are often diametrically opposed. The ancients ate their big meal after dark, and they always ate reclining on couches. Tonight they attacked their swordfish with knives and a variety of little spoons, but no forks—a Byzantine invention.

Not only in the Subura were Romans leery about walking by night. Street crime was probably worse than most cities today, and anyone who could afford it took an armed escort to dinner parties. (You may have noticed that Marcus didn't have a single slave; with Rome's striking inequalities of wealth, a man would have either twenty, or a few thousand, or none at all.) Not only were the streets dangerous, but extremely dark and narrow, with the tall insulae shutting out even the moon. There was no lighting, and no street signs or addresses; it would be easy to get lost even in your own neighbourhood. The main streets, oddly enough, were as busy at night as in the day—thanks to Julius Cæsar, who tried to ease the endless traffic jams by banning all delivery carts during daytime.

The strongest poison ever known
Came from Cæsar's laurel crown.

—William Blake

The Legends   50
The Guesses behind the Myths   51
Rome Conquers Italy and a Bit More   54

History

From Republic to Empire   56
Rome's Middle Age   58
The New Rome   61
The End of Papal Rule   62
Rome in the '90s   64

According to the Romans' own legends, volcanic eruptions forced them down to the Tiber valley sometime about 1000 BC. And that is a perfect introduction to the problems of Roman history—like a million other legends concocted in antiquity, it isn't true. The real beginnings of their city are lost in a Tiber mist. Some finds of pottery around the Capitol go back to 1200 BC. By 900, scattered settlements had sprouted all over Rome's hills. Culturally, these Romans were at the back of the class, but they had two very accomplished neighbours to learn from: the **Greeks**, and more importantly, the **Etruscans**. In the 8th century the Greeks began founding the rich and magnificent cities of Magna Graecia (southern Italy and Sicily) whose merchants traded everywhere along the Tyrrhenian coast. Accounts of the powerful Etruscan nation, which covered modern Tuscany and parts of Campania and North Italy, usually include the adjective 'mysterious'. No one can say for sure where the Etruscans came from, though a possibility is Asia Minor, about 900 BC; their language has yet to be completely deciphered, and their political history and complex, secretive religion have vexed scholars for centuries.

In the 8th century BC, the Etruscan confederation of city-states was an empire that dominated the Italian peninsula. Rome, lying on its main route of communications, became strategically crucial. The Etruscans probably ruled it for much of the 7th and 6th centuries, welding the little villages on the hills into a city.

The Legends

To understand Rome, though, the city's own myths of its beginnings are as important as the elusive facts. For a detailed account, there is Livy, the 1st-century BC historian who provided the most complete account (and himself invented some of it), and his contemporary Virgil. Rome's greatest poet, under the spell of Greek culture, sought to give the new mistress of the world a proper classical background in his *Aeneid*, embellishing the tale of Aeneas, who fled the sack of Troy and found his way to Latium after dallying with the Carthaginian Queen Dido. Livy wanted to emphasize Rome's difference, and also embellished its origins to provide a divine ordination for the city's tremendous destiny.

Livy begins in the ancient Latin capital, Alba Longa (founded, according to Virgil, by Aeneas' son Ascanius) with Numitor, a Latin king whose throne was usurped by his brother Amulius. To preclude contending heirs, Amulius forced Numitor's only daughter, Rhea Sylvia, into service as a Vestal Virgin. Destiny intervened when the god Mars appeared in the Vestals' chambers, leaving her pregnant with twins **Romulus and Remus**. Following one of the world's best known fairytale motifs, Amulius found out and packed the baby twins away in a little basket, like Moses, adrift on the waters. The gods steered them up the Tiber to safe harbour in the Velabrum, the marshes under the Capitoline Hill, where the famous she-wolf looked after the twins until a kindly shepherd took them home. Years later,

Mars appeared again to explain to the grown-up twins their origins and destiny. They travelled to Alba Longa to settle accounts with Amulius, then returned to found the city Mars had commanded. According to Livy, the year was 753 BC.

In another enduring fairytale motif, the brothers soon fell out, like Cain and Abel (for Remus' demise, see Palatine Hill, p. 123). Romulus invited one and all to join with his combative new city. The episode of the Sabine women came soon after, when the Romans, lacking females, resolved to steal some from their neighbours. Romulus was the first of Rome's legendary seven kings. The next, **Numa Pompilius**, was a prophet, who visited a learned nymph named Egeria to learn how to lay down the rules for Rome's cults, priesthoods and auguries. After him came **Tullius Hostilius**, who extended Rome's rule over most of Latium, and **Ancus Martius**, who founded the port of Ostia. The next king, **Tarquinius Priscus**, was an Etruscan, who built Rome into a true city, erecting the Circus Maximus and digging the Cloaca Maxima to drain the area around the Forum.

His successor, according to Livy, was a Latin, Servius Tullius. He began the class division of Roman society into patricians (the Senatorial class) and plebeians, and built his great wall to keep the Etruscans out. Apparently it did not work as planned, for the next king, Tarquinius Superbus (about 534 BC), was an Etruscan, and another great builder. His misfortune was to have a hot-headed son, Tarquinius Sextus, who imposed himself on a virtuous Roman maiden named Lucretia (cf. Shakespeare's Rape of Lucrece). She committed public suicide the next morning, and the enraged Romans, led by Lucius Junius Brutus (later to be the first consul), chased out Tarquin and the Etruscans, and established the Roman Republic before the day was out.

For the next episode, you can follow an even better storyteller than Livy— Macaulay in his stirring epic *Horatius*, about the brave fellow who defended the bridge when Lars Porsena of Clusium and the Etruscan allies came down to recapture the city. As the young republic went from success to success, the patriotic legends continued to multiply: old Cincinnatus accepting the title of Dictator to defeat the neighbouring Aequians, then returning quietly to his farm; the sack by the marauding Gauls in 390, when the cackling of the geese saved the Romans bottled up in their citadel on the Capitol.

The Guesses behind the Myths

Making sense of all this is a problem. Most of the figures mentioned above may well have been historical; the traditional date of 509 for the founding of the Republic was probably fixed later to coincide with the expulsion of the last tyrant from Athens. Servius' Wall, according to the archaeologists, really went up over a century and a half after his legendary reign, in the 370s. And Horatius or not,

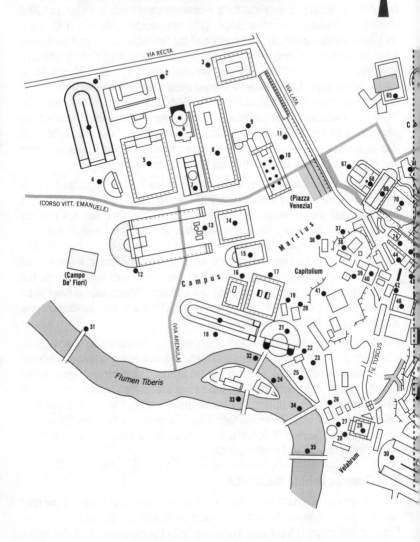

Central Rome 300 AD

N

VIA RECTA

VIA LATA

(CORSO VITT. EMANUELE)

(Piazza Venezia)

(Campo De' Fiori)

Campus

Martius

Capitolium

VIA ARENULA

Flumen Tiberis

V. TUSCUS

Velabrum

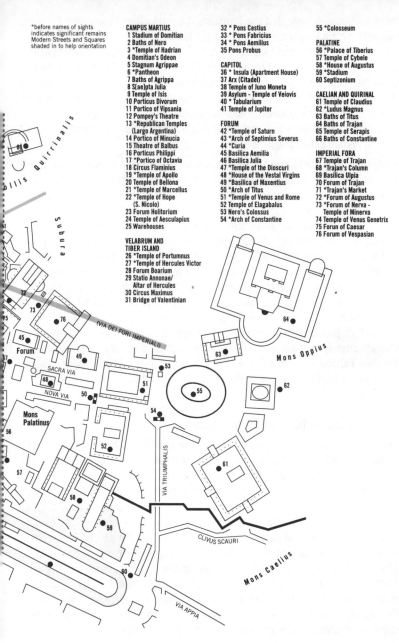

CAMPUS MARTIUS
1 Stadium of Domitian
2 Baths of Nero
3 *Temple of Hadrian
4 Domitian's Odeon
5 Stagnum Agrippae
6 *Pantheon
7 Baths of Agrippa
8 S(ae)pta Julia
9 Temple of Isis
10 Porticus Divorum
11 Portico of Vipsania
12 Pompey's Theatre
13 *Republican Temples
   (Largo Argentina)
14 Portico of Minucia
15 Theatre of Balbus
16 Porticus Philippi
17 *Portico of Octavia
18 Circus Flaminius
19 *Temple of Apollo
20 Temple of Bellona
21 *Temple of Marcellus
22 *Temple of Hope
   (S. Nicolo)
23 Forum Holitorium
24 Temple of Aesculapius
25 Warehouses

**VELABRUM AND
TIBER ISLAND**
26 *Temple of Portumnus
27 *Temple of Hercules Victor
28 Forum Boarium
29 Statio Annonae/
   Altar of Hercules
30 Circus Maximus
31 Bridge of Valentinian

32 * Pons Cestius
33 * Pons Fabricius
34 * Pons Aemilius
35 Pons Probus

CAPITOL
36 * Insula (Apartment House)
37 Arx (Citadel)
38 Temple of Juno Moneta
39 Asylum - Temple of Veiovis
40 * Tabularium
41 Temple of Jupiter

FORUM
42 *Temple of Saturn
43 *Arch of Septimius Severus
44 *Curia
45 Basilica Aemilia
46 Basilica Julia
47 *Temple of the Dioscuri
48 *House of the Vestal Virgins
49 *Basilica of Maxentius
50 *Arch of Titus
51 *Temple of Venus and Rome
52 Temple of Elagabalus
53 Nero's Colossus
54 *Arch of Constantine

55 *Colosseum

PALATINE
56 *Palace of Tiberius
57 Temple of Cybele
58 *House of Augustus
59 *Stadium
60 Septizonium

CAELIAN AND QUIRINAL
61 Temple of Claudius
62 *Ludus Magnus
63 Baths of Titus
64 Baths of Trajan
65 Temple of Serapis
66 Baths of Constantine

IMPERIAL FORA
67 Temple of Trajan
68 *Trajan's Column
69 Basilica Ulpia
70 Forum of Trajan
71 *Trajan's Market
72 *Forum of Augustus
73 *Forum of Nerva -
   Temple of Minerva
74 Temple of Venus Genetrix
75 Forun of Caesar
76 Forum of Vespasian

*before names of sights
indicates significant remains
Modern Streets and Squares
shaded in to help orientation

some historians believe that the Etruscans did retake Rome soon after Tarquin, and held it for a long while. Whenever the Romans finally did break away, they took a powerful Etruscan heritage with them, including their alphabet (with a later Greek influence), and much vocabulary—hundreds of our English words derive from the Etruscan, by way of Latin: person, for example, from an Etruscan word meaning the mask of an actor. The Etruscans also gave the Romans most of their gods and rituals, divination and the taking of auspices, the circus and gladiatorial games; even the lictors' rods (later Mussolini's *fasces*) were an old Etruscan symbol, carried before magistrates as a symbol of authority .

But this growing, half-Etruscan city was already beginning to develop a strong personality of its own. Usually, the Romans expressed their young and carefree souls by waging unending warfare against their neighbours. In the 5th century their city became a formidable rival to its economically declining Etruscan neighbours (the nearest important Etruscan town, **Veii**, was only twelve miles away), while fighting constant campaigns to subjugate the rest of the Latins and tribes even further afield. At home, the militarist fathers of the Republic had to deal with unrest among the lower classes, who did most of the fighting and got to keep few of the spoils. In 494, the plebeians managed to establish a magistracy called the tribunate to look after their interests. In 450, they pulled off perhaps history's first general strike, or 'secession', resulting in the codification and publication of the laws, which previously had been held as a religious secret among the patricians (a very effective way of keeping the law on your side). The result was the famous **Twelve Tables**, in a sense Rome's constitution, drawn up by a temporary junta of ten called the Decemvirate (450) and published on bronze tablets displayed in the Forum.

Rome Conquers Italy, and a Bit More

There was indeed a sack of Rome around the year 390, a brief interruption to Rome's march of conquest. An army of nomadic **Gauls** from the north swooped down on one of their regular raids. When the Romans put up a hard-nosed resistance, the angry Celts took and sacked Rome itself, agreeing to leave only after payment of a stiff tribute. Archaeologists digging today always find a layer of ashes and rubble to record the event. But Rome soon recovered its momentum. Already its arch-enemy Veii had been conquered and razed to the ground. The rest of southern Etruria was Rome's by mid-century, but the Romans needed another fifty years to swallow up the powerful **Samnites** in the mountains to the east. After them, no power in Italy was left to resist the invincible Republic. The frightened Greek cities of the south sought aid from a military adventurer named Pyrrhus of Epirus. He crossed over to Italy and won Pyrrhic victories—never pursuing his advantage—but the Romans caught up with him too, in 272.

Other cities lived by trade or manufactures; Rome, disdaining any sort of honest living, had discovered that continuous small-scale conquest proved much more profitable. Indeed, constant conquest was absolutely necessary to keep the military machine oiled, and province after province was sucked dry to feed Roman avarice and meet the army's budget. The system was working so well, class conflict remained muted, though never completely extinguished—patricians and plebeians alike realized the benefits of working together—and Rome was always able to face its victims with unbroken determination. Its success in the next century was beyond anyone's dreams. In the **Punic Wars** (264–146) the total defeat of rival predator Carthage gave Rome the entire western Mediterranean. Looking eastwards, politically-divided Greece was digested by 168. The equally disunited remnants of Alexander the Great's empire in the east proved easy marks, and by 64 AD Rome's legions were camped on the Cataracts of the Nile, in Jerusalem, and halfway across Asia Minor.

But every success only tended to confirm Rome in the worst side of its character. The old myths about Roman law and virtue can be safely dismissed—Roman rule under the Republic meant an organized, systematic looting that never stopped. An endless stream of money and slaves flowed into the city. Taxation ceased for the relatively small number of Roman citizens, and cheap requisitioned imports of grain ruined most of the farmers, allowing the Roman elite to buy up most of their land and turn Italy into a nation of landed barons and helpless sharecroppers. Many Italian cities actually withered and died in this period, especially those of the Greeks and Etruscans. Country districts became abandoned, their populations fleeing to the only place where work and safety were to be had—in Rome, where the new rich always could use more help, to look after the household while they learned the delights of orgies, gladiatorial combats, and being carried about in the streets by slaves.

Not that Rome's victims failed to resist. A Popular Party did its best to effect reforms, but the new rich of the landed nobility, the 'Optimates', managed to have every one of their leaders murdered. In 133, a remarkable politician named **Tiberius Gracchus** was elected tribune; his plans for land reform earned him assassination the following year. Brother **Gaius Gracchus** went even further, attempting to turn Rome into a genuine democracy, but the Senate had him murdered too. After more of the same, and a disappointing interval of mildly Popular rule under a military strongman named **Gaius Marius** (roughly 100–91), all Italy rose in revolt. The **Social Wars** (92–89), and the famous slaves' rebellion of **Spartacus** (73), both ended as grisly proofs of the Roman elite's monopoly of force. Their privileges were saved, at the cost of permanently deranging the institutions of the Republic.

From Republic to Empire

Optimates and Populists alike realized that the only real power lay with the army, and the last vestiges of the rule of law soon disappeared. After Marius, a reactionary general named **Sulla** made a military coup with the aid of the Senate (82), establishing the bloodiest dictatorship Rome had ever seen. After his death, power passed to the immensely vain but apolitical and intelligent general Pompey, who shared it after 59 in the **First Triumvirate** with a crooked building magnate named Crassus and a young upstart who went into politics to pay his debts, **Julius Cæsar**. Like any aspiring Roman politician, what Cæsar wanted was not a meaningless title of authority in the city , but a military command abroad. He got it, conquered Gaul, crossed the Rubicon in 50 (the worried Senate had forbidden his return to Italy), and defeated Pompey two years later to become unchallenged master of Rome.

Despite repression and incessant civil war, a gradual transformation was coming over the old pirate's nest. The rough and ready appearance of the metropolis slowly blossomed into marbled urbanity, as both Pompey and Cæsar began important building programmes. Both built theatres, an indication of how Greek culture was finally making its way into Rome. Romans began to reflect on the meaning of their republicanism, and on the responsibilities that came with power. This Rome of the 1st century BC could produce a man like **Marcus Tullius Cicero**, who made a name for himself by prosecuting, and convicting, a governor who stole a bit too much from the province he was given. Cicero represented what was left of the Italian middle classes—but too late; his dreams of a stable, constitutional Republic came to naught in the end, caught between his own political ineptitude and the rapacity of his opponents.

And the age produced Cæsar, who took up the popular cause in better style than anyone before, and reformed everything in Rome, even the calendar. His just and decisive government did much to heal the scars of oppression and civil war. His murder in 44 by a clique of Senatorial bitter-enders brought another spell of war; when the dust settled thirteen years later, Cæsar's adopted son Octavian came out on top, and continued his reforms, liberally dispensing Cleopatra's expropriated treasure to grease the way. Personal rule was nicely institutionalized; keeping up the forms of the dead Republic, Octavian occupied most of the offices, modestly referring to himself as princeps ('first citizen'). Less modestly, he had Cæsar declared a god, and renamed himself **Augustus**. For the city, the grandeur of which had long lagged behind its power and wealth, his rule was golden. Augustus transformed 'a city of brick into one of marble'; imposing new temples, basilicas, and theatres sprang up everywhere, especially in the Campus Martius, and the first of the Imperial Fora was begun.

Probably about this time Rome's population passed the million mark, soon surpassing Antioch and Alexandria as the greatest city in the world. Augustus' Rome, governmental and financial metropolis of the West, was also the city of Horace and Virgil, for the first time a cultural centre in its own right. The reigns of future emperors, good or bad, had little effect on the city except to give Romans something to talk about at dinner parties; you can rake over all the dirt in history's first and sleaziest gossip column, Suetonius' Lives of the Cæsars. One big event was the great fire of 23 April 64 AD, under Emperor Nero, in which a quarter of the city went up in flames. Another was the completion of the Colosseum in 81, the definitive monument to Rome's conspicuous consumption, not only of money, but blood.

Still the ultimate predator, Rome produced nothing and consumed everything. No one with any spare denarii would be foolish enough to go into business with them, when the real money was to be made from government, speculation, or real estate. At times most of the population was on the dole—not necessarily because they were poor, but because of the time-honoured tradition of buying citizens' loyalty with cheap food and spectacles. No city, even in our own times, has ever been so unabashedly obsessed with money and the things it can buy; some poets, like Horace, devote much of their attention to accounts of dinner parties and new luxuries from the east, while the more honest ones, like Juvenal, paint a ghoulish, insatiable Rome of unnatural vices and brazen crimes, intrigues and poisons, where 'every street is thronged with gloomy-faced debauchees'.

The empire, in the unparalleled prosperity of the 1st and 2nd centuries, could afford to indulge its wayward capital. While the last monstrous heirs of Augustus—Tiberius, Caligula and Nero—outdid even their subjects, Augustus' disciplined civil service managed to keep the ship of state on an even keel. In the 2nd century, an unbroken string of good emperors—Trajan and Hadrian (both gay Spaniards), and the **Antonines**, Antoninus Pius and Marcus Aurelius—gave the empire sympathetic, effective government and victorious peace, while bestowing on Rome many of its finest monuments. When times got rougher, with the military setbacks and economic crises of the 3rd century, the Mediterranean world began to see that it could no longer support Rome in the manner to which it had become accustomed. And in 275, the threat of invasions caused Emperor Aurelian to give Rome a wall, the first in over 600 years. By that time, the city was already an irrelevant, bloated backwater, and emperors spent most of their time in the east, or up at army headquarters in Mediolanum (Milan). Army recruiters had stopped taking conscripts from the city sometime in the 2nd century—the centurions all said real Romans were too sick and debauched to make decent soldiers.

By 300, Rome's empire had become a shabby, impoverished totalitarian state, a nightmare of taxmen and roughhouse police, run by the army and all but abandoned by its rotten ruling classes. **Constantine**, a cruel but energetic emperor (304–37), did Rome the double indignity of moving the imperial capital to his new foundation, Constantinople, and tossing aside the city's ancient religious traditions by promoting the wealthy and influential cult of the Christians. The last great imperial builder, Constantine's works included an impressive programme of Christian basilicas. By 400, with both the economy and the military in a state of utter collapse, the barbarians were knocking politely at the door. Few Romans could be found to defend the state, and barbarian generals guarded the western empire while its emperors hid out in the impregnable new capital, Ravenna. **Alaric the Goth**, invading Italy in 410, didn't get the tribute the Romans had promised him, so he simply broke in and treated the city to a cautious, respectful sacking. Alaric did little damage, but the news of the sack resounded across the Roman world like the Trump of Doom.

The next visitor, in 452, was **Attila the Hun**. There were no armies to stop him, but the real leader of Rome—Pope Leo I—somehow talked him into leaving the city in peace. **Genseric the Vandal** passed through three years later, a conscientious sacker the long-dead Roman heroes would have appreciated—he stole everything that wasn't nailed down. In 475, Odoacer the Goth pensioned off the last western emperor and Italy became a Gothic kingdom. Under his successor, Theodoric, it was a peaceful and prosperous place, popular mythology notwithstanding. In Rome, chariot races were still on the bill at the Circus Maximus, new churches were built, and the decadent nobility still held on to its immense wealth and privileges. No longer a capital (Theodoric ruled from Ravenna), the city had shrunk ; the Gothic King had to pass laws to keep the Romans from dismantling their own monuments for building stone, and from stealing the gilt and bronze statues. With no new prey to batten on, Rome was beginning to devour itself.

Rome's Middle Age

The serious disasters came not at the hands of barbarians—but of Romans. Eastern Emperor Justinian's invasion of Italy in 538 plunged the entire peninsula into chaos and misery. Rome changed hands several times during the long wars. During King Totila's siege of Rome in 546, when the population may have been down to a few hundreds, the aqueducts were cut and never after repaired; their water flooded the surrounding districts, turning them into malarial swamps. People were forced to abandon their homes on the hills, to camp out among the decaying ruins of the Campus Martius, and to drink the infected waters of the Tiber. They died in their thousands, and Rome never recovered. Recurring plagues and famines, along with the invasion of the truly barbaric Lombards (567) kept the city on the skids, though a number of able and energetic popes did their best to ameliorate the situation—especially **Gregory the Great** (590–604), who brought much relief to the starving Romans, and laid the foundations for the papacy as a temporal power.

Gregory had been the heir of Rome's richest family. It isn't often realized that the well-run and thriving Roman Church of these times was almost entirely a creation of the Roman nobility, and would remain so for centuries. Strangely, almost miraculously, this class managed to shed the drowsiness of its imperial decadence, recapturing some of the iron resolve of the brave days of old. Pooling their resources by donating vast properties to the Church, the nobles exchanged togas for surplices and cassocks, and survived—bringing to their new job the monomania and will to power that had always distinguished them.

Thanks to them, Dark Age Rome never went entirely dark. Crowds of pilgrims still came every year. New churches were built, and decorated with glittering Byzantine mosaics. There were still libraries, and scholars to use them. Especially in the 8th and 9th centuries, under able popes like **Adrian I** and **Leo III**, both great builders, a rebirth of culture and unity seemed to be under way. The popes had found new protectors, the powerful Frankish kings, and when Leo placed an Imperial crown on **Charlemagne**'s head in St Peter's, on Christmas Eve in 800, a partnership was sealed that would change Europe. Oddly enough, Charlemagne wasn't expecting it; the pope sneaked up behind him with the crown while he was praying. Nevertheless, Charlemagne couldn't or wouldn't undo the fait accompli, and the idea was born that Holy Roman Emperors had to get their crown from a Roman pontiff. Besides this brilliant trick, the popes cooked up two outrageous forgeries, the 'Donation of Constantine' and the 'Donation of Pepin', to support their claims to absolute authority over the princes of Christendom. Cæsar's ghost was stirring once more.

Unfortunately, the rapid decline of Frankish power after Charlemagne brought big troubles to Italy once more. Saracen raiders occupied parts of Latium and Campania (one of their bases was a mountain village above Rome called Saracinesco, where their descendants still live) and raided Rome itself in 846, looting St Peter's. In the strife of the terrible 9th century, power in Rome fell to a remarkable pair of ladies, **Theodora** and her daughter **Marozia**. Theodora, who after about 880 assumed the title Senatrix (somehow the old word had come to refer to a single public office), meant to turn back from papal pretensions and found a little state, with her family as dynasts. Marozia, an even more formidable woman, has suffered some sensational character assassination from male chauvinist historians (her career may be one of the sources of the legend of 'Pope Joan').

She dominated Rome, making her lovers and children into popes, until 932, when her son **Alberic** performed a neat coup d'état—not just another change of rulers, but a genuine revolution. For the first time, Rome stood secular and independent. Alberic reformed both Church and state, and pointed the way for Rome to become a free republican comune as other cities all over Italy were doing. The situation became more complicated after his death. In fact the 10th and 11th centuries in Rome were pure anarchy, with nobles like the **Crescenzi** seizing Castel Sant'Angelo and declaring themselves 'Consuls', German emperors making regular expeditions over the Alps to sort things out, and new popes and anti-popes sprouting almost each year. In the 10th century alone, nine popes managed to get themselves murdered.

The banana papacy did not get back on the track until the 1070s, and then it was due largely to the strenuous efforts of a reforming cleric named Hildebrand; he eventually became pope as **Gregory VII** in 1075. Rome's power returned, enough to humble the German emperors and to proclaim the First Crusade in 1097. Along the way, in 1084, the popes' supposed Norman allies under **Robert Guiscard** treated the city to its worst sacking ever. Though the popes were strong enough to meddle in the affairs of all Europe, the 12th century proved almost as confusing and bloody as those before. The 1140s, for example, witnessed the spectacle of a Jewish pope (Anacletus II, head of Rome's powerful Pierleoni family) while the mighty city of the Cæsars was making war on its little neighbour Tivoli, and losing. A sincere monkish reformer appeared, **Arnold of Brescia**, preaching democratic ideals and the divorce of the Church from temporal power. In 1145, his supporters re-established the Roman Republic, complete with Consuls and Senate. Ten years later, he was captured by Emperor Frederick I, and given over to Pope Adrian IV (Nicholas Breakspear, the only English pope) for torture and hanging.

At the century's close, the occupant of St Peter's throne was **Innocent III**, perhaps the most powerful of all popes, able to make his will obeyed everywhere in Europe—excepting occasionally Rome. In the 1200s, popes had to contend not only with determined emperors like Frederick II, and feudal, virtually sovereign Roman families like the legendary **Colonna** and **Orsini**, but also with the Roman people, still trying to keep something of Arnold's Republic alive. For all the troubles, it was a brilliant age for art in Rome, and a time of great prosperity. An especially vile pope, **Boniface VIII** (1294–1303), spoiled it. His high-handed behaviour, trying to fill the shoes of Innocent III, lost the papacy whatever friends it had in Europe. After he died, the French King purchased the election of a French pope, **Clement V**, who packed the Vatican with French cardinals, and then, in 1305, moved the whole show to Avignon.

For Rome, the effect was war, plague and depression all in one. The parasite city that had been living off the pennies of Europe's faithful for so long now found itself cut off from its only source of income, while Orsinis, Colonnas and their imitators raged unchecked in the streets. Much of the city began to look abandoned, as the population dropped to its lowest level in 800 years. To fill the vacuum, there appeared the improbable figure of **Cola di Rienzo**, the self-educated son of a washerwoman, whose musings among the monuments and inscriptions of antiquity fired him with an obsessive passion for returning his city to its former greatness. He meant to accomplish it in the grand old Roman manner, by means of rhetoric. Bending the ears of anyone who would listen, the young orator literally talked Rome into declaring the Republic once more, in May of 1347; the nobles, for all their gangs of warriors, couldn't do a thing to stop it.

Unfortunately, history has shown few examples of power corrupting so quickly, and so absolutely. Rienzo ruled with almost insane conceit and arrogance, claiming dominion for Rome over the entire world. Though the Republic's citizen militia defeated the noble forces, a complete loss of popular support forced Rienzo to abdicate in November of the same year. In 1354, though obese and decayed, he returned and seduced the Romans again. The result was the same, and Rienzo met his end later in the year, torn to pieces by a mob of once-loyal citizens.

Thanks largely to another great persuader, St Catherine of Siena, Pope Gregory XI finally returned to Rome in 1377—though anti-popes remained in Avignon and Pisa for decades. A successful Jubilee Year in 1390 paid for some needed repairs, and Rome was back in business.

The New Rome

The old papacy, before Avignon, had been a simple instrument of the Roman nobility; periods when it was able to achieve real independence were the exception rather than the rule. In the more settled conditions of the 1400s, a new papacy emerged, richer and more sophisticated. Political power, as a guarantee of stability, was always its goal, and a series of talented Renaissance popes saw their best hopes for achieving this in rebuilding Rome. **Martin V** (a Colonna) and **Nicholas V** (1447–55) contributed perhaps the most to this process. By the 1500s it was in full swing. Under **Julius II** (1503–13), the papal domains for the first time were run like a modern state; Julius also laid plans for the rebuilding of St Peter's, beginning the great building programme that was to transform the city. New streets were laid out, especially the Via Giulia and the grand avenues radiating from the Piazza del Popolo; Julius' main architect, Bramante, knocked down medieval Rome with such gay abandon that Raphael nicknamed him 'Ruinante'.

Over the next two centuries, the work continued at a frenetic pace. Besides St Peter's, hundreds of churches were either built or rebuilt, and cardinals and noble families lined the streets with new palaces, imposing if not always beautiful. The new Rome, symbol of the Counter-Reformation and the majesty of the popes, was, however, bought dearly. Besides the destruction by Bramante, buildings that had survived substantially intact for 1500 years were cannibalized for their marble; the popes wantonly ruined more of ancient Rome than Goths or Saracens had ever managed.

In the general prosperity of the time, and despite the Reformation (caused partly by the increased sale of indulgences and Church offices by **Leo X**, the Medici Pope, 1513–22), money poured into Rome as never before. The 'Renaissance popes', from the poisonous Borgia Alexander VI on, have a wonderful reputation as enlightened men of the world and patrons of arts and letters that is largely deserved. On the other hand, each of them ranks among the most cynically corrupt and murderous popes of all time. More than ever, the papacy became a private club among the leading Italian noble houses, devoted entirely to their enrichment and blithely unconcerned with the state of the faith. In the papal auction, it cost millions to get elected—but you knew you would get it back with interest. When the Church's money no longer sufficed for their appetites, they began taxing the economy of the Papal States out of existence. Areas of Lazio that had been relatively prosperous even in the Dark Ages turned into wastelands as exasperated farmers simply abandoned them, and the other cities of Lazio and Umbria were set back centuries in their development. The new Rome was proving as voracious a predator as the old.

Through the previous century the last vestiges of Roman civic liberty had been gradually extinguished. Now, the popes allied themselves alternately with Spain, France or the Emperor to extend their power, decisively contributing to the gradual enslavement of all Italy by foreign powers. In doing so, they reaped a bitter harvest in the 1527 **Sack of Rome**. An out-of-control imperial army, made up of Spaniards, Italians and German Lutherans, occupied the city for almost a year, causing tremendous destruction, while the calamitous Pope **Clement VII** looked on helplessly from Castel Sant'Angelo. Afterwards, the popes were happy to become part of the Imperial-Spanish system. Political repression was fiercer than anywhere else in Italy; the Inquisition was refounded in 1542 by **Paul III**, and book burnings, torture of freethinkers, and executions became more common than in Spain itself.

The End of Papal Rule

By about 1610, there was no Roman foolish enough to get burned at the stake; at the same time workmen were adding the last stones to the cupola of St Peter's. It was the end of an era, but the building continued. A thick accretion of Baroque, some coral and some barnacle, collected over Rome. Bernini made his Piazza Navona fountain in 1650, and the Colonnade for St Peter's 15 years later. The political importance of the popes, however, disappeared with surprising finality.

As Joseph Stalin was later to note, the popes had plenty of Bulls but few divisions; having turned Italy into a political backwater, and exhausted the moral capital of their Church, they drifted into irrelevance in the power politics of modern Europe during the Thirty Years' War and after. Rome was left to enjoy a decadent but rather pleasant twilight. The papacy remained as venal as ever—nearly all the popes managed a grand palace or two for their families. Carnival and fireworks shows were never better. No one in Rome starved, as religious charities began to take on some of the character of the ancient imperial dole, and the worldly Romans learned to polish their lives into the *dolce vita* of a city that had seen it all.

This was the Rome that proved so irresistible to northern Europeans at the beginning of the Grand Tour. Even the Protestants had a good time, and found it easy enough to slide around the religious laws and sleepy Inquisitors. A brief interruption to this pleasant state of affairs came with **Napoleon**'s invasion in 1796, when much of the city's wealth, and tons of its art treasures were methodically carted off to Paris. In 1798, the French once more proclaimed the Roman Republic, and sent the pope packing. Rome later became part of Napoleon's empire, but papal rule was restored in 1815.

The reaction was complete, though not harsh, and Romans seemed not too unhappy about sliding back into the 18th century. But when another Roman Republic appeared in February 1849, at the crest of the 1848 revolutionary wave, the populace responded with surprising fervour. The great revolutionary intriguer, **Giuseppe Mazzini**, took charge, and a Ligurian sailor named **Giuseppe Garibaldi**, with experience in South American guerrilla wars, came to lead the militia. A French army besieged the city; despite a heroic resistance they had the pope propped back on his throne by July.

Napoleon III maintained a garrison to look after the pope, and consequently Rome became the last part of Italy to join the new Italian kingdom. When the Prussians sorted out France in 1870, the opportunity was clear. Italian troops blasted a hole in the old Aurelian Wall near the Porta Pia and cakewalked in. Pius IX, who ironically had decreed Papal Infallibility just the year before, locked himself in the Vatican and pouted; the popes were to be 'prisoners' until the Concordat of 1929. The Italians confiscated most of the monasteries and the pope's Quirinale Palace, knocked down the walls of the Jewish ghetto, and freed the last three woebegone prisoners of the Inquisition.

As capital of the new state, Rome underwent another building boom; new streets like Via del Tritone, Via Vittorio Veneto, and Via Nazionale made circulation a little easier around the seven hills. The bottom fell out of the market for lumber as literally millions of trees were cut down, and the lovely villas and gardens that once encircled the city disappeared under endless blocks of tawdry speculative building (everything round Termini Station, for example). The new Italian kingdom strove mightily to impress the world with gigantic, absurd public buildings and monuments, such as the Altar of the Nation and the Finance Ministry on Via XX Settembre, as big as two Colosseums. More damage was done under Mussolini, who drove wide automobile roads through the picturesque city centre, isolating and sanitizing innumerable ancient ruins.

From the Italian armistice in 1943 until 5 June 1944, Rome found itself on short rations under a rough German occupation. The city's Resistance acquitted itself bravely; as many as 200,000 people—Jews, escaped Allied prisoners and anti-Fascists—were hidden in homes and convents, while Socialist and Communist guerrillas did their best to sabotage the Germans. Their success provoked vicious reprisals like the Fosse Ardeatine massacre, when 335 prisoners from the Regina Coeli prison were murdered in retaliation for a guerrilla bombing. Serious destruction of the city was averted by the careful aim of the Allied air forces (of all the churches, only S. Lorenzo was badly damaged, though homes, hospitals and even the Vatican were occasionally hit), and by the good graces of Adolf Hitler and Feldmarschall von Kesselring, who pulled out their armies and declared Rome an Open City as soon as the Allies approached it.

In the charmed '50s, Rome caught the imagination of the world, if only for the brilliant films of Fellini, de Sica, Visconti and the rest, pouring out of Cinecittà. Mass tourism arrived, and the city continued to dilate unattractively in all directions. By the '70s, the magic illusion of La Dolce Vita was only a memory—with the collapse of the Italian film industry, the government briefly considered selling off Cinecittà for building lots. As Rome's urban problems increased, Italy's 'Years of Lead' made the city a reluctant centre stage for a decade of terrorism and political sleaze, which reached its climax with the kidnapping and murder of Prime Minister Aldo Moro in 1978.

Rome in the '90s

> Rome is inhabited by know-nothings who do not want to be disturbed. They are perfect products of the Church, the type of people who have become so gangrenous in their own secular condition that they believe they can and must live only like this. The Roman is like a grotesque, overgrown child who has the satisfaction of being continually spanked by the Pope.
>
> —*Federico Fellini*

Rome's own newspapers have called it the 'anti-città', a 'mega-factory of poisons', a rancid, uninhabitable city, close behind Naples in the race towards complete social and environmental collapse. Allowances must always be made for Italian journalistic exaggeration, but few Romans would argue the point that their city's quality of life is rapidly deteriorating, and that nothing will be done about it for at least the remainder of the millennium.

At first glance, Rome's problems do not seem overwhelming. Visitors will notice the traffic first, choking the medieval alleys and fouling the air. Crime, though steadily rising, is rarely evident. Even muggings are usually swift – you're far more likely to have a handbag snatched by a pasing Vespa rider than to have it taken at knife point. Drug addiction is a major problem – far worse than it is in Britain. Termini Station and the streets around are full of desolate junkies, and wandering around the city outskirts and parks you increasingly come across areas littered with plastic eggs – heroin containers. As immigrants and refugees from Africa, the Philippines, Bangladesh, Sri Lanka and Eastern Europe flock to the city, membership of neo-fascist groups such as the Fronte del Giovento and Naziskins has swelled. Watching Rome trying to deal with matters of urban development, housing and historical preservation makes a sorry spectacle, rather like meeting Laurel and Hardy in a pastry shop. But every modern city has its troubles. The only insurmountable problem facing Rome is its government. Things were apparently better a few years ago, when the Communists were in charge; buildings got fixed, street festivals filled the summer calendar, and serious plans were undertaken for the city's future.

To most Italians, the Christian Democratic Party is an allegory for Divine Inevitability, in a class with death, the VAT and blocked drains. When they regained power in Rome, as sooner or later they always do, all these initiatives became smothered in a damp caress of good intentions, bureaucratic obfuscation and avuncular incompetence and funding vanished down the plug-hole of corruption. Their approach to governing Rome is a textbook example of the smokescreen tactics political scientists call 'determining the agenda'. They do not care to tackle the traffic problem, so they draw up ever new, more complex schedules of streets closed to non-residential traffic which serves only to create a lucrative market for counterfeit access and parking permits. The latest dream is to turn much of central Rome – from Piazza Venezia to the Via Appia Antica – into an urban park. The funds are there, the plans have been drawn up, and land speculation has begun in suburbs, like Saxa Rubra, destined to become satellite towns of government offices. However, the odds on Rome transforming itself into the ideal city of the third millenium are not high. Despite a much publicized crusade against corruption, and an increasing number of super-grass *mafiosi*, you can nevertheless gamble on the probability that a good many politicians, *mafiosi*, landowners and construction industry magnates will be several billion lire richer by the year 2000.

In part, Rome's problems are a side effect of its queer destiny, a papal Gormeng-hast fated to become capital of a modern European state. The city that craves continual papal spankings, thrown into the First Division with London, Paris and Berlin, found itself constrained to become a cultural capital after 300 years of somnolence. Rome, already the capital of Italian bella figura, could handle the packaging, but never the content. Today it is a city of a hundred galleries, without the slightest hint of art; of famous theatres, without drama, cinema or music; of literary cafés, without a chance of intelligent conversation. Cultural life, as in the 18th century, depends entirely on foreigners and visiting artists. With an assured market for established goods, but an allergy to creativity of any kind, Rome would be hard pressed to match the level of cultural awareness you find in provincial American cities—places like Kansas City, Dallas or Pittsburgh.

Thanks to rent control, a bit of old Rome still lives on in the centre: the sarcastic old codger behind the bar, the saucy market ladies and the weary gents in var-nish-stained vests who restore gaudy Baroque furniture in tiny shops west of Campo de' Fiori. But most of the real Romans have been shunted off to the sub-urbs, to the faceless districts around Via Trionfale and Via Appia Nuova. In a city that has increased in population twentyfold in the last century, authenticity is at a premium. 'I'm a real Roman of the Romans …' someone tells you; later you find out what he means is that his grandfather moved here from Sicily.

Rents are as high as London or New York. The old folks feel under siege in the quarter between the Corso and the Tiber, as speculation drives up land values relentlessly. Everyone wants to live around Piazza Navona, or in Trastevere; leading the invasion is a remarkable sort of Roman yuppie, perhaps an entirely new species of humanity. You'll see them in their special shops, paying L250 000 for an old New York seltzer bottle. You'll see them in the cafés, nursing a scotch for two hours while they peek through their sunglasses to see if anyone is looking at them. If modern Rome has a marketable product, it must be desperate, existen-tial boredom, the sort of numb vacuity that used to inspire French novelists and philosophers, and now only serves to nourish the gilded indolence of a city that has been with us too long.

Political kickbacks have been Rome's middle name since the days of the Caesars, but no one suspected the depth of depravity the *tagentopoli* (kickback city) inves-tigations would uncover; nearly every recycled vampire in the nation's political class is currently under suspicion for diverting funds, mafia connections and even worse. In the referendum of April 1993 Italians overwhelmingly registered their disgust with their political system, and the hard and delicate task of reinventing a new one has just begun. Stay tuned: if Rome can shake loose the crud of milennia it will be a revolution even more amazing than the fall of the Berlin wall.

Roman Art and Architecture

The Etruscans   68

The Romans Learn Building   68

Roman Sculpture, Painting, Mosaics   70

Early Christian and Medieval Art   71

The Renaissance in Rome   73

The End of the Renaissance   75

The Art of the Counter-Reformation   75

The Age of Baroque   77

The Last of Roman Art   79

Perhaps a better title would be 'Art and Architecture in the Service of Rome'. There are three ways of decorating a city: doing it yourself, stealing other peoples' art outright, and taxing or tithing captive provinces to death and hiring away their artists with the proceeds. Rome, through almost all of its eternal story, has preferred the last two.

The Etruscans

Although Rome and Latium stood on the fringes of the Etruscan world, the young city could hardly help being overwhelmed by the presence of a superior culture almost on its doorstep. Along with much of its religion, customs, and its engineering talent, early Rome owed its first art to the enemies from the north. Not that there was ever much of it. For the first five centuries of the city's history, the high point undoubtedly came under the rule of the Etruscan kings—the Tarquins' monumental building programmes, including the first temple of the Capitoline Jupiter, in its time the biggest in Italy. Reconstructions show this lost building as a typical Etruscan work, deriving its form from the Greek temple but with a much more ornate decoration on the frieze and pediment, and perhaps statues along the roofline. Other Etruscan temples, with projecting pediments steeper than the Greek, and an emphasis on the exposed ends of beams and rafters, must have seemed an odd cross between a classical temple and an oriental pagoda.

Thanks to the Villa Giulia National Museum, with finds from all over Etruria, and the wonderful tombs in nearby Cervéteri, Rome can show you much of the best of Etruscan art. Enigmatic, often fantastical, and always intensely vital, Etruria's artistic magpies were able to steal from every style and technique that came out of Greece—from the Archaic, through the Classical and Hellenistic eclecticism—and turn it into something uniquely their own. In their remarkable portrait sculpture (usually, like their architectural decoration, in terracotta), they often excelled even the Greeks. For this, for their love of fresco painting, and for their distinctive 'grotesque' decoration, embodying the Etruscan fancy for the excessive and outlandish, every period of later Roman art is in their debt.

The Romans Learn Building and Just Can't Stop

The greatest builders of antiquity, no less—though even in late imperial times, when it was a question of aesthetics they would usually hire a Greek. In architecture, ancient Roman practicality found its greatest expression. They did not invent the arch, or concrete, or the aqueduct; they learned how to build roads and bridges from the Etruscans. Nevertheless, they perfected all these serviceable things to build works never dreamed of before, combining beauty and utility for their most significant contribution to western culture. Speaking strictly of design, the outstanding fact of Roman building was its conservatism. Under the Republic, Rome adopted Greek architecture wholesale, with a predilection for the more delicate Corinthian order (and a progressive weeding out of Etruscan styles). When the money started rolling in, the Romans began to build in marble; the 2nd century BC Temple of Portunus, still standing by the Tiber, was one of the first examples. But for 400 years, until the height of empire under Trajan and Hadrian, very little changed.

As Rome became the capital of the Mediterranean world, its rulers introduced new building types to embellish it: the series of *imperial fora*, variations on the Greek agora, the first of which was begun by Julius Cæsar; *public baths*, a custom imported from Campania; *colonnaded streets*, as in Syria and Asia Minor; and *theatres*. Unlike Greek theatres, these were enclosed (though not covered), with a semicircular orchestra and columned stage buildings. Theatre buildings were illegal in Republican Rome; Pompey and Cæsar got around the law by adding temples, quadrangles and meeting halls, and claiming the whole as a religious sanctuary. Rome's own contribution was the *basilica*, a large rectangular hall supported on columns, impossibly noisy as a courtroom but still the perfect stage for Romans in their togas to act out their boisterous public life.

In a city of over a million and a half people, some advances in planning and design could be expected. The Forum of Trajan (100–12 AD, by **Apollodorus of Damascus**) makes the work of many modern planners look primitive. Besides providing noble buildings and open space in the crowded city centre, the Forum skilfully combines widely divergent land uses—temples, libraries, government, and a big market—to create the first and finest of large-scale civic centres.

Concrete may not seem a very romantic subject, but in the hands of imperial builders it changed both the theory and practice of architecture. Volcanic sand from the Bay of Naples, used with rubble as a filler, allowed the Romans to cover vast spaces cheaply. Roman concrete lasts almost for ever; it's better than anything in use now. First in the palaces (such as Nero's Golden House), and later in the Pantheon, with its giant concrete dome (128 AD), and in the huge public baths (those of Caracalla and Diocletian were the largest and most elaborate), an increasingly sophisticated use of arches and vaults made the old Greek architecture of columns and lintels obsolete. Concrete seating made the Colosseum and the vast theatres possible, and allowed *insulae*—Roman apartment blocks—to climb six storeys and occasionally more.

Near the empire's end, the tendency towards gigantism becomes an enduring symptom of Roman decadence; the clumsy forms of late monsters like Diocletian's Baths (298–306) and the Basilica of Maxentius (306–10) show a technology far outstripping art, while the nascent Christian Church was failing in its attempts to find an original architectural inspiration for its worship. When Constantine, the last of the big builders, financed Christian foundations around Rome, they all took the form of the basilica—an interesting comment on the early Roman church, that it would choose not a contemplative temple for its gatherings, but a form that to any Roman mind signified temporal authority.

Roman Sculpture, Painting and Mosaics

In the beginning, Romans couldn't have cared less for such stuff. Even after the conquests of the 2nd century BC followed by the methodical looting of the cultured East, it was a long time before Rome would be producing anything of its own. As in architecture, the other arts were dependent for centuries on the Greeks, either by importing artists or copying classical works. Portrait sculpture, inherited from the Etruscans, is the notable exception, with a tradition of almost photographic, warts-and-all busts and funeral reliefs extending well into the imperial centuries. Augustus, who did so much else to decorate Rome, first exploited the possibilities of sculpture as a propaganda tool; the relief scenes of his reign on the Ara Pacis (13 BC) exemplify the clarity and classical restraint Romans preferred. Neither state policy nor private tastes encouraged experimentation, and Rome's sculptors continued to churn out endless copies of celebrated Greek works, even when the originals were on display in the emperor's gardens and temples.

As in architecture, sculptors began to consider new departures only in the confident, self-assured age of the Flavian and Antonine emperors. Some scholars have called the new style in reliefs 'impressionism', with a greater emphasis on effects of light and shadow, at times creating the illusion of depth, and more dynamic, 'unposed' compositions (as on the Arch of Titus or Trajan's Column). More than any other art, sculpture provides a compelling psychological record of Rome's history. In the 3rd century, as that confidence was undergoing its first crisis at the hands of German and Persian invaders, sculpture veers slowly but irreversibly towards the introverted and strange. Already under the late Antonines, the tendency is apparent, with the grim, realistic battle scenes on Marcus Aurelius' column, or the troubled portraits of that emperor himself. Later portraits become even more unsettling, with rigid features and staring eyes, concerned more with psychological depth than outward appearances. Third century reliefs can be either vigorous and queerly contorted, tending towards the abstract, or awkward and stiff, as in the large number of imperial propaganda reliefs (Arch of Constantine), where emperors on campaign or distributing gifts appear in static arrangements of figures, hardly more than symbols, a trend that presages the hieratic Church art of Byzantium and medieval Italy.

In any case, during the 3rd and 4th centuries there was little public art at all. In its brief revival under Constantine, we see how far the process of decay had gone. No work better evokes the Rome of the psychotic, totalitarian late empire than the weird, immense head of Constantine in the Capitoline museum. Gigantism, as in architecture, survived the final disappearance of individuality and genuinely civic art, while the imperial portraits freeze into eerie icons.

Painting and mosaic work were never exposed to the same storm and stress as sculpture. Though both were present from at least the 1st century BC, Romans considered them little more than decoration, and only rarely entrusted to them any serious subjects. Both are a legacy from the Greeks, and both found their way to Rome by way of talented, half-Greek Campania to the south. Painting, in the days of Cæsar and Augustus, usually meant wall frescoes in the homes of the wealthy, with large scenes of gardens (as in the reconstructed room in the National Museum at Diocletian's Baths, which you may be able to see on that magic day when the museum finally opens) or architectural fantasies in the form of window views, making small Roman rooms look brighter and bigger. Mytho-logical scenes were also popular (the careers of Hercules and Dionysus remained favourite subjects for centuries), and there are mentions of 'battle paintings', an early sort of propaganda brought home by victorious generals ready to go into pol-itics; none of these survive. Like the Etruscans, though less ambitiously, Romans liked to paint the walls of their tombs; you can see some in the excavations under St Peter's.

No important advances ever occurred in Roman painting. Skill and grace gradu-ally deteriorated over the centuries; few of the paintings in the Christian catacombs, for example, are anything more than primitive. Mosaics, another import, had their greatest centre at Antioch, in Hellenized Syria, and only became a significant medium at Rome in the 2nd century AD, as painting was declining. Rome is full of simple black and white floor mosaics, but occasionally a virtuoso would turn out a marvellous small scene (like the cats and bunnies at Diocletian's Baths or the debris of a banquet in the Vatican's Gregoriano Profano museum) for a wealthy patron; the tesserae used could be as small as 1/32 inch. Sparkling mosaics of tinted glass chips were also used in fountains and the bottoms of pools, though unfortunately none of this survives. If Rome, too, had been buried under volcanic lava, at whatever period, it is unlikely that much would be found to sur-pass the 2nd and 1st century BC paintings and mosaics discovered at Pompeii.

Early Christian and Medieval Art

Almost from the beginning, Rome's Christians sought to express their faith in art. The cartoon scrawls in the catacombs are no indication of the sophistication they often reached. On dozens of finely carved sarcophagi and statues, dating from the third century on (many are in the Vatican Museums) the figure of Christ is represented as the 'Good Shepherd', a beardless youth with a lamb slung over his shoulder. Occasionally he wears a proper Roman toga. Familiar New Testament scenes are common, along with figures of the early martyrs. The 4th-century building programme financed by Constantine filled Rome with imposing Christian basilicas, though little of the original work remains. The Lateran Baptistry, begun in 315, is the oldest in Christendom; its octagonal shape was copied for baptistries all over Italy for over a thousand years. Sculpture and architecture may have been in decline, but 4th-century mosaic artists were still able to create graceful syntheses of antique art and Christian symbolism, as in Santa Pudenziana church, or the imperial family mausoleum in Via Nomentana, now Santa Costanza.

Through the 5th and early 6th centuries, Christian art—now the only art permitted—changed little in style but broadened its subject matter, including scenes from the Old Testament (as in the Santa Maria Maggiore mosaics) and the Passion of Christ (the Crucifixion on the wooden doors of Santa Sabina may be the oldest one in existence). The new symbolism included the representation of Christ as the Lamb (as in SS Cosma e Damiano), the animal symbols of the four Evangelists, and the four rivers, representing both the 'four rivers of Paradise' and the four Gospels. There was little money, and few artists, to continue after the destructive Greek-Gothic Wars, but the elegant chancel of San Lorenzo, really the original church, begun in 579, shows how the Romans could build even in the worst of times.

Another monument from the advent of the Dark Ages is the mosaics of Sant'Agnese (638). The profound, unearthly gaze of the beautiful St Agnes, and the rich gold background, introduce the Byzantine influence into Roman art. Ravenna, not Rome, was now the artistic centre of Italy, and through it came the formal, mystical art ('hieratic', the Italians call it) of Byzantium. Greek dominance increased in the next three centuries, with an influx of artists fleeing Antioch and Alexandria after the Arab conquests, and from Constantinople itself during the persecutions of the Iconoclast emperors.

An impressive revival of Roman building came in the late 8th century, with peace, relative prosperity, and the enlightened reigns of popes like Hadrian, Leo III and Paschal I. New churches went up—Santa Maria in Cosmedin, Santa Prassede, Santa Maria in Domnica—all decorated with mosaics by Greek artists. The return of hard times after the collapse of the Carolingian Empire put an end to this little Renaissance, and very little was done in Rome until the 1100s.

When Rome began building again, it was largely with native artists, and stylistically there was almost a clean break with the past. The **Cosmati**, perhaps originally a single family of artisans, but eventually a name for a whole school, ground up fragments of coloured glass and precious stone from Rome's ruins and turned them into intricate pavements, altars, paschal candlesticks, pulpits and other decoration, geometrically patterned in styles derived from southern Italy, and ultimately from the Moslem world. Some of the Cosmati school eventually became accomplished sculptors, architects and mosaicists, such as **Pietro Vassalletto**, who built the cloisters at the Lateran and St Paul's (late 12th century) and **Iacopo Torriti** (mosaic of the Coronation of the Virgin at S. Maria Maggiore; late 13th century). One of the Cosmati artists, Pietro Oderisi, even made it to London, to design Henry III's tomb in Westminster Abbey.

Perhaps the greatest Roman artist of the Middle Ages was **Pietro Cavallini** (*c.* 1250–1330), whose new freedom in composition and brilliant talent for expressive portraiture make him a genuine precursor of the Renaissance, equally at home in mosaics (S. Maria in Trastevere) and fresco painting (S. Cecilia). Further nudges towards the Renaissance came from outsiders, often Tuscans, such as the sculptor and architect **Arnolfo di Cambio**; though more famous for Florence's Cathedral and Palazzo della Signoria, he also left considerable work in Rome (in S. Clemente, S. Paolo, St Peter's). Giotto also visited Rome, though almost none of his work at St Peter's survives. Outside influences even went so far as to give Rome a Florentine Gothic church (S. Maria Sopra Minerva, 1280), the one exception to Rome's haughty, almost neurotic avoidance of what at the time was Europe's International Style.

Then came the Babylonian Captivity, in 1308, and with no popes to order the work, and no money from tithes or pilgrims to pay for it, Rome's very promising career as a leader in Italian art came to an abrupt end.

The Renaissance in Rome

Rome had nothing to do with the beginnings of the Renaissance—its first century belonged to Tuscany and to Venice—but with yet another revival of the papacy the city was to have the last word. Almost every Tuscan Renaissance master is represented by something in Rome (minor works of Donatello at St Peter's and the Aracoeli, Botticelli, Ghirlandaio and Perugino in the Sistine Chapel, Masolino at San Clemente, Pinturicchio in the Vatican, Aracoeli, and S. Maria del Popolo, Melozzo da Forlì in the Vatican and S. Croce, among others); they came, however, as cultural missionaries to a city that had been a backwater since 1308. Pius II, the most artistically inclined of the early Renaissance popes, preferred to expend most of his patronage on his native Tuscany. Paul II (1464–71) commissioned many works, including Rome's first proper Renaissance palace, the Palazzo Venezia. Alexander VI (1492–1503), one of the most intelligent of all papal patrons, ordered the Pinturicchio frescoes in his Vatican apartments.

Rome's high Renaissance, though, begins with Julius II (1503–13). **Michelangelo Buonarroti** (1475–1564) had already arrived, to amaze the world of art with his *Pietà* in St Peter's (1499), but the true inauguration of Rome's greatest artistic period was the arrival of **Donato Bramante** (1444–1514), an architect who had already made a name for himself in Milan. In Rome, where the example of the ancients impressed him deeply, he immediately left off the busy, somewhat eccentric style of his youth and began creating a refined classicism that seemed to exemplify the aspirations of the Renaissance more completely than anything that had gone before. This new marriage of the Renaissance and ancient Rome can best be seen at Bramante's *Tempietto* at S. Pietro in Montorio (1503), or at his cloister for S. Maria della Pace (1504). The round Tempietto, the first modern building to depend entirely on the proportions of the classical orders (the Doric, in this case), was the most sophisticated attempt at creating a perfect 'temple', fusing the highest conceptions of faith and art, an ideal taken from the architectural fantasies of early Renaissance paintings (for example, in Perugino's *Donation of the Keys* in the Sistine Chapel).

For painting and sculpture, the High Renaissance meant a greater emphasis on emotion, dynamic movement, and virtuosity. Following in Bramante's footsteps was **Raphael**, Raffaello Sanzio of Urbino (1483–1520), who arrived from Florence in 1508. Learning the grand manner from antique sculpture and the ancient approach to decoration from the paintings in Nero's recently unearthed Golden House, he applied these lessons in the frescoes of the Vatican Stanze (begun 1511), one of the definitive achievements of the age. A versatile artist, Raphael excelled at portraiture, painted mythological frescoes (as in the Villa Farnesina), and was at times capable of almost visionary religious work (the *Liberation of St. Peter* in the Vatican Stanze). He was the most influential painter of his time, with an easy virtuosity and sunny personality that patrons found irresistible—though he would have been mortified to know that his weakness for sweet Madonnas, clouds, putti, and floating holy celebrities was introducing a kitsch element that would plague European sensibilities for the next three centuries.

Michelangelo, unwashed and overworked as ever, spent much of his time sulking over the successes of these two men, whom he claimed stole all their ideas from him. Pope Julius kept him busy enough, with the gargantuan project for his papal tomb that was to bother the artist for much of his life, finally scaled down to a small ensemble, including the famous *Moses*, at S. Pietro in Vincoli. Michelangelo tried to flee his terrible patron in 1506, but Julius snatched him back and put him up on the ceiling of the Sistine Chapel two years later. The artist responded to the unusual commission (ceilings are not exactly the best place for great art, though this one started a fad that would last for centuries) with the most profound and imaginative synthesis of art and faith Renaissance Rome would know.

After Julius came the Medici pope, Leo X, open-handed to artists, though greatly overrated as a patron—thanks largely to Voltaire, who wrote of the 'Age of Leo X' as an unsurpassed golden age of culture. Raphael and Michelangelo kept at their work (at least until 1520, when the former died and the latter returned to Florence). Poetry and humanist scholarship were still fostered at the papal court, but through his reign and that of the other Medici, Clement VII, nothing in art appeared that was as revolutionary as the works done under Julius.

The End of the Renaissance

The Sack of Rome in 1527 brought a rude interruption to artistic endeavours of all kinds. Many of the most promising artists left Rome for ever, including **Rosso Fiorentino** and **Giulio Romano** (one of the rare native Romans, a man who had worked for years as assistant to Raphael). Recovery was swift, though the creative intensity of the years before 1527 was never recaptured. Among the artists who returned to Rome, there was of course Michelangelo, who began the Last Judgement in the Sistine Chapel in 1536. Its sombre tones, not to mention its subject matter, illustrate more clearly than any other work the change in mood that had come over Roman art.

In his later years, Michelangelo produced little sculpture or painting. Pope Paul III, one of the more serious patrons to occupy the papal throne, appointed him architect of St Peter's in 1547—when he was 72. Other late works include the civic centre on the Campidoglio (1547) and Santa Maria degli Angeli (1563). His antagonist, taking up Bramante's old job, was **Antonio da Sangallo the Younger**, most accomplished of a family of Tuscan architects. A more accomplished, though less flamboyant architect than Michelangelo, Sangallo continued the High Renaissance tradition, giving Rome some of its finest buildings (Farnese Palace, 1546).

Tuscan Mannerism, the often eccentric, avant-garde tendency that rebelled against the Olympian high art of the Renaissance, found a place in Rome only for its less shocking exponents: painters such as **Francesco Salviati**, **Perin del Vaga** and **Baldassare Peruzzi** of Siena (1510–63), who besides his paintings contributed original architectural creations like the Villa Farnesina and Palazzo Massimo alle Colonne on Corso Vittorio Emanuele (1537). Two other distinctive architects of this period created fanciful buildings with a touch of Mannerist restlessness—at least in their secular commissions—**Giacomo da Vignola** (Villa Giulia, Palazzo Farnese at Caprarola) and **Pirro Ligorio** (Casino of Pius IV in the Vatican Gardens, 1558; Villa d'Este at Tivoli, 1560). Their works, some of the most delightful and challenging buildings of the Roman Cinquecento, found no one to follow their example in the tough years that followed. The inspiration of the Renaissance was gradually becoming exhausted, just as political conditions were constraining artists to be very, very careful.

The Art of the Counter-Reformation

The decades of the rampant Counter-Reformation and the advent of the Inquisition put a chill on the Italian imagination that would never really be dispelled. In 1563, the final documents of the Council of Trent decreed the new order for art; it was to be conformist and naturalistic, a propaganda tool entirely in the service of the new totalitarian Church, with a touch of Spanish discipline and emotion-alism to remind everyone where the real power lay. Largely under the direction of the Jesuits, a costly building programme was undertaken, with large, extravagant churches meant to overawe the faithful and provide an opulent background for the pageantry and bombastic sermons of the new Catholicism: the Gesù Church (1568), Santa Maria in Vallicella (1575), and Sant'Andrea della Valle (1591), all on Corso Vittorio Emanuele, remain the chief works of the transitional order which past centuries called the 'Jesuit Style'.

The leading architect of the age, **Giacomo della Porta** (Sant'Andrea, façade of the Gesù, Palazzo della Sapienza), earns a place as the last of the Renaissance tra-dition, with a coolly classical style immune to the artistic decay and political stresses of the time. By the end of the 1500s, painting and sculpture were in a bad way, with technically proficient but terminally boring artists like the **Cavaliere d'Arpino** (frescoes in St Peter's dome) holding sway among Roman patrons. **Taddeo Zuccaro** (frescoes at Caprarola) and his brother **Federico** rank among the more serious men who thought Mannerism would last for ever, and sought to steer it towards a stiff, respectable academicism.

Rome itself was ordained to become the urban symbol of the Church resurgent, the most modern, most beautiful city in the world. Under the papacy of Sixtus V (1585–90), **Domenico Fontana** and other architects commenced an epochal planning scheme, uniting the sprawling medieval city with a network of long, straight avenues sighted on obelisks in the major piazzas. Fontana's attempts at architecture, such as the drab Lateran Palace (1607), were less fortunate, but other architects were pointing the way towards the dawning Baroque. **Carlo Maderno**'s façade for Santa Susanna (1603) was one of the first symptoms, though the more conventional façade he designed for St Peter's ten years later has been universally condemned ever since as one of the missed opportunities of Roman art.

Times were right for a change. The militant, intolerant atmosphere of the early Counter-Reformation could never last too long among the worldly aristocrats of Rome, no matter how much mischief they were causing to the rest of Europe, and hedonism and artistic innovation resurfaced under a very thin veneer of piety and propriety. Many of the first challenges came from the painters: first **Annibale Carracci**, who reintroduced mythological subjects, taboo in the early Counter-Reformation terror, along with an intense, dynamic style of presenting them that harks back to Michelangelo's Sistine ceiling (Palazzo Farnese gallery, begun 1597); his greatest follower, a figure whose dramatic altarpieces and ceilings con-tributed much to the birth of the Baroque, was **Guercino** (Casino Ludovisi frescoes, 1621).

Carracci's artistic rival, **Michelangelo Merisi da Caravaggio**, worked in Rome at roughly the same time (1590–1603) before leaving town over the little matter of a homicide. Rome's first certified bohemian (whom modern Italy suavely co-opted by putting his face on a L100, 000 note) might have been the last person to pick a fight with at the tavern, but he was all business at painting. His impeccable draftsmanship, combined with a revolutionary, *tenebroso* use of light and shadow and a new, naturalistic manner of portraying biblical subjects (S. Luigi dei Francesi, S. Maria del Popolo), made him many followers, and inspired many others to find their own approach to breaking out of the High Renaissance strait-jacket.

To Roman opinion, however, the dry, academic painting of the expiring Renaissance was a pinnacle of artistic achievement. And to many later critics, especially in the 1700s, **Guido Reni** (in Rome about 1604–14) and **Domenichino** (1613–31) ranked with Raphael and Michelangelo as the greatest of all time; today the former's brilliantly coloured but often lifeless art, and the latter's vapid classicism hardly ever get a second glance from visitors to Rome's museums.

The Age of Baroque

No one is really sure where the word 'Baroque' originated. One possibility, according to Luigi Barzini in *The Italians*, are the irregular, oversized pearls still called *perle barocche* in Italy. Barzini goes on to explain how 'the term came to be used metaphorically to describe anything pointlessly complicated, otiose, capricious and eccentric ...' Such is the reputation Baroque has acquired in our time. The opprobrium is entirely deserved. Italy was subjected to reactionary priests and despotic tyrants, and art was reduced to mere decoration, forbidden to entertain any thoughts that might be politically dangerous or subversive to Church dogma. But in this captive art there was still talent and will enough for new advances to be made, particularly in architecture.

Plenty of churches, fountains and palaces were still going up in Rome, and there was every opportunity for experimentation. A second landmark, after Maderno's Santa Susanna, was the fountain of the Acqua Paola, built by Flaminio Ponzio in 1610. However, the real breakthrough came in the 1630s, with three great masters who between them inaugurated the Roman High Baroque and determined the course of European architecture for the next century: first **Pietro da Cortona**, with his intricate, flowing façade and dome for SS Martina e Luca; then **Francesco Borromini**, with his earliest and most memorable works, S. Carlo alle Quattro Fontane (1638) and Sant' Ivo (1642), and finally **Gianlorenzo Bernini**, who began the famous colonnades in front of St Peter's in 1656, and the church of Sant'Andrea al Quirinale two years later.

These three men came to architecture from diverse backgrounds, between them exposing something of the range of talents and ambitions of the Baroque movement. Cortona, from the town of Cortona and steeped in the tradition of Florentine Mannerism, began as a painter and designer, already famed for his ceiling frescoes in the Palazzo Barberini (1633–39). Borromini, a profound architect and the son of an architect, came from Lombardy, and brought to Rome the centuries-old tradition of Lombard building skills. The exotic geometry behind his two great churches, mentioned above, was a medieval throwback, repudiating the classical Vitruvian architecture of the Renaissance, but he used it to create amazingly sophisticated forms and spaces. Few architects were able to match this tortured soul's grasp of the art, or the sincere piety that informed it—Borromini himself, in his later career, created nothing as interesting as those first two churches—but everyone who followed did his best to conjure up even more striking and unusual combinations of shapes.

Among the first to catch the fever was Bernini. Neapolitan by birth, with some experience as a playwright and stage designer, Bernini always thought of himself as a sculptor first, and in fact his best known and most original works are decorations, occupying the vague ground between sculpture and architecture: the St Peter's colonnades, the essential statement of Baroque flourish and grandiosity, and the Fountain of the Four Rivers in Piazza Navona (1648). As architect of St Peter's from 1629 on, and the most popular artist in Rome for decades thereafter, Bernini had an opportunity to transform the face of the city afforded to no other man before or since; his churches, palaces and fountains can be seen all over Rome. Other distinctive contributions to the High Baroque came from **Martino Longhi** (SS. Vincenzo ed Anastasio, 1646) and **Carlo Rainaldi** (S. Maria in Campitelli, 1662).

In sculpture, the Baroque meant a new emphasis on cascading drapery and exaggerated poses, typecasting emotion or saintliness or virtue in a way Renaissance artists would have found slightly trashy. Here Bernini led the way, with such works as his early *David* in the Galleria Borghese (1623), the florid papal tombs, equestrian statue of Constantine, and bronze baldachin, all at St Peter's, and the incredible *Ecstasy of St Teresa* in S. Maria della Vittoria (1652). His careful, eloquent portrait sculptures seem hardly to come from the same hand—for apparently the less this self-assured and somewhat arrogant artist was able to follow his fancy, the better. Bernini proved a hard act to follow; the only other Roman Baroque sculptors worthy of mention are the more sober **Alessandro Algardi**, and **Francesco Duquesnoy**, from Brussels, whose modest works, scattered around Rome's museums, often recall something of the freshness and lack of affectation of the early Renaissance.

Painting was on a definite downward spiral, though one usually had to look up to see it. Decorative ceiling frescoes, such as those of Pietro da Cortona, were all the rage, though few artists could bring anything like Cortona's talent to the job, **Andrea Sacchi**'s *Divina Sapienza* fresco (1633) in the Palazzo Barberini being a notable exception. After this, preciosity and tricky illusionism rapidly gained the upper hand, most flagrantly in G. B. Gaulli's ceiling for the Gesù Church (1679) and the Jesuit Andrea Pozzo's *trompe l'oeil* spectacular in Sant'Ignazio (1691). Serious painting was breathing its last, but while you are in Rome's galleries keep a look out for the works of Pier Francesco Mola (1612–68) and two of the more endearing genre painters: scenes of Roman life and ruins by Michelangelo Cerquozzi (1620–60), and the landscapes of Salvator Rosa (1615–73).

The Last of Roman Art

From Rome, the art of the High Baroque reached out to all Europe—just as the last traces of inspiration were dying out in the city itself. The death of Pope Alexander VII (1667) is often mentioned as a convenient turning point, after whom there was less money, and less intelligent patronage. But as the Baroque trudged slowly off to its grave, bad paintings and sculptures were still being cranked out by the hundreds. Ironically, at the time when Rome's artistic powers were reaching their lowest ebb, the popes chose to restore dozens of churches after the degraded tastes of the age, destroying much of Rome's early Christian and medieval artistic patrimony in the process.

At the tail end of the Baroque, Rome's most popular architect was **Carlo Fontana** (S. Marcello in Corso, 1683, plenty of undistinguished palaces, and unrealized plans for extending Piazza San Pietro, even worse than the one finally built by Mussolini). After him, though, Roman architecture bounced back for a brief flurry of surprisingly creative work, beginning with Francesco de Sanctis' Spanish Steps of 1726, and **Filippo Raguzzini**'s lovely, arch-Rococo San Gallicano hospital in Trastevere (1724). Raguzzini also designed the intimate, stage-set ensemble in Piazza Sant'Ignazio (1728). Another accomplished architect to embellish Rome in the 18th century was **Fernando Fuga**, who designed the Palazzo della Consulta (1737) and rebuilt Santa Maria Maggiore (1743). Some things had not changed; all these works continued the Baroque love of the grand gesture—and a hint of stage decoration, nowhere more so than in **Nicola Salvi**'s endearing and utterly Roman Trevi Fountain of 1762.

By this time, a more introspective Rome was looking backwards. Meaningful sculpture and painting were gone for ever, and antiquarianism became a major concern of the few remaining Roman artists, most notably in the endless engravings of **G. B. Piranesi** (1720–78) and in the sketches, drawings, measurements and monologues of the hordes of Grand Tourists from the north. Another symbol of the age was the founding of the Vatican Museums in 1769. By the century's end, what passed for artistic life in Rome was entirely in the hands of foreigners, such as the German Johann Winckelmann, who became the pope's Superintendent of Antiquities in 1763, the Swiss painter Angelica Kauffmann, the French sculptor Jean-Antoine Houdon, the Icelandic sculptor Thorvaldsen. In the train of Napoleon came two Gallicized Italians, the architect Valadier, who gave Piazza del Popolo its present form, and the neo-classical sculptor Antonio Canova.

In the 19th century art in Rome continued to lose ground. The fathers of the new Italy, after 1870, knew in their hearts that liberation and Italian unity would unleash a wave of long-suppressed creativity, and they spent tremendous sums to help it along. They were mistaken. The sepulchral, artless monuments and ministries they imposed on Rome helped ruin the fabric of the city, while providing an enduring reminder of the sterility of the Risorgimento and the corrupt regimes that followed it. The modest revivals of Italian painting—the Italian Impressionists, the Tuscan *Macchiaioli* and the 20th-century Futurists—can all be seen in Rome's Galleria d'Arte Moderna, but few of the artists involved in these movements had anything to do with Rome itself. One exception to this dismal picture is the Roman artist **Giulio Aristide Sartorio** (1860–1932), influenced equally by Michelangelo and contemporary poster art; his masterpiece is the series of frescoes in the parliament chamber at Palazzo Montecitorio. Another exception is the delightful, eccentric neighbourhood of Art Nouveau fantasy houses and flats around Via Dora, just off Piazza Buenos Aires.

Mussolini too wanted his revolution to have its artistic expression. The sort of painting and sculpture his government preferred is best not examined too closely, but his architecture, mashing up Art Deco simplicity with a historical pomposity fit for a Duce, now and then reached beyond the level of the ridiculous (the municipal buildings on Via Petroselli). Rome today is moribund as an art centre, and even architecture has not recovered from the post-Risorgimento, post-Mussolini hangover. There are no first-rate contemporary buildings in Rome. Not few—none. Efforts at planning the city's postwar growth, with satellite towns and housing schemes, resulted in confusion and concrete madness, and the hideous apartment and office blocks of the suburbs (a particularly vile nest of them can be seen along the road to the airport, around Via Magliana). Until recently it seemed impossible that Rome could ever again produce inspired architecture. However, controversial as it is, Paolo Portoghesi's mosque, a playful postmodern extravaganza out near the Villa Ada, could be a sign that the tide is about to turn.

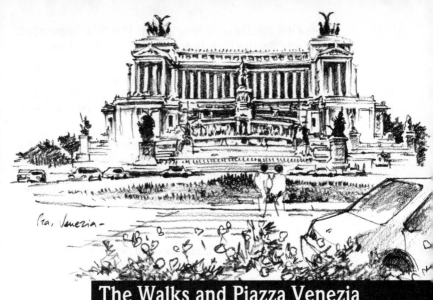

Pza. Venezia

The Walks and Piazza Venezia

Not a few first-time visitors come away from Rome with something less than a good impression. That is to be expected; they stay in some dreary, overpriced hotel near Termini Station, making their obligatory visits to St Peter's and the Forum. They inch down the depressing main thoroughfares in taxis or on overcrowded buses, wondering why they didn't spend their holiday in Paris or Venice again. The real Rome, the Rome you'll enjoy, is tucked away behind those big streets; it has attractions just as worth seeing as those that decorate the postcards in the airport news-stands. To help you find them, this book divides the city into 15 walking tours. Though each inevitably includes a grab-bag of things to see, they fall logically into categories of interest:

Ancient Rome: Walks **I** (Capitol and Tiber), **II** (Forum),
                    III (Caelian Hill) and **XII** (Via Appia Antica)

Medieval Rome: Walks **IV** and **V** (both in Campus Martius)
                    and **XIII** (Trastevere).

Renaissance and Baroque: Walks **VI** and **VII** (Corso and Spanish Steps)
                    and **IX** (Quirinale).

Vatican City: Walks **XIV** (St Peter's and Castel Sant'Angelo)
                    and **XV** (Vatican Museums).

In addition, there are three that do not quite fit in: Walk **VIII** (Villa Borghese park and museums), **X** (Early Christian basilicas) and **XI** (Aventine Hill and Testaccio).

The indispensable walks for an introduction to Rome are **I** and **IV**, with ancient remains more interesting than those in the Forum, and a bit of everything else. They also rank among the most pleasant, with walks **II, III, VII, XII**, and **XIII**. The least fun: **IX** and **X** win the prize. For rainy days, there is **XV**, the world's biggest museum; and to enjoy the best weather, **VIII** and **XII**.

One caveat before you begin: though hours and admission prices are correct at the time of writing, restorations, strikes, inflation or plain old Roman fickleness could change them at any moment. Do as the Romans do, and instead of being frustrated when a museum or church is closed, be pleasantly surprised to find them open.

The start to many walks is **Piazza Venezia**. *Rome has many a fine urban ornament, but Piazza Venezia isn't one of them, and it's a shame to begin with such a traffic-crazed black sheep, reduced to playing vestibule to a manmade glacier called the Altar of the Nation. But Piazza Venezia is the closest thing modern Rome has to a centre, where the bus lines converge and where local Iranians hold their anti-Ayatollah marches.*

The square is named for the **Palazzo Venezia**, the dark, fortress-like palace that occupies the entire west side of the square. A Florentine creation of fine proportions, attributed variously to Giuliano da Maiano or Alberti, it was Rome's first important secular building of the Renaissance (1455); the fun-loving Cardinal Pietro Barbo of Venice (later Paul II) enlarged it a few years later so he could watch the finish of his Carnival horse races from Rome's most famous balcony— the same one used by Mussolini to whip up the 'oceanic' crowds in the piazza (renamed the Forum of the Fascist Empire in those days) and declare war on the United States. In between, the palace was used as a residence for popes, Venetian ambassadors and cardinals, and the Austrian ambassador after the fall of the Venetian Republic.

The **Museo del Palazzo Venezia** (*entrance in Via del Plebiscito; open Mon–Sat 9–7, Sun 9–1, adm L4000*) contains Rome's most important collection of decorative arts. At the time of writing the exhibits have only been partially rearranged: Byzantine jewellery and finely carved ivory triptychs and coffers, especially an 11th century one portraying the life of David; a valuable collection of Florentine *cassoni* (wooden marriage chests), one carved like a medieval cathedral; the 13th-century gilded bronze *Lunette della Mentorella* found near Palestrina; silver work from Abruzzi, paintings by early Renaissance artists

Starnina, Bicci di Lorenzo and Giovanni da Modena and a golden quattrocento Venetian triptych studded with gems. One long hall is devoted to small Renaissance bronzes, the favourite dust magnets of the 16th century, including a club-wielding Venetian Hercules who has a stride and swing uncannily reminiscent of Joe DiMaggio in Yankee Stadium. After home-run Herc come plaster models and sketches by Jacopo Sansovino, Bernini and Algardi and later paintings: a double portrait attributed to Giorgione, works by Guercino, Pietro Novelli, and two small works by Gothic master Pisanello. Waiting to be arranged are the collections of armour, tapestries, and other paintings.

There's almost always a special exhibit in the stately Venetian-opulent halls, including the vast mosaic-floored **Sala del Mappamondo**, with a frescoed map of the world of 1495. This was Mussolini's office, where he routinely rogered anything in a skirt and intimidated out of favour male visitors by making them walk 60 feet in silence to his desk. Another of his tricks was to leave the lights burning all night so passing Romans would think he was working late.

> Adjacent to the palazzo, in Piazza San Marco, the ancient church of **San Marco** was incorporated into Palazzo Venezia by Paul II; Leon Battista Alberti and Giuliano da Maiano gave it an elegant new portico and loggia from which the pope would give his blessing. This is the most convenient place to see an example of one of Rome's glories—mosaics from the Dark Ages.

Founded in 336 by Pope Mark, San Marco is one of Rome's oldest titular churches, traditionally that of the cardinal from Venice. Popes have revamped it constantly since, but always preserved its ancient basilica form. The beautiful mosaic (833) in the apse shows one of these pontiffs, Gregory IV, holding a model of his version of the church while being introduced to Christ by Pope Mark; along the bottom caper white llama-horses. When Cardinal Pietro Barbo built the Palazzo Venezia he rebuilt San Marco, adding its ornate gilded ceiling and the Cosmati pavement, still partially visible. The rest was Baroqued over in the 18th century; the chapel just right of the high altar has a painting of Pope Mark by Melozzo da Forli.

> On the west end of Piazza San Marco stands the **Palazzetto Venezia** (mid-15th century). This formerly stood in Piazza Venezia, and was moved to reveal the Vittoriano in all its blazing enormity. It has what many believe is the loveliest Renaissance courtyard in Rome, though to see it you have to make a special request at no. 49. Just to the right, rather forgotten now in its corner, is a large bust of the well endowed 'Madama Lucrezia' (a recycled statue of Isis) who since the 15th century has been Rome's only female 'talking statue' in the style of Pasquino.

Mussolini wasn't the only celebrity to spend time in Piazza Venezia. On the corner of the Corso, the **Palazzo Bonaparte** now houses a café, but between 1815 and 1836 its chief resident was Napoleon's mother, Letizia Bonaparte, who had her boy's eagle emblazoned on the façade; Pius VII, the very pope Napoleon had exiled, had welcomed her to Rome, perhaps partly because she offered to lend him money at an interest rate that undercut the city's banks. Among the medieval alleys under the Capitol, cleared away to form a stage for the Vittoriano, was the home and studio of Michelangelo, where he died in 1564 (commemorated by a plaque on the phoney-Renaissance insurance company opposite Palazzo Venezia). But if he were still nearby, what would he, as founder of modern artistic egomania, have thought of the boondoggle that replaced his old home?

Risorgimento Italy's own self-inflicted satire, the **Vittorio Emanuele II Monument** (or Vittoriano, or Altar of the Nation) was erected between 1885 and 1911 in honour of Italian unity, an airy concept that the Italians have tried vainly to secure with this giant paperweight, one of the world's greatest apotheoses of kitsch, 500 ft long and 200 ft high. Giuseppe Sacconi's design, a unique combination of typewriter, wedding cake, and dentures which the architect envisioned as a 'public container', was chosen out of 95 entries in an international competition, while the glaring white *botticino* marble of Brescia, comes, understandably enough, from the home district of Prime Minister Giuseppe Zanardelli, who commissioned the project. Unlike traditional Roman travertine, it refuses to 'drink the sun' and mellow, but rather bleaches ever brighter; like 'The Blob' the monument grew to nightmarish proportions, until it hid the Capitol and Forum and distorted the surroundings all the way to St Peter's, so the pope, holed up in the Vatican, could look out over the city and feel its glacial chill. In one of history's most devastating backhand compliments, Kaiser Wilhelm called the Vittoriano the 'maximum expression of Latin genius'.

Lately its guardians have been very peevish about letting people roam over its arctic wastes to enjoy the superb views from the top or inspect its complex sculptural allegory. In the centre of it all, the modest virtues of Vittorio Emanuele II have earned him a 12m bronze equestrian statue, perhaps the world's largest, bleeding his blue-green guts out over the immaculate white. Underneath, Italy's Unknown Soldier from World War I sleeps peacefully with a round-the-clock guard. Even if there's no admission to the monument, you can see, on the left, the remains of the Republican tomb of tipsy-sounding C. Publicus Bibulus that once marked the beginning of the Via Flaminia.

Few living souls have penetrated the vast, mildewing bowels of the Vittoriano, where models and plaster casts of its statuary collect dust under some fine turn-of-the-century mosaics. Intrepid explorers have noted a long-forgotten museum of the Risorgimento tucked in one corner; a tiny **museum-sanctuary of Marine Flags** on the left side, may be breached between 9.30 and 1.30.

I: Capitoline Hill and Tiber Banks

Aracœli

Santa Maria d'Aracoeli   91
Campidoglio   92
Capitoline Museums   94
Santa Maria in Cosmedin   98
Temples of Vesta and Fortuna Virilis   99
Piazza di Campitelli   101
Portico of Octavia   101
Tiber Island   103

Start: *Piazza Venezia.*

Finish: *Tiber Island.*

Walking Time: *3 hours, not counting the Capitoline Museums, where there is enough to keep you entertained for at least two more.*

At first glance, it would seem that the areas in this walk could not have less in common: the Capitoline Hill, mystic centre of Rome and the Roman world; the ancient and medieval market districts around it; the serene Tiber island; the Jewish Ghetto. Though there *are* some stretches of car-packed tarmac here (notably Via del Teatro di Marcello, Piazza Bocca della Verità and the Lungotevere) the various quarters in between are connected by a certain atmosphere, a quietness. This is the invisible Rome; we put it first because it has the most surprises to offer the first-time visitor. The unspeakable Vittoriano hides the Capitol completely; many tourists leave Rome never dreaming such a place exists. The Tiber boulevards and Via del Teatro di Marcello carry their hordes of traffic around and through the neighbourhoods, but few stop to look.

Yet perhaps it is this very quietness, the benign neglect that keeps the heart of Rome from being transformed into a tourist preserve, that makes this walk the place to start for anyone who really wants to know the city. Along the way you'll pass the Goddess Roma herself, and the spot where Romulus and Remus landed. There is Rome's finest museum of antique art, and its best preserved temples, along with samplings from most of the centuries since they were built.

Trying to do this walk in the same day as Walk II, the Forum and Palatine, would be a heavy load, but it nicely rounds out the heart of the ancient city. Combining it with IV, V or VI, medieval and Renaissance Rome, or XIII, Trastevere, would be easier on your feet. Unlike many of the walks, this one is good for the afternoon—the Capitoline Museums will be closed, but you can save this for a special Saturday evening treat, when the *palazzi* are lit up like ballrooms.

---

lunch/cafés

Until you get to the Ghetto, restaurants and even cafés are few: a picnic on the Capitol is a possibility, at the pretty viewpoint called the Belvedere Tarpeo—but the spot is small and often crowded.

La Dolce Roma, Via del Portico d'Ottavia 20B. Closed Sun pm and all day Mon. Open 7–1.30 and 4–8. Austro-Hungarian bakery which produces a sinfully appetising (and pricey) selection of cakes and cookies, ranging from carrot cake and choc-chip cookies to apple strudel and yogurt cake. Pumpkin pie in season.

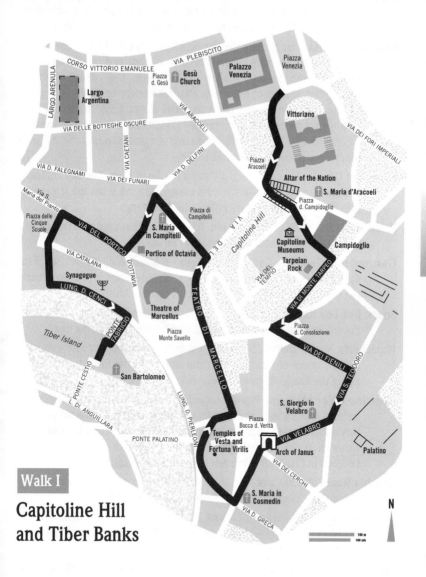

CORSO VITTORIO EMANUELE

VIA PLEBISCITO

Piazza Venezia

Palazzo Venezia

Piazza d. Gesù

Gesù Church

Largo Argentina

LARGO ARENULA

VIA ARACOELI

Vittoriano

VIA DEI FORI IMPERIALI

VIA DELLE BOTTEGHE OSCURE

VIA CAETANI

VIA D. FALEGNAMI

VIA D. DELFINI

VIA DEI FUNARI

Piazza Aracoeli

Altar of the Nation

S. Maria d'Aracoeli

Via S. Maria del Pianto

Piazza delle Cinque Scuole

VIA DEL PORTICO

Piazza di Campitelli

S. Maria in Campitelli

Piazza d. Campidoglio

Capitoline Hill

Capitoline Museums

Campidoglio

VIA CATALANA

D'OTTAVIA

Portico of Octavia

VIA DEL TEMPIO

Tarpeian Rock

Synagogue

LUNG. D. CENCI

Theatre of Marcellus

TEATRO DI MARCELLO

VIA DI MONTE TARPEO

Tiber Island

PONTE FABRICIO

Piazza Monte Savello

Piazza d. Consolazione

VIA DEI FIENILI

PONTE CESTIO

San Bartolomeo

VIA S. TEODORO

L. DI ANGUILLARA

LUNG. D. PIERLEONI

S. Giorgio in Velabro

PONTE PALATINO

Piazza Bocca d. Verità

Temples of Vesta and Fortuna Virilis

Arch of Janus

VIA VELABRO

Palatino

Palatino

VIA DEI CERCHI

Walk I

Capitoline Hill and Tiber Banks

S. Maria in Cosmedin

VIA D. GRECA

N

100 m
100 yds

Da Bleve, Via di S. Maria del Pianto 9A–11. Closed Sun. Open 8 am–8 pm. A traditional *enoteca* (wine shop) which serves light lunches to gastronomes (smoked fish, cheeses, cured meats, salads and the like) from Mon–Fri.

Sora Margherita, Piazza delle Cinque Scuole 30, ✆ 686 4002. Closed Sun. Open lunchtimes only. There's no sign outside this utterly authentic Roman/Jewish trattoria—follow your nose to the delicious smells wafting through a door hung with plastic streamers, and join the regulars in a lunch of home-made *agnolotti, pasta e ceci, bucatini con cacio,* or *all'amatriciana* depending on the day. Traditional *secondi* too—such as *pajata, baccalà al sugo* and *trippa alla romana.* Cakes from the local bakery (see below) for dessert; L18,000.

Forno del Ghetto, Via del Portico d'Ottavia 2. Closed Mon. The best fruitcake in Rome, created in a tiny Jewish bakery. Around 5 pm the street outside is packed with people contentedly munching.

Pizza al Taglio, Via S. Maria del Pianto 65. Open mid-morning till 8 pm. Closed Sun. Pizza slices and fizzy Chardonnay on tap.

Gastronomia-Gelateria-Caffè, Via del Teatro di Marcello 42. Closed Sat. Standard sandwiches and *tavola calda* fare, outside tables for Fiat-watchers, but the only spot to rest after the Capitol and Velabrum.

Snack Bar-Tea Room, Piazza Aracoeli 15. Closed Sun. Better sandwiches and hot snacks than most places around here (which is not saying much).

Pizzicheria, Via de' Delfini 25. Modest, old-fashioned *alimentari* where you can join the queue of locals at lunchtime for sandwiches made to order from any of the hams, cheeses and salamis in the fridge.

Angelino a Tor Margana, Piazza Margana 37. Closed Sun. A rather expensive trattoria cashing in on the facts that (1) it's been going since the last century and (2) that Goethe is alleged to have dined with a woman here. However, it's on a lovely quiet piazza and in summer you can eat outside. L60,000 but half that if you just have pasta, wine and salad.

Vecchia Roma, Piazza Campitelli 18, ✆ 656 4604. Closed Wed. Elegant restaurant and excellent, traditional Roman cooking; L70,000.

Da Giggetto, Via del Portico d'Ottavia 20, ✆ 656 1105. Closed Mon. Reliable Jewish/Roman fare—artichokes, *pajata* and the like, eaten outside in summer; L40,000.

Piperno, Via Monte de'Cenci 9, ✆ 6880 6629. Closed Sun eve and all day Mon. Longstanding temple of Jewish-Roman cuisine; L75,000.

Il Portico, Via del Portico d'Ottavia 1, ✆ 6830 7937. Closed Sat lunch and Sun eve. Gentile restaurant in the core of the Ghetto, serving good, non-kosher Jewish/Roman fare; L50,000.

Alberto Pica, Via della Seggiola 12. Closed Sun. A short diversion—but worth it for some of the best fruit ice creams and sorbets in Rome. Pity about the sour service.

> *The Capitol was the head of the world, where the consuls and senators abode to govern the Earth ... all adorned with gold and silver and brass and costly stones, to be a mirror to all nations. And it was therefore called Golden Capitol, because it excelled in wisdom and beauty before all the realms of the world.*

> —the 12th-century guide, *Mirabilia Urbis Romae*

None of the above is really true, but by the time a monkish chronicler compiled the *Mirabilia Urbis*, the **Capitoline Hill** had completely passed into legend. Rome did not begin here, nor did the hill ever serve as a seat of government in ancient times. But so entangled is this smallest and steepest mount with Rome's state myths and its presiding deities, that for all the citizens of the empire it was indeed the *caput* of the world they knew.

According to the historian Dionysius of Halicarnassus, workers digging the foundations for King Tarquin's original Temple of Jupiter found the head of a freshly slain man, dripping blood. Unable to get an explanation from the local soothsayers, Tarquin turned to the Etruscan oracles, who assured him that the prodigy meant that Rome was ordained by fate to be 'head' of all Italy. Another story had the name coming from *Caput Tollii*, the head of a mythical hero Tollius; either way, the tale follows a recurring motif in myth—like the head of the ancient god Bran buried under the Tower of London, that keeps England from harm.

The archaeologists' story is that sometime in the 7th century, the hill became a joint religious sanctuary for the scattered communities on the other Roman hills. Tarquin's great Temple of Jupiter (traditionally 590 BC) became the chief shrine of the state religion, replaced several times in the following centuries. Like most of the other temples on the hill, it disappeared almost without a trace during the Dark Ages, when the former hub of the Roman world became known as Monte Caprino—Goat Hill. The Capitol's long-delayed reappearance in history came in the 1140s, during Arnold of Brescia's republican revolution, when the Romans refounded the Senate and built a fortified palace for its meetings. Throughout the

Middle Ages, this new Capitol was the symbol of popular aspirations, and often of resistance against the popes.

> *Nowadays, you'll have to get around the looming hulk of the Vittoriano to even see it. In antiquity, the main approaches to the hill were on the south side, facing the Forum; since medieval times, when the centre of Roman life shifted to the Campus Martius, new ascents were created from the north. Standing behind the Vittoriano on **Via Teatro di Marcello** (you can thank Mussolini for this pitiless autobahn, doing its best to spoil the neighbourhood), you will see three flights of steps, one leading up steeply to the Aracoeli Church, another, the graceful **Cordonata** leading up to Michelangelo's Campidoglio, with Rome's city hall and the Capitoline Museums, and a minor, bush-flanked flight in between. But first look behind you, towards the little alley called Via della Tribuna di Tor de' Specchi, and the monastery of the same name. There isn't much to see, but the name—the **Tower of Mirrors**—recalls one of the most fascinating medieval legends of the Capitol.*

Somehow, in the confusion of the Dark Ages, the great poet Virgil became transmuted into Master Virgil, a consummate sorcerer whose magic helped the emperors rule the world. In Naples, where the real Virgil is buried, he built the famous Castel dell'Ovo, balanced on an eggshell in the bay, and got credit for the long Roman road tunnel at Fuorigrotta, along with the bronze fly and bronze horse that once perched atop the city gates, magically repelling invaders. In Rome, he was associated with every ancient marvel. Besides tales of magic talking statues and buried treasures, there was the tower Virgil built for the emperor, covered with mirrors facing every point of the compass. Whenever a province was threatened with invasion or revolt, the danger would appear beforehand, reflected in the mirrors, and the emperor would know how to deal with it.

> *To the left of the Aracoeli staircase, there is a jumble of ancient brick and masonry that most visitors never notice—the best surviving example of an insula in Rome.*

Originally six storeys tall, reconstructions of it in the Museum of Roman Civilization show a building that would look perfectly at home on any modern street, with a row of shops on the ground floor (now under the street level) and large windows on the mezzanine that may have been a wealthy residence or offices. The incongruous little steeple and frescoed apse on the side belonged to the church of San Biagio, built into the half-occupied ruin in the Middle Ages. The foot of these stairs is a fatal spot in Rome's history. In 121 BC a gang of senators and their clients and slaves murdered the great reformer Tiberius Gracchus here; in 1354 the scene was repeated when Cola di Rienzo, trying to escape Rome in disguise, was recognized by the rings on his fingers and torn to pieces by a mob of the citizens he had so grievously betrayed.

> *It doesn't matter which way you go up, but be sure to swivel round at the top for a wonderful view of Roman rooftops. Rienzo himself built the left-hand stair, and was the first to climb it; half-way up is a very flattering statue of the 'Last Tribune', on a base of random antique fragments (it seems like a view inside Rienzo's brain). While he ruled Rome, the church of **Santa Maria d'Aracoeli** (open daily at 7 am and 4 pm–3.30 pm in winter) was the meeting place of the reconstituted 'Senate'.*

Originally built in the 6th or 7th century, the 'altar of Heaven' commemorates the legend that the ancient Sibyl of Tivoli prophesied the coming of Jesus and told Augustus to build a temple here to the 'first born of God'. Until quite recently, people believed this to have been the site of the Temple of Jupiter. Edward Gibbon thought so, and while 'musing over the ruins' here he resolved to write the story of Rome's fall. So did Marcantonio Colonna, who celebrated the last old-fashioned Triumph here after helping the Spaniards and Venetians beat the Turks at Lepanto in 1571. In fact, this was the site of the *Arx*, Rome's first citadel, where the honking of the geese, warning of a surprise night attack, saved the besieged Romans during the Gaulish sack of 390 BC. For centuries thereafter, the Romans commemorated the event each year by leading a goose in a chariot on a triumphal parade through the Forum (and with typically gentle Roman humour, they crucified a dog in memory of the sleeping citadel watchdogs). Later, the site held the temple of Juno Moneta. The title translates as 'warning' or 'admonishing' (in memory of the geese), but for us it means the origin of our words *mint* and *money*; the Roman state mint and treasury were included in the temple complex. Some of Juno's columns found their way into the original church. Though rebuilt in the 1200s and again in 1575, no one was ever able to give it a façade; its stark brick wall with the tiny rose windows, looming over the stairs, is still somehow one of the memorable landmarks of Rome. Beyond it, the gaudily decorated interior makes a striking contrast, hung with ballroom chandeliers under a gilt ceiling. On one of the columns on the left side of the nave, you can see the inscription *a cubiculo Augustorum*—it came from Augustus' apartments on the Palatine.

Near the entrance are three Renaissance tombs, including that of Giovanni Crivelli, by Donatello—not a very representative work of the greatest Renaissance sculptor, and badly worn down from too many centuries on the floor, but one of his only two works in Rome (the other is in St Peter's). Another tomb, that of the astronomer Lodovico Margani by Sansovino, stands opposite the main door. In the first chapel of the right aisle is the series of frescoes by Pinturicchio on the **Life of St Bernard of Siena**; brilliantly coloured and drawn with a careful attention to detail (note the fantasy architecture on the left, and the charming band of angel musicians), they rank among the finest early Renaissance cycles in Rome. Nearby, beyond the grotesque giant figure of Pope Gregory XIII, the *tomb of Luca Savelli* is probably by Arnolfo di Cambio, the great medieval sculptor-architect who designed Florence's Cathedral and Palazzo Vecchio. As was common in the antiquity-haunted Rome of the Middle Ages, Arnolfo built the tomb around an ancient sarcophagus.

Besides the contributions of the Renaissance Tuscans, the Aracoeli has some fine embellishments by the medieval Cosmati family and their followers: the pavement and the lovely pair of pulpits (*ambones*), and in the right transept, the *Tomb of Matteo di Acquasparta*, with a painting by Pietro Cavallini. The most celebrated miracle-working icon in Rome, and perhaps the only one who still makes house calls, resides in the second chapel of the right aisle: the *Santo Bambino* (Holy Child), carved by angels in olive wood from the Garden of Gethsemane, and completely covered in gold and jewels. The Bambino is often taken out, as a last resort, to the sickbeds of the desperately ill (according to Dickens, who witnessed such an occasion, its sudden appearance often succeeded in scaring them to death) and it receives letters from troubled souls the world over. Every year around Christmas, delegations of Roman children pay their respects to the image, reciting the poems and songs they have composed in its honour.

In the left aisle, besides monuments to Popes Leo X and Paul III—neither of whom is buried here—there is a painting of St Anthony by another early Renaissance Florentine, Benozzo Gozzoli (2nd chapel), and an unusual 16th-century allegory of the Virgin, drawn from the Book of Revelation (1st chapel).

> *Although you can cross directly from the church to **Piazza del Campidoglio**, it's worth running back down the steps to approach the piazza up the Cordonata. Designed by Michelangelo, it's an effortless climb, up a ramp crossed with shallow ridges —tone versions of ropes traditionally laid across hilly paths to help animals climb up them (hence the name: cordon = rope). As you climb, the Campidoglio slowly comes into view, a miniature open-air museum of Roman sculpture.*

The two big fellows at the top of the stair are the **Dioscuri** (the heavenly twins, Castor and Pollux). The first striking thing about them is a bizarre resemblance to Princess Diana; the second, their peculiar headgear. These odd caps (which they always sport in classical art) recall the eggshell from which they were born, after Zeus in the form of a swan ravished their mother Leda. Keeping them company are stone images of triumphs, milestones from the Appian Way, and statues of Constantine and Constans, though their most famous neighbour, gilded bronze equestrian **Marcus Aurelius**, has now, after years of restoration, been placed behind a glass screen in the courtyard of the Palazzo del Museo Capitolino, so you can't see it till you buy a ticket. See below.

Mottled with gold and verdigris, the benign and serious image of the philosopher-emperor represents Rome at its best; it survived destruction only because the Christians believed it was really Constantine. It stood for centuries in front of the pope's palace at the Lateran; Michelangelo moved it here when he redesigned the Campidoglio in 1538. An old Roman superstition holds that the world will come to an end when the last bit of gold flakes off. Fortunately, thanks to the restorers and his new glass cage, that doesn't look too imminent.

> *The only relic of the statue of **Marcus Aurelius** left in the piazza is the pedestal, designed by Michelangelo, who was also responsible for the lovely geometric pattern in the pavement around it. His designs for the **Palazzo Senatorio**, and the flanking **Palazzo dei Conservatori** and **Palazzo del Museo Capitolino**, now comprising the **Capitoline Museums**, were much tinkered with by later architects, but the ensemble came out as planned—as fine a civic centre as any town could desire.*

The **Palazzo Senatorio**, Rome's city hall, occupies the site of the medieval Senate House; its tower is almost a copy of its medieval predecessor, where a big bell hung to summon the citizens to war or to assemblies, imitating the practice of the free trading cities of Tuscany and north Italy. Below Michelangelo's elegant staircase, the **Goddess Roma** herself gazes over the piazza; she was originally a statue of Minerva, perhaps transformed when the empire evolved the artificial cult of the deified Roma. The building has seen more than its share of history; Mazzini and Garibaldi's Roman Republic was born here in the revolutions of 1848, and the present Italian Republic was declared after the plebiscite in 1946; it was also the birthplace of the European Community, upon the signing of the Treaty of Rome here in 1957. The building is closed to casual visitors, but they let everyone in on Rome's birthday, 21 April. You might also sneak in with a wedding party; between the Campidoglio, for the secular, and the Aracoeli, for the faithful, this is the nuptial showcase of Rome.

The palace rests on the massive foundations of the **Tabularium**, the Roman state archive; these can be seen better from the Forum. The piazza, in ancient times a depression between the temples of Juno and Jupiter, was known as the *Asylum*, from a tradition that Romulus offered refuge here to any criminals or fugitives that wanted to join his new robber camp. Beneath the pavement, ruins of the area still exist (not open to visitors), including those of the Temple of Veiovis, the shadowy 'god of night thunder', a mysterious infernal alter ego of Jove.

*Both of the other palaces on the piazza are part of the **Capitoline Museums**, the best-kept and richest collection of Roman art and relics (open Tues–Sat 9–1.30, Sun 9–1; also evenings, Tues and Sat 5–8 pm; April–Sept, Sat evenings 8.30 pm–11; closed Mon; adm L10,000, but free last Sun of each month).*

The **Palazzo Nuovo** (1655) on the north side of the square houses the greatest sculptures, many donated by Sixtus IV in 1471, before there was a Vatican museum to contain the papal hoard. In the courtyard, along with magnficent Marcus, is the huge, vaguely sinister form of 'Marforio', a 2nd-century AD river god. Before being imprisoned in a fountain, Marforio sprawled at the foot of the Capitol where, as one of Rome's 'talking statues', he exchanged witticisms with Pasquino. Next to see are two famous sarcophagi, one carved with a vigorous battle between the Romans and Gauls; the other, an unusual double sarcophagus of the 3rd century AD, has scenes of the life of Achilles.

Other marble celebrities are gathered on the first floor; beginning with the *Dying Gaul*, a copy of a bronze made in Pergamon in the 3rd century BC, commemorating Attalos I's defeat of the Gauls—surely the most poignant and noble work a nation ever created in memory of a defeated foe. Next, the graceful *Young Satyr*, a copy of Praxiteles' original, inspired Hawthorne's *The Marble Faun*, the book every traveller in the 19th century brought to read in Rome; a Hellenistic *Eros and Psyche* that inspired many later baubles; the red marble *Laughing Silenus*, a copy of a Hellenistic work; *Infant Hercules*, wrestling with a snake, said to be a portrait of Caracalla already ugly at the tender age of five. Two rooms are lined with busts of philosophers (Homer, Socrates, Pythagoras and other leading lights) and emperors, where the Roman fascination with realism is striking—unlike the idealizing Greeks, the Romans wanted to be remembered with all their flaws intact, creating unflattering marble 'photographs' in which Augustus comes out fairly august; Caracalla with his sideburns looks like a Victorian robber baron and Elagabalus like the child molester he probably was.

Among the emperors sits a fine statue of *Helena*, mother of Constantine, and on the walls are two exquisite bas-reliefs of Endymion and Perseus rescuing Andromeda. Two expressive statues of old women stand out—one terrified and one tipsy. The voluptuous *Capitoline Venus* is so steamy she gets a room to herself; an excellent Roman copy of Praxiteles' *Aphrodite of Cnidos,* which so aroused at least one ancient Greek that he sexually assaulted it; the statue was discovered in the 17th century where its owner, fearing the Christians' prudish axes, had carefully walled it up for safekeeping. The 'Room of Doves' is named after two charming works: a jewel-like mosaic from Hadrian's villa and a statue of a little girl sheltering a dove in her hands.

*Save your ticket for the rest of the museum across the piazza in the **Palazzo dei Conservatori**, rebuilt in 1564 after a design by Michelangelo.*

Dominating the courtyard like lost props from a Fellini movie are the giant head, foot, and pointing hand from a colossal statue of Constantine found in the Basilica of Maxentius (the rest of him was apparently made of wood, dressed in sheets of bronze); here, too, is an inscription from the Arch of Claudius (51 AD) celebrating his conquest of Britain, and reliefs of other Roman conquests taken from the temple of Hadrian in Piazza di Pietra. Inside are more triumphal reliefs from the **Arch of Marcus Aurelius**—some of the finest ever done in Rome, including scenes of the emperor's clemency and piety, and his victorious receptions in Rome. Marcus always looks a little worried in these, perhaps considering his good-for-nothing son Commodus and the empire he would inherit, more than ever sunk into corruption and excess.

Among the bronzes is the famous **Capitoline Wolf**, an Etruscan work of the 6th century BC, to which Antonio Pollaiuolo added the suckling twins in 1510; the *Spinario*, a 1st-century BC bronze of a boy pulling a thorn from his foot; a beautiful but uncomfortable bronze bed, a litter, a reconstructed chariot (used to transport images of the gods to the Circus games), a hermaphrodite, a horse and half a bull. The late Empire works are often in a kitsch style recalling the 1964 New York World's Fair: especially another swollen head, hand, and globe (of Constans II), and another ball from the top of the Vatican Obelisk, once believed to contain the ashes of Julius Cæsar and used for target practice in the 1527 Sack of Rome.

One room contains statues, some made in the 'archaic' fashion popular in the 1st century AD; another has imported Attic vases of the 6th century BC, one with pictures of Achilles playing dice with Ajax and another with Odysseus and the Cyclops. More recent efforts include statues of *Charles of Anjou* by Arnolfo di Cambio, *Innocent X* by Algardi, and *Urban VIII* by Bernini. A passage leads past a musty tufa wall of the 6th-century BC Temple of Jupiter Best and Greatest (see below) to the **New Wing**, with Republican art, including some of the earliest Roman frescoes ever discovered (3rd century BC), a relief of Marcus Curtius hurtling into the abyss, mosaics, friezes, and a 5th-century BC *Apollo the Archer.* The exhibits continue in the 'Museo Nuovo' in Palazzo Caffarelli, off the tufa wall passage: look especially for the Hellenistic statue of the *Muse Polyhymnia*, one of the loveliest pieces in the museum; also more good Roman busts and reproductions of Greek art.

The **Pinacoteca** on the second floor has a small but diverse collection of paintings: from the 14th century, a series of panels on New Testament scenes; a beautiful but anonymous 16th-century *Madonna, Child, and Saints*; Guercino's vast *Burial of S. Petronilla* (1622) painted for St Peter's, with a gaping tomb in the foreground from which mysterious hands emerge to support the saint's body, while above she is welcomed into heaven. Another, even more influential Baroque painting in its day was Pietro da Cortona's *Rape of the Sabines* (1629), with its romantic-antique detail and twisting, sculptural groups of figures. Caravaggio contributes two works: *The Fortune teller*, predicting adventure to a young man (a self-portrait?) and the *Young St John*, in a never-before-seen-pose, a painting lost in a long gallery of coy 18th-century china shepherdesses and monkey musicians in powdered wigs.

There's also a giant gilt bronze Hercules, found in the Forum Boarium, and a medley of Venetian art: masculine portraits by Gentile and Giovanni Bellini; Mary Magdalenes by Veronese and Tintoretto; an *Adulteress* by Palma Vecchio, and Lorenzo Lotto's sly *Gentleman with a Crossbow*. There's a copy of Jacopino del Conte's Portrait of Michelangelo, perhaps the best-known likeness of the artist; some cocky Dutchmen from Van Dyck; an eerie Witch by proto-romantic Salvator Rosa; rosy-cheeked Romulus and Remus by Rubens; and disdainful of his fellow paintings, Velazquez's *Portrait of a Gentleman,* thought by some to be Bernini.

> *To descend, take the street just to the right of the Capitol steps, behind the Palazzo dei Conservatori and through the eerie stillness of the Capitol. The southern end is largely a park, planted with pines and laurel, and a few cedars of Lebanon (lately it has become central Rome's gay pick-up area). Fragments of the* **Temple of Jupiter** *can be seen, including a large relief of a quadriga, through a gate, in the gardens on Via di Villa Caffarelli.*

Before the Etruscans came to dominate Rome, Mars apparently was the city's chief deity; throughout the centuries, when victorious generals finished their triumphal parades at the foot of this temple, they had their faces painted red to 'imitate Mars'. When King Tarquin the Proud built the first Temple of Jupiter Best and Greatest, he was expressing in stone an unrecorded but very important religious revolution. As in Etruscan temples, this one (and all its successors) took the classical Greek form, but with three chambers instead of one, perhaps originally dedicated to the triad of Jupiter, Juno and Minerva (Tinia, Uni and Menvra to the Etruscans).

The fragments of the cornice are from the last Temple, rebuilt by Domitian after a fire in 80 AD. Even under the empire, rubber-stamp consuls and other magistrates of ancient fame would come here to receive their insignia of office. Every year the Senate held its first meeting in the Temple, making the appropriate sacrifices, and on certain occasions the images of the three gods were carried through Rome in solemn procession—just as Italians today parade their Madonnas and saints on holy days. The 'Golden' Capitol, so called for its gilded roof, was not the largest temple ever built in Rome (that of Venus and Rome surpassed it), but shining atop its hill it would have been the city's most conspicuous landmark. Emperor Honorius' general, the Vandal Stilicho, made off with the gilt bronze roof and the golden doors and statues to pay his army, but the records are silent as to how the temple came to disappear so completely—though as the chief symbol of the old religion, the Christians were probably anxious to be rid of it.

> *To leave the Capitol, return to the piazza and take Via del Campidoglio (at the right-hand side of the Palazzo del Senatorio) which runs downhill into Via di Monte Tarpeo. From here there are stupendous views over the Roman Forum. The steep cliffs on this part of the hill are generally believed to be the famous **Tarpeian Rock**, from which the Romans tossed condemned criminals.*

Tarpeia, after whom it is named, was an early Roman maiden who betrayed the Capitol to the Sabines (they smashed her to pulp with their shields by way of thanks; no one liked a traitor in those days). Some scholars still argue over the rock's location, holding it to be either on the north slopes (now under the Vittoriano) or on the west.

> *At the bottom of the hill, **Santa Maria della Consolazione**, on the piazza of the same name, sports an early Baroque façade by Longhi and Roman Mannerist frescoes by Taddeo Zuccari (usually closed). Rome's first settlement may have existed here, in the marshy area called the **Velabrum**, the legendary spot where Romulus and Remus' basket washed up and where the she-wolf found them. Like all of Rome south of the Capitol and Forum, this quiet, almost deserted area is full of old churches, all with something of interest but usually always closed. On the west side of the piazza a short flight of steps leads up to Via dei Fienili, which takes you up to Via S. Teodoro.*

The circular **San Teodoro** (closed) was built into the slope of the Palatine, over the ruins of a state grain storehouse. Behind it, the massive substructure of the Palace of Tiberius makes an impressive sight along the slopes of the Palatine.

> *Next, head down Via di S. Teodoro and around the corner into Via Velabro.*

S. Giorgio in Velabro is an elegant, simple interior of the 7th century but, following a bomb explosion in 1993, the portico has been destroyed and the apse by Pietro Cavallini damaged. Attached to the side, the **Arcus Argentarium** was built in 204 AD by the moneychangers of Rome in honour of Septimius Severus and his family—you can still make out the figures of the emperor, his wife, Julia

Domna, and his son Caracalla underneath the arch. The blank space next to Caracalla was occupied by a relief of his brother Geta, until Caracalla murdered him. Geta instantly became a non-person, and his portrait, like the inscription on the Arch of Septimius Severus, was effaced. On the outer wall, under the cornice, is a hale and hearty relief of Hercules in his lion's skin.

The moneychangers had plenty of business on this spot; it was the Forum Boarium, early Rome's cattle market, and though it's hard to imagine cows tramping through the Urbs in imperial times, plenty of market business was still being transacted in the arch's shade. The nearby stretch of the Tiber was always lined with docks.

> *Via Velabro opens into* **Piazza Bocca della Verità**, *passing another monument of the cattle market, the bulky* **Arch of Janus**.

This one was built in honour of Constantine, or perhaps Constans II; its form, and the woeful fragments of older monuments snatched off to decorate it, testify to the decadence of the age. Of the figures on the keystones of the four arches, the standing ones were Janus and the Goddess Roma, the seated ones Ceres and Minerva. Around the corner is **S. Giovanni Decollato** ('St John with the head chopped off'; in the sack of Rome in 1527 soldiers reputedly used the Baptist's head for a football). Have a look inside if it's open, for some unusual Mannerist frescoes by Salviati, Vasari, Ligorio, and others.

> *The piazza, facing the Tiber, would be one of the loveliest spots in Rome without its usual fierce traffic. Facing the two ancient temples on the river bank is another early church, one of the best preserved in Rome,* **Santa Maria in Cosmedin** *(open 9–12 and 3–5).*

In the 8th century, this was the centre of the *Schola Graeca*, the Greek neighbourhood of Rome, its ranks swelled by refugees from Iconoclast persecutions in the East. They must have loved their holy images dearly; the church Pope Adrian I rebuilt for them in the 770s soon acquired the appellation *in Cosmedin* (meaning 'decorated', from the same Greek root as our word *cosmetics*—and also, oddly enough *cosmos*). The church's best known ornament is a marble disc that probably began life as a lid for a well or cistern. Carved with the ghostly face of a man, it was built into the façade of the medieval church to become the **Bocca della Verità**—the mouth of truth, that gives the piazza its name. Romans would come here to swear oaths, test the chastity of their wives, and close business deals. If you tell a lie with your hand in the image's mouth, he will bite it off. Go ahead and try it.

A fortuitous restoration of the 1890s peeled off the Baroque façade imposed by a well-meaning cardinal in 1741, leaving the exterior much as it was in the Middle

Ages, but without the mosaics or paintings that must originally have covered it. Inside, decorations include some excellent Cosmati work: pavement, candlesticks, choir screen, and bishop's throne, all dating from the 12th-century rebuilding that gave the church its tall and lovely campanile. The Gothic *baldacchino* over the altar came later (*c.* 1290) but it too was the work of a descendant of the Cosmati. Among the more ancient remains are the recycled columns in the nave, and columns from an altar of Hercules in the crypt (possibly to commemorate his slaying of the giant Cacus here—see Palatine Hill). The medieval mosaics in the apse are very faded, but there is a lovely 8th-century mosaic of the *Adoration of the Magi* (detached) in a room off the right aisle. Little else remains of the Greek church, excepting perhaps the odd marble latticework on the west wall, and the ceiling painted with stars—almost too faded to see, but the Greek original must have glittered with a bright blue and gold firmament.

Like S. Teodoro, and several other early Roman churches, this one had its beginnings as a chapel of a *diaconicon*—one of the pope's combination supply centres, military stores and charity distribution points. Gregory the Great probably began the system, commandeering the old warehouses to reorganize the food supply for Rome's beleaguered populace in the 590s. This centre, only a stone's throw from the Circus Maximus, had been the bread of the Bread and Circuses—the *Statio Annonae*, headquarters of the imperial dole. Around the walls of the church are embedded 17 impressive columns from the *Annonae*, and near the door you will see a pair of round stones—the market's standard weights.

> To see the two best preserved pagan temples in Rome, you wouldn't look in the Forum or on the Palatine, but in this unlikely spot (where few visitors ever do find them). Across Via Petroselli, on the other side of the piazza, stand the round **Temple of Vesta** and the **Temple of Fortuna Virilis**.

Or so they've been named—both attributions are in fact mistaken guesses by early archaeologists. Vesta's, so called because its round shape reminded them of the Vestal Virgins' shrine in the Forum, was probably dedicated to Hercules Victor (2nd century BC; one of the very first marble buildings in Rome, built by a Greek architect), and connected to the altar under S. Maria in Cosmedin. Its cornice and domed roof are long gone. The other, originally much older, was rebuilt about the same time. It seems to have honoured Portunus, a god of harbours; this stretch of river was Rome's first port (and perhaps there was a connection with the safe landing of Romulus and Remus). Both temples, like the Pantheon, only survived thanks to their reconsecration as Christian churches.

> *Lean over the Tiber Embankment here to see the mouth of King Tarquin's famous sewer, the **Cloaca Maxima**, still efficiently draining the Forum area after 2400 years.*

The present tunnel, wide enough to drive two carriages through, is from the 2nd century BC. The Etruscans may get a bit too much credit for engineering here—their original was probably only an open ditch. Just beyond the next bridge, the Ponte Palatino, stand the sorrowful remains of Rome's first stone bridge, the Pons Aemilius, built in 142 BC. Now better known as the **Ponte Rotto**—the broken bridge—it was already collapsing in the 1500s when the popes started raiding its stone, inexplicably leaving the lone arch in midstream. Originally there were seven, a good indicator of how much wider the Tiber was, with its shallow banks, before the building of the Embankments.

> *Head back across Piazza Bocca della Verità to have a look at the **House of the Crescenzi** in the northwest corner.*

Incorporating fragments scavenged from every sort of ancient building, it's one of the best examples of Rome's magpie school of architecture. It was built around 1100 for the powerful Crescenzi clan, descendants of former Castel Sant'Angelo dwellers and pontiff-killers Theodora and Marozia. The younger generation was conscious enough of Rome's great past to attempt this imitation of a classical noble dwelling—also conscious of the need to make it a strong fortress for defence.

> *Continue back towards the Capitol on Via Petroselli, passing on the right some recent excavations in what may be the oldest inhabited corner of Rome, the **Sacred Area of Sant'Omobono**.*

Over the fence, you'll see the foundations of 5th-century BC 'twin temples' to Fortuna and to Mater Matuta (the former under the church of Sant'Omobono). Some fragments of pottery here go back as far as 1100 BC. Across the street is the church of **San Nicola in Carcere**, built over the ruins of temples to Janus, Juno, and Spes (Hope) and last remodelled by Della Porta in 1599; the columns of the temples are still in plain view, helping to hold up the walls.

> *This area, full of temples in ancient times, continued the densely populated string of markets, warehouses and docks along the Tiber; it was the **Forum Holitarium,** the marketplace for fruit and vegetables. Sitting incongruously next to it—but the market noise would have died down before showtime—is the weathered hulk of the **Theatre of Marcellus.***

Julius Cæsar, the sort of Roman who might have appreciated real theatre, began the work; he planned it big (15,000 seats) to upstage Pompey, whose own theatre in the Campus Martius was just being completed. Augustus finished it in 23 BC, dedicating it to his son-in-law Marcellus, who had just died. Despite the poets of the Latin New Comedy, serious theatre never really caught on in Rome, and very soon degenerated into bloody spectacles differing little from the shows at the Colosseum (see Pompey's Theatre, p. 175). By 235, the public had decided they liked them better in the amphitheatre, and this huge pile was abandoned. In the age of Constantine the Romans were carting off its stones to repair the bridges.

In the Dark Ages, noble families turned the ruin into a fortress; its strategic location dominated both the Tiber and the southern approaches to the shrunken city. For whatever reason, it changed hands often; Fabii, Caetani, Savelli, Pierlioni, and Orsini all controlled it at one time or another. The Savelli commissioned Baldassare Peruzzi to add some Renaissance style to the upper storeys, now fashionable apartments. Mussolini's dismal archaeologists cleared the surrounding buildings and excavated the foundations; before that, the half-sunken ruin with little shops hiding under the great arches was one of the picturesque sights of the city.

> *Walking around the north side of the theatre, you pass three elegant standing columns which belonged to the* **Temple of Apollo***, a 5th-century original rebuilt in 33* BC. *Just beyond, Via Montanara opens into long, narrow Piazza di Campitelli, the centre of the medieval rione of the same name—a corruption of Capitolinum.* **Santa Maria in Campitelli** *(1663–7) is the star of the piazza's Baroque ensemble.*

This is the masterpiece of Carlo Rainaldi, introducing North Italian elements to the Roman Baroque, in the complex façade (very like his earlier S. Andrea della Valle) and the striking interior, where carefully placed pairs of columns shape the main axis into an unusual perspectivist effect.

> *Pass behind the church, down narrow Via Trib. Campitelli, and head on straight through the small brick archway that was medieval Rome's fishmarket. Then turn around and look back to see another of Rome's surprises, the well-preserved façade of the* **Portico of Octavia***.*

What you see, the columned propylaeum or entrance, is only a small part of the original, built by Augustus and named after his sister; behind it stretched a great square colonnade of some 300 columns, enclosing twin temples to Jupiter and Juno. There was also a library, and some celebrated works of Greek sculpture for decoration. The unusual thing about such a complex is its setting, at the edge of the hurly-burly of the Roman markets. It would not have seemed strange to a Roman, accustomed to crowds and noise, with every facet of urban life jumbled together. The ancient fishmarket was here too, the Forum Piscarium, and if there were no stands inside the complex itself, the fish and their aroma were certainly close enough to distract the priests in the temples and the scholars at their desks.

In the Middle Ages, though the fish remained, the neighbourhood acquired a different destiny, as the home of the city's Jewish community. Much reduced from ancient times, when some 30–50,000 Jews populated both sides of the Tiber in this district, the community has survived every sort of persecution and hard times.

> Walk down **Via del Portico d'Ottavia**, the main street, and do not be surprised to find at least a faint resemblance to a street on New York's Lower East Side: Jewish restaurants and bakeries, clothing wholesalers and workshops on the back streets. The four broad city blocks south of the street, bordered by Piazza delle Cinque Scuole (ex Via del Progresso, in case you have an old map) and the Tiber, were the site of the **Jewish Ghetto**.

It is something of a misconception that ghettos are a relic of the bad old Middle Ages. In Italy at least, systematic, carefully planned persecution is a relatively recent phenomenon. That Counter-Reformation charmer, Paul IV, the father of the Inquisition, decreed that Jews should be locked up in a Ghetto only in 1555. He also forced them to wear distinctive clothing, and attend sermons for their conversion, and limited their livelihood to the trade in used clothes and old iron. Within this four-block area as many as 5000 people lived, in an anthill-like maze of tall tenements and narrow alleys. Behind the Ghetto walls, which were locked at dusk, few non-Jews ever penetrated, other than society ladies sneaking in incognito to visit the renowned Jewish fortune-tellers.

Though all sources agree on the degradation of the closely-packed Ghetto, it had its advantages: a refuge, physical and psychological, from common bigotry, and fixed rents in perpetuity. In 1870, almost one of the first acts of the new Italian Kingdom after the liberation of Rome was to tear down the Ghetto Walls. Since then the Jewish community has largely moved on to other neighbourhoods, and the land has been completely cleared for new streets and buildings.

> Via del Portico d'Ottavia is an ancient street, with remains of several old Roman and medieval buildings built into later structures.

The most outlandish is the richly decorated façade of the **House of Laurentius Manlius**, carved with patriotic inscriptions and portraits of the family. Manlius is trying to fool us; he isn't an ancient Roman at all, but a Renaissance admirer named Lorenzo Manilio who built it in 1468—or year 2221 of the founding of Rome, as the Latin inscriptions attest.

> Heading across Piazza delle Cinque Scuole, you pass the rear of **Palazzo Cenci**, home of Shelley's sad heroine Beatrice (who paid thugs to kill her father after he violated her, and was executed for it); to the left on

*ruins of the Ghetto in the 1870s. Pope John Paul II paid a historic visit here in April 1986, the first modern pope to make such an ecumenical gesture. There is a small **museum** with historical and ritual objects (daily exc Fri pm and Sat, 9.30–2 and 3–5, Sun 10–12; L4000).*

*Across from it, facing the Tiber, is a lonely little church with a faded Christian fresco and Hebrew inscription above the door. **San Gregorio** was one of the places where Ghetto Jews were compelled to attend mass; the inscription uses a quotation from Isaiah (65.1.2) to reproach them for not converting.*

*The graceful bridge with the two arches opposite the Synagogue is the oldest surviving one in Rome, the **Pons Fabricius**, begun in 62 BC. It leads to the **Tiber Island**.*

The little island with the tapering ends suggests a ship anchored in the river, and the ancient Romans used the thought to create a fond landmark, building a big stone prow and stern for it (remains of which can still be seen on the downstream side), and an obelisk in the middle for a mast. Most of the island is covered by a hospital—now, as always, for the Tiber Island has been dedicated to medicine since 289 BC. Legend states that after a plague in 293, the Sibylline Books directed the Romans to seek aid from the famous Temple of Aesculapius in Epidauros. The Greek God of Healing sent one of his snakes (those serpents that twine around the staff of Aesculapius, a medical symbol to this day) into the Romans' ship where it coiled around the mast. Amazed at the prodigy, the Romans sailed home, where the serpent slid off the ship and swam up-river to this spot. A temple to the god was founded, connected to a famous hospital.

Classical medicine (at least until the time of Galen, the great Roman scientist and physician of the 2nd century) depended heavily on the psychological side of healing; it would drive a modern doctor crazy. There were dream cures, requiring physicians or priests to appear to drugged patients in the guise of Aesculapius, holy serpents to apply to wounds, hypnotism and water from the sacred well. No one knows if a hospital survived here through the Dark Ages, but there was something like one in medieval times; the present **Ospedale Fatebenefratelli** ('Do well, brothers') dates from 1538. Despite its venerable appearance, it is a thoroughly up-to-date institution today.

*Opposite the hospital, built over the ruins of Aesculapius' temple, is the church of **San Bartolomeo**.*

Emperor Otto III built it in the late 900s, in honour of his friend St Adelbert, patron of Bohemia. The high altar is recycled from one of the greatest status symbols an ancient Roman could own—a porphyry bathtub; in front of it, the covered medieval well is probably the font of the ancient hospital's sacred spring, carved with images of Christ and St Adelbert. In the chapel to the right, the expressive fresco of the Madonna and Child (with two pet Byzantine lions) dates from the founding of the church. One of the monks here, Padre Martini, is a notable sculptor, and the church is well endowed with his elegantly ascetic semi-abstract works.

From the Tiber Island, where the walk ends, it's a short walk over to the centre of Trastevere (with lots of nice places to eat, drink and people-watch), or back to Piazza Venezia. The no. 23 bus, following the east bank of the Tiber, takes you up near Castel Sant'Angelo and the Vatican. The second oldest complete Roman bridge, (30 BC) **Pons Cestius** much restored, leads to the centre of Trastevere— a good place to go if it's time for lunch (see p. 343-5 and Walk XIII—or back to Piazza Venezia. The no. 23 bus takes you up near Castel Sant' Angelo and the Vatican.

i fori romani

II: Forum, Palatine and Colosseum

Trajan's Column	109
The Imperial Fora	111
Mamertine Prison	112
Roman Forum	113
Palatine Hill	123
Colosseum	131
Santa Francesca Romana	133

Start: *Piazza Venezia, near Trajan's Column.*

Finish: *Via dei Fori Imperiali, a short distance from the Colosseum.*

Walking Time: *If you really hoof it, you can see the centre of ancient Rome in about five hours, though be kind to yourself and give it most of a day.*

> *Thou stranger, which for Rome in Rome here seekest,*
> *And nought of Rome in Rome perceiv'st at all,*
> *These same olde walls, old arches, which thou seest,*
> *Olde palaces, is that which Rome men call.*
> *Behold what wreake, what ruine, and what wast,*
> *And how that she, which with her mightie powre*
> *Tam'd all the world, hath tam'd herselfe at last,*
> *The prey of Time, which all things doth devowre.*
> *Rome, living, was the world's sole ornament,*
> *And dead, is now the world's sole moniment.*

Spenser, *The Ruines of Rome*

Spenser never visited Rome, but like many Elizabethans he loved to indulge in the melancholy of wreake and ruine, nowhere more striking than in the fossil heart of the ancient empire—its famous seats of government and temples of the Forum, the imperial residence on the Palatine hill, and the brooding shell of the Colosseum. Much of what had awed travellers and conquerors 1500 years ago is now the world's most glorified rubble, poignantly setting off the few columns and arches that have survived a cannibalizing citizenry, far too familiar with Rome's past to have any respect for the sanctity of its remains. The most famous buildings of the empire were enthusiastically consigned to the dustbin of history and their building stone to homes and churches, their magnificent marbles to the maw of the lime kiln. The Roman Forum became the *Campo Vaccino*, or Cow Pasture; the Palatine, residence of emperors, was planted with gardens; the Via Sacra, the road of golden triumphs of conquest, was renamed Via Fabatosta, or Street of Roast Beans; and nature forgave the Colosseum its enormities by strewing it with wild flowers and exotic plants. History's dust was so deep that scholars even argued that the Roman Forum was actually located elsewhere.

For Rome's dreamy-eyed lovers, these romantic, ivy-wreathed ruins among the cow pats were far more evocative than the sterile archaeological pits that the Forum and Palatine have become. In response, the tendency in recent years has been to step back, plant trees, and let the grass grow between the stones, making this walk through the very core of ancient Rome a treat for the eye as well as

Roman Forum, Palatine and Colosseum

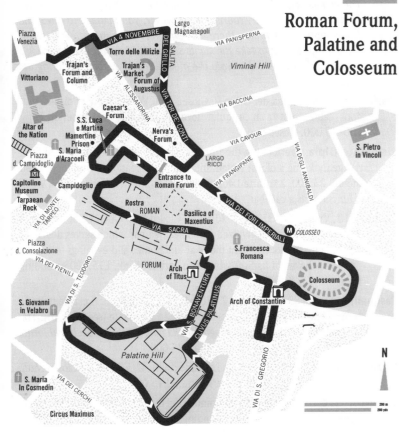

Piazza Venezia

VIA 4 NOVEMBRE

Torre delle Milizie

Largo Magnanapoli

SALITA DEL GRILLO

VIA PANISPERNA

Viminal Hill

Trajan's Forum and Column

Trajan's Market

Forum of Augustus

VIA ALESSANDRINA

VIA TOR DE' CONTI

VIA BACCINA

Vittoriano

Caesar's Forum

S.S. Luca e Martina

Mamertine Prison

S. Maria d'Aracoeli

Nerva's Forum

VIA CAVOUR

S. Pietro in Vincoli

Altar of the Nation

Piazza d. Campidoglio

LARGO RICCI

VIA FRANGIPANE

VIA DEGLI ANNIBALDI

Capitoline Museum

Campidoglio

Entrance to Roman Forum

Tarpaean Rock

VIA DI MONTE TARPEO

Rostra

ROMAN

VIA SACRA

Basilica of Maxentius

VIA DEI FORI IMPERIALI

M COLOSSEO

Piazza d. Consolazione

VIA DEI FIENILI

FORUM

S.Francesca Romana

VIA DI S. TEODORO

Arch of Titus

Colosseum

S. Giovanni in Velabro

VIA S. BONAVENTURA

CLIVUS PALATINUS

Arch of Constantine

Palatine Hill

VIA DI S. GREGORIO

N

S. Maria In Cosmedin

VIA DEI CERCHI

Circus Maximus

200 m
200 yds

for your historical imagination. Bring plenty of the latter, along with a pair of comfortable shoes and a bottle of wine to tantalize the thirsty ghosts. Or better yet, plan a picnic (discreetly, as the guards may not approve) on the Palatine gardens, over the ruins of Caligula's dining-room. In summer, start as early as possible to avoid heat stroke; there's little shade in the Forum, though the groves of the Palatine gardens are a fine refuge from the afternoon sun. Beware the shorter hours on Sunday and Tuesday!

The archaeological zone is full of dire eateries, cashing in on the droves of famished, foot-weary tourists. If, however, you manage to reach the Colosseum by lunchtime, there are some very pleasant retreats nearby, though if you want to take the sights slowly, the best option is to pack a picnic. Whatever you do, avoid the mobile snack wagons cluttering the roadsides.

Mario's Hostaria, Piazza del Grillo 9. Closed Sun. Wide variety of dishes, outdoor tables and a nice quiet location behind the Imperial Fora; L30–35,000, closed Sun.

Ristorante Ulpia, overlooking the Imperial fora, ℂ 678 9980. Closed Sun. Allegedly Rome's oldest restaurant, beautiful location, awful food; fixed menu L25,000; à la carte L40,000.Instead, come between 4 and 7, when it functions as a café-bar.

Cavour 313, Via Cavour 313, ℂ 678 5496. Closed Sun. Open 12.30–2.30 and 7.30 pm–1.30 am. A civilized wood-beamed bar which serves delicious, high quality snacks and light meals at lunchtimes and evenings to accompany whichever of its 500 wines you care to drink. L15,000 excluding wine.

Pasqualino, Via dei SS Quattro 66, ℂ 700 4576. Closed Mon. A classic trattoria convenient for both the Colosseum and San Clemente (see Walk III). Traditional Roman dishes like *spaghetti alla carbonara, abbacchio al forno, saltimbocca* and *trippa alla romana*; L35,000.

Pizza Forum, Via di San Giovanni in Laterano 34–8, ℂ 700 2515. Closed Mon. Neopolitan pizza in a theme-park forum; L15,000.

Ulderico, Via di San Giovanni in Laterano 106, ℂ 735 724. Closed Sun. Good honest tratt fare, in surroundings unchanged since the fifties; L25–30,000.

Caffè Martini, Piazza del Colosseo 3B, ℂ 700 4431. Closed Wed. With its grubby table-cloths, multilingual menu (advertising capricious pizza) and a soundtrack of roaring traffic, the Martini looks like the kind of place to avoid at all costs. In fact, it serves an extremely good (and cheap) lasagne.

Bar Pasticceria, Via di San Giovanni in Laterano 44. Nothing special, but the pleasantest of the many snack bars around here. *Tavola calda* at lunchtime, along with *pizza romana* and sandwiches.

Turn your back on the maelstrom of Piazza Venezia, watch out for thieving gipsy kids, and take a brief look at the twinned domed churches overlooking Trajan's Forum. The first, Santa Maria di Loreto, is a High Renaissance bauble begun by Antonio da Sangallo, crowned by a pretty lantern by Giacomo del Duca from 1582. If it's open, pop in to see François Duquesnoy's statue of **S. Susanna**, *his highly influential 1633 masterpiece that unites classical grace and beauty with a gentle naturalisma Baroque alternative model to Bernini's twists and shouts. The second church,* **SS. Nome di Maria** *was added to balance the picture in the 18th century. This is the best spot to see what you can of* **Trajan's Column**, *since the enclosed pit around it has been closed for years.*

Built of marble drums 100 Roman feet high, the column (perhaps designed by Trajan himself) commemorates the emperor's two victorious campaigns in Dacia (modern Romania, 101–2 and 105–6 AD), the subject of the magnificent sculptural frieze, 200 m long, that winds around the column and was originally painted as brightly as a barbershop pole. The sculptors, anonymous but some of Rome's finest, expertly hid the drum joinings and the 43 windows that light the internal spiral stair leading to the viewing platform on top (now closed). When Trajan died suddenly in Cilicia, his successor Hadrian brought his ashes back to Rome and buried them at the foot of the column. Never before had anyone been interred within the sacred limits of the *pomerium*; Hadrian explained that, after all, Trajan was no mere mortal, but a god.

The scrolling reliefs were designed to be read from the balconies of two libraries, one Greek, one Roman, flanking the column. From ground level making sense of the reliefs is not easy (though you can see casts at eye-level in EUR's Museum of Roman Civilization). Trajan's column survived centuries of rapacious Romans mainly because it was a profitable tourist attraction in the Middle Ages, and connected to a pious tale; Gregory the Great, strolling one day through the forum, noticed the relief on the column showing Trajan dismounting to grant justice to a poor widow. The good Pope wept to think of such a good man condemned to suffer eternal torment for merely being a pagan, and as he wept, a voice in St Peter's announced that his request for Trajan's salvation had been granted, adding, however, that he had better not make such requests too often! The area around the column became sacred, and was used as a cemetery. The legend continues that when Trajan was exhumed there, his tongue was miraculously alive in his skull, to tell of his salvation from hell. In 1588 a statue of St Peter was placed on top of the column as if to rubberstamp as much of this as you care to believe.

After the pious emperor's death, Hadrian added a massive **Temple of Trajan**, located where the twin churches now stand, though it was so thoroughly quarried that only part of one great granite column survives. The broken columns and fragments of marble pavement you see in front of the column mark the **Basilica Ulpia** (named for Trajan's family) one of the largest basilicas in Rome, extending across the entire width of the forum.

> *Take stepped Via Magnanapoli to Via Quattro Novembre and turn right for* **Trojan's Forum,** *nowadays entered via Trajan's slendid semicircular multistorey markets. Open Tues–Sat, 9–1.30; Sun 9-1; but sometimes open longer hours when there are exhibitions in the market; closed Mon; adm L3000.*

Begun in 107 AD, Trajan's Forum the grandest of the five imperial fora, was the Rockefeller Center of the Empire, a huge project of impeccable design by Apollodorus of Damascus. In building it, Trajan completed the twofold plan begun by that urban visionary, Julius Cæsar, when he added the first 'imperial forum': to eliminate crowding in the Roman Forum and to link southern Rome to the Campus Martius by lopping off a spur of the Quirinale. This was no mean achievement in the pre-bulldozer era, especially when you consider that the height of Trajan's column marks the original ground level. The forum and marketplace he built in the new space awed contemporaries, and the nobility of its architecture inspired noble acts: here slaves were freed, Hadrian and Aurelian burned lists of state debtors and political prisoners, and Marcus Aurelius auctioned off the emperor's personal treasures to avoid raising new war taxes. When Constantine saw it for the first time he sadly conceded that nothing he could build in his new 'Rome' on the Bosphorus would equal the work of Trajan.

> *The modern entrance gives access to the second floor of the hemicycle, built into the side of the Quirinale.*

Originally it faced a matching hemicyclical wall, screening the forum, and now completely destroyed. This was the Harrod's or Macy's of ancient times, lacking only escalators; 150 booths in all, now utterly bare, but 1700 years ago stocking, it is thought, wine and oil on the ground and first floors; imports, pepper and spices on the second (even in the Middle Ages this floor remained the lane of pepper sellers, the flagstone-paved Via Biberatica); on the third floor was the hall of the 'Congiaria', or welfare office, where food and money were distributed to the needy; and on the fourth, fresh fish were kept alive in two ponds, one filled with sea water piped in from Ostia, and the other fed with fresh water from an aqueduct; among them there might have been a mollusc or two from Colchester, delivered express by oyster-relay along the Roman roads. The market owes its preservation to its conversion into a convent, while the southern edge was used as a castle. A mighty reminder of this is the knobby, medieval **Torre delle**

Milizie built on a Byzantine base over the hemicycle; according to one anachronistic tradition, it was from its splendid vantage point that Nero fiddled while Rome burned.

> Steps lead down to the ground floor of the hemicycle and the once porticoed forum, of which lazy cats are the main feature today. From the corner, a tunnel (now closed, and used for storing archaeological bits and pieces) cuts under the street to the second enclosure.
>
> If the idea of treading where Augustus trod thrills you, try to get permission before leaving Trajan's Markets to visit the Forum of Augustus and the Casa dei Cavalieri di Rodi. Leaving the markets, continue a few steps up Via Quattro Novembre to Largo Magnanapoli, address of an unheralded Baroque gem: **SS. Domenico e Sisto** finely positioned on top of Rome's first grand Baroque stair (1654). If it happens to be open, you can ponder Domenico Maria Canuti's ceiling fresco of the **Apotheosis of St Dominic** (1674) in which one of the sternest members of the heavenly hierarchy rockets to grace in a curlicue stage set. From SS. Domenico e Sisto, head down picturesque Salita del Grillo, under the handsome 'bridge of sighs' that links the Grillo palace with the 13th-century **Torre del Grillo**, another urban castle of Rome's battling barons. In Piazza del Grillo is the entrance to the **Forum of Augustus**, built soon after Octavian changed his name.

The vast wall that begins here and continues down the street once protected the forum from the teeming, fire-ridden slum of Subura, and the wide stair and a few columns from the **Temple of Mars Ultor** (Avenging Mars), which Cæsar vowed to the god while driving Brutus and Cassius to suicide during the Battle of Philippi. The temple became a kind of imperial reliquary, containing Cæsar's sword among its mementoes. Of the forum's two basilicas, only a few suggestive fragments remain; the **Casa dei Cavalieri di Rodi** was built over another building in the forum in the 12th century. Now owned by the Knights of Rhodes, it preserves the Augustan atrium as its chapel, a portico, and three ancient shops housing the **Antiquarium of the Forum of Augustus**.

> From Piazza del Grillo, Via Tor de' Conti continues past the Subura wall to the tremendous stump of 12th-century **Torre de' Conti**, which Petrarch described as the mightiest in Rome.

Lightning and earthquakes have since lopped off most of its storeys; and its base is faced with black and white stripes, a common decoration in northern Italy but rare in Rome. It covers part of **Vespasian's Forum**, built in 70 AD with booty from the Jewish wars, while nearly all the rest is under Via dei Fori Imperiali, the wide street in front of the Torre de' Conti, built by Mussolini in the 1930s so he could see the Colosseum from his window in Palazzo Venezia. Its fate is one of the most hotly debated topics in Rome; the Fascist government performed only a perfunctory excavation of the fora of Augustus, Nerva, and Vespasian before filling them in to construct the road, and archaeologists would love to tear it up and investigate, even though the prospect of turning the entire city centre into a lifeless dig appals everyone else.

Some excavations have begun in the **Forum of Nerva**, a narrow corridor with a temple of Minerva at one end. The latest excavations are on the far side of Via dei Fori Imperiali—at the time of writing they were down to the medieval layer. Two beautiful Corinthian columns survive from the temple, topped by reliefs of the goddess. The carved entablature has a frieze illustrating the myth of Arachne, who challenged the goddess' weaving art and was zapped into a spider; the ensemble, known as the *Colonnacce*, served for years as a bakery.

> *To atone for burying their fora, Mussolini placed statues of the emperors in front of their works along Via dei Fori Imperiali. After Trajan, cross the big street to peer down into the enclave of the first of the imperial fora, the* **Forum of Cæsar**.

It was built by Julius Cæsar after he redesigned the Roman Forum. Its temple, of which only the base and three re-erected columns remain, was dedicated to his ancestress, Venus Genetrix, the goddess of love, and contained statues of the famous lovers, Cæsar and Cleopatra. Twelve columns survive of a later basilica added by the indefatigable Trajan.

> *Behind Cæsar's Forum, is the little church of* **San Giuseppe dei Falegnami** *(1598), built over the* **Mamertine Prison** *(open 9–12.30 and 2–6.30) of horrible memory.*

The Mamertine was actually the more pleasant upper floor of the hideous dark dungeon called the Tullianum, possibly part of a tholos tomb of the legendary hero Tullus. The only entrance to the Tullianum was a hole in the floor (now there's a modern stairway) and the only exit was death and a drain that led into the Cloaca Maxima for the convenient disposal of corpses. Important captives, after being paraded in chains in their conqueror's triumph through the Forum, were taken here to be slain. Vercingetorix was strangled, but Jugurtha, the unrepentant North African, was tossed into the Tullianum to starve to death. Famous political prisoners included the Catiline conspirators and according to tradition, St Peter, though as a non-citizen he wasn't important enough to be slain here; the relief over the altar portrays him baptizing his gaoler.

> *Opposite the prison stands one of Rome's most innovative Baroque churches,* **San Luca e Santa Martina**, *built in the 7th century on the*

site of the Secretarium Senatus (a tribunal to judge erring senators, built by the late emperors), and rebuilt by Pietro da Cortona in 1635–50.

St Luke is the patron of painters, and Pietro, in remodelling the ancient crypt to build his own tomb, was surprised to find the body of S. Martina lost among the artists. The church was rededicated, and Pietro hired to rebuild it. To keep both saints happy, he created a double-decker façade, half for each saint, which curves in a rich play of Florentine Mannerist motifs, a theme continued in the Greek cross plan of the interior. Unlike Bernini and the Roman school, Pietro disdained the use of colour to highlight the vigorous lines of the walls, which seem to ebb and flow with columns, mouldings, and decorative motifs. The drum and cupola, viewed either from within or without, continue the play of soft and rigid forms in a highly original manner that inaugurated the best of Roman High Baroque.

From the steps of SS. Luca e Martina you have a fine view over the **Roman Forum**. *Will something funny happen on your way there? Something nasty very well might. On either side of the entrance, 100 yards down Via dei Fori Imperiali, lurk a band of Fagin's children, as permanent as the ruins themselves, one inevitably armed with a piece of cardboard to thrust in your face while the others pick your pocket (if you snarl and make a noisy stand, they'll soon back off).*

The Roman Forum and Palatine are included in the same ticket (open summer Wed–Sat and Mon 9–6; Tues 9–1; Sun 9–12; winter Wed–Sat and Mon 9–3; Tue 9–1; Sun 9–12. Exit one hour after last entry time. Adm L10,000).

For a place that once was the centre of the Mediterranean world and saw so much history, it is a strangely quiet, empty place. Cats keep it clear of the king-sized rats who rule subterranean Rome, which has countless entrances in the Forum. Originally a sodden valley lying between the Capitoline and Palatine hills, the area was first used as a graveyard by the surrounding Iron Age hill dwellers, who called it the forum, a word that meant 'outside' the walls (like the Italian *fuori*). According to legend it became the tribes' common ground and shared marketplace when Romulus made peace with the Sabines near the Lapis Niger; and it has always been the sacred symbol of the founding of the united city of Rome.

During the seven centuries of the republic the Forum was the heartbeat of Rome, its political, religious, legal, and commercial centre; a modern Italian piazza, where an orator could address the city's representatives, senators, and people. By the 2nd century AD, it had lost most of its importance; the Sacred Way became the haunt of idlers, fortune-tellers, and tourists from Gaul or Egypt who would gawk at the sight of a Vestal Virgin or togaed senator ambling to the Curia. Power had shifted to the imperial palace on the Palatine, commerce to Trajan's more up-

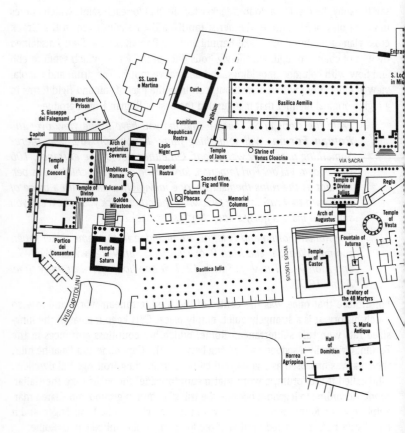

Labels visible on map:

SS. Luca e Martina

Curia

Mamertine Prison

S. Giuseppe dei Falegnami

Capitol

Temple of Concord

Comitium

Republican Rostra

Arch of Septimius Severus

Umbilicus Romae

Lapis Niger

Basilica Aemilia

Argiletum

Imperial Rostra

Temple of Janus

Shrine of Venus Cloacina

VIA SACRA

Temple of Divine Julius

Regia

Vulcanal

Temple of Divine Vespasian

Golden Milestone

Sacred Olive, Fig and Vine

Column of Phocas

Memorial Columns

Tabularium

Portico dei Consentes

Temple of Saturn

Arch of Augustus

Temple of Vesta

Fountain of Juturna

Temple of Castor

Basilica Julia

VICUS TUSCUS

IVUS CAPITOLINU

Oratory of the 40 Martyrs

S. Maria Antiqua

Hall of Domitian

Horrea Agrippina

Entra[nce]

S. Lo[renzo] in Mi[randa]

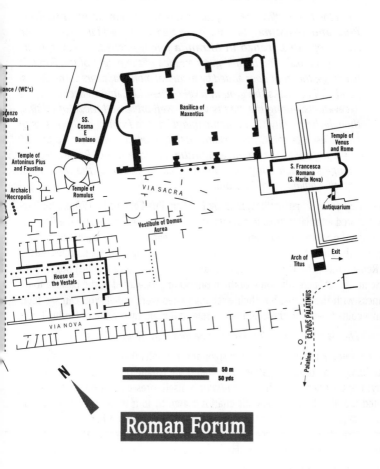

ance / (WC's)

ocenzo
isanda

Temple of
Antoninus Pius
and Faustina

Archaic
Necropolis

SS.
Cosma
E
Damiano

Temple of
Romulus

Basilica of
Maxentius

VIA SACRA

Temple of
Venus
and Rome

S. Francesca
Romana
(S. Maria Nova)

Antiquarium

Vestibule of Domus
Aurea

House of
the Vestals

Arch of
Titus

Exit

VIA NOVA

CLIVUS PALATINUS

Palatine

N

50 m
50 yds

Roman Forum

to-date market. Temples (most of them used as art museums) and memorials enclosed the once spacious square, strewn with ranks of statues and monuments that gave it the appearance of a king-size modern Roman souvenir stand.

> *From the ticket office the ramp descends to the* **Temple of Antoninus Pius and Faustina** *(141 AD) converted in the Middle Ages to the church of* **San Lorenzo in Miranda** *(rarely opened, however, by its gloomy monks). The temple gives an idea of the height of the Forum's buildings; the front door added by medieval monks appears surreally suspended, but marks the ground level of the old Campo Vaccino before excavations. Along the side is a fine, well-preserved frieze of griffins; though the mighty Corinthian columns at the front bear the marks of chains used by the Christians attempting to pull them down. To the left of the ramp was the* **Basilica Aemilia,** *headquarters of Rome's money-changers, which Pliny the Younger classed as one of the three most beautiful buildings in the world.*

It was the Forum's first basilica, built by M. Aemilius Lepidus in 179 BC, but lavishly restored after later fires; fragments of its republican-era reliefs (of the Romans abducting the Sabine women and the Sabines preparing to kill Tarpeia) have been placed in the corner. Although nearly completely scavenged for its marbles during the Renaissance, the Basilica's decline (at least according to legend) began with Alaric in 410. Apparently some of the moneychangers waited in the basilica to do business with the Goths, but their exchange rates were unfair; you can see their bronze coins fused into the coloured marble pavement by the fire of Gothic fury.

> *The Basilica faces* **Via Sacra** *or Sacred Way, Rome's most ancient road.*

It seems remarkably narrow for the splendid triumphs that once passed along it; try to imagine all of Rome gathered to watch the parade of victorious legions, the booty, the prisoners, and the *triumphator* himself, dressed in a purple toga, face painted red like the god Mars, his chariot drawn by four white horses, accompanied by a slave who constantly repeated in his ear: 'Remember that you are a man'. More often, though, the Sacred Way would see the likes of Horace, absent-mindedly strolling along with a slave; and even more often, Horace's Bore, the spiritual father of so many Romans down to this day, who glued himself to the poet, endlessly singing his own praises in the hopes of scaring up an introduction to the poet's wealthy patron Mæcenas. Poor Horace feared he would be talked to death before he was suddenly rescued by a man who was suing the Bore in court that very morning and suspected him of trying to escape.

In front of the Basilica Aemilia a bare round foundation marks the site of the **Shrine of Venus Cloacina**, near the lid of the Cloaca Maxima (and who, you may ask, worshipped this Venus of the Drains? Plumbers?). Equally perverse in its own way is the tale of Virginia, said to have taken place here: the maiden was about to be seduced by the deceiver Appius Claudius Crassinus, when her father Virginus stabbed her to save her chastity. Like the story of the Rape of Lucrezia, it was piously repeated to drill Roman women in the virtue of chastity.

*Closer to the Argiletum stood the now vanished **Temple of Janus**, the two doors of which stood open when Rome was at war and closed in times of peace, which history declares happened only three times in a thousand years. Just east of the Basilica Aemilia, the Sacred Way met the thronging **Argiletum**, an important street lined with bookshops.*

*The open space between the Argiletum and the Senate House was the **Comitium**, the centre of civic life during the republic.*

Here the representatives of the city's 30 neighbourhoods (the Comitia Curiata) met to cast their votes. Scant remains of the **Republican Rostra** were found here, dating from 338 BC; the name rostra for speaking platforms came from the iron beaks of captured ships which were used to adorn them.

*Here, too, is the austere, tawny brick **Curia**, or Senate House, built by Julius Cæsar, and rebuilt by Diocletian after a fire in 283 AD—by that time the emperors rarely visited Rome, and it was a mere sop to let her senators prattle away on whatever topic they chose. Gothic King Theodoric rebuilt it for the last time, and the senators were probably still prattling into the 600s.*

The Curia, minus its marble facings and decorations, was found intact under the 7th-century church of Sant'Adriano. Unfortunately owing to staff shortages the Curia is rarely open, but if it *is*, it's well worth popping inside to see the original pavement, the steps where the senators sat in marble seats, and a set of reliefs called the **Plutei of Trajan**, found near the Column of Phocas and depicting lively scenes of the Forum itself. When the Gauls invaded Rome in 390 BC, they entered an earlier edition of this building, to find what appeared to be statues of Senators, so motionlessly did they sit in their full senate regalia, ivory wands in hand. One of the Gauls summoned the courage to pull one of their beards, to see if they were real; the senator whacked him with his wand, whereupon he and all of his fellows were massacred.

On one end of the Curia is the base for the famous golden statue of Victory, the reigning deity of the Senate and the subject of another instructive anecdote. The statue was removed by the Christians, replaced by Julian the Apostate, and removed again by Gratian (380s) when it became the rallying point for die-hard pagans among the patricians, led by the aristocratic orator Symmachus. 'These rites have repelled Hannibal from the city and the Gauls from the Capitol', he wrote in his petition to the emperor, asking that the statue be returned in the name of freedom of religion. He was answered by the eloquent St Ambrose, and by 394 Victory had disappeared for good. When Alaric sacked Rome 16 years later the pagans grumbled their inevitable I-told-you-so, only to be put down by another saint, Augustine, in his *City of God.*

> *In front of the Curia, in the ancient Comitium, is the Forum's most venerable relic, the* **Lapis Niger***, named for the slab of fractured black marble that marked the tomb of Romulus.*

It may have originally been a chthonic shrine to the forging god of fire, Vulcan. Under the slab a chamber was discovered (reached by a modern stair behind one of Rome's numerous eternally locked gates) containing an altar of tufa with the ashes of massive sacrifices, a broken column, and a stele inscribed with one of the most ancient Latin inscriptions ever discovered (6th century BC), written down and up and down again in a style called 'boustrophedic', warning against profaning the sacred site.

> *'Geta sit divus dum non sit vivus'* *(Geta may be a god as long as he's a dead one) Caracalla grimly jested after slaying his brother the co-emperor, a murder unintentionally recorded on the* **Arch of Septimius Severus***, erected in 203 AD in honour of their father's tenth year in power.*

The marble reliefs record some rather trivial victories over the Arabs and Parthians, and a notable artistic decline since the Arch of Titus; conservative Romans of the time must have strongly resented this upstart African Severus planting his monument in such an important spot, between the Comitium and the Capitol. The inscription on the arch also commemorated his sons, but after Geta's murder Caracalla had his name removed from the fourth line and replaced with an inscription glorifying himself. Time dislodged both sets of bronze letters, making it possible to read the original and edited versions.

The area to the left, behind the rostra, is fenced off, and the best view of what lies behind is from Via di Monte Tarpeia on the Capitoline. To the left of the arch stood the **Umbilicus Romae**, the conical brick 'navel of Rome' (at 9 ft high, a definite 'outie') marking the centre of the city; to the left of this, under a shelter, is the **Vulcanal**, an altar carved in the living rock, and along with the Lapis Niger, the most ancient monument in the Forum. A bit beyond the curved steps of the **Imperial Rostra** (rebuilt here by Cæsar to replace the Republican Rostra near the Curia) stood the **Golden Milestone**. This was actually a bronze column, erected by Augustus, from which all the roads of the empire symbolically began, and from which all distances in the empire were calculated.

*Between Severus' arch and the Capitol stood the **Temple of Concord**, of which only the platform remains; this was reconstructed by Tiberius from a republican original celebrating the peace—now enforced by the emperors—between patricians and plebeians. Next to this are the three elegant corner columns from the **Temple of Divine Vespasian** (79AD; a fitting memorial to the emperor who died laughing: 'My goodness,' he exclaimed, 'I think I am about to become a god.') To the left of Vespasian's temple, on the other side of the Clivus Capitolinus (the extension of the Sacred Way) are the eight grey and red columns from the portico of the **Temple of Saturn**.*

This is one of the Forum's oldest temples (479 BC) dedicated to the ancient Etruscan god of purification against blight, although later Saturn was associated with the origins of agriculture and the 'Golden Age'. The cult statue in the temple was filled with olive oil, and from 17–23 December, it was the centre of the Saturnalia festivities, a holiday that combined much of the rituals of our Christmas and Carnival. A huge sum of gold was secretly stored here, with the provision that it only be used if the Gauls re-invaded Rome. Cæsar, who always needed cash, purloined it with the excuse that thanks to him there would be no more Gallic troubles (though as spendthrifts go, he was a tiddler compared to Mark Antony, who managed to spend the equivalent of $5 billion in his lifetime, with much less to show for it). The columns date from the Senate's rebuilding of 284 AD, done so clumsily that one was put in upside down.

*Behind the Temple of Saturn and left of the Temple of Vespasian are 12 columns from the **Portico of the Dei Consentes**, dedicated to the 12 Olympian gods; restored in 367 AD, during the reign of Julian the Apostate, it was the last work on a pagan temple in Rome. Behind you stands the last monument erected in the Forum in ancient times, the **Column of Phocas**.*

In 608, the exarch Smaragdus robbed the column from an older building to honour the Byzantine usurper, Nikephorus Phocas, probably as a thank–you present for giving the Pantheon to Pope Boniface IV. As the silt of centuries covered its base, its identity was forgotten, which many, like Byron ('Thou nameless column with the buried base!') found as evocative as its sharp-fluted beauty. The Duchess of Devonshire ruined their romance by having it excavated. The brick wall next to the column was the **Imperial Rostra**, moved here from the Comitium by Julius Cæsar.

*Closing the south end of the Forum stood the vast **Basilica Julia**, begun by Julius Cæsar in 54 BC as a pendant to the Basilica Aemilia. Augustus completed it, though what you see are the bare roots of a 305 rebuilding.*

The four tribunals of the Centumviri tried civil cases here, and as the Romans had one of history's worst cases of litigation fever, it was one of the noisiest places of the Forum, as lawyers struggled to outshout other lawyers presenting their cases elsewhere in the basilica. Idlers, or perhaps defendants waiting their turn at court carved the game boards you can still see in the steps.

> *In front of the Basilica Julia, just beyond the Column of Phocas, are a fig tree, olive, and vine, symbols of Italian agriculture, replanted where they stood in ancient times. Lacking is the statue of Marsyas, the musician who challenged Apollo to a hoedown, lost, and was flayed by the god; it was apparently a warning against presumption. Next to the trees is the irregular-shaped pavement of the* **Lacus Curtius**.

The Lacus was a pond before the forum was drained, and a place made holy in 445 BC, when lightning blasted a fissure in the pavement. But most famously, it marks the site of one of Rome's favourite legends. In 362 BC, according to Livy, a bottomless abyss suddenly opened in the Forum, and nothing the Romans could do could fill it up again. The Sibyls were consulted, and gave the answer: it would never close until 'the thing the Romans held most precious' was thrown in. A young Consul, Marcus Curtius, took this to mean a Roman citizen and a soldier. Dressed in full armour, he mounted his horse, dedicated his death to the gods, and rode into the chasm, and the crack closed over him. A noble story, apparently the result of later Roman romancing over the human sacrifices that once took place on the spot.

> *To the left of Basilica Julia, across the ancient Vicus Tuscus (Etruscan Lane and once the resort of Etruscan rent-boys), stand the three grand columns of the* **Temple of Castor**, *the mortal twin of the Dioscuri, the brothers of Helen of Troy and patrons of the cavalry.*

The Dioscuri were the first gods to be bribed away by the Romans from their enemies, in this case from the Latin tribes that they fought at the Battle of Lake Regillus in 496 BC. The odds were against the Romans, whose cavalry was woefully inadequate, but in the heat of the battle they offered Castor and Pollux, the chief gods of the Latins, a huge temple if they would change sides. The Twins apparently couldn't resist the offer, and were seen in the Forum shortly afterwards, battle-stained with sweating horses, which they watered in the fountain of Juturna near the Temple of Vesta. 'And like a blast, away they passed/And no man saw them more' as Macaulay put it. The Romans built their temple on the spot, and it became the meeting place of Rome's Equites (knights, but later the class of businessmen), who had their safe-deposit boxes in the basement, along with the standards and measures of the empire.

*In the fenced-off area just to the east of the temple is a reconstructed shrine to the healing waters of the Lacus Juturnae. Behind this, the **Oratory of the Forty Martyrs** commemorates soldiers who were forced to wade into an icy lake in Armenia; it preserves some of its 8th-century frescoes. Far better preserved are the excellent 7th- and 8th-century Byzantine frescoes in **Santa Maria Antiqua**, just south of the oratory, the oldest church in the Forum. It's rarely if ever open; though you could try asking in the Forum Antiquarium (see below).*

*Walk back to the front of the Temple of Castor; the **Arch of Augustus** once crossed over the street, symbolically linking the basilica with the **Temple of Julius Cæsar**, marked by its large altar.*

Here Cæsar's body was brought after his assassination in Pompey's theatre; here Mark Antony read his will and incited friends, Romans and countrymen to cremate the body on the spot, in spite of the religious prohibitions. Augustus built the temple to Divine Julius 15 years later, and decorated the altar with the prow of Antony and Cleopatra's ship. The bare altar has survived, marking the spot where Cæsar lay.

*East of it stood the **Regia**, the oldest cult building of the Forum (7th century BC).*

The office of the Chief Priest or Pontifex Maximus, the Regia was closely identified with Mars, the chief god of the Romans before the Etruscans introduced Jupiter. Mars' shields and spears were kept here, and if the spears rattled on their own it was an ill omen indeed. To help prevent such calamities the Pontifex Maximus presided over the ancient rite of the October Horse, when a horse race would be held along the Sacred Way, though the prize for the winning pony was a real booby: immediate decapitation. Its blood, used for purification ceremonies, was given to the Vestal Virgins; its genitals were dedicated to Mars; its skeleton used for special juju to protect the city; and its head was fought over viciously by the residents of the Via Sacra and Subura for the honour of nailing it up in their quarter.

*The Pontifex Maximus was the only male ever allowed to enter the **Temple of Vesta**, located just across the Via Nova.*

Votive offerings to the hearth goddess date the first temple back to 575 BC, and the pretty circular edifice (partially reconstructed in the 1930s) was designed to recall the original Latin hut, where the ancient kings' daughters had the task of keeping the tribe's fire alight. The rites of the Vestal Virgins were equally consciously archaic; they were, after all, the guardians of Rome's soul and sacred totems. The embers of their temple's sacred fire had been brought from Vesta's temple in Troy by Aeneas, and if a negligent Vestal let it go out, she would be flogged by the Pontifex Maximus, while the rest of the superstitious city awaited calamity (few sleepy Vestals were caught in imperial times—the Romans had just invented matches). Vesta's temple also contained Rome's seven holiest of holies preserving in themselves the nation's safety and very existence: the Palladium (a wooden statue of Pallas Athene which fell from heaven and was also brought by Aeneas from Troy), a terracotta chariot from Veii, the ashes of Orestes, a needle used by the mother of gods, the shields of the Salii (the 12 Leaping Priests of Mars), the sceptre of Priam, and the veil of Ilione. The Vestals protected these for 1100 years, and when the imperial pervert Elagabalus tried to steal them for his Temple of the Sun, the Virgins outwitted him with substitutes. Knowledge of their ultimate fate perished with the last Vestal.

> *Adjacent is the **House of the Vestals**, now the charming rose garden of the Forum, with its three pools that once adorned the centre of its rectangular two-storey courtyard.*

The similarity between the Vestals and the sisters of the Church are probably no accident: their house was like a cloister, forbidden to all men except the Pontifex Maximus; their hair was cut when they entered the order, and they wore long robes and a veil, which you can see in the mostly decapitated 3rd century AD statues in the court (the one statue with her head intact but name effaced is believed to be the Vestal Claudia, who became a Christian). There were only six Vestals at a time, all from patrician families and chosen between the ages of six and ten. They would spend the next 30 years of their lives in this large cloister; the first decade learning the austere and complex rites, the second ten practising them, and the third in teaching novices, after which they were free to do as they liked, though a majority preferred to stay on until they died.

For the Vestals enjoyed great honour and privileges, as women second only to the Empress herself: if they came across a condemned prisoner, they could stay his execution; they could ride about in chariots in the city, in daytime. They had front row seats in the Circus and Colosseum, and were in charge of all wills and treaties; the eldest Vestal could demand an audience with an emperor at will. They were, however, bound by the strictest vows of chastity; the punishment for breaking these was being buried alive (the penalty for incest under Roman law) in what is now Piazza dell'Indipendenza. Since it was sacrilege to starve a priestess, the poor sinners would be given a lamp, a loaf, and a pitcher of water before the door above was closed forever; some 20 are believed to have died so cruelly, and as far as anyone knows, they're still there under the piazza's heaving traffic.

> *Across from the House of the Vestals, up the Via Sacra, is a short row of rooms, sunk well below the level of the Forum's other buildings. It's believed to be a Republican-era brothel. Alongside is the circular*

Temple of Romulus, a mysterious place, perhaps built in 309 AD by Maxentius in memory of his young son Romulus. Later used as the vestibule of SS. Cosma e Damiano (see below), – it is one of the best preserved buildings in the Forum, with its original bronze doors on their original hinges, the ancient lock still opened by the original key. Next to this loom the three immense vaults of the Basilica of Maxentius.

Begun by Maxentius in 306, it was completed by his arch-rival Constantine, who installed the colossal statue of himself (naturally), now amputated in the Capitoline Museum. The Basilica was some 300 ft long, with a nave and two aisles, of which only the north aisle still stands, as well as part of the apse and (just outside the 20th-century fence) a porphyry portico added by Constantine. The audacity of its soaring barrel vaults was studied by Bramante and Michelangelo for the design of St Peter's; the last of its mighty Corinthian columns now stands in front of S. Maria Maggiore.

At the corner of the basilica is S. Francesca Romana, built into the Temple of Venus and Rome. The church can only be entered from Via dei Fori Imperiali (see below), but next to its 1163 campanile (in the Romanesque party style, decorated with coloured circles) the convent contains the Forum Antiquarium.

The old-fashioned displays include models and furniture of the various Iron Age necropolises excavated in the Forum's lowest levels, from the days when Rome was a cluster of hill villages, of which some cremated their dead, and others buried them. Upstairs are friezes, sculptures, inscriptions, and reliefs found in the Forum, and a fresco of the Virgin with saints originally in S. Maria Antiqua.

Nearby, crowning the summit of the Sacred Way (the Clivus Sacer) is the Arch of Titus, which no true Jew ever passes through.

Erected by Domitian in 81 AD, the arch commemorates the victories of his father Vespasian and brother Titus over the rebellious Jews, one of the fiercest struggles Rome ever had to fight; the reliefs within the arch proper show a triumphal procession carrying off the treasure from the Holy of Holies in the Temple, including the seven-branch candlestick and the altar, which were deposited in Vespasian's Temple of Peace. Whatever eventually became of them is a subject of considerable dispute. Roman Jews believe they were eventually thrown in the Tiber; another story has them hidden along with Alaric, who carried them off in 410— when he died in Calabria, soon after the sack, his men buried him along with his loot in a secret place, then diverted the river Busento over it.

A road leads up from the Arch of Titus to the Palatine Hill, the site of the imperial residences that went on to give the word 'palace' to nearly

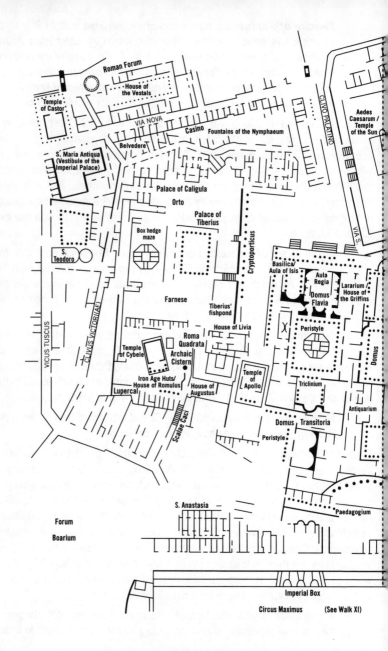

Roman Forum

Temple of Castor

House of the Vestals

VIA NOVA

Casino   Fountains of the Nymphaeum

CLIVO PALATINO

Aedes Caesarum / Temple of the Sun

Belvedere

S. Maria Antiqua (Vestibule of the Imperial Palace)

Palace of Caligula

Orto

Palace of Tiberius

Cryptoporticus

VIA S.

Box hedge maze

Basilica/ Aula of Isis

Aula Regia

Lararium/ House of the Griffins

T

S. Teodoro

Domus Flavia

Farnese

Tiberius' fishpond

House of Livia

Peristyle

X

Domus

VICUS TUSCUS

CLIVUS VICTORIAE

Roma Quadrata

Temple of Cybele

Archaic Cistern

Iron Age Huts/ House of Romulus

Lupercal

House of Augustus

Temple of Apollo

Triclinium

Scalae Caci

Antiquarium

Domus Transitoria

Peristyle

Forum

Boarium

S. Anastasia

Paedagogium

Imperial Box

Circus Maximus   (See Walk XI)

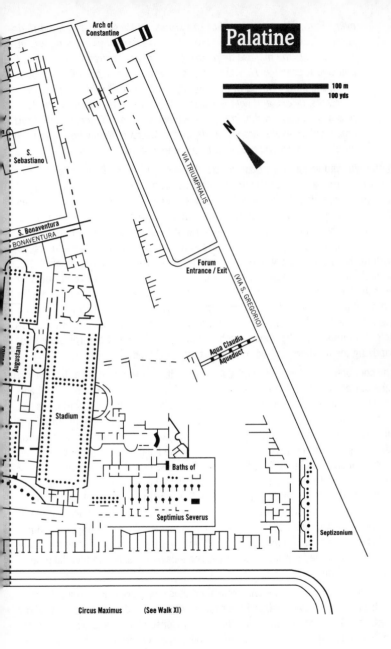

Palatine

100 m
100 yds

N

Arch of Constantine

S. Sebastiano

S. Bonaventura
BONAVENTURA

VIA TRIUMPHALIS

Forum
Entrance / Exit

(VIA S. GREGORIO)

Aqua Claudia
Aqueduct

Augustana

Stadium

Baths of

Septimius Severus

Septizonium

Circus Maximus   (See Walk XI)

every European language. But the stones of these palaces keep their secrets well; the ruins of the Forum seem elementary in comparison. Look at it as 'the malaise de pierre of a number of extremely odd and ill-adjusted Cæsars' as H. V. Morton says, or as a landscape of picturesque ruins, the kind beloved in the 18th century, planted with parasol pines, cypresses, ilexes, and wild flowers. At any given time a third of the Palatine will be obscured by the archaeologist's net and fence; some of this crazy quilt of vaults, arches, walls, and columns is simply unsafe to walk around in. What you really want to see will probably be closed.

Both myth and archaeology confirm that Rome began on the Palatine, perhaps in the 9th century BC; the city's birthday on 21 April was originally the feast day of the hill's namesake, the shepherd god Pales. One of Pales' followers discovered the foundling sons of Mars, Romulus and Remus, suckling wolf-flavoured milk on the hill, and brought them up as his own. But it hardly ended their wolfish behaviour. Remus, when he grew up, established himself on the Aventine, and argued with his twin over the name of the new city they meant to found. 'Roma!' 'No, Rema!' they shouted back and forth, until Romulus saw the twelve vultures fly over the Palatine while Remus only saw six fly over his hill. Romulus declared his extra vultures indicated the gods' favour, and began to build Rome's first walls on the Palatine, later known as *Roma Quadrata*. To show his disdain for their puny height, Remus leapt the walls; and his twin, goaded beyond control, slew him, baptizing the newborn city with his own brother's blood.

The cool breezes enjoyed by the Palatine made it an elite residence in later years: Cicero, Catullus, and Antony called it home; Augustus was born on the hill and lived here simply all his life, modestly pretending he didn't rule the world. His less worthy successors, almost in proportion to their inability, had no qualms about building themselves magnificent palaces, and when they ran out of hill they added huge substructures (the main feature of the Palatine today) to support even more rooms. The biggest builders were: Tiberius, whose palace is now mostly covered by the Farnese Gardens; crazy Caligula, who extended it and built a catwalk over the Forum to the Capitol, so he'd never have to rub elbows with the masses; Nero, who built a new palace, the Domus Transitoria, which burned in the fire of 64 AD, whereupon he used the bits that survived as mere outbuildings for his even grander Domus Aurea, extending over the Esquiline. Domitian, however, is responsible for much of what you see today: official and residential palaces and the stadium.

Although abandoned by the emperors after Diocletian, Rome kept the palaces in repair in case they ever changed their minds. Odoacer and Theodoric made short stays, as did Byzantine Emperors Phocas and Constans II, the latter here on his ten-day pillaging spree. Several medieval popes called it home before the ensemble became a building inspector's nightmare; the last genuine emperors to visit were German Ottos, in the 900s.

> *At the top of the lane leading up from the Forum is the shady **Orti Farnesiani** and garden pavilion.*

In the 1550s, Pope Paul III's grandson, Alessandro Farnese, purchased the palace of Tiberius, dug for statues, then filled the ruins with rubble and hired Vignola to lay out a classical garden that extended down the Palatine slope to the House of the Vestals. After centuries of weeds and neglect, the great archaeologist of the Forum, Giacomo Boni (1859–1925) replanted the trees and hedges, creating a charming oasis in the centre of ancient and modern Rome. At the highest point stands the **casino**, added by Rainaldi in the 17th century. There are excellent views over the Forum from the belvedere terrace built on top of great arches of the substructures; these were added in the 3rd century AD as guard rooms for the Praetorians. At some point in strolling through the gardens you may pass over the spot where they stabbed Caligula, or where they found his uncle Claudius hiding behind a curtain, expecting to be slain instead of proclaimed the new emperor. It set a catastrophic precedent; from then on, arms and not the decision of the Senate would choose the master of the world.

> *Steps by the side of the casino descend to the creeper-dripping fountains of the **Nymphaeum** and, around the corner, Nero's remarkable **Cryptoporticus.***

This half-submerged vaulted passageway, partially decorated with stuccoes, was built to connect the Palatine with the Domus Aurea. Stretching 130 m, it may well have served the imperial household as a cool promenade in the summer; it extends past **Tiberius' fishpond** (all that remains of his palace above ground) back to the House of Livia (see below). In the middle of the gardens box hedges have been planted, following the shape of the *impluvium* in the Domus Augustana.

> *South of the Farnese gardens are the romantic, ilex-shaded ruins of the podium and sanctuary of the **Temple of Cybele** (Magna Mater), dedicated in 191 BC according to the instructions in the Sibylline Books.*

Earlier, one of the Sibyls had warned the Romans that they could never hope to defeat Hannibal without the lumpy black image (perhaps a meteorite) that represented Cybele, the Phrygian Mother of the Gods, in her principal temple at Pessinus. What the Phrygians had to say about this is unrecorded, but the Romans somehow obtained the image, won the Second Punic War, and built this temple; in April games called the *Ludi Megalenses* were dedicated in honour of the goddess. Her cult, one of the first oriental religions to reach Rome, was as popular with the masses as it was offensive to conservative Romans, who disapproved of its orgies and the self-castration of its priests, in imitation of Cybele's consort Attis.

The temple is last mentioned in the 4th century, when Serena, the wife of the Vandal General Stilicho, visited it in the company of one of the last Vestal Virgins, and removed the beautiful necklace from Cybele's image (perhaps the same one you see today) and placed it on her own neck. The Vestal put a curse on Serena for her sacrilege, and not long after she was strangled by the Senate for collusion with the Goths.

> *South of the temple, protected by corrugated iron roofs, are traces of the tufa walls of* **Roma Quadrata** *and the 9th-century BC village, including the holes used to plant the roof poles of the huts and channels dug in the rock to carry the rain. The traditional '***Casa di Romulus***' was maintained here for centuries as a kind of museum piece, and in the same area of the slope, two famous cave-dens.*

One, the **Lupercal** (which no-one has actually found yet), was in the sacred grove of the god Lupercus, where the she-wolf suckled the twins. It is best known for another kinky festival, the *Lupercalia* (15 February), in which priests clad in goat skins pranced around the hill whipping everyone they encountered, purifying them; and bestowing fertility, a rite that attracted many women. The second cave belonged to the flame-belching giant Cacus, who decorated it with human skulls (another reminder of early Rome's human sacrifices); a sharply declining path before one of the gates in the tufa walls of *Roma Quadrata* was named **Scalae Caci** after him. Cacus lived in the time of legendary King Evander, an exile from Arcadia who came to Rome 60 years before the Trojan War and brought the Latins their alphabet. He welcomed Hercules to Rome as the hero was driving Geryon's cattle home from Spain; but when Hercules left the herd overnight in the Forum Boarium, Cacus slipped down and carried some of them off. When Hercules found him, a terrible wrestling match ensued (a favourite subject of Renaissance sculptors) in which Cacus scorched Hercules' bare behind and Hercules smashed Cacus' face to pulp. The Greek hero (afterwards known as 'Great black bottom') is also said to have freed Evander from a tribute owed the Etruscans, and to have halted the practice of tossing men into the Tiber each May, forcing the Romans to substitute dummies made from bulrushes.

> *East of the Scalae Caci are the ruined rooms of the* **House of Augustus,** *painted with bright frescoes though not open to the public. But just beyond in the rooms of the* **House of Livia** *you can see delicately-painted scenes of the same period: of Hermes, Io, and Argus; a street scene; and a faded Polyphemus pursuing Galatea.*

Lead pipes found within (and now hung along the wall) labelled 'Iulia Augusta' identified the house with Augustus' wife, but now it is believed the rooms formed part of Augustus' house. Later emperors left it intact in honour of his memory.

Less remains of Augustus' famous **Temple of Apollo**, vowed to the god just before the Battle of Actium, and in its day celebrated for its rare marbles and beautiful carvings; it burned in 363, and according to some, the Sibylline Books then lodged inside burned with it.

> *One of the more ill-adjusted Cæsars was Domitian, who built the* ***Domus Flavia****, the* ***Domus Augustana****, and the* ***Stadium*** *on the east end of the Palatine, housing himself in splendid paranoia.*

Domitian was obsessed with death, especially his own, and had the walls of the courtyard of the **Domus Flavia**, the emperor's official residence, lined with slabs of shiny mica from Cappadocia, in which he would be able to see assassins trying to sneak up from behind, bearing the dagger that was to kill him in the end. The rooms of the palace are located around this large peristyle with an octagonal maze-shaped impluvium in the centre: the **Aula Regia**, or emperor's throne room; the **Basilica**, in the north corner, perhaps used as an auditorium, linked by an extension to the Cryptoporticus; and the so-called **Lararium**, which is more likely to have been home to the Preatorian Guard than househould gods (Lares). More interesting than the meagre decoration remaining in these, however, are the rooms from the republican era found below: the **Aula of Isis**, under the Basilica, and the **House of the Griffins**, under the Lararium, with wall paintings and stuccoes of griffins. On the opposite side of the peristyle is the large dining room, the **Triclinium**, paved with coloured marbles, which have unfortunately been covered with a protective layer of gravel. The room is so-named because the diners reclined three to a couch, though the emperor himself dined apart, on the podium. Domitian held the most bizarre banquet on record here, when he draped the hall in black and for place cards used tombstones; funeral cakes, usually offered to the dead, were served, while for entertainment Domitian told tales of violent death, which the guests themselves expected at any moment. But it was all just Domitian's little joke, and instead of the sword they were given presents. Elagabalus liked the odd prank in the Triclinium as well; if the dinner threatened to fall flat, he would set panthers and tigers upon his guests to liven things up.

> *By the time Domitian wanted to build on the Palatine, there was virtually no room left, so in order to create space for a new palace his architect, Rabirius, cut a step out of the side of the hill and used the excavated soil to fill in the cleft between the two peaks. In the process, various earlier buildings were buried, and some day, you may be able to visit them.*

Beyond, to the east, is Domitian's **Domus Augustana**, the private residence of the emperors, built on the two levels of Rabirius's 'step'. From the sunken courtyard (closed to the public) a passage led to the imperial box over the Circus Maximus. Two other peristyles, one open and one surrounded by rooms (one converted into a chapel in the 4th century) are on the upper level. A former convent building in between houses the **Palatine Antiquarium**, usually closed; it contains detached frescoes, fragments of pavement, statues, and the infamous 3rd century *Graffito of Alexamenos*, discovered in the Paedagogium, in which a boy is shown with a crucified figure with a donkey's head and the caption: 'Alexamenos worships his god'. The **Paedagogium**, or pages' school, was located to the south, overlooking the great hollow of the Circus Maximus. Until recently, the **Altar to the Unknown God** stood near the Paedagogium; even though the Romans worshipped every god they could find, they feared to inadvertently offend one they may have neglected to invite to the party, like the bad fairy in Sleeping Beauty.

For more intimate sports, Domitian built a small **Stadium** east of the Domus Augustana, with a two-storey portico scooped into the side, from which the imperial family could watch in comfort. In latter years the emperors may have converted the stadium into a garden; the stubby stone oval enclosure at the far end was built by Theodoric, for reasons unknown. Around the back of the stadium's exedra are the remains of the **Baths of Severus**, supported by the great substructures visible from the Circus Maximus; the water came by way of Domitian's aqueduct.

> From the Stadium a path, the Clivus Palatinus, descends back to the Arch of Titus and the path to the Forum's back entrance on Via S. Gregorio. On your left, rising up on the levelled mound of the Velian hill, are the massive ruins of the **Temple of Venus and Rome**.

This unusual double-feature was built and perhaps designed by the dilettante emperor Hadrian over the vestibule of Nero's Golden House—in the face of objections by his architect, Apollodorus,who dared to point out that if the statues seated in the niches stood up, they would bang their heads on the roof. It had two doors: facing the Forum was the side dedicated to Immortal Rome (now part of the church of S. Francesca Romana); facing the Colosseum was the entrance to the sanctuary of Venus. One of the last pagan temples to close, it survived until Pope Honorius I tore off its bronze roof for the original St Peter's. Some columns have been re-erected; its twin cellae still stand in the centre, back to back.

> From the Forum's exit, turn left on Via S. Gregorio, the ancient Triumphal Way of Rome's *generalissimo*s, who would turn up to the Forum's Sacred Way near the **Arch of Constantine**, erected in 315 AD in honour of Constantine's victory over rival Maxentius at the Milvian Bridge.

According to Christian tradition, it was before this battle that Constantine had his vision of the cross and was instructed to fight under its sign. Much is made out of the seemingly fence-sitting inscription crediting 'the inspiration of the Deity' for his victory, though by that point all emperors were divine and he was surely referring to himself rather than Christ or Jove. The Arch is attractive, covered with fine bas-reliefs and medallions, but Constantine, however divine he might have been, had nothing to do with them—nearly all were stolen from other structures, in an attempt to link his regime with the past glories of divine Rome. The medallions on the arch's flanks, of the sinking moon in her chariot and the rising sun, are believed to be late works, though the Romans rarely mustered such charm and grace in their decline.

> *In between the arch and the Colosseum stood until 1936 the remains of a shamelessly phallic fountain called the Meta Sudans (the 'sweating meta' for its resemblance to a conical turning post in a circus). Only the memory remains of the other monument that stood nearby, the gilt Colossus of Nero, at 120 ft the largest bronze statue ever made, transported here by 24 elephants from the vestibule of the Golden House after Nero's death. It was renamed after the sun god, and its head frequently changed to match those of the reigning emperor, but what eventually became of this glowering golden giant is a Roman mystery. It did, however, lend its name to the neighbouring Flavian Amphitheatre, which has come down to posterity as the **Colosseum.***

Earthquakes and pillage, subsidence, pollution and the vibrations of traffic—metro line B runs below it—have taken their toll on the fabric of the Colosseum, and in September 1992 a major restoration programme swung into action. Financed by the Banca di Roma to the tune of 20 million pounds, with the promise of more funds if they prove to be necessary, the first stage will last four years. The monument will be repaired and cleaned, the problem of subsidence will be tackled, and eventually the arena floor, removed during the 19th-century excavations, will be replaced. There are also more ambitious plans—to divert the traffic, sink the metro line lower and even to deviate the water table—so the work is likely to last for at least a decade. So far it appears that the Colosseum will remain open to the public (*9 am–one hour before sunset; Wed and Sun 9–1 free; adm L6000 to upper levels*).

The ruin to beat all ruins, it is perhaps Rome's greatest marvel, breathtaking and beautifully built—for the pure delight in watching the cruellest torture and slaughter of men and animals. As vast as it is, what you see is less than half of the original structure, the bare skeleton of a travertine oval once a third of a mile in circumference.The Colosseum was called the Flavian Amphitheatre after the family of emperors who built it, beginning with Vespasian in 72 AD. Vespasian, the first post-Julian emperor to reign for more than a minute, was a self-made man who had to build popular support for his dynasty. One of his more successful public relations efforts was to return Nero's pleasure gardens to public use, then to out-do his predecessors by erecting the world's largest amphitheatre in the middle of Nero's lake—an astounding engineering feat that required what must be the Sistine Chapel of drains as well as foundations that go down several tiers of arches beneath the surface.

Yet Vespasian and his son Titus were, if nothing else, practical men. The massive amount of labour required to build the Colosseum was performed by Jewish slaves, brought here for the purpose after the suppression of their revolt. The lake was selected as its location, not for the mere sake of showing off, but because it was the perfect site—accessible from the Forum and Esquiline, Palatine, and Caelian hills, yet isolated enough to maintain crowd control. Some 50,000 thumbs could go down at once inside, and Vespasian's engineers provided 76 numbered entrances with free-flowing corridors to the seats, enabling all ticket-holders to be in position for the first round of death in only ten minutes. All modern stadiums have copied its general plan, and all have envied the unique adjustable awning that once covered the stands, protecting the crowds from the baking sun. Manipulated with poles (the sockets of which still remain) the awning was manned by a detachment of sailors from Cape Misenum (the Roman naval headquarters, near Naples); they also crewed the miniature galleys in the frequent mock sea battles, easily enough staged in the Colosseum by closing off its drains.

In the year 80, Titus opened the amphitheatre with a gala massacre of 5000 animals, roughly one every 10 seconds; the Romans' appetite for such sport led to the extinction of the native elephant and lion of North Africa and Arabia. Although it appears unlikely that Christians were ever thrown to the lions here (the Colosseum, after all, was built after Nero, the arch martyr-maker), there were plenty of other games to make it perhaps the most sadistic and best-organized perversity in all history. Nearly every primitive society indulged in human sacrifice in its darkest days, but the Romans were the only ones to make a sport of it once it had lost its religious purpose. The earliest gladiatorial contests were first noted among the Samnites around 400 BC; the Etruscans are said to have held prototypical combats; and tradition has it they were introduced to Rome during the First Punic War 'to boost morale' and make Romans better soldiers by rendering them indifferent to the sight of death. It worked. Indifferent and utterly brutalized, the Roman crowd's chief interest in the show was the outcome of their wagers. Later emperors introduced new displays to make the odds more interesting—men versus animals, lions versus elephants, women versus dwarfs, sea battles, and even genuine athletics, a Greek import the Romans never much cared for. The emperor and other important people had front row seats in marble, while the rest of the concrete seats (now all eroded away) were divided by wealth and social class; women were confined to the uppermost reaches. An exception were the Vestals, who sat near the emperor, a privilege the younger, more sensitive girls didn't always appreciate; occasionally they had to be escorted further back, along

one of the 160 vertical passages between the seats appropriately called *vomitoria.*
If it's open, the view from the top ranks is unforgettable, both looking across the
Roman Forum towards the city and gazing down what seems to be the corrugated
cone of a man-made volcano.

In the 8th century, the Venerable Bede recorded a favourite Latin proverb of
Rome's Saxon pilgrims, best known in Byron's translation from *Childe Harold:*

> *While stands the Coliseum, Rome shall stand;*
> *When falls the Coliseum, Rome shall fall;*
> *And when Rome falls—the world.*

Which, however, didn't prevent the Romans from trying to tear it apart. Although
it was quickly repaired after several fires caused by lightning, earthquakes in the
Dark Ages turned the outer ring of arches, once filled with statues and embell-
ished with bronze shields, into a quarry that Renaissance popes used to build the
Palazzo Venezia, Palazzo Barberini, a few other palaces and bridges and part of St
Peter's. Their job had been made easier by Constans II, who in 664 looted the
metal clamps that held the travertine skeleton together, leaving the holes that
pockmark the exterior today. The plunder stopped only in 1744, when Benedict
XIV consecrated the Colosseum to its supposed Christian martyrs and set up the
Stations of the Cross in the arena; later Popes, especially Leo XII in 1825, prevented further crumbling of the outer walls with the familiar sloping smooth
buttresses. The confusing labyrinth of walls and passages in the arena contained
cages for the wild beasts and mechanisms for the more elaborate spectacles; in
ancient times these were covered with a wooden floor and sand (*arena*), which
kept the gladiators from slipping and soaked up the blood. The excavation of the
arena in the 19th century gravely offended romantics who loved to contemplate
the mighty ruin by moonlight; strange humours were said to rise from the uncovered marshy depths, the 'Roman fever' that killed Henry James's poor susceptible
Daisy Miller. Although the surrounding haze of electric light has cooled the old
romance, the Colosseum is specially floodlit so that the shadows in its arches
become endless tunnels of dark and mystery, sinister enough to be haunted by the
fiery demons that arose when sculptor Benvenuto Cellini and a renegade priest
conjured them in a seance one midnight in 1534. Cellini, in his *Autobiography*, is
full of bluff, but he wasn't the only one who believed in the fiends; in 1522, a bull
was sacrificed to them during a plague that even the saints couldn't end.

> *From here, walk back along Via dei Fori Imperiali, towards Piazza*
> *Venezia, shrugging off pickpockets and fortune-tellers to visit the churches*
> *inaccessible from the Forum, beginning with a ramp on the left, leading*
> *to **Santa Francesca Romana** (Santa Maria Nova) (10–12 and 3.30–5.*
> *Later in summer), once the titular church of Cardinal Cesare Borgia.*

Built into the portico of the Temple of Venus and Rome, the church began (8th century) as a shrine dedicated to SS. Peter and Paul, for its most holy relic: the paving stones from the Via Sacra bearing the knee prints of the two saints. Peter and Paul had to do some very weighty praying to bag their rival Simon Magus. The sorcerer had challenged them to a magic duel to prove who had the most power. Simon at first seemed to get the better of them by soaring over the Forum, but the saints asked God to make him fall, and he crashed to his death nearby. Grope your way through the dim candlelit church to the right transept where the alleged knee prints, are incorporated into the wall.

In the same transept, there's a late Renaissance monument to Gregory XI, the Pope who returned to Rome from Avignon in 1377 and regretted every minute of it, but died before he could go back to France. The monument, showing a merry St Catherine of Siena leading the Pope home, was paid for by the grateful people of Rome. In the crypt you can pay your respects to the shrouded skeleton of the only native Roman to found a religious order, S. Francesca Romana who founded the Oblates for lady nuns in the 15th century, and who has been appointed patron saint of motorists; on 9 March, her feast day, the Piazzale del Colosseo is packed solid with Fiats come for her blessing.

S. Francesca Romana has three lovely Madonnas: a 12th-century mosaic of the Madonna and saints in the apse; a painting of the same century over the altar; and the Madonna that was discovered beneath it, a unique easel painting of the 6th century. The painting, of an eerie, strangely distorted Madonna with elongated nose and gigantic eyes, is now kept in the sacristy.

> *From S. Francesca the pavement passes the outer wall of the Basilica of Maxentius, on which Mussolini placed four stone maps illustrating the expansion (but not the decline) of the Roman Empire. The next church, Santi Cosma e Damiano (open 8–1 and 4–6.30), was built over the library of Vespasian's forum.*

Converted to a church in 527 and rebuilt in 1632, it preserves the beautiful gold ground mosaics of the 6th century that influenced many subsequent Roman artists. In the triumphal arch are the Lamb, angels and symbols of the Evangelists and in the apse, SS. Peter and Paul introducing Cosmas and Damian (two doctors from the Middle East) to Christ, with twelve lambs symbolizing the Apostles, and four rivers, for the Gospels. Signs point the way to an elaborate 18th-century Neapolitan *presepio*, or Christmas crib, which you can illuminate with coins.

> *The walk ends on Via dei Fori Imperiali. Walk along to the Ristorante Ulpia for an early evening drink on its terrace or jump on bus 81 or 87 which will take you to Corso Rinascimento, a 30 second walk from Piazza Navona, where you can recover in one of the cafés.*

San Clemente and Mithraeum	139
Santi Quattro Coronati	141
Santa Maria in Domnica	142
Villa Celimontana	143
Santi Giovanni e Paolo	144
Baths of Caracalla	146

Start: ⓜ *Colosseum. Take bus 85 or 87 to the Colosseum from Piazza Venezia, 81 from the Vatican, Piazza del Risorgimento, or else the B line of the Metropolitana.*
Finish: *At the Baths of Caracalla.*
Walking Time: *3–3½ hours.*

III: San Clemente and the Caelian Hill

Caralla —

This walk is for explorers. You'll be traversing an area that had in late imperial days a population of several hundred thousand, including some of the most fashionable quarters of the city. Today, except for the little neighbourhood around San Clemente, it is almost entirely empty. When the besieging Goths cut the aqueducts in the Greek-Gothic wars of the 530s, property values dropped a bit for the wealthy villas and apartment blocks on Rome's southern hills. As the population gradually moved down to the Campus Martius, the area became abandoned, leaving behind monumental ruins and some of the most important early Christian churches, sitting among vineyards and cow pastures.

Somehow, the area escaped the post-1870 speculative building boom that ruined so much of Rome. The top of the Caelian Hill particularly remains one of the most tranquil and beautiful sections of the city, a Roman fantasy of cypresses and parasol pines. Plans are afoot to turn it into a sort of archaeological park, connecting the Forum and Palatine Hill with the monuments along the Via Appia Antica. The money has been appropriated, but it will be several years before something starts to happen.

This walk is best in the morning, when its seldom-visited churches are open, and goes nicely with no. XII: the Appian Way (though the Museum of the Walls usually closes at 1.30) or Walk X: Ancient Churches and Big Basilicas.

Don't go if it threatens to rain; there are few opportunities for shelter along the way.

---

lunch/cafés

You won't find many restaurants or snack bars along this route, though if you decide to go in the afternoon you could begin with lunch at Cavour 313, Ulderico, Pizza Forum or Pasqualino, listed in Walk II. If you do the walk in the morning you could end up with lunch in one of these places, by catching bus 118 from Via delle Terme di Caracalla back to the Colosseum. The best option, however, weather permitting, is to pack a picnic (you could buy provisions at the morning street market on Via delle Santi Quattro) and stop halfway through in the lovely Villa Celimontana park.

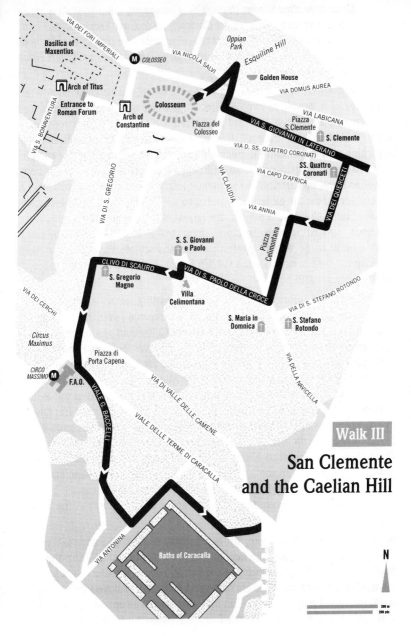

Walk III

San Clemente
and the Caelian Hill

N

If you have already been through the Colosseum, take the shallow stair at the eastern end of Piazza del Colosseo up to Colle Oppio, a spur of the Esquiline Hill. Near the top (and we mention this only in case it should ever reopen), is the entrance to what is left of Nero's Golden House (Domus Aurea).

Nero may not have started Rome's great fire of 64 AD, but he knew how to take advantage of it, buying or expropriating huge tracts of burned properties for a palace to end all palaces. 'At last I am lodged like a man!', Nero is reported to have said when he moved in. Covering nearly a quarter of central Rome, stretching over most of the Esquiline, Palatine and Caelian Hills, the complex included extensive gardens and an artificial lake (where the Colosseum is now), as well as baths, menageries, and an avenue with triple colonnades a mile long. At the entrance, near the eastern approaches to the Forum, stood a 120-foot gilded statue of (who else?) Nero himself, the largest ever made in antiquity; from this 'colossus', surpassing even the more famous one at Rhodes, the nearby Colosseum took its name. All the greatest painters and sculptors available were kept working full time to decorate the Golden House, though work stopped abruptly upon Nero's death in 68.

To the honest emperors that followed, this sprawling symbol of vulgar tyranny was not the best possible advertisement for the imperial government. Vespasian and Titus cleared much of the ground for the Colosseum and other buildings, Hadrian built the Temple of Venus and Rome in its vestibule, and Trajan demolished most of the palace itself for his baths on the Esquiline. The very location of the fabled Golden House was forgotten by the Middle Ages, but in the 1490s, one wing was accidentally discovered, a section that Trajan had saved to use as foundations for the baths. Renaissance artists flocked to see the delicate, fanciful paintings on its walls, the same sort of purely decorative faces, twining foliage and fantasy pavilions common in the villas of Pompeii. In one of the long corridors there is an arch, inscribed with the names of many visiting artists, including Raphael's assistant, Giovanni da Udine. Raphael and his circle were impresssed enough with this style of decoration (called *grottesche*, or grotesques, from this 'grotto' in which they were first seen) to copy it in such places as the Vatican Loggie.

Another work of art found here, just as influential in the Renaissance as the paintings, was dug up in 1506, the famous *Laocoön*, mentioned by Pliny and other ancient authors. Though probably only a Roman copy of an older Greek work, its discovery became an artistic event of the first magnitude. Michelangelo praised it, Julius II snapped it up for the Vatican Palace (where it can be seen today) and as it was carried through the streets, the Romans showered it with flowers. The contorted, suffering forms of the Trojan priest and his sons, with Apollo's serpents coiling around them, were for centuries considered one of the greatest works of all time.

> *Above the Golden House, the large park of Colle Oppio is littered every-where with remains of the **Baths of Trajan**.*

Built in 109 by Apollodorus, the master architect who also laid out Trajan's Forum, this was the first of the truly monumental bath complexes, its plan copied by all those that followed. It has never been excavated, and nowadays the city's homeless sleep beneath its vaults; old men while away their afternoons playing cards, after lunching in the local soup kitchen; Muslims come to pray. The park has consequently become a target for Rome's fascist extremists, who were recently responsible for the murder of two North African immigrants here.

> *Leave Colle Oppio, heading across busy Via Labicana, south on Piazza del Colosseo; right across from the Colosseum you will see the ruins of the **Ludus Magnus**, an imposing quadrangle with a small arena where the gladiators trained, and where emperors who really enjoyed that sort of thing would put on private shows. Turn left on Via di San Giovanni, then continue straight to **San Clemente** (open 9–12.30 and 3.30–6), the major attraction on this walk and a sight no visitor to Rome should miss.*

With four levels of building, shrines of two religions, works of art from almost all of the last 20 centuries, along with a subterranean street and some good old solid Roman engineering, San Clemente offers a unique lesson in Rome's many-layered history. The site, including many 1st-century buildings, apparently became Christian property in the early 300s; about 375, one of the first big Christian building projects was begun over the older foundations, a basilica dedicated to St Clement, the third pope (inscriptions record the property as belonging to a certain T. Flavius Clemens, so perhaps there was a family connection). Burned along with the rest of the neighbourhood in the Norman sack of 1084, the church was soon after rebuilt over the remains of the original, which was filled in with soil and rubble. It remained unknown until 1857, when the prior, Father Joseph Mulhooly, started excavations on his own initiative. Some 40 years and scores of wagon-loads of debris later, the ancient basilica was cleared, and the lower levels discovered.

Usually only the side entrance is open, but in front of the church, along with the plain late Baroque façade added in the 1700s, is a medieval *quadroporticus*, one of the few left in Rome—a survival of an ancient building style more common in south Italy; most of the early Christian basilicas had one, a square colonnaded courtyard leading to the main door. Inside, the eye is immediately attracted to the exquisite *schola cantorum* (choir screen) that fills the centre of the church, carved in the 6th and 7th centuries and saved from the original building. The early Cosmatesque pavement and *baldacchino* over the altar date from the rebuilding. The anchor on it is a symbol of St Clement, who supposedly was tied to one to make sure he drowned. In the apse, 12th-century frescoes detail the *Triumph of the Cross*—note the twelve doves, representing the Apostles, and the four rivers of Paradise springing from the foot of the cross. Below it are some fine frescoes of saints from the 1300s, and a tabernacle from the same period by Arnolfo di Cambio.

In the **left aisle**, near the side entrance, there is a chapel with a beautiful series of frescoes on the *Life of St Catherine* by Masolino (1420s; perhaps assisted by his precocious pupil Masaccio), one of your few chances in Rome to experience the vivid, revolutionary painting of the Florentine early Renaissance— just revealed after a lengthy restoration. Along with St Catherine (on the left wall) there is a Crucifixion and portraits of the Apostles, Evangelists, and Doctors of the Church. In the **sacristy**, just before the stair down to the **Lower Church**, there is a souvenir stand with posters and slides of the paintings below, rare works of the 9th–11th centuries. Take a look at them, for the actual frescoes are not in nearly as good a shape—every year sees them a little more faded. The stairway, lined with a jumble of fragments from the different ages of the church, leads down to the narthex, with 11th-century frescoes of the life of St Clement. The Lower Church itself was somewhat larger than its medieval successor, though the space is broken up by piers and walls added to support what is above. Frescoes on the wall facing the narthex include scenes of the life of Jesus and the Ascension (9th century); in a niche on the right-hand wall is a portrait that may be, intriguingly, either the Virgin Mary or the notorious Byzantine Empress Theodora. On the opposite wall, more 9th-century frescoes tell the typically ingenuous saint story of Sisinius—but are remarkable for the inscriptions below, perhaps the oldest in the Italian language.

On one of the supporting walls is a little plaque erected by, of all people, Mr Todor Zhivkov, former Chairman of the Bulgarian Communist Party. And not without reason. From this church, in the 10th century, SS. Cyril and Methodius were sent out to convert the Slavs. They made a good job of it, and also invented the Cyrillic alphabet to translate the Bible into Old Slavonic, creating the first written works in any Slavic language. San Clemente has a long history of missionary work to exotic places. The first two bishops of New York came from the Irish college next door.

Climb down another level (the steps are near the right wall) for the 1st-century AD block housing the **Mithraeum**. Of at least a dozen temples of Mithras discovered in Rome, this is by far the most accessible and best preserved. Mithraism was a mystery religion, imported from Persia, which as late as the 300s could probably claim more adherents in Rome than Christianity. Heavily soaked in astrology and the blood of bulls, the religion based itself on the myth of a sun hero, Mithras; other features included a heavy dose of ethics, initiations involving trials by fire, ice, hunger and thirst, and a surprising number of similarities in ritual and myth to Christianity. Mithraism was a men-only cult which appealed especially to soldiers; the exclusion of women, and lack of followers among the ruling classes, eventually doomed it. The Christians stamped it out as soon as they could after achieving power in Rome.

This Mithraeum was one of the larger complexes, built into the block in the 2nd or 3rd century. After an antechamber with an ornamental stucco ceiling, there is the 'triclinium', with an altar portraying—as always on Mithraic altars—Mithras dispatching a white bull with a knife. The room gets its name because the form, and the benches lining the walls, suggest it was used for ritual suppers. Originally the ceiling was decorated with stucco reliefs representing the constellations, with narrow shafts of light through the roof for the stars. Adjacent to this is another chamber with a better-preserved ceiling, believed to be a school where boys were instructed in the religion before their initiations.

And still there is one more level below, foundations of Republican-era buildings that burned in Nero's great fire. These have never been excavated, but from the Mithraeum you can walk out into a 1900-year-old Roman alley, now some 30 feet below street level. At the end of it (where the excavations stopped), you will hear water rushing below. No one knows if this outlet of the eerie sub-Roma of underground lakes, caves and buildings is an ancient sewer or an underground stream, but according to one story a child fell into it during a school outing a hundred years ago; they found him, barely alive, in open country several miles from the city.

> *From the front of San Clemente, take Via dei Querceti, then first left, Via dei SS Quattro. The fortress-like church here is* **Santi Quattro Coronati** *(open Mon–Fri 9–12 and 4–6, Sun;Capella di San Silvestro closes at 11 am).*

Like San Clemente, the original church was destroyed in the 1084 Norman sack. When Paschal II rebuilt it, around 1111, he made the church and its abbey into a veritable castle, with some of the thickest walls in Rome. The entrance, under a campanile that is really a defence tower, leads to another *quadroporticus*, and then a second court, once occupied by the nave of the original church. The interior, restored by various hands over the centuries, has a *matroneum*, one of the last to be built in Rome, and some fragmentary medieval frescoes. The large apse, with Baroque frescoes by Giovanni San Giovanni, survives from the original building—and gives an idea how much larger it was than what you see now.

Ring the bell near the door in the left aisle, and a nun will admit you to the peaceful medieval cloister, its walls lined with fascinating bits of the pre–1084 decoration: neo-Celtic reliefs and other such barbaric stuff; one little plaque may be Rome's oldest surviving stick-no-bills sign—*applicar non licet.* Off the cloister, the small **Chapel of Santa Barbara** has more remains of medieval frescoes, and lovely ancient capitals recycled to support the brick vaulting. Much better preserved frescoes can be seen in the **Chapel of San Silvestro**, off the second courtyard in front of the church (ask the nun to let you in). These scenes (*c.* 1246) chronicle a very important part of Church mythology, the story of the sainted Pope Sylvester, how he cured Emperor Constantine of leprosy, and how in return the Emperor bestowed temporal authority over the West on the papacy—the Donation of Constantine, all a fairy tale, but the basis of the popes' claim to absolute authority over the centuries.

> *Head back to Via dei Querceti and walk up the hill, crossing Via Capo d'Africa (a street that has kept its name since ancient times, perhaps from a memory of Jugurtha or some other captured African prince. Via dei Querceti recalls that the Caelian was originally the Mons Querquetulanus, from the oak forest that covered it). At the top of Via dei Querceti, take Via Annia to the right, and then left on to Piazza Celimontana.*

> *The ruins to the right, at the end of the piazza (fenced off and impossible to see), were the outer wall of the* **Temple of Claudius,** *a huge quadrangle full of gardens with the temple (now vanished) at its centre. Claudius' wife Agrippina built it on his death in 54 AD, and Nero thought so much of his imperial father-in-law that he turned the place into a pleasure garden for his Golden House.*

> *Adjacent* **Piazza Navicella** *takes its name from the little ancient stone boat, probably an ex-voto offering by sailors to the goddess Isis. It was discovered in the time of Pope Leo X, who had it incorporated into the fountain here. Behind it is* **Santa Maria in Domnica** *(8.30–12 and 4–6), an early 9th-century church restored, like the Navicella, by Leo X.*

In the simple interior, bathed in a golden light and lined with ancient granite columns, the climax are the lovely, Ravenna-style mosaics in the apse, added around 820 under Pope Paschal I—he is the fellow you see kneeling at the foot of the enthroned Madonna, wearing a square nimbus instead of a halo, this, according to the artistic conventions of the time, because he was still alive.

(Vanity or not, Paschal was canonized later. This pope was a special friend of the English in Rome. When the wooden Anglo-Saxon Borgo caught fire in the 820s, he ran out barefoot at midnight from the Vatican to help put it out, then contributed the money for its rebuilding.) Above Mary, on the triumphal arch, Jesus is flanked by the Apostles, arranged like a chorus line among the mosaic flowers; the figures below represent Moses and Elijah.

No one ever mentions this church's very singular ceiling. Ferdinand de' Medici, Grand Duke of Tuscany and part-time alchemist, added it in honour of his kinsman Leo X. Replete with cryptic inscriptions about the 'mystic rose' and 'tower of David', along with plenty of arcane symbolism, in which the Navicella itself is a recurring theme (sometimes as the Ark)—we don't know what to make of it either.

> *Across the piazza (entrance on Via Santo Stefano Rotondo to the left) is the huge round church of **Santo Stefano Rotondo** (open Mon–Fri 8.20–12.20), built about 470.*

The round shape has made many scholars think it was built over a meat market—the Macellum Magnum of Nero (round market buildings were common, as at Pompeii and Pozzuoli near Naples). It must have been built over something, for remains of another Mithraeum have recently been found underneath. Another opinion has it designed after the round Church of the Holy Sepulchre Constantine erected in Jerusalem. Perhaps the biggest of all early Christian churches (before the outer ring of columns had to be pulled down in the 1400s, it was over 200 ft in diameter), it's a wonderfully peaceful, harmonious church, though the serenity is somewhat spoiled by the thoroughly perverse frescoes of martyrdoms, added in the 1580s, which cover its walls.

> *Stretching behind S. Stefano, you see impressive remains of the **Aqua Claudia (Claudian Aqueduct)**, its long, tall arcades designed to bring water to the highest points of the city. Head back to Piazza Navicella and under the **Arch of Dolabella**, site of an old gate, rebuilt in 10 AD (Dolabella was Consul in that year) and later used to carry the Aqua Claudia over the road. To the left, **San Tommaso in Formis** has a mosaic of 1218 above the door (behind a gate in the wall, usually locked. If you're keen to see it, arrange a visit by phoning © 342 059 between 1 and 2 or 8 and 9 pm).*

> ***Via di San Paolo della Croce*** *runs down from the Arch, almost a village lane, bounded on one side by the gardens of a large Passionist monastery, and on the other by the extensive **Villa Celimontana**, the most beautiful and agreeable park in this part of Rome. The southern*

end of the park has a small obelisk dedicated to Isis, twin to the one in front of the Pantheon. A nobleman named Ciriaco Mattei moved it here in 1582, as part of an odd plan to build a classical Circus on what was then his family villa gardens.

*All along Via di San Paolo della Croce, lurking behind the high walls, you can catch the occasional glimpse of the Aqua Claudia; to an ancient visitor this would have been as conspicuous a demonstration of Roman engineering as the bridges or the Pantheon, zigzagging behind the villas and smart insulae of the Caelian on three levels of brick arches, finally adding a fourth, higher than the top of the Colosseum, as it crossed the Triumphal Way (see below) to bring water up to the Palatine hill. Via di San Paolo ends at the pretty piazza in front of another remarkable early church, **Santi Giovanni e Paolo** (open 9–11.30 and 4–6).*

Though there was a Christian centre here as early as 400, incorporating older apartment buildings, the present building is from the 11th–12th centuries, rebuilt after the Norman sack. One of the few medieval buildings to escape the attentions of the Baroque spoilers, it remains largely as it was built, with a tall and graceful detached campanile, an Ionic portico (later partially enclosed) and an arcaded Romanesque apse. The exterior was faithfully restored in 1950 under the direction of its titular cardinal Francis Spellman, Archbishop of Neoboracum—New York in Latin, as you'll see it written on the plaque in the portico.

The Baroque had its way with the interior, but the real treasures are underneath. Some 70 years ago, one of the Passionist fathers in the adjacent monastery, digging just on instinct, discovered the Roman apartments now called the **House of SS. John and Paul** (closed for restorations), after the two 4th-century martyrs honoured in the church above. Cardinal Spellman also oversaw the rest of the excavations, uncovering a lavish abode with its own baths, a library and a wine cellar. Many of the rooms are painted, some later ones with Christian subjects, and one exceptional mythological scene of the 3rd century, most likely representing *Persephone* (or perhaps Achilles' mother Thetis) and another divinity, reclining on a couch while little cupids sail by.

* **Clivo di Scauro**, another ancient street that has kept its name (Clivus Scaurus, after a Republican consul named Aemilius Scaurus) for all these centuries, continues down the opposite slope of the Caelian, passing remains of many ancient buildings: first the arches, now facing the piazza, that covered a row of Roman shops, then the side wall of an insula, built into the church and propped up by the arches over the street, and finally, to the left at the end of the street, ruins of perhaps the last library ever built in ancient Rome. The **Library of Agapetus** was*

begun as late as 535, when Pope Agapetus I and the learned ministers of Gothic King Theodoric were planning to start a new Roman university—plans that disappeared in the tragic Greek-Gothic War that began the same year.

One of the last of the wealthy Romans to keep up a villa on the Caelian was Pope Gregory the Great. Upon his election in 590, in the prostrate, devastated Rome that followed the wars and the Lombard invasion, Gregory donated a third of his wealth to the Church and its relief efforts. His mansion, behind the Library of Agapetus, became a monastery, where Gregory continued to live. From here he reorganized Rome and its Church, and from here he sent St Augustine out to convert the heathen Angles and Saxons.

*This villa-monastery—perhaps the one site in Rome most worth excavating—still lies below the surface; all that remains now is the church of **San Gregorio Magno** (8–12.30 and 4–6.30) completely rebuilt in the 1620s, with a fine façade by Giovan Battista Soria that is one of the first landmarks of the emerging Baroque. It too will be under restoration (until the end of 1993), as are the three small chapels to the left of it on Clivo di Scauro, dedicated to S. Silvia, S. Andrea and S. Barbara. Built over parts of Gregory's monastery, they are full of Baroque frescoes—notably S. Silvia, with an Angel Choir that could make even a sceptic appreciate the work of Guido Reni.*

*Turn left at the foot of the steps onto the Salita di San Gregorio, running above busy Via di San Gregorio, laid out by Mussolini to follow the ancient Triumphal Way between the Caelian and the Palatine. On the Palatine side, absolutely nothing is now left of the famous **Septizonium**.*

Sixtus V carted away its psychedelic marbles for a new chapel in S. Maria Maggiore, but this unusual building, created by Septimius Severus in 203 AD, was one of the sights of ancient Rome. A tall, shallow structure with three storeys of columns, rather like a nymphaeum or the stage building of a Roman theatre, no one has yet guessed its purpose, if it had one. Its name comes from the 'seven zones' into which it was divided, probably symbolizing the seven planets.

*Here Via di San Gregorio opens into Piazza di Porta Capena. To the right was the **Circus Maximus** (see Walk XI, pp. 245-56) , and to the left there is a forlorn little Renaissance pavilion called **La Vignola**, lost among the speeding traffic. Straight ahead stands the newest and oddest of Rome's obelisks, stolen by Mussolini from the Ethiopian holy city of Axum and put up along the new Triumphal Way as a symbol of Italy's* *new imperial pretensions. The **Obelisk of Axum** is probably really a funeral monument from the 4th century; no one in Italy has since considered that it might be a nice gesture to give it back. The clean, modern building behind, standing at the beginning of Via delle Terme di Caracalla, was intended to be Mussolini's Ministry of Africa. Still unfinished at the end of the war, it has found a better use as home to the United Nations food organization, **FAO**. Further along Via delle Terme di Caracalla is the entrance to the **Baths of Caracalla.***

Alexander Severus finished the baths that Caracalla started, but somehow it is fitting that this grand symbol of Roman opulence should be associated with this most decadent of emperors. The sprawling complex, covering some 27¼ acres, could service over 2000 bathers at a time, though tens of thousands more could have made themselves comfortable among the gardens, exercise yards, swimming pools and libraries. Its marble basins were salvaged to hold fountains all over Rome, and its works of art (like the famous Farnese Hercules, now in Naples) take pride of place in many Italian museums. Closed after the aqueducts were cut during the Gothic siege of 546, the baths were gradually abandoned, leaving for us only the giant arches of the central halls, and weirdly eroded brick and concrete forms that give a faint clue to the original layout. Some large mosaics have been restored and displayed around the central building, and beneath the outer wall near the entrance is the largest Mithraeum yet discovered in Rome; you may be able to persuade one of the guards to take you down to see it.

This is not the most enlightening of Roman ruins to visit, but it is one of the best known, thanks largely to the summer opera season begun here in Mussolini's time. A large tunnel, built to bring in the tons of firewood necessary for the baths, runs from here to the Palazzo Venezia; Mussolini liked to drive his Alfa roadster through it, popping up magically on stage, car and all, for the opera's opening festivities.

If you have the stamina to go on to Walk X take the 118 bus from the Baths back to the Colosseum, where X begins at nearby S. Pietro in Vincoli. Also from the Baths, the no. 90 bus can bring you back to Piazza Venezia, passing the Palatine, Circus Maximus, and the ancient temples still standing in Piazza Bocca della Verità.

Santa Maria Sopra Minerva	151
Pantheon	152
Piazza di Sant'Eustachio	154
Sant'Ivo	155
Sant'Agostino	156
Via dell'Orso	156
Santa Maria della Pace	158
Piazza Navona	158

Start: *If you're not staying in the area, catch a bus down to Piazza Venezia. If you are, simply navigate your way along the centro storico's alleyways to Piazza della Minerva.*

IV: Pantheon and Piazza Navona

Finish: *Piazza Navona or Via dei Coronari.*
Walking Time: *2 ½–3 hours.*

Pza Navona –
fontana del Nettuno

This walk, and the two that follow, cover the broad bend in the Tiber that surrounds what, for lack of a better name, is often called simply 'old Rome'—it's hardly the oldest part, but a typical irony in this venerable city that its brightest, most alive, most ingratiating quarter should be the crumbling old medieval flatlands. There's no neighbourhood like this one, not in Rome or any other city. The seat of the Italian government is here (really in Walk VI), and you may find your tour occasionally interrupted by speeding blue Lancias and Alfas full of diplomats and ministers, accompanied by a noisy gaggle of Carabinieri. The Pantheon is here too, and a score of other monuments—politicians, journalists, cats, artists, trendies, fruit vendors, Dominicans and Jesuits, tons of tourists, all heaped together in what would otherwise be a peaceful and normal residential quarter. There's room for everyone; the tight web of narrow medieval alleys and pint-sized *piazze*, inscrutable and almost indecipherable to the first-time visitor, makes the neighbourhood seem bigger (and more tranquil) than it really is.

To ancient Rome this bend in the river was the **Campus Martius**, the field of Mars, where the first citizens of the republic drilled and practised their swordplay, also where they came to stand up and be counted on election day. The growing city eventually covered it all with theatres and temples, public buildings and *insulae*; in the 600s, with the all-important aqueducts out of service, what was left of Rome's population began straggling down here, where drinkable (just barely!) water from the Tiber was readily available.

See
P. 3

Combine Walk V with this one, for a complete day's tour of the sweetest corner of Rome, or cross over to Trastevere for the afternoon (Walk XIII) and stay for dinner. All the other walks in the centre (I,II,VI,VII) are also possibilities. This one is almost entirely outdoors, with no big museums to slow you down.

Lazy folk might like to know about minibus 119, which creeps along the twisting streets following a circular route: Pantheon—Piazza di S. Eustachio—Piazza delle Cinque Lune—Tiber—Via di Ripetta—Via del Babuino—Via del Tritone—Pantheon.

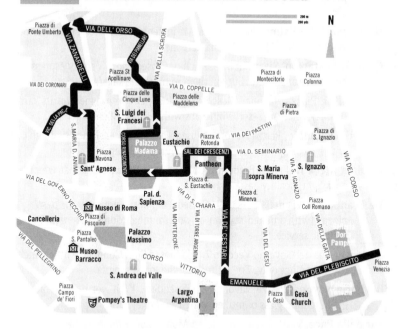

lunch/cafés

Bar della Rotonda, Piazza della Rotonda, tables in front of Pantheon, good coffee.

Tazza d'Oro, Via degli Orfani, just off Piazza della Rotonda. Not much to look at, but the latest contender for Rome's best cup of java (and coffee *granita* topped with cream), with many loyal supporters.

Pizza al taglio, 82 Via della Minerva off Piazza della Rotonda; good pizza, *suppli* and sandwiches.

Pizza al taglio, Via del Governo Vecchio 28. Closed Thurs pm in winter, Sat pm in summer and Sun all year round. Open 8–2 (prompt!) and 5–8. Unbeatable pizza bread sandwiches made to order—choose your own filling from the bowls of *ricotta*, *mozzarella*, tomato, *rughetta*, tuna, *bresaola*, *prosciutto*...laid out on the bar. Be ready to elbow your way to the front of the queue.

La Montecarlo, Vicolo Savelli 12, closed Mon in winter. Exuberant, engagingly chaotic pizzeria.

Caffè Capranica, Via in Aquiro, just north of the Pantheon. Not much atmosphere, but a good, popular *tavola calda*, serving Rome's best try at a real breakfast.

Gelateria della Palma, Piazza della Maddalena, deluxe ice cream parlours; wacky flavours like fig and mascarpone.

Caffè S. Eustachio, Piazza di S. Eustachio. Closed Mon. Velvety espresso and heavenly cappuccino, but tell them to mind the sugar.

Tre Scalini, Piazza Navona. Closed Wed. Justifiably renowned for its *tartufo* (truffle) ice cream—served in slabs with a smear of cream.

Caffè di Colombie, Piazza Navona. Closed Thur in winter. Fancy sit-down café, with a close-up view of the Quattro Fiume fountain.

Insalata Ricca II, Piazza Pasquino. Closed Mon. Deluxe salad bar which also does light, healthy pasta dishes.

Da Francesco, Via della Fossa 29. Closed Tue. Serve yourself *antipasti*, great pizzas (with smoked salmon or *porcini* mushrooms and *rughetta*) and amiable service.

Il Piccolo, Via del Governo Vecchio 74–5. Closed Sun. Conducive little wine bar open evenings only. Try the fruits of the forest sangria.

Bevitoria Navona, Piazza Navona 72. Closed Sun. Well worth a visit on a cold evening for a glass of mulled wine (*vin brûlé*).

Bar della Pace, Via della Pace 5. Closed Mon. Snooty *fin-de-siècle* bar; elitist in the evenings, but a pleasant retreat during the day. L10,000 a cappuccino.

Cul de Sac I, Piazza Pasquino 73. Closed Mon. Italian cheese, salamis and cured meats, along with salads, home-made pâtés and soups in the doyenne of Rome's wine bars.

---

*If you're beginning at Piazza Venezia, take any of the streets off Corso Vittorio Emanuele towards the north—**Via della Gatta**, named after the tiny stone cat (found in a Temple of Isis) stranded high up on the cornice of one of the palazzi; **Via del Gesù**, where the same mad monk who built the water clock in the Pincio left another one just like it (courtyard of the palazzo at no. 62); on **Via dei Cestari**, though, you'll have a chance to check out the latest in clerical fashions and liturgical apparatus. This has been the street of religious goods shops since the Middle Ages, though the smiling bambi-eyed mannequins dressed as nuns and displays of the latest in convent nightwear in the show windows are probably more recent innovations.*

*At the end of Via dei Cestari, in Piazza di Minerva, you'll find a work of Bernini (1667), a winsome, grinning **elephant** supporting on its back a modest Egyptian obelisk, found in the ruins of the same Temple of Isis that provided the cat. Supposedly this elephant is Bernini's tribute to the wisdom of his patron, Pope Alexander VI.*

*Behind it is **Santa Maria sopra Minerva** (open 7–12 and 4–7), whose august façade is likely to be concealed behind scaffolding until at least the end of 1993.*

It was the Florentine church in Rome, and the dowdy austerity of its exterior is as evocative of the Florentine sensibility as the quirky Gothic inside. Fra Ristoro and Fra Sisto, the architects of Florence's great S. Maria Novella, built it in the same style, beginning in the 1280s. The church's name refers to a temple of Minerva that occupied the spot before the original Santa Maria was built, in the 9th century. Besides its Florentine associations, this was the church of the Dominicans, and of the Inquisition; the 'monks of the Minerva' were as dear to the Romans as toothache, and on several occasions in the 1500s the church and its adjacent monastery (where Galileo was tried) only narrowly escaped destruction at the hands of a mob.

The Gothic interior should perhaps not be taken too seriously; much of it was redone in a somewhat fanciful 1840s restoration. In any case it's almost unique in Rome, a city that has entertained no Gothic thoughts since the days of Alaric and Totila.

In the left aisle, 3rd chapel, is a small altarpiece, perhaps the work of Perugino. The best art is in the **transepts**, with solid ranks of chapels along the east wall in the Florentine manner: in the 2nd left of the altar, the delicate **Tomb of Giovanni Arberini**, by that much-neglected quattrocento sculptor Agostino di Duccio; the central relief, a battle of Hercules with the Nemean lion, is thought to be an ancient Roman work. Just left of the altar is the **Tomb of Fra Angelico**, Dominican monk and great Florentine artist who died in Rome in 1455.

Leo X and Clement VII, the Medici popes, are buried in the apse: though unless you dare pass behind the altar, you can only just glimpse their tombs. Both contributed much to the decoration of this church, and not surprisingly at least one of their commissions went to fellow Florentine Michelangelo; his **Christ bearing the Cross** (not to mention a skewered bronze loin-cloth), near the altar, is a memorable work, with all of the Michelangelesque intensity and none of the neurotic excess.

Under the altar itself is buried St Catherine of Siena, who talked Pope Gregory XI into returning to Rome from Avignon in 1377, thus ending the so-called 'Baby-

Ionian Captivity' and rescuing Rome from its most serious period of decline.

In the 2nd chapel of the right transept, the **Carafa Chapel**, you can pay your respects to the foulest, bloodiest pope of them all, Paul IV (1555–9), father of the Inquisition. Besides the pope's tomb, there is some fine quattrocento decorative sculptural work by Mino da Fiesole and Verrocchio (both Florentines) and above all the great series of frescoes on the **Life of St Thomas Aquinas** by Filippino Lippi (1480s), some of his best work outside Florence. On the wall to the left of the chapel, Giovanni Cosmati contributed one of the loveliest—and seemingly most comfortable—tombs any cleric has ever enjoyed. But for the golden mosaic of the Madonna, it would be easy to mistake this precocious work, the **Tomb of Guillaume Durand** (1296) for something from the best of the Renaissance.

> *The original Temple of Minerva formed part of one of the first and largest imperial building complexes, begun in the reign of Augustus by his great general Cornelius Agrippa, and rebuilt under Hadrian. In Republican days, the Saepta was the field (roughly between the Pantheon and Via Sant'Ignazio) where citizens came to cast their votes in the annual elections. The emperors made it into Rome's favourite promenade, famous gardens, with a lagoon, surrounded by a portico that sheltered Rome's classier art auctioneers and antique dealers, along with the Minerva temple and some libraries.*

> *To the west stretched the Baths of Agrippa, the first such facility in Rome (remains of which can be seen built into later buildings around this area, as on Via Arco della Ciambella).*

> *Behind the baths, just a block north of Piazza Minerva, the centrepiece of the project still stands, the best preserved, most perfect monument of the ancient world. Despite the inscription mentioning Agrippa on the pediment, the **Pantheon** as we see it today was almost entirely reconstructed under Hadrian in 128 AD (open daily exc Mon, 9–2, Sun 9–1, longer hours in summer, adm free).*

The 2nd-century writer Dio Cassius leaves us a rather cryptic anecdote concerning Hadrian: as a youth, the future emperor could not resist butting in with his opinions whenever Trajan and Apollodorus were discussing their new building programmes. On one occasion, the great architect from Damascus is reported to have told Hadrian to 'go off and draw pumpkins'. Perhaps this is exactly what he did—tradition has it that Hadrian himself contributed the basic plan for the remodelled Pantheon.

Though certainly built to last, its survival to our day is a result of two strokes of good luck: first, being converted to a Christian church in 609 (the first time a pagan temple was converted in Rome) and second, in 734, when Pope Gregory III had the good sense to plate the concrete dome with lead. Originally, the dome was glittering gilded bronze inside and out. Byzantine Emperor Constans II, passing through in 667, stole the exterior plating and most of the rest of the bronze statues and fittings in Rome—to be melted down into coins back in Constantinople. In the Dark Ages, when so much else was lost, the Pantheon became an important symbol to the Romans of their ancient greatness; the popes always took good care of it, even in the worst of times. Today, though hardly ever used for services, the Pantheon is still officially a church—S. Maria ad Martyres—so there's no admission fee.

Before going inside, consider the virtuoso architectural tricks incorporated by Hadrian's architects. At first sight, the building may seem perilously unsound; there is no way a simple brick cylindrical wall could support such a heavy, shallow dome—obviously the whole thing should have tumbled down long ago. The explanation lies in the uniquely elegant design; the once-gilded dome really isn't a dome at all—the real one is hiding underneath, a perfect hemisphere of cast concrete that rests on a solid ring wall over 22 ft thick. It was the biggest piece of concrete ever attempted before the 20th century. The ribbed dome you see outside consists of simple courses of cantilevered brick, effectively almost weightless.

A portico of colossal granite columns (used as a fishmarket in the Middle Ages) leads to a pair of equally huge bronze doors—Hadrian's originals, restored in the 1560s. No matter how many times you've seen it in pictures, the interior of the Pantheon remains one of the most astounding sights of Rome, between the immense dome (43 m, slightly larger than St. Peter's), the sunlight pouring through the oculus at the top, and the rich coloured marble fittings below. No other ancient building in Italy has kept its interior so perfectly preserved. All that is missing are the original statues.

The building was planned as a meditation on the twelve Olympian gods of classical Greece; their images stood in the niches spaced along the circular wall, along with statues of Augustus and Hadrian, and in the centre, illuminated by the sun every afternoon around midsummer, that of Jove Ultor, the Avenging Jupiter, patron of Augustus' methodical revenge for his adoptive father Cæsar. (If this book were being written in Hadrian's time, we would have called attention to the statue of Venus, wearing for earrings two great English pearls that Cæsar once gave to Cleopatra.)

As it is, the interior has enough to say about Roman opulence in the palmy days of empire—one suspects that every director of Roman costume epics since Cecil B.

DeMille has drawn some inspiration from it. The Pantheon's worst enemy in its nearly two millennia of existence, Gianlorenzo Bernini, talked Pope Urban VIII into letting him loot the bronze ceiling for the gaudy baldachin he was planning for the high altar of St Peter's—supposedly there was enough left over to make the Pope 60 new cannons. As if that were not indignity enough for the old temple, Bernini was sure he could improve the work of Hadrian's architects by adding a pair of Baroque spires flanking the dome; 'Bernini's asses' ears', as they were known to generations of Romans, were removed in a restoration of 1883.

Not much inside the Pantheon would make you think it was still a church, though there is an Annunciation attributed to Melozzo da Forli on the left of the entrance. Over the years there was a half-hearted intention to make the place into a pantheon of famous Italians; around the walls you will see the tombs of Raphael, Baldassare Peruzzi, and Italy's first two kings, Vittorio Emanuele II and Umberto I.

Before you go any further, there are two popular cafés in front of the Pantheon where you can contemplate the famous façade in one of old Rome's prettiest and most characteristic squares, **Piazza della Rotonda**.

The obligatory obelisk in the centre, erected in 1575, was yet another find from that Temple of Isis— originally the complex may have had a dozen of them. Isis, the transcendent Egyptian goddess, always had plenty of devotees in Rome (Apuleius' *Golden Ass* was written in her honour); one of the most fervent was Emperor Domitian, who built the temple, roughly where Piazza del Collegio Romano is today.

If you don't need to sit down yet, persevere for another two blocks, down Salita dei Crescenzi and left on Via S. Eustachio, to **Piazza di S. Eustachio.**

Sant' Eustachio church, with the bronze stag's head on top, suffered a thorough Baroquing in the 1700s, but keeps its campanile of 1196. One of the first Roman martyrs, St Eustace was a soldier who, while hunting, had a vision of the Holy Cross—between the antlers of a stag, like Saint Hubert of France.

The giant **fountain basin** *on the western edge of the piazza came from the Baths of Caracalla.*

It may seem sleepy enough now, but in the Middle Ages this piazza was a busy market right in the centre of Rome. Sometime about the 1300s the area became headquarters for the English community in Rome. Sant'Eustachio was one of their churches; the other, its outlandish cupola peeking over the square, is hiding inside the bulky palace just to *the west, the **Palazzo di Sapienza**, home of Rome's old papal university, founded in 1303 as the 'Archiginnasio Romano'.*

Tourists have been overlooking it for 300 years, little suspecting that one of the most imaginative pieces of Baroque excess in Italy was concealed inside: Borromini's masterpiece, **Sant'Ivo** (1642–50) (*open Sunday mornings only for a trendy guitar-strumming service*).

Both a tunnel opening off Via della Dogana Vecchia and the main entrance on Corso del Rinascimento lead into an impeccably elegant Renaissance courtyard, the work of Giacomo della Porta.

He also contributed the façade of Sant'Ivo, at the far end of the court, but everything behind it is Borromini's, a unique, hexagonal chapel topped by a swirling spiral lantern. There's a little obscure symbolism present: supposedly the hexagon recalls the bee symbol of the Barberinis, in honour of Borromini's employer, Urban VIII. In its present state, painted a uniform dull white, Sant'Ivo loses much in first impressions. What remains is the bare bones of Borromini's remarkable geometrical conception, a complex space unified by a repetition of rhythms in threes—architecture in waltz time.

*Continuing north along Via del Dogana Vecchia, you'll pass the big frowsy block called **Palazzo Madama** (not open to the public).*

Its history is typical of a Roman palace; a papal treasurer bought up the property in the late 1400s, including a tower fortress of the ancient Crescenzi family, and converted the whole into a single structure. Later the the Orsini picked it up, and lost it as part of the dowry when Lorenzo de' Medici married Clarice Orsini. Their son, Giovanni, lived here briefly before becoming Pope Leo X (and following ancient tradition the Roman mob sacked it thoroughly upon news of his election). Emperor Charles V parked one of his illegitimate daughters here, Margaret of Parma; as a love child, the only title this girl had was Madama—hence the palace's name. Later owners, in the 1700s, tacked on the inevitable assembly-line Baroque façade (facing Corso del Rinascimento), though the part overlooking Via del Dogana Vecchia sports natty hula-hooped columns and miserable masks. As with most Roman palaces, nobody gives it a second look today, except maybe to admire the overdressed Carabinieri at the entrances. For Madama's palace was the property of the Pope in 1870, and the new Italian state was happy to snatch it up. It's been the home of the Italian Senate ever since.

*After Palazzo Madama, turn right on Via del Salvatore to the next block and the church of **San Luigi dei Francesi** (open 7.30–2.30 and 3.30–7; closed Thurs pm), designed, like the exterior of Sant'Ivo, by della Porta (c. 1520).*

The French national church in Rome was begun at the time when France was contending the domination of all Italy with Spain, and both nations were working hard to expand their influence in every sphere. A thorough plastering of late Baroque inside leaves little but historical associations to attract a visit; there are French memorials everywhere, including Renaissance frescoes on the conversion of Clovis and the Franks, and a big slab in the south aisle for the troops who fell attacking Garibaldi and the Roman Republic in 1849 (Rome never bears grudges about things like this).

As with so many of Rome's smaller churches, this one has one real attraction: three paintings by Caravaggio on the *Vocation, Inspiration and Martyrdom of St Matthew*, all recently restored. As always, when you hear the name Caravaggio you should instinctively check your pockets to see if you have change for the lighting machine. These works were done late in the artist's career, about 1600; only a few islands of light in the surrounding blackness are enough to make the austere figures into something magical (especially the *Vocation*, in which Matthew hears the call while collecting taxes).

> *Take Via della Scrofa two streets to the north, then left, for another church with one great work, the plain Renaissance (1480s)* **Sant'Agostino** *(open 7.45–12 and 4.30–7.30).*

On the third column of the left nave, the portrait of a muscle-bound *Isaiah* is an unusually macho work by Raphael (1512). The other prophets, and most of the rest of the abundant frescoes, are by a 19th-century Roman artist named Gagliardi. Beneath Isaiah, there is a fine statue of the Madonna with St Anne by Sansovino, and the first chapel on the left aisle has another Caravaggio (i.e. reach for your purse), the *Madonna of Loreto.* Before you leave, don't miss the Junoesque *Madonna del Parto* against the back wall, credited with the power to help women conceive and give birth. It's inevitably surrounded by glinting ex-votos and vases of fresh flowers from those she's helped.

> *Follow the alley behind the church, Via dei Pianellari, and you'll find yourself on one of the most picturesque corners of old Rome,* **Via dell'Orso***, with its medieval* **Frangipane Tower** *and trailing vines.*

In the neighbourhood, it is better known as the 'Monkey Tower', for the pet chimp of the 1700s who picked up his master's newborn baby and climbed to the top. The family promised the Virgin Mary a candle burning for ever if only she would talk this midget King Kong into coming down—of course she did, and you can see the candle today on the little shrine up on the tower.

> *The church in the middle of this narrow lane is the Baroque* **Sant'Antonio dei Portoghesi***, with one of Rome's most lavish Baroque interiors, heavily encrusted with precious marbles and gilt.*

Along Bear Street, note the antique sculptural fragments— lions and hares—built into the old houses; at the end of the street, a restaurant called the Osteria dell'Orso keeps up the name and occupies the building of what long ago was Rome's best-known hotel, host to many famous figures in the 17th and 18th centuries; the building dates from 1460, and it has been imaginatively restored. Piazza di Ponte Umberto, up the steps, has a view across the Tiber of the extravagantly awful **Palazzo della Giustizia** *and up towards the Vatican and Castel Sant'Angelo. If it has reopened, you could pass some time at one of Rome's smallest museums, the* **Museo Napoleonico**.

This museum-palace contains a weird collection of family memorabilia and neoclassical bric-à-brac, including portraits by David and Gerard, sculptures by Canova and Thorvaldsen, political cartoons, gowns, cameos, board games sent to the Emperor on St Helena, and a hopeful drawing of 'St Napoleon' made for his mum, who like any Italian mother knew her son deserved canonization at the very least. The little imperialist, for his part, found the concept of Rome as irresistible as its art treasures were portable; he dubbed his baby eaglet the King of Rome, and you can see his milk teeth here, and some of his dilettante sketches, which were donated by a later owner to Mussolini. One room is dedicated to the family Venus, Pauline Bonaparte Borghese, and displays her little shoes and a cast of her shapely breast.

Via Zanardelli leads south towards Piazza Navona. At the end of the street you are in Piazza di Tor Sanguigna, and just to the right is the beginning of Via dei Coronari and its scores of antique shops (see Shopping). For now, take the little alley to the left of it, Via di Tor Sanguigna; the curve of this street and its adjacent piazza (where Benvenuto Cellini claimed to have dispatched a policeman with a long Pistoian dagger) follows the outside of Domitian's stadium, now Piazza Navona. On this part of the exterior (at no. 16) you can see all that is left of the original building, including one of the gates, excavated from under later buildings. The street ends in another of the national churches, the German **Santa Maria dell'Anima**.

From the front, you can inspect the ponderous façade by Giuliano da Sangallo, uncle of the more famous Antonio. Being German did not save it from the Lutheran *Landsknechten* during the sack of 1527; the church was burnt, only a few years after Sangallo finished it, and most of what you see now was done in the 1800s. To get inside, go around the back along Vicolo della Pace to Via della Pace, where a door at number 20 on the left leads into a delightful small courtyard, with the church entrance on the other side.

This church, too, has only one real attraction: Baldassare Peruzzi's excellent Renaissance *Tomb of Hadrian VI*, the dour reforming pope from Utrecht who delighted the Romans by lasting only one year. It stands just to the right of the altar, near a faded fresco of the Holy Family by Giulio Romano; almost all the rest of the interior is from the 19th century.

> *While you're on this back alley (Vicolo della Pace), look around—it offers a back view of one of the most original architectural projects ever attempted (and never finished) in Rome, **Santa Maria della Pace** (open 10–12 and 4–6; enter via the cloisters on Arco della Pace), a church that contains great works by Raphael and many others. After years of restoration, Santa Maria della Pace is at last open, though the dome and choir are still full of scaffolding.*

It was founded in 1484 by Sixtus IV. In 1656, Pope Alexander VII commissioned Pietro da Cortona for the job of redoing the façade and the surrounding piazza; the exuberant ceiling painter gave him a plan that was startling, even eccentric. Though the asymmetric piazza was never completed, the church façade itself, with its clever interplay of concave and convex forms, is enough to give at least something of Cortona's intentions. Even as it is, the small space in front of Santa Maria succeeds as well as any church in Rome in creating the 'stage set' effect the decorous Baroque age always strove for.

The cloister was Bramante's first work in Rome, cool, restrained, and quintessentially Renaissance. Inside, Raphael's *Sibyls* grace the Chigi chapel, and next door, delicate stuccoes by Sangallo the Younger frame the Cesi chapel. Above the high altar is a fine fresco of the Virgin with SS. Bridget and Catherine by Peruzzi.

> *By day, you would not notice that these quiet streets around S. Maria della Pace form the trendiest area in Rome; home to pricey cafés like Bar della Pace and the recently opened Bramante, packed in the evenings with the city's media crowd and **jeunesse dorée**.*
>
> ***Piazza Navona*** *is only a block away, back towards Santa Maria dell'Anima and through the narrow passage called Via dei Lorenesi. Like most of the streets that lead into the piazza, this one was originally one of the entrances into Domitian's stadium; one of the others, **Via Agonale**, recalls the athletes who once entered through it for the races, (the name of the piazza itself was originally 'in Agone', from the Greek for athlete), and later 'n'Agona'.*
>
> *Today, with Bernini's famous fountains and the dim, old-fashioned street lighting, the piazza is a vortex of Roman charm, favoured as much by Roman trendies as the tourists, lined with cafés and full of weary artists*

*waiting to do snap portraits of all comers. Many of the other artists are
fakes—they trace from photos, and mass-produce scenes of Rome, etc.
The Romans insist they're all Neapolitans. Often you'll see the cherubic
smiles of Italian TV celebrities, filming a spot in front of the fountains, or
pallid models being photographed for the fashion ads. Still a circus,
though of a different sort.*

On entering the piazza the distinctive shape is readily apparent, a classical Greek
stadium, 276 m long, with a curve at one end. Genuine athletics, as opposed to
the bloodier chariot races and gladiatorial games, never really caught on in Rome.
And the deranged Domitian seems hardly the sort of emperor to have promoted
them. Nevertheless, he began the work, in 85 AD, for the annual games he
planned to hold in honour of Capitoline Jove. By the Middle Ages, the 'field of
athletes' was a rather empty corner of Rome, with vineyards and barns among the
still substantial ruins. With Rome's rebirth in the 15th century it became a marketplace (later moved to Campo dei Fiori), though not until the time of Pope
Innocent X (1644–55) did it become the elegant square we see today.

The Piazza saw more than its share of Baroque spectacles. Its construction
allowed it to be flooded for mock sea battles, or for skating in the coldest winters.
It has long been the home of the Toy Fair, lasting through Christmas until
Epiphany—traditionally the old witch called the Befana brings children (and the
national lottery winners) their presents on Twelfth Night. Now, with the advent
of commercial Christmas, most little Italian crumbsnatchers get presents twice.

*Innocent's dream house, the 1644 **Palazzo Pamphili**, occupies the
southwest corner of the square. Now the Brazilian Embassy, it has an
interior by Borromini and frescoes by Pietro da Cortona—but the only
part you are likely to see is the annexe, where frequent cultural
exhibitions are held. Next door, Borromini also contributed the façade of
Sant'Agnese in Agone (theoretically open Mon–Sat 5–7 pm and Sun
10–1 pm; but don't count on it.).*

This church, intended to be one of the showpieces of the Baroque, never really
came together as planned. The original centralized Greek cross design, by the
Rainaldis, would have projected into the piazza. Borromini, called in to revise the
work, solved the problem by shortening the apses on the main axis—his subtle
illusionistic effects make some people leave here thinking the round dome above
them is really elliptical. His façade, squeezing all this in to make it look good from
the street, is a quiet triumph; the convex front makes a perfect setting for the
dome and towers. It is perhaps the way the façade of St Peter's should have been
built, a fact not lost on architects of the time.

If you do pass by when Sant'Agnese is open, step inside its bold interior, full of Borrominesque artifice; the distribution of pillars makes the shallower apses appear equal to the longer ones. Many of the structural elements are hidden by a jungle of decoration, including the funeral monument of Innocent X. Underneath are the uninteresting remains of the original Dark Age Oratory of St Agnes, built into Domitian's stadium, where the pious virgin was flung naked into a brothel— her punishment for refusing to marry—and instantly grew long tresses to hide her charms.

For many Piazza Navona is simply the background for the **Bernini Fountains***, one of the peaks of Baroque sculpture and sensibility.*

The central **Fountain of the Rivers** (1651), with its massive sculptures and obelisk, has become one of the symbols of Rome. As in all of Bernini's work, there is some flaccid allegory behind the composition: besides an allusion to the four rivers of Paradise, the anthropomorphized rivers (Nile, Ganges, Danube, and the Rio de la Plata) represent the four corners of the world enlightened and dominated by Pope Innocent X; the dove atop the obelisk was a family symbol. In the sculpture itself though (executed by his students), Bernini for once transcends the bombast and simple-mindedness of the Baroque. The powerful, expressive figures growing out of the jagged mass of travertine, the vivid portrayal of natural elements—rocks, tropical plants, seashells—and the brilliant use of the water itself as a sculptural element (a trick Bernini probably invented) combine to make this something unique in the chilly, awful 1600s—a sign of life in the land of the dead.

The supposed rivalry between Bernini and Borromini plays a big part in Roman artistic folklore. Tour guides always tell their credulous charges how Bernini made the figures of the rivers seem to be recoiling in horror from Borromini's Sant'Agnese across the street, and how the angels on top of the church return the compliment by refusing even to look at the fountain. Another story has Borromini spreading the rumour that his enemy's obelisk was improperly erected, and about to fall. When the authorities put the question to Bernini, he led them to the fountain, climbed up, and tied a piece of string around the obelisk; after attaching the other end of the string to a nearby building, he went laughing all the way home.

The obelisk, as you might have guessed by now, is from Domitian's Temple of Isis. Roman emperors commissioned obelisks as often as they stole them; the hieroglyphics on this one record Domitian's devotion to the goddess (he built another such temple in Benevento, where there is a wonderful statue of the Emperor in Egyptian costume). Isis herself, at least the cult image from the temple, can be seen in front of San Marco, just off Piazza Venezia; discovered during the Renaissance and placed there, she became one of the political talking statues, 'Madama Lucrezia'.

Of the two smaller fountains, the one at the northern end of the Piazza was added in the 19th century. The southern fountain, however, is another dramatic design by Bernini, the **Fontana del Moro**—not really a Moor at all, but a sort of marine divinity chasing a dolphin.

> *This walk officially ends here, but if your feet aren't too sore, and the cafés of Piazza Navona can't tempt you to stay, there are some other corners of this neighbourhood to see. For starters, just outside the southwestern corner of the piazza is another small square with a quiet, forlorn protagonist of Rome's history, **Pasquino**, best known of the 'talking statues' that have contributed witty pasquinades on current affairs since ancient times (see under Topics, p.36).*

Scholars believe this talkative, though faceless fellow was originally a statue of Menelaus or some other Homeric hero that once decorated Domitian's circus. Apart from the occasional teenage revolutionary manifesto plastered to his base, and a speech bubble sprayed on the wall behind Pasquino hasn't had much to say lately—just when Rome needs him most.

> *Pressing on west towards the Tiber, you will encounter quiet streets of Renaissance palaces: Via del Governo Vecchio and Via dei Banchi Nuovi, the main streets of the neighbourhood before the Corso was laid out, and part of the papal processional route to and from the Vatican. The slight rise in the land to the north isn't really even much of a hill—it's entirely artificial, made of ruins and debris—but in Rome it is ennobled as Monte Giordano, medieval headquarters of the battling Orsini family. All that remains of their huge fortified compound has been incorporated into the 18th-century **Palazzo Taverna**, with a pretty fountain in its courtyard. **Via dei Coronari**, lined with antique and artisans' shops selling everything from Baroque cherubs to Tiffany lamps. This ancient street redesigned (like the Via Giulia) under Julius II is worth a look even if you're not interested in antiques. It too has its share of Renaissance buildings, including the one at no. 122 that once belonged to Raphael. Halfway down this street, is **San Salvatore in Lauro** with a Palladian style interior with gilded featherish capitals and a black Madonna and Child wrapped in an embroidered gown. To get back to Piazza Venezia or Termini, or across to the Vatican cut down to Corso Vittorio Emanuele and squeeze onto bus 64.*

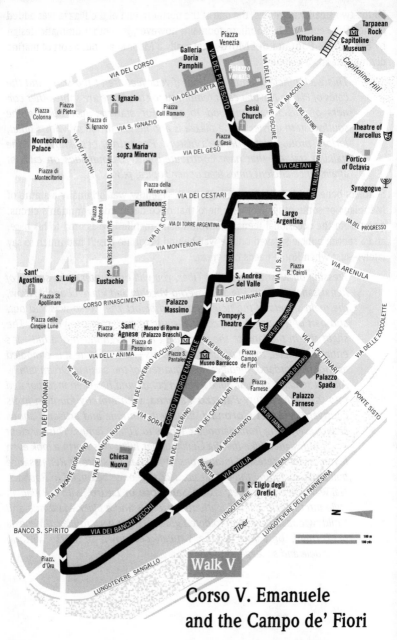

Walk V

Corso V. Emanuele
and the Campo de' Fiori

Vic Giulia

V: Corso V. Emanuele–Campo de' Fiori

Gesù Church   165
Largo Argentina Temples   167
Sant'Andrea della Valle   168
Chiesa Nuova   170
Via Giulia   171
Palazzo Farnese   172
Spada Gallery   174
Campo de' Fiori   176

Start: *Piazza Venezia. Bus nos. 46, 62, and 64 take you along Corso Vittorio Emanuele; nos. 23 and 65 follow the Tiber; the 65 also goes up Via Arenula, and back to Piazza Venezia.*

Finish: *Campo de' Fiori.*

Walking Time: *about 2½–3 hours.*

This is the lower half of the Campus Martius—medieval Rome, with the same warrens of twisting, ochre alleys you saw in Walk IV, crowded with market barrows and Baroque baubles, noisy children, convivial *trattorie* and antique restorers sanding frilly old tallboys in front of their tiny shops. Before reaching the good parts—and this pleasant old quarter is full of surprises—you must spend some time on the **Corso Vittorio Emanuele**, a grim, treeless boulevard bloated with traffic, exactly the sort of street you should avoid. But in the 1870s, when the planners of the new Italy extended this street through the chaos of old Rome out towards the Vatican, they aligned it carefully to gobble up some old streets, and create a new address for several of Rome's Renaissance and Baroque landmarks.

Besides the Corso, very little has changed here since the 1500s. For many—and this neighbourhood is very trendy now among Romans and foreign residents alike—this is its great attraction: a slice of the real Rome, easy and informal, where the refined palaces of Via Giulia and Piazza Farnese exist side by side with the Campo de'Fiori market vendors. Once off the Corso, you'll be relatively safe from traffic, and ready to explore some of the most joyful corners Rome has to offer.

This is a fine walk to do in the morning, when the Spada gallery is open and the market in Campo de'Fiori is at its best. This walk follows Walk IV nicely, and is also convenient to VI, XIII and I.

---

lunch/cafés

Bella Napoli, Corso Vittorio Emanuele II 252. Closed Sat. *Sfogliatella* (pastries filled with lemon-spiked ricotta) and other Neapolitan specialities, good *cornetti* and milky cappuccino.

Bar Peru, Via Monserrato 46. Closed Sun. A local bar where you can sit free of charge in the company of punkish schoolkids playing truant, fruit machines and guitar. Good, stiff, frothy cappuccino, warm *cornetti*, and a fridge full of yogurt if you're watching the calories.

Pasticceria Farnese, Via de' Baullari (corner with Piazza Farnese). Closed Sun. Civilized bar popular with businessmen and beautiful people. Scrumptious custard *cornetti* and *pizza romana*.

Il Fornaio, Via de' Baullari 5. Closed Thurs pm and Sun. Superior bakery selling excellent *pizza al taglio*.

Il Forno, Campo de'Fiori 22. Closed Sun. The source of most of the slices of *pizza bianca* you'll see being munched in the streets around.

Pizza al Taglio, Campo de' Fiori 39. Closed Sun. Succulent take-away pizza and a good range of *tavola calda* dishes.

Fiori di Campo, Campo de' Fiori. Closed Sun. Opens with the market at 6 am, and closes in the early hours. OK sandwiches and great *frullati*, and seats outside for watching the life of the piazza.

Mekong, Corso V. Emanuele 333. Closed Tues. Vietnamese restaurant with a L22,000 set lunch menu.

Pierluigi, Piazza de' Ricci, off Via Monserrato. Closed Mon. Good antipasti, surprising pasta dishes and grilled fish, on a flaking piazza. L30–35,000.

Moretta, Vicolo della Moretta, on the corner of Via Monserrato 32. Closed Sun. Famous for *farfalle*.

Nuova Shanghai, Via dei Giubbonari, off Campo de'Fiori; excellent Chinese, with a L10,000 set lunch menu.

Costanza, Piazza Paradiso 65. Wonderful pasta and rice dishes.

From Piazza Venezia, begin towards the west down Via del Plebiscito, the beginning of the Corso V. E., past the side entrance of Palazzo Venezia (Luigi Barzini in the '30s here 'stumbled on one of the darkest state secrets of the time' when he found out, from a soldier to whom he had given a lift, that the dictator spent much of his day in the courtyard, talking to the drivers and doormen). Via del Plebiscito terminates in Piazza del Gesù, home to three of the most powerful organizations in Rome: the national headquarters of the Christian Democratic Party, a freemasons' lodge and the **Gesù Church** *(open 6.30–12.30 and 4–7.15), one-time nerve centre of the DC's Jesuit predecessors. An old Roman story has the Wind and the Devil out walking this way. In front of the Gesù, the Devil announces he has an errand inside with the subtle brothers; going inside, he is never seen again, and the wind waits for him to this day, swirling vacantly around the dreary piazza.*

Alessandro Farnese, a descendant of Paul III, footed the enormous bills for this church between 1568 and 1575. Its precedent-setting design (the façade by della Porta, the interior by Vignola) took the most dramatic elements from High Renaissance architecture and distilled them even further into a confectionary new style that perfectly expressed the theatrical, anti-intellectual approach to Christian ritual born in the terror of the Counter-Reformation. Contemporary observers called it the 'Jesuit style', and though ephemeral, it proved to be an important stepping-stone on the way to the Baroque.

Modern visitors usually have little patience with such a church; ill cared-for over the years, its busy decoration in stone, paint and plaster now seems to be made of dirty ice cream. Try to imagine it clean and new, full of candles and flowers, with a Renaissance congregation echoing hosannas to the sounding brass of a polished Jesuit sermon. Look at the *trompe l'oeil* ceiling by Baciccio (Gian Battista Gaulli) where writhing plaster bodies pasted on the corners complement the vertiginous painted angels above, all seemingly in the process of being vacuumed up into heaven through a hole in the clouds. The title of this work is the *Adoration of the Name of Jesus*, and it proved to be one of the most influential frescoes of the Roman high Baroque. Little of the painting in the side aisles is of interest, blackened and waiting for a restoration that may never come. In the left transept, the **Tomb of St Ignatius**, founder of the Jesuits, exults in its panoply of marble, gold and bronze. The original statue of Ignatius was melted down in the French Revolution, but its replacement, under a sculptural group of the Trinity, includes a globe that is said to be the largest piece of lapis lazuli on this planet.

> *From Piazza del Gesù, dodging the police guarding the DC headquarters and barmen bearing trays of cappuccini to breakfasting politicians, head-down Via Celsa to the busy* **Via delle Botteghe Oscure.**

It's been known as the 'street of the dark shops' since ancient times, when a double row of arcades concealed its merchants' wares. In the Italian newspapers, when you read 'Via delle Botteghe Oscure', you know that the writer is referring to the PDS, the former Communist Party, which has its offices just to the right, a block away from their Democristiano nemesis

> *Take a quick detour left down Via dei Caetani. At* **no. 6C***, look inside the doorway for a display of archaeological plans and photographs, detailing the* **Theatre of Balbus** *being excavated inside the courtyard.*

This 1st-century BC complex, including a temple and quadrangle (its columns made the 'dark shops' dark), was covered by the Convent of St Catherine in the Middle Ages. Today excavations are suspended for lack of funds, but if you peep in you can just see the layout of Lucius Cornelius Balbus' stage building.

> *Just south of no. 6, note the big bronze plaque in honour of Aldo Moro, the progressive Prime Minister kidnapped and murdered by the Red Brigade—on whose orders, we may never know. The car containing Moro's body was discovered here in May 1978 after 55 days of captivity. If the door of 32 is open, walk inside to see a courtyard extravagantly studded with statues, busts and friezes.*

> *On the corner, facing Via dei Funari, **Santa Caterina dei Funari** has one of the most ornate of all 16th-century façades (by Guidetto Guidetti, 1564); inside are fancy frescoes to match, by Federico Zuccari and others.*

In a way, this neglected church is a landmark; better than any other in Rome, it can show you the fizzling out of the Renaissance, in a period when virtuosity came so easily that inspiration, even if such a thing were still possible, was no longer much of a concern.

> *From here, a right turn along Via dei Funari takes you to Piazza Mattei and the **Fontana delle Tartarughe**, one of the prettiest and best-loved fountains of Rome. Too many cooks couldn't spoil this turtly broth; from an original design by della Porta, Taddeo Landini sculpted the central figure, and Bernini added the tortoises. Turn right up Via Paganica, to the end of Via delle Botteghe Oscure, opening on to **Largo Argentina**, an open square where a tidy row of **Republican-era temples** was unearthed and partially restored in the '20s.*

This is a good pile of ruins to explore with your eyes, entirely visible below you, though never open. It isn't hard to see the difference between the pavement of travertine, added by Emperor Domitian after a fire in 80 AD, and the earlier surface of brownish tufa from about 240 BC. All originally faced a courtyard to the east, under Via S. Nicola dei Cesarini. Looking west, and starting from the right by the bus stops: a temple of Juturna, dedicated during the Punic Wars, and converted to a church of St Nicholas (now demolished) in the Middle Ages; behind it are ruins of a monumental public latrine of the Imperial age (toilets like this had plenty of fancy marble, but no stalls; the uninhibited gentlemen of ancient Rome liked to relax and talk over business while they unburdened themselves); next, a small building with the offices of the water authorities and the distributors of public grain; then a round temple of Fortune, dedicated after the defeat of the last Celtic raiders in 101 BC; next, furthest to the left, is the oldest, a small temple of Feronia from the 4th century BC; lastly, a modest domestic temple to the *Lari Permarini* dedicated in 179 BC. Part of it is still buried under adjacent Via Florida. The **Torre Papita**, a medieval tower fortress, was discovered among the old buildings demolished in the '20s restored and placed on the edge of the site.

> *Just behind that public latrine, on the east side of the square, the **Teatro Argentina** is thought to mark the spot where Julius Cæsar was assassinated. It has also witnessed the first performances of many great operas.*

Rossini's *Barber of Seville* flopped badly here on the first night, in 1816, driving the composer to despair in his nearby lodgings; he didn't know that his enemy,

Pauline Bonaparte, had packed the house with hecklers. The second night, however, the audience changed its mind, and went in a body to Rossini's house, in a torchlight procession, to tell him how much they liked it. The Argentina hasn't been used for opera for years, but it plays an important role in Rome's theatre scene as the home of the Teatro di Roma repertory company.

Around the corner, on Via del Sudario, the **Casa di Burcardo** at no.44 has a peculiar northern air about it, no surprise considering Burcardo was really a Burckhardt, a German who worked for Pope Alexander VI, and kept a meticulous record of events at the papal court—including the outrageous Borgia banquets. He built this house in 1503. The Italian Society of Writers and Editors occupies it now with a small Museum of Roman Theatre (closed indefinitely for restoration).

> *Via del Sudario leads to Piazza Vidoni where one of Rome's four 'talking statues,* **Abate Luigi***, is dwarfed by the wall of* **Sant'Andrea della Valle** *(open 7.30–12 and 4.30–7).*

This Counter-Reformation creation was begun in 1591. A number of architects had a hand in it before its completion in the 1660s: Carlo Maderno designed the dome, Rome's second-tallest, and also the little fountain across the Corso, while the general plan was by Giacomo della Porta. The rhythmic façade from the 1660s is by Carlo Rainaldi, perhaps after Maderno's original design.

After the Gesù, Sant'Andrea's interior may be a little disappointing. Under Maderno's big dome, Giovanni Lanfranco pointed the way towards the Gesù's ceiling pyrotechnics with his frantic fresco of the *Virgin in Glory* (1625–7). Few of the hundreds of contorted figures in it can still be made out; as yet no one has threatened to restore it. At about the same time, Domenichino contributed paintings of the four evangelists at the dome's pendentives, and scenes from the life of St Andrew (he whose innovative crucifixion contributed the saltire cross to the Union Jack) around the apse. Two popes are buried here, Pius II (d.1464) and III (d.1503), both of the Piccolomini family in Siena, and both great patrons of the arts—after the work they commissioned all over Tuscany, their simple tombs high on the walls at the end of the nave seem hardly fitting.

> *This part of the Campus Martius, in antiquity, seems to have been entirely devoted to good times. Where Sant'Andrea stands, the Romans had an artificial lake, created by Augustus' friend, Agrippa (hence* **della Valle***, for the depression that survived until recent times). The colonnades of Pompey's theatre were just a few steps away (see below), and across the Corso, the curve of the street follows the seats of Domitian's* **Odeon***, a little theatre built as part of his stadium complex (see Piazza Navona, Walk IV). Domitian's Greek Games, the* **Agon Capitolinus***,*

also included musical competitions. Romans weren't impressed, and the idea died along with the emperor.

*Baldassare Peruzzi's masterpiece, the **Palazzo Massimo alle Colonne** (1536), follows the Odeon's curve. Blackened as it is by the traffic soot, it's hard to appreciate this unusual design, created for a haughty and murderous family that claimed to trace its nobility back to ancient Rome. The squat Doric columns around the entrance, and the ornate windows, make this one of the most idiosyncratic palaces in Rome, one more admired than really influential in its time.*

*Here the Corso opens into **Piazza San Pantaleo**, named after the small church with the blank 19th-century façade.*

San Pantaleo (or Pantaleone) is Rome's answer to Naples' famous patron, San Gennaro. Like Gennaro, Pantaleo left a phial of his blood that miraculously liquefies and boils every year, on 27 July. But what really makes Neapolitans envious is Pantaleo's habit of giving out lottery numbers. Pray to the saint alone, in your bedroom, for three nights; on the third night, leave a pencil and paper on the nightstand, and during the night the portly saint will climb through your window and write down a winning number—but being the prankster he is, he will hide it carefully somewhere in the house.

*Next to his church, the gaily painted banner of the **Museo di Roma** belies its intractable nature—Rome's most elusive museum.*

The collection, including portraits, old views of the city, and pieces of demolished buildings (including surprises like the mosaics from the original St Peter's) is said to be a fine one, but few people, even Romans, have ever seen it. Locked in some Kafkaesque dispute between the city and a state ministry, the museum has been closed for years, with no end to the problem in sight. The building that houses it, the **Palazzo Braschi** (c. 1795), is notable only as the last big family palace to be built on the profits of the papacy. By the early 1700s, large scale papal graft was a dying tradition, but Gianangelo Braschi of Cesena, as Pius VI, revived the old style just in time for the French Revolution; his comeuppance came in 1798, when Napoleon's troops packed him off to exile in France.

Special exhibitions are frequently held here; watch for posters at the entrance.

Two of this city's finest palaces, just across the street, also sprang up on this charmed corner of Papal Rome. The first is an elegant, complex design by Antonio da Sangallo the Younger (an excellent Tuscan Renaissance architect, who also gave Rome the nearby Palazzo Farnese—see below). The heraldic lilies on the decoration, similar to those on the arms of the Farnese, gave the palace its familiar, entirely mistaken name,

> *the Piccola Farnesina—in fact they are emblems of the French cardinal who had the place built in 1523. Today the building is the **Museo Barracco** (open Tue—at 9–1.30 pm; Sun 9–1 pm., Tue and Thur also 5–8 pm, adm L3750), an important collection of classical sculpture.*

A private collector, Senator Giovanni Barracco, assembled this remarkable collection, and gave it to the city; it contains more great sculpture from ancient Greece than any other in Italy (except perhaps the Vatican), along with an Egyptian room, some fine Assyrian reliefs, Roman and early Christian art.

> *The other palace, just to the west, weighs in at about thirty times the bulk of the Piccola Farnesina, though still managing to carry itself with the same Renaissance grace. Many have judged the **Palazzo della Cancelleria** (1480s) (not generally open to the public, but sometimes used as a venue for classical concerts) to be the best palace in Rome.*

No one knows for sure which architects should have the credit; it is believed Bramante had some hand in designing the stately double arcade of the courtyard. Cardinal Raffaele Riario, nephew of Pope Sixtus IV, won the money to build it in one night's card playing. His luck must have turned on him; a later pope acquired the place, and used it as a home for the papal government bureaucracy; the Cancelleria still houses some Vatican offices.

> *Continuing down the smoky Corso, you'll find the third of the boulevard's important churches, Santa Maria in Vallicella, better known as the **Chiesa Nuova** (open 8–12 and 4.30–7).*

Gregory XIII, in 1575, had this church rebuilt for St Philip Neri, the unconventional, irascible holy man who has been declared Patron Saint of Rome. Founder of the Roman Oratory, Philip was quite a character, with something of the Zen Buddhist in him—a remarkable contrast with the iron clerics and inquisitors that dominated Rome in that grim age. He forbade his followers any sort of philosophical speculation or dialectic, instead making them sing and write poetry. Two of his favourite pastimes were insulting the pope and embarrassing initiates, making them walk through Rome with foxtails sewn to their coats to learn humility.

Inevitably, Philip's sincere faith and modesty were translated into Roman monumentality. Neither the church nor its decoration is especially noteworthy, except perhaps the ceiling frescoes by Pietro da Cortona: the *Life and Apotheosis of Aeneas*, of all subjects, in diaphanous Baroque pastels. The sacristan might show you more works by da Cortona, as well as Rubens and Guido Reni, in the sacristy and in St Philip's rooms nearby. This church perhaps represents the gentler side of the Counter-Reformation, a proto-Baroque version of the spacious simple Franciscan buildings of the 1200s, built for praying and singing; the most prominent features are the two great glorious gilt organs on either side of the nave.

Adjacent to the church, most of the large complex of the Philippine fathers was designed by Borromini, including a pretty clock tower (long hidden behind scaffolding) and the idiosyncratic façade of the **Philippine Oratory**, where Philip's congregation held its concerts and where the musical form known as the *oratorio* was developed. Today the complex houses the **Biblioteca Vallicelliana**, the greatest library for Rome's history and antiquities.

> *From here, cross the Corso and take Vicolo Cellini, or narrow Via dei Cartari a block south to Via dei Banchi Vecchi. Head right on this street, passing at no. 24 the* **Casa Crivelli***, known familiarly to the Romans as the 'Doll's House' (1538), a small palace covered with relief grotesques and trophies—armoured torsos on sticks, the sort of bizarre, arrogant-looking imperial art you would associate with the reign of Charles V. And indeed, the owner of the house decorated it in honour of the Emperor's visit in 1538. The street, lined with antique shops, returns you to the Corso; turn left on Via dei Cimatori, and continue a block to Piazza d'Oro and the large church of* **San Giovanni dei Fiorentini***— the Florentine church in Rome, begun by the Medici Pope Leo X.*

Restoration of its façade has just begun, but once it is complete be sure not to miss the jiving ecclesiasts balancing on its cornice. It's a stately enough building, though something of a hotch-potch of all the architects who had a hand in it: Jacopo Sansovino, Sangallo the Younger, and della Porta among others spent time trying to satisfy their fickle papal patrons. Ironically though, for all that Florentine artists contributed to Rome's High Renaissance, this church has not one work worth a detour inside.

> **Via Giulia** *begins in front of this church—not much to see, at first glance, but persevere a few blocks for a lesson in the subtler mood of the Renaissance aesthetic.*

Pope Julius II laid it out in 1508 and naturally named it after himself; long before Corso Vittorio Emanuele was dreamt of, this street was intended to be the main route from the centre of Rome to St Peter's. Bramante planned it, straight and narrow, in contrast with the winding lanes of the medieval city, and every future architect kept closely to the restrained, classical air of the developing streetscape.

> *Many among the newly rich of the papal elite built palaces along Via Giulia, along with some of the more fashionable artists, such as Raphael. At* **no. 79** *is the house Sangallo the Younger built for himself; before the unification of Italy it served as the Tuscan Embassy. Like the other palaces,* **no. 52** *(corner of Via del Gonfalone) has iron grilles on the windows—a fashion that probably came from Spain. This one, however, has*

*some excuse for them, being the **Model Prison** built in the 1650s. There is a **Museum of Criminology** inside (entrance on Via del Gonfalone), supposedly full of old papal torture instruments and such; keep an eye peeled—it's rumoured to be reopening shortly.*

*A little further down, you'll have your choice of digressions at Via della Barchetta. To the right, you reach the Tiber and **Sant'Eligio degli Orefici** (open 10.30 am only, except on Wed and Sat; ring at the porter's bell around the corner).*

Still the property of the Roman goldsmiths, who built it in 1516, the original design, an austere Greek-cross plan, is attributed to Raphael, perhaps his only foray into architecture. Baldassare Peruzzi and others saw it through completion.

*A left turn up Via della Barchetta takes you to Via Monserrato and the Spanish church of **Santa Maria di Monserrato**, another work of Sangallo the Younger. The Spanish Borgia pope, Alexander VI, is buried here, along with Alfonso XIII, the king who went into exile when the Spanish Republic was declared in 1931. It's rarely open.*

*Via Giulia's landmark is an archway covered with vines, neatly dividing the street in two. Near it, you'll see the church of **Santa Maria dell'Orazione e della Morte**, with a lovely 1737 façade by Fernando Fuga, the Rococo follower of Borromini. The Compagnia della Buona Morte, a confraternity dedicated to burials of the poor, had its headquarters here. Near the entrance, with its cheerful sculptural work, notice the sgraffito plaque with the coin slot and the leering skeleton; the inscription invites contributions for 'the poor snatched up in the Campagna' during the plague of 1694. A little further down the street is the outlandish fountain called the **Mascherone**, with a big grotesque face and basin recovered from an ancient fountain.*

*Returning to the arch, take Via dei Farnesi up to the Piazza Farnese, with its twin fountains spurting from giant Farnese lilies into ancient tubs taken from the Baths of Caracalla. It's a perfect setting for the most magnificent of all High Renaissance palaces in Rome, the **Palazzo Farnese**. Since the 1870s this has been the French Embassy, and special permission from them is required to get in—call the Cultural Section of the Embassy © 6565241 for details.*

Street, square and palace are all named after the most spectacularly rapacious predators that ever ruled papal Rome. Alessandro Farnese, the scion of an obscure noble family from northern Lazio, worked his way up through the church hierarchy in the late 1400s. His great good fortune was to have a willing and irresistible sister, Giulia (she of the famous nude statue in St Peter's). Alessandro set her up with Pope Alexander VI (the fellow buried around the corner) and the family's fortune was made. Unlike most of the families that built palaces off Church money, Farnese managed to begin his even before his election as Pope Paul III—on the income from his 16 absentee bishoprics.

When Alessandro became Pope, Giuliano da Sangallo had to modify the plans a bit; now there was booty enough to make the family hideaway the grandest palace in Europe. No expense of other peoples' money was spared; the builders looted tons of building stone from the Colosseum and other ancient ruins, while Pasquino and the other 'talking statues' were hung with endless pasquinades mocking a pigginess unheard of even in Rome. When Sangallo died, the vast pile was entrusted to Michelangelo, who continued the imperiously elegant design on the upper storey and added the heavy cornice. Among the works of art inside that you may never get to see is a famous series of mythological frescoes by Annibale Carracci, one of the masterpieces of late Mannerism (finished 1603). These vigorous scenes, variations on the theme of all-conquering love, were considered by Italians of the Baroque centuries to be among the greatest paintings of all time.

The little archway over Via Giulia is also Michelangelo's, an approach to the bridge Farnese intended to build just for himself across the Tiber, connecting the palace with the Villa Farnesina (see Trastevere); not content with two sumptuous palaces in Rome, Alessandro and his successors planted others all over Italy, including a truly colossal one in Caprarola, north of Rome. They also extracted a duchy for themselves out of the Papal State, that of Parma. This particular Farnese palace was not complete until 1589; after 1635 there were no Farnesi around to enjoy it, and the place passed into the hands of the Bourbons.

While the Farnesi inhabited it, this palace and square were the epicentre of aristocratic Rome; the family staged every sort of spectacle for the entertainment of the Romans: masques and mock triumphs, bullfights, water pageants, even races of carnival floats pulled by water buffaloes. It still looks the part—the most elegant Renaissance backdrop in Rome.

> *On the corner of Via dei Baullari, you can stop for a coffee and eavesdrop on the French diplomats at the trendy **Pasticceria Farnese**. Looking down that street, just ahead you'll be able to see the bright umbrellas and noisy street life of Rome's marketplace, the Campo de'Fiori. It may be just what you're looking for after the terrors of the Corso and the aristocratic quiet of Via Giulia. Sorry, not yet: there's one more palace on this walk, and it's full of Baroque art.*

> *The building of the Farnese palace brought up the level of the entire neighbourhood, especially on the adjacent streets: Via Monserrato, to*

> the north, and Vico de'Venti—Via Capo di Ferro—Via San Paolo to the
> south. Take this irascible street, insisting on changing its name every
> block, and you'll soon come to a palace that is smaller, but just as stun-
> ning in its way as the Farnese, the **Palazzo Spada**. For anyone who
> feels obliged to see just one of the patrician art collections of Rome, this
> might be the one. The collection has its charms (open Tues–Sat 9–7,
> Sun 9–1, adm L4000, entrance is through the courtyard to the rear, then
> inside a little door to the left and up the spiral staircase), but the building
> itself is the real attraction.

Built in 1540 for a wealthy cardinal, it was picked up by an even wealthier one in
the 1600s: Bernardino Spada, who left the collection and gave the building its
current name. Most of the palace is now home to the Italian Council of State.

You can't miss this palace—it has the most outrageously ornate façade in Rome,
guarded by a row of statues representing antique Roman worthies, interspersed
with reliefs of dogs gazing fondly at posts. The lovely courtyard is decorated by
some excellent, fanciful reliefs of mythological scenes (maybe the work of an
undeservedly obscure Renaissance artist named Giulio Mazzoni) and by bored
Carabinieri posing for each other. Look official enough, and you can sneak past
them, up the stairway on the right to Cardinal Spada's state rooms: a corridor
with more stucco reliefs by Mazzoni, some delightful ceiling frescoes by Bolognese artists A. Mitelli and M. Colonna, and one room with decoration entirely
devoted to a complex ceiling sundial that gives the time around the world, deci-
pherable perhaps if you have a good working knowledge of physics and Latin, but
enjoyable in any case. The Grand Council Chamber has a statue of Pompey,
according to legend the one from Pompey's Theatre, at the foot of which Cæsar
was assassinated.

If you find the museum they may seem surprised to see you; visitors are often as
rare as new acquisitions. The works are not labelled, but each room has a small
stack of photocopied guides that can identify them for you. **Room I** is rather tiresome, with portraits more often than not of Cardinal Spada. **Room II** has more
portraits, with a fine *Visitation* by Andrea del Sarto (which makes a fascinating
comparison with the more famous Visitation by his pupil, Pontormo), some works
of Renaissance painters from Umbria (rare in Rome) and a Titian or two.

Room III has the Baroque art, more portraits of Spada and ancient Roman sculpture; much more interesting though, are the *terrestrial and celestial globes* of the
famous Dutch astronomer and geographer Caelius (1622), a complete com-
pendium of the increased knowledge gained from Galileo and the Age of
Exploration. **Room IV** holds the best pictures: the classicizing work of Orazio

Gentileschi and his precocious daughter Artemisia (a follower of Caravaggio who contributes a fine *Santa Cecilia*); some naive but historically informative paintings by an earnest Baroque genre painter, Michelangelo Cerquozzi (*Masaniello's Revolt in Naples*); and best of all a relief of *Divine and Profane Love* by François Duquesnoy, an artist to look out for, one of the few in Rome to maintain the early Renaissance's common sense and careful line in the miasma of the Baroque.

Before you leave the Spada, just outside the entrance to the museum, in the garden, Cardinal Spada's friend Borromini added the best visual trick of the century—better than Sant'Ignazio's *trompe l'oeil* ceiling. An opening in the walls reveals a long colonnade leading to a garden—walk through it and you will see that the passage is a quarter the length it seemed to be, and the statue at the vanishing point only a fraction of the size you thought it was when you first saw it.

> *Beyond the palace, take any of the alleys on the left and you will arrive at* **Via dei Giubbonari***, the shopping street of the Campo de'Fiori and one of the liveliest streets in all Rome. You can buy some of the best cheap clothes in the city here, or just listen to buskers and watch the neighbourhood crowd go by. But for now, keep heading north, down Via dei Chiavari, towards the oddest-shaped block in Rome. One side of it, the narrow semicircle, is Via di Grotta Pinta, with its little repertory theatre and restaurant; the other, the broad curve facing Campo de'Fiori, includes Via del Biscione and the Albergo Sole, among many other venerable buildings. This block is built directly over the ruins of* **Pompey's Theatre***, the first permanent theatre building in Rome.*

There's nothing above ground to see of it, unless you dine in the cellar of *da Pancrazio's* or stay at the *Hotel Teatro di Pompeo*, both built among the foundation stones. Via di Grotta Pinta, bounded by a tall, curving wall, was roughly the orchestra, and the curve around Via del Biscione follows the outer boundary of the *cavea*, the semicircle of seats, with room for perhaps as many as 40,000. Greek theatre was still something of a novelty when Pompey returned from the east after mopping up the Cilician pirates in 61 BC. But drama could wait—apparently the opening of the place included games where 500 lions were slaughtered. Some drama was undoubtedly seen, though in the later empire novel abominations were developed for the delectation of the well-to-do crowds: one-man celebrity shows with a little cross-dressing, nudity and stylized live sex, eastern music and grand panache at the finale; or perhaps the ancient snuff shows, plays where condemned criminals took the part of those about to die and were really killed on stage. One of the few plays that could still draw an audience in imperial times was Catullus' *Laureolus*, if only because the villain got tortured and crucified at the end. Usually the drama was chopped down to mere vignettes, to allow more time for the torturing. When wealthy refugees from the first sack of Rome, in 410, arrived at Carthage, their first thought, according to the chroniclers, was of what was on at the theatres.

In Pompey's time, the prudish Republic had an ordinance against permanent theatres. Pompey got round it by dedicating the entire construction as a temple; in fact, he built a small temple of the Victorious Venus right on top of the seats, above the site where the modern Farnese Theatre (on Campo de'Fiori) grinds out its second-run thrillers. The complex included a quadrangle that extended as far as the Republican temples on Largo Argentina. Somewhere in this complex (the archaeologists disagree just where), Pompey built a small meeting hall. In the spring of 44 BC, while the Senate House in the Forum was undergoing restorations, the Senate met here—perhaps around the corner of Via del Sudario and Via Monte della Farina. Wherever, it was the spot where Cæsar was murdered.

> *After a long morning's walk, here you are on* **Campo de'Fiori**. *If it's still before one o'clock, the fish and vegetables will be out for your inspection—though the early birds got the best of them.*

It's 7.30 am, as the slick Italian TV interviewer sticks his microphone into the face of a tired old woman, asking cheerfully: 'What are these you're selling, *signora*?' 'Christ!,' she replies, 'they're *tomatoes*; haven't you ever seen tomatoes before?' It isn't easy being the last bastion of reality in a deranged town like Rome, but Campo de'Fiori carries on as best it can. The food is good and fresh, and the neighbourhood folk—young trendies, foreigners, honest workmen, or tenth-generation Roman poor who only hang on here because of rent control—really appreciate it.

Snooty Piazza Farnese is only a block away, and in the other direction the motorized divisions of Corso Vittorio Emanuele threaten you with an abrupt flattening. Enjoy this little oasis while you can. Negotiate some mussels and spiralling Roman broccoli, if you've got a kitchen, or else watch the locals do it. This is a good democratic piazza, though in the bad old days the popes used it as the site for the executions of heretics. In its centre stands a statue of **Giordano Bruno**, the foolhardy scholar and, alleged spy avowed natural magician, one of the first to take the new Copernican system to its logical extremes. After travelling through Europe, thoroughly confusing the English and French, he allowed himself to be captured by the Catholic secret police, and was burned at the stake in this square in 1600. It wasn't his scientific opinions that got Bruno into trouble, contrary to popular belief, though they were mentioned in the indictment. The Church incinerated him for proposing a 'natural religion' that included both Christianity and magic. But as the hero of Italian freethinkers, he earned a monument from the new Italian kingdom directly after the liberation of Rome from papal rule.

VI: Around the Corso

Galleria Colonna	180
Galleria Doria Pamphili	183
Sant'Ignazio	185
Temple of Hadrian	186
Piazza Colonna	187
Trevi Fountain	188

Start: *Piazza Venezia. If you're travelling by bus nos. 64, 65 or 170, get off on Via IV Novembre, and turn right up Via della Pilotta.*

Finish: *Around the Trevi Fountain.*

Walking Time: *1–1½ hours not counting museums.*

Here in Rome's busy centre, the centuries have left a varied batch of attractions: an emperor's memorial column and half of a mighty temple, some Rococo frippery and three somewhat neglected monuments of the Baroque. This walk is also part of the Campus Martius, and its medieval streets differ little from those around the Pantheon and Campo de' Fiori. These days, they find themselves hard pressed to maintain their ochre medieval conviviality, oppressed as they are by their great, dreary neighbour, the **Corso**. This famous street goes back to ancient Rome; then its name was *Via Lata*—Broad Street—an important thoroughfare that led northwards to the Via Flaminia, spanned by the triumphal arches of Tiberius and Claudius (both gone, the latter demolished in the 1500s). After acquiring some kinks and narrows in the Middle Ages, it was made broad and straight once more by the Renaissance popes, beginning in the 1450s.

The Corso—and all the other boulevards in Italy named after it—got its name in the last three centuries of papal rule, when the wild horse races of the Roman Carnival thundered down it towards the finish at Piazza Venezia. Modern Roman drivers do a good imitation every day, filling the long cavern with smoke and muscling mere pedestrians onto the narrow broken pavements. Often the street is closed to traffic for short periods—then, just when you start to feel safe, they pull down the barriers and a snarling tidal wave of traffic pours in, blasting non-motorized folk into oblivion by the score.

Walk IX, the Quirinale, follows on nicely, though remember its churches won't be open until mid-afternoon. Alternatively head north to Piazza di Spagna to do Walk VII or buy some ritzy shoes. As for the two galleries on this trip, the better of them, the Doria Pamphili, is open Tues–Fri–Sat–Mon mornings, the other, the sumptuous Colonna, on Saturday mornings only—but on that day the third museum, the Accademia, is closed.

lunch/cafés

You won't starve in this busy area, full of cafés and snack bars of all kinds—but watch out for touristy restaurants. Ice cream fiends prepare to enter a gelato heaven.

Around the Corso

Pizza Bar Italian Fast Food, Via delle Muratte 93. Closed Sat. Basic self-service bar just round the corner from the Trevi where you can sit outside for no extra charge.

Forno, Via delle Muratte 8. Closed Thurs pm and Sun in winter and open daily in summer. Deli-bakery on the corner of Piazza di Trevi selling delicious, reasonably priced sandwiches, pizza slices and cold cans of fizz and beer.

Gelateria A Cecere, Via del Lavatore 84. Excellent home-made ice cream: the speciality is a soft, decadently rich, zabaglione.

Pizza Fantasy, Via di Pietra 79; large choice of good pizza *al taglio*, along with a *tavola calda*. Sit inside or out.

La Meridiana, Via Campo Marzio, just behind Montecitorio Palace; one of the best *tavole calde* in the city—quiches, pizza, salads—along with tempting cakes and pastries.

Giolitti, Via Ufficio del Vicario 40. Closed Mon. Divine ice creams. Eat outside or indulge in a sundae in the fading splendour of its parlour.

Trattoria al Gallinaccio, Vicolo del Gallinaccio off Largo del Tritone; closed Sun. Specializes in dishes with artichokes; L30-35,000.

Al Moro, Vicolo delle Bollette 13. Closed Sun. Reserve in advance for excellent Roman and provincial cooking; L60,000.

Golden Crown, Via in Arcione 85. Closed Mon. Chinese; L25,000.

Al Piccolo Arancio, Via Scanderbeg 112. Closed Mon. Old hosteria under talented young management. L45–50,000.

---

*Once more, we begin at the Piazza Venezia. The first attraction is just for fun, and only if you're in the right mood for it; leave the piazza by its broad extension, Via Battisti, to the east, and one block down you'll encounter Rome's woebegone but endearing **Wax Museum** (daily, 9–9 pm; adm L5000).*

It's a family-run operation, in a corner of the old Palazzo Colonna block, where the young folks can be seen after school dusting off the statues and spraying around cans of room freshener. There's more than just wax: a genuine gas chamber and an electric chair, for example, and a fine display of ceramic dinosaurs. Among the figures represented, all with wonderfully big ears, are a Roman rock band, the Big Three at Yalta, the Seven Dwarfs, and the famous charlatan Cagliostro predicting to Marie Antoinette her end—with a fishbowl for a crystal ball. The biggest tableau portrays the last meeting of the Grand Council of Fascism, on 25 July 1943, with dozens of nasty blackshirts who haven't yet mentioned to Mussolini that the king was about to have him arrested and packed off in an ambulance. A natty fellow in a 1920s suit, looking on in the background, is identified as 'Lord Byron, a famous English poet'.

*In the Middle Ages, when the Colonna family was the most powerful feudal faction in Rome, they usually took the Ghibelline side in scuffles against the popes and their great enemies, the Orsini. In 1424, however, they elected a pope of their own, Martin V (Oddone Colonna), and used the papal bonanza to begin a huge new family compound, the Palazzo Colonna. Rebuilt in the 1700s, there is more size than art in the building. Also by the 1700s, however, the family that was once so martial and quarrelsome had settled down to be quiet aristocratic collectors of art. The result, the **Galleria Colonna**, is a hoard of late Renaissance and Baroque painting (Sat only, 9–1; adm L5000; entrance at the back on Via della Pilotta). Like the Galleria Doria Pamphili, this is an exercise*

*in fleecing tourists. The paintings are not labelled, but they'll be glad to
sell you a fat book to guide you through.*

The first room, after the vestibule at the top of the stairs, features portraits of various Colonnas, along with polished, languishing Venuses by Florentine Mannerist
artists Bronzino and Salviati, and the Roman fantasies of the 1400s Florentine Bartolommeo di Giovanni; certainly the most arresting painting is a *Temptation of St
Anthony* by an unknown follower of Hieronymus Bosch, with monsters, ladies,
mysterious fish and bagpipe-birds, the subconscious of the holy hermit laid out for
all to see.

Next comes the glorious, gilded Great Hall, with ceiling frescoes representing the
apotheosis of Marcantonio Colonna, and scenes of the Battle of Lepanto, a naval
defeat of the Turks in 1571, where Colonna played a small role; paintings include
a flaccid *Assumption* by Rubens, more Colonnas, and a *Madonna del Soccorso* of
the Umbrian artist L'Alunno—a familiar subject in Umbrian art, with the Devil
trying to steal a baby, and the Madonna ready to whack him with a big club.

The third room, the Hall of the Desks, takes its name from two serious pieces of
furniture, one cabinet covered with intricately carved ivory panels, reproducing
works of Michelangelo and Raphael, the other in *pietra dura* arabesques, with
bronze statuettes of the muses. We owe the ceiling, a powdered fairyland of battles, putti, terrible Turks, voluptuous maidens, and dreamy pink and blue boats,
to Sebastiano Ricci, a happy 18th-century virtuoso better known in Venice than
his Roman birthplace. This too supposedly has something to do with the Battle of
Lepanto, but you may be content with enjoying it as perhaps the most colourful
and unabashedly joyful ceiling in all Rome. Underneath, Gaspard Dughet left a
memorable series of enchanted Baroque landscapes.

The ceiling in the fourth room deals with the *Apotheosis of Martin V*, the only
Colonna to become a pope. Pier Francesco Mola contributes a solemn, almost
Impressionist *Cain and Abel*, and Guido Reni an *Angel Gabriel*. Next comes the
Throne Room, where a chair (turned to the wall) is kept ready just in case some
pope should drop in for a visit. On the wall is a beautiful portolan map of Europe
from the 1500s that belonged to Marcantonio Colonna (note how Britain is
almost *terra incognita*).

The sixth and last room is named after Maria Mancini. Perhaps better known as a
once-famous brand of cigars, the real Maria was the niece of Cardinal Mazarin,
the fellow who ran France for much of the 17th century. His father, who must
have been a remarkable fellow himself, had been the Colonna's butler. He
somehow married into the family (and on the death of his wife, picked up another
among the Colonna's arch rivals, the Orsini); his granddaughter Maria married

Prince Colonna himself. The paintings include an eloquent, shadowy *Moses* by Guercino, and a Madonna from the workshop of Botticelli; Maria herself appears in a portrait by Caspar Netscher.

From the museum, you can look across Via della Pilotta into the other half of the Colonna estate, a shady block-long garden (no admittance) strewn with ruins of one of ancient Rome's most impressive exotic shrines, Caracalla's Temple of Serapis (65 ft columns, all marble; one piece of marble from the roof is the biggest ever found in Rome—over 100 tons). Finding a private garden like this in the centre of a city is something that could only happen in Rome—it's charming, but it could never have survived in any country with an honest tax system.

> *Circumnavigating the Colonna will bring you back to Piazza SS. Apostoli; before you go on, you might care to take a look at the venerable church of **SS. Apostoli** (open 7–12 and 4–7), encased in the bulk of the palace like a pearl in a Rococo oyster.*

Emperor Justinian's favourite eunuch—Narses, the general who whipped the Goths and reconquered Italy for the empire—built it in 560. After an unfortunate rebuilding in 1702 (destroying fine Renaissance frescoes) and a new façade by Napoleon's architect, Valadier, this historic building shows little of its origins. In the portico, added under Julius II, is an 1807 tomb by Canova, two Byzantine lions and a relief of a Roman imperial eagle, found in the Forum of Trajan.

SS. Apostoli belongs to the Franciscan Friars Minor, who look after it well—the cleanest statues and squeakiest floors in all Rome. Leopold II, the kind and liberal Duke of Tuscany who allowed himself to be overthrown in 1859, obligingly getting out of the way of the Risorgimento, is buried here, as is Clementina Sobieski, the wife of the pretender James III, and the famous Greek scholar Cardinal Bessarione; the latter gave the church a fine 15th-century Greek Madonna, which can be seen in the first chapel on the right aisle. Thoroughly Baroqued by Fontana in the early 1700s, nothing inside would make you guess the church is 1400 years old, though there are two lovely Renaissance tombs flanking the high altar. That on the right may have been designed by Michelangelo; the other is from the school of Andrea Bregno, who contributed another one himself, that of Raffaello della Rovere, Julius II's father. It's down in the crypt.

> *Across the narrow piazza, the 1665 **Palazzo Odescalchi** sports a façade by Bernini. At the end of the piazza, **Palazzo Muti** was the Roman abode of exiled James III, the Old Chevalier, a gift of the pope in 1719. Bonny Prince Charlie was born here, and despite his great expectations, died here as well. Via SS. Apostoli takes you back to the Corso; on the other side, the continuation is called Via Lata, a memory of the*

*ancient Roman street. It passes first, on the Corso, the church of **S. Maria in Via Lata**, with a heavy, solemnly classical façade by Pietro da Cortona that could use a good wash; the palace next door, with a very likeable ornate Rococo façade (by Gabriele Valvassori, 1734) is just part of the mammoth **Palazzo Doria Pamphili**, covering most of this large city block. Across the Corso, continuing down Via Lata, you'll see on the right a weathered fountain relief of a man holding a cask, known to Romans as **Il Facchino**, the porter; one tradition claims he is Martin Luther, while another says he was a celebrated local drunk. Just beyond him opens Piazza del Collegio Romano.*

The **Collegio Romano** (north side of the square, built 1585) was the equivalent of the war ministry of the Jesuits, the 'storm troopers of Christ', founded by its third General, St Francis Borgia; after the Risorgimento, the building was used to store the priceless hoard of books and manuscripts garnered by the state from Italy's disestablished monastic institutions; there they rotted until the 1880s when a scholar found his butter wrapped in a letter signed by Columbus—the porter had sold manuscripts by the hundredweight as scrap paper to buy wine!

*An insignificant door in the corner is the back door of the Doria Pamphili compound, and the entrance to the sumptuous **Doria Pamphili Gallery and Palace**, containing one of Rome's best surviving private collections of art (Piazza del Collegio Romano 1a, open Tues, Fri, Sat & Sun, 10–1; L5000; palace tours (at 11 am and noon) L3000).*

The Doria half of this well-upholstered Roman family hails from Genoa, heirs of Admiral Andrea Doria; the Pamphili (or 'Pamphilj' as they like to affect) began their great fortune as perhaps the rawest money grubbers ever to win the papal sweepstakes. Their kinsman, the mean, prudish, and singularly unloved Innocent X (elected in 1644; see Topics: ten worst popes) was henpecked by his piggy, shrewish sister-in-law Olimpia Maidalchini, who visited the Pope on his deathbed only to steal one last box of coins he had managed until then to hide from her. Although the Doria Pamphili as a family improved with age—the popular, anti-fascist Prince Filippo Doria Pamphili was named Mayor of Rome after the Liberation in 1944—the uncharitable spirit of Olimpia lingers in the Galleria: *if you want to identify the paintings, you have to shell out another L4,000 for the museum guide. (But the weeded selection below should suffice.)*

The Doria Pamphili palace is organic architecture, its rococo façade hiding the building and rebuildings of centuries. Acquired in 1659, its main purpose was to show off the family's collection, for if Innocent X and Olimpia had no scruples, they at least had a taste for art. In the first arm of the gallery look for: 10. Titian's dire-sounding *Spain Succouring Religion*; 20. Correggio's sketch for *The Allegory of Virtue*; 23. a sombre *Double Portrait of two Venetians*, by Raphael; 29. Titian's *Salome*, coyly cradling the Baptist's head on a dish; 40. Caravaggio's *Maddalena*, with her vanities spilled on the floor and 42. *Rest on the Flight into Egypt*, one of his most tender paintings, where the Virgin and Child sleep while Joseph holds up the musical score for an angel playing a lullaby; 46. Lo Spagnoletto's *St Jerome* in its own little chamber, and then 1. Algardi's *Bust of Olimpia Maidalchini*, a portrait with all the charm of a stout, hooded cobra. In the adjacent **Salone Aldobrandini** are 16th-century tapestries of the Battle of Lepanto, Guercino's violently tenebroso *Herminia finds wounded Tancred* and a good collection of pseudo- and classical sculpture: Odysseus hiding under the ram's belly, a merry centaur snapping his fingers at the world, and the relief labelled II. *Fighting Putti* by François Duquesnoy. Back in the main gallery: 117. a 17th-century Rembrandt forgery, believed to be by Luca Giordano, who could paint in any style he chose and unfortunately usually chose his own.

The second gallery holds little allure but Room II has 174 and 176. *The Birth and Marriage of the Virgin* with Islamic touches, by the 15th-century Sienese Giovanni di Paolo; 185. a good copy of Bellini's *Circumcision of Christ*; 191. Frangipane's *Christ and Veronica* in a modern zoom shot; 200. Parmigianino's windblown *Nativity* and 207. his *Madonna*; 203. a bleak *St Jerome* by Beccafumi; 216 and 217 by Lodovico Mazzolino (d. 1530) whose primary colours stand out in the century of *sfumato*. Room IV is devoted to the Dutch and Flemish: 237. Thomas de Keyser's *Portrait of a woman*; 262. *Aeneas conducted by the Sibyl into hell*, complete with flying lobster, by an imitator of Jan Breughel, who painted in person 278. *The Creation of Man* and 280. *Vision of St John on Patmos*; 317. *Battle in the Bay of Naples* is a fine work by Pieter Breughel the Elder.

At the end of the 18th-century Gallery of Mirrors is a cabinet with the showpiece of the collection, Velazquez's *Portrait of Innocent X* (1650), so accurately portraying the Pope's weak and suspicious nature that Innocent himself remarked that it was 'Too true, too true'. Bernini's more flattering bust of the Pope, also in the cabinet, seems vacuous in comparison. The last arm of the gallery contains 17th-century landscapes, 342, 346, 348, 351, and 352 by Claude Lorraine.

The guided tours of the palace's lavish **Private Apartments**, still used now and then by the family, includes the Winter Garden with ancient busts, elegant board games and an 18th-century children's sledge and sedan chair; the Smoking Room, surely one of the cosiest rooms ever to find its way into any Italian palazzo (there isn't even a word for cosy in Italian; this was built for a homesick English bride); the Andrea Doria room has memorabilia and two portraits of the great admiral by

Sebastiano del Piombo as well as Lorenzo Lotto's fine *Portrait of a Gentleman*. In the Green Salone are a huge 15th-century Tournai tapestry of the *Legend of Alexander the Great*, 40 years in the weaving, Filippo Lippi's *Annunciation*, with a beautiful Renaissance angel, a *Holy Family* by Beccafumi and *Deposition* by Hans Memling. The second set of rooms surrounds the delightful Ballroom; the Chapel has two bodies from the catacombs; in the Yellow Room are tapestries of the months, made for Louis XIV, and two Ming vases; the charming Venetian-style Green Room and Red Room with four allegories by Pieter Breughel the Elder complete the tour.

> From here return to the piazza and take Via Sant'Ignazio north a block to a relic of the Jesuits. But before entering **Sant'Ignazio**, (open 7.30–12 and 4–7.15) have a look at **Piazza di Sant'Ignazio** in front, a delightful late Baroque confection of oddly shaped and exotically decorated apartment blocks, created in 1728 and still, though a little dingy, one of the most successful architectural ensembles in Rome; architect Filippino Raguzzini made it a treat for the eye by a subtle plan, playing three ellipses (incorporating the curving façades of the buildings) against the monumental, serious façade of the church.

That façade (currently shrouded in scaffolding), is not a bad one; it was designed by a Jesuit mathematician and dilettante architect named Padre Orazio Grassi; the church was begun in 1626 to celebrate the canonization of the Jesuits' founder (the military, somewhat disturbing character Ignatius of Loyola, buried in the nearby Gesù Church—see Walk V). Once inside, gird your imagination and prepare for some of the Baroque's dizziest ceiling pyrotechnics. Another Jesuit, Padre Andrea Pozzo, conjured up this *Allegory of the Missionary Work of the Jesuits* (1694), full of charming detail; saved souls of every race and colour take flight and soar up to heaven, following in the train of a smiling Pied Piper Jesus. To the eye, this Jesus seems several times as high as the ceiling of the church; here Pozzo created the trickiest of all Baroque feats of *trompe l'oeil*, making another storey of heavy arches and columns—all made of nothing but paint—rise above the nave, with an open, limitless heaven beyond that.

Pozzo also contributed the dome—not a dome at all of course, but a flat disc of paint made to look like one (with all the Order's other projects, there wasn't money enough for a real cupola). The trick works perfectly when the light is on, and when you view it from the circle set into the floor near the centre of the nave. The political ramifications of all this should not be lost on us; the Jesuits did not indulge such fancies because they were incurable dreamers. To the bullied and overawed crowds of the Baroque city, paintings like this were an ingenious reminder that truth was whatever the Jesuits said it was.

*Now cross the piazza, and duck behind the Baroque apartments into
either of the narrow streets named Via del Burrò. Both will take you into
Piazza di Pietra to inspect the back wall of the Roman Stock Exchange.*

No stock changes hands at this **Borsa** any more (they do that in Milan), but the
wall is one of the seldom-noticed, most complete relics of antiquity: an entire cella
wall and colonnade of the huge **Temple of Hadrian**, a good example of the best
2nd-century style, dedicated in 145 by Hadrian's adopted son and successor,
Antoninus Pius.

*At the west end of the piazza another alley, Via della Guglia, waits to
carry you north into a broad square full of cars, with a weary obelisk and
a large, nondescript palace with a clock on top. It could be a museum or
library, or municipal offices or even the Ministry of Superfluous Paperwork, but in fact the **Palazzo Montecitorio** is nothing less than the
seat of the Chamber of Deputies.*

Few major nations would tolerate such a modest setting for their political holy-of-
holies—but think as an Italian would. There are any number of things worthy of
architectural pomp and circumstance, even dead politicians sometimes, but certainly never, ever live ones. To the average Italian, elected officials deserve the
same respect as used-car salesmen, Mormon missionaries, and cockroaches.

Bernini constructed this palace for a noble family in 1650. Confiscated from the
pope and handed over to the politicians in 1870, it was expanded and given a
new façade in 1918. Under Mussolini, it held a rubber-stamp parliament called
the 'Chamber of the Fasces and Corporations'. Inside, the remodellings left some
fine Art Nouveau details, including a great coloured glass skylight and the huge,
remarkable **frescoes** by Giulio Aristide Sartorio (1908–12), a circular frieze
around the parliament chamber that represents Italian civilization in 5000 square
feet of allegorical ladies, horses and writhing youths. Sartorio, who later made one
of Italy's first feature-length movies (*Il Mistero di Galatea*, 1920), an artist who
deserves to be better known, here borrows his monumental approach to the
human form, and his liking for pale greens and purples, from Michelangelo's Sistine ceiling. You'll never see them without special permission; it's hardly
surprising that a government in which parliamentarians are still allowed to vote in
secret wants to keep the public eye out of its business as much as possible. If you
really want to see a parliamentary session, and Sartorio's frescoes, try applying at
the rear of the palace, no. 24 Piazza del Parlamento.

The **obelisk** in front, a 4th-century BC work from Heliopolis, came to Rome in
Augustus' time along with the one in Piazza del Popolo. Augustus took it to his
spacious gardens (kept as a public park, though later emperors sold it off to

building speculators); it was erected, not far from its present location, to form the gnomon of a gigantic sundial, with time and date markers all over the park. On Augustus' birthday, its shadow fell over the Ara Pacis (see Walk VII), originally located nearby. Augustus' Greek-Egyptian astronomers designed it for him, the same gentlemen who kept his calendar, and who ordained the census that made Mary and Joseph travel to Bethlehem.

> Back towards the Corso, Montecitorio's neighbour **Palazzo Chigi** is the most expensive hotel in Italy—the Prime Minister's residence, and on the average it has known at least one new occupant a year since the founding of the Republic. Palazzo Wedekind opposite, now home of the Socialists and of *Il Tempo* newspaper, was Fascist Party headquarters during the Mussolini years. Both palaces face the opening on the Corso called Piazza Colonna: nothing to do with the Colonna family, but with the piazza's landmark, the **Marcus Aurelius column** (180–93 AD).

Rome's stoic philosopher Emperor would not have appreciated the expenditure of public funds on such a bauble, but his son Commodus returned to conventional behaviour by commissioning this expensive monument to Marcus' relatively modest victories over the Germans and Sarmatians. Built in imitation of Trajan's column, it has the same spiral bands of battle scenes—only more realistic ones, more concerned with the horrors of war than the serene, Olympian tableaux of Trajan's day (some casts can be seen up close in the Museum of Roman Civilization at EUR). Originally capped by a statue of the emperor and his wife, a 1589 restoration saw them replaced with a figure of St Paul. As in Trajan's column, this one has a spiral stair inside (never open) leading 97 ft to the top.

> Across the Corso, on one of the busiest corners of Rome, the **Galleria Colonna** is Rome's modest answer to the glorious Belle Epoque glass arcades of Milan and Naples.

> This is the beginning of Rome's shopping district, and just across the street the equally modest **La Rinascente** is anxious to point out to you that it is Rome's only department store (Romans, just don't like such new-fangled innovations; La Rinascente is a branch of a Milan firm).

> **Via del Tritone** begins here, connecting the Corso with Piazza Barberini; the Triton fountain there gives it its name (see Walk IX). The only easy crossing from the plain of the Campus Martius up into the hills, it is a main route today just as its predecessor was in ancient times, choked with traffic and lined with shops that seem to be offering drastic sales the whole year round.

> If you're interested in ancient Rome, or if you have a letter to mail, inter-

*rupt this walk for a digression across Via del Tritone into **Piazza di San Silvestro** and Rome's **Main Post Office**, where a superfluity of employees are ready either to do you surprising favours or to give you fits about anything you wish to send overseas, all depending on the luck of the draw. In the lobby, a beautiful map in ceramic tiles gives you a relatively accurate directory of every important building in ancient Rome, based on a Renaissance print.*

Piazza di San Silvestro conceals some secrets underneath. Archaeologists long disputed its location, but today the general consensus says that this was the location of the last great pagan temple built in Rome, Emperor Aurelian's 273 AD **Temple of the Invincible Sun**. No trace of it remains, perhaps because the Christians found it too close competition. Throughout the centuries of Empire, religious tendencies consistently favoured some form of monotheism. Aurelian, combining philosophical monotheism with Syrian Greek solar mysticism (as in the famous temple of Baalbek) and with the time-honoured eastern tradition of emperor-worship, made the Cult of *Sol Invictus* the official religion of the Roman Empire. When Christianity captured the leadership of the empire, it patterned its own practices closely on this cult, and re-invented its holidays to smooth the religious transition—25 December, a date close to the winter solstice, had been for imperial believers the Birthday of the Sun.

*Next to the Post Office, a medieval campanile with a bronze cock on top is all there is of **San Silvestro**, an ancient church, to have survived a 17th-century rebuilding. The church has long been associated with the English community in Rome.*

*All the allure of Via de' Condotti and big-league Roman shopping awaits you to the north (see Walk VII). But one of Rome's best loved sights is just two blocks away. Go back across Via del Tritone, then down diagonal Via del Mortaro and south on Via Poli, then find a L100 lire piece, turn your back, and throw it in the **Trevi Fountain**.*

If you wanted to avoid the Trevi Fountain because of its corny connotations, we must politely disagree. Hollywood in the '50s may have done its worst (*Roman Holiday* and *Three Coins in the Fountain*) to trash this quiet corner of Rome, and it may well be surrounded by gawking camera-bugs twelve months of the year. Nevertheless, this is one of the most lovable creations of the cynical, relaxed Rome of the papal twilight. Tucked unobtrusively among a nest of twisting alleys, it comes as one of Rome's nicest surprises when you finally find it. Scholars believe Pietro da Cortona first had the idea of combining a fountain with a palace façade (often falsely attributed to Bernini). Clement XII's architect, Nicola Salvi, oversaw its building from 1732 to his death in 1762; all the time he spent among the mists and damp finally killed him.

The water you see is the *Acqua Vergine*, with the reputation of being Rome's sweetest since Augustus built the aqueduct in 19 BC. Cut off during Totila's siege in the Greek-Gothic Wars, the aqueduct was not repaired until the 1400s; a simple Renaissance basin was enough to commemorate its conclusion until the reign of Benedict XII. Salvi's design, carried out by a number of sculptors, follows the popular marine mythology fancy of the age: two tritons blowing conch shells conduct Neptune's chariot, flanked by figures representing Abundance and Health (ironically for poor old Salvi). The result is so much like a theatre set that later architects added rows of seats for people who enjoy sitting and watching it.

The story about throwing a coin over your shoulder into the fountain to ensure your return to Rome seems to be true. Every day, hundreds of Japanese tourists do it, and every day Rome gets more tourists from Japan. The coins get raked out every week or so, and supposedly they go to charities. There doesn't seem to be any law against fishing them out yourself—but try telling that to a Roman cop. By day, the Trevi is too busy to be fun; come back at night when the hordes have passed on, and the waters and sea gods are beautifully illuminated.

> Across the Trevi's piazza, **Santi Vincenzo ed Anastasio** *(1646) squats like a Baroque toad, mulling over the macabre secret within.*

In the days when the popes lived at the nearby Quirinal Palace, this was their parish church. Nobody knows exactly why, but from about 1600 to 1903, almost all the popes bequeathed their hearts and entrails to this church; they are kept in marble urns down in the crypt. A neighbourhood boy, the famous Cardinal Mazarin, built it, (see above, Colonna Palace). Calling his church a toad may be a bit unfair to the architect, Martino Longhi; his façade, with its muscular ranks of columns, is one of the boldest statements of the High Baroque.

> From the right of the fountain, Via della Stamperia curves northwards towards Via del Tritone, passing two small museums. On the left is the **Calcografia Nazionale**, perhaps the largest collection of prints and etchings in the world. (Open daily exc Sun, 9–1; free.)

Begun in 1738, the collection includes over 20 000 plates from copper engravings, and endless books of the actual prints. The most famous are of course the engravings of G. B. Piranesi: his mysterious and unsettling series of fantasy dungeons, the *Carceri*, and hundreds of views of ancient and modern Rome. The museum keeps only a small number of its treasures on display, in changing exhibitions on the ground floor, but all the rest can be seen in the library upstairs upon request. It's a great way to while away an hour or so—all you need to get access to the prints is some ID. *They will also make copies for you, some from the original plates; the charge is usually about L50–100,000.*

> *And on the right, the **Accademia di San Luca** (Mon, Wed and Fri, and the last Sun of each month 10–1; adm free).*

Although in business since 1577, Rome's artistic academy only moved to this address in the '30s, when its old home was cleared to make way for Via dei Fori Imperiali. In 1577, at the tail end of the Renaissance, academies were sprouting all over Italy. Partly because of the restrictive atmosphere of the Counter-Reformation, artistic individualism was going out of fashion, and new institutions like this one seemed, both to rulers and their favoured artists, the best way to train future generations in the rules of the safe, conformist art they believed in.

Nevertheless, this Academy's gallery contains a few choice works—particularly the portraits, serene, worldly-wise old Romans who would make jolly company at any dinner party, doubly welcome if they could bring along all that delectable seafood from the 18th-century still-life paintings. In room 1, there is a fresco fragment by Raphael, a lovely though perplexed *putto* that seems to be asking 'why am I here, under glass?' Works attributed to Titian include a *St Jerome* and two contemporary portraits. In room 2, the Cavaliere d'Arpino, who has taken a lot of abuse in this book, answers his critics with a delightful *Perseus and Andromeda*. Florence contributes examples of its early Renaissance style, including a colourful, typically Florentine *Annunciation* from the school of Lorenzo di Credi.

The next three rooms and the main hall contain 18th–19th-century painting: plenty of foreigners, especially Italianized Dutchmen, as in the classic Roman landscapes of Giovanni van Bloemen and Gaspare Vanvitelli (Van Wittel); also works by the grand lady of the late 18th-century Roman art world, Angelica Kauffmann, including a self-portrait. In room 5, Salvatore Rosa offers some *studies of the cat*, in which you will recognize the arch expression of the Roman puss. Best of all, in the main hall, is the most sensuous and memorable *Venus* of all the Venuses in Rome, by Guercino. And finally, if you couldn't get into Palazzo Montecitorio to see the frescoes of Aristide Sartorio, on the stair going out take some time to consider his luminous, colossal *Monte Circeo*, a vision from the enchanted, malarial wilds of Lazio's southern coast.

> *This is the end, but if you're heading back towards the Corso, do it by way of Via Marco Minghetti, for a look at the little 1900s arcade called the **Galleria Sciarra**.*

This nearly forgotten monument of the *Italietta* ('Little Italy', a slightly derogatory word historians use for the utterly pleasant turn-of-the-century Italy of ice cream and Puccini operas) has a glass roof and winsome Art Nouveau murals of bourgeois and feminine Virtues.

VII: Spanish Steps–Piazza del Popolo

Pza di Spagna

Piazza di Spagna   194
Keats–Shelley Memorial House   195
Trinità dei Monti   196
Villa Medici   196
S. Andrea delle Fratte   197
S. Lorenzo in Lucina   198
Mausoleum of Augustus   199
Ara Pacis   199
Santa Maria del Popolo   202

Start: Ⓜ *Spagna. Or bus 56 or 60 to the foot of Via Due Macelli from Piazza Venezia.*

Finish: *Piazza del Popolo near* Ⓜ *Flaminio.*

Walking Time: *2 hours, not counting window shopping.*

Theatrical, dream-like, and delighting in artifice, Baroque and high fashion are a marriage made in Italy—and nowhere more strikingly than in the neighbourhood around Piazza di Spagna, with Rome's swishiest shopping district and two of its most delightful Baroque squares. This architectural *bella figura* reaches an irresistible climax in the Spanish Steps, a sensuous cascade of travertine with a luminous sunken boat at the foot, a grandstand of fallen empire, where young pilgrims from around the world posture like hopeful starlets in a Hollywood diner, waiting for something that never happens.

Crowds of foreigners are nothing new here, at least not since the Renaissance. The Spanish and French have long had institutions around the Piazza di Spagna; Lombards, Greeks, Dalmatians and Burgundians left their churches and street names; Flemish painters, cosmopolitan literati and Bohemians of all nationalities brought it artistic distinction, and so many Brits checked into its inexpensive inns and flats in the 18th and 19th centuries that this quarter was nicknamed the English ghetto. These days only the czars of high fashion and 'good taste' can afford the rents, where the price tags contain enough 0s to make an omelette; this is where people-fanciers can watch the rich and the flakey strut their stuff, and study the degrees of polite disdain in shop assistants. But it is one of the few corners of the Big Parasite where the Romans endeavour to create something, even if it's only as ephemeral as style.

Save this walk for a fair weather treat: of all the walks in this book, this is the least taxing, both mentally and physi-cally; its charm and interest are immediate. Tuesday and Friday mornings will find everything open, but weekday afternoons, except Monday, are nearly as good, making sure that you reach the Ara Pacis before 4. Sundays and Monday mornings are dead, dead, dead.

---

lunch/cafés

Babington's Tea Rooms, Piazza di Spagna 23 (right next to the steps). Closed Thur. Opened in 1896 by an English spinster who thought what Romans needed most was a cup of tea like mum makes. Scones, crumpets, English breakfast in an uncosy English setting; prices make you do a double-take.

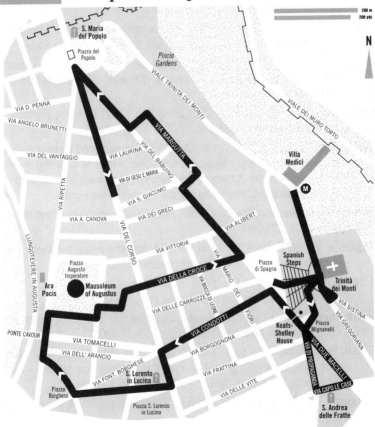

Ciampini al Café du Jardin, in front of Villa Medici. Open summer only. Closed Tue. Outdoor tables only, lovely views over Rome, velvety truffle ice cream.

Alla Rampa, Piazza Mignanelli. Closed Sun and Mon lunchtimes. Outdoor tables in quiet square; Italian, seafood; L60,000.

Fior Fiori, Via della Croce 16. Excellent *pizza al taglio*. Closed Sun.

Cose Fritte, Via di Ripetta 3. Deep-fried fare, from pineapple rings to peppers.

Vanni, Via della Frattina 94. Closed Mon. Good sandwiches, great cakes and delicious salads, most entertainingly consumed at outside tables as you watch the beautiful people floating by.

Dolci e Doni, Via delle Carrozze 86. Closed Mon. Stylish, civilized tea room; delectable savouries and scrumptious cakes. Ideal for a restful lunch or mid-afternoon treat.

Edy, Vicolo del Babuino 2. Closed Sun. Amiable family-run trattoria. Memorable *tagliatelle* with ricotta and artichokes and the best *tiramisù* in Rome.

McDonald's, Piazza di Spagna 46/47. Marble and fountains provide a classical setting for your Big Mac, 700 seats and blue-lit nightclub bathrooms; L10,000.

Sogo Asahi, Via di Propaganda 22. Closed Sun. Good Japanese restaurant; fixed lunch menu for L25,000.

Caffè Greco, Via Condotti 86, closed Sun. A charming period piece opened in the early 1700s and last redecorated in 1860. Service is appalling, and the food scarcely better. Sit where Casanova flirted, Ludwig of Bavaria raved, and Keats coughed. Prepare to splutter yourself at the prices.

Birreria Viennese, Via della Croce 21. Closed Wed. Rome's oldest rathskeller, since 1939; L25,000.

Angelo's, Via della Croce 30. Closed Sun. Bright and noisy, but that's how Romans like it. Bar, ice cream, light lunches; L10,000.

Il Re degli Amici, Via della Croce 33b. Closed Mon. Dates back to 1939. Good grilled meat daily and fish on Tues and Fri; L60,000.

Beltramme, Via della Croce 39. Closed Sun. Jovial, studiously unaffected trattoria, which has been here since 1889; L30–35,000.

Fratelli Roffi Isabelli, Via della Croce 76. Closed Sun. A beautiful 19th-century-style wine shop (also grappa and olive oil), where you can buy by the bottle or by the glass at the bar.

Margutta, Via Margutta 119. Closed Sun. Trendy people eating pricey veggie fare; L40–50,000.

Rosati, Piazza del Popolo 4. Closed Tues. One of the prettiest Liberty-style cafés in Rome with tasty and original cocktails, and celebrated homemade sweets, pastries and cakes, and fine views over the square; restaurant upstairs; L60,000.

---

*Even the most experienced old Rome hand envies every visitor's virgin sighting of the **Piazza di Spagna**, with charms enough to disarm the most chaste Baroqueophobe.*

For a pretty square is like a melody; and what could be more lyrical than the ochre, pink, salmon, and russets of the 18th-century palaces along its butterfly-winged confines, crossed by the languid silhouettes of slender palms. Then these part like a curtain to reveal the rippling Rococo theatrics of the **Scalinata di Trinità dei Monti**, better known in English as the **Spanish Steps**, which must niggle the French, since they paid Francesco De Sanctis to build them in 1725. Almost immediately after, Romans hoping to pick up jobs as artists' models would come to pose on this unique stage dressed like Madonnas or Cæsars; when tourists began bringing cameras they donned peasant costumes for a lira a shot.

In May the steps are frocked with banks of pink azaleas, but there are always flowers in the stand at the foot of the steps, by the leaking marble barge of the **Fontana della Barcaccia** (1629), believed to be the last work by Bernini's dad Pietro, whose ingenious solution to the problem of low water pressure of the Acqua Vergine was to sink the fountain below ground level. The inspiration may have been the stupendous Tiber flood of Christmas Day, 1598, that stranded a similar barge on the Pincio Hill.

> When Spain and France were at war, Piazza di Spagna would be divided to form a temporary 'Piazza di Francia' to keep belligerents apart. The English presence was less quarrelsome and more poetic. Byron, who could pen 'Oh Rome! my country! city of the soul!', then actually spend less than a month there, lodged at Piazza di Spagna 66. John Keats stayed only a bit longer, but it is his ghost that wanly flits over the boisterous pageantry of the square, fondly remembered in the **Keats–Shelley Memorial House**, no. 26, (9–1 and 2.30–5.30, closed Sat and Sun, adm L4000) just to the right of the Steps.

The flat was rented by the young artist Joseph Severn, who invited his friend John Keats to stay with him in September 1820. Keats was suffering from consumption and unkind literary criticism in the *Quarterly Review*. His doctor ordered a change of climate, but winter in Rome wasn't the answer, and he died anyway on 23 February 1821, aged 25, comforted to the last by the faithful Severn. Shelley composed *Adonais* in his memory, but Byron's obituary was more terse:

> 'Who killed John Keats?'
> 'I,' said the Quarterly,
> 'So savage and tartarly
> It was one of my feats.'

Since 1909 the house has been a library and memorial to Keats and Shelley, who also died young, drowned near Viareggio, with a volume by Keats in his pocket; highlights include Byron's carnival mask, Shelley's charred jawbone in a jug, a lock of Keats' hair and his death mask, and what is touted as the 'most sacred relic of English literature', a silver scallop reliquary once owned by Pius V (who excommunicated Queen Elizabeth), containing strands of Milton's and Elizabeth Barrett Browning's hair, worn by Addison, Dr. Johnson, Leigh Hunt, and Robert Browning. Beyond these Romantic memories, the main interest lies in the books and numerous reprinted articles and essays on the poets liberally scattered through the rooms.

> The steps lend a graceful majesty to the simple French church at the summit, **Trinità dei Monti** (open 9.30–12.30 and 4–6), the conventual church of the Minims, founded in 1493 by Louis XII, with a late 16th-century façade by Domenico Fontana (if you don't feel like walking, take the Metropolitana escalator).

It contains two fine paintings by Daniele da Volterra, Michelangelo's star pupil: a faded *Assumption* in the right aisle, and in the left, a vigorous but damaged *Descent from the Cross*, which Poussin rated as one of the three greatest paintings of all time. Behind the grille in the transept are colourful frescoes by Raphael's best pupil, Giulio Romano, and Perin del Vaga.

> The **Obelisk** in front of the church is a 2nd-century Roman model from the Gardens of Sallust. Like a **meta** in the circus, it and the obelisk in the Pincio Gardens (see Walk VIII marked the length of the most fashionable passeggiata of the 18th and 19th centuries, where a pale John Keats met Napoleon's vampy sister Pauline in one of history's more awkward coincidences. Walk up it to see the mighty bulwarks of the **Villa Medici** (guided tours of the gardens 1 Mar–31 May and 6–25 Oct on Sun mornings every half hour from 10 to 12.30).

Built in 1540, it was remodelled to Medici taste by Florentine Mannerist Ammannati, who added a magnificent decorative collage of Roman antiquities to the garden façade. Galileo, under the discreet protection of the Medici Grand Dukes, stayed here under house arrest by the Inquisition (1630–3); Napoleon purchased it in 1801 and made it the seat of the French Academy. Frequent exhibitions are held here. In front of the villa the round fountain has a Roman basin and a spout made from a cannonball shot from Castel Sant'Angelo by madcap Queen Christina—her way of saying that she would be a little late for an appointment.

> If you want a break, continue along Viale Trinità dei Monti to the Pincio Gardens (see p.208). Otherwise wander back past Trinità dei Monti to Via Sistina and Via Gregoriana, where the **Palazzetto Zuccari** is wedged in the angle.

Built in the 16th century by Federico Zuccari, its striking rounded loggia was added later by the quirky Baroque architect Juvarra. Zuccari, however, is responsible for door and windows in the main façade on Via Gregoriana, framed with hideous genie faces with gawping hell-mouths that offer a sneak preview of Bomarzo's Monster Park, one of Rome's more intriguing day trips. From 1749–52 Sir Joshua Reynolds lodged here, while Turner had his studio down the stair at the top of the street, at Piazza Mignanelli 12.

Towering erect above Piazza Mignanelli is the **Column of the Immaculata** commemorating the proclamation by Pius IX in 1854 of the Immaculate Conception of the Virgin Mary, a dogma first mentioned in the Koran, of all places. On 8 December, when the pope comes to pray by the column, Roman firemen climb their ladders to place a wreath on the head of the Madonna's statue.

> *Promoting this and other Catholic dogma is the job of the ecclesiastical PR-men based in the **Collegio di Propaganda Fide** at the top of Via di Propaganda. If the Spanish Steps are Baroque at its most graceful, the Collegio is Baroque at its most claustrophobic. Walk down Via di Propaganda to see its principal façade, by Borromini (1622).*

Borromini is nowhere more disconcerting; the looming Collegio seems ready to pounce and crush passers-by. Architectural psychologists, if there are such people, can ponder the fact that he committed suicide shortly after designing it.

> *Borromini was also responsible for the fantastical tower atop the old Scots church of **Sant'Andrea delle Fratte** (6.30–12.30 and 4–7.30) at the foot of Via di Propaganda.*

Unfortunately the architect never had a chance to finish more than the delicate tower, with its delicate cherub-herms and spiky crowned curly scroll ornament, meant to offer a contrast to the heavy buttressed dome. The interior, covered with plush frescoes, has two of Bernini's original 'Breezy Maniacs' from the Ponte Sant'Angelo as well as the tomb of Swiss painter Angelica Kauffmann.

> *Head back to Piazza di Spagna, past the **Palazzo di Spagna,** since 1622 the Spanish Embassy to the Holy See.*
>
> *It stands at the head of the glit-and-glam grid of Rome's most celebrated shopping district, a woof and warp of immaculate consumption that extends back to the Corso. Turn left down **Via Condotti,** which, in spite of its humble name, referring to its underground pipes that carry the Acqua Vergine, is now the most glamorous street of them all.*

When the rents were still reasonable Tennyson, and later Thackeray, lived across from the Caffè Greco, the latter as he wrote *The Rose and the Ring,* while the biggest Italophiles of them all, the Brownings, lived around the corner at Via Bocca di Leone 43. And what would Rome be without the monumental costume epics of Hollywood, its main rival in fakery and dreams? *Quo Vadis?*, one of the greats, was based on the book written by Polish Nobel prize-winner Henryk Sienkiewicz in the Hotel d'Inghilterra, Via Bocca di Leone 14.

> *Via Condotti gives on to Largo Goldoni; just to the right on the Corso you can see the splendidly restored façade of the national church of the Lombards, **San Carlo in Corso**, with a fine dome by Pietro da Cortona (1668) and an unusual combination of screening columns around the drum. From Largo Goldoni, however, turn left, past Ammannati's vast **Palazzo Ruspoli** and right to the piazza of the titular church of **San Lorenzo in Lucina** (open 7.45–12.10 and 4.30–7.45), founded in the garden of a Roman matron named Lucina in the 4th century.*

The portico and campanile date from a rebuilding in the 1100s, while the interior is all Baroque. S. Lorenzo's chief relic is a portion of St Laurence's gridiron, in the first chapel on the right, while a bit further on is its celebrity tomb, of Nicolas Poussin, who died in Rome in 1665; the tomb, by Lemoyne, was commissioned by Chateaubriand and has a bust of the painter and a relief of his famous painting *Et in Arcadia Ego*. The fourth chapel on the right contains the tomb of Innocent X's goateed doctor Gabriele Fonseca, by Bernini, in the pious jack-in-the-box style, his head popping out of the wall to participate symbolically in the mass. The *Crucifixion* by Reni over the altar is one of the Divine Guido's few startling works, with a touch of Daliesque religious kitsch in the lone glowing figure of Christ in the foreground, against a dark and dingy world. As you leave, look into the rococo chapel near the door, where the font is topped by what is believed to be the model for Bramante's original plan for St Peter's.

> *From Piazza S. Lorenzo, Via del Leone leads to Largo Fontanella Borghese and from there into Piazza Borghese, site of Rome's daily old print market and Vignola's **Palazzo Borghese**.*

A Mannerist *tour de force* nicknamed the 'harpsichord of Rome' after its quaint shape, it was purchased by Camillo Borghese, the future Pope Paul V. The palace became famous for the lavish entertainments held in its lovely courtyard and on the riverside terrace, the harpsichord's 'keyboard', now housing a carpet warehouse; from here the perspective of the palace's curve is most striking.

> *There is another curve here, too, the Tiber's first bend in the city. Long ago this was the site of the busy landing stage called Porto di Ripetta, as exuberantly rococo as the Spanish Steps, where goods from the country-side were unloaded until the Tiber embankment made it all a memory*

*(to see what it was like, look at the painting in the foyer of Via di Ripetta 73, just beyond the Mausoleum). Many of the dockworkers were Dalmatian (**Schiavoni**), who arrived in Rome as refugees after the battle of Kossovo in 1389; their church **San Girolamo degli Schiavoni** (rebuilt by Martino Longhi in the 1580s, with a late Renaissance façade) is just to the right along Via di Ripetta. **San Rocco**, the next church, just before Augustus' Mausoleum, was built for the Tiber innkeepers and boatmen by Pope Alexander VI and given a sleepy neoclassical façade by Valadier.*

*Whatever life the neighbourhood retained after the destruction of the port was obliterated by Mussolini's **Piazza Augusto Imperatore**, an envelope of ponderous Fascist architecture enclosing the **Mausoleum of Augustus**, where it is rumoured that the Duce himself intended to be interred.*

> *Look round: You see a little supper room;*
> *But from my window, lo! great Cæsar's tomb!*
> *And the great dead themselves, with jovial breath*
> *Bid you be merry and remember death.*

—Martial

But there's no longer anything jovial about the pathetic cylinder of shabby brick, once covered in white marble and topped with diminishing arcaded cylinders, its summit crowned by a golden statue of Augustus and planted with cypresses, its entrance flanked by two obelisks. The ashes of all the Julian emperors except Nero were interred here, in the middle of what were Augustus' enormous gardens. After the centuries despoiled the tomb of its riches, the Colonnas turned the hulk into one of their fortresses. Further indignities were in store. Until 1823, when the Pope forbade them, bullfights were extremely popular in Rome, and a certain Spanish entrepreneur found the circular enclosure perfect for the *toreros*. After that, the tomb was used as a concert hall, until Mussolini had it excavated and planted with cypresses, restoring as much of its original appearance as possible. Beyond that, no one knows what to do with it; it sits locked up and forlorn.

*Mussolini's attempts to link his regime symbolically to imperial Rome scarred the city with bombastic fascist pomposity, but in the case of the celebrated **Ara Pacis** (Altar of Peace: open Oct–Mar 9–1, closed Mon; April–Sept 9–1.30, Tues, Thurs and Sat also 4–7 closed Mon; L3750) next to the Mausoleum on the Tiber embankment, he returned to Rome a lost work of great historical importance and a proper memorial for Augustus, a beautiful evocation of the Romans at their most noble.*

Sheltered by a modern glass pavilion, the Ara Pacis was voted by the Senate to Augustus on 4 July 13 BC on his return from Spain and Gaul; it was completed in 9 BC and dedicated to the peace of the Empire; so he wrote in his autobiographical *Res Gestae Augusti*, part of which is engraved on the wall of the pavilion. After centuries of civil war and conquests, Peace must have seemed like the only god the Romans couldn't tempt over to their side—until Augustus willed it.

The altar was originally located under the Palazzo Fiano in Piazza S. Lorenzo in Lucina. Fragments of superb reliefs were first discovered there in 1525, and snapped up by collectors like the Medici, though no one knew what monument they belonged to. In the 19th century, during restoration work on the palace's foundations, more slabs were discovered, and it dawned on archaeologists that they formed part of the celebrated Ara Pacis. But to remove any other sections would have endangered the palace, and nothing else was done until 1937, when Mussolini took the extraordinary measure of having the ground water frozen to support the palace while completing the excavation. Missing sections and casts were gathered from various museums of Europe, and the altar was reassembled here.

Restored in the 1980s, it is enclosed by a sanctuary decorated with some of the finest reliefs ever made by Roman artists, influenced by the lyrical lines of Hellenistic art. Acanthus-leaf patterns adorn the façade, along with two reliefs, of Aeneas sacrificing to the Penates (household gods) and a much damaged scene of the Lupercalia, or feast of Pan; on the back façade is a lovely allegory of the earth goddess Tellus, or perhaps Peace, with two toddlers, and a damaged portrait of the goddess Roma. Along the flanks we see the procession through the Campus Martius dedicating this very altar: leading the procession on the right side are the *lictors*, originally 12 in number, holding their *fasces*, the symbol of authority, followed by the tall, handsome, but half-ruined figure of Augustus and the *flamines*, priests in curious T-top bonnets who would light the sacrificial fires; then Augustus' son-in-law Agrippa, the Empress Livia, and Augustus' daughter, Julia, and her husband Tiberius, accompanied by the young Germanicus and Claudius, and followed by friends of the family. On the Tiber side the procession includes the priests, senators, magistrates, and the Pontifex Maximus (with his head covered), whose office would soon be assumed by the emperor himself. If you wish to identify everyone there is a useful booklet on sale with a key.

> *From the Mausoleum, narrow Via della Tribuna di S. Carlo leads around the back of the big church to the **Largo dei Lombardi**, with stalls selling books and prints. From here walk up busy Via della Croce, with its food shops, to staid **Via del Babuino**, or 'Baboon street', originally Via Clementina.*

One of its ornaments was a fountain statue of Silenus by Giacomo della Porta, so ugly that the Romans named it the Baboon. Although the statue was long hidden through embarrassment, it has since resurfaced in all its mouldering, leprous glory, ludicrously topped with a new head and covered with loony graffiti, in front of the Greek Catholic church of **Sant'Atanasio** (to the left, at the corner of Via dei Greci). By 1581 the whole street was named after this ape, except for the section near Piazza del Popolo that went by the even more ignoble title of Borghetto Pidocchioso ('Fleabag alley'). Although within the Aurelian wall, this corner of Rome was covered with ornamental gardens in antiquity and vegetable plots in the Middle Ages, and it remained rural until it caught the eye of the late Renaissance popes; Rubens and Poussin are only the most famous of the foreign artists who had studios with the fleas and baboon.

> The next church down Via del Babuino is the Anglican church, **All Saints**, a pretty neo-Gothic building of 1882 by G.E. Street, with a bright white spire poking above the roofs like 'a summer hat worn out of season' (open mornings except Thurs).

> From here, take little Vicolo Babuino back to **Via Margutta**, a lane parallel to Via del Babuino, skirting the Pincio and long the refuge of Rome's artsy-bohemians. Though the high cost of trendiness has forced the artists elsewhere, a few galleries remain; large outdoor exhibits perk up the street in spring and autumn though the paintings are usually frightful

> From Via Margutta, walk back along Via del Babuino to Rome's magnificent front door, the **Piazza del Popolo**, where travellers descending along the Via Flaminia enter the Aurelian walls.

No city has a better introduction, but it only attained its present form, depicted on the walls of half the pizza parlours in the world, after a long evolution. Its name has nothing to do with democracy, a Greek concept that never really caught on in Rome, but comes from the *popolus*, or hamlet, which stood here in the Middle Ages amongst the fields. The modern Corso, or Via Lata, was always there, leading straight to the Capitol and Forum; Leo X added Via di Ripetta as an express route to the Vatican for pilgrims (presumably so they could buy his indulgences before their pockets were picked by too many other Romans); a bit later, for symmetry's sake and the 1525 Jubilee, Clement VII added Via del Babuino, leading to Piazza di Spagna. These three streets, fanning out from Piazza del Popolo, are Rome's 'Trident', and Sixtus V and his architect Domenico Fontana erected the great **Obelisk** of Pharaoh Ramses II to punctuate the view from the boulevards. This obelisk is 3200 years old, but like all obelisks it looks mysteriously brand new; Augustus carried it off from Heliopolis and planted it in the Circus Maximus. In the late 17th century Cardinal Gastaldi added the two little domed churches to emphasize the Trident, **Santa Maria dei Miracoli** and **Santa Maria in Montesanto** by Carlo Rainaldi, Bernini and Fontana; unless you look closely, you miss Rainaldi's main achievement—making two differently shaped churches look like twins. In 1814 Napoleon, reserving Rome for his last great triumph, had Valadier give the square its current oval shape; he also added the four Egyptian lions, spitting razor-sharp wedges of water around the obelisk. The monumental three arches of the **Porta del Popolo** were designed in the 16th century, in alignment with the Trident; Alexander VII had the internal façade adapted as a triumphal arch to welcome Queen Christina in 1655. In the old days Piazza del Popolo was not only the main gate to the city, but the centre of Rome's crazy carnival; this, too, being obsolete, the piazza seems to be awaiting a new identity.

> On the far side of Piazza del Popolo, tucked next to the gate, is one of Rome's finest art churches, **Santa Maria del Popolo** (7–12.30 and 4–7.30).

Long ago its site was the garden and tombs of the Domitia, where Nero's nurse and mistress furtively buried his unloved ashes. Walnut trees were planted on his grave, and soon everyone in Rome knew the stories of how the emperor's ghost haunted the grove, sending out demons—in the form of flocks of ravens that nested there—to perform deeds of evil. In 1099 Pope Paschal II cut down the walnuts and scattered the ashes, and to complete the exorcism built a chapel over the site. Sixtus IV had it rebuilt, enlarged, and given a Renaissance façade by Andrea Bregno in the 1470s; Bernini later Baroqued the interior.

But what S. Maria is best known for is its Renaissance art, beginning with the first chapel to the right, frescoed by Pinturicchio in the 1480s, with a lovely pastel *Nativity* to complement its two Renaissance tombs, the one on the left by Mino da Fiesole and Andrea Bregno. The second chapel, Capella Cybo, is a colourful *pietra dura* work by Carlo Fontana (1687); the third, by Pinturicchio or his school, is frescoed with scenes from the Virgin's life. In the right transept, there's a fine tabernacle by Bregno, paid for by Alexander VI, framing a Sienese painting of the Madonna.

Walk behind the altar to see the **Tribune**, by Bramante and financed by Julius II (1509), which incorporates some of the architect's original plans for the choir in St Peter's, with its coffered barrel vault and shell niches. The elegant frescoes in the vault, of golden Sibyls, Evangelists, and Doctors of the Church, framed by grotesques, are by Pinturicchio; the stained glass is by the all-time master of that art, Guillaume de Marcillat (1509), and the two beautifully carved tombs of sleeping cardinals Ascanio Sforza (brother of Milan boss Ludovico il Moro) and Girolamo Basso are early cinquecento works by Andrea Sansovino. On the high altar in front is a highly venerated icon of the Madonna, attributed to a 13th-century St Luke.

In the left transept, next to the choir, the **Cerasi Chapel** offers an opportunity to compare paintings by Rome's leading artistic rivals of the seicento, Annibale Carracci and Michelangelo da Caravaggio; this was the only project they worked on together. But Carracci's *Assumption of the Virgin*, even though the Virgin dramatically bursts from the tomb, seems hopelessly vacuous next to the psychological intensity of Caravaggio's two masterpieces, *The Crucifixion of St Peter* and *Paul on the road to Damascus*—in both the figures are brought right up to the forefront of the canvas and lit by a highly artificial but extremely effective lighting that heightens the sense of inner illumination. Caravaggio had no use for conventional iconography; in the painting of St Paul there is no sign of any supernatural agency, but only sympathetic gazes from the horse and attendant.

In the left aisle the mood changes again with the **Chigi Chapel**, designed by Raphael for Renaissance banking tycoon Agostino Chigi. A good friend of Julius II, Chigi was described in a papal bull as hoping in his chapel 'to convert earthly things into heavenly', and to oblige him Raphael went back to eternal forms of the Eternal City; the Chigi Chapel is, if nothing else, a personal-sized Pantheon, with mosaics of God the Father in the oculus of the dome and figures of the planets, describing Chigi's horoscope. Planned to achieve an austere perfection in its decoration as well as its geometry, the project was brought to abrupt halt by the death of both Raphael and Chigi in 1520, and it was finished by Bernini and Lorenzetto, on orders of the Chigi Pope Alexander VII. The pyramid tombs, of Agostino and his brother were made according to Raphael's design, as was the statue of Jonah emerging from the whale's mouth to the left of the altar, executed by Lorenzetto; Bernini added the figure of Habakkuk on the right. The altarpiece, the *Birth of the Virgin* is by Sebastiano del Piombo, while Salviati painted the frescoes of the Creation and Fall.

As you leave, don't miss the very different attempt at immortality erected in 1672 by a certain G.B. Chisleni, who wanted posterity to think of him as a praying skeleton (a bust of what he looked like with his skin on is on top); in between are bronze reliefs of a larva and moth, symbolizing the metamorphosis of the soul.

There are a couple of diversions just down the Corso, between the twin churches. If it has reopened, you can visit the **Goethe Museum,** *in the Corso (no. 20), where the poet lived from 1786 to 1788 and wrote the letters and diaries that became part of his* Italian Journey. *A bit further south, on the right, stands* **San Giacomo degli Incurabili** *with a façade by Maderno and a large oval interior; its name refers to the syphilitic patients admitted to the adjacent hospital. Across the Corso, yet another church,* **Gesù e Maria** *was used to take the idea of Bernini's tomb of Fonseca in S. Lorenzo in Lucina one step further, into the nave itself: animated statues of the Bolognetti family chat and worship from their tombs atop the confessionals in a fine colour-coordinated High Baroque interior.*

From Piazza del Popolo you can catch bus 90 or 90B back to Piazza Venezia, little bus 119 to the Pantheon, or, from nearby Passeggiata di Ripetta, bus 81 to Piazza del Risorgimento near the Vatican.

The Pincio Gardens 208

Galleria Nazionale d'Arte Moderna 209

Villa Giulia/Etruscan Museum 210

Zoo 212

Galleria Borghese 212

Start: *Piazza del Popolo:* Ⓜ *Flaminio or bus 90B or 95 from Piazza Venezia.*

Finish: *Porta Pinciana at the head of Via Veneto.*

Walking Time: *1½ hours for a mere stroll through the park.*

VIII: The Villa Borghese

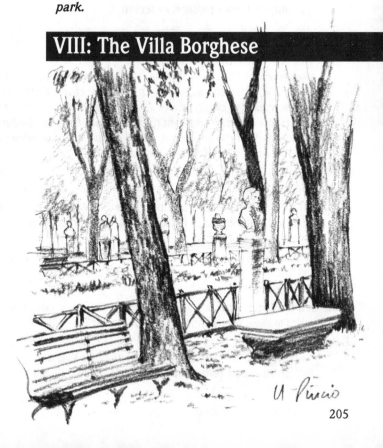

Il Pincio

The beautiful gardens of the Villa Borghese, where the pines of Rome seem their most pinishly Roman, can be either the perfect antidote to Baroque fever or a day's worth of sights in itself. Linger long in its shady groves, though, and you may find as H. V. Morton, that the shadows are haunted by retired pagan gods and classical ghosts, who feel at home here,while the city they knew has undergone a thousand transformations.

This walk is best done on any morning but Monday when its museums are closed. It could follow—or precede—a prowl through the 'Trident' just below (Walk VII), and is perfect for a picnic. It may be a jog to see all three museums in one day: save time by hiring a bicycle from the round, unlabelled medievalish hut just above the Muro Torto, off Viale dell'Obelisco in the Pincio gardens (L5000 an hour, with your passport as security).

---

lunch/cafés

*Not too much choice, though there are bars at both the Galleria Borghese and Galleria Nazionale dell'Arte Moderne and a restaurant inside the zoo. Otherwise there are few places to eat near the Villa Borghese. Bring a picnic, or walk for five minutes or so east to Via Salaria and Piazza Fiume. If you want to picnic, stock up at the brilliant food shops just off Piazza del Popolo, on Via di Ripetta. Try the **alimentari** at 233, the bakery at 7a and the wine shop at 19.*

Caffè Fiume, Via Salaria 57. Closed Sun. Art Nouveau café with a mouth-watering selection of sandwiches, salads and hot dishes at lunchtime.

Pizza Italia, Corso Italia 103 (just below Piazza Fiume). Closed Sun. Superior *pizza al taglio* specializing in cold toppings like smoked salmon and salad or mozzarella and rocket.

Casina Valadier (1817), up on the Pincio. Closed Mon. The food is unimaginative and ludicrously expensive (L150,000) but the view over Rome from the upper terrace is superb.

Caffè dell'Orologio. Open summer only. The Pincio's water clock has outdoor tables to linger over a drink.

Relais Le Jardin in the Hotel Lord Byron, Via Giuseppe De Notaris 5, ✆ 322 4541. Closed Sun. Ten minutes walk north of the Villa Giulia. One of the two or three best restaurants in all Rome; L130,000 and up. Book in advance.

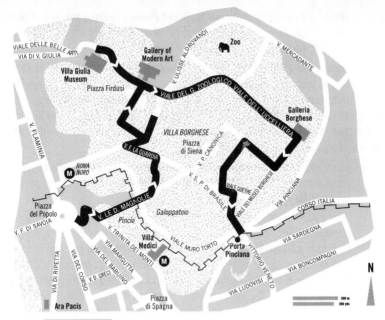

Walk VIII The Villa Borghese

The heights around the Muro Torto have been planted with gardens since the days of the Republic, when Monte Pincio was known as the 'hill of gardens' or *Collis Hortulorum*. The most famous gardens belonged to the Villa of Lucullus, the 1st-century BC general and epicure, who conquered Mithridates of Pontus in Northern Anatolia and brought back, among his trophies, the first cherries to Europe. His gardens later became the retreat of Claudius' third wife, Messalina, who murdered the owner and after publicly 'marrying' her lover, was later murdered here herself by the troops of her outraged husband.

In 1605, the first of Rome's princely cardinal-nephews, Scipione Borghese (nephew of Paul V), set a new standard in nepotism with the acquisition of the vast estates outside Porta Pinciana, creating for himself a Lucullus-style retreat to entertain his friends and house his growing art collection. In 1773, Scipione's heir Prince Marcantonio Borghese had the formal Italian gardens redesigned all'inglese by Scotsman Jacob Moore; the next Borghese, Camillo, brother-in-law of Napoleon, added the occasional neoclassical touch. In 1901 the state purchased the garden and Borghese palazzina, and linked them with the Pincio and Villa Giulia to create Rome's most accessible and popular public park.

Walk up to the Pincio from Piazza del Popolo, leaving the helter-skel-
tering traffic behind at the Salita del Pincio, a footpath which climbs up
through trees to the park's belvedere.

One of the uncanonical hills of Rome, the **Pincio** is best known as THE place to
watch the sun set over the city, with the sun-finger obelisk of the Piazza del
Popolo in the foreground and the dome of St Peter's on the horizon melting in the
twilight to the bells of the Angelus. The formal gardens of the Pincio were laid out
by Valadier in 1814 and throughout the 19th century Rome's fops and belles
posed and postured here each evening.

From the belvedere, turn right and walk past the Casina Valadier for a
view, through the bars of the gate, of the celebrated 16th-century garden
*of the **Villa Medici** (see Walk VII).*

In the early 1980s an atavistic vandal decapitated the scores of busts of
famous Italians, lending the Pincio a weird, surreal touch in its hundreds
*of empty pedestals. The equally unadorned **Obelisk** in central Viale*
dell'Obelisco, to the right of Casina Valadier, was brought from the tomb
of Hadrian's darling Antinous, who was drowned in the Nile while
saving Hadrian's life and deified by imperial decree. Walk down Viale
dell'Obelisco and turn left on Viale dell'Orologio for one of Rome's more
*quirky fountains, the rusto-romantic **Water Clock**, designed by a*
Dominican priest named Embriago for the Paris Exhibition of 1867. Viale
*dell'Obelisco then crosses over the **Muro Torto**, or crooked wall.*

The Muro Torto was the only section of the Aurelian wall Belisarius didn't repair,
for the Romans assured him that St Peter himself would defend it, and apparently
they were right, for it was never assaulted. Later this area was the cemetery for
prostitutes, thieves, and actors; a tradition recalled by the merry whores in
Fellini's *Nights of Cabiria* who waited for clients cruising the sunken highway,
Viale del Muro Torto.

Cross the bridge over Viale del Muro Torto on to a traffic-free lane lined
*with magnolias; off to the right you can see the circuit of the **Galoppa-**
***toio**, where the sight of grazing horses and trotting Italians is a pleasant*
surprise in the middle of Rome. Cut diagonally across to the left, past the
large round fountain to Viale Fiorello La Guardia, named for the kind
New York mayor who read the comics over the radio during newspaper
*strikes, to the **Portico Egiziano**, a bus stop fit for a pharaoh, originally a*
neoclassical conceit built by Camillo Borghese. Just beyond is a rock-
bound fountain dedicated to Aesculapius, though the good god of
healing is better served further on: turn right at the fountain on Viale

*Esculapio, then turn right again though another Borghese gate, and you'll find the charming neoclassical **Temple of Aesculapius** on the shores of a romantic lakelet. If you want to do as the Romans do, hire a rowboat and smooch among the nattering ducks or gaze fondly at your beloved over a coke at the nearby caff; otherwise head back through the gate down Viale Madama Letizia, and to the right down the steps into oval Piazza Firdusi, adorned with two giant goblet fountains, supported by flowering fascii and encircled by tortoises ready to tumble exhausted into the basin. Piazza Firdusi overlooks busy Viale delle Belle Arti and the elephantine bulk of one of Rome's more inexcusable buildings, the 1911* **Galleria Nazionale d'Arte Moderna** *(open 9–7, Sun 9–1, closed Mon; adm L8000).*

The museum contains one of Italy's most important hoards of 19th- and 20th-century art. At the time of writing the collection is being rearranged and only the 20th-century collection on the ground floor is open.

Paintings and sculptures of the 20th century fill the ground floor, beginning with four colourful Art Nouveau panels by Galileo Chini (1914), designer of opera sets for Puccini and the throne room of the King of Siam. The panels, with their oriental influence, make an interesting comparison with Gustav Klimt's more Byzantine *Three Ages of Woman*. There are paintings by Cézanne, Modigliani, and a shimmering pointillist view of the *Villa Borghese* by Giacomo Balla, one of the fathers of contemporary Italian art. Balla's style changed dramatically after he became a signatory of the 1910 Futurist Manifesto. Rebelling against the weight of Italian history and tradition—even to the point of wanting to abolish spaghetti—the Futurists propounded a new Italy, dynamic, technological, and above all, speedy; where the Cubists probed the structure of an object (as in Braque's 1911 *Still Life*), the Futurist artists sent it hurtling through space to startle the spectator (Balla's 1913 *Ponte della velocità*; also his menacing 1915 *Insidie di guerra* and Ferruccio Ferrazzi's fauvist, swirling *Carrosello*). The talented Umberto Boccioni, who like many Futurists died in World War I, combined the tenets of Futurism and Cubism in *Cavallo + Cavaliere + caseggiato* (1914) and in sculpture (the grinning/grimacing *Ritratto antigrazioso*).

The post-war reaction of the '20s is represented by works of Mondrian, Duchamp, Schwitters, and in Italy by the Metaphysical School, founded in Ferrara, questioning perceptions of reality with haunting, motionless, ambiguous scenes populated with the lifeless but human forms of mannequins by Giorgio de Chirico (*Ettore e Andromaca*) and Carlo Carrà (*Ovale delle apparizioni*). In a similar metaphysical vein is the Italian sculpture of the '20s and '30s on the first veranda, its phalanx of famous and unknown portrait busts gazing back en masse at the spectator. From the '30s are paintings by Kandinsky, Miró, Maurice Utrillo, some dull abstract Italians, weird historically minded Fascists (i.e. *Bacchus at the inn*); and most interestingly, the 'Magic Realism' of Filippo de Pisis, Antonio Donghi (*Il Tevere*) and Mario Broglio (*La Rusticana* and the pale *La Sorgente*), who achieve an uncanniness through simple, everyday objects and scenes. Just off the second veranda, don't miss the room of 20th-century prints, especially those from the '20s and '30s by Bruno da Osino (1888–1962) and Disertori Benevenuto (1887–1969). Other works, to be arranged, are by Van Gogh, Monet, Degas, Felice Casorati, Paul Klee, Jan Arp and Max Ernst.

Sometime, perhaps, the 19th-century collection will reopen. Highlights include the often delightful Tuscan Impressionists (*Macchiaioli*), led by Giovanni Fattori, Silvestro Lega, and Telemaco Signorini; the *Bois de Boulogne* by Paris-based Giuseppe de Nittis; two amazing and enormous melodramas by Aristide Sartorio, with the Gorgon and Diana of Ephesus in the lead roles; and fine sculptures by Medardo Rosso. Among the non-Italians, look for Dante Gabriele Rossetti's *Portrait of Mrs William Morris* (1874) and prints and drawings by Goya, Blake, Hogarth, Renoir, Toulouse-Lautrec, Géricault, Delacroix, Millet, Corot, Munch, Whistler, Burne-Jones, Rodin, Manet, Beardsley, and William Morris.

> *Leaving the museum, head right down Viale delle Belle Arti which sweeps down to the **Villa Giulia**, the pleasure dome of Julius III (1550–5), a pope fond of antique statues, young boys, large onions from Gaeta, and above all parties. It now houses Italy's most important Etruscan museum. Open 9–7, Sun 9–1 (extended in summer) closed Mon, adm L8000.*

To entertain his guests like a true Roman, Julius III hired Vignola, Vasari, and Ammannati, with Michelangelo as consultant, to create a villa and garden, fountains and statuary, as graceful a Mannerist conceit as could ever be. Although stripped of most of its ornaments and 300 ancient and Renaissance statues by more prudish popes, the villa is still a delight, heavily rusticated on the outside like an oyster, secreting a pearl of a semicircular portico, with ceiling frescoes of trellises, vines, and birds. The most charming innovation of all, the **Nymphaeum**, was designed by Vignola, sunk into the garden to take the clear waters of the Acqua Vergine and provide a cool refuge from the summer heat.

After serving as a papal guest house for Queen Christina and other VIPs, the villa in 1889 became the **Museo Nazionale Etrusco**—a great place to learn about the Romans' shadowy predecessors, their mentors, and later rivals. Enter their realm just beyond the left portico, where you are greeted by two rare archaic Etruscan sculptures, of a centaur and a youth riding a sea monster, from the 6th century BC. These, like nearly all the other exhibits in the museum, were discovered in tombs, but are rarely morbid; few people ever smiled at the Grim Reaper like the Etruscans, who preferred to face eternity reclining on a banquet couch, like the perfectly charming couple on the terracotta *Sarcofago dei Sposi* from Cerveteri (6th century BC), who by their expressive, elegant gestures seem disconcertingly to be discussing you, the viewer.

From the Temple of Portonaccio at Veio come their equally elegant cousins, giant terracotta statues of *Apollo and Hercules*, believed to be by Vulca, the one Etruscan sculptor whose name has come down to us, famed for his work in the Temple of Capitoline Jupiter for Tarquin the Proud. Elsewhere, the Etruscans bridge the centuries with their effortless, endearing talent for portraiture in terracotta ex-votos (some of children), for nuttiness (the extremely tall and thin 'blade' figures), and for the vase paintings by the imaginative and occasionally risqué 'Pittore di Micali' of Vulci, master of the winged willies in the Vatican's Etruscan collection.

The Etruscans were superb metalworkers, casting bronze incense burners in the form of overcrowded chariots and cremation urns shaped like huts, and most magnificently of all, the **Chigi Vase** (7th century BC) embellished with hunting scenes and a Judgement of Paris. Their gold jewellery has rarely been matched in its intricate filigree and painstaking miniaturism, able to squeeze 50 golden rams in a square inch of brooch; compare it to the lovely baubles in the **Castellani Collection** (Room 22, open upon request), displaying gold from the Minoans (1400 BC) to the pre-Columbian civilizations. The Etruscans often buried their warriors with their armour, and in one case, at least, with a **chariot** and two horses, whose skeletons surprisingly are no larger than Great Danes.

Other rooms contain beautiful Greek kraters and amphorae with mythological scenes, and Etruscan versions of the same; some of the best are from the Ager Faliscus (Rooms 23–27), the area between Lake Bracciano and the Tiber, inhabited by the Falisci, cousins to the Latins but influenced by the Etruscans, and famous for their ceramics and terracottas; don't miss the plate with a war elephant and her baby, painted in the 3rd century, inspired by Pyrrhus' Pyrrhic victories in South Italy.

In the grounds is a life-sized reproduction of the colourful and ornate **Temple of Alatri** built in 1891, but now closed owing to its fragile condition. Near the entrance there's a newly arranged room of artefacts from Pyrgi, the port of Cerveteri (open by request); it includes a beautiful high relief of *The Seven Against Thebes* and laminated gold inscriptions in Etruscan and Phoenician from the 5th century BC when Etruria and Carthage were allies against the Greeks.

*Backtrack up Viale delle Belle Arti to Viale del Giardino Zoologico for Rome's zoo, a good 15-minute trek (you can save shoe leather by catching a tram (30 or 19) from the Villa Giulia to the top of Viale del Giardino Zoologico). The **Zoo** (daily 8.30–5 pm, till 6 on summer Sats and Suns; adm L10,000, free for anyone under 3 ft 6ins) lies behind a charming elephant-headed doorway, although the statuary on the gate above, of bullies clobbering the very creatures you are about to see, rather betrays the initial impression.*

Founded in 1911, the zoo contains all the usual zoo residents in a pretty garden setting; this being Italy, even the camels don't smell. Besides land creatures, there's an aquarium which will set you back another *L2500*, and on the north side of the zoo, in Via Aldovrandi 18, the **Museo Civico di Zoologia** *(9–1, free to zoo visitors)*, with stuffed critters; also here are the **African Museum** and **Shell Museum** in the same building, but rarely open. The real show stoppers, however, are two clownish young African elephants who like to squirt passers-by with pachyderm-flavoured water from their pool.

*From the zoo's entrance the Viale dell'Uccelliera leads directly past the ochre, swarmingly decorated 'secret' (i.e. enclosed) **gardens and aviary** of the **Palazzina Borghese** of Cardinal Scipione Borghese, built between 1608–15 by Flaminio Ponzio and Giovanni Vasanzio (Jan van Zanten).*

Like the Villa Giulia, it was not built as a residence, but in the mode of an ancient *villa suburbana*, for entertaining. The well-padded Scipione was famed for his lavish banquets, and in its original form his palazzina was covered with an equally lavish feast of Mannerist reliefs, statues and baubles, all whisked away in the early 19th century. An inkling of his taste remains in these secret gardens, with Borghese dragons, grotesque masks, floral reliefs etc.

*The Palazzina itself, despite its unkempt garden and crumpled fences, contains one of Rome's greatest patrician collections, the **Galleria Borghese**. At the time of writing the building is undergoing a major restoration and only the Gallery's ground floor is open (Tues–Sat 9–7, Sun 9–1, closed Mon, last entrance 30 min before closing; adm L4000). The first floor collection has been temporarily moved to San Michele a Ripa, Via San Michele a Ripa, 22 (Tues–Sat 9–7, Sun/Mon 9–1; adm L4000).*

Despite the family name, Borghese taste was anything but bourgeois. The exquisitely cultivated Scipione not only advised his uncle Paul V on artistic matters, but with papal pin money amassed one of the world's greatest private collections of sculpture and paintings. Later members of the family added to the collection, much of which has landed in the Louvre, thanks to Prince Camillo Borghese, who donated or sold a large portion of it to his brother-in-law Napoleon. The Italian state purchased what remained in 1902.

The **Ground Floor** stars the Borghese's marble men and marble women; Scipione was the first to discover the precocious talent of Gianlorenzo Bernini, and the sculptor produced many of his earliest works for the cardinal. These statuary groups of mythological subjects date from the early 1620s, before Bernini got religion, and they break new ground, for better or worse, in the contrived drama of their virtuoso *figura serpentinata* poses, each portrayed in the most intense, climactic moments of their stories. Looking at them, you may think, as many have before you, that Bernini was the Michelangelo of the day (though as F. Marion Crawford drily put it, 'no one has yet been bold enough, or foolish enough, to call Michelangelo the Bernini of the sixteenth century.')

The statuary in each room lent its theme to the grand 18th-century décor of Prince Marcantonio, who had a weakness for brightly coloured, mildly *trompe l'oeil* ceiling frescoes. The rooms are prominently numbered, and begin with the most notorious **Room I** where Canova's sculpture of Pauline Bonaparte Borghese reclines half-nude as Venus under a ceiling portraying the *Judgement of Paris*. When asked by an acquaintance how ever she could have posed nearly naked, Pauline replied that it wasn't so hard because 'the artist had a furnace in his studio'. Although serenely neoclassical, Napoleon's sister is one of Rome's spicier tomatoes (she had the statue made shortly after marrying Prince Camillo Borghese, to please him); but as saucy as she was, she was minute—the statue is life-sized. Connoisseurs may want to compare her breasts with the cast in the Napoleon Museum. In **Room II** Bernini's *David* (modestly bearing the 25-year-old sculptor's own features) is about to discharge his loaded sling, though his set look of determination is mocked by the playful putti of the ceiling frescoes. Sharing the room are fine sarcophagus panels illustrating the Labours of Hercules.

Room III is designed around another hot piece of marble, Bernini's *Daphne and Apollo*, the former in the act of turning into a laurel tree to avoid the embraces of the god. **Room IV** the large *Sala degli Imperatori* is a chilly cynosure of 18th-century design, the 17th-century alabaster and porphyry busts of the emperors in perfect chromatic accord with the precious marbles of the floor, pillars, and ceiling, all looking icily at Bernini's *Rape of Proserpina*, the goddess struggling in Pluto's arms, though perhaps not as desperately as she might have done.

Room V contains a replica of the famous Hellenistic Hermaphrodite, the inspiration of the Hermaphrodite Room; **Room VI** features *Aeneas and Anchises*, carved by young Bernini with his father Pietro; Aeneas is carrying his father out of burning Troy, while the older man clutches the Palladium. The Egyptian room, **Room VII** is actually built around an archaic Greek statue of a young girl. **Room VIII** contains the gallery's finest ancient sculpture, the *Dancing Faun*, restored by Thorvaldsen. Beyond this is the **Salone**, crowned by a fresco of Marcus Furius Camillus breaking the treaty with the Gauls and a relief of Marco Curzio leaping the abyss. Set into the floor are rather grisly 3rd-century AD mosaics of gladiatorial scenes from Torronuova. There's a bar in the adjacent portico if you need liquid support at this point.

Sometime, somehow, the treasure trove of paintings upstairs will reopen. Among the celebrated works are Raphael's Manneristic *Deposition* (1507), inspired by Leonardo and Michelangelo and filched with papal aid from a church in Perugia; also his *Lady and the Unicorn*, believed to a portrait of his fiancée Maddalena Strozzi; Titian's *Sacred and Profane Love*, the beautifully coloured, ambiguous masterpiece of his youth, in which the two women have the same face; Correggio's melting, erotic *Danae*; Madonnas by Giovanni Bellini, Andrea del Sarto, Perugino, Piero di Cosimo and Caravaggio (the latter with a serpent); here, too, is one of his most important early works, the *Boy with a Fruit Basket* and *David with Goliath's head*. There are excellent portraits by two masters of the genre, Lorenzo Lotto and Antonello da Messina, whose *Italian gentlemen* is a prototype of the genre; and Dosso Dossi's mysterious *Circe*, contemplating her next spell. Among the sculpture, don't miss Bernini's portrait busts of Cardinal Scipione Borghese (mouth partly open as he inhales his next asthmatic breath) and Paul V, and his model for the curly flowing equestrian statue of Louis XIV (now known as Quintus Curtius Rufus, located at Versailles) and Algardi's statue of *Sleep*—a slumbering boy with a sleepy dormouse.

*From the Gallery, walk back around the aluminium fence to the Viale del Museo Borghese, which will take you past a monument to Lord Byron (paid for by the Queen Mother in 1959) down to the fortified **Porta Pinciana** and the indigestible movable feast of Via Veneto (see Walk IX). Or, if you'd rather, take a detour west in the garden to the **Piazza di Siena**, which at the beginning of May hosts one of Italy's largest horse shows (the rest of the year, joggers canter around). From here, signs point the way back to the Pincio or Piazza di Spagna.*

To get back to Piazza Venezia from Porta Pinciana continue 100 m down Via Veneto and catch bus no.56.

Palazzo Quirinale	218
Sant'Andrea	218
San Carlino	219
Palazzo Barberini	220
Via Vittorio Veneto	222
Baths of Diocletian	224
Termini Station	226

Start: *Piazza del Quirinale, a short walk from the Trevi Fountain.*

Finish: *near Termini station.*

Walking Time: *2 ½ hours at the most, with one big museum.*

IX: Quirinale, Via Veneto, Diocletian

fontain
delle Api

A disproportionate helping of Roman unpleasantness is concentrated in this walk, but it has its attractions, especially for lovers of the Baroque and of the bizarre: beginning with one of the dreariest and longest palaces in Italy, past the competing masterpieces of Bernini and Borromini, through a massive hoard of Baroque art, then over to inspect the artistically arranged bones of 4,000 dead monks and the melancholy sycamores of the once-fashionable Via Veneto. Next comes the worst-run major museum in Europe *(closed Monday)*, where a magnificent collection of antique art is jealously kept out of our sight. Finally, we leave you at the mercies of the mad, the addicts and the gypsies who surround Termini Station.

No buses pass through the Quirinale to disturb the President of Italy's sleep, so you have to take bus 57, 64, 65, 70, 75, 81, 170 along Via Nazionale to Via IV Novembre, and walk up Via XXIV Maggio.

---

lunch/cafés

Not many choices here; detour two blocks over to Via Nazionale if you need a quick hit of espresso or a limp pizza. Don't expect to find anything good near Termini Station either, though there are restaurants and bars in profusion. For other nearby restaurants, see Walk VI for those around the Trevi Fountain.

Al Piccolo Arancio, Via Scanderbeg 112 (see Walk VI); L45–50,000.

Colline Emiliane, Via degli Avignonesi 22. Closed Fri. Highly rated Emilia-Romagnan cusine; L50–55,000.

Enoteca Nibbi, Via Emilia 42. Closed Sat and Sun. Upmarket stand-up bar where business folk flock at lunchtime for a glass of wine and fresh sandwiches made to order.

Peppone, Via Emilia 60. Closed Sun. Serious, old fashioned restaurant popular with business people; L55–60,000.

Da Giovanni, Via Salandra 1. Closed Sun. Honest old trat, wide choice of simple favourites; L20–30,000.

Cantina Cantarini, Piazza Sallustio 12, Via XX Settembre. Closed Sun. Book ahead (© 485 528) as the Marches-style food is extremely popular.

Trimani, Via Cernaia 37B. Closed Sun. Scrumptious light lunches in a smart wine bar five minutes' walk from Termini station.

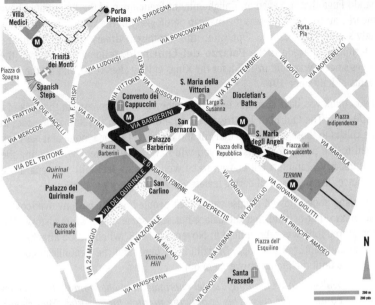

The Quirinale is the highest of the Roman hills. According to Roman mythology it was occupied by the Sabines in the time of Titus Tatius, when the rape of the Sabine women occurred. Its name may come either from Cures, the name of the Sabine settlement, or from Quirinus, a title of Romulus—Romans as late as the Middle Ages liked to refer to themselves romantically as the 'Quirites'. In Classical Rome, the hill was always a quiet residential neighbourhood, with a number of odd religious sanctuaries—to personified Hope and Fortune, to Venus Erigena from Sicily, to Mithras and the Egyptian god Serapis. None of them, as far as is known, ever did anything to depress property values or attract the attentions of the police.

So great was the abandonment of the hill in the Middle Ages that even its name was forgotten. 'Monte Cavallo', the farmers and shepherds of medieval Rome called it, from the half-buried horses' heads, projecting above the ground in the area. These were dug up in the 1500s, along with broken remains of the **Dioscuri**, imperial-era copies of a Greek sculptural ensemble of Castor and Pollux. Renaissance wags reassembled them and carved upon them the lying inscriptions claiming to be a 'work of Phidias' and a 'work of Praxiteles'. Pius VI added the obelisk to complete the new monument, along with a basin that, appropriately enough, formerly served as a horse trough in the Forum.

Behind them is the 1739 **Palazzo della Consultà**, a stately Rococo work by Fernando Fuga that not even an Enlightenment Frenchman of the time would have sneered at; it now witnesses the madcap pettifoggery of the Corte Costituzionale, Italy's Supreme Court. Opposite, the promised dreary palace with the interminable façade is the **Palazzo del Quirinale**, residence of most of the popes since it was built in 1574, for the Kings of Italy after 1870, and for the Presidents of Italy since 1947.

If you think you have seen this ensemble somewhere before, look at the back of a L500 coin. The Quirinale is a treasure house of art, from the Roman frescoes in the cellars to those of Melozzo da Forli and Pietro da Cortona; none of it has been open to the public for years, and you will have to be content with eyeing the bejewelled Carabinieri (all chosen to be well over six feet tall) who guard the entrances from any sort of daring malefactor who might try to break in.

Kings and popes showed themselves to their people from the balcony overlooking the piazza, but beyond that the palace has seen some action in its history. The Roman republic was reborn here in November 1848, when a mob attacked the palace and captured the pope. Mazzini lived here, and the Republican council met here until the French drove them out.

> Walking down the long Via del Quirinale, it might seem that the palace continues for ever. This is only the **manica lunga**—the 'long sleeve' designed by Bernini, a palace wing a sixth of a mile long, and two rooms deep.

> On the right side of the street, you will soon have a chance to pledge your final allegiance to, or perfect your disdain for the Baroque, with two provocative masterpieces that have excited much critical comment and a discreet popular interest over the last three centuries. The first is Bernini's **Sant' Andrea al Quirinale** (open 8–12 and 4–7, closed Tues).

This church (1658–70) deserves a little of your time, a building that can compel an objective look even from sworn enemies of the Baroque. Bernini's *tour de force* involves architectural forms hardly seen before or since, ideas never really understood by his contemporaries. There is really no façade at all, only a remarkably elegant classical portal embraced by a semi-elliptical wall; inside is an elliptical building that reverses the scheme you thought you saw at the entrance; a unique oval space surrounded by eight side chapels, still emphasizing the main altar, uniting the interior with a bold elliptical cornice and a decorative scheme including maritime motifs that remind us constantly of the fisherman St Andrew. A cleverly placed window allows a shaft of light to fall over the high altar.

Sant'Andrea is a small, aristocratic building, full of family symbols of the wealthy Roman clerics who paid for it; remove the altar and it could just as easily be a ball-room as a church. Its rich columns of red *cottanello* marble from Sicily and trim in almost every other variety of expensive stone, commemorate the Jesuits who commissioned it, with their philosophy that the glory of heaven could best be imparted to the faithful by the glory of worldly opulence. The best of the decoration is the stucco putti and angels by Antonio Raggi around the dome; not really angels at all they seem, but stray mythological creatures caught in a very Catholic century, looking for a lost mythology.

> *Borromini has his say at the corner of Via delle Quattro Fontane, with the church of* **San Carlino** *or San Carlo alle Quattro Fontane (1646), open 9–12.30 and 4–6, closed Sat pm and all day Sun. Façade undergoing restoration, but due to be revealed shortly.*

At first, this may seem to be a High Baroque showpiece much like Sant'Andrea, but despite the classical pediments and Corinthan columns inside, these two creations have surprisingly little in common. Bernini, though perhaps inspired by his rival's work to a greater freedom of form, chose to stick closer to the book, planning his church by the proportions of the classical Orders and carefully maintaining the distinction between architectural elements and the sculptural decoration. Borromini never used the Orders, preferring to revive the constructive geometry of the medieval cathedral builders; San Carlino, with its undulating shapes and ellipses, is by far the most complex building in Rome—but if you were as clever as Borromini, you could prove every point in its design with a compass and straight-edge.

To the eye, however, this tiny church seems more a sculptural fantasy than a bundle of mathematics. And this blurring of boundaries between sculpture and architecture is also at the heart of Borromini's art. This is true of the interior as a whole, a continuous space where it is difficult to rest the eye on any particular part, and also in the details: the unusual geometrical coffering on the dome, and on the façade, where a pair of angel wings forms an arch to frame the statue of San Carlo (St Charles Borromeo, bishop of Milan and one of the protagonists of the Counter-Reformation). This façade, completed only in 1668, was Borromini's last work, just as the interior was his first; together they sum up his achievement as the most creative master of the Roman Baroque.

There are some other virtues to point out: a very unusual crypt, with curves echoing the church above, and a small cloister, also designed by Borromini. The entire complex is a lesson in economy, how to get the best use out of a small and irregular plot of land. There is a story, probably apocryphal, that Borromini planned San Carlino to be the same size as one of the four great piers of St Peter's; in fact the dimensions are very close.

> *One of the constraints on Borromini's façade was to make it fit in with the **Quattro Fontane** (1593), four fountains built into the street corner that represent the Tiber and the Aniene, Strength and Fidelity. The street crossing Via del Quirinale here, Via delle Quattro Fontane, was one of the grand boulevards of Sixtus V's planning scheme; down one end you can see the obelisk of Trinitá dei Monti, down the other, that of S. Maria Maggiore. Turn left here, to see what became of the profits of the papacy for the 1620s and '30s.*

> *Urban VIII was pope then, and Rome's artists were kept busy building and embellishing his family preserve, the **Palazzo Barberini**. Now owned by the state, the Palazzo houses the **Galleria Nazionale d'Arte Antica**, an odd name for a few medieval pictures and plenty from the late Renaissance and later, sometimes upstaged by the effusive original decoration. The building itself is, and will be for some time, sheathed in scaffolding, but the gallery remains open (9–2, Sun 9–1, closed Mon; last entry 30 min before closing; adm).*

The unusual design is primarily by Carlo Maderno, an outsize country villa with three storeys of arcades; the windows of the upper floor are a famous innovation, made to match the size of those of the *piano nobile* by a perspectivist illusion. After Maderno's death the palace was finished by Bernini (who added the theatrical square stair on the left) and the more imaginative Borromini (the oval spiral stair to the right, and the windows on the upper floor of the façade).

Once up Bernini's stair, the gallery begins sedately with a 13th-century Tuscan *Crucifixion* and a few choice quattrocento works—an old-fashioned *Madonna* by Neri di Bicci; two paintings by Filippo Lippi: an *Annunciation* with a lovely Renaissance angel, and a Madonna with an ugly Bambino; a triptych by Fra Angelico; an unusually studious *Maddalena* by Piero di Cosimo; *Madonna and Saints* by Umbrian artist L'Alunno, one of his better works, especially St Jerome with his specs and pussycat lion, asking to be stroked; a sombre *S. Nicola da Tolentino* by Perugino. After these works, Andrea del Sarto's *Holy Family* and Beccafumi's *Madonna, Child, and St John* startle with their Mannerists' more-lifelike-than-life colours and light. Here, too, is the Gallery's most famous painting, Raphael's portrait of a courtesan, which everyone would like to believe is his beloved baker's girl, *La Fornarina*. It was painted in the year of his death which, according to popular rumour, resulted from a fever caused by her demanding passion. In the same room is a *Rape of the Sabines* by an artist nicknamed for more curious passions, Il Sodoma; also a *portrait of Stefano Colonna* by Bronzino.

Note the ceiling of **Room VII**, with its fresco by Andrea Sacchi called *The Triumph of Divine Knowledge* (1633), where the enthroned Virgin looks down on the round earth in a Baroque attempt to create a new astronomy. There are paintings by Titian (*Venus and Adonis*, a copy of the painting in the Prado), Tintoretto, two small but busy El Grecos (more Mannerist than any Italian Mannerist could dream) and Garofalo's fantastical *Picus transformed into a woodpecker.*

The inevitable Counter-Reformation blast of the mindless and mawkish is shut up in the next rooms. Only the bizarre really stand out in the crowd—works like Jacopino del Conte's *Deposition;* Il Mastelletta's dark and elongated forms in *Christ by a lake;* then comes Caravaggio (*Narcissus* and *Judith and Holofernes*) and his numerous followers. Press on for more seicento treats: playful Poussin's *Bacchanale of putti;* Guido Reni's famous *Portrait of a Girl,* which has always been presumed to be the ill-fated Beatrice Cenci, though apparently Reni never saw her; Guercino's *Et in Arcadia Ego,* a must for French occultists and Merovingian conspiracy addicts; Quentin Metsys' *Erasmus;* Holbein's *Henry VIII* (1540, painted on the day of his marriage to Anne of Cleves), and the 'curious perspectives' of Jean François Niceron (1613–46), who took the Renaissance science of artificial perspective to a mad extreme, painting portraits that seem to have been stretched around the rim of a goldfish bowl.

The **Gran Salone**, the restoration of which should be complete by the time you read this, comes as a grand finale, its ceiling embellished by Pietro da Cortona's overwhelming *Triumph of Divine Providence* (1633–39), one of the Baroque masterpieces of Rome, set in an illusionistic architectural framework, only to then explode beyond its limits. The depth and complexity of the imagery was intended to apotheosize that big spender, Urban VIII; the three bees flying in formation from Divine Providence towards the tiara and laurel wreath are from the Barberini coat of arms much in evidence elsewhere in the palace.

The upper floor offers no relief for the footsore, but instead works from that numbing dark age of painting, the 1700s (but good views of Rome by Pannini and Van Wittel, and other works by Fragonard, Boucher, Guardi, and Canaletto). It was a delightful period for interior decoration, however, as can be seen in the frescoed **Barberini apartments**, with period furnishings, Meissen china, costumes, Chinese porcelain, and the Barberini toddlers' carriage.

*Walk to the foot of Via delle Quattro Fontane and **Piazza Barberini**.*

If it's possible to feel sorry for any marble child of Bernini, it would have to be the marine god in his **Fontana del Tritone**(1637), gamely blowing his shell through the buzz of traffic. This busy crossroads is named after the Florentine family that gave Rome Urban VIII, whose coat of arms and papal tiara are entwined in the tails of the sea-creatures supporting the triton. He's honoured too in the piazza's second fountain, the **Fontana delle Api**(1644), from which three huge Barberini bees slake their thirst. Most of the piazza is really the roof of the Barberini's underground stables, now a forgotten grotto inhabited by the biggest and fiercest rats in Rome.

*From here, head north up the shady, curving **Via Vittorio Veneto**, the stage background for Roman society since it was first laid out.*

Few parts of Rome have become as grievously mangled in the last two centuries as this one. In papal Rome, this area was the edge of the city, and everything to the east was villas and gardens. First came Via del Tritone, in the 19th century, opening the area to development, and the villas and gardens soon disappeared, victims of the post-1870 speculative boom. Perhaps the greatest casualty was the Villa Ludovisi, an extensive wooded preserve that was one of the beauty spots of Rome. Romans loved the poetic justice that overtook the family that sold it to the speculators. They built a mammoth palace on Via Veneto with the proceeds—now the US Embassy, but soon found they had created a neighbourhood too dear even for them; the tax man ruined them and snatched away their palace not long after. This neighbourhood, known since 1885 as the aristocratic 'Ludovisi District', with the Via Veneto as its centre, was just in time to claim the ornate Grand Hotels, mansions and cafés of the Belle Epoque. Our own century added Via Barberini, lined with Mussolini-style airline offices and banks, perhaps the most gruesome street in Rome.

Via Veneto really caught the world's attention in the 1950s, thanks to a fortunate convergence of Italy's newfound talent for making movies and the postwar tourist boom. With Roberto Rossellini and Ingrid Bergman likely to turn up at the next table of the Café de Paris, and the first hordes of *paparazzi* combing the street to see who among the international film set was flirting with whom, the life epitomized by Fellini's *La Dolce Vita* was in full swing. One step behind the *paparazzi* came the Americans. Just as Piazza di Spagna was the English headquarters on the Grand Tour, so Via Veneto became the American Rome in the days of bulky Kodaks and Hawaiian sportshirts. Even now, perhaps owing to the presence of the gargantuan, well-fortified US Embassy (gained after 1945 in a trade-off for some tons of war surplus), the street has an American air about it, as if any minute fleets of '59 Cadillacs with lofty tailfins could come gliding around the bend.

Unfortunately, the *dolce vita* in Rome faded away long ago, and today's Via Veneto is as fashionable as pointy sunglasses and Capri pants. First-time visitors do not often know this, and the street still does a grandstand business vacuuming out the pockets of package tourists.

*These days, the best show on Via Veneto is the one in the basement of the **Convento dei Cappuccini** at the southern end of the street.*

Cardinal Antonio Barberini must have been a strange bird. While Baroque was blooming, and while his relatives were rolling in the loot from Urban VIII's papacy, he devoted himself to the construction of this monastic house and its austere church, **Santa Maria della Concezione**; here you can see his tomb, with the inscription 'Here lies dust, ashes, nothing'.

The real treat, however, lies downstairs, the **Capuchin Cemetery** (*door to the right of the church, open daily 9–12, 3–6; obligatory 'donation'*), a joyous celebration of Death unequalled this side of Palermo (where there are some even better Capuchin catacombs). A French Capuchin, back in 1528, came up with the idea; his brethren kept at it until 1870, turning the church crypt into five glorious chapels decorated in Baroque frippery—entirely made of human bones and skulls, with a few whole Capuchins wired up to the walls in period dress. Some 4000 monks contributed their remains for the work. It is not without artistic merit. Somehow mouldering bones and Baroque go very well together; shoulder-blades and vertebrae especially can be used for some attractive patterns. All this rests on a floor of dirt brought specially from Jerusalem. Visit on the first Sunday of October, and by the grace of Pope Paul VI you'll earn a special indulgence.

> *Retrace your steps through Piazza Barberini, and take the aforementioned Via Barberini (sorry!) into Largo S. Susanna and its three churches. **Santa Susanna**, with its façade by Maderno, was the prototypical work of the Baroque (1603), and is now the American national church. As it was being restored in 1992, Roman ruins were unearthed beneath the sacristy. **San Bernardo**, on the other side of the piazza, was built into one of the circular halls, probably used as a temple, that stood at the corners of Diocletian's Baths (see below); but the church most people come to see is **Santa Maria della Vittoria** (open 6.30–12 and 4.30–7.30).*

The victory this church commemorates is a sad one, the 1620 Battle of White Mountain, during the Thirty Years' War, where the religious and political freedom of the Czechs was snuffed out by the Catholic armies, an enslavement of an entire nation that was to last 298 years. Such a feat deserved the finest foolishness Baroque had to offer, and this is one of the most decorated churches in Rome. Giovan Battista Soria added the façade. Most of the interior is by Bernini and his pupils, the highlight being the ornate **Cornaro Chapel**, a kind of stage set squeezed into a shallow space; Bernini had once worked as a stage designer, and here he carries the conceit as far as to include members of the Venetian Cornaro family sitting in theatre boxes along the sides.

The show in this case is Bernini's remarkable sculpture of the *Ecstasy of St Teresa*, with a smirking angel about to drive a burning arrow into the soulfully agitated girl's heart (this is the vision Teresa had in Avila, Spain, in 1537, that started her on her career as a contemplative mystic and monastic reformer). You may take this as advertised, an illustration of 'divine love and mystic ecstasy', but nothing could be more cynically Baroque than taking an ostensibly religious subject and tossing in a dose of refined titillation. Not for nothing is Rome called the Eternal City; poor Teresa has been 5 seconds away from climax for over 300 years.

> Another bit of premature Baroque stands next to the church: the fountain of the **Acqua Felice**, built in 1587 for the reopening of the ancient aqueduct by Pope Sixtus V. The big gruesome fellow in the middle is Moses, by a sculptor named Prospero Antichi who was absolutely sure he could upstage Michelangelo's Moses, and do it even bigger. On the map, you can see the outline of the **Baths of Diocletian** preserved in the surrounding streets—from Via XX Settembre to Piazza dei Cinquecento, between Piazza della Repubblica and Via Volturno.

The biggest and one of the last of Rome's baths, it cost the dour Illyrian emperor enormous sums to build it in 298, when the empire was nearly bankrupt and his price-fixing, debased coinage and high taxes were crushing the life out of Europe.

> Walk a block south, to **Piazza della Repubblica**, where Rome's post-1870 planners came up with one of their very rare good ideas; the semicircular piazza is still often called Piazza dell'Esedra, and its curve follows the exedra of the baths, where ancient Romans could exercise and pursue their favourite ball games. The main entrance was where Via Nazionale enters the piazza, aligned directly with the vast central hall, now converted into the church of **Santa Maria degli Angeli**.

Michelangelo designed the interior, one of his less impressive attempts at architecture, and considerable tinkering by later architects, such as Vanvitelli, did nothing to improve it. Nevertheless, the original form of the hall stands out clearly; Michelangelo's respect for the ancients kept him from making any great changes to the form of the building. It remains the best example we have of the architecture of the late empire: short on aesthetics but long on engineering, with soaring concrete vaulting and gabled roofs. Much of the rest of the baths survives: the octagonal hall, now across Via Cernaia, converted into a planetarium, and the other ruins stretching up that street. The baths were well-preserved enough until modern times; the popes used their rambling spaces for centuries to house monasteries, granaries and even prisons. After about 1600 they began quarrying the stone, and huge areas of the original buildings disappeared.

> Besides the church, Michelangelo also built a pair of cloisters for the adjacent Carthusian monastery. These, along with other surviving rooms

Baths of Diocletian

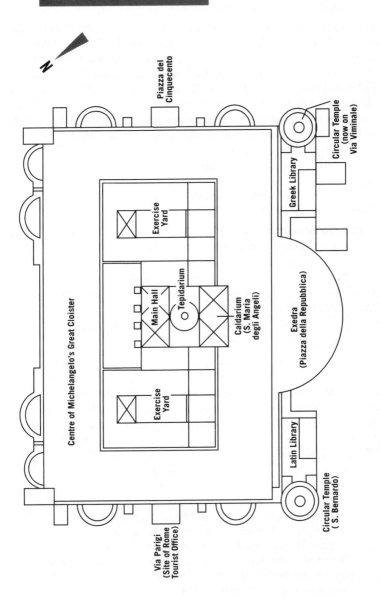

N

Piazza del Cinquecento

Circular Temple (now on Via Viminale)

Greek Library

Exercise Yard

Tepidarium

Main Hall

Caldarium (S. Maria degli Angeli)

Centre of Michelangelo's Great Cloister

Exedra (Piazza della Republica)

Exercise Yard

Latin Library

Circular Temple (S. Bernardo)

Via Parigi (Site of Rome Tourist Office)

*of the baths, now house the **Museo Nazionale Romano**. The entrance is on the south side of the complex, facing Piazza dei Cinquecento (9–2, Sun 9–1, closed Mon; L3000).*

Perhaps the greatest collection of Roman art and relics, for years most of it has been closed, awaiting 'restorations' that may never be finished. Few state museums in Italy could be called well-run, but this one is a scandal. After a century of existence, most of its exhibits are not even labelled yet; the small bit you are allowed to see is presided over by slovenly louts who can hardly be called away from their football magazines and cigarettes to turn on the lights. Downstairs, all that's open is the monumental cloister attributed to Michelangelo (if so, it would be his last work) and lined with antique statues. Most of these are Roman copies of Greek works, or copies of copies. At present your L3000 buys a chance to see the so-called **Ludovisi Throne**, with an exquisite relief of Aphrodite rising from the sea, and an athletic discus thrower, a superb copy of an ancient Greek work by Myron. It was sold to Hitler in 1938, but returned to Italy by Germany ten years later.

The **Palazzo Massimo** opposite Termini has long been earmarked as the museum's new home. It's been restored and painted a nauseous shade of peach), but exactly when the collection will be moved there is anybody's guess. When it does reopen, the treasures should include some exquisite Roman frescoes, from a villa in Trastevere (where Cleopatra may have stayed) and from Augustus' wife Livia's country residence.

*The end of this walk is the biggest square in Rome, creepy, disorienting **Piazza dei Cinquecento**.*

The piazza is named not after Rome's Renaissance century, but in memory of the 500 soldiers who died at Dogali, Ethiopia in 1887, a battle that so embarrassed the nation that it decided it had to conquer the country to save face; this led to an even bigger disaster at Adowa nine years later before they finally gave up. A sample of Rome's low life is on permanent display, sprawled around the northern fringes of the piazza. On Sundays, the city's Philippino population do their best to instil a note of festivity, gathering for picnics among the revving buses.

*At the southern end, there is **Termini Station** (named after the baths), begun by Mussolini though not finished until after the war. Perhaps the busiest station in Europe, the building itself is one of modern Rome's very few architectural triumphs. The postwar architects threw out Mussolini's planned façade of tired neoclassical colonnades, replacing it with a bold cantilevered roof projecting over the ticket hall and taxi area. The result is well planned and functional in every respect—if only there were somewhere to sit down. To the left, near the main entrance, is a surviving corner of the **Servian Wall**.*

Mosé

X: Ancient Churches / Big Basilicas

San Pietro in Vincoli (Michelangelo's *Moses*) 230
Santa Prassede   232
Santa Maria Maggiore   233
Museo Nazionale Orientale   237
San Giovanni in Laterano   237
Santa Croce   242
Museum of Instruments   242
San Lorenzo fuori le Mura   244

Start: Ⓜ *Cavour.*

Finish: *San Lorenzo, from where bus 492 will take you back to Piazza Venezia, Largo Argentina and Piazza Risorgimento near the Vatican.*

Walking Time: *4–5 hours, depending on how long you linger in the churches.*

Ancient Churches and Big Basilicas

Tramping from church to church through this dismal neighbour-hood will make you feel like a real *romero*, or medieval pilgrim, anxious to earn some divine dividends in the Bank of Grace. It includes four of the Seven Churches of Rome, and four others of venerable antiquity, located on the Esquiline Hill and along the fringes of Aurelian's eastern wall, where the earliest Christian communities lived. By the Middle Ages they stood picturesquely remote in open countryside, and only in the 19th and 20th centuries has the city grown to swallow them once more, creating holy islands in the doldrums of speculative sprawl.

To rephrase an old pop song, 'Purgatory is here on earth', and much of it is concentrated in this backside of Rome. It is infected with the terminal ugliness of everything within a mile of Termini station: the noise, dirt, gypsies, junkies, and solid masses of automobiles are an infernal cocktail brewed by Beelzebub himself. Any sinner who foots this walk deserves whatever indulgence the Church has decreed. Yet for all that, its rewards are of this world as well as the next. Step inside the cool incense-scented

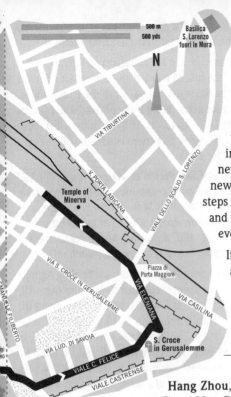

500 m
500 yds

Basilica
S. Lorenzo
fuori le Mura

N

VIA TIBURTINA

V. PORTA LABICANA

VIALE DELLO SCALO S. LORENZO

Temple of
Minerva

VIA S. CROCE IN GERUSALEMME

VIA EMANUELE FILIBERTO

Piazza di
Porta Maggiore

VIA ELENIANA

VIA CASILINA

VIA LUD. DI SAVOIA

S. Croce
in Gerusalemme

VIALE C. FELICE

VIALE CASTRENSE

darkness of a basilica, and as your eyes adjust to the light, you'll find some of the most beautiful things in Rome: richly-coloured, golden mosaics, shimmering and as magical as fairy tale illustrations, their sainted figures living in a fresh, springtime Never-never Rome that makes the cheap newness and cacophony only a few steps away seem shabby, tiresome, and a hurlyburly waste of just about everything good and fair.

If you do begin the walk mid-afternoon, when all the churches are open, you could stay in the San Lorenzo area for drinks and dinner (see listings pp.342-3)

lunch/cafés

Hang Zhou, Via di S. Martino ai Monti 33/C. Closed Mon. Fill up on Chinese food for L25,000.

Trattoria ai Monti, Via di S. Vito 13/a, just off Via Carlo Alberto. Closed Tues. Far above average trat fare; L40,000.

Cicilardone, Via Merulana 77. Closed Mon, Sun eve. Intimate, Italian; L50,000.

Cannavota, Piazza di S. Giovanni in Laterano. Closed Wed. The gourmet choice on this walk; specializes in fish and seafood; L40–50,000.

Bar Camilloni, Via A Depretis 77a. *Tavola calda* and *fredda* popular with office workers at lunchtime.

Roscioni, Via Principe Amedeo 17 (corner of Via Cavour). Delicious cakes.

Cottini, Via Merulana 286–7. Large, modern self-service near S. Maria Maggiore.

G Fassi (Palazzo del Freddo), Via Principe Eugenio 65–7. Closed Mon. Ten minutes' walk from Piazza Vittorio Emanuele. Fantastic fruit ice creams, milkshakes and sundaes made to century-old recipes and served in an airy 1920s ice cream parlour. Hot chocolate in winter.

*From the Metro station walk down Via Cavour to **Via di S. Francesco di Paola**, the unholy stair on the left that passes under a palace.*

This was once a steep little street, where, in 534 BC, Tullia purposefully drove her chariot over the corpse of the father she helped murder, the ancient king Servius Tullius. The stair is also known as the Salita dei Borgia, for in the palace above, Vanozza Cattanei held a garden party for her sons the Duke of Gandia and Cesare Borgia, in June 1497, after which the Duke was found belly-up in the Tiber (odds are, it was Cesare who did him in, but there's no better Get-Out-of-Jail-Free card than having a pope like Alexander VI for a dad).

*The steps lead up to the piazza of **San Pietro in Vincoli** (open 7–12.30 and 3.30–6), with its Renaissance portico and souvenir hawkers, whose predecessors predate even Michelangelo's Moses; for this was long one of the main pilgrimage churches in Rome. The nave has been undergoing restoration for some time, and, according to the sacristan, will never be finished until tourists begin to pay to see the church.*

The name 'St Peter in Chains' is derived from the manacles used by King Agrippa I in Jerusalem to bind Peter, which miraculously separated to free him (Acts XII, 1–13). In 440 the relics were given to Empress Eudoxia, wife of Valentinian III, who founded this church. It was practically rebuilt in 1475 by Sixtus IV who added the fine portico; and its titular cardinal Giuliano della Rovere touched it up as well, not knowing that one day he would be Pope Julius II and his tomb by Michelangelo—what was to be the 'greatest monument in the world'—would end up here and not in St Peter's. The 'tragedy of a tomb' as the artist bitterly called it, was to have 40 figures in a massive tabernacle, but disputes with the strong-willed Julius, the Sistine Chapel frescoes, and commissions from subsequent popes prevented Michelangelo from ever completing more than the highly individualistic and powerful figure of **Moses**, perhaps the closest anyone has ever come to capturing prophetic vision in stone, even if the end result bears an uncanny resemblance to Charlton Heston. The director of *The Ten Commandments*, Cecil B. DeMille, was also struck by the likeness. 'If it's good enough for Michelangelo, it's good enough for me,' he decided, after scribbling a beard on a photograph of the actor.

Under Moses's arm are the tablets inscribed with the Ten Commandments; his glance is furious because the Israelites are worshipping the golden calf; his 'horns' apparently come from the sculptor's reading of the Vulgate translated into Latin by St Jerome, in which the saint made a grievous error, describing Moses as *cornutum* ('horned') instead of 'radiant' as in the original Hebrew. Michelangelo signed this work, not with his name, but with his profile, formed by the upper part of the beard. Michelangelo also had a hand in the figures of Rachel and Leah on either side of Moses, but the rest of the tomb is by his students, not all of them so gifted; if Moses looks like Heston, the reclining effigy of Julius II could pass for the Caterpillar in *Alice in Wonderland.*

The famous chains, enclosed in a gilt and glass casket, may be seen in the chapel of the Confessio; in the Dark Ages pilgrims would queue for filings, one of the most potent holy relics to be had in Rome; for the virtuous the filings came right off, but the chains refused to yield a splinter for real sinners. Besides the chains, the Confessio holds a 4th-century sarcophagus, believed to have held the remains of the seven Maccabees, whose gruesome martyrdoms prefigured those of the Christians (Maccabees II,7). A 7th-century mosaic of St Sebastian (a rare portrayal as an old man with a beard) is well preserved in the left aisle, next to the macabre Hallowe'en tomb of Cardinal Aldobrandino.

> *From S. Pietro in Vincoli, turn right along narrow Via delle Sette Sale, criss-crossing the Esquiline, and passing on your right the Parco di Traiano on Colle Oppio. Follow the wall of the park, until you emerge on Via delle Terme di Traiano, with the brick hulks of the* **Baths of Trajan** *on your right; these were designed by Apollodorus of Damascus and incorporate some of Nero's Golden House. The* **Sette Sale,** *an enormous vaulted structure built as the reservoir for the baths, are behind the high walls of Palazzo Brancaccio. It's a popular place for wedding receptions, and you can often wander without problem into its opulent gardens from the entrance on Viale Monte Oppio. Just beyond, on the other side of the road, is the little piazza of* **San Martino ai Monti** *(open 7–12 and 4–7).*

S. Martino's 17th-century appearance evolved from one of Rome's most ancient titular churches, the 3rd-century *Titulus Equitius.* In the next century it was rededicated to St Martin of Tours by Pope St Sylvester, whose life was so uneventful that a more exciting one was invented for him. This included curing Constantine of leprosy and slaying a dragon that slid out of a crack in the Forum. Its wide, spacious interior is decorated with faded frescoes of Roman landscapes and scenes from the life of Elijah, painted in the 1640s by Poussin's brother-in-law Gaspar Dughet. In the left aisle, near the altar, note the rare fresco of the interior of Old St Peter's, complete with its giant pine cone, while towards the door another scene portrays the interior of St John Lateran in its pre-Borromini days. The priest, who is usually around in the morning, can let you into the grey netherworld of the ancient Titulus Equitius, under the crypt (though beware the treacherous steps going down); it contains a badly restored mosaic with the face of Pope Sylvester surrounded by what looks like mouldy ricotta. There are also some patches of fresco, tomb slabs, and pretty sculpted fragments.

*From S. Martino, turn left down Via Equizia past the ancient stone walls of the **titulus** under S. Martino. Via Equizia continues into Piazza di S. Martino, with its two medieval towers restored to look spanking new. Cross the road and take a sharp right turn, in front of the bike and scooter shop, down Via di S. Martino ai Monti, then turn left on Via di S. Prassede. Make sure you have at least two L500 coins, then enter, on the left, the modest pink doorway of the ancient church of **Santa Prassede**, the masterpiece of Rome's Carolingian Renaissance (open daily 7–12 and 4–6.30).*

Santa Prassede was built in 822 by Pope Paschal I, two decades after Charlemagne visited the city. Paschal hoped to create an edifice that would be compared to the magnificent ruins that lay on every side—from which he borrowed some beautiful columns (near the sanctuary) and pieces of architrave. But Paschal was not your typical Roman magpie: to embellish his churches he imported artists from Byzantium who brought with them the latest advances in mosaic work and painting. By this time the last lingering naturalism of the late classical period had vanished—not because Byzantine artists had forgotten how, but because they preferred to work in a less realistic, more spiritual vocabulary. In the triumphal arch these 9th-century mosaics portray New Jerusalem, Christ and the saints; in the apse SS. Peter and Paul introduce the sisters SS. Prassede and Pudenziana to Christ. The figures, though stylized, evoke a certain tenderness in the way the Apostles lay their hands on the shoulders of the two women.

Save your other L500 coin to illuminate the jewel of Santa Prassede, the right aisle's **Chapel of San Zeno**, or 'Garden of Paradise' built as a mausoleum for the Pope's mother Theodora. Gold-ground mosaics completely cover this little square vaulted chamber, of Christ Pantocrator, saints, Theodora (the lady with the square halo), and some very dignified, classical angels who look as if they never heard about the fall of Rome. Tradition holds that the piece of jasper in the corner shrine, bedecked with plastic flowers, is a fragment of the column where Christ was scourged. On a pillar outside the chapel is the bust and memorial of Santoni, carved by a 19-year-old Bernini.

The **Confessio** contains the relics of the sisters Prassede and Pudenziana, who, according to legend, hosted St Peter when he first came to Rome, and were especially known for giving refuge to Christians. The Church has now decided that they never existed, though the remains of some 30 massacred bodies were indeed discovered in a well (marked by the slab of porphyry in the Cosmatesque pavement). The corpse of the fictional Prassede is buried with the sponge she used to carefully mop up their blood.

*Continue along Via di S. Prassede into **Piazza di Santa Maria Maggiore**, marked by the sole mighty column to have survived from the Forum's Basilica of Maxentius.*

*In ancient times a temple of the mother goddess Juno Lucina stood here; when the 431 Council of Ephesus proclaimed Mary 'the Mother of God', it was the logical place to build her a church, too—the greatest of all Rome's Mary churches, **Santa Maria Maggiore**, an ancient basilica hidden behind Ferdinando Fuga's elegant, 18th-century shadow-filled façade and its incongruous **campanile**, tallest and fairest in Rome, a brightly decorated relic from the 1380s (open all day, every day) .*

Of the four Patriarchal Basilicas, Santa Maria Maggiore has best preserved its medieval appearance. Try to come at least once after nightfall, when the upper floor of Fuga's loggia is illuminated, and you can see the 12th-century mosaics from the medieval façade, telling the legend of the church's founding: on 4 August 352, the Virgin appeared simultaneously to a wealthy Christian and to Pope Liberius, directing them to build a church on the Esquiline. The two found the exact spot Mary wanted by a miraculous snowfall that neatly outlined the shape required. This porch, before Fuga added his façade, was long the favourite place to burn heretical books, as the Church decided such literary sacrifices were particularly pleasing to the Virgin.

S. Maria Maggiore's elegant basilican nave is almost unchanged since its construction by Pope Sixtus III in the 5th century, with the exception of the coffered ceiling by Renaissance architect Giuliano da Sangallo, gilded with the first gold brought back from the New World by Columbus—a gift to Alexander VI from King Ferdinand. Above the columns runs a remarkable cycle of 36 5th-century mosaic panels of Old Testament scenes, while the triumphal arch shows mostly apocryphal scenes of the youth of Christ. They are unfortunately a bit hard to see, unless you have binoculars; try to arrive at noon, when the light is brightest. The floor, of fine Cosmatesque work, dates from the 12th century.

Two enormous chapels were added to the Basilica's aisles by popes who feared that if they left it to posterity to build them the memorials they deserved, they wouldn't get any. The first, in the right aisle, is the sumptuous **Sistine Chapel** of Sixtus V, designed by Domenico Fontana in 1585 and built, literally, of the coloured marbles of the ancient Septizonium, which the Pope cannibalized into oblivion as part of his policy to convert pagan Rome into Christian Rome. But in his eagerness to build himself a really special chapel, the Pope inadvertently destroyed one of Christian Rome's most venerated treasures as well: Santa Maria Maggiore's *Presepio*, or Christmas crib, which since the 6th or 7th century stood

Santa Maria Maggiore

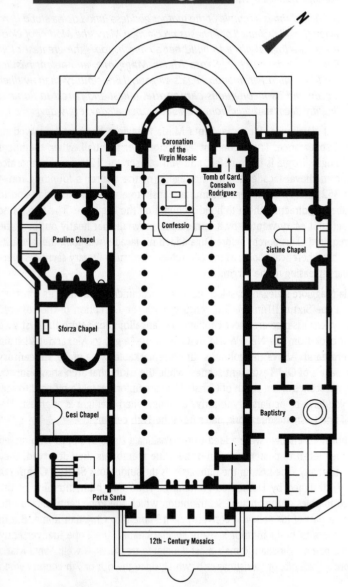

Coronation
of the
Virgin Mosaic

Tomb of Card.
Consalvo
Rodriguez

Confessio

Pauline Chapel

Sistine Chapel

Sforza Chapel

Cesi Chapel

Baptistry

Porta Santa

12th - Century Mosaics

outside the Basilica, in a grotto simulating Bethlehem's stable. Lined with precious mosaics and containing 13th-century crib figures by the great Arnolfo di Cambio, it was the place where the pope traditionally said Christmas Eve Mass (as Hildebrand did in 1075 when armed thugs suddenly burst in and dragged him off by the hair to the tower of their Ghibelline boss Cencius. When the people learned next morning where their Pope had been taken, they stoned the tower until he was released—whereupon he returned to finish the mass). But Sixtus V ordered Domenico Fontana to move the *Presepio* into his chapel, and despite all the architect's careful preparations (after all, this was the man who moved the Vatican obelisk) it collapsed and broke into bits. Only Arnolfo's charming figures of Joseph, the Magi, and animals survive (the Mary and Jesus are 16th-century replacements), locked away in the crypt beneath the wooden canopy, which is shaped like an ideal Renaissance temple and supported by four angels. If you can find a sacristan, you may persuade him to open the gate.

The Borghese pope, Paul V, bears the onus for the hyper-decorated **Pauline Chapel**, across the nave of Sixtus' pile, though to his credit nothing was destroyed to build his precious inanity. An altar of semi-precious stone holds an ancient and highly venerated icon of the Madonna and Child known as the *Salus Populi Romani*, painted by angels. This is the place to come on 5 August, when during mass white petals fall like snow from the dome in memory of the basilica's legendary founding.

Fuga designed the porphyry-pillared baldacchino over the altar; below in the Confessio a colossal, ungainly statue of Pius IX kneels in prayer before the basilica's chief relic, five pieces of wood bound with iron said to be nothing less than the genuine manger from Bethlehem. Shimmering above the altar is the magnificent apse mosaic of *The Coronation of the Virgin*, made in 1295 by Iacopo Torriti, who is believed to have reproduced the subject of Sixtus III's original, honouring Mary's new divine status. To the right of the apse is the most beautiful tomb in the church, of 13th-century Cardinal Consalvo Rodriguez, by Giovanni Cosmati.

> *The basilica's rear façade is currently behind scaffolding, but once the work is complete be sure to leave by the exit just beyond the Cardinal's tomb and walk down the magnificent ripple of steps. The **Obelisk** at the bottom, in Piazza dell'Esquilino, came from the Mausoleum of Augustus. Walk past it to the far end of the piazza and turn left on Via Urbana for **Santa Pudenziana** (open 8.30–12 and 3–6) dedicated to the mythical sister of St Prassede.*

The ground level has risen 23 steps since the church was built over a room of a Roman bath sometime in the 4th century. According to tradition, this is the location of the house where the sisters entertained St Peter; its chief relic is half of the table where he would celebrate mass. The present façade with faded frescoes is 19th century, though conserving two ancient columns and a medieval relief of the holy sister over the door. Rather disappointingly the interior has been restored often, at one point cutting off a section of S. Pudenziana's beautiful claim to fame, its apse adorned with the earliest Christian mosaic in Rome (390). Artists had yet to decide on the familiar iconography of the saints; here all have become honorary Romans, especially the Apostles in their senatorial togas. SS. Pudenziana and Prassede stand with laurel wreaths, ready to crown SS. Peter and Paul, while Christ, enthroned in the centre, sits in what looks like Jupiter's throne before a classical city.

> *Retrace your steps back round S. Maria Maggiore and down Via Carlo Alberto (the busy street to the left, aiming straight at the front façade). On the right side of the street, behind the church of S. Vito, is the* **Arch of Gallienus***, originally a gate in the Servian wall, dedicated to Gallienus in 262 AD. Further down Via Carlo Alberto is Rome's biggest, busiest, smelliest market square,* **Piazza Vittorio Emanuele***, surrounded with 19th-century porticoes.*

Here, on any weekday morning, you will see Rome's gypsies trading stolen clothes and purses for vegetables. The garbage-blown garden in the centre is a favourite siesta flop for Rome's down and out; local merchants and residents have been exerting themselves for years, trying to persuade the city to clean up some of the faeces and needles, so far without much success. It has a ruined fountain from the time of Alexander Severus, in ancient Baroque; nearby stands a fenced-in brick mass that once held the marble **Trophies of Marius** (later moved to the Campidoglio).

> *Directly behind this, in the northernmost corner, is the* **Porta Magica***.*

The 'Magic Door' is all that survives of the Villa Palombara. The story goes that an alchemist once found hospitality with the *marchese* who owned it, and in return left a small lump of gold and a page of magic formulas. In 1653, after years of trying to decipher this recipe for the 'Great Work', the *marchese* had the magic page carved on to a door of his villa, putting it at the disposal of all. Now broken, you can barely discern the symbols of the planets and the mysterious inscriptions in Latin and Hebrew. A typical one, over Mars reads: 'He who burns with water and washes with fire makes a heaven of earth and of heaven a precious land.'

> *From the west corner of this dire piazza, take Via Leopardi, built, like everything in the immediate environs, over the Gardens of Maecenas, Augustus' fabulously wealthy minister and patron of the arts.*

Earlier, during the republic this land was haunted by witches, and was used to bury paupers and crucify slaves, whose skeletons were left rattling on their crosses; Maecenas and other plutocrats built their villas over the troubled grounds to exorcize the spooks.

> *Where Via Leopardi widens into Largo Leopardi is the newly roofed* **Auditorium of Maecenas** *(open 9–1.30, Sun 9–1, closed Mon; April–Sept also open Tues, Thurs and Sat 4–7; L3750) or perhaps his Nymphaeum, with an apse and tiered seats, where Virgil, Horace, and other great poets may have recited their latest works to their patron.*

> *From here, cross Via Merulana. Just to the left, at Via Merulana 248 is the* **Museo Nazionale Orientale**, *one of the few places in the world that tries to answer the question posed by Edward Lear in one of his greatest poems: 'Who or why, or which, or* **what**, *Is the Akond of SWAT?' It's closed for restoration, but due to be reopened in the near future. Lear fans can phone them © 735 946, for the latest news.*

The finds from SWAT, in northeast Pakistan, are fascinating. There Hellenistic, Buddhist, and Hindu influences combined to create sensuous and graceful reliefs from the 1st–5th centuries AD, of dashing fellows with big moustaches and Carmen Miranda costumes, and women with hourglass figures outlined in delicate draperies. There are strange and colourful hundred-armed gods from Tibet; 14th-century Last Judgement scenes, armour and helmets from Japan; Chinese porcelains, bronzes, and funeral statues; 9th–16th-century Islamic ceramics; ancient gold and silver art of Parthia, showing the hellenizing influence of Alexander the Great; bronze idols from Luristan (1500–700 BC); and 3rd millennium BC pots with Paul Klee animals from Tepe Siyalk in Iran.

> *From the museum it's a shady but otherwise unrewarding 15-minute hike (or short hop on bus 93) south on Via Merulana to the Patriarchal Basilica of* **San Giovanni in Laterano** *(St John Lateran); nothing less than the 'Mother and Head Church of Rome and the World', the first church founded by Constantine, and still the city's cathedral. (There is some bomb damage to the frescoes in the portico, but it is not serious.)*

Lying just within the Aurelian Wall, the site originally belonged to a patrician named Plautinius Lateranus, executed by Nero for plotting against him; the property, however, maintained the family name even when it passed to Fausta, the wife of Constantine (*Domus Faustae in Laterano*). Constantine, after 19 years of marriage, had Fausta smothered in a hot bath, but in the meantime he used her palace (the site of the present baptistry) for a church council with Pope Miltiades in 313. It became a cult centre for the new religion, and soon all the surrounding land was donated by Constantine to Rome's Christians; St John's itself was built over the barracks of the emperor's personal guard. When building it, the Christians chose one of the forms they knew best—a basilica—which with its five naves was designed to stand up to the architecture of the pagans. As it contained the *cathedra*, or chair of Rome's bishop, it became the city's *cathedral*. And although nothing remains of the original structure (sacks by Vandals and Normans, two earthquakes and several fires have seen to that) it has all along maintained the same basilican form that inspired countless later churches.

The Lateran was the chief papal residence before Avignon, and was regarded as the Vatican is today. Popes were crowned here until the 19th century. Charlemagne came here to be baptized in 774. Five Councils of the Church were held here in the Middle Ages. But there have been other moments that the Church would prefer to forget, especially the 897 posthumous trial of Pope Formosus. The Romans were notorious for mocking dead popes, but this was an extreme case, especially since the sick charade was acted out in the basilica by Formosus' successor and arch-enemy, Stephen VII, who had the grinning corpse exhumed and dressed in full pontifical regalia. The papal lawyer drilled the mummy with questions. Formosus, though given time to respond, failed to defend himself. Declaring him an usurper, Stephen cut three fingers from his benedicting hand, and tossed the rest of him in the Tiber.

The church building itself has suffered its ups and downs, too. When Boniface VIII declared the first Jubilee in 1300 it was the wonder of the age, and the priests with their long rakes couldn't scrape in the pilgrims' donations fast enough. By 1350, when papal finances demanded another Jubilee year, Petrarch mourned that 'the mother of all churches stands without a roof, exposed to wind and rain'. It was collapsing again just before the 1650 Jubilee, when Innocent X ordered Borromini to repair the interior; the façade needed to be replaced in the 1730s, and was the subject of a competition, in which Alessandro Galilei eventually triumphed over his 22 competitors with a stretched out version of Maderno's façade for St Peter's, striking for the deep chiaroscuro in its arches. Along the roof a giant Baroque Christ and saints model the latest in marble draperies. The central bronze door originally hung in the Senate House in the Forum; to the right is the Porta Santa, opened only in Holy Years; and to the left stands a whopping great statue of Constantine, carted here from his baths on the Quirinale.

Borromini's solution to reinforcing the basilica's structure was to fill in the spaces between the pillars, creating massive piers with alcoves for more overgrown 18th-century Apostles, glaring down at puny humanity like Roman emperors of old. The intricate, geometric Cosmati floor is matched by the rich ceiling by Daniele da Volterra. Although sheer size is the main effect, there are occasional details worth looking for: Giotto's fresco of *Boniface VIII's Jubilee*, just behind the first

San Giovanni in Laterano

(St John Lateran)

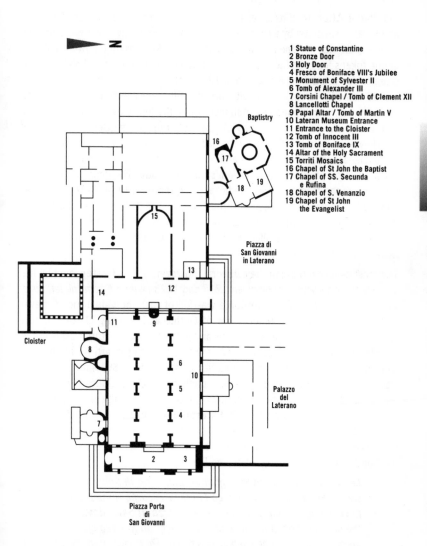

N

1 Statue of Constantine
2 Bronze Door
3 Holy Door
4 Fresco of Boniface VIII's Jubilee
5 Monument of Sylvester II
6 Tomb of Alexander III
7 Corsini Chapel / Tomb of Clement XII
8 Lancellotti Chapel
9 Papal Altar / Tomb of Martin V
10 Lateran Museum Entrance
11 Entrance to the Cloister
12 Tomb of Innocent III
13 Tomb of Boniface IX
14 Altar of the Holy Sacrament
15 Torriti Mosaics
16 Chapel of St John the Baptist
17 Chapel of SS. Secunda
   e Rufina
18 Chapel of S. Venanzio
19 Chapel of St John
   the Evangelist

Baptistry

Piazza di
San Giovanni
in Laterano

Cloister

Palazzo
del
Laterano

Piazza Porta
di
San Giovanni

pier on the right, and on the next pier a Hungarian-made 1909 memorial to Pope Sylvester II (see also S. Croce, below), who crowned St Stephen, first king of Hungary, in 1001. The memorial incorporates part of his original tombstone, said to sweat and rattle when a pope is about to die. The other chapels contain plenty of carefree Baroque, with some Jesuit-style cut-out saints.

The **Papal Altar**, with its silver reliquaries said to contain the heads of SS. Paul and Peter, is sheltered by a festive Gothic baldacchino. In the Confessio is the fine bronze tomb slab of Pope Martin V, on whom the Romans drop flowers and telephone tokens for good luck. The apse had to be reconstructed in 1885, and the mosaics you see now are a copy of a 13th-century copy by two Iacopos, Torriti and da Camerino, from a much older original; the scene shows a dove descending on the Cross, worshipped by a reindeer, while the four Gospels flow like rivers and the Virgin and saints stand by. At the end of the left transept is the Altar of the Holy Sacrament (1600), sheltering half of St Peter's communion table, from S. Pudenziana; the bronze columns and lintel are said to have been melted down from the ships' prows from the Forum's Imperial rostra. The right transept holds the tomb of the most powerful medieval pope, Innocent III (d. 1216), who was poisoned in Perugia (some suspect through his slippers, though in the morning he was found in the cathedral stark naked). His remains were brought here in 1891; frescoes tell the story of his life. The 14th-century Cosmatesque tomb of Boniface IX is in the chapel to the right.

The most beautiful thing in the cathedral, however, is the **cloister**, built by the Vassalletti (father and son) between 1215 and 1223 (*entered from the left aisle, open 9–5, adm L1000*). Once Rome was full of such individualistic medieval jewels, well outside the mainstream of Gothic and reviving classicism; this cloister, with its pairs of spiral columns and glittering 13th-century Cosmatesque mosaics, is the most striking survival of this lost chapter in art. All around the cloister walls, fragments from the earlier incarnations of St John's have been assembled, a wistful collection of broken pretty things that includes an interesting tomb of a 13th-century bishop by Arnolfo di Cambio. Across the nave, in the right aisle, is the entrance to the small **Lateran museum** (*9–1 and 2.20–4.30; L2000*), laden with ecclesiastical finery and pomp—golden vestments, golden reliquaries, and so on; the best piece is a 14th-century gilded silver cross called the Constantiniana, depicting Adam and Eve.

Leave the basilica from the right transept, or north front, with its impressive 1586 façade by Domenico Fontana, incorporating two earlier bell towers in its design. This gives on to **Piazza di San Giovanni,** *base for the tallest* **Obelisk** *in the world, just over 100 ft of red granite from the Temple of Ammon at Thebes, erected by Thothmes IV in the 15th cen-*

*tury BC and stolen by Constantius II in 357 for the Circus Maximus. In the piazza's southwest corner is the **Baptistry of St John**, nothing less than the first one in Christendom, built by Constantine in the 320s in an octagonal form copied by baptistries throughout Italy. Open 9–1, 3–5.*

And it was in this holy place that Cola di Rienzo went over the top, even by Roman standards; after a bath in the baptismal font, he spent the night in vigil and emerged in the morning dressed like a Liberace in golden spurs, self-christened as 'Knight Nicolas, Friend of the World'. It feels ancient, but like St Peter's, it magically repels dust. The green basalt basin, where Rienzo took his presumptuous bath, is surrounded by eight porphyry columns, and there are two famous bronze doors on either side: one set from 1196, etched with scenes of how the Lateran basilica appeared at the time, opens into the **Chapel of St John the Evangelist**, with alabaster columns by the altar and an exquisite 5th-century mosaic with birds and flowers in the vault; the other doors, traditionally from the Baths of Caracalla (though they may be original to the Baptistry), 'sing' with a low, harmonic sound when slowly opened. The baptistry has two other chapels, **SS. Secunda and Rufina** with another exquisite 5th-century mosaic, of vines on a blue ground, and the **Chapel of S. Venanzio** with mosaics of Dalmatian saints made in the 640s, a time when artistic rigor mortis had already begun to set in.

*Opposite the Baptistry, adjoining the Basilica, is the **Lateran Palace** (no adm), address of the popes before they became voluntary 'Babylonian Captives' in Avignon in 1309. After the massive fire of 1309, which destroyed church and palace, it remained a ruin until 1586 when Sixtus V had it rebuilt by Domenico Fontana. On the east of the piazza are two holy relics that survived flames, **Scala Santa** and **Sancta Sanctorum** (winter 6.15–12.15 and 3–6, summer 6.15–12.15 and 3.30–7.15).*

The Scala Santa is the legendary stair from Pontius Pilate's palace in Jerusalem, descended by Christ after his judgement and brought to Rome by Constantine's mother, St Helena. Serious pilgrims ascend them on their knees—the only way permitted, ever since 1510, when Martin Luther crawled halfway up and heard a little voice saying 'The just shall live by faith, not by pilgrimage, not by penance', whereupon he did the unthinkable; he stood up and walked back down. At the top of the stairs is the Holy of Holies, the **Sancta Sanctorum**, or Chapel of St Lawrence, built in 1278 as the pope's private chapel . Through the locked gate you can see a miraculous 'handless' portrait of Jesus, painted by angels, frescoes attributed to Pietro Cavallini, and a mosaic of Christ, perhaps by the Cosmati.

*East of the Scala Santa is a **Tribune** erected by Fuga in 1743 to house copies of mosaics from the great dining hall, or **Triclinium** of the medieval palace. Across the lawn is **Porta Asinara**, one of Rome's best*

preserved ancient gates, and nearby **Porta di San Giovanni**, *rebuilt in
1564. Follow this stretch of the Aurelian wall east, or take tram 13, 30 or
30 along Viale Carlo Felice, which after five blocks widens into a piazza
before the charming rococo façade of* **Santa Croce in Gerusalemme**
(7–12.30, 3.30–7) another of the Seven Churches of Rome.

According to tradition, Constantine's mother Helen not only found Pilate's stair in
Jerusalem, but the True Cross as well, and brought a piece of it back to her palace,
later converted into S. Croce in Gerusalemme. In Roman legend it is linked to
Gerbert (Sylvester II), the pope of the dread millennium, which everyone believed
would be the end of the world. The election of the Frankish Gerbert, educated in
the Muslim schools of Toledo, was a fearful portent; one of the few real scholars
of the day and inventor of a hydraulic organ, he was believed to be a wizard. He
reputedly owned a prophetic bronze head (like the Templars three centuries later)
which told him, among other things, that he would die in 'Jerusalem', and in
1003, while saying mass in this church, he dropped dead.

S. Croce was rebuilt in 1144 (the date of the campanile) and in 1744, when
Domenico Gregorini and Pietro Passalacqua added the bold convex façade and
oval vestibule. The Cosmati pavement dates from the first rebuilding; the gaudy
quattrocento fresco in the apse, of St Helen finding the Cross, is by Antoniazzo
Romano; the tomb below, of Charles V's confessor Cardinal Quiñones, is by
Jacopo Sansovino; the delicate baldacchino is from the 1600s. Steps from the right
aisle lead down into the **Chapel of St Helen** (built over St Helen's bedroom),
the jewel of S. Croce, with a gorgeous Renaissance vault mosaic of an avuncular
Christ designed by Melozzo da Forli in 1494. The statue of St Helen was converted from a Juno found in Ostia. Off the left aisle is the **Cappella della Croce**,
built in 1930 to shelter pieces of the True Cross, a larger chunk from the Cross of
the Good Thief, and the genuine finger St Thomas stuck in Christ's side.

> *To the left of S. Croce are the old Granatieri Barracks, built around a
> large 4th-century hall called the Temple of Venus and Cupid, and now
> housing three museums: the* **Historical Museum of the Infantry**
> *(daily 9.30–12, closed Aug; free);* **Museum of the Grenadiers of Sar-
> dinia** *(open Tues, Thurs, Sat 10–12, free); and in the barracks, the*
> **Museum of Instruments** *(open Mon–Sat 9–1.30; L2000) .*

The museum houses musical instruments that once belonged to tenor Evan Gorga
(d. 1957), famous as *La Bohème's* first Rodolfo. But an obsession for collecting
took over his operatic career, and these instruments (only one of his 30 collections, purchased by the state when he declared bankruptcy) have ended here:
trumpets, lutes, viols, and lap organs that look as if they had just been lifted from
Renaissance paintings, the golden 16th-century Barberini harp, and one of the
three surviving pianofortes by Bartolomeo Cristofori, signed and dated 1722, 12

years after he invented the instrument. There are folk instruments from around the world, some made of armadillo shells and jawbones; also hurdy-gurdies, ocarinas, music boxes, portable harpsichords, and early record players. Recordings are provided, though the speakers aren't always turned on; do ask if they're not.

> From Piazza S. Croce, bear left along Via Eleniana into bustling, tram-filled **Piazza di Porta Maggiore**. From here you could either catch tram 30 up to San Lorenzo, or, if you really want to punish yourself, have a wander round the sights of this ghastly neighbourhood.

The arches along Via Eleniana are part of the Aqua Claudia, an aqueduct begun by Caligula and completed by Claudius in 52 AD, carrying spring water from Subiaco 68 km away to slake Rome's thirst. This aqueduct, and the even longer Anio Novus, were incorporated, one on top of the other, into Aurelius' Porta Prenestina, now known as **Porta Maggiore**, arching over a section of the ancient Via Prenestina, for Palestrina. Even more peculiar is the great block of travertine, carved with circles to symbolize bread pans. This is the **Baker's Tomb** (30 BC), built for a certain Marcus Virgilius Eurysaces, who earned his fortune by supplying to the state the more nutritious half of the daily bread-and-circus. In the frieze you can see the deceased in his toga, directing his slaves in their work.

> On the far side of the piazza, directly below the railway line (modern Via Prenestina 17) is the entrance to one of Rome's most remarkable sights, the **Underground Basilica of Porta Maggiore** (closed to regular admission; phone Ripartizione X © 6710 2070 for details).

Discovered only in 1916 while work was being done on the main line into Termini station, the Basilica, unlike Rome's other ruins, was never quarried or covered with the debris of centuries—it was built underground for a secret, possibly illegal religious sect in the 1st century AD, and not long after, closed up and forgotten. Its elegant stucco reliefs are fascinating; scholars, unable to decipher the sect's beliefs from the décor, call them 'neo-Pythagorean'. Its form, intriguingly, is that adapted by later churches, with a nave, two aisles, an apse, a porch.

> There are more treats in store for cultural masochists: walk back along the tracks on Via Giolitti to the dismally situated and misnamed **Temple of Minerva Medica**. A large ten-sided structure from the 4th century, it is believed to have been a nymphaeum in the Gardens of Licinius; its dome, before caving in, inspired many artists of the Renaissance. Further down Via Giolitti, on the right, is **Santa Bibiana** (1625).

The church was a proving ground for two of Rome's Baroque trinity. Bernini's Palladio-inspired façade was his first architectural work, and the pious, rapt statue of S. Bibiana above the altar his first religious commission. To the left, above the arches, are Pietro da Cortona's vibrant frescoes of the saint's life, his first important work in Rome, especially the one showing Bibiana refusing to sacrifice to idols.

> *Sensible folk will by now be on tram 30 heading north to yet another of the Seven Churches of Rome, the* **Basilica of San Lorenzo fuori le Mura** *(if you're still around here, catch the tram at Piazza Porta Maggiore). The basilica (open 6.45–12 and 3–6.30, summer 3.30–7.30) is wedged between Campo Verano Cemetery, where all Rome's Catholics eventually go, and Mussolini's unremittingly dull University City.*

Lawrence was a 3rd-century deacon with spunk; when commanded by the Roman authorities to hand over the treasures of the Church, he produced all the sick and destitute people he could round up. 'Grill this wise guy,' the Roman police sergeant must have growled, and his minions obeyed—literally. But as they toasted him on the gridiron, Lawrence kept his sense of humour. 'You can turn me over now,' he told his tormentors. 'I'm done on this side.' Even the worst Romans, battened on gladiators' blood, had to admire the courage of such martyrs, which, in no little way, led to their own acceptance of the new religion.

Lawrence's poor body was interred in the catacombs here, and in the 4th century a cemetery basilica was dedicated to him by Constantine; a second church, dedicated to the Madonna, was built nearby in 440; and in 1216, in response to the increased number of pilgrims visiting the basilica, Pope Honorius III stuck the churches together by chopping off their apses, which gives the basilica its extraordinary form. None of this is apparent from the façade, with its medieval portico rebuilt after the war (when S. Lorenzo had the misfortune to be the only church bombed in Rome), decorated with 13th-century frescoes on the life of St Lawrence and Manzù's tomb of Italy's post-war leader, Alcide de Gasperi.

The nave of the basilica, formerly the church of the Madonna, has a Cosmatesque pavement, pulpit, paschal candlestick, episcopal throne, and other 12th-century furnishings, though the mosaic on the inside of the triumphal arch dates back to the 6th century and shows Pope Pelagius II offering the basilica to Christ. The long chancel that begins here was once the nave of Pelagius' older basilica, with its beautiful Corinthian columns and embroidered marble windows. SS. Lawrence, Stephen, and Justin are buried in the crypt under the altar, while in the chancel is the 'medieval' tomb of Pio Nono (Pius IX, d. 1878); after spending his last eight years a self-made prisoner in the Vatican, he was probably glad to get out, even as a corpse. The fine old cloister, beyond the sacristy of Pelagius' basilica, is lined with a hotch-potch of ancient columns and fragments of sarcophagi. From the basilica you can visit the **Catacombs of S. Cyriaca**, where Lawrence originally lay, *open 3–5.30* if enough people are interested, though they offer little unless you're a true catacomb fiend.

Circus Maximus	248
Santa Sabina	249
Santa Prisca	251
San Saba	252
Pyramid	253
Protestant Cemetery	253
Monte Testaccio	254
San Paolo fuori le Mura	255

Start: Ⓜ *Circo Massimo. Or bus 90, 90B or 94 from Piazza Venezia to the first stop along Circus Maximus.*
Finish: *San Paolo fuori le Mura, close to* Ⓜ *S. Paolo.*

XI: The Aventine to San Paolo

Walking Time: *Three hours, including a bus or metro ride from Piramide to S. Paolo fuori le Mura.*

Tomba di Keats

The Aventine is one of the few places in Rome where you can hear birds singing, where old villas, churches, convents, and flats amid lofty pines and tidy gardens enjoy a rare tranquillity on nearly traffic-less streets.The mood, however, changes abruptly as you descend towards Porta San Paolo and Testaccio, still one of the city's more entrenched proletarian neighbourhoods. Its hectic, rundown charms are becoming increasingly popular among Roman trendies—little theatres and new restaurants are opening up, and rents are rising—all hoping that one of Rome's biggest un-happenings, the conversion of the neighbourhood's landmark slaughterhouse into a massive cultural centre, will one day be more than a kiss to build a dream on.

A good walk for a Monday morning when the museums are closed; or for a Sunday, combining an early morning visit to Porta Portese market just over the Tiber with the 10 am Gregorian chant at Sant' Anselmo. It fits in well with an afternoon jaunt to Ostia Antica (see p.398-407) or with a late morning excursion to EUR (p.333-5).

lunch/cafés

Aim to be in Testaccio for lunch, as it holds this walk's best eateries, along with an excellent morning food market.

Lo Scoppettaro, Lungotevere di Testaccio 7, ✆ 574 2408. Closed Tues. Traditional Testaccio tratt—so lots of offal—but pasta for the queasy; L40,000.

Caffè de la Seme e la Foglia, Via Galvini 18, corner Via Zabaglia. Closed Sun. Trendy little jazz-playing café popular with students from the nearby music school. Excellent sandwiches.

Piccolo Alpino, Via Orazio Antinori 5, ✆ 574 1386. Closed Mon. Chaotic family-run pizzeria/trattoria justifiably famous for its *fettuccine* with mushrooms, peas and cream; L25,000.

Gennargentu, Via Ostiense 21–23, ✆ 575 9817. Closed Mon. Open evenings only from 6 pm. Sardinian pizzeria famous for its *pizza al Gennargentu*, with *salsiccia*, mozzarella and tomato; L15,000.

Apuleius, Via Tempio di Diana 15, Roman specialities and seafood in 1st-century AD Roman house; L70,000.

Rosticceria di Pietro, P. Porta di S. Paolo 6. Closed Tues. Italian fastfood; L12,000.

Da Felice, Via di Mastro Giorgio 29. Closed Sun. Authentic, unprettified tratt near Testaccio's market; L25,000.

Il Canestro, Via Luca della Robbia 47. Closed Sun. Restaurant above a wholefood shop; vegetarian, macrobiotic lunches and dinners; L30–40,000.

The Aventine to San Paolo Fuori le Mura

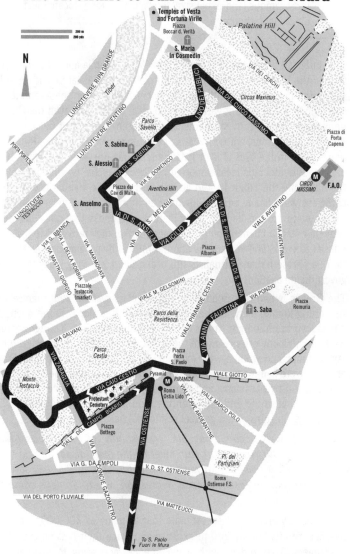

I Carmini Burana, Via Luca della Robbia 15. Closed Wed. An old *enoteca* converted into a trendy restaurant; L40,000.

Checchino dal 1887, Via di Monte Testaccio 30. Closed Sun eve and Mon. The most famous (and expensive) Testaccio trattoria, located just outside the old slaughterhouse.

In Republican times, the depression of the Vallis Murcia and its Circus Maximus formed the boundary between the high rollers on the Palatine and what Juvenal called 'the mob of Remus', the solidly plebeian quarter on the Aventine hill. The psychological distance, however, was so great as to make even the Circus Maximus seem like a penny sideshow, beginning in the days of those nasty twins, Romulus and Remus, whose Aventine cause ended on the point of Romulus' Palatine dagger. In the eyes of later Palatine residents, the Aventine was a hotbed of dangerous democratic ideas imported by Greek merchants, who lived just below the hill along the Tiber. In 494 BC, when the double standards of the Palatine patricians were finally written down for all to see on the Twelve Tables, the plebeians were so appalled by their blatant unfairness that they invented that venerable Italian phenomenon, the general strike; they retreated to the Aventine, refused to work, and vowed one another mutual help—the first 'Aventine Secession', a phrase Italian journalists still use when a left-wing party walks out of a government coalition.

The Greeks, when not eroding the Roman class system, kept themselves busy subverting Roman piety. In the hidden caves on the slopes of the Aventine they introduced the midnight rituals of Dionysos and Bacchus. Though secret, their wild, often bloody orgies came to the attention of the Senate and in 186 BC thousands of men and women were executed for participating in the rites. From then on, men were banned from taking part. In the imperial age, the old plebeian hill was usurped by patricians, and rents have remained high ever since. But you could say that in the end the Aventine won the battle of the hills—while the Palatine lies in ruins, it is a genteel residential neighbourhood.

> *This walk begins along the 'grandstands' of the **Circus Maximus**, which for fans of **Ben Hur** must be the most disappointing ruin in all Rome: it was too convenient a quarry, and all that has survived is a banked, horseshoe-shaped depression, where Romans come to walk their dogs.*

But in its day archaeologists estimate that as many as 300,000 Romans could squeeze into its 600 by 200 m expanse and place their bets on their favourite charioteers. They did so with a vehemence, according to Juvenal's famous passage: 'Now that no one buys our votes, the public has long since cast off its cares; the people that once bestowed commands, consulships, legions and all else, now meddles no more and longs eagerly for just two things—bread and circuses.' Since the Cæsars had to provide for an estimated 150,000 idlers, it was their insurance against revolt. But in the time of the first kings the horse races held between the Palatine and Aventine had a religious significance; the pounding of hooves apparently awoke the powers of the underworld, promoting fertility and appeasing the spirits of the dead; the competitive aspect brought out the courage of warriors, who worshipped the agriculture-war-god Mars. The Etruscan king Tarquinius Superbus built the first stands around the old course, and a temple dedicated to the fertility goddess Ceres on the Palatine, overlooking the Circus.

Early piety soon went by the boards. Jérôme Carcopino writes how the Roman crowd found 'in the circus itself a miniature projection of the universe and, as it were, an epitome of its destiny'. In the astrological symbolism of the race, the obelisk on the central *spina* ('backbone') symbolized the sun; the 12 starting stalls of the chariots, or *carceres*, became the 12 symbols of the zodiac; the seven laps, measured by seven wooden eggs, and later seven bronze dolphins, evoked the planets or days of the week. Augustus added the imperial box (*pulvinar*) linked to his house on the Palatine, the prototype of the famous *kathisma* of the Byzantine emperors in Constantinople's Hippodrome. Beneath this, in the massive *cavea*, the first tier of seats was of marble (for Senators), the second of wood, and the third was standing room only, though unlike the Colosseum the sexes were not separated; Ovid recommends a day at the races to pick up girls or husbands. There would be plenty of time for making passes as well as bets; from the time of Caligula it was usual to have 24 races spread through the day, some with two-horsed chariots (*bigae*), or with acrobatic jockeys leaping from one horse to another, though always it was the four-horsed chariots, the *quadrigae* that were the most exciting—and costly. To finance the men and horses, there grew up four factions, each represented by a colour: the Whites and Greens, and Reds and Blues (often the favourites of the Emperors), who had their stables and headquarters around Campo de' Fiori. The emperors also had to deal with the unhappiness of punters who lost, placating them with gimmicks like 'the hail of eatables' and free raffle tickets.

> From the Circus Maximus, walk up rose-scented Clivo dei Publicii to Via di S. Sabina and the pretty orange trees and parasol pines of **Parco Savello**. After enjoying the excellent view from the park, exit through the door in the corner to Piazza Pietro d'Illiria, with a glowering mask fountain in the wall and what many people consider the loveliest church in Rome, the early Christian basilica of **Santa Sabina**. (Open 6.30–12.45 and 3.30–7.)

In ancient times this was the site of the temple of Juno Regina, the patroness of Rome's Etruscan arch-rival Veii, who was seduced into changing sides in 392 BC. According to tradition, Sabina, who lived nearby, was a Roman matron converted to Christianity by her Greek slave Seriphia. They were martyred together, and in 425 a Dalmatian priest named Pietro d'Illiria built this basilica. In 1219 Pope Honorius III gave it to the fiery St Dominic, and the Dominicans have held on to it ever since, restoring it to its original appearance in 1936. The 15th-century portico houses ancient sarcophagi (the waving lines symbolize eternal life) and what may be the oldest wooden church doors in the world, carved from cypress in the 5th century with parallel reliefs of Old and New Testament scenes, made with consummate devotion and a creeping forgetfulness of the proportions of the human body.

The beauty within S. Sabina is that of a pure, contemplative simplicity, so rare in Rome that it takes a moment to adjust; the eye, instinctively by this point, expects at least a little Baroque curlicue or eyeball-rolling saint *somewhere*. The ceiling is of simple wood, supported by 24 beautiful Corinthian columns, probably from the temple of Juno, linked by arches decorated with discrete marble inlay. The delicate windows, illuminating the nave with a soft, magical light, were reconstructed from 9th-century fragments; their glass, as in the originals, is really a mineral called selenite. A portion of the 5th-century mosaic inscription remains over the door, referring to the founder, with allegories of the churches of the Jews and Gentiles who have converted to the new faith. In the floor of the nave is Rome's only mosaic tomb (c. 1300), and the painting in the apse by Taddeo Zuccari, the only jarring note, is believed to represent the same subject as the original mosaics. A chapel in the left aisle contains Sassoferrato's almost anti-Baroque 1643 *Madonna del Rosario*, painted with pre-Raphaelite clearness. By the door, on a pedestal, sits the black 'martyr's stone' that the devil hurled at St Dominic, though his aim was off. If there are any Dominicans around, you can ask them about it, or better yet, ask to see S. Sabina's beautiful cloister (1225).

> From the basilica, continue right on Via S. Sabina to the next church, grimy **Sant'Alessio** (open 8.30–12 and 3.30–5 (6 in summer), almost as old as Santa Sabina but completely remodelled in the 18th century, preserving only its intricately worked bell tower outside and sections of fine Cosmatesque pavement in its pastel interior. To the left of the door is one of Rome's more curious chapels, hung with the stair that St Alexis fell down (not one of the more exciting martyrdoms!). Proceed down Via S. Sabina to Giambattista Piranesi's delightfully quirky **Piazza dei Cavalieri di Malta**, lined with baby obelisks and classical trophies, surrounded by a dark wall of cypresses. Peep through the bronze-lined

keyhole, at the monumental entrance of the **Priory of the Sovereign Order of Malta** for the famous view of St Peter's, framed at the end of a tree-lined path. The gate will open only with advance permission from the Order's headquarters at Via de' Condotti 68.

In the Roaring '900s it was probably just as hard to get in, for this was the home of Rome's big boss, Alberic, who watched over his fief from this commanding spot over the Tiber. In the 1100s it was bought by the Templars, and when they were suppressed for heresy in 1312, it was inherited by the Knights Hospitallers of St John, later to become the Knights of Malta. The Knights no longer wait for the popes to unleash them against Saracen and Turk; since they left Malta, this social club for old nobles bestirs itself to assist hospitals, its original job during the Crusades. The Priory, with its lovely gardens, is the residence of the Grand Master (currently a kinsman of Winston Churchill), and of the Order's ambassadors to Italy and the Vatican City—which seems like an enormous state in comparison. The Knights, however, get their own car number plates (S.M.O.M.), and the Aventine is a good place to see their modern-day squires, the chauffeurs, awaiting them double-parked. The real reason for visiting the Priory is to see Piranesi's other attempt at architecture, **S. Maria del Priorato**, a fancy rococo ornament emblazoned with knightly motifs that makes you wish he had been given more commissions.

In the southeast corner of the square is the neo-Lombard **Sant'Anselmo** *(open daily 8 am–7.30 pm), the Benedictine seminary church and one of the best places in Rome to hear Gregorian chant (Sun at 9.30 am); it also has a 3rd-century black and white mosaic of Orpheus in the cloister, though you will probably never be allowed to see it.*

From outside the church take Via di Porta Lavernale to Piazza di Sant'Anselmo, then Via di S. Anselmo (just past the hotel) to Via Icilio. Now turn left through the gardens of Piazza Albina for Piazza di S. Prisca.

Not a trace remains of the famous Temple of Diana that Servius Tullius built here in 540 BC to steal Nemi's thunder as a cult centre for the Latin people. Diana, in her turn, was upstaged here by the more personal religions practised at **Santa Prisca**, *on the north side of the piazza. Open 8–12 and 4–7; if closed ring at the parish house on the left.*

The church occupies the site where Prisca and Aquila, a married couple mentioned in a letter by St Paul, entertained St Peter. In the 2nd century a sanctuary was built next to their house—not dedicated to the saints but to their most obdurate pagan rival, the Persian god Mithras. In the year 400, with Christianity the victorious cult, the Mithraeum was vandalized, covered up by the new church, and only rediscovered in 1958. The early Christians would be appalled to learn that the Mithraeum is now S. Prisca's chief claim to fame, and would perhaps take secret delight in the fact that access is possible only with special permission. The stucco statues of Mithras slaying the bull and a reclining Saturn (made from an amphora) that they hacked to bits have been carefully put back together, and the rare frescoes they axed have been restored. On the right wall is a scene of the highest Roman sacrifice, that of a bull, ram, and pig, called the *suovetaurilia*; on the left wall, a procession of initiates and a sacrificial feast. One room, believed to have been a nymphaeum, contains pieces of glass, stucco reliefs, and ceramics.

*To reach the next church, take Via di S. Prisca down to busy Viale Aventino (you could catch bus 94 although it is only a ten-minute walk); cross when you dare, and continue straight on for Via di S. Saba; as you do, brave a look down Viale Aventino to the equestrian **statue of Scanderbeg**, the national hero of Albania, in his pointy Scanderbeg cap; he visited Rome in 1466 and was hailed as a hero for his guerrilla fight against the Turks (really a Greek named George Castrioti, the Turks called him after Alexander the Great—**Iskander Bey**—for his bravery. In Rome he lived on what is now Via Scanderbeg, near Piazza Quirinale). Via di S. Saba leads up to the hill's second summit, or 'Little Aventine' and the intriguing medieval church of **San Saba** (7–12 and 3.30–6.30).*

When the Arabs invaded Syria and Jordan in the 7th century, as many monks as could fled to Italy; in Rome they built a monastery and S. Saba, in the Greek style, with three apses. Much has been added since: the delightful quattrocento loggia, which shelters a curious relief of a knight and falcon, perhaps made by the first monks; the door, from the early 1200s by Master Jacopo, the head of the Cosmati tribe, who also worked on the superb mosaic floor. The centre apse has a lovely baldacchino, and in the triumphal arch, a Renaissance painting of the Annunciation; in the truncated fourth aisle are frescoes on the life of St Nicolas, from the 1200s; detached 7th-century frescoes from the original church can be seen in the corridor leading to the sacristy.

*Behind San Saba is Piazza Bernini, the humble, litter-blown centre of the Little Aventine, which lacks the patrician quality of its bigger sister. There's little reason to linger—there is a little market and a couple of snack bars; from the front of S. Saba, take Via Annia Faustina, lined with blocks of flats, down to Viale Giotto and one of the best-preserved gates in the Aurelian wall, the Porta Ostiense, renamed **Porta San Paolo** long after St Paul walked through it on his way to execution. While the inner side of the gate is Roman, the outside face was reconstructed by Belisarius in the 6th century. If you can fight the traffic to the gatehouse,* *you'll find the little* **Museo della Via Ostiense** *(open Mon–Sat 9–1; L4000), with scale models of Imperial-era Ostia, frescoes from a painted tomb and plaster casts of milestones and tombs from the ancient road. Looming beyond the gate is one of Rome's oddities, the* **Pyramid of Gaius Cestius***, built in 12 BC by a wealthy praetor and tribune of the people.*

Cestius spent some time in Egypt when the Romans were in the midst of their post-Cleopatra craze, carrying off obelisks and immersing themselves in the cult of Isis. Cestius went one step further, and in terms of terrestrial immortality, he made a sound choice, for while the tombs of the emperors themselves have suffered countless indignities, his pyramid survives intact, even if it was built, as the inscription claims, in a manner that any self-respecting Egyptian would have disdained. The pile is made of brick, covered with white marble from Luni, and completed in only 330 days.

Aurelian incorporated the pyramid in his wall, and the English and German communities incorporated the wall into their **Protestant Cemetery** *or Cimiterio Acattolico (ring at the gate at Via Caio Cestio 6, around the corner from the pyramid. Open Mar–Sep 8–11.30 and 3.20–5.30; Oct–Feb 8–11.30 and 2.20–4.30; closed Wed.) Don't worry too much about the sheet of rules warning of rabid cats.*

The Romans have become rather sentimental about this most romantic and loveliest of graveyards, and often quote Shelley's preface to Adonais: 'The Cemetery is an open space among the ruines, covered in winter with violets and daisies. It might make one in love with death to know that one should be buried in so sweet a place.' But throughout the 19th century, burials had to made at night, by torchlight, for fear that the mourners would be harmed by the intolerant populace; and until 1870 neither crosses nor inscriptions referring to heaven were permitted, on the grounds that no salvation was possible outside the Church.

Only a handful of people came to watch Keats' (1796–1821) burial in the lovely lawn of the Old Cemetery, to the left as you enter. 'Here lies one whose name was writ in water' is the epitaph he composed for himself in his sad and bitter last days, believing his poetry a failure; entombed with him are the letters from his sweetheart Fanny, which, once he knew he was dying, he could no longer bear to open. Buried next to him is his friend Severn, who survived him by 65 years. Shelley, whose description of the cemetery was prophetic, drowned the year after Keats died; his ashes lie next to the grave of his friend Trelawny, under the Aurelian wall with the inscription 'Cor cordium' (heart of hearts) and a verse from *The Tempest*. A map given by the caretaker will help you locate the other 'Acatholics' buried here: Goethe's only son, Julius; J. Addington Symonds, the Renaissance historian; Antonio Gramsci, philosopher and founder of the Italian Communist party; and the American sculptor William Story, who sculpted the 'Angel of Grief' despairing over his wife's tomb.

> *Continue down Via Caio Cestio to Via N. Zabaglia. Just to the left is the quiet* **Rome British Military Cemetery** *(daily 8–12 and 1–4), a touching memorial to 429 British troops killed during the liberation of Rome. To the right rises the uncanny weed-tonsured bulge of Rome's youngest and most peculiar hill,* **Monte Testaccio***. Access is officially forbidden unless you have permission from Ripartizione X.*

Norfolk, Virginia's Mt Trashmore may be the biggest mountain of rubbish, but Monte Testaccio was the first. Testae means 'potsherds' in Latin, and that is what Testaccio is made of; nothing but broken amphorae (mostly used to bring cheap wine from Spain) which Tiber longshoremen mysteriously but systematically piled here, behind the ancient warehouse district of Marmorata. If nothing else, Monte Testaccio is the world's biggest monument to the butter-fingered: over the centuries enough amphorae were broken to build a mound 35 m high and 1000 m round, covering seven city blocks. Its strangeness has attracted both extremes of the human condition: the pious would come here to perform the Stations of the Cross, while the not-so-pious came for low-life fun and the Testaccio games, a wild urban rodeo with live pig slicing and other sports. Rome's communal wine cellars were dug into Monte Testaccio's flanks, for the densely-packed potsherds were found to maintain an even temperature year round.

> *Nowadays Monte Testaccio has as many car-repair grottoes as wine cellars, though in spite of (or because of) its seediness clubs and theatres are beginning to sprout here and there, as revealed by a stroll around the hill on Via di Monte Testaccio. The Tiber side of Via di Monte Testaccio is blocked by the massive buildings of the old slaughterhouse, the* **Ex-Mattatoio***, entered by way of an impressive 1889 gate crowned by a bronco-busting angel.*

The city has big plans to make this into a Roman Beaubourg, with theatres and auditoriums, exhibitions space, libraries, and restaurants, each plan more exciting and unfinished than the last. In the meantime it houses an old people's day centre and stables for the carriage horses, and hosts the occasional rave or rock gig.

> *From here, follow the mighty Aurelian wall back to Piazza San Paolo. The station at the end of the piazza is for the train to Ostia (see p. 398) and the Metro to the Colosseum or EUR; the FS Ostiense Station is just behind in Piazzale dei Partigiani (the former Piazza Adolf Hitler). This*

walk, however, continues by bus from the top of Via Ostiense, (no. 23 or 673), passing through a mile of gas-works and industrial-commercial sprawl.

*In the Dark Ages this stretch of road was one of the marvels of Rome, sheltered by a 1.5 km portico, supported by 800 marble columns, built by Pope John VIII in the 870s to shelter pilgrims between Porta S. Paolo and **San Paolo fuori le Mura**, (St Paul's Outside the Walls) and around the basilica a separate walled suburb grew up , 'Giovannipoli'.*

The colossal portico may as well have been constructed of breadcrumbs for all that has survived; Giovannipoli, pummelled by the Normans in 1084 and every other roughneck coming up the Tiber, was given its *coup de grâce* in an 1823 fire that began when two roofers, horsing around on top of St Paul's, spilled a bucket of hot coals. One fell forgotten in a gutter, and in the night the most beautiful of the four Patriarchal Basilicas and its suburb went up like a torch.

When condemned, St Paul, as a Roman citizen, merited the relatively painless death of decapitation along the road to Ostia. According to an embarrassing tradition, his head bounced three times, bringing forth three springs, now occupied by the Abbazia delle Tre Fontane (in EUR). Paul's head ended up in the Lateran, while over the grave of his trunk Constantine built the first shrine. Theodosius and his children, Honorius and Galla Placidia, erected a basilica over the site, and over the years it was as frequently restored and embellished as it was pillaged. It became the special church of the kings of England, who were honorary canons here until the Reformation; the abbots of St Paul's were automatically made Knights of the Garter. The nearly total reconstruction in the early 19th century followed the outline of the original basilica, making it the second largest church in Rome.

The entrance faces the Tiber, through a massive but pointless courtyard called the Quadriporticus, relieved by four tall palms and the gold of the 19th-century mosaic on the façade that blazes in the setting sun; in the middle a giant marble St Paul, sword in hand, seems ready to thump any art critics. On the right, one of the few things to survive the fire, is the original bronze **Holy Door** with panels inlaid in silver, brought from Constantinople in the 11th century. The long, long nave, lined with a double forest of granite columns, glossy marbles, and polished stones, has the cool, solemn majesty of an ice palace, although there are critics who say its shiny newness better evokes the feel of an original basilica than any other. The famous frieze along the nave and aisles has mosaic portraits of all 265 popes, from St Peter on; the first 40 are survivors from the fire. According to Roman tradition, the world will end when there is no room for a new pope's portrait, and as there are only eight spaces left after John Paul II, you may just as well go for the high-calorie *gelato* you passed up yesterday.

The **Triumphal Arch**, adorned with mosaics paid for by Galla Placidia in the 5th century, survived the fire. Art Deco is not would you expect from those times, but these bear an uncanny resemblance to Roosevelt's public works murals of the early '30s: a severe-looking Christ in the centre circle, worshipped by winged symbols of the Evangelists, two angels with pointers, and the Elders of the Apocalypse bearing crowns, all posed as if for the last number of a Hollywood musical. Underneath, porphyry columns support another relic of the original church, the ornate 1285 baldacchino by Arnolfo di Cambio, built over the confessio containing the tomb of St Paul. Whether or not Paul's remains are still there is a matter of debate; his bronze sarcophagus was looted by the Saracens in 846, when they picked up some five tons of gold and silver treasure from St Paul's and St Peter's, all of which went down to Davy Jones' locker off Sicily's coast. If the confessio is open, you can see the inscription PAULO APOSTOLO MART, carved in a stone slab pierced by two holes for the purpose of inserting cloth to be made sacred by the proximity of his relics. Just to the right of the altar is a massive, fantastically medieval Paschal Candlestick from the 12th century. The mosaics in the apse with a giant Byzantine Christ and smaller saints were made by Venetian artisans in 1220.

The short transepts, covered with precious marbles, are closed by altars of malachite and lapis lazuli donated by Czar Nicholas I, one of many heads-of-state who contributed to the rebuilding; even Mohammed Ali of Egypt sent a precious column or two. Of the chapels, only the one just to the left of the apse survived the flames; designed by Carlo Maderno, it houses a fine 13th-century Crucifix and the altar where St Ignatius and his followers took the formal vows that made the Jesuits a religious order. Off the right transept are the lovely **Cloisters**, finished in 1208 and similar to those of St John Lateran, with their glittering mosaics and columns that delightfully shun symmetry. The basilica's little **Pinacoteca** contains a copy of the stone slab over St Paul's tomb along with a souvenir stand and some highly missable art.

If you want to continue exploring, head onwards to the Abbazia delle Tre Fontane (see p.335) on bus 223 or do the Via Appia walk (XII) backwards. Take bus 766 from the side of St Pauls to its terminus in Via Ardeatina, walk a few steps south to the crossroads with Via di Tor Carbone, and take the 765 east to the point where it crosses the Via Appia. Alternatively catch bus 170 from outside the basilica to Piazza Venezia via Trastevere.

San Giovanni a Porta Latina   261

Museo delle Mura   263

Catacombs of St Calixtus   264

Mausoleum of the Fosse Ardeatine   265

Catacombs of St Domitilla   266

Catacombs of St Sebastiano   266

Circus of Maxentius   267

Tomb of Cecilia Metella   268

Via Appia Antica   268

Start: *Piazzale Numa Pompilio, by bus no.90 from Piazza Venezia; 92 from Termini Station; 118 from Colosseum.*

XII: Via Appia Antica

Via Appia Antica

Via Appia Antica, the 'Queen of Roads' has, like many a queen, a public and a private personality. The public one that most people see is the two mile stretch nearest Rome, a shooting gallery with pedestrians for targets, where tour buses drop trippers at the catacombs. The second, the more personal, carries on past the last catacomb, cutting straight and true across the Roman *campagna* into the horizon. This is the Appian Way that her lovers remember, beautiful and haunting, where parasol pines, acanthus, and wild flowers create an ideal classical background for ancient tombs and villas, their bricks blasted by time into hollow shells and forlorn stumps, to say nothing of the four-wheeled love-nests parked along its verges. Where marching legions, ox carts, and imperial pony-express riders once created the world's first traffic jams, the silence is only broken by a distant cicada, the droning of a lazy fly—or groans emerging from a steamy-windowed Fiat.

There's no easy way to see the most beautiful parts of the Appia Antica; ideally, hire a bike. To see everything on foot would require an entire day, the most comfortable walking shoes you own, and a healthy constitution. Otherwise, allow five hours by foot and bus to see at least one of the three catacombs, the other sights, and some of the ancient road. Details on transport back to the centre are given at the end of the walk.

Note: Besides the three catacombs open to the public, there are two others—the Jewish Catacombs, Via Appia Antica 119A, and the Catacombs of Pretestato, Via Appia Pignatelli 1—that are only open by request from the pope's archaeologists (Ponteficio Istituto di Archeologia Sacra, Via Napoleone III 1, ℰ 735 824).

lunch/cafés

Sorry, no gourmet road food, but typical Roman and Italian dishes that taste better for being al fresco. The classical stretch of Via Appia Antica is a glorious place for a picnic. Buy provisons at the Appia's only alimentari—just beyond the junction with Via Cecilia Metella.

Nameless Trattoria, Via Appia Antica 68. Lunch only. Closed Mon. Opposite Domine Quo Vadis? Full of locals; *gnocchi* and *pasta e fagioli*; L25,000.

Orazio, Via di Porta Latina 5. Closed Tues. Garden terrace; good grilled dishes; moderate prices.

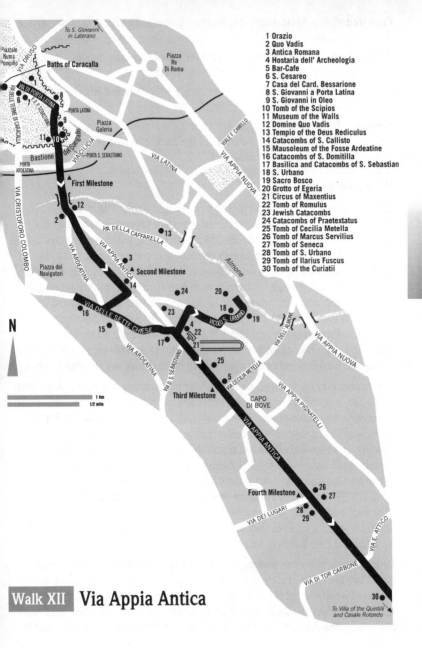

1 Orazio
2 Quo Vadis
3 Antica Romana
4 Hostaria dell' Archeologia
5 Bar-Cafe
6 S. Cesareo
7 Casa del Card. Bessarione
8 S. Giovanni a Porta Latina
9 S. Giovanni in Oleo
10 Tomb of the Scipios
11 Museum of the Walls
12 Domine Quo Vadis
13 Tempio of the Deus Rediculus
14 Catacombs of S. Callisto
15 Mausoleum of the Fosse Ardeatine
16 Catacombs of S. Domitilla
17 Basilica and Catacombs of S. Sebastian
18 S. Urbano
19 Sacro Bosco
20 Grotto of Egeria
21 Circus of Maxentius
22 Tomb of Romulus
23 Jewish Catacombs
24 Catacombs of Praetextatus
25 Tomb of Cecilia Metella
26 Tomb of Marcus Servilius
27 Tomb of Seneca
28 Tomb of S. Urbano
29 Tomb of Ilarius Fuscus
30 Tomb of the Curiatii

Walk XII Via Appia Antica

Quo Vadis?, Via Appia Antica 38. Standard pastas and chops on a pretty terrace; moderate.

Antica Roma, Via Appia Antica 87. Your chance to dine outside among the evocative ruins of a columbarium; moderate.

Hostaria dell'Archeologia, Via Appia Antica 139. Pasta and grills under masses of wistaria; moderate.

No-name bar, corner Via Appia Antica and Via di Cecilia Metella. Cold buffet, sandwiches and tables outside in the back, run by a garrulous old man; get your cold picnic drinks here.

Via Appia Antica

The Via Appia Antica was built in 312 BC by Consul Appius Claudius the blind, in those distant days when a wealthy citizen thought it his civic duty to contribute to the good of the state. It originally linked Rome to Capua, and was later extended to the port of Brindisi, making it Rome's chief route of conquest in the East. By 4th-century BC standards it was a superhighway, 4 m wide, with two wide pavements on either side, and though built primarily to move armies as quickly as possible, it was soon lined with inns, workshops, farms, villas, tombs, catacombs, and on one unhappy occasion, by 4000 crosses bearing the followers of Spartacus. When Hadrian had it repaved, it cost him 190,000 *sestercii* (about £430,000) a Roman mile—and that's non-union labour. Yet after 1750 years large sections of flagstone paving still remain, a record our modern road builders may have trouble matching.

The Appian Way these days is best known for its catacombs and tombs. According to Roman law, inherited from the Etruscans, all burials had to be outside the *pomerium*, the sacred ground of the city itself, and like all consular roads the Via Appia was soon crowded with cemeteries and the elaborate mausoleums of the wealthy. Later the early Christian community built some of its most extensive catacombs here—the word itself is believed to come from the catacombs of San Sebastiano, located near a dip (*ad catacumbas*) in the road. The Christians called them simply cemeteries. Popular romance and modern cinema notwithstanding, they were never places of refuge from persecution or anything else; as cruel as the ancient Romans could be, they regarded bodies, even of executed 'criminals', as inviolate and their tombs as sacred.

Later Romans, as you've probably noticed by now, lacked any qualms their ancestors may have had and so, you may well ask, why is the Via Appia Antica so well preserved when the rest of extramural Rome has been mercilessly buried under tons of concrete? The catacombs, a main pilgrimage destination in the Dark Ages, were first pillaged by the Goths and the Lombards, and then by relic hunters; after the

Saracen raid of 847, the whole Via Appia declined, and became infested with cut-throats and malaria. The catacombs were abandoned and forgotten (with the exception of the Catacombs of San Sebastian), and honest traffic on the Via Appia was reduced even further by the toll gate erected in 1300 by the Caetani family in the tomb of Cecilia Metella. To get around them, the Via Appia Nuova was constructed, and the Via Appia Antica was left to push up weeds until the 19th century. The great archaeologist Giambattista De Rossi rediscovered the lost catacombs of St Calixtus in 1850, while the sculptor Antonio Canova deserves the credit for the innovative idea of leaving the tombs, or at least casts, along the road where they were found instead of carting them off to rot in a museum. Recently it has been announced that the whole area will some day be preserved as part of an urban park.

With the baths of Caracalla up on your right, walk south from Piazzale Numa Pompilio to the narrow fork in the road; the one on the right is Via di Porta San Sebastiano. Just beyond the fork is the ancient church of **San Cesareo in Palatio**, *though you'll be lucky to find it open.*

The discovery of a great black and white mosaic of 2nd-century sea monsters suggests that S. Cesareo was built over a Roman bath. In the late 16th century it was given a façade by Giacomo della Porta and an exquisite wooden ceiling of gold and blue, which colourfully complements the Cosmatesque choir, ambo and altar.

Next door is a peaceful little garden and 15th-century villa, known as the **Casa del Cardinale Bessarione**.

The Greek Cardinal Bessarione (d. 1472) was a great humanist, diplomat, and scholar who came to Rome during the luckless Ecumenical Council called by Pope Eugenius IV, to reconcile the Eastern and Western Churches. Bessarione stayed on in Italy, translated many works from Greek to Latin and wrote on Plato. Although charmingly preserved inside, with frescoes and Renaissance furniture (after being hidden for centuries under the fixtures of an inn), the villa hasn't been open for donkey's years.

From here, cross over the grass to the left fork, Via di Porta Latina, a walled country lane that about 450 m on, leads back to a little cul-de-sac on the left, the site of **San Giovanni a Porta Latina** *(9.30–12.30 and 3–7), a delightful country church often in demand for weddings.*

Built in the 5th century by St Gelasius I, and fiddled with often after, what you see today is essentially 12th century, with a fine husky campanile, a Romanesque portico, and a charming, richly carved marble well; within, it has three apses in the Greek style, and some curiously diaphanous 12th-century frescoes, lit by three lacy selenite windows.

Just before the Porta Latina is the little octagonal chapel of **San Giovanni in Oleo,** *'St John in Oil', built in the early 16th century and attributed to Bramante. It marks the site of the strange story of an attempt by the authorities to deep-fry the good saint, from which he emerged 'refreshed'. The disappointed Romans let him go. The chapel, never open, has a pretty frieze added by its restorer, Borromini.*

To the right of the chapel is the entrance to one of Rome's quieter public gardens, which you can cut across for Via di Porta S. Sebastiano, turning right as you leave the park to see if the **Sepolcro degli Scipioni**, the family tomb of the Scipios, has been reopened. If the restoration isn't complete you might be able to arrange to see it by phoning Ripartizione X, ✆ 6710 2070.

Discovered in 1780 under a 3rd-century house, the tomb is one of the oldest on the Via Appia, built around 290 BC. It was melancholy enough to ignite Byron's romantic imagination in *Childe Harold*:

> *Niobe of nations! there she stands*
> *Childless and crownless, in her voiceless woe,*
> *An empty urn within her withered hands,*
> *Whose sacred dust was scattered long ago;*
> *The Scipios' tomb contains no ashes now;*
> *The very sepulchres lie tenantless*
> *Of their heroic dwellers.*

In truth it never did contain ashes; the Scipios claimed descent from the gods, and instead of cremation they were entombed in marble sarcophagi. The best one (replaced by a cast) is of the tomb's builder, Consul L. Cornelius Scipio Barbatus, conqueror of the Samnites, whose grandsons were Rome's generals in Spain during the 2nd Punic War, and whose great-grandson, Scipio Africanus, defeated Hannibal at Zama, bringing that war to a close. A brilliant, charismatic, and humane individualist when the rest of the Romans were stolid conformists, Scipio Africanus was the first Roman leader to stand out, a kind of proto-Cæsar, and his remarkable family (including his brother, Scipio Asiaticus, who introduced Eastern luxuries and dancing girls to Rome, and Cornelia, his daughter and Rome's first liberated woman, mother of the revolutionary Gracchi) were round pegs in a square empire. The ultra-conservative Cato (a hero to modern conservatives, though one of the most nauseatingly cruel figures in Rome's cruel history) forced Scipio Africanus into retirement, and he died in 183 BC near Naples, shunned by an ungrateful Rome. Hence he was not buried here, though many of his kin are; and like the mausoleums of the Cæsars, it exudes tristesse.

A small Christian **catacomb** branches off from the gloomy halls of the Scipios' tomb; in front, steps lead down to a wonderful mossy, fern-festooned **Colum-barium**, its dovecote niches still holding a few urns. This, however, pales next to the the 1st-century AD **Columbarium of Pomponius Hylas**, nothing less than the most luxurious columbarium ever discovered, embellished with wonderfully preserved mosaics, stucco, and frescoes. Once again, to gain access, you have to twist the arms of the folk at Ripartizione X.

Pomponius Hylas himself is believed by archaeologists to have been a kind of Roman cemetery plot salesman, and you can just imagine him in a checked toga, intoning: 'Hurry, hurry, hurry, the best niches are going fast …'.

> *Continue down Via Porta S. Sebastiano, through the **Arch of Drusus**, which once carried an aqueduct; beyond stands the mightiest gate surviving in the Aurelian Wall, **Porta San Sebastiano**, originally the Porta Appia; Honorius, Belisarius, and Narses restored and fortifed it, and now its twin canister towers contain the **Museo delle Mura**. Open 9–1.30, Tues and Thurs, staffing levels permitting, also 4–7, closed Mon; L3750.*

Exhibits tell the story of the Aurelian walls and Via Appia Antica; among the more interesting items is an ancient country calendar called the *Menologium Rusticum Colutianum*. Best of all, this is your chance to play Roman patrol along the wall, as far as the powerful **Bastione del Sangallo** built by Antonio da Sangallo the Younger; as this corner of the city is rural—you can just see the Vittoriano rearing up on the horizon—this section of walls offers the quaint illusion of still defending Rome from its greatest enemy: the endless traffic spewing along the boulevards just outside.

> *Beyond the gate (be sure to glance back as you leave, to see its best side) the **Via Appia Antica** stretches uninvitingly ahead. There's a 118 bus stop just before the gate, which can save you a couple of kilometres of fumes, and stops at the entrance of the Catacombs of St Calixtus (don't get off at the sign for the parking lot!); alternatively, persevere past the run-down bars and petrol stations, trying to pick out traces of ancient tombs in the grimy walls. In a kilometre you'll arrive at a triple fork in the road; just before it, to the left of the Appian way, is the little church of **Domine Quo Vadis?**(1637). Open 7.30 am–6.45 pm.*

The tale goes that Peter, in fleeing from the dangers of Rome, met Christ here coming the other way. 'Whither goest thou, Lord?' Peter asked. 'I am going to Rome to be crucified once more,' was the reply. As the vision departed the shamed Apostle turned back, soon to face his own crucifixion in Nero's Circus. The curious footprints inside, said to be Christ's, are actually a cast of a pagan ex-voto found in the Catacombs of S. Sebastiano.

> *The fork to the right is Via Ardeatina; the middle road, as marked, leads to the parking lot of St Calixtus, while Via Appia Antica continues to the left. To see one of Rome's more obscure sights, the **Temple of the Deus Rediculus**, press on down Via Appia Antica 100 m, turning left at Via della Caffarella, continuing, now on an unmade track, to a farm with a pretty terracotta and jonquil-hued temple (no access) in its grounds.*

This 2nd-century AD 'temple' (which was never dedicated to the gods of ridicule, as it sounds, or even, as once believed, to the gods who turned back Hannibal) was actually the tomb of Annia Regilla, the wife of perhaps the wealthiest man in antiquity, Herodes Atticus, whose vast villa occupied the next two miles or so just beyond the Via Appia. Herodes made his fortune à la Arabian Nights—his father found a buried treasure under the Acropolis in Athens, and he married a wealthy heiress. Cultured and educated, he was Marcus Aurelius' professor of rhetoric and the great benefactor of Athens, erecting a number of public buildings. When his wife Annia died in childbirth, his grief was proverbial; and he built in his gardens a rich tomb of contrasting colours of brick and stucco decoration that has survived remarkably intact.

> *From here, retrace your steps to the above crossroads; those travelling by foot, bike, or car, should turn up at the pretty road to the catacombs' parking lot, to avoid a ghastly stretch of Via Appia; if you're on bus 118 continue to the gate of the **Catacombs of St Calixtus**, the first official Christian cemetery in Rome, and burial place of the first bishops of Rome. Open for guided tours only, winter 8.30–12 and 2.30–5, summer 8.30–12 and 2.30–6, closed Wed; L6000.*

St Calixtus is the most visited of the catacombs, and becomes surreal at peak efficiency, when all seven different language groups are conducted on a synchronized dance through the labyrinth, the Germans padding past one way, the French arguing just beyond the next wall, while echoes of Polish drift down from above. Although all the catacombs have their unique points of interest, the truth is, once you've seen one, you've seen them all, and you'll find a more appropriately dead atmosphere in the equally interesting Catacombs of Domitilla (see below).

But why did the early Christians create these enormous termitaries? Few other Mediterranean cities have catacombs (Naples, Syracuse, Malta, and the Greek island of Milos are among those that do), and all exist thanks to tufa or some other easily excavated rock. There may also have been a problem of space; everyone wanted to be near a martyr in the hopes of preferential treatment at the pearly gates. And when the galleries became too long—some go on for kilometres—they added another floor below, and another, and another; St Calixtus, the largest, has five levels, and has yet to be completely explored. Most of the burials were in simple shelves carved in the walls, called *locali*, or in the floors, where the shrouded bodies would be laid, and sealed with a marble or terracotta slab; and it's a sad comment on the infant mortality of the day to see row upon row of tiny *locali*. The *arcosolia* are a bit fancier, topped by an arch and often decorated with the bits of painting or stucco that constitute the catacombs' chief interest, representing the earliest stages of official Christian iconography. Artistic standards weren't very high, though this reflects more on the dire state of late Roman imagination than on the Christians. Most elaborate of all are the *cubicula*, or family vaults.

St Calixtus was appointed caretaker of this cemetery by Pope Zephyrinus before he himself became pope, and it was used into the 4th century. The main attraction is the **Crypt of the Popes**, where the first bishops of Rome were interred after their martyrdoms: SS. Pontianus, Anterus, Fabian, Lucius, and Eutychianus, whose names are preserved in Greek inscriptions, and it is assumed, on the basis of an inscription placed here in their memory by Pope St Damasus, that other martyred popes were buried here as well—SS. Stephen I, Dionysius, and Felix I, and Sixtus II, who was killed in this very cemetery in the persecution of Valerian. Next to it is the **Crypt of Santa Cecilia**, where her body originally lay before Pope Paschal I moved it to the church of S. Cecilia in 821; it contains a copy of Stefano Maderno's famous statue of the saint. The tour takes in the other highlights of the second floor—including the fascinating 3rd-century **Crypts of the Sacraments** and two mummies in glass cases.

> *From St Calixtus, you can return to the Via Appia and catch the 118 to San Sebastiano or beyond (see below), or continue south along the private rural road to S. Sebastiano, skipping another stretch of the still unlovely Via Appia, or take the road west to Via Ardeatina; this last route will bring you just above the most harrowing memorial on this walk, the stark **Mausoleum of the Fosse Ardeatine**.*

On 23 March 1944 the Italian Resistance killed 32 German soldiers in Rome, and the next day, in reprisal, the Nazis rounded up 335 innocents, and shot and buried them here in a sand pit under a tall tufa cliff. As soon as the Germans retreated, the bodies were recovered and identified, and re-buried together; the chapels carved in the tufa corridors have been compared to the catacombs.

> *From Fosse Ardeatine, turn left at the busy intersection to Via delle Sette Chiese (the old pilgrimage route to San Paolo Outside the Walls); a ½ km walk from the crossroads (beware of speeding traffic and blind corners)*

*leads to the **Catacombs of St Domitilla** (on the left at 283). Guided tours from 8.30–12 and 2.30–5, closed Tues; L6000.*

The Catacombs of Domitilla are nearly as large as St Calixtus, and are even older. St Domitilla was the Christian niece of Domitian's sister, and she and her two servants Nereus and Achilleus were buried here in what was originally part of a pagan *hypogeum*, which included a cemetery of the imperial Flavian family. Over the tombs of SS. Nereus and Achilleus a basilica was built in the 4th century, with a rare bas-relief showing the martyrdom of St Achilleus; adjoining is the **Chapel of St Petronilla**, with a fresco of the saint believed to have been the adopted daughter of St Peter. There are hundreds of inscriptions, and some interesting paintings, including one of a beardless young Jesus teaching his apostles, all wearing togas, while underneath is a scene of a warehouse; also an early scene of the Epiphany, the Raising of Lazarus, and in the *cubiculum* of Diogenes, a portrait of St Paul.

*Backtrack along shady but busy Via delle Sette Chiese, which after 1½ km will return you to Via Appia Antica, and just to the right, the **Basilica of San Sebastiano**, one of the Seven Churches of Rome. Open 9–12 and 2.30–5.*

In the 3rd century, during the persecution of Valerian, the Christians feared even for the safety of their dead martyrs, and brought the relics of SS. Paul and Peter from their original tombs to be temporarily interred here; under Diocletian's persecutions, a young officer in the imperial household named Sebastian was tied to a tree and pumped full of arrows. He recovered, only to be martyred again and laid out in these same catacombs. Thus rendered twice holy, a basilica was built over their tombs in the 4th century, and was called SS. Apostoli. But 500 years later the Romans forgot why, and renamed it for Sebastian, whom artists always portray as the most handsome and dashing of saints, whose charms were especially potent against the plague. They were less successful in maintaining his basilica in repair; in 1612 Cardinal Scipio Borghese paid Flaminio Ponzio and Giovanni Vasanzio to rebuild it. Exciting it isn't, but in the chapel on the right are the original set of the footprints in Domine Quo Vadis?, and across the nave, a marble *S. Sebastiano* by Antonio Giorgetti after a design by Bernini, full of such languid pathos that he seems in love with his own death.

*A door to the left of the basilica leads down into the **Catacombs of San Sebastiano**, or, properly, the Cemetery of San Sebastiano 'ad catacumbas'. Guided tours 8.30–12, 2.30–5, closed Thurs; L6000.*

As the only catacombs to have remained open through the centuries, these galleries have suffered the most from relic pirates. But they are among the most interesting. The burial ground was originally pagan, from the time of Trajan, but once the remains of the two apostles were brought here, the Christians began to bury their dead nearby and hold funerary banquets to honour Peter and Paul and benefit the poor, a meal known as a *refrigerium*. These took place in the *triclinium* located under the basilica, which the Christians built over the mausoleums of the pagans sometime around the year 250; inscriptions on the walls refer to the Apostles, confirming the tradition that their relics were here, at least for 40 years. Paintings in the *arcosolia* include a unique manger scene, and there are some charming frescoes in one of the pagan tombs, the **Hypogeum of Clodius Hermes**. The ambulatory of the 4th-century basilica has been converted into a museum, with a model of the complex, inscriptions found in the catacombs, and some fascinating early Christian sarcophagi, especially one belonging to a certain Lot.

> *From S. Sebastiano, continue 100 m along the Via Appia to the narrow Vicolo della Basilica; turn right and continue to busy Via Appia Pignatelli, which links Via Appia Antica to Via Appia Nuova. Turn right and walk 200 m to Vicolo S. Urbano (on the left), a little lane that ends at the gate of a villa guarded by vicious dogs; if you're lucky, the caretaker will be about to let you in to see the charming little church of **Sant'Urbano**.*

Sant'Urbano was originally a garden temple in the vast estates of Herodes Atticus, and its columns are perfectly preserved in the walls of the church. The conversion took place relatively late, in the 10th century, and inside are rare frescoes from 1011, depicting New Testament scenes, and the lives of contemporaries S. Cecilia and Pope St Urban who reputedly hid out in this area during the persecutions.

> *Even if you're repulsed by gate and dogs, take the narrow path to the right around the villa walls, and tramp along it through a field that soon reveals a slice of the old Roman **campagna**. The three trees on the ridge to the right are all that remains of the **Sacro Bosco**, or Sacred Wood, where tradition has it that King Numa Pompilius had his encounters with the nymph Egeria. The path continues down and around to her secret home, the so-called **Grotto of Egeria**.*

Cool and dark, mossy and mouldering, watered by a trickling stream and hung with draperies of ivy, this artificial grotto with crumbling niches and a headless statue of a reclining nymph, was one of the favourite excursions of Romantic tourists of the 18th and 19th centuries. The very few people who come these days are either junkies or the more actively romantic.

> *Retrace your steps to the Via Appia Antica, and turn left down to the **Circus of Maxentius**, the last of the great Roman race tracks and the*

best preserved. Open Tues–Sat 9–1.30 and Sun 9–1; April–Sep also Tues, Thurs, Sat 4–7, last entrance 30 min before closing; L3750.

Almost a quarter of a mile long, capable of holding 18,000 spectators, it was part of a villa complex built by Emperor Maxentius in 309. Its late date meant it saw little action, although the builders incorporated all the latest circus technology in its construction, the starting stalls for chariots arranged at an angle to make the race as fair as possible, the vaults over the stands lightened by inserting amphorae in the masonry. Its distant reaches, down the vast lawn, must be the quietest corner in Rome; the obelisk that once stood in its *spina* (Maxentius stole it from Domitian's Temple of Isis) has gone off to become a celebrity in Piazza Navona.

Next to the Circus, surrounded by looming walls, is the round **Tomb of Romulus**, Maxentius' young son, topped by an old farm house. In its vestibule are remains of frescoes, one of which seems to be a joust; below, the hollow doughnut of a tomb is as shadowy, dank, and empty as the rest.

> *On a low hill, dominating this stretch of road is the Appian Way's most famous monument, the **Tomb of Cecilia Metella**. Open Tues–Sat 9 am to between 4 and 7 pm, depending on when it gets dark. Sun and Mon open 9 am–1pm; currently free.*

Cecilia Metella was the daughter-in-law of the wealthy triumvir Crassus, who made a mountain of *sestercii* by following the fire brigades through Rome to buy up the land for his property speculation. Of Cecilia little is known but that her family must have loved her dearly to build a tomb nearly as big as those of some emperors. Its beautiful ox-head frieze gave the name Capo di Bove to the neighbourhood, which in the 13th century came under the control of the Caetani, the family of Boniface VIII. The Caetani added the crenellations to Cecilia's tomb, making it the castle keep of their fortified toll booth; ruins of their castle and Gothic church moulder across the road. You can walk down into the steep core of the empty tomb; a courtyard contains fragments of other tombs found along the road.

> *Just beyond the Tomb of Cecilia Metella, most of the traffic and bus 118 veer off for Via Appia Nuova. The next kilometre of Via Appia Antica, shaded with plane trees, has a number of ancient memorials:*

On the right is the so-called **Heroic Relief** of a naked man with a cape thrown over his shoulder. Just beyond, on the left, is the **Tomb of Marcus Servilius**, a 3D jigsaw puzzled together by Canova, who embedded fragments of rosettes, stylized vegetation and an inscription in a brick cuboid. A little further on, also on the left, is the supposed **Tomb of Seneca**, with a lion's head peeking through a curtain of ivy. Condemned to die by his old pupil, Nero, he slit his wrists in a nearby villa, and calmly continued to dictate to his weeping secretary, while his equally stoic wife quietly bled her life away in the next room. The cast of the tomb shows a relief of the dying Atys; also on the left is the **Tomb of Pompeus Sixtus** featuring a relief of a mother and child. Beyond, a right turn along **Via Lugari** leads to the scant ruins of a villa, passing the 'Tomb of St Urban' (virtually invisible behind a high walll and screen of cypresses). Back on the Appia, you soon come to the **Tomb of Ilarius Fuscus** on the right, with five portrait busts.

> *Beyond the crossing with Via Erode Attico/Tor di Carbone, the Via Appia Antica comes into its own as the 'queen of roads'—peaceful, sun drenched, dotted with cypresses and parasol pines, voluptuous with wild flowers in the spring, surrounded by some of the last unspoilt fields and hills of the classic Roman **campagna**; any moment you expect a chariot to come racing up from Brindisi with the news of the legionaries' latest conquest. Large sections of the Via Appia's original pavement have been uncovered, enormous stones softened and smoothed by time and ancient travellers. It is one of the most attractive places in all Rome, especially the spot just ahead where the engineers made a bend in the road to avoid th e ancient tower-crowned 'Tomb of the Curiatii'. Further on are two mounds called the **Tombs of the Horatii** and next, on the left, comes one of the highlights: the splendid ruins of the **Villa of the Quintilii**.*

Dating from the early 2nd century AD, this enormous villa belonged to the soldiers and agricultural writers Condianus and Maximus Quintilius, who ran it as a magnificent model farm—so magnificent that it was coveted by the awful Emperor Commodus. To get his hands on their property he had them proscribed and killed. At the villa's main entrance on the Via Appia are the ruins of a Nymphaeum, later converted into a castle; beyond, among the sheep pastures, are remains of an aqueduct, a hippodrome, and a cryptoporticus; further to the east, near Via Appia Nuova, are even more impressive walls and arcades, and a small amphitheatre. It is currently allegedly undergoing restoration—though there's usually no one about. If you're prepared to squeeze through or climb over a gate, access is not impossible.

> *Beyond, just before the sixth milestone, is the largest tomb on the entire road, the **Casale Rotondo**, a massive round republican tomb, later enlarged, and now topped by a house and garden. Beyond this Via Appia Antica, still dotted with scattered tombs and towers, is travelled largely by men heading to the whores who sit huddled over braziers at the road-side. The next road to the left leads to Via Appia Nuova, near the Capannelle Race track.*

*How you return to central Rome depends on where you decide to end—
you could continue 20 km to the Alban Hills. If you stop near the tomb of
Cecilia Metella or before, bus 118 will return you to the Colosseum. If
you continue another mile, bus 765 on Via Erode Attico/Tor di Carbone,
which crosses the Via Appia Antica near the fourth milestone, can take
you east to ⓂArco di Travertino, a stop on Metro A; if you take it to the
west, you'll end up at Ⓜ EUR Fermi on metro line B. If you walk down
to the Casale Rotondo, near the sixth milestone, the nearest buses are a
further 1 km walk to Via Appia Nuova; bus 214 passes the Cinecittà
Metro stop, at the crossroads of Via Tuscolana; alternatively, bus 664 follows Via Appia Nuova north to the Colli Albani station.*

Santa Cecilia	276
San Francesco a Ripa	277
Santa Maria inTrastevere	278
Folklore Museum	279
Palazzo Corsini	280
Villa Farnesina	281
Janiculum Hill	282
Bramante's Tempietto	283

Start: *Piazza Gioacchino Belli. Bus 56, 60, 718, 719 from Piazza Venezia via Largo Argentina.*

Finish: *Via della Lungara, from where you can nip back across the river to Campo de' Fiori.*

XIII: Trastevere

Tempietto

In every city that has ever had a river flowing through it, it's the same story. The Left Bank, Shakespeare's Southwark, Buda and Pest, Brooklyn: once over the bridge everything is different. Often, as in Brooklyn, the odd bit across the river conserves the old ways and look of the city better than any other. The people of Trastevere hold Rome's best try at a real neighbourhood festival each July, the *Festa dei Noiantri* (roughly 'we ourselves' in dialect); in a city full of recent migrants they claim to be the only real Romans left. Indeed, neighbourhood historians like to trace the origins of the community to the imperial sailors kept in Rome to work the great canvas awning at the Colosseum and man the ships for the mock sea battles.

Trastevere ('across the Tiber') has become a very trendy spot these days; in the evenings it fills up with Roman tourists from the other side to dine at its many restaurants and take a stroll around the romantic environs of Piazza S. Maria in Trastevere. But being fashionable hasn't changed the place too much; Italian rent control, as much as the strong attachment of the old-time residents, keeps Trastevere sane and serene.

Mostly outdoors, this walk is more for exploring old streets and squares than museums and churches—though make sure not to miss S. Maria in Trastevere and the Folklore Museum (closed Monday). Any of the centre Walks (I, II, III, IV) can be done on the same day, or else Walk VI (the Aventine) or, thanks to the tram to the Colosseum, Walks III and X. If you take the optional extension over the Janiculum, you can go from there and see St Peter's in the afternoon.

---

lunch/cafés

La Canonica, Vicolo del Piede. Closed Mon. Seafood and fish outside in a quiet piazza; L40–50,000.

Da Lucia, Vicolo del Mattonato 2B. Closed Mon. Roman, with a difference; renowned for its *spaghetti alla gricia* with cheese, pepper and bacon; L35,000.

Bar S. Calisto. Piazza S. Calisto. Closed Sun. A good, cheap place to lunch—bring your own from one of the *pizza al taglio* outlets on Via di San Francesco a Ripa and sit outside for as long as you want. Demi-mondish crowd at night.

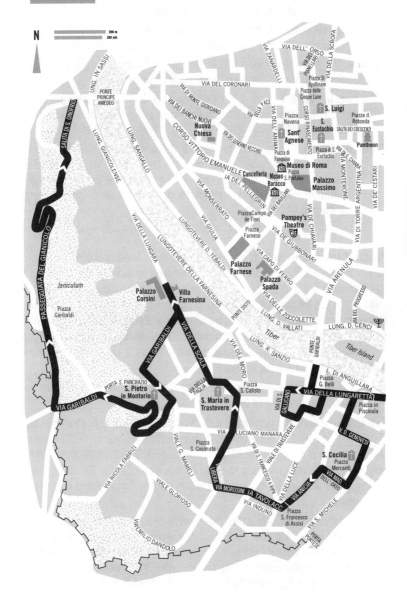

N

200 m
200 yds

UNG. IN SASSI

SALITA DI S. ONOFRIO

PONTE
PRINCIPE
AMEDEO

LUNG. GIANICOLENSE

LUNG. SANGALLO

VIA DI MONTE GIORDANO

VIA DEI BANCHI NUOVI

Nuova
Chiesa

VIA DEL CORONARI

VIA DEL GOVERNO VECCHIO

VIA DELLA PACE

CORSO VITTORIO EMANUELE

VIA DELL' ORSO

VIA DEI PIANELLARI

VIA ZANARDELLI

VIA DELLA SCROFA

Piazza S.
Apollinare
Piazza delle
Cinque Lune

S. Luigi

Piazza
Navona

Sant'
Agnese

S.
Eustachio

Piazza d.
Rotonda

SALITA DEI CRESCENZI

Piazza di S.
Eustachio

VIA DI S. CHIARA

VIA DI S. EUSTACHIO

Pantheon

Cancelleria

VIA DEL PELLEGRINO

Piazza di
Pasquino

Museo di Roma

Museo
Baracco

Piazza
S. Pantaleo

Palazzo
Massimo

Palazzo
Massimo

VIA MONTERONE

VIA DE CESTARI

VIA MONSERRATO

VIA GIULIA

PiazzaCampo
de' Fiori

Piazza
Farnese

LUNGOTEVERE DE' TEBALDI

LUNGOTEVERE DELLA FARNESINA

Pompey's
Theatre

VIA DE GIUBBONARI

VIA DE' CHIAVARI

VIA DE' BAULARI

VIA DI TORRE ARGENTINA

Palazzo
Farnese

VIA CAPO DI FERRO

Palazzo
Spada

VIA DELLE ZOCCOLETTE

Palazzo
Corsini

Villa
Farnesina

Janiculum

Piazza
Garibaldi

PASSEGGIATA DEL GIANICOLO

VIA DELLA LUNGARA

PONTE SISTO

LUNG. DI. VALLATI

Tiber

LUNG. R. SANZIO

VIA ARENULA

VIA DEL PROGRESSO

LUNG. D. CENCI

Tiber Island

PONTE GARIBALDI

L. DI ANGUILLARA

Piazza
G. Belli

VIA GARIBALDI

VIA DELLA SCALA

VIA DEL MORO

VIA DI S.
DOROTEA

Piazza
S. Calisto

VIA DELLA LUNGARETTA

Piazza in
Piscinula

PORTA S. PANCRAZIO

S. Pietro
in Montorio

VIA GARIBALDI

S. Maria in
Trastevere

VIA DI S. GALLICANO

V. D. GENOVESI

VIA LUCIANO MANARA

VIALE G. MAMELI

VIA NICOLA FABRIZI

Piazza
S. Cosimato

VIA DI S. FRANCESCO A RIPA

VIALE DI TRASTEVERE

VIA DELLA LUCE

S. Cecilia

Piazza
Mercanti

VIA MAD.
DELL'ORTO

VIALE GLORIOSO

LIBERTA

VIA MOROSINI

1A TAVOLACCI

VIA ANICIA

VIA S. MICHELE

VIA INDUNO

VIA EMILIO DANDOLO

Piazza
S. Francesco
di Assisi

PORTA
PORTESE

San Michele aveva un Gallo, Via di San Francesco a Ripa 73. Closed Sat lunch and Sun. Recently opened wine bar with delicious light meals, including unusual salads and palate-zinging *secondi.*

Osteria dell'Aquila, Via Natale del Grande 4. Closed Tues. Abruzzese specialities created by three sisters still giggling like schoolgirls in their seventies.

Cecere, Via di San Francesco a Ripa 20. Closed Thurs. Gelateria famed for its hedonistic zabaglione ices. Good *cornetti* for breakfast, too.

Il Generale, Via del Moro 1A. Closed Sat eve and Sun. Authentic trattoria where you can eat the city's best *penne alla primavera* in summer, outside in a small courtyard.

Caffè di Marzio, Piazza di Santa Maria in Trastevere 14B. Closed Mon. Outside tables which look directly onto the façade of S. Maria in Trastevere. Good for a sandwich lunch or lingering drink. The gardens on the Janiculum make a lovely picnic spot, though you'll have to carry everything up the hill.

Piazza Gioacchino Belli is named after the most famous of Rome's 19th-century 'Romanesco' dialect poets. That's Signor Belli looking dapper in his top hat, atop the monument in the piazza's centre; a relief on the back of its pedestal portrays a fond old Roman scene, a group of citizens gathered to read some political satire pinned on to the 'talking statue' Pasquino. **Palazzo Anguillara**, with its medieval defence tower, was built in the 1200s; an ambitious modern restoration did its best to make the palace look the part. Today it houses an institute and library devoted to the work of Dante.

> *To the south, the piazza flows into Viale di Trastevere, a modern boulevard that bisects this old quarter.*

San Crisogono, at the beginning of the Viale, has a rather sober Baroque façade (by G. B. Soria, 1623) and a typical Roman portico (Fontana, 1702) covering a largely medieval church. The 13th-century campanile survives, along with the pavement inside and mosaics in the apse by followers of Pietro Cavallini. Down in the crypt, the body of the original 5th-century church, fragments of medieval frescoes remain.

> *From the right side of the the church, head down Via della Lungaretta, then left on Via di S. Gallicano, to see a remarkable building by Rome's most imaginative 18th-century architect, the **Ospedale San Gallicano** by Filippo Raguzzini, a long, low complex of that certain brand of Rococo that inspired so many buildings in Spain, Florida and southern California*

around the turn of the century. Now, back on Viale di Trastevere, cross the boulevard and continue down the little street opposite San Criso-gono, Via della VII Coorte, the name of which is explained by the presence here of the **World's Oldest Police Station.**

The small building with the papal arms (now closed) was built only in the last century, but imagine the surprise of the papal gendarmes when archaeologists in 1866 discovered beneath it the *excubitorium* of the 7th cohort of ancient Rome's police—like the modern Carabinieri, the Roman *vigiles* were technically part of the army, and organized in cohorts and centuries. Conscripts probably often wished they had been sent to the German frontier; besides doing the night watch on pitch-dark streets full of desperadoes, they had to double as firemen, and help pull down collapsed buildings.

Trastevere, divided by its Viale, has a split personality. Everything to the west, old as it is, seems well kept and occasionally elegant; the side you're on now, a little ragged, is full of the warehouses and workshops that indicate that this has always been a proletarian, seafaring neigh-bourhood, with pockets of alleys that have changed little in 500 years.

Turn left on Via Montefiore, and right on Via della Lungaretta, to see some of these around **Piazza in Piscinula,** *a square that probably takes its name from the pool of an ancient baths complex on the site.*

Tiny **San Benedetto**, in the corner of the piazza, has one of the oldest campanili in Rome (c. 1090) and a fresco inside picturing St Benedict, the 6th-century father of Christian monasticism who may have lived here. Opposite, the frowning medieval palace (13–14th centuries) studded with antique fragments—one of the most evocative and best-preserved of such buildings in Rome—is the **Casa dei Mattei**, original home of one of Rome's most quarrelsome noble families.

A tour of the area, passing many 14th- and 15th-century houses (much of old Rome still looked like this a hundred years ago) will take you up Via dell'Arco dei Tolomei on the south side of the piazza, through the rugged brick **Arch of the Tolomei***, then continuing straight ahead down Via Anicia, named after the wealthiest family of the late Roman Empire. The Anicii once owned most of this neighbourhood; both St Benedict and Gregory the Great were related to them. Turn left at Via dei Genovesi and then right at Via di S. Cecilia.*

One street down, **Piazza dei Mercanti** *hardly seems impressive now, though the 'Merchants' Square', like the Tolomei's Arch (they were a great medieval banking family of Siena) and Via dei Genovesi (named after the church and hospice of the Genoese sailors on it), recall the days* *when Trastevere with its river docks was the business district of Rome. Facing the piazza, behind an imposing 12th-century quadroporticus, stands the church of Santa Cecilia (open 10–12 and 4–6, though the frosty nuns are not among the Church's best time-keepers).*

One of the most popular early martyrs, the wealthy Cecilia is said to have had her house on this site. The bad old Romans tried to pressure-cook her in the *caldarium* of her own baths, without success, whereupon they determined to chop her head off—she still hung on for three days after that. (By law, Roman axemen were allowed only three strikes; the one charged with Cecilia must have been sent back to the minor leagues after such a dismal performance.) Apparently no church was built on the site until the 820s; almost nothing from the original can be seen, though the walls and columns remain, hidden under a complete 18th-century rebuilding. It wasn't a bad job, replacing the old gallery with clerestory windows to create a light, airy interior; the frescoes are inoffensive, at best. Connected to a convent, the church is well-scrubbed, with piped-in hymns to remind us that Cecilia is the patroness of music. The rebuilders spared a fine 9th-century apse mosaic, a bit archaic in the Ravenna style; Pope Paschal, who built the church, appears in the square halo, offering the building to Christ. The two cities on the ends of the mosaic possibly represent Jerusalem and Bethlehem.

Below the mosaic, the high altar is graced with a glorious Gothic *baldacchino* by Arnolfo di Cambio. The saint, moved here from the catacombs by Pope Paschal when he built the church, was dug up again in 1599, for reasons not entirely clear; the pose of her uncorrupted body is captured exactly in the lovely statue by Stefano Maderna, under the high altar. Other survivals include some medieval frescoes of St Cecilia's martyrdom, in the first chapel on the right, and the Renaissance **Tomb of Cardinal Forteguerri** by Mino da Fiesole near the door; on the opposite tomb, that of an English titular cardinal, Adam Easton, who died in 1398, can be seen the coat of arms of the Plantagenets.

Down in the crypt (ask the sacristan), besides some flashy neo-Byzantine decoration of the 1900s, you can see the tombs of Cecilia and other saints, along with rooms from what may have been the saint's home (some with mosaics).

The Rococo restorers may have done one very serious disservice to Roman art. Much of the church was originally covered by frescoes by Pietro Cavallini, perhaps his finest work. Ask at the adjacent cloister, and you can see fragments of his **Last Judgement**, later recovered and detached from the walls. No one else, in Italy or anywhere in Europe, was capable of anything like this work in the year 1293. The careful, naturalistic draughtsmanship, and intensely spiritual expression (especially in the figure of Christ himself) make the greatest evidence for considering Cavallini, along with Giotto, as one of the precocious antecedents of the Renaissance.

> *Now, south on Via di San Michele, and right on Via della Madonna dell'Orto: at the end of this street, facing Via Anicia,* **Santa Maria dell'Orto** *has a queer façade topped by little obelisks.*

Not too interesting to look at, in this city of 901 churches, but a landmark of a strange interlude in the progress of the expiring Renaissance. Vignola, that restless and underrated architect from Modena, built it in 1566; its façade, spare and strange, but skilful and correct according to the architectural canons of the age, records a modest reaction against the busy and overdecorated work of the High Renaissance. This tendency was even more pronounced in Spain, where Juan de Herrera had inaugurated the *estilo desornamentado* three years earlier with his design for El Escorial. Herrera too was notoriously fond of obelisks.

> *Turn left on Via Anicia, passing drab barracks and Mussolini apartment houses, on the way to* **San Francesco a Ripa** *(Mon–Sat 7–12 and 4–7; Sun 7–1 and 4–7.30), one of the first Franciscan churches in Rome.*

This church has two treasures, the squirming, erotic statue of the *Beata Ludovica Albertoni* by Bernini, in the last chapel on the left, expressing divine ecstasy with the same Hollywood spirituality as his famous *Santa Teresa* in S. Maria della Vittoria (see Walk IX); and the cell in the adjacent cloister where St Francis stayed in 1219, while trying to persuade the pope to reform the Church. The thoroughly Baroqued cell (ask the sacristan to let you see it) includes a 13th-century painting believed to be a likeness of Francis himself. *Ripa*, incidentally, was the old name for Trastevere's *rione*.

> *Just behind the church, the Porta Portese flea market fills the surrounding streets on Sunday mornings. Any other time, there's nothing to see; take Via Tavolacci, just south of the church, recross Viale di Trastevere, and continue down Via Morosini, past the big, post-1870 Education Ministry, a building that hardly seems at home, stuck here in the middle of Trastevere (the grim building you passed on Via Tavolacci was its annexe, the Palace of Exams). A right turn on to Via Roma Libera takes you to* **San Cosimato**, *presiding over Trastevere's street market, on Piazza di San Cosimato. The church, built in the 10th century and remodelled in 1475, is usually closed, but you can see the lovely 12th-century cloister next door, now part of a hospital.*

> *Finally, to the north, Via di S. Cosimato takes you to the peaceful, completely lovable heart of the district,* **Piazza di S. Maria in Trastevere**—*no traffic, no Baroque, no obelisks, only children (a rarity*

*in Rome) playing ball and a few cafés. Behind Fontana's fountain, with an ancient Roman basin, you'll see the only church in all Rome that has retained its complete medieval appearance, **Santa Maria in Trastevere** (open 7–12.40 and 3–7).*

It may be the oldest church in Rome, and the first dedicated to the Virgin Mary. An old legend had it that on the day of Christ's birth, a spring of olive oil—an Italian housewife's dream—miraculously gushed up from this spot, flowing down to the Tiber. There may have been a Christian building here as early as 220, but the building you see now was begun by Pope Julius I in 337, and rebuilt in the 1140s. Carlo Fontana built the portico, probably replacing an earlier, simpler one. Above it, the beautiful 12th-century gold-ground mosaic on the façade shows how most important medieval Roman churches were decorated; this is the only one to survive time and the Baroque rebuilders. Mary in the centre is flanked by ten maidens with lamps who probably represent the Wise and Foolish Virgins (from Jesus' parable, Matthew 25, 1–14); the exquisite palm trees below were a symbolic 'tree of life' in some early Christian art, and quite common in some Islamic work. Palms weren't grown in Rome in the Middle Ages, part of the case for ascribing this mosaic to artists from the Greek East.

The portico, full of inscriptions and early Christian decorative panels, leads to an interior with an excellent Cosmati pavement (much restored), accented with deep red porphyry and green *verde antico*. Many of the massive nave columns came from the Baths of Caracalla, and some of the capitals atop them are especially fine. Like the pavement, the pretty Cosmatesque spiral candlestick, choir screen, tabernacle and throne owe more to the 19th century than to their medieval originals—by that time the pendulum of Roman taste had swung completely back, and instead of covering churches in Baroque plaster, the pope and cardinals were often trying their best to imaginatively recreate the Middle Ages.

The **apse mosaics** are among Rome's best, done at the same time as those on the exterior. The enthroned Virgin sits among Jesus and the saints, with Isaiah, Jeremiah, and the symbols of the Evangelists on the surrounding triumphal arch. Note the caged birds underneath them—a charming conceit, reminding the faithful how Jesus imprisoned his own spirit in an earthly body to redeem the sins of the world. The rich colouring, and nervous, yet controlled line of these mosaics reflect the classical revival in Byzantium, an influence to which the Italians (however much they hate to admit it) owe much of their own advances in late medieval and Renaissance art. How well they learned their lessons can be seen in the mosaic **scenes from the life of Mary** below, another masterpiece by Pietro Cavallini (1290) to complement his paintings a few blocks away at Santa Cecilia.

To the left of the altar, the pleasant, airy **Altemps Chapel** has frescoes of 1588 portraying the Council of Trent. In the left aisle, the **Chapel of S. Girolamo** is an elaborate late Baroque fancy (Ant. Gherardi, 1680s), a little theatre lit by its own small cupola. At the entrance to the sacristy are two small ancient mosaics.

> *Take Via della Paglia, to the right of the church, into Piazza di Sant'Egidio, where an unassuming former convent has been converted into an interesting but little-known tribute to the Eternal City's not so distant past, the* **Folklore Museum of Rome.** *Open weekdays 9–1.30, Tues and Thurs also 5–7.30, Sun 9–12.30, closed Mon; L3000.*

You can read all you like about Rome in the last centuries of papal rule, the timeless, retrograde city that captivated the northerners on the Grand Tour, but this is the only place to see it come to life, with a unique collection of prints and paintings from the last century of papal rule. A British artist named P. Sandby starts the fun with a series of Hogarthian prints of the old Roman Carnival, with colour and incident unthinkable in the staid Rome of today. Others include scenes from the fish market at the Portico d'Ottavia, public scribes scratching out *billets doux* and government forms for the illiterate, housewives doing the wash in the Acqua Vergine fountain, and picturesque *ciociari*, peasants from southern Lazio, so called for their wooden clogs, or *ciocie*, posed around a half-buried Porta San Lorenzo—until the archaeologists got seriously to work in the 1800s, most of the ancient monuments projected from the centuries' accumulation of soil like so many marble and travertine spring posies.

Some amazing pictures record the fireworks and illuminations of old Rome, the greatest shows any 19th-century Italian city had to offer. Until quite recently, a strange community of workers called the *Sanpietrini*, inheriting their jobs from their fathers, had charge of keeping up St Peter's and the Castel Sant'Angelo; for papal festivals, they would clamber over the castle and St Peter's dome, placing strings of oil lamps to light the outlines of the buildings against the night sky, while their fellows below set off giant Catherine wheels and, of course, Roman candles.

Beyond these, there are casts of Pasquino and the Bocca della Verità, and every other fond old Roman landmark, a series of life-sized tableaux with waxwork figures, portraying Roman shops, taverns and homes from long ago, and—quite inexplicably to the foreign visitor—the reconstructed quarters of one of the last and most beloved of Roman dialect poets, Trilussa (Carlo Salustri, d. 1950). Trilussa's works can be found in any good Roman bookstore; though not the sort of stuff likely to be found in anthologies or poetry courses, they comment blithely on the passing Roman scene, with some pointed satire reserved for Mussolini and the fascists (and not at all hard to read if you know some Italian). Trilussa seems to have been interested in everything, and on a slow day the curators will be glad to point out his funny mythological paintings, bug collections, and other clutter. Keep an eye open for the special exhibitions in the lower floor of this museum.

> *Piazza Sant'Egidio leads into Via della Scala, continuing north towards the Vatican.* **Santa Maria della Scala,** *on the left, serves the adjacent Carmelite monastery, and has had a reputation in the practice of medicine for centuries. The monks run a completely modern and up-to-date pharmacy, facing the square, but if you ask, they'll be glad to take you up for a look at the old one, a genuine 18th-century Roman pharmacy with pretty majolica jars full of exotic herbal cures.*

> *Via della Scala continues north, passing under the* **Porta Settimiana,** *a gate of the Aurelian wall rebuilt under Pope Alexander VI; here the street changes its name to Via della Lungara. For you, it's back to the culture torture. It could be worse; just after the arch stands an anonymous building with one of the best collections of ancient sculpture and Etruscan paintings in Rome. The Museo Torlonia, however, acquired by the state in 1977, still awaits its reopening, lost in a maze of bureaucratic difficulties. That leaves the* **Palazzo Corsini** *(Tues–Sat 9–7, Sun 9–1; L6000) one block to the north, sharing the collection of the 'National Museum of Antique Art' with the Palazzo Barberini (see Walk IX).*

It's a small, attractive museum hardly ever troubled with visitors. The palazzo, one of the more ambitious creations of 18th-century Rome, turns its back on Via della Lungara, waiting for a grander façade facing the Janiculum that was never built. The Corsini were bankers, and relatives of more than one 17th-century pope, one of the last families to make it big off the centuries-old papal banking racket. Queen Christina lived here for a while, as did Napoleon's mother, Letizia Bonaparte; the back of the palace suffered considerable damage during the French attacks against the Roman Republic in 1849; after Napoleon III's armies breached the Janiculum walls, this part of Trastevere found itself in the front line.

You enter through the quiet courtyard, then up the stair, decorated with miscellaneous ancient sculptures and neoclassical works of the Napoleonic era. In the first room, there is a little model of how the palace was meant to look; it would have been the grandest in Rome, or at least the biggest. The paintings are typical Roman museum fare, largely Italian artists, with a few Flemish, ranging from the late 1500s through the Baroque. Murillo's *Madonna and Child* stands out, one of the pious Spaniard's less saccharine attempts. The second room is devoted to the northerners, with two Breughel winter scenes and some overripe Rubens: a *Madonna* and a *St Sebastian*. Followers of Caravaggio occupy rooms three and four, including one fine painting of *John the Baptist*, a copy made by the master himself of the work in the Capitoline Pinacoteca. Room five was Queen Christina's bedroom; she died here in 1689. This and the last two rooms contain works of Mattia Preti (a striking *Martyrdom of St Bartholomew*), Pier Francesco Mola, Guido Reni, Carlo Dolci, Guercino (one of the *Et in Arcadia Ego* paintings), Luca Giordano and Salvator Rosa, who wins the prize for fright and gore with his *Prometheus*, complete with hungry eagle.

> Behind the palace, the Corsini grounds have become Rome's **Botanical Gardens** *(entrance on Via Corsini; summer Mon–Sat 9–7, Sun 10–7; winter Mon–Sat 9–1, Sun 10–7; L2000). There is little to see besides some tall palms, but it's your best chance for some rest and shade. Across the street from the Corsini, another papal banker created a smaller but more memorable pleasure dome, now known as the* **Villa Farnesina**. *Open daily exc Sun, 9–1, free.*

The Chigi family came originally from Siena. Banker Agostino Chigi hit the big jackpot in the early 1500s, at the beginning of the great Renaissance orgy of Roman acquisitiveness, by winning the papal account. Other families, most notably the Medici of Florence, had already made their fortunes in this way (the most recent, of course, was the late Michele Sindona); the Chigi never became Grand Dukes like the Medici, but for conspicuous consumption nobody could beat them. In the gilded reign of Leo X, nouveau riche Agostino's Trastevere villa was the cynosure of Rome, with cardinals, poets, princes, tremendous courtesans and fashionable artists over for dinner almost every night. The best story about Agostino has him hosting banquets on the riverbank, with the servants tossing the gold and silver plates into the Tiber after each course to show off. Of course there was a net at the bottom, to retrieve the loot afterwards.

Baldassare Peruzzi, another Sienese, designed the villa in 1508 and helped decorate it with his paintings, along with Raphael and Sebastiano del Piombo. After decades of the high life, the Chigi found themselves overdrawn, and sold the property to the Farnese family. The Bourbons of Naples held it for a while, and since the '20s it has served as home for the *Accademia dei Lincei*, a scientific circle founded in the early 1600s (Galileo was an early member).

For visitors, the prime attraction will be Raphael's famous fresco on the ground floor, of *Galatea*, daintily riding the waves like a marine Venus; Cupids aiming rather dangerous-looking arrows float above. Raphael's elegant mythological fantasy, just the sort of thing Renaissance bankers and cardinals preferred, sets the tone for the rest of the villa's frescoes. The architect, Peruzzi, added the ceiling frescoes of astronomical constellations, and the semicircular paintings below are vignetttes from Ovid's *Metamorphoses* by Sebastiano del Piombo.

In the other room on the ground floor, the Loggia of Cupid and Psyche, Raphael's pupils, including Giulio Romano, contributed a series of paintings from Apuleius' *Golden Ass*. Upstairs, the main hall of the villa is an eccentric masterpiece of Peruzzi, the *Salone delle Prospettive; trompe l'oeil* archways enclose mock window views of Roman vistas, a rare chance to see what Trastevere and the Vatican Borgo looked like in the 16th century. Nearby is Agostino Chigi's own bedroom. Il Sodoma did this room, the Sienese painter whose name reflects contemporary opinion crediting him with every sort of vice—really he was a good family man, devoted entirely to his pet badger and the rest of his sizeable menagerie. He was also one of the greatest artists of his time, who never got over the shock when his frescoes in the Vatican were destroyed by Julius II, to be replaced by the smoother, sweeter, more fashionable art of Raphael. His major work here is a large scene of the *Marriage of Alexander the Great and Roxana*.

> *Via della Lungara continues northwards towards the Vatican, passing the* **Regina Coeli Prison**, *Rome's main lockup for centuries, and the scene of some memorable Nazi atrocities in 1943–4; the prisoners murdered in the Fosse Ardeatina, in reprisal for partisan activities, were taken from here. This is the end of the Trastevere walk, though if you have any steam left, we have a nice long climb and another mile or so of walking for you to consider:*

The Janiculum Hill

Monte Gianicolo to modern Rome, the trans-Tiberine Janiculum has always been the odd man out among Rome's hills—the biggest, though not even one of the canonical Seven, and not even included within the city walls (a branch of the fortifications, following the crest of the Janiculum, was built strictly out of defensive necessity). In latter days most of the hill has been preserved as parks. It's worth a climb for the views over Rome, and also for one very special building—the Tempietto of Bramante, the most characteristic work of the Roman High Renaissance.

> *To begin, you will have to retrace your steps through the Porta Settimiana. Just after it, to the right,* **Via Garibaldi** *begins its snaking climb up the Janiculum's southern slope, passing the church of* **Santa Maria dei Sette Dolori**, *with an unfinished façade by Borromini. After a left turn, and some 400 yards of climbing, Via Garibaldi takes you to* **San Pietro in Montorio** *(open 9–12 and 4–7), an ancient church rebuilt at the behest of Ferdinand and Isabella of Spain in the 1480s.*

And a good choice it was for the Spaniards. Today's students at the adjacent Spanish Academy enjoy one of the most peaceful corners of Rome, with the best views over the city. One of the Academy's more recent students was King Juan

Carlos, who still remembers his days on the Janiculum with affection, and drops in for a visit every now and then. In the church, the most noteworthy painting is a *Flagellation of Christ* by Sebastiano del Piombo, in the first chapel on the right. The next chapel's ceiling has a *Coronation of the Virgin* by Peruzzi; two chapels further on, Florentine Mannerism makes one of its rare appearances in Rome, with sculptural work by Ammannati and a fresco of St Paul by Giorgio Vasari. Under the high altar are buried two troublesome Irish earls, Hugh O'Neill and Roderick O'Donnell, unsuccessful Catholic rebels against King James I.

Bramante's now grubby **Tempietto** can be seen in the little courtyard to the right of the church. Do not think that this ambitious attempt at perfect architecture was intentionally tucked away in an obscure spot; at the time (about 1501) this was believed to be the exact location of St Peter's upside-down crucifixion, making it one of the most important pilgrimage sites in Rome. But at the climax of the Renaissance, somehow this holy ground acquired a monument steeped in pagan antiquity. Bramante was the first modern architect to recapture entirely the Doric order from Vitruvius' ancient textbook. His tiny temple, only large enough for a few worshippers at a time, stands as a unique monument to the Renaissance ideal of expressing the inexpressible in architecture.

Everything is sliced down to basic principles, without a trace of Gothic bravura or the free-spirited experimentation of the early Renaissance. The perfect symmetry of the sixteen-columned, radial temple proclaims its abject submission to a simple ideal. Bramante wished to build as the ancients did, and he sacrificed all the experience of the medieval centuries to erect his impeccable little cylinder. The clumsy hulk of St Peter's only emphasizes the impotence of an architecture that sought to translate its perfection to larger sizes. Michelangelo and his successors, dilettante architects that they were, could never have built this, but only mock its form into shapeless gigantism.

> *Across the road from this exhilarating, perhaps disturbing building, is the brazenly fascist* **Monument to the Fallen of 1849–1870**, *a chill travertine pavilion (1941) with battle scenes of the Risorgimento wars and imbecile patriotic inscriptions from Gabriele D'Annunzio. There was some talk of moving Garibaldi's remains here from his last home, in Sardinia, before the war intervened. Continue up the hill to the* **Acqua Paola**, *a fine miniature Trevi Fountain built under Paul V, where you can pause for breath and the view.*

The papal works followed Trajan's Aqueduct, bringing into Rome the waters of Lake Bracciano; in ancient times, near this spot, they powered ranks of mills that ground Rome's flour. The columns of Paul's fountain come from the façade of the original St Peter's.

> *A little further up is the **Largo di Porta San Pancrazio,** an open space in the wall, where Urban VIII's original Porta San Pancrazio had to be rebuilt after the battles of 1849.*

In ancient times, the gate was the beginning of the Via Aurelia, the great consular road that travelled up Italy's coast and into Gaul. For three months, April–June 1849, this part of the wall was the front line, contested between Garibaldi's volunteers and the French army sent to prop the pope back on his throne. It was the Risorgimento's finest hour. Waves of French assaults fell back before Garibaldi's men, supported by volunteers from all over Europe, republican idealists—some from the nobility— brigades of students, and fierce Trastevere working men armed only with knives. Roman military bands played the 'Marseillaise' to remind the French of the shameful mission on which the republican government in Paris had sent them. Finally, under intense artillery bombardment and heavy losses, the French smashed their way in on the last day of June, ending the Roman Republic and closing the book on Italy's wave of 1848 revolutions. The gate building houses a small **museum** of the Risorgimento (*open Tues, Wed, Thurs, 9–12*).

> *Continuing northwards along the crest of the hill, take the Passeggiata di Gianicolo to the right, inside the Aurelian wall. 'Passeggiata' is something of a misnomer, as traffic is heavy and the road runs through a forlorn park of handkerchief-patch lawns, decorated with busts of the fallen heroes of 1849. At the next bastion in the walls the road opens into Piazzale Garibaldi, a fine viewpoint adorned with tourist clutter including a miniature puppet show (closed Wed). There's a huge bronze equestrian Garibaldi in the piazza, but even better is the equally massive bronze **equestrian Mrs Garibaldi** a little further on.*

The remarkable Anita, who is buried underneath, certainly did her part through all the battles of 1849—even though she was pregnant; the statue has her galloping towards destiny with a pistol in one hand, and cradling her baby in the other. The Brazilians erected it to honour their brave daughter; Garibaldi had brought her home to Italy after fighting in the South American wars of independence.

> *Just beyond is a lighthouse, a perplexing gift to Rome from the Argentinians. Descending towards the Vatican, take a short cut down the **Rampa della Quercia** from the far end of the belvedere, past a dead tree trunk known as Tasso's oak because the poet apparently used to sit beneath it. Rejoining the main road, it's a short walk downhill to **Sant'Onofrio** (open mornings only), a monastic foundation of 1419. The church has frescoes by Annibale Caracci and Antoniazzo Romano. Opposite, Salita di S. Onofrio continues down to the Borgo and the bulk of the ancient hospital of S. Spirito; the Vatican lies a few blocks away.*

Castel St. Angelo

XIV: Vatican City and the Borgo

St Peter's	291
Vatican City and Gardens	302
Via della Conciliazione	302
Castel S. Angelo	303
Museum of Dead Souls	307

Start: *Via dei Corridori, terminus of bus 64 from Termini.*
Finish: *Castel Sant'Angelo.*
Walking Time: *Half a day; all day with Vatican Museums.*

The Pope does nothing on a small scale; by a mystery of the faith, the world's smallest country contains the world's largest museum, piazza, and church. If cruel destiny decrees that you must see the Vatican Museums, St Peter's, and Castel Sant'Angelo all in one day, make it a Monday (when all the state museums are closed anyway). It is the only day that Castel Sant'Angelo is open in the afternoon, and if you've had the foresight to book an afternoon tour of the Ancient Necropolis under St Peter's you can even, with some fancy footwork, fit that in too (see Vatican practicalities, pp.24-5) though our publisher refuses to be liable for any blisters or fallen arches you may sustain in the process. Remember the dress code: no shorts, sleeveless blouses or tee shirts.

The one attraction that even the saints in heaven couldn't squeeze into a single day itinerary is the three hour morning tour of Vatican City (though from the dome you get a bird's eye view of the little state and its gardens). If it's not Monday, make sure to start early in the Vatican Museums, and leave by 11.30 for Castel Sant'Angelo, as it closes at 1 pm. Or in the summer, begin with Castel Sant'Angelo and St Peter's, have an early lunch, and then move on to the cool corridors of the Vatican museums (open afternoons during Holy Week and July, August and September). Ideally, you'll be able to return two or three times—especially to the museums—to prevent total sensory breakdown. If you happen to be in Rome on the last Sunday of the month, take advantage of papal charity—the Vatican museums are free.

If you've begun this day with the Vatican Museums (convenient for Ⓜ Ottaviano) you have the option of reaching Piazza San Pietro either by the little Vatican bus (L2000), which takes the short cut through the Vatican Gardens every half hour, or by foot, following the walls along Viale Vaticano, Via Leone IV, and Via della Porta Angelica.

lunch/cafés

There are lots of pleasant places to snack on Borgo Pio, along with groceries, delis and fruit shops if you want to picnic. Avoid the places along Viale Vaticano. Some are quite a walk from St Peter's—we've included them in case you need to escape ecclesiastica and tourists.

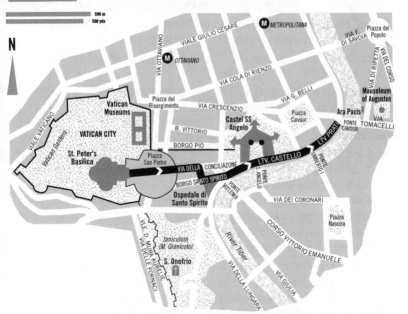

Da Giovanni, Via della Lungara 44. Closed Sun. Closer to the Trastevere walk, but an ideal escape if you don't mind a ten-minute walk. Basic tratt serving legendarily cheap nosh. Popular with guards from the nearby Regina Coeli prison; L15–18,000.

Charango, Via di Sant'Ononfrio. Closed Mon. Latin-American snacks; L15,000

Enoteca Costantini, Piazza Cavour 16. Closed Sun. Gorgeous wine bar serving snacks for gastronomes; L15,000 excluding wine.

Abruzzese, Via de' Gracchi 27. Closed Mon. Amicable Abruzzese trattoria with a fixed L20,000 lunch menu.

La Madonella, Via Tunisi 27–9. Closed Mon. Basic tratt for budget Sardinian lunches. Less than L20,000.

Osteria dell'Angelo, Via G Bettolo 24, closed Sat lunch and Sun. Authentic Roman fare; L35–40,000.

Antico Forno, Borgo Pio 8. Closed Thurs. Unusual *pizza al taglio*—try *tartufo* (truffle) and mozzarella.

Taverna Negma, Borgo Vittorio 92. Closed Tues. Couscous, both North African and Sicilian; L40,000,

Franchi, Via Cola di Rienzo 202. Closed Sun. An excellent 'gastronomia' but no tables— picnic in the park next to Castel Sant'Angelo; L15,000.

Fantini, Piazza della Unità 12 (part of Via dei Gracchi). Café good for a light lunch or ice cream, *frullati* and *frappés;* L10–15,000.

Il Ragno d'Oro, Via Silla 26. Closed Sun. Good Italian homecooking; L35–40,000.

San Luigi, Via Mocenigo 10. Closed Sun. Gourmet dishes based on traditional Southern Italian recipes; L75,000.

Vatican City

Vatican, curiously, means 'prophecy', for it was on this eighth hill of Rome that King Numa received tips on religion from the Sibyls. But as it was on the wrong side of the Tiber the land was cheap, and Caligula used it to build his personal circus, later known as Nero's; here St Peter was crucified upside down, at his own request, so that his martyrdom would not resemble Christ's. He was buried in a nearby cemetery, on a spot that has been hallowed ever since. It has been the chief residence of Peter's successors since the late 14th century.

'The Papacy is not other than the Ghost of the Deceased Roman Empire, sitting crowned upon the grave thereof,' said Thomas Hobbes, though since Hobbes this imperial ectoplasm has been confined like an afrit in a magic lamp. Better known as the independent state of Vatican City (pop. around 1000), it was the papacy's consolation prize negotiated in the 1929 Lateran Concordat. But the temporal power of the popes had been in decline for centuries; the old Papal States by the 18th century were the worst run in Europe, kept 'alive only because the earth refuses to swallow them', as Goethe put it. Unfortunately, thanks to Mussolini, much of the evil of the Papal States has been concentrated in a country the size of a golf course—one where the duffers don't always count all their strokes. For instead of creating a realm of the spirit, as Vatican brochures would like you to believe, members of the Curia who run Vatican City have used its sovereignty (read unaccountability) to create the Corporate Papacy, the world's last real autocracy, with a tiny tax haven all its own. The scandal of Vatican finances, Mafia connections, the laundering of drug money through the Vatican Bank, and the circumstances surrounding the sudden death of John Paul I have been so unsavoury that the government across the Tiber has responded by steadily decreasing the Church's role in the state, legalizing divorce and abortion, making religious instruction optional in schools, taxing Vatican profits from the stock market, and taking away Roman Catholicism's special status as the official religion of Italy. Ask any Roman about it, and you'll get an earful. It's one reason why the city has one of the lowest percentages of church attendance in Italy—'Faith is made here and believed elsewhere', is an old Roman saying.

Yet as you stroll among the merry crowds of pilgrims and tourists chattering in every known language, remember Boccaccio's story in the Decameron, of two friends who live in Paris, one Christian and one Jewish, the former constantly pestering the other to convert. Finally the Jew agrees, on the condition that he first visits Rome, to see if the life and habits of the pope and his cardinals were evidence of the superiority of their faith. The Christian naturally despairs, but off the Jew goes to Rome, returning with the expected tale of a thousand abominations, declaring that the pontiff and the rest were 'doing their level best to reduce the Christian religion to nought and drive it from the face of the earth'. That the faith could survive and prosper with such sharks in charge was enough to convince him that it must indeed be holy and genuine, and he converted immediately.

Vatican City is surrounded by a high wall, designed by Michelangelo; its only public entrances are through St Peter's Square and the Vatican Museums. Swiss Guards (still recruited from the four Catholic cantons), dressed in a scaled-down version of the striped suits designed by either Michelangelo or Raphael, stand ready to smite you with their halberds if you try to push your way in elsewhere. The Vatican has its own stamps and postal service, which make it a tidy profit; it is also, like every postal system in the galaxy, more efficient than the Posta Italiana. The official language in Vatican City is Latin, though its own semi-official daily newspaper, *L'Osservatore Romano,* is in Italian (with a weekly digest in English) and its Vatican Radio broadcasts in 26 languages.

Borgo

Another set of walls, originally built by Leo IV after the Saracen raid in 846, surrounds the Borgo, the small neighbourhood in the shadow of St Peter's. The word comes from the Anglo-Saxon burgh, or town, founded in the early 8th century by Anglo-Saxon kings and pilgrims. They were soon followed by the Franks and Frisians, who each built their own schola as a school and a hostel to protect their pilgrims from the wiles of Roman innkeepers. Today the Borgo, numbed by the predominance of its self-contained institutions, retains few memories of its English origins beyond its street names and the mediocrity of its restaurants. But it, too, has a mastodonic landmark of its own—the Castel Sant'Angelo.

Piazza San Pietro

Not even all the photographs you've seen can quite prepare you for **Piazza San Pietro**, *where 'small is beautiful' is dashed as heresy. The gigantic proportions force you to suspend your normal visual belief; all is so superscale that only by constant reference to the measurements of man, a mere tiddlywink next to St Peter's 350 ft long façade, can you begin to digest its outrageous size.*

Someone has calculated that there is room for about 300,000 people in the piazza, with no crowding. Few have ever noticed Bernini's little joke on antiquity; the open space almost exactly matches the size and dimensions of the Colosseum. And as Norwood Young wrote, in the 1901 *Story of Rome*, the intention of the architects is not dissimilar—to overawe and crush the individual. 'But now I feel the cold scrutiny of Bernini's self-complacent columns,' writes Mr Young. 'Their long octopus arms ready to encircle me, while the body of the monster waits eyeing me from the distance. I cannot escape.' Bernini would prefer us to see his **Colonnade**, with its 284 massive columns and statues of 140 saints, as 'the arms of the Church embracing the world'. Stand on either of the two dark stones at the foci of the elliptical piazza, and you will see the forest of columns resolve into neat rows, a subtly impressive optical effect like the hole in the dome of the Pantheon. Bernini designed the Colonnade so that the nobility could drive their carriages underneath to St Peter's, sheltered from sun or rain.

Flanked by two lovely fountains, luxuriantly spraying water all over the pavement—the one on the right by Carlo Maderno (1614), and the other, copied from it in 1667—the Vatican **Obelisk**, though only average-size for an obelisk, is one of the most fantastical relics in all Rome. It comes from Heliopolis, the Egyptian city founded as a capital and cult centre by Ikhnaton, the half-legendary Pharaoh and religious reformer who, according to Sigmund Freud and others, founded the first monotheistic religion, influencing Moses and all who came after. It arrived here apparently by divine coincidence; originally in the *spina* of Nero's Circus Vaticanus, it overlooked the martyrdom of St Peter. For a millennium and a half it remained in place, just to the left of the present basilica, until Sixtus V had it moved, accompanied by one of the city's favourite (and like most, probably fabricated) anecdotes:

Sixtus V was no stuck-in-the-*sedia-gestatoria* pope, but a man of action, the only one, Queen Elizabeth I claimed, half-jokingly, who was worthy of her hand. One of his pet projects was to humble the ancient pagans of Rome, whose monuments, even in ruins, still threatened to overshadow the grandeur of the Church. In 1586, he ordered Domenico Fontana to move the obelisk to the piazza, to show how puny this heathen ornament was in comparison to the Biggest Church in the World. The problem was, no one could remember how to move an obelisk. Fontana made careful, elaborate plans (Sixtus hinted that failure meant the chopping block), and on 18 Sept 900 men, 150 horses, and 47 cranes creaked into action. A vast crowd had gathered to watch the procedure, but the Pope insisted on perfect silence (underlined by the presence of a gallows) so the workmen could hear Fontana's orders. Slowly the obelisk was hauled upright by the ropes, then hesitated, the ropes too taut with the strain to finish the task. Suddenly the silence was broken by a Ligurian sailor's cry, 'Water on the ropes!' saving the obelisk and Fontana's neck. Sixtus showed his gratitude by giving the sailor's hometown of Bordighera the monopoly of supplying palm fronds to the Vatican on Palm Sunday. Originally the obelisk was topped by a golden ball, believed to contain the ashes of Julius Cæsar (though empty when cracked open); now it has an iron cross, containing a sliver of the True Cross.

> *Off to the right of the square is a confusing cluster of buildings, the Vatican palaces, built over the years to satisfy some of the bigger papal egos. Modern popes don't take up much room; since 1903, when the newly-elected Pius X refused to move from the servants' quarters of the* **Apostolic Palace** *(the tallest building) where he stayed during the conclave, the popes have chosen to live there, behind the last two windows on the right, on the top floor.*

The stories of Pius' simplicity do much to counter the tons of travertine bombast: one story goes that a nun prone to leg cramps asked to borrow Pius' old woollen stockings, and came back declaring a miracle, for the stockings had completely cured her pains. 'How extraordinary!' the Pope replied. 'They never did anything for me.'

> *On Sunday at noon John Paul II appears at the window and blesses the crowd in the piazza.*

> *The gallery along the right, the* **Corridore del Bernini,** *leads to the great* **Bronze Door,** *the ceremonial entrance to the Vatican for visiting dignitaries; it leads to the Scala Regia. On the left side are the Vatican information office (where you may book the Vatican Gardens tour), the bus stop for the Vatican Museums, post office, lavatories, and first aid station. At the end is the* **Arco delle Campane,** *under St Peter's bells, guarded by the Swiss; if you're booking to see the necropolis, just tell them 'Ufficio degli Scavi'.*

St Peter's

> *Looming over all is the massive façade of the* **Basilica of St Peter.** *(Open daily 7 am–7 pm.) Mr Young compares it to the great Gothic Cathedrals: '"Come," say Milan, Amiens, Cologne, York, "come and worship God with me. See how comely it is to do so." But Rome says, "See how grand and powerful I am, and how contemptible you are."'*

Old St Peter's was much cosier. Begun by Constantine over the Apostle's tomb in 324, it was a richly decorated basilica, in form much like St Paul's Outside the Walls, full of gold and mosaics, with a vast porch of marble and bronze in front, and a lofty campanile topped by the famous golden cockerel that everyone believed would some day crow to announce the end of the world. This St Peter's, where Charlemagne and Frederick II received their imperial crowns, was falling to pieces by the 1400s, conveniently in time for the popes and artists of the Renaissance to plan a replacement. The first to do so was Nicholas V, who, in about 1450, conceived an almost Neronian building programme for the Vatican, ten times as large as anything his ancestors could have contemplated—a complex that would have stretched all the way to Castel Sant'Angelo. It was not until Julius II realized that there was not enough room in the basilica for his planned tomb that he commissioned Bramante to demolish the old church and begin the new. His original plan called for a great dome over a central Greek cross. Michelangelo, who took over the work in 1546, basically agreed, and if he had had his way St Peter's might indeed have become the crowning achievement of Renaissance art everyone hoped it would be.

Unfortunately, despite nearly 200 years of construction and an expenditure of £460,000,000, too many popes and too many architects created instead of a masterpiece a monster of compromise. Raphael, who took over as architect after Bramante's death (nicknaming his former mentor 'Ruinante' for his summary demolition of much that was sacred and preservable in the old basilica) opted for a Latin cross. A number of architects succeeded him; Peruzzi returning to the Greek cross of Bramante, followed by Antonio da Sangallo the Younger, another advocate of the Latin Cross. Paul III then summoned Michelangelo, aged 72, who reluctantly took over the mess, on the condition that the pope gave him a free hand (in return, he worked for free, too), whereupon he demolished everything da Sangallo had built and started afresh on Bramante's lines, though changing his plans for a Pantheon-type dome to a higher cupola modelled on Brunelleschi's dome on Florence Cathedral. But even this was reshaped by one of his successors, Giacomo della Porta, who completed it in 1590.

The most substantial tinkering came in 1605, when Paul V and his committee of cardinals decided on a Latin cross after all. Carlo Maderno was given the task of demolishing the portico of the old basilica to extend the nave, which had the unforeseen effect of blocking out the view of the dome, and he designed the façade (1612) with Paul V's name blazoned on top. But Maderno shouldn't be blamed for its disproportionate width: Bernini, who was in charge of decorating the interior, had the bright idea of adding twin campaniles to the flanks which were such a dismal failure that they were levelled to the same height as Maderno's façade. In the centre is the balcony from which the pope gives his Urbi et Orbi blessing at Easter and Christmas. On 18 Nov 1626, the supposed 1300th anniversary of the original basilica, Urban VIII consecrated the new St Peter's.

*Step inside, hopefully past the security men and the dress code bouncers without trouble, and into the **Portico.***

Some of the best art in St Peter's is in the Portico, beginning with the oldest and hardest to see, Giotto's 1298 mosaic of Christ walking on water, called the *Navicella*, located in the tympanum over the central door; this has been so often moved and restored almost nothing remains of the original. At the extreme right end of the portico is Bernini's equestrian statue of *Constantine*, showing the emperor staring at the vision of the cross. There are five sets of bronze doors leading into the basilica, the work of some of Italy's leading modern sculptors. From right to left they are: the **Holy Door**, opened only in Holy Years (1950, by Vico Consorti); the next, by Venanzio Crocetti (1968); the famous central doors, from Old St Peter's, made by Antonio Filarete (1439–45), with scenes from the life of Pope Eugenius IV, who held an ecumenical council in Florence in 1441, an attempt to reconcile the differences between the Eastern and Western Churches in face of the mutual Turkish threat; you can recognize Emperor John Palaeologos by his pointy hat, while Ethiopian monks pay homage to Eugenius. Crudely carved on the other side of the right door, at the bottom, Filarete and his workmen may be seen dancing with their tools below an inscription in pidgin Latin. The next set of doors to the left are by Giacomo Manzù (1963), with harrowing scenes of death and martyrdoms and victims torn like paper bags; on the back of these Manzù cast a scene from the Vatican Second Ecumenical Council, of Pope John XXIII conversing with a cardinal from Tanzania—a reference to Filarete's doors. The last set of doors, by Luciano Minguzzi (1977), includes a charming hedgehog. The plodding equestrian statue at the left end is of Charlemagne, by Cornacchini, giving the portico two knights in case any of the giant marble saints ever want to play chess. The floor of the portico is by the indefatigable Bernini, embedded with the giant coat of arms of John XXIII by Manzù to commemorate the Second Vatican Council of 1962.

Most people find the **interior** disappointing, again partly because your eyes are confused by its scale; its proportions, as everyone said a hundred years ago, are so harmonious you don't notice how large it is, but probably no architect who ever lived could have found a solution to making such a vast barn visually stimulating. Bernini, in charge of decorating the interior, made it into a holy Grand Central Station, full of stone saints and angels, keeping an eye on the big clocks overhead as they wait for trains to Paradise. Up the middle of the nave, bronze markers showing the length of other proud cathedrals prove how each fails miserably to measure up—the fact that they aren't accurate, and make Milan Cathedral some 20 m too small, proves (at least to the Milanese) that the duplicity of the Romans

St Peter's

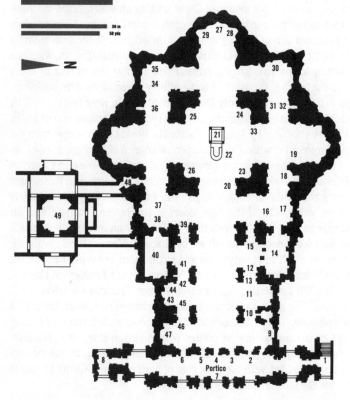

50 m
50 yds

N

Portico

1 Statue of Constantine / Scala Regia
2 Holy Door
3 Crocetti's Door
4 Filarete's Door
5 Manzù Door
6 Minguzzi's Door
7 Giotto's Navicella
8 Statue of Charlemagne
9 Michelangelo's Pietà
10 Queen Christina Monument
11 Cappella di S. Sebastiano
12 Countess Matilda Monument
13 Innocent XII Monument
14 Cappella del Smo. Sacramento
15 Gregory XIII Monument
16 Cappella Gregoriana
17 Madonna del Soccorso
18 Lift up to Dome

19 Altar of St Wenceslas
20 Statue of St Peter
21 High Altar / Bernini's
   Baldacchino
22 Confessio
23 St Longinus / Entrance
   to Grottoes
24 St Helen
25 St Veronica
26 St Andrew
27 Tribune / Cathedra of St Peter
28 Urban VIII Monument
29 Paul III Monument
30 Guercino's St Petronillar
31 Altar of the Navicella
32 Clement XIII Monument
33 St Bruno
34 Cappella della Colonna

35 Leo the Great Tomb
36 Alexander VII Monument
37 Cappella Clementina
38 Pius VII Monument
39 Leo XI Monument
40 Cappella del Coro
41 Innocent VIII Monument
42 Pius X Monument
43 Cappella della Presentazione
44 John XXIII Monument
45 Clementina Sobieska Monument / stairs
   and down lift from dome
46 Monument to the Last Stuarts
47 Baptistry
48 Pius VIII Monument / entrance to
   St Peter's Treasury
49 Sacristy

knows no bounds. The round porphyry stone in the pavement near the central door marks the place by the altar of the old basilica where emperors would kneel to be crowned.

The Pietà

The best work of art is right in front, in the first chapel on the right: Michelangelo's famous *Pietà*, now restored and hard to see behind the glass that protects it from future madmen. Finished in 1499, when he was only 25, the statue helped make Michelangelo's reputation. Its smooth and elegant figures, with the realities of death and grief sublimated on some ethereal plane known only to saints and artists, marked a turning point in religious art—from here, the beautiful, unreal art of the religious Baroque was the logical next step. The *Pietà* is the only work Michelangelo ever signed (on the band of the Virgin's garment); he added it after overhearing a group of tourists from Milan who thought the *Pietà* was the work of a fellow Milanese.

Michelangelo sculpted the *Pietà* for the French ambassador; significantly, none of the art made to order for St Peter's can match it. By the time the basilica was finished, the great artists of the Renaissance were dead, and whatever glories they may have contributed have been replaced by assembly-line Baroque statues and huge Counter-Reformation paintings, in turn replaced by 'more eternal' mosaic copies. The cold feeling is made more oppressive by the ranks of papal funerary monuments with ghoulish Baroque effigies, like Babylonian potentates in their beehive tiaras, their fat fingers laden with rings while voluptuous female allegories pose dutifully below.

The Right Aisle

Two of the few memorials to real women may be seen in the right aisle: in the arch after the *Pietà* is a **Monument to Queen Christina of Sweden**, topped by a large, flattering portrait of the frowzy monarch, who at one point embarrassed her papal sponsors by falling in love with a nun; and in the next chapel, the **Cappella di San Sebastiano**, Bernini's **Monument to Countess Matilda of Tuscany**, the great benefactress of the temporal papacy who died in 1115, and whose remains were brought here from Mantua in 1635. The pride of the next chapel, the **Cappella del Santissimo Sacramento**, is its iron grille by Borromini; on the altar the ciborium by Bernini is a miniature copy of Bramante's Tempietto of S. Pietro in Montorio. In the next arch an allegorical figure of Courage lifts the cover of the sarcophagus of the **Monument of Gregory XIII** by Camillo Rusconi (1723), to reveal an allegory of Gregory's calendar reforms and, underneath, a hobgoblin of a dragon. Beyond, the **Cappella Gregoriana** defines the original, pre-Maderno limits of St Peter's; it was designed by Michelangelo. The altar painting of the *Madonna del Soccorso* is an 11th-century relic from the old basilica. In the next arch is the lift up to the roof (see below).

The right transept contains three altars, the one on the right dedicated to good King Wenceslas (of Bohemia), the same who 'looked out on the Feast of Stephen'. Around the enormous pier sits the famous bronze **Statue of St Peter**, its extended foot worn away by the kisses of the faithful (a 50-day indulgence per smack, according to Pius IX). Its date is a mystery: long believed to belong to the 5th century, made from the bronze of the statue of Capitoline Jove, it was later assumed to be a 13th-century work by Arnolfo di Cambio, though the latest scholarship has reverted to the original date; it may have been part of the tomb of Emperor Honorius, which later became the French monastery of St Martin, just to the left of St Peter's: early Christians, like ancient Romans, often added statues of a personal divine intercessor to help them through the beyond. On 29 June, the feast day of SS. Peter and Paul, the statue is dressed up in full pontifical garb.

The High Altar and the Dome

The **High Altar**, where only the Pope may celebrate mass, is sheltered by Bernini's celebrated **Baldacchino** (1633), cast from bronze looted from the Pantheon roof by his Barberini patron, Urban VIII. The canopy is as tall as the Farnese Palace, to give a hint of its scale, and in form resembles the baldacchino of old St Peter's, with its twisted columns and hangings (though now made of bronze). Barberini bees swarm over it as if it were real barley sugar, and on the pedestals supporting the columns, incorporated into coats of arms, are seven female faces expressing labour pains, and lastly a happy baby's face; Urban VIII commissioned the baldacchino as an ex-voto for the safe deliverance of a favourite niece from a dangerous pregnancy. But even the world's biggest canopy shrinks under the world's biggest **Dome** (the Pantheon's shallow dome is about 6 ft wider, and there are two even bigger ones in Malta, but if inverted this one could hold the most soup). Decorated with a minestrone of religious mosaics spooned on by the tedious Cavaliere d'Arpino, it is a dizzy 352 ft to the top. By the time of Michelangelo's death it was completed only so far as the drum, where 7-ft high letters spell out the words of Christ to Peter: 'Tu es Petrus ...' The horseshoe-shaped **Confessio**, designed by Maderno and perpetually lit by 95 lamps, contains, behind the grille, a shaft leading down to the tomb of St Peter through which the woollen *pallia* (the long strips of cloth that bishops wear around their necks) are lowered to be sanctified. It was when workmen were lowering the floor in the crypt below the Confessio in 1939 that the ancient cemetery was discovered, along with the presumed relics of St Peter (see the Ancient Necropolis, below).

The four massive **Piers** supporting the dome are graced by mastodonic statues of saints associated with St Peter's most treasured relics. These relics used to be publicly displayed during Holy Week from the piers' upper balconies, each of these adorned with a pair of columns from old St Peter's—six of which were brought from Byzantium by Constantine, while the others are copies made shortly after. Nearest the bronze statue of St Peter is *St Longinus* (statue by Bernini) whose relic is the lance that Longinus, a Roman soldier, used to pierce the side of Christ; underneath is the entrance to the Vatican Grottoes (see below). Also on the right is *St Helen* (whose relic is a piece of the True Cross); across from here is *St Veronica*, whose handkerchief preserves an imprint of Christ's features; and last of all is *St Andrew*, by Duquesnoy, whose relic was his head, but that has recently been returned to the church in Patras, Greece, from which the Despot of Morea grabbed it in the 15th century.

The Tribune

Meant to be seen under the baldacchino from the moment you enter is Bernini's **Tribune**, a gaudy 1665 work encasing St Peter's *cathedra*, the chair from which the Apostle was said to have delivered his first sermon to the Romans. Bernini's first training was in the theatre, and this is one of his smash hits, with a multimedia cast of gilt bronze, coloured marbles and stucco, illuminated by a glowing window with a dove emblem that forms an integral part of the composition.

This part of the basilica is usually roped off, but if you have binoculars and are prepared to engage in various bodily contortions, you may just be able to see Bernini's **Monument of Urban VIII** (begun in 1628) to the right of Bernini's throne. Here again the sculptor effectively uses different materials and colours: the Pope, jauntily waving from the afterlife, and Death, penning his epitaph, are in dark bronze, while the more worldly figures of Charity and Justice are of white marble. To the left is Guglielmo della Porta's notorious 1575 **Monument of Paul III**, flanked by figures of Prudence (modelled on the Pope's mother) and Justice, a portrait of his sister, the lovely Giulia Farnese, who as Alexander VI's mistress did her part in advancing Paul's career. Originally the statue was nude; the story goes that its beauty drove a Spanish student to distraction, until one night he hid in the basilica to make love to it. In the morning he was found dead at its side, and since then it has worn metal draperies.

To the right of the tribune, around the Pier of St Helena, is the **Cappella San Michele**, with a mosaic of Guercino's *St Petronilla* (original in the Capitoline museum); behind, on the pier itself, is the **Altar of the Navicella** by Lanfranco, inspired by Giotto's mosaic in the portico; directly across from it is Canova's neoclassical **Monument of Clement XIII**. Continue around the pier for

Michelangelo Slodtz's 1744 *St Bruno*, where the bald, effeminate saint is shown gracefully refusing a bishop's mitre.

The Left Aisle

Backtrack across Bernini's Tribune to the left aisle; behind the Pier of St Veronica is the **Cappella della Colonna**, named after a column from the old basilica, painted with a much venerated picture of the Virgin. The chapel contains the **Tomb of Leo the Great**, with Algardi's relief of St Leo halting the advance of Attila the Hun (the pope is said to have threatened Attila with a fatal nosebleed if he should enter Rome, but since Attila couldn't understand Latin, we see SS. Peter and Paul translating). In the next arch is Bernini's **Monument of Alexander VII**, a late work that juxtaposes the serenely praying pope with Death, popping out of the curtains below, waving a warning hourglass. Across the left transept is the **Cappella Clementina**, decorated by Giacomo della Porta and containing the **Monument of Pius VII** (1823) by Thorvaldsen, the only Protestant to contribute to St Peter's, and probably also the only Icelander.

Beyond, in the arch, is Algardi's **Monument of Leo XI**, whose pontificate lasted only 27 days; the relief shows him as a cardinal watching Henry IV abjure Protestantism. In the next arch, beyond the ornate **Cappella del Coro** is Antonio Pollaiuolo's bronze **Monument to Innocent VIII** (1492), the only survivor from the old basilica, with its good-humoured papal effigy of Innocent blessing with a smile and holding the blade of Longinus' spear, given him by Sultan Bayazit II, while below another effigy represents Innocent in death. Across is the **Monument of St Pius X**, whose tomb is in the next chapel, the **Cappella della Presentazione**. Next on the right is Emilio Greco's **Monument of John XXIII**. The following arch is dedicated to the last Stuarts: up on the right, the **Monument of Clementina Sobieska**, wife of the Old Pretender and granddaughter of the saviour of Vienna, and here called 'Queen of Great Britain, France, and Ireland,' while on the left, Canova's pyramid-shaped **Monument of the Old and Young Pretenders and Henry, Cardinal of York** was paid for by George IV. The **Baptistry** contains an ancient font made of Emperor Otto II's sarcophagus lid turned upside-down, with a metal cover by Carlo Fontana.

> *There's still more: the Treasury, Grottoes, and Dome. Just before the left transept and under the monument of Pius VIII is the entrance to St Peter's Treasury (9–5.30, L3000), containing a choice selection of the bits that the Saracens, Normans, Spaniards and Napoleon didn't steal.*

Near the entrance are two famous relics from the old basilica: the golden cockerel that Leo IV set atop the campanile, whose cock-a-doodle will announce the end of the world, and the beautiful twisted **Colonna Santa**, of Parian marble, traditionally the column on which Christ leaned while disputing with the doctors in the Temple—in the Middle Ages exorcists would place their patients against it to chase out the devil. The bejewelled **Vatican Cross** was given to St Peter's by Justin II in 578, and has portraits of the emperor and empress on the back, who raise their arms as if to say 'Surprise!'; in the same room is the so-called **Dalmatic of Charlemagne**, which tradition claims he wore during his coronation, though it dates from the 11th century (even then, a rare enough example of Byzantine ceremonial dress). Equally intriguing is a 1974 copy of **St Peter's Chair**, the original of the one enclosed in Bernini's Baroque confection, though chances are slim that Peter ever sat in it, as it was donated to the basilica in 875 by Charles the Bald. The upper part is Carolingian, while the lower half, from the 3rd century, surprisingly decorated with fine ivory reliefs of the Labours of Hercules.

Beyond is a lovely marble tabernacle (1435) by Donatello, saved from the old basilica; it frames a much revered painting of the *Madonna della Febbre*, invoked against malaria. The **Tomb of Sixtus IV** by Antonio Pollaiuolo (1493) is a masterpiece of bronze casting, with its fine effigy of the sleeping Pope and the allegories of the Seven Virtues and ten Sciences that adorn its sides; it can be viewed from the platform above. This is followed by a 14th-century Giottesque fresco of SS. Peter and Paul, found in the crypt; a 13th-century bust reliquary of St Luke; a key of St Peter's tomb (one of many copies made; after a time in the sacred keyhole it would become one of the most prized relics a pilgrim could obtain); Sixtus IV's ring; choir antiphonies embellished with beautiful grotesques; the gilded bronze SS. Peter and Paul by Torrigiano (most famous in Italy for having broken Michelangelo's nose); a pair of enormous candelabra attributed to Cellini; the jewelled tiara used to crown the ancient statue of St Peter, followed by chalices and other Church paraphernalia studded with precious stones, much of it given to the popes since Napoleon; and lastly, the remarkable **Sarcophagus of Junius Bassus**, prefect of Rome in 359; the reliefs portray both Old and New Testament scenes and baby Bacchuses.

> *The entrance to the crypt of St Peter's, or **Sacred Grottoes** is usually by way of the stair by the Pier of St Longinus. The Grottoes, on the floor level of the old basilica, follow the floor plan of the basilica above, and are lined with tombs: a full house, with a pair of queens, 20 popes, and an emperor (open except when the pope is in the basilica, Oct–April 7–5; May–Sept 7–6; free adm).*

The horseshoe-shaped **Grotte Nuove**, built 1534–46 under the area of St Peter's altar, are called 'new' because their decoration is more recent. Most beautiful here is the Renaissance **Tomb of Paul II**, on which Mino da Fiesole and Giovanni Dalmata laboured for ten years without finishing. Further along, placed in the wall, are lovely marble reliefs from the baldacchino made for Sixtus IV. In the centre of the horseshoe, directly under the High Altar and over the 'Trophy of Gaius' (the 3rd-century shrine built around St Peter's tomb), is the **Cappella Clementina** (1605); if the lights are on in the necropolis below, you can see a section of it in a gap to the left of the altar.

The adjoining **Grotte Vecchie** were built at the same time that Maderno extended the nave. The central altar has another exquisite Renaissance work, a relief of *Christ in Majesty* from the tomb of Nicholas V, by Giovanni Dalmata (1450s). In the area under St Peter's right aisle are the simple tombs of John XXIII (always covered with flowers), John Paul I, and Paul VI, while those of Christina of Sweden and Charlotte of Cyprus face each other. Canova's large statue of praying **Pius VI**, formerly in the Confessio, was moved to the end of the Grottoes in 1980. The Old Pretender, Bonny Prince Charlie, and Henry, Cardinal of York are in the left aisle, as is the English pope, Adrian IV, in a 3rd-century sarcophagus (no one brings *him* pretty flowers—the Romans remember him best for burning Arnold of Brescia). Off the left aisle are a few rooms used to house fragments of the old basilica.

> *To ascend St Peter's **Dome**, one of Rome's biggest thrills and chills (especially if you suffer from vertigo), leave the basilica and join the queue on the far right-hand side. Open Oct–Apr 8–5, May–Sept 8–6; adm L4000, L5000 by lift (worthwhile since it's another 200 steps from the roof to the top of the dome).*

The lift leaves you on the roof, a strange world of domes on wavy pavement, where you can measure yourself against the saintly titans who will look over Piazza San Pietro until kingdom come; here, too, is a souvenir shop, post office, coke machine, WCs, and buildings of the *Sanpietrini*, the workmen in charge of maintaining the fabric of the basilica. In the old days the *Sanpietrini* not only worked on the roof, but lived here with their families, producing sons who scoffed at heights and who would later inherit their jobs.

Although recent cupolas cast a shadow on St Peter's superlatives (visitors from New Orleans find it downright puny next to their Superdome) it can still claim to be the largest brick dome in existence. Stairs within the dome lead up to the **First Gallery**, for a death-defying view 53 m above the floor of St Peter's that brings home, more than anything, the basilica's scale. A narrower stair, tilted for the curve in the dome, continues up to the **Second Gallery** 73 m up, but this is closed to the public. An even narrower spiral stair continues the rest of the way up to the terrace under the lantern, from where, on a clear day, all Rome, much of the *campagna*, and the Tyrhennian coast lie spread out at your feet. The golden ball high overhead, which looks like a marble from below, is actually big enough to hold 16 people.

> *In 1939, when Pius XII ordered the Sanpietrini to lower the floor of the Sacred Grottoes and prepare a tomb for Pius XI, the workmen discovered not only the floor of the Constantinian Basilica, but below this, signs of an ancient tomb. Although its existence has been documented since Bramante's day, Pius XII was the first pope to consent to an exploration of the area (previous popes had superstitiously feared to disturb the bones, or worse yet, to learn that the Saracens in 846 had stolen St Peter's relics after all). All during the war, the secret excavations continued, uncovering one of the most remarkable sights in all Rome: the* **Ancient Necropolis of St Peter's**, *a pristine street of pagan and early Christian tombs built around that of the Apostle.*
>
> *Lack of space and the delicate condition of the tombs and frescoes permit only 15 people or so to enter at a time. In the off season, you may be able to get on an English-speaking tour at a moment's notice, but try to book as far in advance as possible (see p.25; adm L10,000. The 1 ½-hour tours meet by the Uffizio degli Scavi (excavations office), open Mon–Sat 9–12 and 2–5, under the Arco delle Campane, and descend through the Sacred Grottoes to the level of the ancient tombs.*

Apparently the pagan tombs originally overlooked the Vatican Circus, so the dead could enjoy the games even in the afterlife. The guides know their subject well and take you past the delightful, brightly-painted tombs lined with niches for urns, described by H.V. Morton as 'little sitting-rooms for the soul'. The burials date from 150–300 AD; the Christians, naturally, are near St Peter; one tomb has what is believed to be the earliest Christian mosaic ever found—Christ depicted as the sun god Helios.

Deep under the High Altar the excavations revealed the red walls of a monument-shrine, or *ædicula*, believed to be the so-called 'trophy of Gaius' (built around 160 AD, and described by the priest Gaius around the year 200). When constructing St Peter's basilica, Constantine enclosed the 'trophy of Gaius' in marble and porphyry, filled in the surrounding tombs, and laboriously excavated a section of the Vatican hill to ensure that this spot would be under the altar. Physical evidence was found of the Saracens' raid, and in the ædicula, a hole which probably contained St Peter's bronze casket. But outside the ædicula were found the headless bones of an elderly, strongly built man; graffiti on the wall above invoke the aid of St Peter. After years of consideration, Paul VI announced that these bones were indeed the relics of St Peter. Jammed around are the tombs of Christians anxious to be buried near the Apostle.

No one is quite sure how far the street of pagan tombs extends—perhaps to Castel Sant'Angelo. To excavate any further would undermine the basilica, and besides, as the guide will tell you: 'the rest are pagans, so why bother?'

Vatican City and Gardens

The three-hour guided tours of Vatican City and the Gardens begin from in front of the tourist office. Book in advance, showing your ID; tours begin at 10 am; daily except Sun and Wed in summer; Sat only in winter; L15,000.

After a short bus ride through the Arco delle Campane, past the 8th-century German cemetery (where you'll be buried for free if you drop dead during the tour) and a plaque marking the original site of the obelisk, you'll see the Vatican railway station, used for bringing in goods to be sold tax free in the Vatican supermarket. It was used only once by a pope, when John XXIII went to Assisi (jet-age John Paul II prefers the heliport near the west wall) and is said to be fitted with a choir loft and organ. Go ahead and laugh, but it was an extremely liberal move to have it built in the first place; popes originally forbade railways in the Papal States for fear that passengers would snog in the tunnels! Next are various office palazzi, the mosaic workshop, and the Ethiopian Seminary, where the Pope sheltered students during Mussolini's imperial adventures. The well manicured grounds are planted with fine specimens of exotic trees and roses, with beds arranged in 16th-century Italian garden geometry. One section is set aside for something no Polish pope could do without—cabbages. The most beautiful building is Pirro Ligorio and Peruzzi's **Casino of Pius IV** (1558–62), a jewel-like summer pavilion where popes and their cardinals could engage in elegant conversation.

*As you leave Piazza San Pietro, note the building to the left of Bernini's Colonnade: this is the **Palazzo del Sant'Uffizio**, or Holy Office, or Inquisition. The same kind of perversely reasoned force that it once used to stamp out heresy was employed in 1936–50 to bulldoze two pleasant old lanes of the Borgo to create **Via della Conciliazione**, planned as a triumphal way to St Peter's, and an opportunity to view the famous dome. Critics have always complained that it ruined one of the best surprises in Rome, that of suddenly stumbling upon Bernini's grand piazza. Worst of all, its bossy airs make Via della Conciliazione an uncomfortably sterile no man's land, a perfect runway for the squadrons of jumbo tourist buses descending on St Peter's.*

*Via della Conciliazione has mediocre cafés, bookshops, and souvenir shops with 3-D winking Jesuses, and three Renaissance palazzi salvaged by Mussolini's new 'Ruinantes': the **Palazzo dei Convertendi**, on the* *left at **no. 34,** where Raphael died of love and exhaustion and an ill-advised bleeding by his surgeons, reassembled here in the 1930s from its original site in Via Scossacavalli; in the next block, no. 30, **Palazzo Torlonia**, a 1504 mini-Cancelleria palace by Andrea Bregno, headquarters of Rome's richest banking family; and opposite, at no. 33, the **Palazzo dei Penitenzieri**, built in the 1470s and now a hotel.*

*Turn right after this palace on Via Scossacavalli to Borgo Santo Spirito, site of the church of **Santo Spirito in Sassia**. 'Sassia' as in Saxony: though rebuilt after the Sack of Rome, with a façade by Antonio da Sangallo the Younger, it was founded in the 9th century to serve the Borgo's Anglo-Saxon community. Next to it is the **Ospedale di Santo Spirito in Sassia**, the successor to the Schola Anglorum.*

Founded by King Ina of Wessex in 717, it was the largest and best run of the Borgo's national school-hospices. Unfortunately, it was made of wood, and went up like a torch in the great fire of 847 (depicted in Raphael's Stanze in the Vatican). Seven years later, King Ethelwolf came with his son, the future Alfred the Great, and rebuilt the Schola, funding it and the pope by a voluntary contribution of his subjects known as Peter's Pence—which soon became a mandatory hearth tax until abolished by Henry VIII (curiously, a fortune in Plantagenet-era silver pennies was discovered in 1883, hidden in the House of the Vestal Virgins). Among the most famous pilgrims to have stayed in the Borgo were Macbeth, who came in 1050 with a guilty conscience, and the half-legendary Tannhauser, who came in the 13th century and was refused absolution for his love of Venus. But by the time he arrived (walking the whole way with his eyes shut, to deny himself the beauty of Italy), the English had let their Schola decline to such a state that Innocent III had it converted into a hospital (1204). It was rebuilt in 1473 as Rome's main home for foundlings—an improvement on the old practice of leaving unwanted children on the banks of the Tiber. You can still see the lazy Susan in the façade, where until the mid-19th century infants could be anonymously dropped.

Castel Sant'Angelo

*Just up the Tiber from the long wards of Santo Spirito looms Castel Sant'Angelo, but before going in, note the unusual wall that links the fortress with the Vatican like a stone umbilical cord. Rome is full of aqueducts but this one is a pope-a-duct, the famous **Covered Passageway** used by St Peter's successors since 1277 to escape to the castle when things became too hot to handle. You can see the windows along the top; try to imagine glimpses of the pale Clement VII fleeing down the* *passage during the Sack of Rome, his robes flying and prelates racing desperately behind for the safety of **Castel Sant'Angelo**, the ancient Mausoleum of Hadrian. Open 9–1, Sun 9–12, Mon 2–6.30 (winter 2–5.30); adm L8000.*

Hadrian thought he couldn't go wrong when he designed this new tomb for the emperors in 138, three years before his own death. He placed it on the uninhabited bank of the pestilential Tiber, where the imperial megalomania would cause no resentment, and he built it solidly to defend his memory against Time itself. Instead, his last resting place has seen more blood, treachery, and turmoil than any in Rome; his ashes were still warm in the urn when Aurelian made it a bulwark in his walls, inaugurating its history as Rome's chief citadel and dungeon.

Hadrian's original design harked back to Augustus' Mausoleum, though on a pharaonic scale, consisting of a massive 89 m solid square base topped by a cylinder 64 m in diameter and 20 m high, made of travertine with a white Parian marble veneer. Like a giant planter, cypresses grew out of its top, while at the very summit of the tower stood a gilded quadriga driven by a colossal statue of Hadrian (now replaced by the bronze angel). The emperor was a great art collector, and beautiful statues adorned the sides; these, whether made by Praxiteles or Roman assembly-line chisels, were used as ammunition in 537, when Belisarius' besieged troops were holed up inside the mausoleum: a rain of marble gods that persuaded the Goths to give up the attack. Some 50 years later, when the even deadlier plague besieged Rome, Pope Gregory the Great was leading a procession through the city, praying for divine mercy, when he had a vision of St Michael on top of the mausoleum, sheathing his sword to announce the end of the pestilence. Henceforth it was known as Castel Sant'Angelo.

For a thousand years the master of Castel Sant'Angelo was the master of Rome. There would be no papacy, perhaps, without it, at least not in its present form. With rebellions of some sort occurring on average every two years before 1400, the popes often had recourse to this place of safety. It last saw action in the Sack of 1527, when according to Cellini's *Autobiography* he personally saved the castle and Clement VII from the crazed Lutherans, while back at the Vatican the valiant Swiss Guard were slain to a man. For several months the Pope and his followers watched helplessly as Rome burned; Clement eventually escaped, disguised as a servant. Subsequent popes, fearing similar long stays, had the castle's interiors fashionably decorated, but mostly they found it a convenient prison and torture chamber for the likes of Cellini, Beatrice Cenci, and Giordano Bruno. Opera-goers will recognize it from the last act of Puccini's *Tosca*, when Cavaradossi's foul murder makes Tosca literally go over the top (in a memorable early performance in New York, the soprano leapt from the stage set Castel

Sant'Angelo to an over-taut trampoline, and bounced back on stage, to wild applause). In 1992 a TV production of the opera was shot on location in Rome at precisely the times specified in Puccini's score and broadcast live to 107 countries. At 5 am Rome time, millions watched as the TV Tosca leapt to her death. Actually her fall was a mere six feet to a pile of cushions.

Nothing very humorous ever happened for real in the castle; from 1849 to 70 it was occupied by French troops, and by the Italians until 1901, when it underwent a 30-year restoration and was opened as a museum.

Still, there is something uncanny about Castel Sant'Angelo. It exhales the musty air of one of evolution's mistakes, a muscle-bound dinosaur or ungainly iron-clad ship run aground behind a frilly Baroque bridge. For all the torture and death that stain its bowels it tells no ghost stories. But come back at twilight, when it becomes a malignant vortex for swarms of sparrows that blacken the sky; the parasol pines in its moat-cum-garden vibrate with their wings; their twittering thunder drowns even Rome's traffic. (Significantly, their other evening rendezvous is in front of Termini Station!)

> *At the entrance of Castel Sant'Angelo, steps descend to the **vestibule**, with four models of the mausoleum's previous incarnations. Straight on is the shaft of fat and lazy Leo X's man-powered lift, which no longer works, so turn right, and walk up Hadrian's sombrely impressive **spiral ramp**, which still preserves patches of its original floor mosaic.*

Four ventilation shafts rose up through the earthen tumulus; the third one was converted into a dread prison in the Middle Ages. The ramp leads to a bridge that passes over the gloomy, stripped bare **sepulchral chamber**, where the ashes of the emperors were kept. This bridge was built in 1822 to replace a drawbridge, which could be pulled up to isolate the papal apartments in case of siege. The **Stair of Alexander VI** continues up to the left, to the **Court of the Angel**, named for Raffaello da Montelupo's marble angel, whose position atop the castle was usurped by van Verschaffelt's bronze Michael in 1753. The court is decorated with piles of cannon balls, and Michelangelo's façade of the **Chapel of Leo X**, perhaps Il Divino's most obscure work (directly across the court, by the stair of Urban VIII). To the right are a row of old guard rooms, housing a **Museum of Weapons and Armour** featuring Stone Age arrowheads, fancy Renaissance metal suits, and overstretched 18th-century rifles. A door on the left leads into the two **Rooms of Clement VIII**, with an ornate stucco chimneypiece; the **Hall of Justice**, reached through a second doorway near the Chapel of Leo X, is directly over the tomb chamber and was used as the seat of Rome's tribunal in the 16th–17th centuries; it contains a fresco of the Angel of Justice by Perin del Vaga.

Giving on to this room is the **Sala dell'Apollo**, painted with grotesques for Paul III. Beyond this are the two small **Rooms of Clement VII**, where he lived during the Sack of Rome, the first decorated with a frieze by Giulio Romano. They are now used as a small art gallery, with a triptych by Giotto's best pupil, Taddeo Gaddi; Montagna's *Madonna and Child* and Signorelli's *Madonna and Saints*.

*A passageway leads into the **Courtyard of Alexander VI**, with a pretty Renaissance well-head bearing the Borgia arms and a large catapult ready to fire.*

In Alexander's time the courtyard was used for theatrical performances. A small stair leads up to the **Bathroom of Clement VII**, the most charming corner of the castle with its colourful frescoes and stuccoes by Giulio Romano, where the miserable pope could forget his troubles in a hot bath. The semi-circular two-storey building enclosing this was formerly used as prisons, which seem luxurious compared to the cramped and dreadful **Historic Prisons**, down the steps from the courtyard. Skeletons discovered just beneath the floor confirmed the stories of prisoners tortured to death or murdered in their cells. Also down at this level are the vast **Oil Stores**, holding over 20,000 litres for frying the prisoners' meals or pouring on the heads of assailants. The adjacent rooms were for storing grain, though the popes later used them to store excess political prisoners.

*Walk back up to Alexander VI's courtyard, and from there up to the **Loggia of Paul III**, designed by Antonio da Sangallo the Younger.*

There are excellent views from here and the other galleries that encircle the castle, a restored cell of a political prisoner of the 1830s, and a most welcome and panoramic bar. A few steps lead up from the Loggia of Paul III to the main Papal Apartments, decorated for Paul III, beginning with the lavishly stuccoed **Sala Paolina**, painted by Perin del Vaga and Pellegrino Tibaldi. Note the *trompe l'oeil* fresco of a doorway, through which a black-robed courtier appears to be entering. The next room, the **Camera del Perseo** is decorated with a frieze on the myth of Perseus by Perin del Vaga and furnished in 16th-century style; the **Camera di Amore e Psyche**, also painted by Perin del Vaga, is arranged as a bedroom of the same period.

Return to the Sala Paolina, from which a curved corridor painted with grotesques leads to the ornate **Library**; beyond this are two more rooms, the **Camera dell'Adriano** with frescoes of the Mausoleum of Hadrian, and **Camera dei Festoni**, with paintings by Dosso Dossi (*Bacchanal*) and Lorenzo Lotto (*St Jerome* and *Madonna and saints*). From the Library a stair leads up to three little rooms called the **Cagliostra**, with more paintings, so named for the greatest con man of the 18th century, the Count of Cagliostro. Also from the Library, a small passage leads into the circular core of the castle, the **Room of the Secret Archives**, lined with walnut cupboards where the popes stored their treasure until 1870, when it was moved to the Vatican for safe-keeping.

From here, a Roman-era stair built in the thickness of the wall leads up to another circular room, with military memorabilia. Above this is the **Terrace** under the great bronze angel, the scene of the last act of *Tosca*, with a famous view of St Peter's and the rest of Rome. The large bell here, the *Campana della Misericordia*, was only rung when a prisoner was executed in the castle.

> *Dark, too, is the history of Castel Sant'Angelo's bridge **Ponte Sant'-Angelo**, Hadrian's Pons Aelius, built in 134 to link his Mausoleum to the city (the three central arches are Hadrian's, the other two were added with the Tiber Embankments).*

While a solid stillness hangs over the rest of Rome, the famous angels of Ponte Sant'Angelo battle a perpetual Baroque hurricane to display the symbols of Christ's passion; **Bernini's Breezy Maniacs** they were dubbed almost immediately after they appeared in 1688, sculpted to Bernini's design by students. They replace the rows of gallows erected for the Jubilee of 1500, when 18 swinging corpses formed a memorable welcome to Rome, though the death toll was worse in the 1450 Jubilee, when 200 pilgrims were crushed to death in a panic on the bridge. Previously the right bank of the bridge was occupied by the horrible Tor di Nona, a prison tower favoured for night-time executions; both this and Castel Sant'Angelo had permanent nooses on display and they were rarely vacant.

> *Pious souls may skip the rest of this walk and have a Campari. Doubting Thomases, unconvinced by St Peter's and the rest, should continue up the Tiber from Castel Sant'Angelo, along Lungotevere Castello, past the cheerfully-named fascisti **Casa Madre dei Mutilati** and the corrugated aluminium fence that surrounds the **Palazzo di Giustizia**(1910), a bombastic travertine fruitcake that has been on the verge of collapse since 1970; the few unfortunates working there always seem to be glancing over their shoulders.*

> *Persist, you sceptic, past the next bridge, where the street becomes Lungotevere Prati and enter the neo-Gothic **Sacro Cuore del Suffragio**(no. 12) and its **Museum of Purgatory, or of the Souls of the Dead** in the sacristy; you may have to ask the sacristan to unlock it (open 7.30–11.15 am and 5–6.30 pm). Its one dingy display case contains bits of cloth and faded prayer books singed by the burning hands of souls from Purgatory. A handout explains each story; some dead people do the darndest things!*

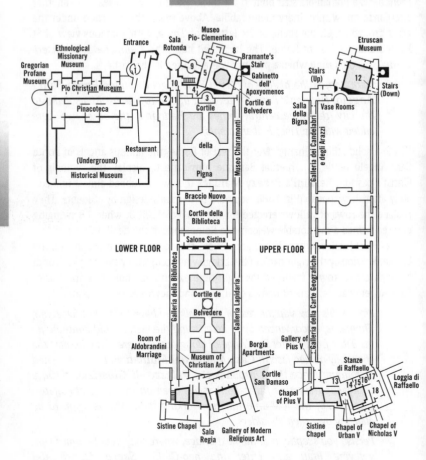

The Vatican Museums

LOWER FLOOR

Ethnological Missionary Museum

Gregorian Profane Museum

Pio Christian Museum

Pinacoteca

Restaurant

(Underground)

Historical Museum

Entrance

Sala Rotonda

Museo Pio-Clementino

Bramante's Stair

Gabinetto dell' Apoxyomenos

Cortile di Belvedere

Cortile della Pigna

Museo Chiaramonti

Braccio Nuovo

Cortile della Biblioteca

Salone Sistina

Galleria della Biblioteca

Cortile de Belvedere

Galleria Lapidaria

Room of Aldobrandini Marriage

Museum of Christian Art

Borgia Apartments

Cortile San Damaso

Chapel of Pius V

Sistine Chapel

Sala Regia

Gallery of Modern Religious Art

UPPER FLOOR

Etruscan Museum

Stairs (Up)

Stairs (Down)

Salla della Bigna

Galleria del Candelabri e degli Arazzi

Vase Rooms

Galleria della Carte Geografiche

Gallery of Pius V

Stanze di Raffaello

Loggia di Raffaello

Sistine Chapel

Chapel of Urban V

Chapel of Nicholas V

1 Spiral
2 Quattro Cancelli
3 La Pigna
4 Egyptian Museum
5 Animal Room
6 Gallery of Statues
7 Mask Room
8 Gallery of Busts
9 Hall of the Muses

10 Hall of the Greek Cross
11 Museum of Pagan Antiquities
12 Rooms of Greek Originals
13 Hall of Immaculate Conception
14 Stanza del Incendio
15 Stanza della Segnatura
16 Stanza di Eliodoro
17 Sala di Costantino
18 Sala dei Chiaro Scuri

The Museums	310
Raphael Stanze	315
Borgia Apartment	318
Sistine Chapel	319

Start: *At the entrance to the Vatican Museums on Viale Vaticano.*

Walking Time: *1 hour (for a sprint to the Sistine Chapel) to 5 hours (for a jog around every museum).*

XV: The Vatican Museums

Musei Vaticani

Although 99 per cent indoors, this is one of the longest walks in this book and when and how you tackle the world's biggest museum will partly depend on when you come (see Walk XIV for suggestions on how to combine the museums with St Peter's and Castel Sant'Angelo).To reach the Museum entrance either take the Metro A to Ottaviano and walk down Via Ottaviano, turning right at the second block (Via Germanico, which soon turns into Viale Vaticano). Alternatively, from Piazza San Pietro (see Walk XIV), walk 10 minutes north along the walls of Vatican City until you come to the entrance; or catch the minibus in front of the tourist information office. It leaves every half hour until 2 pm.

The Museum hours are Mon–Sat 8.45–1.45; Easter period and July, Aug and Sept Mon–Sat 8.45–4.45. Last entrance 45 minutes before closing. Closed Sun except last Sun of each month (winter 8.45–1.45, summer 8.45–4.45) when it's free (and packed with Romans); otherwise, adm L12,000, a pretty penny, but the Pope gives good value for money: 12 museums, a couple of miles of galleries, the Sistine Chapel, the Raphael Stanze, and the Borgia Apartment.

Unfortunately for you, there isn't much dull museum clutter to pass over lightly, and seeing all 7 km of exhibits would take a lifetime. On the bright side, the Pope sees to it that his museum is managed more thoughtfully than anything run by the Italian state and it recently won an EC award for its arrangements for people with disabilities. There are two special routes for people in wheelchairs—just ask the guards at the entrance, and they'll get things organized.

To control the crowds, the Vatican has imposed a choice of four colour-coded one-way itineraries that will thread you through the labyrinth in the amount of time you care to spend, from 90 min (A: a jog down to the Sistine Chapel and back) to 5 hours (D: yellow, which takes in everything). Itinerary B (3 hours) includes the Etruscan Museum, the Sistine Chapel, the Pinacoteca, and the old Lateran Museums; itinerary C (3½ hours) takes in most of the classical sculpture (except the Etruscans) and all the great Renaissance frescoes, and no one cares if you tack on the Pinacoteca, too. In practice, the guards don't mind too much if you duck under the rails, but will enforce the one-way rule if it's full.

The Vatican Museums' Cafeteria is the one place in Italy where you can't get a decent cup of coffee. The plastic pasta would make even the faithless consider fasting. See Walk XIV for suggestions.

*Don't be discouraged as you squeeze down the dangerously narrow pavement, past the shiny denizens of the tour group demi-monde; within the Vatican Museums all is tidy and almost rational. An impressive double spiral ramp of steps (1932, by Giuseppe Momo) takes you up to the gallery level and the Museums' main crossroads, the **Atrio dei Quattro Cancelli**; from here a door leads into the museums' most striking feature, the **Cortile del Belvedere**, enclosed by twin half-mile long galleries. Designed by Bramante for Julius II as a great outdoor auditorium, the courtyard has since been subdivided. The section you can now see is the **Cortile della Pigna** (named for the monstrously large bronze pine cone, originally part of a fountain by the Temple of Isis, and later a landmark on the Portico of Old St Peter's) by the **Braccio Nuovo**. If you want to see the fabulous collection of antique sculpture (Itineraries C & D) you must first pass through the **Egyptian Museum**.*

Founded by Gregory XVI in the 1830s and housed in earnest, phoney Egyptian rooms, it has the usual mummies, sarcophagi, figurines, monumental statues of gods and pharaohs (the sandstone *bust of Mentuhotep II* in the hemicycle overlooking the Cortile della Pigna, is one of the finest and also the oldest in the museum, *c.* 2040 BC). Keeping him company are some bizarre Egyptian deities—baboonish Thot with chin on knees and a cooky grin, and the pot-bellied moonfaced Bes. Most people walk right through **Room III** without realizing that its contents are Roman imitations of Egyptian art, nearly all made for Hadrian's Villa at Tivoli; so pop back and have a look: the presence of little wolf-headed gods in togas and a marble Egyptianized statue of his beloved Antinous gives it away, if nothing else.

*The next museum, the **Chiaramonti Sculpture Gallery** is down the stair to the right from the Egyptian Museum.*

This long, dead-end gallery jam-packed with busts, reliefs, and statues—Greek originals, Roman copies, and Roman originals—was founded by Pius VII and arranged by Canova. It occupies half of Bramante's east gallery and probably should be skipped if you're pressed for time or not a serious student of ancient art. Otherwise, it's worth a stroll for the nightmarish hypnosis of being watched by a

1000-foot double row of blank eyeballs. A 5th-century BC Greek bust of Athena in section XVI, startles with her keen gaze of ivory and semi-precious stones; she at least can see you, she knows you're really looking for Apollo Belvedere, though you should really hang on for ten minutes and take a wander down the **Braccio Nuovo**. It was built in 1822 as an extension of the Chiaramonti Gallery, and graced with a number of celebrated works: a fine copy of the *Wounded Amazon*, Polycletus' prize winner in a 5th-century competition in Ephesus; a copy of a famous 3rd-century statue of the orator *Demosthenes*, whose marble mouth betrays his stutter; a Hellenistic statue of *The Nile*, who reclines like Goliath near a little sphinx, with 16 lilliputian children (the 16 cubits the Nile rises when flooded); and nearby, a noble bust of the young Marcus Aurelius (no. 94), and a not-so-noble one of Mark Antony (89). Beyond is the central hall with the *Giustiniani Athena*, an excellent copy of a famous 4th-century BC work; a fine portrait bust of Philip the Arab (Emperor in 121); the *Doryphoros*, or spear thrower, a copy of a Greek original by Polycletus, a work famous for its study of human proportions; the lovely *Modesty*, actually the Greek mother of the Muses, Mnemosyne (Memory); and the handsome *Augustus of Prima Porta*, found at Livia's villa at Prima Porta, and considered the finest portrait of the emperor. He wears a beautifully carved cuirass, showing the king of Parthia returning to Tiberius the Roman military insignia captured from Crassus in 53 BC; the Cupid on the dolphin refers to the Julian family's Venusian ancestry. The only detail lacking is his elevator sandals (usually hidden by his long toga; Augustus was only 5ft 7in).

> *When you've had your fill, walk back through the Chiaramonti and up the steps to the Pio Clementino, containing the Vatican's most celebrated classical sculpture and its most irritating plaster fig leaves.*

The first prize is the 3rd-century BC Etruscan-influenced *Sarcophagus of L. Cornelius Scipio*, taken from the Tomb of the Scipios; the second, in Room X, is an excellent Roman copy of Lysippus' 4th-century bronze *Apoxyomenos* (the 'Scraper'), the weary athlete scraping oil from his body after his game. Beyond is the **Octagonal Court of the Belvedere**, which lent the marble *Apollo Belvedere* his name; this is a 2nd-century copy of Leochares' bronze statue that once stood in the Athenian Agora, and shows the young god, long held as the paragon of male beauty, looking after an arrow he has just shot. Clockwise, he is followed by an original relief from Augustus' Ara Pacis, and beyond, the famous *Laocoön*, discovered near Nero's Golden House in 1506 and immediately recognized as the famous group described by Pliny the Elder. Sculpted *c.*50 BC by the Rhodian sculptors Agesander and his sons Polydoros and Athenodoros, this most violent and contorted of all Hellenistic sculpture portrays the Trojan priest of

Apollo, Laocoön, with his two young sons struggling desperately in the constricting coils of the sea serpents sent by Apollo as punishment for telling the truth about Greeks bearing gifts. A photo of a plaster cast shows how the group appeared for centuries, according to Michelangelo's idea; the present reconstruction came about when Laocoön's original arm was found in a pawn shop. Next, guarding the exit, are two Hellenistic hounds from Pergamon, and beyond them a Roman copy of Praxiteles' beautiful *Hermes* and a *Perseus*, carrying the head of Medusa, by the neoclassical sculptor Canova, who made it to compensate for some of the ancient pieces carted off by Napoleon.

A door between the hounds fittingly leads into a delightful bronze and marble zoo. Some of the animals are antique (the sow, the camel head, Meleager, a young marble god who wouldn't look out of place pestering females on the Spanish Steps, with his dog and boar's head, and Mithras slaying a bull while a scorpion goes for its testicles) but the rest were made in the 18th century for Pius VI, by sculptor Francesco Antonio Franzoni. The colourful mosaics of animals are from Hadrian's villa in Tivoli.

The **Gallery of Statues** (Room V) has two fine copies of Praxiteles' work: *Apollo Sauroktonos* (the god about to kill a lizard) and the *Resting Satyr*; the so-called *Eros of Centocelle* (no. 250), a copy of a 4th-century BC Greek statue, a charming work said to represent Thanatos, or Death; the *Sleeping Ariadne*, a copy of a Hellenistic original, with the famous 2nd-century AD *Barberini Candelabra* on either side, found in Hadrian's villa, where they were used to support flaming lamps.

At the end of the Gallery of Statues is the **Gallery of Busts** (often closed), featuring portraits of Caracalla, the ugly brute (292), Julius Cæsar, Augustus as a youth (273), the fair Antinous (357) and the seated *Jupiter Verospi*. Backtracking through the Gallery of Statues you might find the **Gabinetto delle Maschere** open, named after the brightly coloured theatrical mask mosaics from Hadrian's villa; it contains one of the best copies of Praxiteles' *Venus of Cnidus* (4th-century BC), the famous nude commissioned by the people of Kos and rejected for its voluptuous nudity, a prudery not shared by the Cnidians, who set it up in a seaside temple as a tourist attraction.

Backtrack further, through the animal room to the great octagonal **Sala delle Muse**, where Roman copies of 4th-century BC Greek muses, Apollo, Greek philosophers and writers (Homer, Socrates, Plato, Euripides, etc.) gaze upon the taut, muscled *Torso del Belvedere* in the centre, signed by Apollonius of Athens (1st century BC), found in the Campo dei Fiori, snapped up by Julius II, and much studied by Michelangelo.

The next room, the **Sala Rotonda** is a neoclassical copy of the Pantheon, built around an enormous porphyry basin from the Golden House; the floor is paved with the Mosaic of Otricoli, representing a battle of Greeks and centaurs, and a sea fight between the mermen. Among the busts of the emperors is the magnificent head of *Jupiter of Otricoli* (539) next to a serenely beautiful *Antinous* dressed as Bacchus, much studied by Bernini and other sculptors in Rome; beside him stands *Demeter*, or Ceres, a fine copy of a 5th-century BC original, and next to her towers a gilded bronze *Hercules* with a tiny ET-like head, originally in Pompey's Theatre. Room I, the **Hall of the Greek Cross** has two remarkable porphyry sarcophagi, of St Helen (with nary a Christian symbol in sight among the Roman soldiers, war-captives and phallic missiles) and the less warlike tomb (with palaeo-Christian symbols of peacocks, grapes, etc.) of Constantia, the nasty daughter or grand-daughter of Constantine, brought here from the church of S. Costanza.

> *Outside the Hall of the Greek Cross the Simonetti Staircase leads up to the Gallery of the Candelabra (see below) past the inevitably locked **Sala della Biga**. Peep through the iron gate into a small domed hall built for a 1st-century AD biga, or two-horse chariot, which was reconstructed by Fanzoni, who added the inner horse; the chariot may have been a votive offering to Ceres. Up another flight of stairs is the **Gregorian Etruscan Museum**, founded in 1837 by Gregory XVI and too good to skip.*

The collection, currently being rearranged, was mostly unearthed in Southern Etruria, the land of the old Papal States, and features the **Regolini-Galassi Tomb** from the 7th century BC, discovered near Caere and reconstructed here, with its fine golden ornaments and tomb furniture for two, a warrior and a priest of considerable standing. Elsewhere you can see fine bronzes, especially the 4th-century *Mars of Todi*, influenced by the Greeks; along with beautifully engraved mirrors and boxes (*cistae*) for toiletries, some charming examples of the Etruscan knack for portraiture. The Greeks never cared for it, though they would probably have approved of Bramante's elegant stair, which can be seen from one of the next rooms; each column is of a slightly different length (a kind of entasis, as the Greeks used in building the Parthenon) in this case to create the illusion of a perfect spiral.

Room XII, of the Greek Originals, houses superb works from the 5th century BC: a head of Athena, fragments from the Parthenon friezes, and loveliest of all, the *funeral stele of a young athlete with his servant*. The two floors of the Hemicycle, embracing the mighty pine cone in the court, are home to an outstanding collection of vases imported by the Etruscans from Greece in the 7th–5th centuries BC: the black-figured amphora of *Achilles and Ajax playing dice*, signed by Exekias; the famous kylix by Duris, of *Oedipus solving the riddle of the Sphinx*; and upstairs, a hydria of *Apollo of Delphi on a tripod* and a jug with a *Scene of a cock-*

fight. Other vases on display, from Magna Grecia and Etruria, make interesting comparisons.

> *Head back down the stairs to begin the quarter mile walk down Bra-*
> *mante's gallery to the old papal apartments and Sistine Chapel. The*
> *popes decorated the interlinking galleries in various styles, which the*
> *popes have had decorated in various styles, beginning with the **Gallery***
> ***of the Candelabra,** named for the ancient marble pairs of candelabra*
> *that stand sentry among its sculpture, with some especially good sar-*
> *cophagus reliefs. The next section, the **Gallery of the Tapestries** is*
> *hung with 16th-century tapestries woven to designs by the 'New School'*
> *of Raphael—works by his pupils after his death, many based on his draw-*
> *ings. Next comes the equally long **Gallery of Maps,** with colourful*
> *sixteenth century frescoes of Italy's regions and cities and papal territo-*
> *ries by a Dominican monk and cartographer Ignazio Danti, painted for*
> *Gregory XIII, best known for reforming Caesar's calendar. The last bit of*
> *corridor is the **Gallery of Pius V,** with 15th-century tapestries from*
> *Tournai, including a Last Supper represented as a Renaissance dinner*
> *party; the **Sobieski room,** with a painting of the Polish king who came*
> *to the relief of Turk-besieged Vienna in 1683; and lastly, the **Hall of the***
> ***Immaculate Conception.** Beyond are the famous **Stanze of***
> ***Raphael.***

These small rooms were built by Nicholas V as his private apartments and were originally frescoed by Piero della Francesca, Andrea del Castagno and Benedetto Bonfigli; when Julius II was elected, he hired Signorelli, Sodoma, Lorenzo Lotto, Perugino, and Peruzzi to finish the decoration. Yet this unique trove of Renaissance art was utterly destroyed when Julius was smitten by the 26-year-old Raphael—as if there wasn't enough empty wall space left to fresco! But the pope wanted nothing less than the most up-to-date interior decoration available, and the sweetheart of the Renaissance obliged by painting some of his greatest masterpieces. Though a mind-boggling egomaniac, Julius II had whatever mixture of bullying, kindness, and coaxing it took to get the very best from his artists.

Raphael began the Stanze in 1508 and left them unfinished at his death in 1520. Yet in these four little rooms you can trace his progress over his years in Rome, if at least you're prepared to skip back and forth to see them in the order in which they were painted. The official route begins with the Stanza di Costantino, and runs through the Stanza di Eliodoro and Stanza della Segnatura to the Stanza dell'Incendio. You should begin with the **Stanza della Segnatura** (where the pope signed his bulls) which contains the very quintessence of the High Renaissance in its celebrated frescoes. These were Raphael's first works for Julius

II (1508–11), and done entirely by his hand. On the long wall, his first fresco, the *Disputation on the Holy Sacrament* glorifies the triumph of religious truth, and masterfully portrays two zones; the heavenly one shows God the Father, Christ, the Virgin, John the Baptist, and an intermingling of figures from the Old and New Testaments (the latter with haloes). On the terrestrial sphere, grouped around the altar with a monstrance of the Host, are the Doctors of the Church, popes, bishops, and the faithful, including, on the far left, Fra Angelico, and Dante (with a laurel crown) on the right, and Savonarola, made to play the bad guy in the black hat.

Opposite is the great *School of Athens* or the triumph of philosophical truth, a painting that has become a symbol for the Renaissance itself. Set in an imaginary temple, suggested by Raphael's mentor Bramante and by the Baths of Diocletian, the fresco depicts the greatest philosophers and scholars, separated into two camps on either side of the central figures of Plato, holding a copy of *Timaeus* (perhaps with Leonardo da Vinci's features, though Leonardo's interest in nature would make him more of an Aristotelian) and Aristotle, holding his *Ethics*. On Plato's side it's easy to find the snub-nosed Socrates making a point with Alcibiades, dressed in armour, next to the shorter figure of Xenophon. On the far left, in bearded profile, is Zeno, near Epicurus crowned with vine leaves; in the forefront sits Pythagoras, writing down his harmonic scale with Averroes in a turban and bald Empedocles looking on. Julius had Raphael add his young hostage, Federigo Gonzaga, seated behind Averroes, and his nephew, Francesco Maria della Rovere, the fair youth in white. No one is quite sure of the identity of the prominent figure with one foot on a block of marble; but the seated figure to the right is Heraclitus, the great pessimist, who didn't appear in the original cartoon and was added by Raphael after half of the scaffolding was taken down from the Sistine Chapel ceiling. Like everyone else in Rome he was astonished, and he paid Michelangelo the sincerest of compliments by painting the philosopher in his style.

On Aristotle's side, Diogenes the cynic sprawls on the steps, while in the foreground is Euclid, with Bramante's features, teaching his students; to the right, wearing a crown (a confusion with the Hellenistic dynasty in Egypt) and holding a terrestrial sphere, is the back of Ptolemy, facing Zoroaster, holding a celestial sphere. To his right stand Raphael himself and Sodoma, the older man in a cap.

Above the window is *Parnassus*, representing Beauty, with Apollo playing his violin for the Muses and the poets, including on the left Homer, Dante, Virgil, and Sappho, and on the right Ovid and Boccaccio, and seated, Horace and Pindar. Across are the *Virtues of Fortitude, Temperance, and Prudence*, by Raphael, and below, symbolic of Law, *Justinian delivering the Pendects* by Perin del Vaga, who also had a hand in *Gregory IX handing the Decretals to Raymond de Penafort* (the Pope actually a portrait of Julius II).

The **Stanza di Eliodoro**, the next room, was painted by Raphael in 1512–14 with subjects chosen by Julius II. The compositions are more dramatic, more richly coloured: the marvellous *Deliverance of St Peter*, with its striking night lighting, shows the angel entering the prison, unchaining St Peter, and leading him in the escape. On the main wall is the *Expulsion of Heliodorus from the Temple*, which gave the room its name; the incident portrayed (of King Seleucus' treasurer Heliodorus attempting to seize the treasure of the Temple, and chased out by a horseman and angels) is from the Apocrypha (Maccabees II, 3), and refers to Julius II's battles to expel foreign powers from the Papal States; Julius may be seen, watching the scene from his litter. The *Mass of Bolsena*, over the window, represents the miracle of 1263, when a priest who doubted the truth of transubstantiation celebrated mass and found the Host bleeding; Julius II, in a fine portrait, is seen kneeling on the right. The fourth fresco, of the *Meeting of St Leo and Attila*, lacks the verve of the others, and is mostly by Raphael's assistants, who had to change St Leo's face from a portrait of Julius II to Leo X when the latter pope was elected. Leo X had already been portrayed among the cardinals, so the same fat face appears twice, enough to spoil any painting.

*Now nip back to the **Stanza dell'Incendio** (the papal dining room).*

By this time (1514–17) Leo X was pope, and he chose the subject of the great fire in the Borgo, in 847, which stopped when the saintly Leo IV made the sign of the cross. This was designed by Raphael and painted by his pupils, and shows his tendency towards Mannerism: grand gestures, greater emphasis on the human body as a means of expression, often in difficult poses, and the use of more violent colours. Leo IV has Leo X's fat features; the fresco refers to his efforts to end the flames of war in Italy. The other frescoes in the room, with far more pupil than Raphael in them, show Leo X playing Leo III at the *Coronation of Charlemagne* and Leo IV in the *Victory over the Saracens*, both alluding to related events in the life of Leo X. The ceiling, by Raphael's master Perugino, is the only original fresco to survive.

The last room, the **Stanza di Costantino** was painted after Raphael's death by Giulio Romano and other pupils; only the *Victory of Constantine over Maxentius* was done after the master's sketches. Beyond this are the **Loggie di Raffaello** (now only open to scholars with permission) which Raphael built after Bramante's death, also contributing designs for half of the scenes from the Old Testament (hence the 'Bible of Raphael' in contrast with the Sistine Chapel, the 'Bible of Michelangelo'). Executed by his students, especially Giovanni da Udine, the loggie are especially interesting for their grotesque borders, inspired by Raphael's visit to Nero's Golden House.

Also off the Stanza di Costantino is the **Sala dei Palafrenieri** (better known as the **Sala dei Chiarascuri** for its monochrome Raphael-school frescoes) with a beautiful carved ceiling glorifying the Medici, and beyond that, a memory of an earlier, simpler and more pious age, the small **Chapel of Nicholas V**. This was closed off and forgotten until someone, counting the windows of the Vatican palace, noted that there was an extra one; inside are rarefied, pastel frescoes by Fra Angelico, on the lives of SS. Stephen (above) and Lawrence (below).

> *Now walk back (sorry!) to the Stanza dell'Incendio, where a door leads into the **Chapel of Urban VIII**, lavishly decorated by Pietro da Cortona; a stair leads down to the **Appartamento Borgia** and **Gallery of Modern Religious Art**. If you're running out of time, you can go straight to the Sistine Chapel from here.*

Although the 'Borgia Apartment' in the popular mind may conjure up a Chamber of Horrors, it is actually one of the most delightful corners of the Vatican, intimate and embellished with all the colours of spring. The rooms were frescoed in 1492–5 for Alexander VI by Pinturicchio (whose name means 'rich painter' for his use of gold and expensive colours), a Renaissance reactionary who rejected the innovations in colour and composition of contemporaries like Leonardo and Piero della Francesca. Sprinkled throughout are Borgia family symbols of the bull, twin crowns of Aragon, and flaming pennant. A sample of Pope Paul VI's modern art displayed in the little rooms couldn't be more incongruous; Pinturicchio's room of Sibyls is next to a room full of copes designed by Matisse. Rooms III and IV are by Pinturicchio's pupils; Room IV, by Antonio da Viterbo, was Alexander's study, where his daughter Lucrezia would help him with his correspondence, and where his hidden treasure was discovered after his death. The next room (often roped off), with scenes of the saints, is Pinturicchio's masterpiece. According to tradition, the large fresco of the *Disputation of St Catherine of Alexandria and Emperor Maximian* portrays the fair and much calumnied Lucrezia Borgia as St Catherine and Prince Djem, ambitious brother of Sultan Beyazit II, as the oriental soldier on the right; the Sultan paid Alexander to keep him as a 'guest' until, wearied of his company, the pope had him poisoned. Above the far door is a portrait of Alexander VI's mistress, Giulia Farnese. In the next room, of the Mysteries of the Faith, Alexander VI's richly robed, unflattered self appears in the scene of the Resurrection, with a young Roman bearing the features of his eldest son, the Duke of Gandia, and a soldier believed to be the awful Cesare. The ceiling of the last room collapsed on Alexander's head and almost killed him; Leo X ordered the new beautiful, frescoed and stuccoed ceiling from Perin del Vaga and Giovanni da Udine.

> *From here it's a long march to the Sistine Chapel through the Vatican's game attempt to prove that modern religious art exists (more by sheer acreage than anything else). But there are a few pearls hidden in the gaudy sea of kitsch, among them some curious works by Chagall, Picasso, Kokoschka, Feininger, Munch, Francis Bacon, Siqueiros and many, many more, and some genuinely beautiful paintings—American Charles Burchfield's* **Eye of God in the Woods** *and the fairy-tale paintings of Yugoslavs Ivan Lackovic and Ivan Vecenaj. At the end, join the throng heading for the* **Sistine Chapel,** *which has been one of Rome's chief tourist attractions ever since the day in 1512 when the weary, paint-spattered Michelangelo finally unlocked the door. (Of course the one time not to come is during a conclave, when the cardinals are sealed inside until they elect a new pope.)*

What some people would claim as the greatest achievement in art, ever, by a single artist, a work of consummate vision and genius, may have been the result of petty jealousy and intrigue. According to Vasari's *Lives of the Artists*, Bramante talked Pope Julius into sending his rival Michelangelo up to the ceiling of the ungainly barn of a chapel built by his della Rovere kinsman, Sixtus IV. Some of the finest painters of the Renaissance had already decorated the walls with a beautiful series on the Old Testament, but the vast ceiling had only a simple pattern of stars. Bramante hoped Michelangelo would refuse the commission and anger the pig-headed Pope, or else fritter away the time he needed to work on the tomb.

Michelangelo hated the idea, but Julius was adamant, and in 1508, he reluctantly agreed to get out his brushes. The Pope, like most Renaissance patrons, required only some virtuoso interior decoration: until then, ceiling frescoes had been simple small-scale decorations. Julius envisaged something similar, only somewhat bigger (40 m by 13 m, equal to the wall surface of 4 ½ average suburban bungalows). No one can say what drove Michelangelo to create a masterpiece instead: the fear of wasting his time, the challenge of an impossible task, or maybe just to spite Bramante and Julius—he exasperated the Pope by making him wait four long years, and refused all demands that he hire some assistants. 'When will you finish?' railed Julius. 'When I can,' the equally stubborn Michelangelo invariably replied. The Pope was ready to hurl him off the scaffolding when Michelangelo finally agreed to forego the highlights in gold and blue and let Julius show Rome and the world what he had got for his 3000 ducats: no mere illustrations from the Scriptures, but the way the Old Testament looks in the deepest recesses of the imagination.

Centuries of candle smoke slowly darkened Michelangelo's masterpiece, as well as incidents like that which occurred at the conclave that elected John Paul I, when clouds of black smoke meant to issue from the chimney backed up into the chapel, nearly suffocating the 111 cardinals. Now that the restorers (financed by a Japanese television network) have finished their controversial cleaning of the ceiling, it is more startling than ever. Michelangelo's true colours have been revealed—bright yellows, sea-green, and purple, with dramatic shadows—colours no interior decorator would ever dream of using. He totally eschewed stage props; one of the tenets of his art was that complex ideas could be expressed by the portrayal of the human body alone. Perhaps the inspiration that kept Michelangelo suffering on the ceiling (and the physical hardship, in the heat and cold, was extreme; it is said that after painting he could only read letters by holding them over his head) was the chance of distilling from the book of Genesis and his own genius an entirely new vocabulary of images, Christian and intellectual. His most original innovation, the famous nude youths, or *Ignudi*, may well represent forms he despaired of ever having the time to sculpt; they also serve as a unique perspective device, and like the rest of the ceiling's programme, probably have a deeper, secret meaning that would take years of inspired wondering to decipher. Michelangelo's style became more daring and confident as he painted; compare *The Intoxication of Noah*, where he began, with the impressionistic *Separation of Light and Darkness* by the altar. Most rubberneckers (and after looking up for a while, you'll wish your neck really was made of rubber) direct their attention to the all too famous scene of the *Creation of Man*, perhaps the only representation of God the Father ever painted that escapes being merely ridiculous. Here, one might suspect that the figure is really some ageing Florentine artist, and that Michelangelo only forgot to paint the brush in his hand. Along the sides are six-toed prophets and powerful Russian masseuse Sibyls (Michelangelo never had much use for women, even as models); in the lunettes over the windows are figures of the forerunners of Christ.

The magnificent, supremely confident spirit of the High Renaissance in first bloom, when man was the measure of all things and man was a giant, never recovered from the shock of the Sack of Rome. Seven years after that brutal event, in 1534 (22 years after the ceiling), Paul III commissioned Michelangelo to paint the harrowing *Last Judgement* on the altar wall; its utter disenchantment with the world is in violent contrast with the ceiling. The saints swarming around the beardless, implacable Christ demand vengeance on humanity for their martyrdoms, while angels come hurtling over, bearing the Cross, the crown of thorns, the pillar from Pilate's palace as if to remind Christ of his own passion. Only the Virgin shows any sign of pity, but she shrinks back against her son, unable to intervene (though curiously, Michelangelo's preliminary sketches show her actively imploring mercy). Just below and to the right of Christ gestures a furious St Bartholomew (a portrait of Pietro Aretino, Renaissance satirist and one of Michelangelo's bitter critics. He clutches a skin with the features of the artist he had 'flayed'). To the right below him, isolated from the angels sounding the trumpets of doom, and from another group beating the condemned down to hell, is perhaps the most famous vision of despair in art, the damned soul, hugging himself, one eye uncovered and open wide in a horror beyond words; he is made doubly effective by being the only figure in the whole composition to gaze out at the viewer.

At the time of writing, restoration, also financed by Nippon, is in progress on its turgid candle-darkened surface and the fresco will remain covered until 1994. It appears, however, that the delicate question of whether or not to remove the 'breeches' from the nude figures added by Daniele da Volterra (on orders from Pius IV, in 1564, the year of Michelangelo's death) has been decided. It is rumoured that the restorers discovered there was nothing but bare plaster beneath the breeches! Presumably da Volterra scraped off the painted genitalia. Just as well for him that the master was dead—the prudish Biagio da Cesena, Paul III's secretary, dared to criticize the nudity while the artist was alive and ended up being painted in hell as Midas (entwined in a serpent's coils, with asses' ears). When he complained to the Pope, he received the famous reply, that had Michelangelo placed him in Purgatory he could have helped, but over Hell he had no influence.

Try to pull your eyes away from Michelangelo to take in the lovely Cosmatesque-like floor, the marble screen by Mino da Fiesole, Giovanni Dalmata, and Andrea Bregno, and the frescoes of the lives of Moses and Christ along the walls. Among the finest are Botticelli's *The Burning Bush, Moses driving the Midianites from the well, and the Daughters of Jethro*, the maidens full of Botticellian grace, and the *Punishment of Korah, Dathan, and Abiram*, set in Rome, before the Arch of Constantine and the then-standing ruins of the Septizonium. On the other side is Ghirlandaio's *Calling of Peter and Andrew* and Perugino's *Christ donating the keys to St Peter*, set before an ideal Renaissance temple.

> *There are two famous rooms off the Sistine Chapel, Bernini's and Paul Brill's **Sala Ducale** and the **Sala Paolina**, with two of Michelangelo's last frescoes, though to see them you need special permission from the governor of Vatican City.*
>
> *From the Sistine you enter the lower floor of Bramante's long corridor, the **Library Gallery**, lined with the cupboards holding some of the Vat-*

ican Library's million books, and tens of thousands of manuscripts and incunabula. The core of the collection dates back to the humanist Pope Nicholas V.

The most precious and secret were removed in 1983 to a bunker some 40 feet underground, but many unique possessions are on display, such as the 16th-century maps in the **Gallery of Urban VIII**, and Bramante's wooden machine for stamping the papal seal, or *bollo,* on documents (hence 'bull') and a fresco showing the erection of the obelisk in Piazza S. Pietro in 1585, an operation masterminded by Sixtus V's favourite architect, Domenico Fontana. Fontana was also responsible for the enormous, lavishly decorated **Salone Sistina**, cutting across the old Courtyard of the Belvedere.

*Eventually you'll find yourself back at the Quattro Cancelli where you entered the museum. But there's another mile to go; follow the signs to the left for the **Pinacoteca**. On the way you can stop at the gruesome Vatican cafeteria for a cup of American coffee, an overpriced snack, and a pee (free). Then gird your tired eyes for Rome's finest collection of paintings.*

These are arranged in chronological order, beginning with Byzantines and medieval Italians, including Margaritone d'Arezzo's *St Francis of Assisi*, a near-contemporary portrait, and the elegant Bernardo Daddi's paintings on *The Life of St Stephen*, and the lightbulb-shaped *Universal Judgement* (11th century) signed by Giovanni and Niccolò of Rome, who invented much of their own iconography. In Room II centre stage is given to the *Stefaneschi Triptych*, by Giotto and assistants, taken from the Confessio of Old St Peter's, portraying the martyrdoms of SS. Peter and Paul on either side of the enthroned Christ (note the donor, Cardinal Stefaneschi, kneeling to the left). Sharing the same room are beauiful works by early Tuscan masters Daddi, Simone Martini, Pietro Lorenzetti, Lorenzo Monaco, and Gentile da Fabriano. In Room III are Fra Angelico's brightly coloured *Scenes from the life of St Nicholas of Bari* and a triptych by the more worldly monk, Filippo Lippi; Room IV is dedicated to Melozzo da Forli, with his charming frescoes of angel musicians from SS. Apostoli, and the famous *Sixtus IV conferring the Vatican librarianship on the humanist Platina*, with the Pope's nephew, the future Julius II, standing between Platina and the Pope.

Rooms V and VI house 15th-century paintings and polyptychs, including a fine *Pietà* by Carlo Crivelli; room VII is devoted to the Umbrians, especially Perugino's *Madonna enthroned with saints* and a work by Raphael's father, Giovanni Santi, which hardly prepares you for Room VIII, dedicated to the works of his son: the *Coronation of the Virgin*, painted at age 20; the *Madonna di Foligno*, painted for

Sigismondo Conti of Foligno as an ex-voto, after he survived a cannonball hitting his house; and Raphael's last painting, the *Transfiguration*, unfinished at his death and placed on his bier; the bottom section, showing the dramatic healing of a mad boy, was completed to his design by his students, Giulio Romano and Francesco Penni. Also in this room are the tapestries woven in Brussels after Raphael's cartoons and originally hung in the Sistine Chapel.

Room IX contains Rome's only work by Leonardo da Vinci, an unfinished monochrome *St Jerome*, and a lovely *Pietà* by Giovanni Bellini. In the next rooms are later works, of which Caravaggio's *Deposition* is the most striking, where again the viewer is drawn uncannily into the scene by the gaze of a figure. Also look for one of the finest of Domenichino's paintings, the *Communion of S. Girolamo*; Poussin's surgical *Martyrdom of S. Erasmo*; Titian's *Madonna dei Frari* (where the artist placed his name between the saints and the Madonna), and his *Portrait of Doge Niccolò Marcello* in the last room.

> *Next (and last) on the agenda are the three ex-Lateran museums, which John XXIII relocated when the Lateran palace became the offices of the Vicariate of Rome. The ultramodern building (opened in 1970), is located near the cafeteria entrance and begins with **Museo Gregoriano Profano**, housing Roman and Greek sculpture and mosaics, much of it in the eclectic, academic neo-Attic style.*

Founded by Gregory XVI to house Vatican overflow, this museum has a copy of Myron's 5th-century *Marsyas*; a handsome statue of *Sophocles*, a copy of a 4th-century work and the *Heraclitus Mosaic*, found on the Aventine and depicting the remains of what must have been a pretty wild banquet. One of the loveliest ladies in the whole Vatican is the headless *Chiaramonti Niobid*, a Roman copy of a 4th-century Greek original; she is followed by Roman portrait busts and statues, and two snoozing *Sileni*. The intriguing *Tomb of the Haterii* is thought to show the funeral of a member of a family of construction workers. They had no qualms about using the sad occasion to advertise their business—the tomb is covered with reliefs of the buildings (including the Colosseum) which they worked on, and a natty Roman crane. The next section contains a fascinating collection of pagan sarcophagi, decorated with reliefs ranging from the *Triumph of Bacchus* to the *Myth of Orestes*. As you go upstairs, be sure to look down on the *Mosaic of Athletes* found in the Baths of Caracalla, a black marble stag, and fine Roman bas-reliefs.

> *The rest of the upper floor contains the **Museo Pio Cristiano**, with sarcopohagi, inscriptions, and statues found in the catacombs, of prime importance to the study of the evolution of Christianity in Rome.*

Among the statues is the famous *Good Shepherd* from the 3rd century, showing a young, beardless Christ, inspired by the Hermes Kriophorus in the Museo Barracco, and a statue of the martyred doctor St Hippolytus, with the dates of Easter for the years 222–334 carved on the side. On the balcony is part of the tombstone of Abericus, bishop of Hierapolis, who lived in the 2nd century, describing his journeys to Rome and through the Middle East.

*And lastly, the vast **Museo Missionario Etnologico**, founded in 1927 by Pius XI, fills the basement, featuring fascinating displays on local cultures, religions, and arts from around the world. Among the most curious displays are native adaptations of Christian iconography; others illustrate the Church's missionary activities, along with beautiful carvings from South America and Polynesia.*

Monte Mario   326
Foro Italico   326
Parioli and Villa Ada   327
Via Nomentana/Sant'Agnese fuori le Mura 328
The Viminale and Via Nazionale   331
Città Universitaria   331
Cinecittà   332
EUR   333
Villa Doria Pamphili   335

Peripheral Attractions

Some city sights have refused to fit into the walks. Anyone who wants to visit a catacomb but hates large guided tours should head to those of Priscilla or below the churches of Sant'Agnese fuori le Mura and San Pancrazio; there are escapes from the city at the Abbazia delle Tre Fontane and the Villa Pamphili and Villa Ada parks; while ice cream fiends should target Parioli, and lovers of Fascist-era architecture, EUR. They are listed below, more or less clockwise, beginning from the northwest.

Monte Mario

No buses up here, so take a taxi or walk from the 90 or 90B bus-stop at Piazzale Maresciallo Giardino.

Beyond the Prati quarter to the north, the Tiber curves in to meet the slopes of Monte Mario, one of the highest of Rome's hills, crowned with broadcasting antennas and the brutal Hilton Hotel. Up on top, besides an abundance of cypresses, there is the **Villa Stuart**, a retreat for England's Royal Pretenders in the 1700s, and the **Villa Madama**, built for Pope Clement VII by Raphael and Giulio Romano. The Italian government keeps this place as a home for visiting premiers, kings, and sheikhs, which is a pity; Romano's frescoes inside are some of the most original in Rome. It can be visited with permission from the Foreign Ministry (but just try and get it). At the top of the hill, the **Astronomical Observatory** has a small scientific museum said to be quite interesting—but it's been closed for years.

The Foro Italico

Any number of buses come up this way from Piazzale Flaminia, and there is also the 32 from Piazza del Risorgimento near the Vatican, and the (infrequent) 186, from the Lateran—Colosseum—Piazza Venezia—Corso del Rinascimento.

Its original name was Foro Mussolini, but for some reason, in the late '40s the city decided to change it. Mussolini had planned to snare the Olympics like his friend Hitler, and began a huge sports complex upstream along the Tiber to celebrate the games with proper Fascist solemnity. The result, mouldering though it may be, rivals the best of Roman Baroque for pure kitsch entertainment. We can only regret that Mussolini never got to finish it. The final plan called for, among other ornaments, a 250-foot statue of the Dictator himself, dressed as Hercules.

At the entrance, on Lungotevere Marasciallo Diaz, a 55-foot obelisk proclaims MUSSOLINI DUX, in letters too big to ever be effaced. The 'Forum' behind it, now used as a roller-skating track by the neighbourhood children, is paved with black-and-white mosaics of heroic athletes in various sports, interspersed with scenes of Italian soldiers bayonetting Ethiopians. Beyond, more mosaics and inscriptions celebrate the mystic creative force of Fascism, set among borders with the endlessly repeated words 'Duce' and 'Balilla' (this was the Fascist Youth group, members of which were tricked into doing most of the work here).

To the right of the Forum, the sunken **Marble Stadium** was to be the site of the games. Knowing Mussolini, one shouldn't be surprised that this monstrosity is really built of travertine; the sixty colossal stone athletes around the top of the oval are impressive nevertheless. Rome finally did get the Olympics, in 1960, and built the even bigger **Stadio Olympico** for them, the huge geometric steel spider just to the left of the Forum. Twenty years after its completion, it started falling to pieces. The city is rebuilding it, one section at a time, and meanwhile it serves as home to the understandably nervous fans of the Roma football club, still trying to climb back to the top of the Italian first division after many years of mediocrity. Some of the other buildings, including the travertine-trimmed raspberry Piscina (swimming pool) and Palazzo di Scherma (fencing hall), are modest examples of the sunnier side of Mussolini architecture.

The rest of the Olympic complex lies across the Tiber, off Viale Flaminia, including the domed, American-style **Palazzetto dello Sport**, a striking steel and concrete dome by the famed architect-engineer Pier Luigi Nervi. Behind it, the creepy modern **Olympic Village** is now just another middle-class neighbourhood plagued with drugs, prostitution and crime.

In the newspapers, when you see the 'Farnesina' mentioned, you will know they mean the Italian Foreign Ministry, hidden away from the public eye in their modern building behind the Marble Stadium. Rome already has enough Farnesinas, but this one takes its name from its street address, on Via Macchia di Farnesina. Just upstream from it stands the famous **Milvian Bridge**, better known to Romans as Ponte Molle. Built about 109 BC, and restored endlessly since, it holds a place in history from the battle of 312 AD, where Constantine defeated rival Emperor Maxentius; the night before, Constantine had had his famous dream of the cross, hearing the words 'In this sign you shall conquer'. In fact the battle took place a mile or so upstream, but the defeated Maxentius drowned in the Tiber here while trying to flee.

Parioli and Villa Ada

To see the Catacombs of Priscilla, the closest buses are the 56, from Piazza Sonnino in Trastevere—Via Arenula—Corso—Via del Tritone—Via Veneto—Via Tagliamento—Via Nemorense; the 57 from Porta S. Paolo—Lungotevere Aventino—Piazza Venezia—Via Nazionale—Via Salaria; and the 319 from Termini Station. For all three, get off at Via di Priscilla and walk back west towards Via Salaria.

Parioli also holds two of the city's best gelaterias: Bar San Filippo, Via di Villa San Filippo 8/10, serving delectable chocolate, marron glacé and zabaglione ices, and Duse, round the corner on Via Eleonora Duse, which includes bitter chocolate, date and maracuja in its repertoire.

Parioli is the name for the huge area north of Villa Borghese, home to Rome's nouveau riche, their sports-car driving offspring and Philippina maids. It's a numb and grey district of villas and curving boulevards. The large **Villa Ada** borders it to the east, formerly Villa Savoia, a hunting preserve for King Vittorio Emanuele III. It is now partly a public park, and partly the Egyptian Embassy. The Egyptians had a lot to do with the building of Rome's first and only **Mosque**, designed by post-modern architect, Paolo Portoghesi, and now, after eight years, finally nearing completion. It's on Via Forte Antenne, near the **Acqua Acetosa**, a fountain designed by Bernini.

Catacombs of Priscilla

*There are at least a dozen catacombs in this part of the city, all but one on private land and never open to visitors. The exception, however, is the largest and oldest of them all, the **Catacombs of Priscilla** (open daily exc Mon, 8.30–12, 2.30–5; in summer until 6; adm L6000).*

Priscilla, the founder of the cemetery, belonged to a wealthy Senatorial family of the 1st century AD, the Acilii; their estate occupied most of the neighbourhood, and their villa may have been directly connected to the catacombs. Greatly expanded in the 3rd and 4th centuries, the place had become a sort of society catacomb after 300, and several popes are buried here. As such, it has some good paintings—familiar scenes like the drowning of Jonah, and Jesus as the Good Shepherd, along with a 3rd-century fresco of a mother and baby, long thought to be the earliest surviving image of the Madonna and Child. It is actually now thought to be simply a portrait of two of the catacomb's occupants. The 'Greek Chapel', where funeral services were held, may have been a cryptoporticus from the Acilii villa; besides some stucco decoration it has well-preserved frescoes, including one behind the altar that may represent an early Christian *agape*, or ritual banquet.

Around Via Nomentana

The 36 bus follows Via Nomentana to Sant'Agnese from Termini Station; the 60 follows the same route, from Piazza Sonnino in Trastevere— Largo Argentina—Piazza Venezia—Via del Tritone.

Rome's main route towards the northeast begins as Via Quirinale—Via XX Settembre. After Largo S. Susanna, and the church of S. Maria della Vittoria (Walk IX), it passes the thousand foot-long **Finance Ministry**, biggest of all the white elephants built by the new Italian Kingdom after 1870. A few blocks down, the street passes through the Aurelian wall at **Porta Pia**, flanked by the modern British Embassy and a villa that was once home to Pauline Bonaparte. The gate was known as Porta Nomentana until Pope Pius IV had it rebuilt in 1561— Michelangelo designed it, without taking the task too seriously.

Outside it, at the beginning of Via Nomentana, stands a big ferocious monument to the Italian *Bersaglieri* (sharpshooters), the army's elite corps. They had one of their brighter moments here on 20 September 1870, when, facing half-hearted resistance from papal troops, they blew a hole in the wall and liberated Rome, completing Italian unification. The famous *breccia* (breach) can be seen a bit to the north of the gate. There is a small museum devoted to the Bersaglieri inside Porta Pia.

Via Nomentana is one of Rome's flashier boulevards, lined with trees and boutiques. Several old villas survive, some of them converted into hotels; one of the largest, the Villa Torlonia, was Mussolini's residence for most of his dictatorship.

Sant'Agnese fuori le Mura

About a mile beyond Porta Pia, the lovely early Christian complex of Sant' Agnese fuori le Mura (7 am–noon and 4–8 pm) sits inconspicuously on the left.

Saint Agnes, who met her theatrical end on Piazza Navona (see Walk IV) was buried here, in the Via Nomentana catacombs, in about 350. As one of the most popular early martyrs, representing Christian chastity despite the recorded fact that she never bathed, her tomb became a pilgrimage for Roman women, and the first church over the catacombs was probably built soon after the reign of Constantine. Completely rebuilt in 625, it has suffered every sort of tinkering, repair and improvement in the last 400 years. Much of it was necessary—Sant'Agnese witnessed one of the last great papal miracles in 1855, when the floor collapsed right under Pius IX. Divine Providence, humourless as ever, scotched this perfect opportunity for a pontifical pratfall; while everyone else tumbled into the basement, Pius floated in the air for a bit, then settled gently down to earth. Small wonder that Pius, some years later, would declare himself Infallible.

All around the narthex and the rear of the church, early Christian reliefs and inscriptions have been arranged as in a museum. The elegant columns and capitals were recycled from ancient buildings; above them, the Greek-style *matroneum* (women's gallery) survives from the 625 rebuilding. Above the Cosmatesque altar, containing the remains of St Agnes, the apse has one of the simplest and most beautiful ancient mosaics in Rome. The serene figure of Agnes, in rich Byzantine court dress, is flanked by the church's two builders, Popes Symmachus and Honorius. If the sacristan is around, and you can get together a group of four or more, you can visit the 3rd–6th century **catacombs** below—no paintings, but one of the simpler and more peaceful catacombs in Rome. Also one of the smaller ones—a mere 7 km of tunnels.

The sacristan will also show you an exceptional jewel of late Roman art, tucked away behind Sant'Agnese, in a park where the neighbourhood kids play football over the catacombs. Circular **Santa Costanza** isn't very impressive from the outside. Its portico and marble decoration disappeared centuries ago, but its vaults are graced with exquisite mosaics, geometric and floral designs combining both Christian and pagan motifs. According to Church history, Emperor Constantine was persuaded to build Sant'Agnese by his pious daughter Constantia, who retired here as a nun and had the circular Santa Costanza built as her mausoleum. If anything, this fairy tale is a comment on Church history. The sainted Constantia, whether Christian or not, seems to have been as naturally vicious as the rest of Constantine's family. Never a nun, but the scheming wife of a tyrannous provincial governor, she is recorded by the reliable contemporary historian Ammianus Marcellinus as 'insatiable as [her husband, Gallus] in her thirst for human blood'.

A nice story became necessary when the mausoleum was converted to a baptistry, some time in the 4th century. The mosaic, with a tremendous variety of images, has more of Bacchus in it than Jesus Christ: vines and vintage scenes, Cupids, birds and creatures of the sea, a mirror, and amphorae. Originally the dome had even better mosaics, also with Bacchic scenes; these were senselessly destroyed by Paul V in 1622.

Further along Via Nomentana, towards Monte Sacro (no one knows how this hill got its name) the old Nomentana diverges from the modern road, crossing the little River Aniene on the **Ponte Nomentano**, built by the invading Greek armies from Constantinople in 552, and covered with a fortress by some extortionist baron in the Middle Ages.

And if you are spending time in these modern quarters of the city, **Via Salaria** north of Porta Pia is one of Rome's biggest shopping districts. On the corner of Via di Villa Albani, the **Villa Torlonia** (don't confuse it with the two other Villa Torlonias on Via Nomentana and in Trastevere) was a monument to the last family to make it big off papal banking, in the 1700s. Since its acquisition by the state, the grounds have become run down and overgrown, and the villa, with an excellent collection of ancient art, is closed to the public with no reopening planned or even imagined. The rather sad, equally overgrown ruin across Via Salaria from the entrance is the **Mausoleum of Lucilius Peto**, from the time of Augustus.

Along Viale Regina Margherita, another important thoroughfare, you can stop at Piazza Buenos Aires to tour the marvellously overripe villas and *palazzi* of the **Coppedé Quarter**. Built after World War I, when Art Nouveau was going out of fashion everywhere else, these few blocks of architectural madness take the style to its wildest extremes. The best parts are along Via Dora, a block east of the Viale, with its fairy-castle apartment blocks arched over the street, and Via Brenta, with mock-medieval villas that Dante might have imagined in Paradise.

The Viminale and Via Nazionale

Only in Rome, perhaps, would the heart of the modern city be of peripheral interest. Via Nazionale is that gruesome main thoroughfare linking Termini Station with Piazza Venezia, cutting its tiresome way between the Quirinale and the Viminale hills (if the Seven Hills were Disney's Seven Dwarfs, the Viminale would be 'Sleepy'). It has Rome's **Teatro d'Opera**, at Via Viminale and Torino, near Piazza della Repubblica (1880, enlarged by Marcello Piacentini in the 1930s); the vast Ministry of the Interior, in the 1920 Palazzo Viminale; and behind the Ministry, the prettily situated church of **San Lorenzo in Panisperna** on Via Panisperna, marking the alleged site of Lawrence's martyrdom, and containing an oversize fresco of the saint on the grill within.

From S. Lorenzo, Via Milano will take you back to Via Nazionale. Near the corner is the grand, recently renovated **Palazzo dell'Esposizione** of the 1870s. It hosts some good contemporary art and photography exhibitions, and has an arts cinema, excellent design shop, a pleasant café and rooftop restaurant.

On the other side of the Palazzo dell'Esposizione, the church of **San Vitale** hides timidly below the street level, evidence of just how much the valleys between Rome's hills have been filled in. Though built in 416, almost nothing original remains inside, though there is a pair of fine 17th-century wooden doors, carved by a talented but anonymous Jesuit.

Further down Via Nazionale is the **Palazzo Rospigliosi**, built by Cardinal Scipio Borghese over the Baths of Constantine, and later the residence of Cardinal Mazarin. On the first floor (entrance on XXIV Maggio 43), the **Galleria Pallavicini** has a collection of Italian paintings from the 15th–18th centuries (open by permission from Princess Pallavicini); the adjacent **Casino dell'Aurora**, frescoed by Guido Reni with a famous scene of Aurora and the sun, was near the top of the list of sights for any 19th-century traveller. *The princess opens it on the first of each month, from 10–12 and 3–5, though it occasionally hosts temporary art exhibitions.*

Città Universitaria

Ⓜ *Policlinico or Castro Pretorio (Line B), or bus 9 or 310 from Termini.*

Another grey area, just west of Piazza San Lorenzo, this is the new home built for the University of Rome in the 1930s to replace its cramped quarters in the Palazzo della Sapienza. Fifty years have been enough to make this 'University City' look shabby and anonymous; even the thousands of students find little reason to hang about after classes. The monumental entrance on Viale delle Scienze, leading to the University 'Forum', wears the sad, worried look of great but disappointed expectations.

Near the University is the equally vast **Policlinico** (1893), Rome's training hospital; and on Viale Castro Pretorio, the **Biblioteca Nazionale Centrale**, Italy's National Library, with some 2,500,000 volumes inherited from the Collegio Romano and other suppressed monasteries, built in the 1970s over the ruins of the Praetorian Barracks, sections of which may still be seen. Augustus founded the Praetorian Guard as a 'bodyguard', some 10,000 strong; as troops were not allowed in Rome, their barracks were located here just outside the city, in a permanent camp built under Tiberius. It wasn't long before the arrangement backfired, and the Praetorians controlled the emperor instead of vice versa, beginning with the murder of Caligula. When Aurelian built his wall he had to make a special bulge to incorporate the barracks.

From Viale Castro Pretorio you can wander back towards Termini along Via S. Martino della Battaglia, and stop for a drink at the bar on the west side of **Piazza dell'Indipendenza** to admire the frescoes of old Buffalo, New York and the Erie Canal painted on the walls (the present owners don't know why). It becomes even more incongruous when you consider that under your feet is the ancient **Campus Sceleratus**, the field where Vestal Virgins who lost their qualification for the job were buried alive; they are are still there under the traffic.

Cinecittà

🅜 *Cinecittà (Line A) or bus 650 from Piazza S. Giovanni in Laterano.*

For film buffs, the studios of Cinecittà are the biggest non-sight in Rome; of Italy's 'Hollywood' you can only see the gate, surrounded by spooky, crime-ridden suburbia. No tours of the famous colossal sets, no museum of its history or even movie paraphernalia, no cinematèque showing its classics, no festival to promote its current efforts. Perhaps memories of the bad old days linger too strongly—for Cinecittà was inaugurated by Mussolini in 1937, and he lavished vast sums to make it an advanced, experimental studio. 'Cinema is our strongest weapon' he said, almost exactly repeating Lenin's words of 1918.

Not surprisingly, the first six years saw Cinecittà produce millions of feet of distorted historical films, heroic war movies, and flimsy, diverting pictures that for some reason are called 'white telephone' comedies. Its success as a psychological 'weapon' may be gauged by the fact that a mob sacked it in 1943, causing great damage; most of the surviving equipment was sent to Venice and 'misplaced'.

Cinecittà was transformed by the Allies into a camp for the homeless, but the film skills remained in Rome, and the neo-realist reaction to fascist propaganda began immediately with Roberto Rossellini's *Rome, Open City*, shot on a shoestring budget in 1945.

Cinecittà was rebuilt, to become a land of dreams for millions of Italians in the late '40s and '50s, a period nostalgically evoked in Fellini's *Intervista*. Every morning the gate would be swarming with would-be film stars, in the way the Spanish Steps used to attract thousands of would-be artists' models. The natural Roman urge to gigantism made Cinecittà a favourite for filming American colossals like *Quo Vadis?*, *Cleopatra*, *Ben Hur*, and *War and Peace*—Italian craftsmen make the biggest and most impressive movie sets in the world. Rising costs saw such a serious decline in the late '60s and '70s that the city seriously considered knocking Cinecittà down to build more horrible cement block housing. Ironically, the fact that television began to make use of the facilities put the studio back in the black, and of late it has once more been specializing in big international films: Bertolucci's *The Last Emperor*, Sergio Leone's *Once Upon a Time in America*, Jean-Jacques Annaud's *The Name of the Rose*, Terry Gilliam's *The Baron of Münchenchausen*, and Coppola's *Godfather III*.

EUR and the Tre Fontane

> *The easiest and quickest way to EUR is to take the Metropolitana B to the end of the line; alternatively, buses 223 or 707 from St Paul's Basilica, or the unremittingly unscenic 93 from Termini or S. Giovanni in Laterano. Bus 707 passes near the entrance of LUNEUR park.*

By the late '30s, Mussolini was proud enough of his accomplishments to plan a world's fair to show humanity the fruits of fascism. Its theme was to be the Progress of Civilization, measured from the invention of the wheel up to the invention of the Corporate State. A vast area south of Rome was cleared and transformed into a grid of wide boulevards broken by parks and a long artificial lagoon. Huge Mussolini-style pavilions and colonnades were begun, and a design was accepted for a tremendous aluminium arch—like the famous one in St Louis, but many times bigger—that would overspread the entire fairgrounds, a fake rainbow, a fascist symbol of hope. War intervening, the arch never appeared, and the Esposizione Universale di Roma never came off. After 1945 the Italians tried to make the best of it, turning EUR into a model satellite city and trade centre on the lines of La Défense in Paris. The result will derange your senses as much as it does the average Roman's, a chilly nightmare of modernism with fascist-land street names like the Boulevard of Humanism, Boulevard of Electronics, and the Boulevard of Social Security. These can be either as haunted and void of life as a De Chirico painting, or immensely wide speedways where the few foolish pedestrians are mowed down like ducks in a shooting gallery. The post-war glass skyscrapers looming over them make the crumbling old Mussolini buildings look positively cosy and cheerful.

Still, for those who can appreciate the well-landscaped macabre, EUR can be fun. Some of the older corners reveal giant fascist mosaics of heroic miners, soldiers, assembly-line workers, and mothers, and at the end of Viale della Civiltà del Lavoro, you can have a look at the modest masterpiece of Mussolini architecture and EUR's most striking landmark, the almost elegant **Palazzo della Civiltà del Lavoro**. Liberal, post-war Italy has rarely, if ever, been able to conceive anything with such a sure sense of design and a feeling for history. Of course some Roman malcontents call it the 'Square Colosseum'.

The only fun reason to come to EUR is to take a spin on the old-fashioned rides in Rome's permanent fun fair, **LUNEUR Park**; the only serious reason is to see its museums, especially the **Museo della Civiltà Romana**, located in a fascist-Art Deco Temple of Karnak at the end of Piazza Giovanni Agnelli—the name is a reminder that Fiat footed the construction bill. (*Open 9–1.30, Tues and Thurs also 4–7, closed Mon; adm L4000.*) The museum was born from the 1911 archaeological show, and was housed in this exposition building to celebrate Emperor Augustus' bi-millennium in 1937. Models of ancient buildings help to evoke the Rome of the Cæsars, especially the great **Plastico di Roma**, a 1:250 scale model of 4th-century Rome, with every building present within the Aurelian walls, a great place to seed your imagination with 'the grandeur that was Rome'. Scholarship of the last 50 years would quibble on a few of the details: the *insulae*, or apartment buildings, should be taller than shown, the Circus Flaminius is missing, and Aurelian's Temple of the Sun is in the wrong place. Other exhibits include models of Roman furniture, musical instruments, sundials, surgical tools, reliefs of various shops, and a series of casts made from Trajan's Column in 1861—your chance to examine its magnificent reliefs up close. The last room charts the history of the museum itself, including some interesting old photos of Rome. Check before you go that the sections you want to see are open.

Near vast Piazza Marconi, the colonnaded heart of EUR, there are three smaller museums: in the northeast corner, the **Museo delle Arti e delle Tradizioni Popolari** (*Piazza Marconi 8, open 9–2, Sun 9–1, adm L4000*), with ethnographic displays of Italian life. On the southeast corner of the colonnade, entered at Viale Lincoln 1, the fascinating **Museo Preistorico Etnografico** (open 9–2, Sun 9–1, L6000) is the ideal place to learn about pre-Roman Italy, from the Stone to the Iron Ages—Etruscan tomb finds, Sardinian bronze figures, and ceramic works, arranged geographically. In the same building, at Viale Lincoln 3, the **Museo dell'Alto Medioevo** (*9–2, Sun 9–1, free*) attempts to shed a bit of light on the 5th–11th centuries; the age may have been dark, but the jewellery at least sparkled.

Other sites in EUR include the massive church and dome of **SS. Pietro e Paolo**, which is just as well seen from a distance, and the park around the Lago Artificiale, with its Japanese cherry trees and bridges leading to the **Palazzo dello**

Sport, designed by Pier Luigi Nervi and Marcello Piacentini for the 1960 Olympics, crowned by a striking rib-vaulted dome 100 m in diameter.

A kilometre east of LUNEUR park on Via delle Tre Fontane, and predating EUR by 1300 years is the **Abbazia delle Tre Fontane** (open all day apart from lunchtime) founded by refugee monks from Syria on the traditional site of St Paul's martyrdom. The three fountains of its name supposedly sprang forth on the three places where the saintly head rebounded. A miracle, but not the long distance record for holy noggins; that belongs to an obscure 3rd-century Florentine saint named Minias, whose severed head bounced nearly a kilometre—uphill—from the chopper's block. St Bernard lodged here while visiting Rome in 1138–40, and wrote of the inhabitants: 'Who is ignorant of the vanity and arrogance of the Romans? Dexterous in mischief, they have never learnt the science of doing good. Odious to earth and heaven, impious to God, seditious among themselves ... Adulation and calumny, perfidy and treason, are the familiar arts of their policy ...' Some things never change, though Bernard's vision may have been coloured by the fact that the Tre Fontane was a famous swampbed of malaria; Rahere, King Henry II's jester, came down with the sickness during a stay here, and vowed to build a church in London if he were cured; thus the origins of St Bartholomew the Great, and its hospital, named after San Bartolomeo on the Tiber Island .

In the 19th century, Trappists came to live in the dismal place and sucked the swamps dry with groves of eucalyptus, from which they distil a humdinger of a liqueur. Now one of the more serene garden corners of Rome, there are three churches to visit: **SS. Vincenzo ed Anastasio**, founded by Honorius I in 625, rebuilt in 1221 by Honorius III, and preserving its original appearance. To the right, the octagonal **S. Maria Scala Coeli** (the 'Stairway to Heaven') was so named for a vision of St Bernard. While praying for a departed friend, the soul suddenly appeared before him, ascending from purgatory to paradise thanks to his good offices. The crypt preserves the Cosmatesque altar on which the vision appeared. The third church, **San Paolo alle Tre Fontane** dates from the 5th century, but was rebuilt by Giacomo della Porta in 1599; St Paul was supposed to have been bound to the column on the right. The prettiest things inside are two mosaic pavements from Ostia Antica.

Around Villa Doria Pamphili

Bus 44 from Piazza Venezia, or bus 75 from Piazza dei Cinquecento pass down Viale Trastevere, near Villa Doria Pamphili; bus 31 from Trastevere Station goes through the park itself.

Villa Doria Pamphili, Rome's largest public park, was originally laid out by Algardi for one of the insatiable kinsmen of Innocent X. It is a pretty place full of tall parasol pines, with fine views over Rome; underneath it is apparently riddled with catacombs, built along the Via Aurelia, the main road along Italy's coast into Gaul. The only ones open for visits are the **Catacombs of San Pancrazio** (*open 9.30–12 and 4.30–6 for a minimum of four people*), entered from the church of the same name, on Via San Pancrazio. Pancrazio was martyred at the age of twelve in 304, and is thus the patron of neophytes. His catacomb, although mostly destroyed, is of interest for its oriental inscriptions; Trastevere was once home to many immigrants from the east. The church of **San Pancrazio**, though built in the 7th century, is covered by a boring Baroque mask.

Eating Out	338
Food	339
Wine	340
Prices	340
Restaurants:	342
S. Maria Maggiore and the Lateran	342
Termini and San Lorenzo	342
Trastevere	343
Corso/Trevi Fountain	345
Spanish Steps/Piazza del Popolo	346
Around Via Veneto/Piazza Barberini	347
Forum and Colosseum	348
Testaccio	348
Piazza Navona/Pantheo	349
Ghetto/Piazza Bocca della Verità	350
Around Campo de'Fiori	351
Vatican/Prati	352

Food and Drink

In many ways Rome is one of the best cities in Italy for dining out, not only for the variety of its restaurants, but for the local custom of making dinner the main event of the evening. Most of Rome's nightlife is in its trattorias, especially in the warmer months, when everyone sits out in the piazza. The passing carnival of nations, the itinerant musicians, the splashing of a fountain, and the delightful coolness and moonlight after a long hot day is one of the city's greatest charms. While Roman cuisine itself hasn't been the same since the ban on nightingales' tongues, as the capital the city has attracted chefs from nearly every region in the country, offering a variety of restaurants unique in Italy; and as people from all over the world settle here, there are, unusually for conservative Italy, a fair number of non-Italian restaurants—including 300 Chinese.

Eating Out

To eat like a Roman means a stop at a bar for a quick stand-up breakfast of coffee (usually a *cappuccino* or *caffè latte*) and a warm *cornetto* ('horn', like a croissant, empty, or filled with custard, raisins or jam) or a *brioche* (a flaky pastry with chocolate inside). You can stop for refills as often as necessary, though around noon it's time to move on to an *aperitivo* of some sort: a Campari, some kind of vermouth (Italians prefer something bitter, to whet the appetite) or perhaps a fruit juice.

Between 1 and 2 is time for lunch (*pranzo*; most restaurants open at 12 and stop serving at around 2:30 or 3). This is traditionally the biggest meal of the day in Italy, though in practice many Romans prefer to grab a quick meal in a cafeteria-buffet or *tavola calda* (a selection of hot, prepared foods) rather than commute home. But most will have some form of pasta (rather than in the evening, when it tends to sit on the all-important stomach), a main meat or fish course, a salad or vegetable, wine or water, and fruit, followed by a coffee in a nearby bar (the stomach conscious will have a *digestivo* to aid gastric action, perhaps a traditional anise-flavoured sambuco, with *tre mosche* ('three flies' or coffee beans), an amaretto, a Strega (made from saffron), a Fernet-Branca (made from mysterious herbs), or a Scotch. Late afternoon snacks (at 5 or 6 pm) would be an ice cream in the summer, or a *suppli* (a deep-fried rice croquette, usually with mozzarella inside), a slice of pizza (*a taglio*), or one of a hundred varieties of *tramezzino*, or finger sandwiches, washed down with a glass of beer or wine.

Romans eat dinner (*cena*) any time after 8 or 9 pm, always caught between the desire to go late and that of finding a table at their favourite restaurant in Trastevere or around Piazza Navona. A plate of *antipasti* and a pizza is a popular (and economical) supper, as is having a light meal in one of the burgeoning number of wine bars or *enoteche*; but there are always plenty of Romans ordering three- and four-course dinners. Flasks of the house wine, usually from the Castelli Romani, help fill out the evening. Last stop: another bar, another coffee (to help you sleep!) perhaps 'corrected' with a shot of grappa or brandy.

Food

Traditional Roman specialities tend to be simple, almost rustic, making use of inexpensive ingredients that are produced locally; pickled swan hearts and imported fish gut sauce went out with the Cæsars. Now the most famous Roman first course, or *primo,* is *spaghetti* or *bucatini* (thin tubes) *all'amatriciana,* with a sauce of salt pork, tomatoes, chilli peppers, topped with grated *pecorino* (sharp sheep cheese). *Spaghetti alla carbonara,* another popular dish, features bacon, eggs, garlic, cheese and pepper (tradition says it was invented by American GIs, who topped spaghetti with their breakfast rations). Other local specialities include *fettuccine al burro* (cholesterol heaven: ribbon egg noodles, with a double dose of butter, cream, and Parmesan cheese); *penne all'arrabiata* ('angry quills', with tomato sauce and lots of chilli pepper); *gnocchi di patate* (potato dumplings with butter or meat sauce, a favourite on Thursdays), or the much harder to find *gnocchi alla romana,* made of semolina and baked in the oven; *stracciatella* (broth with eggs, semolina, Parmesan cheese); *spaghetti ad aglio e olio* (with garlic, olive oil, chilli pepper and parsley).

Typical Roman meat courses (*secondo*) are headed by the famous 'jump-in-the-mouth' *saltimbocca alla romana* (veal scallops with ham and sage, cooked in butter and white wine). For heartier fare, try *trippa alla romana* (tripe stewed with onions, carrots, mint, meat sauce and Parmesan), or *coda alla vaccinara* (stewed ox tail), or *involtini al sugo* (rolled veal cutlets filled with ham, celery, and cheese and cooked in tomato sauce). *Pajata,* for intrepid diners only, is veal intestine with its mother's milk clotted inside, dressed up with garlic, chilli peppers, tomatoes, and white wine. Popular, but often expensive, is *abbacchio alla scottadito,* lamb chops 'burn the finger' grilled over a flame. *Tordi matti* are a kind of grilled *involtini.* Seafood is expensive; traditional dishes are *anguillette in umido* (stewed baby eels from Lake Bracciano) and *filetti di baccalà* (dried cod fried in batter), and *seppiette con i carciofi* (cuttlefish with artichokes).

The Roman campagna produces tender, purple 'Roman' artichokes, used in *carciofi alla giudea* (artichokes fried in oil), the famous side dish or *contorno,* one of many adopted from the Jews. A *misticanza* is a green salad composed of wild and domestic greens. In the winter try Roman cauliflower, which grows in beautiful pale green spirals (but tastes pretty much like regular cauliflower). A typical dessert (also Jewish in origin) is *crostata di ricotta*, a tart filled with cream, ricotta, cinnamon and bits of chocolate; or *zuppa inglese alla romana*, the local version of trifle. The classic Roman cheese is *pecorino*, made from sheep's milk; *caciotta romana* comes from a mixture of cow's and sheep's milk.

Wine

Wine in Rome usually means a white Castelli Romani, most famously *Frascati*, which inspired the Trastevere's dialect poet Trilussa to rhapsodize: *'Dentro 'sta boccia trovi er bonumore/che canta l'inni e t'imbandiera er còre'* (something like: 'in a mouthful there's such good humour/that sings hymns and decks your heart with banners'). Straw-coloured, dry, and clear, Frascati, like all the Castelli wines, is the perfect accompaniment to Roman cooking. Other white wines worth trying from the region are *Marino*, like Frascati a DOC wine; also *Colli Albani*, from near Castel Gandolfo, a pale gold in colour, soft and fruity; *Colli Lanuvini*, from south of Lake Nemi, good for fish and antipasti; and *Velletri*, both a white and a dry tannic ruby red, a friend to pasta, and roast and grilled meats. The other regions around Rome produce a fair complement of vini: a full-bodied red wine and a slightly bitter, dry and aromatic white from *Cervéteri*; *Zagarolo*, a soft, harmonic white wine famous during the Renaissance; *Monte Compatri Colonna*, from the Zagarolo-Colonna area, another white that should be served quite cool with dishes like *fettuccine al burro*. Harder to find are *Torre Ercolana*, *Fiorano* (red or white), and the red *Castel San Giorgio*. If none of these wines please, Rome is a great place to find thousands of wines from all other corners of Italy, some as inexpensive. On the whole, the *vino della casa* is usually cheap and drinkable, though it's advisable, if you're quaffing cheap wine, to do as the Romans do and dilute it with water to avoid a morning-after headache.

Prices

'The more you spend the worse you eat,' is an old Roman saying, though the city's restaurants are doing their utmost to keep prices rising above the Italian average. The humble, inexpensive *vini e cucina*, a mainstay of working-class Rome, are an endangered species. Watch out for tourist traps—those places near a major sight with a 'tourist menu' almost always mean mediocrity. Rome also has some quite expensive joints that could best be described as parodies of old, famous establishments; they advertise heavily, and aren't hard to smell out. The Romans have another pessimistic saying—that in a lovely setting you'll eat like a dog; it's true that many places with pretty outside gardens lose their ambition in the kitchen. Hotel restaurants, especially those in the deluxe class, can be very, very good but fiendishly expensive, where you can easily drop L150,000. The old distinctions between a *ristorante*, *trattoria*, and *osteria* have become confused—some of Rome's swankiest eating places are trattorias or osterias. Unfortunately the old habit of posting prices in the window has fallen out of fashion, so it's difficult to judge prices, though generally the fancier the fittings, the fancier the *conto* at the end, though neither price nor décor have anything to do with the quality of the food. When you eat out, mentally add to the bill the bread and cover charge (*pane e coperto*, usually L2000–3000, but can be a lot more in swanky restaurants) and a 15 per cent service charge. This is usually included in the bill (*servizio compreso*); if it says *servizio non compreso* you'll have to do your own arithmetic. An additional small tip is expected for good service.

Finally, note that when a restaurant advertises a fixed-price menu (*menu turistico*), you won't see a trace of it inside—memorize what you want before you go in. Secondly, many of the places that take food seriously offer a *menu degustazione*—a set-price gourmet meal that allows you to taste whatever seasonal delicacies the chef has whipped up. Both are cheaper than if you had ordered à la carte. When you leave a restaurant you should be given a receipt (if not, the owners are tax-dodging), which by law you must hold on to until you're 60 metres from the door or risk an ambush from the tax police.

The prices listed below are for an average meal (antipasto, first and second courses, dessert, and wine) per person. If you order seafood or truffles, the price will be considerably higher; with some discretion (and drinking the house wine only) it could be considerably less. Remember too to flick back to the Walks listings for recommended wine bars, *gelaterie* and cafés.

> **luxury:** L100–150,000
>
> **expensive:** L60–100,000
>
> **moderate:** L40–60,000
>
> **inexpensive:** L25–40,000
>
> **cheap:** under L25,000
>
> **Credit cards:** AE=American Express, DC=Diner's Club

Restaurants

moderate

Cannavota, Piazza S. Giovanni in Laterano, ✆ 775 007. *Closed Wed*. (AE, DC) Specializes in fish and seafood. The chef has a way with fresh scampi, clams, and other fruits of the sea, both in antipasti and generous pasta dishes. Good value, charming service.

Cicilardone, Via Merulana 77, ✆ 733 806. *Closed Sun pm and Mon.* Reserve. Excellent home-made pasta dishes, such as *maltagliati* with ricotta and tomato and spaghetti with *cacio* (a kind of cheese) and pepper. The *secondi* are less good, though the *pezza pazza*, pieces of (literally) mad beef in a piquant sauce, is interesting. Lively atmosphere, aided by a good wine selection.

inexpensive

Monti, Via S. Vito 13a, on the corner of Via Carlo Alberto, ✆ 733 285. *Closed Tues.* Roman. A small, friendly trattoria where you dine with the TV for company. Olive ascotane, homemade pasta and excellent grilled meats.

cheap

Mar Rosso, Via Conte Verde 62, ✆ 730 702. *Closed Tues.* Popular Ethiopian restaurant where you can dine at low tables and eat with your fingers, or more conventionally at higher tables with a knife and fork. Hot, spicy food.

Termini and San Lorenzo

inexpensive

Tram Tram, Via de' Reti 44-6, ✆ 490 416. *Closed Mon.* The best of San Lorenzo's trendy new restaurants. More-ish seafood lasagne, scrumptious *involtini*, and a good range of main course salads. There's also a bar for pre and post dinner drinks.

Hosteria La Famiglia, Via Gaeta 66, ✆ 494 0622. *Closed Sat.* An Abruzzese trattoria popular with Rome's jolly, arty communists (who work across the road organizing the city's summer feast of culture). Home-made fettuccine, along with standard *secondi* like *melanzane alla parmigiana* (aubergines baked with parmesan) and *cotaletta alla milanese* (veal cutlet fried in breadcrumbs).

Pommidoro, Piazza dei Sanniti 44. ✆ 445 2692. *Closed Sun.* A classic San Lorenzo trattoria popular with the neighbourhood's intellectuals and artists, serving Roman dishes cooked by the talented wife of the owner. Good pasta dishes (like spaghetti *alla verdura* or *all'amatriciana*) and equally good meat and fish grilled *alla brace*. Outdoor tables in good weather.

Trimani, Via Cernaia 37B. ✆ 446 9630. *Closed Sun.* A haven of sanity in the Termini area to which intellectuals and businessmen with demanding tastebuds flock at lunchtime - though it's also worth frequenting in the evenings. Salads such as borlotti beans with tuna and onion, quiches, smoked fish, wild boar salami, a wide selection of regional cheeses and an utterly unforgettable *caprese* (buffalo mozzarella with tomato and fresh basil) served with dark rustic bread and a saucer of luscious green olive oil. Desserts include chestnut mousse, and there's a mind-boggling range of wines. A set lunch (glass of wine, a selection of cheeses and salamis and a desert) for L19,500.

cheap

Formula 1, Via degli Equi 13. ✆ 445 3866. *Evenings only. Closed Sun.* An old, amicable pizzeria popular with students in the nearby university. And deservedly so. Great pizza (including a good veggie option, *all'Ortolana*, with peppers, aubergines and courgettes) as are the deep fried courgette flowers and *suppli al telefono* (rice balls with a knob of mozzarella in the centre which forms a 'telephone' cable when you bite into it). Tables outside in good weather.

Le Maschere, Via degli Umbri 8-14. ✆ 445 3805. *Evenings only. Closed Mon.* Another excellent studenty San Lorenzo pizzeria, run by Calabrians. If you like your pizza pungent, try *estimata*, with hot peppers, garlic, anchovies and oregano, if you don't, *la Maschere* comes with mozzarella, mushroooms, olives and onion. A good selection of *bruschette*, along with highly praised *suppli* and deep-fried *baccalà* on Fridays. Tables outside in good weather.

Africa, Via Gaeta 26, ✆ 494 1077. *Closed Mon.* Eritrean specialities along with Italo-Eritrean combos like spaghetti with hot spicy sauce.

Trastevere

luxury

Alberto Ciarla, Piazza S. Cosimato 40, ✆ 581 8668. *Closed Sun.* (AE, Visa,DC; reservations suggested.) This flash candlelit fairyland of seafood is unique in Rome not only for its variety of sea creatures, but for the variety of methods of preparation: if you can't decide, try the less expensive *menu degustazione.*

Tentativo di Descrizione di un Banchetto di Roma, Via della Luce 5, ✆ 589 5234. *Closed Sun.* (AE, Visa, DC; reservations essential.) Very elegant, if slightly clinical shrine to *nuova cucina* with a menu of perfectly cooked and presented dishes which change with the seasons. Considered very chic.

expensive

Cul de Sac II, Vicolo dell'Atleta 21, ✆ 581 3324. *Closed Mon and lunchtimes except on Sun.* A former wine bar which now ranks among the best new-wave restaurants in the city. A memorable wine list, intelligently inventive dishes and courteous service. Reserve in advance.

Checco er Carettiere, Via Benedetta 10, ✆ 581 7018. *Closed Sun eve and Mon.* (AE, Visa, DC.) One of Trastevere's oldest inns, with well-prepared versions of popular Roman specialities like *coda alla vaccinara* and seafood. Famous for making even tripe taste good; the fish is just right.

Carlo Menta, Via della Lungaretta 101, ✆ 580 3733. *Closed Mon.* Gastronomes adore it; sensitive souls blanch at the bordello-style decor; the paranoid are convinced that every other diner is a mafioso; and the irreverent will simply giggle at the tinkling piano and campish medallion-wearing proprietor, who nervously answers the door in this exclusive fish restaurant. An experience.

Paris in Trastevere, Piazza S. Callisto 7a, ✆ 581 378. *Closed Sun eve and Mon.* (AE, Visa, DC.) Memorable Roman/Jewish cuisine. Try the home-made *gnocchetti* with fish sauce, the *fritto misto* and the excellent vegetable dishes; tables outside in the piazza in summer.

moderate

Ciak, Vicolo del Cinque 21, ✆ 589 4774. *Closed Mon. Eves only.* Il Ciak's flaming fiery furnace makes it an ideal place to go on a cold winter's night. Hearty Tuscan fare like *ribollita* (a thick soup), polenta with hare or wild boar sauce, and thick Florentine and wild boar steaks grilled over the fire. Very popular, so reserve a table.

La Canonica, Vicolo del Piede, behind S. Maria in Trastevere, ✆ 580 3845. *Closed Mon.* A touristy restaurant with a cluttered mock-rustic dining room. The fresh seafood is good, however, and prices are reasonable. Some interesting dishes too – smoked swordfish wotj rugjetta, and among the *contorni puntarella con salsa di asciughe.* Lovely, peaceful outside tables.

Da Cencia, Piazza S. Rufina, (Via della Lungaretta 67) ✆ 581 2670. *Closed Sun.* One of Trastevere's lobsters-in-the-tank seafood palaces. With outside tables. Come for lunch and a modest but surprising all-seafood L50,000 menu.

inexpensive

San Michele aveva un Gallo, Via San Francesco a Ripa 73, ✆ 588 2870. *Closed Sat lunch and Sun.* One of Trastevere's new-wave wine bars, whose clinical cream walls, exposed beams and confrontational lighting resolutely shun romance - they show up every blemish on your companion's complexion! However, the food is light and imaginative, and as bottles of wine start at L10,000 you can induce a more flattering, soft-focused vision of the world without breaking the bank.

Osteria dell'Aquila, Via Natale del Grande 4, ✆ 581 0924. *Closed Tues.* An authentic Roman/Abruzzese restaurant and pizzeria, run for 30 years by three sisters. Neopolitan pizza, and home-made *gnocchi, fettucine* and *tiramisù.*

La Parolaccia, Vicolo del Cinque 3, © 580 3633. *Closed eves and Wed.* Should you happen to have the perverse desire to have a meal accompanied with insults and curses, or simply wish to broaden your Italian vocabulary, this is the place to come. *Parolaccia* means swearword, and waiters are employed for their sleazy verbal repertoire. A Roman institution, but don't expect too much of the food.

Sorya Mahal, Piazza Trilussa s/n © 589 4554. *Evenings only. Closed Sun.* Probably Rome's best Indian restaurant (though it doesn't have a great deal of competition). However, with excellent service, a pretty garden for summer eating, and an entire vegetarian menu, even die-hard aficionados of Brick Lane and Rusholme shouldn't be disappointed. The set veggie menu (L20,000) includes dahl, spiced cauliflower and a pea and mushroom curry, while fish-lovers and carnivores can plump for lemon chicken, prawn korma, rogan josh, and swordfish tandoori. Poppadums, pakoras and samosas too, along with lassi and a (small, but carefully chosen) selection of wines.

Da Umberto, Piazza La Malva s/n. *Closed Wed .* An affable restaurant which serves excellent game and meat dishes, so a good place to come if you want an autumnal treat of wild boar (*cinghiale*), pheasant (*fagiano*) or hare (*lepre*).

Da Lucia, Vicolo del Mattonato 2B, © 580 3601. *Closed Mon.* Hidden on a back street (off the lower end of Via Garibaldi), but worth seeking out for some of the best real Roman cooking this side of the river. Menu changes daily. Try *spaghetti alla gricia* (with cheese, pepper and bacon) and on Fridays, *baccalà con zibibbo e pinoli* (salt cod with raisins and pine-nuts).

Da Augusto, Piazza de' Renzi 15, © 580 3798. *Closed Sun.* A classic Trastevere trattoria, now in danger of becoming a parody of itself. Habitués squeeze past the tightly packed tables, exchange insults with Augusto, grab a sheet of paper from the shelf at the back, lay their own table, place their order, and usually end up collecting their own wine and food from the kitchen hatch. The food's not bad, prices are low, and in good weather you can eat outside.

Il Generale, Vicolo del Moro 1A, © 580, 3769. *Closed Sat eve and all day Sun.* An authentic little trattoria where you can warm up on a cold day with *cicoria con fava* (Italian chicory with fava bean stew) or linger in a tiny courtyard in summer over *penne primavera* (penne tossed with basil, raw tomato and mozzarella). Drinkable house wine, but splash out on Brolio Chianti.

Corso/Trevi Fountain

moderate

Al Piccolo Arancio. Via Scanderbeg 112, © 678 6139. *Closed Mon.* A find, if you *can* find it (Via Scanderbeg runs off Via della Dataria, just southeast of the Trevi Fountain). This is an old hostaria, done up brightly by a serious new owner. Imaginative: try zucchini flower, mozzarella and artichoke fritters, ravioli stuffed with ricotta in a cream and orange sauce, or *orechiette* with baby broccoli.

Al Moro, Vicolo delle Bollette 13, © 678 3495. *Closed Sun.* Reserve. Popular with politicians and businessmen who come for super fresh food and daily specials depending on market availability, prepared with an authentic Roman touch.Great pasta dishes and wonderful baccalà. Bill may tip into the expensive category.

inexpensive

Trattoria al Gallinaccio, Vicolo del Gallinaccio, © 679 0945. *Closed Sun.* Inconspicuous trattoria off Largo del Tritone. The place to go if you like artichokes—over the pasta, on the scallopine, and of course by themselves *alla Romana*.

Golden Crown, Via Arcione 85, © 678 9831. Closed Mon. (AE, Visa; reservations suggested.) Authentic cuisine from Hong Kong.

Spanish Steps/Piazza del Popolo

luxury

Relais le Jardin, Via G. Notaris 5, © 322 4541. *Closed Sun.* (AE, Visa, DC; reserve.) Elegant, haute cuisine. An extra-special occasion for most mortals.

El Toulà, Via della Lupa 29b, © 687 3498. Closed Sat lunch and Sun. (AE, Visa, DC; reservations required.) Chic, and serving some of the finest food in Rome, with plenty of swank; the high bills include a pay-to-see-and-be-seen tax.

expensive

Alfredo all'Augustea l'Originale, Piazza Augusto Imperatore, © 687 8615. *Closed Sun.* One of several heirs of the creator of *fettuccine alfredo* with triple butter, now a slightly smug relic of the *dolce vita* days. Outdoor dining in summer.

Dal Bolognese, Piazza del Popolo 1/2 © 361 1426. *Closed Mon.* Upmarket Emilia-Romagnan restaurant, popular with wealthy tourists and Roman carnivores. Excellent *bollito misto*.

moderate

Il Re degli Amici, Via della Croce 33b, © 679 5380. *Closed Mon.* (AE, Mastercard,Visa, DC) Tues and Fri fresh fish (grilled meat the rest of the week) served in art-filled rooms. Expensive pizza in the evening.

Alla Rampa, Piazza Mignanelli 18, © 678 2621. *Closed Mon lunch and Sun.* Italian, simple and good, and amazingly quiet for the proximity of the Spanish Steps, though the service can be rushed. Lots of tables in the piazza.

Mario, Via della Vite 55, © 678 3818. *Closed Sun.* Tuscan (AE, Visa, DC.) *Crostini* (liver canapés), *ribollita* (thick, mostly cabbage soup), *bistecca alla fiorentina*, Chianti, and all the old favourites from the land of the bean-eaters.

Sogo Asahi, Via di Propaganda 22, © 678 3942. *Closed Sun.* (AE, Visa, DC.) Wonderful Japanese restaurant frequented little by Westerners. Excellent value lunch menu (L25,000), but dinners can fall into the expensive category.

Margutta, Via Margutta 119, © 678 6033. *Closed Sun.* One of Rome's few vegetarian restaurants. Rather chic and somewhat overpriced by US and UK standards.

Birreria Viennese, Via della Croce 21, © 679 5569. *Closed Wed.* (AE, Visa, DC.) Traditional Austro-Hungarian fare: beer and sausages, goulash, sauerkraut, wienerschnitzel and Sachertorte (though watch some of the prices). The fixed price tourist menu falls into the inexpensive category.

inexpensive

Edy, Vicolo del Babuino 4, © 678 4331. *Closed Sun.* A lovely family-run trattoria, romantically candlelit in the evenings, and serving a memorable fettuccine with ricotta and artichokes and one of the best *tiramisùs* you're ever likely to taste.

Beltramme, Via della Croce 39 (no tel). *Closed Sun.* There's no name on this simple trattoria, bravely holding its own on one of the chicest streets in town—look for the sign 'Fiaschetteria' above a door with a dingy net curtain. All the old favourites, from *pasta e ceci* and *fettuccine* to *pajata*, tripe and ox tail; determinedly unpretentious and a good place to meet the locals.

Around Via Veneto/Piazza Barberini

expensive

Andrea, Via Sardegna 26, © 493 707. *Closed Sun.* (All major credit cards; reservations recommended.) Well worth a splurge for beautifully prepared dishes made from the best quality ingredients. Mouthwatering antipasti, an unforgettable lobster stew (*l'astice alla catalana*) and skilful pasta dishes.

George's, Via Marche 7, © 484 575. *Closed Sun.* (All major credit cards; reservations recommended.) A *dolce vita* era classic which is still posh and elegant, with a gorgeous garden terrace, refined service, tinkling piano, and extensive wine list.

moderate

Colline Emiliane, Via degli Avignonesi 22, © 475 7538. *Closed Fri.* Emilia-Romagnan food is reckoned by Italians to be the best in the country, and in Rome there's no better place to sample it than Colline Emiliane. Classic dishes include *tortelloni di zucca* (pumpkin), lasagne verde and, for offal-lovers, an impressive *bollito misto* (beef tongue, calf cheek and pigs trotters). In autumn there are dishes laced with truffles, though obviously these bump the price up.

Taverna Flavia, Via Flavia 9/1, ℰ 474 5214. *Closed Sat lunch and Sun.* (All major credit cards.) An old favourite of the Cinecittà set. Specialities include *penne alla Flavia* (with peas and mushrooms), a salad spiked with truffles and gruyère, and ossobucco with risotto.

Tempio di Bacco, Via Lombardia 36–38, ℰ 475 4625. *Closed Sat.* (All major credit cards.) One of the oldest trattorias in the area, with a tasty and varied menu according to the season and fresh fish on Tues and Fri.

inexpensive

Cantina Cantarini, Piazza Sallustio 12, ℰ 485 528. *Closed Sun.* All major credit cards. A century-old trattoria serving good honest fare with a touch of the Marche region. Reserve in advance, even at lunchtime. Mon–Thurs meat dishes, Fri–Sat seafood.

Forum and Colosseum

inexpensive

Pasqualino, Via dei SS Quattro 66, ℰ 700 4576. *Closed Mon.* A venerable old tratt dishing up classic Roman fare such as *spaghetti alla carbonara*, *abbacchio al forno*, *saltimbocca* and *trippa alla romana.*

Cavour 313 Via Cavour 313, ℰ 678 5496. *Closed Sun.* A mellow wood-beamed bar converted from an old wine shop. Mouthwatering (and lengthy menu) of snacks, all made with top-notch ingredients, along with 500 wines.

Ulderico, Via di San Giovanni in Laterano 106, ℰ 735 924. Closed Sun. Good honest tratt fare, in surroundings unchanged since the fifties.

cheap

Pizza Forum, Via di San Giovanni in Laterano 34–8, ℰ 700 2515. *Closed Mon.* Another place you'd assume to be best avoided, kitted out as a theme-park version of an ancient forum, with fish-tank lighting to boot. Forget aesthetics for half an hour, and go inside for a good Neopolitan style pizza (thicker bases than their Roman cousins).

Testaccio

expensive

Checchino dal 1887, Via di Monte Testaccio 30, ℰ 574 6318. *Closed Sun eve and Mon.* (All major credit cards; reservations recommended.) In a traditional, naturally air-conditioned Testaccio wine cave, you can dine on Rome's most authentic and best-prepared local specialities, a perfect match for one of the city's best wine cellars. Order the *menu degustazione* for a memorable repast.

Dolce Vita da Luisa, Lungotevere Pietrapapa 51, ℰ 557 9865. *Eves only, closed Mon.* (AE, DC). Actually across the Tiber, but a good and popular bet for its more imaginative fish dishes. Open until 2am.

Lo Scoppetaro, Lungotevere Testaccio 7, ✆ 574 2408. *Closed Tues.* Wood veneer
walls adorned with racing photos and the occasional lipstick smeared wine-
glass notwithstanding, this is one of the most popular of Testaccio's offal
temples, attracting besuited businessmen as well as proletarian locals. There's
no menu— dishes are reeled off by the waiter at top speed. The speciality is
rigatoni con pajata (pasta with veal intestine) but if this doesn't appeal, try the
perfectly cooked pasta *alla carbonara* or *matriciana.*

inexpensive

I Carmini Burana, Via Luca della Robbia 15, ✆ 574 2500. *Eves only, closed Wed.*
Affordable *nuova cucina* with lots of seasonal vegetables.

cheap

Augustarello, Via G. Branca 100, ✆ 574 6585. *Closed Sun.* Old family restaurant
stubbornly refuses to lighten true Roman fare or adapt to modern tastes.

Da Felice, Via Mastro Giorgio 29, ✆ 574 6800. *Closed Sun.* Since 1935, despite the
lack of a sign on the door, the few tables at Felice's have been full of admirers
of the home-style Roman cuisine, gnocchi, tripe, *pajata*, each served on its
appointed day. Arrive before 1 at lunchtime and 8 in the evenings to be sure
of a table, and don't be surprised to be treated brusquely.

Piccolo Alpino, Via Orazio Antinori 5, ✆ 574 1386. *Closed Mon.* A jovial family-
run trattoria-pizzeria, well known for its fettucine with mushrooms, peas and
cream, and haphazard service.

Gennargentu, Via Ostiense 21-23, ✆ 575 9817. *Closed Mon.* Open evenings only.
Sardinian pizzeria known for its pizza al Gennargentu (with sausage, mozzarella and tomato) which you can wash down with Sardinian wine. Desserts
are Sardinian too –notably *seada*, a sweet cheese fritter served with honey.

Piazza Navona/Pantheon

luxury

La Rosetta, Via della Rosetta 9, ✆ 6830 8841. *Closed Sat and Sun.* (Visa, DC.) An
upmarket classic specializing in seafood and Sicilian cuisine.

Papà Giovanni, Via dei Sediari 4, ✆ 686 5308. *Closed Sun.* (Visa, Mastercard.) Must
reserve. Brick walls, bottles, postcards—and some of the most heavenly (though
devilishly expensive) food in Rome, entirely based on availability in the market.

moderate

L'Eau Vive, Via Monterone 85, ✆ 654 1095. *Closed Sun.*(AE,Visa,DC.) In a 16th-
century palace, this is operated by the Christian Virgins of Catholic Missionary
Action through Work, whose work is waitressing in national costume to the
movers and shakers from the Vatican and Christian Democrat party. Daily specials from anywhere in the world; solemn music; French wines.

Tre Maghi, Piazza Pasquino 77-8, ℂ 654 7704. *Closed Sun.* A hip New Age (though not veggie) restaurant in which dishes are inspired by seasons and the signs of the zodiac. Some utterly delicious pasta dishes, along with imaginative salads and desserts to die for. Some memorable wines as well.

L'Orso 80, Via dell'Orso 33, ℂ 656 4904. *Closed Mon.* (AE, Visa, DC.) Popular, family-run, not imaginative perhaps, but delicious antipasti, pasta, and meat dishes, and what more could you want?

cheap

Il Leoncino, Via del Leoncino 28, ℂ 687 6306. *Closed Wed.* Old-fashioned pizzeria in the heart of the *centro storico*, but largely bypassed by tourists. Chaotic, of course, with harrassed waiters, so choose your pizza from the menu board before you sit down.

La Montecarlo, Vicolo Savelli 12, ℂ 686 1877. *Closed Wed in winter, open daily in summer.* Though it makes Leoncino seem tranquil, it's worth putting up with sitting elbow to elbow with your neighbours and ducking as plates of pizza, chairs and tables are whipped over your head, for the brilliant pizzas. There's plenty of time while you're queuing to peruse the menu board. Tables outside in summer.

Da Francesco, Via della Fossa 29. *Closed Tues.* Affable staff and a kitchen which stays open till after midnight makes this a great place for a late night dinner. The pizza is excellent—try it with smoked salmon, or with rocket and porcini mushrooms. Tables outside in summer.

Navona Notte, Via del Teatro Pace 44. Pizza with oysters depending on availability, at other times worth remembering if you get the munchies in the small hours as it stays open till 3 or 4am.

L'Antico Carbonaro, Vicolo di Monte Vecchio 27, ℂ 687 9471. *Closed Wed.* Though it's best known for the brusque irony of its owner, the food at L'Antico Carbonaro makes it worth a visit, even if your Italian's not up to the banter. Brilliant pasta with artichokes.

Ghetto/Piazza Bocca della Verità

expensive

Piperno, Monte de' Cenci 9, ℂ 6880 6629. *Closed Sun eve and Mon.* Hearty, very filling Jewish-Roman cuisine and good wines; you may need an evening stroll to work off the *crostata di ricotta*.

Vecchia Roma, Piazza Campitelli 18, ℂ 656 4604. *Closed Wed.* Reservations advised. A serene place to sit out in the evening and try bruschetta with artichokes and capers, gnocchi with borlotti beans, bacon and tomato, *maltagliati* (literally badly cut pasta) with broccoli, garlic, hot pepper and parmesan, or beef fillet in brandy sauce with foie gras and radicchio. Desserts are excellent.

Evangelista, Via delle Zoccolette 11, ✆ 687 5810. *Closed Sun; evenings only.* (Visa; reserve.) *The* place in Rome to eat artichokes, prepared in a variety of ways, but most famously beaten flat and fried (*al mattone*). The *primi* and *secondi* menus are always changing, but tend to be unusual, making subtle use of game and offal, and Sicilian/Arabic sweets.

Il Portico, Via del Portico d'Ottavia s/n, ✆ 6830.7937. *Closed Sat lunch and Sun eve.* A gentile restaurant in the heart of the ghetto; non-kosher Judeo/Roman fare: mixed vegetable fritters, fried *baccalà* and *carciofi alla giudea.*

Da Giggetto, Via Portico d'Ottavia 21, ✆ 656 1105. *Closed Mon.* Roman-Jewish dishes, served outside in summer by the Portico d'Ottavia. Wonderful *carciofi alla giudea*, *rigatoni con pajata* for the unsqueamish, and standards like *spaghetti alla carbonara* and *penne all'arrabiata* for those who prefer not to eat calf intestines.

Around Campo de' Fiori

luxury

Patrizia e Roberto del Pianeta Terra, Via Arco del Monte 94, ✆ 656 9893. *Closed Mon.* (AE, DC; reservations recommended.) The name says it all. Frightfully precious restaurant in a elegant old palace: sophisticated food, exquisite wines and formal service from pairs of synchronized waiters.

expensive

Girone VI, Vicolo Sinibaldi 2, near Piazza Argentina, ✆ 654 2831. *Closed Sun, open eves only.* (All major credit cards.) Superb Ligurian food: first courses with fresh herbs, imaginative *secondi*, wonderful desserts. In a tranquil little alley.

Taverna Giulia, Vicolo dell'Oro, ✆ 656 9768. Closed Tues. (AE, Visa, DC.) Tasty Ligurian dishes in a 15th-century house.

moderate

La Carbonara, Campo de' Fiori 23, ✆ 686 4783. *Closed Tue.* The most upmarket of Campo de' Fiori's restaurants, frequented by PDS party members as well as scores of tourists. Roman classics like frittered brains and artichokes as well as tagliolini with porcini mushrooms, artichokes or clams. Best visited in good weather, as half the fun is sitting outside and watching the streetlife.

Costanza, Piazza del Paradiso 65, ✆ 656 1717. *Closed Sun.* (AE, Visa.) A romantic place, with a courtyard for summer dining, serving the best of several Italian regions, including a divine risotto with zucchini flowers and ravioli stuffed with artichokes. Cocky waiters though.

Il Drappo, Vicolo del Malpasso, ✆ 687 7365. *Closed Sun.* (Reserve.) Both traditional and innovative dishes from the island of Sardinia in a pretty candle-lit setting.

Thien Kim, Via Giulia 201, ✆ 654 7832. *Closed Sun.* (AE.) A charming, civilized Vietnamese restaurant, with good duck dishes.

Osteria Romanesca, Campo de' Fiori 40. *Closed Mon.* A matey trattoria where the owner bums cigarettes off clients, throws amiable insults at passing neighbours, and saves the Campo's oddballs from starvation by feeding them in return for a few hours' casual work. No frills Roman fare, with prices to match.

Nello e Walter, Via del Pellegrino 107, © 686 9361. *Closed Mon.* In summer sit outside on picturesque Via del Pellegrino. Excellent pasta with seafood.

Pierluigi, Piazza de'Ricci, on Via Monserrato, © 686 1302. *Closed Mon.* A tempting array of antipasti, seafood and delicious pasta dishes. Another good place to eat in summer—outside on a mellow old piazza.

Moretta, Vicolo della Moretta, on the corner of Via Monserrato 32. *Closed Sun.* Pretty trattoria specializing in farfalle (pasta butterflies with cream, spinach, tomato and pepper sauce) and seafood; outdoor tables.

cheap

'Baccalà', Largo dei Librari 88, off Via dei Giubbonari, © 656 4018. *Closed Sun.* From 5–10 pm the finest codfish fillets in Rome (and little else), to eat on the spot with a glass of wine, on outside tables in summer, or to take away.

Nuova Shanghai, Via dei Giubbonari 52, just off Campo de' Fiori. *Closed Sun.* One of the best Chinese places in Rome. L10,000 lunch menu.

Vatican /Prati

expensive

San Luigi, Via Mocenigo 10 (near the Vatican Museums), © 302 0704. *Closed Sun.* (AE, Visa.) Intimate, 19th-century décor, featuring dishes from *gnocchetti verdi* (made of potatoes and broccoli) with clams, liver with honey, and a salad of rocket, pears, parmesan and black truffles.

Tullio is a seafood restaurant on a Tiber barge moored below Lungotevere Mellini, on the north side of Ponte Cavour. A treat for a special summer night out.

moderate

Osteria dell'Angelo, Via G Bettolo 24, *closed Sat lunch and Sun.* Highly rated tratt run by a former rugby player. Authentic Roman dishes.

inexpensive

Taverna Negma, Borgo Vittorio 92, © 656 5143. *Closed Wed.* (AE, DC.) Good Arabian tabbuleh, falafel and kebabs and Rome's best couscous cooked by a family from Salerno.

cheap

Abruzzese, Via de' Gracchi 27. *Closed Mon.* Family run tratt, serving Abruzzese dishes like *maccheroni alla chitarra*.

La Madonella, Via Tunisi 27–9. *Closed Mon.* Basic Sardinian trattoria behind the Andrea Doria market. Full meals under l20,000.

Hotels:	355
Aventine Hill	355
Campo de'Fiori/Piazza Navona/Pantheon	356

Where to Stay

Forum and Colosseum	357
Spanish Steps/Piazza del Popolo	358
Near St Peter's and Prati	360
Near Termini and S. Maria Maggiore	361
Via Vittorio Veneto and environs	363
Trastevere	363
Coppodé	364
Students	364
Religious Institutions	365
Campsites	365
Residential Hotels	366

For a city that has been entertaining crowds of visitors for the last 2,000 years, Rome does not seem to have acquired any special flair for accommodating them. Hotels here are neither better nor worse than anywhere else in Italy. From Belle Epoque palaces on Via Veneto to grimy hovels on the wrong side of Termini Station, little is truly distinctive; places with a history, a famous view, or quiet gardens to shut out the noise are few and far between (and usually so well known that you can never book too soon in advance). Rome has been rated the noisiest capital city in Europe—a score of decibels higher than EEC standards think is good for your health. If you can, avoid main streets, avoid the Termini Station area, and aim for something on a medieval lane in central Rome—it will probably be quieter than a hotel in the suburbs. If you're staying for a week or more, Rome's Hotel-Residences—flats to let for a minimum of a week or a month—may be good value (the most central ones are listed below). At the other end of the scale are the numerous hostels for pilgrims and students, many run by religious orders. Because of puny lifts and stairs, accommodation accessible to the handicapped is almost entirely limited to Rome's five and four star hotels; those that don't follow this rule will be so designated.

The price categories used below refer to rates for double rooms with bathroom (without bathroom in the case of budget hotels) and were appropriate at the time of writing. As a rule, rates rise by around 10 per cent every year at Easter. Single rooms are roughly two-thirds the price of a double. Adding an **extra bed** to a room will add 35 per cent to the bill. If you show up asking for a single, and all that's left is a double, by law the hotel should let you have it for ⅔ the rate—but usually they will try to charge you 100 per cent. Taxes and service charges are included in the given rates, though some hotels charge extra for air conditioning (around L25,000 per day), and some may try to make you swallow hefty breakfast charges. Rooms listed without bath mean that the lavatory and shower are in the hall—in cheaper establishments you may have to pay an extra L3000 or so to have a shower. Prices are by law listed on the door of each room and any discrepancies in your disfavour could be reported to the tourist office in Via Parigi (but don't expect much). Rome has no high or low season; when more than one price is listed it means that some rooms are nicer than others.

Extra luxury: over L500,000	**Moderate:** L125–200,000
Luxury: L300–500,000	**Inexpensive:** L75–125,000
Expensive: L200–300,000	**Cheap:** under L75,000

Because the Italian post is unreliable and Rome can be crowded at unexpected times, the best thing to do when booking is to telephone and make sure a room is available before sending a deposit, if one is required. (The prefix for Rome is 06, and you'll find that hotel clerks in Rome speak English, except in some of the cheaper places.) Be sure to request a quiet room.

Remember, though, that telephone numbers in Rome are in the process of changing: if you can't get through to a hotel, or get a recorded message which you can't understand, phone directory enquiries (12) in Italy, or, in Britain, international directory enquiries, 153.

If you turn up without a reservation, head to *Enjoy Rome*, Via Varese 39, ℂ 445 1843, where you'll get a friendlier welcome and more personal service than you would at either of the tourist offices. It's a five- to ten-minute walk north of Termini.

Note: this list of hotels is very select, and it omits, not unintentionally, some of the best-known establishments in Rome. It was designed to give readers a choice of the quietest, most serendipitous places, in the best locations. Admittedly, covering hotels is a difficult job—first impressions are often misleading. If you find us mistaken on any point, or if we have left out something good, we would like to know about it.

Aventine Hill

One of the prettiest, coolest, and quietest corners in Rome, with safe street parking for motorists. A bit inconvenient (bus 94 is the Aventine's link with Piazza Venezia) but bars and restaurants are not too far away in Testaccio (see Walk XI) or Trastevere.

moderate

- ★★★ **Sant' Anselmo,** Piazza Sant' Anselmo 2, 00153, ℂ 578 3214, fax 578 3604. A former villa, with a bar and garden to sit outside. Exquisite decor.

- ★★★ **Villa San Pio,** Via Sant'Anselmo 19, 00153, ℂ 574 5231, fax 574 3547. Another glorious Aventine villa with a gorgeous, secluded statue-studded garden. Run by the same folk as the Sant'Anselmo and Aventino.

- ★★ **Domus Aventina**, Via S. Prisca 11–b, 00153, ℂ 574 6135. A recently refurbished hotel in a former convent, very quiet and right next to the church of Santa Prisca.

inexpensive

- ★★ **Aventino,** Via S. Domenico 10, 00153, ℂ 574 5232, fax 578 3604. Yet another Aventine villa—not as stylish as its elder sisters, but the rooms are adequate and the garden is lovely.

Anyone serious about experiencing this city at its best should consider spending time in its oldest and most convivial neighbourhoods; unfortunately there isn't a wide choice of hotels. The most modern is the new Holiday Inn near the Pantheon. Otherwise try to book one of the following well in advance of your departure.

luxury

✶✶✶✶✶ **Holiday Inn,** Crowne Plaza Minerva, Piazza della Minerva 69, 00186, ✆ 684 1888, fax 679 4165. A 17th-century palazzo for visiting ecclesiasts, stunningly revamped by post-modern architect Paolo Portoghesi. Large bedrooms (in which kids under nineteen sharing with parents stay for free) and wittily kitted out public rooms. Brilliant views from the rooftop terrace.

✶✶✶✶ **Raphael,** Largo di Febo 2, 00186, ✆ 650 881, fax 687 8993. Very near Piazza Navona, a vine-covered old charmer, beautifully decorated with antiques and art. Bettino Craxi had himself a penthouse built on top, and many other important politicians stay here too, so the place is always full of cops. Try to get one of the top floor rooms for the lovely views.

✶✶✶✶ **Sole al Pantheon,** Via del Pantheon 63, 00186, ✆ 678 0441, fax 684 0689. A small hotel a block from the Pantheon, mentioned as an inn in the 15th century—Ariosto slept here. Charmingly renovated.

moderate

✶✶✶ **Del Senato,** Piazza della Rotonda 73, 00186, ✆ 679 3231, fax 684 0297. Charmless but comfortable, air-conditioned, with some rooms facing the Pantheon.

✶✶✶ **Portoghesi,** Via dei Portoghesi 1, 00186, ✆ 686 4231, fax 687 6976. A small, well-kept hotel on a quiet but central street north of Piazza Navona, with the option of air conditioning.

✶✶✶ **Teatro di Pompeo**, Largo del Pallaro 8, 00186, ✆ 687 2812/6830 0170, fax 654 5531. The most upmarket hotel around Campo de' Fiori. Twelve beamed bedrooms, and a breakfast room under the vaults of Pompey's Theatre.

✶✶ **Due Torri,** Vicolo del Leonetto 23 (just north of Via del Orso), 00186, ✆ 654 0956, on a tiny street, but with a garage and comfortable rooms.

inexpensive

✶✶ **Campo de' Fiori,** Via del Biscione 6, 00186, ✆ 654 0865 (new number 6880 6865), fax 687 6003. A feverishly revamped hotel featuring a hall-of-mirrors corridor, and theme park bedrooms (the kitchiest of which boasts a bathroom roofed with hewn logs). Vertiginous views from the roof garden.

★★ **Piccolo,** Via dei Chiavari 32, 00186 (near Campo de' Fiori), © 654 2560 (new © 6880 2560). A charming little hotel on a quiet street; showers off the hall.

★★ **Pomezia,** Via dei Chiavari 12, 00186, © 686 1371. Immaculate rooms in a pleasant, friendly little hotel.

★★ **Della Lunetta,** Piazza del Paradiso 68, 00186, © 686 1080, fax 689 2028. Near Campo de' Fiori, fairly large, and nice, quiet rooms.

★★ **Sole,** Via del Biscione 76, 00186, © 654 0873 (new © 6880 6873), fax 689 3787. Near Campo de' Fiori, on the foundations of Pompey's Theatre rises the not very bright but endearing Sun, a family-run favourite of backpackers, grandparents and everyone in between. Ask for a room facing the upstairs courtyard. Garage and TV room. Book in advance.

★★ **Rinascimento,** Via del Pellegrino 122, 00186, © 687 4813, fax 683 3518. Just west of Campo de' Fiori, 13 very pleasant rooms with bathroom (don't worry; 13 isn't unlucky in Italy—it's 17 you have to watch out for). Optional air conditioning.

★ **Navona,** Via dei Sediari 8, 00186, © 686 4203. As with the others, worth it for the location rather than the intrinsic quality of its 18 rooms. Friendly owners from Down Under.

★★ **Abruzzi,** Piazza della Rotonda 69, 00186, © 679 2021 is directly across the square from the Pantheon. The rooms in the back without the view aren't so great, but at least they're quiet. A bit ragged, but amenable.

★ **Mimosa,** Via S. Chiara 61, 00186, © 654 1753. Near the Pantheon. 10 rooms on a quiet street overlooking a carabinieri barracks.

★ **Pensione Primavera,** Piazza San Pantaleo 3, 00186, © 654 3109. A little known pensione with eight simple rooms set back from Corso Vittorio Emanuele a couple of minute's walk from both Piazza Navona and Campo de' Fiori.

Forum and Colosseum

The area can be a bit noisy during the day, but it's very convenient for the sights and public transport. At night it quietens down considerably—there are very few fun restaurants or bars nearby.

★★★★ **Forum,** Via Tor de' Conti 25, 00184, ✆ 679 2446, fax 678 6479. The only really luxury establishment near the centre of ancient Rome, dignified and somewhat old-fashioned, with a unique view over the ruins from the rooftop bar and restaurant—also air conditioning, TV, and a garage. No wheelchair access.

inexpensive

★★ **Casa Kolbe,** Via S. Teodoro 44 (south of the Forum and west of the Palatine), 00186, ✆ 679 4974, fax 684 1550. Large rooms in a former monastery in one of Rome's most central but remote corners, with a garden, bar, and restaurant to retreat from the rigours of Rome. Handicapped access.

★★ **Nerva,** Via Tor de' Conti 3, 00184, ✆ 678 1835. A view straight onto Augustus' great Subura wall for those keen on ancient masonry. A small hotel with shabby but comfortable rooms, with friendly new owners who are about to renovate.

★ **Perugia,** Via del Colosseo 7, 00184, ✆ 679 7200. Small, fairly quiet hotel near the Colosseum and the park of Monte Oppio.

★ **Romano,** Largo Corrado Ricci 32, 00184, ✆ 679 5851. Simple accommodation across from the Forum.

Spanish Steps/Piazza del Popolo

This has been a favourite lodging place for foreigners for the past 300 years, and it still is trendy today; if you don't book early you won't find a room anywhere in the neighbourhood. Metro and bus connections make it very convenient, and the Villa Borghese is close by (see Walk VII).

For something different, there's one self-catering flat in the **Keats House** next to the Spanish Steps, owned by Britain's Landmark Trust (✆ (062882) 5925). There is room for four people, and prices average at £950 per week, although you can also book for shorter periods (minimum three nights).

extra luxury

★★★★★ **Hassler-Villa Medici,** Piazza Trinità dei Monti 6, 00187, ✆ 678 2651, fax 678 9991. This is Rome's swankiest and best appointed hotel, perfectly located on top of the Spanish Steps; every luxury, and a famous roof-top restaurant with a famous view. In fair weather the garden courtyard becomes the breakfast room; air conditioning, private garage, etc.

★★★★ **Hotel de la Ville,** Via Sistina 69, 00187, ✆ 67331, fax 678 4213. The Hassler's larger neighbour, and also has a great view from the roof and upper floors; air conditioned, TV, garage.

★★★★ **Hotel d'Inghilterra,** Via Bocca di Leone 14, 00187 (on the corner of Via Condotti) ✆ 672 161, fax 684 0828. The d'Inghilterra opened its doors in 1850 but has been smartened up since. Henry James, Felix Mendelssohn, the king of Portugal, and Ernest Hemingway checked in here before it had air conditioning and colour TV.

★★★★ **Valadier,** Via della Fontanella 15, 00187, ✆ 361 0592, fax 320 1558. Smarmy nightclub-style decor for would-be seducers, and bedrooms with mirrored ceilings and padded walls for those who succeed.

expensive

★★★ **Scalinata di Spagna,** Piazza Trinità dei Monti 17, 00187, ✆ 684 00986 fax 684 0598. A small, friendly family run hotel at the top of the Spanish Steps, patronized by the occasional discerning film or soap star. Pleasant bedrooms (some with coffered ceilings and a couple with private roof terraces) and a homely dining room where guests breakfast together at a polished wooden table in the company of a parrot. Book months in advance. Some rooms fall into moderate price category.

★★★ **Croce di Malta**, Via Borgognona 28, 00187, ✆ 679 5482 fax 678 0675. Good location on one of the designer shopping streets, and smart bedrooms, some of which have opulent carved furniture and voluptuous candelabra. No breakfast, but plenty of pleasant cafés in the neighbourhood.

moderate

★★★ **Mozart,** Via dei Greci 23, 00187, ✆ 684 0041, fax 678 4271. A lovely little place on a quiet cobbled street. Stone-flagged entrance hall, small flowery rooms with parquet floors, and a pleasant café next door for breakfast or lunch.

★★★ **Carriage.** Via delle Carrozze 36, 00187, ✆ 699 0124, fax 678 8279. A small hotel with a 1600s décor, air conditioned, and fitted with TVs, ideally placed for bouts of designer retail therapy in the Condotti boutiques. Ask for a room at the top so you can have access to the roof terrace.

★★★ **Gregoriana,** Via Gregoriana 18, 00187, ✆ 679 4269, fax 678 4258. A former convent with 19 rooms and corridors papered in unconvential leopard-skin print. Air conditioning available, radio in room, friendly staff.

★★★ **Fontana,** Piazza di Trevi 96, 00187, ✆ 678 6113. Air conditioning, and some rooms with view of the Trevi Fountain.

★★★ **Manfredi,** Via Margutta 61, 00187, ✆ 320 7712. Pretty rooms with fabric-covered walls and tastefully decorated public areas. Small, friendly and run by a charming family. Some rooms fall into the inexpensive category.

inexpensive

★★ **Homs,** Via della Vite 71, 00187, ✆ 679 2976, fax 678 0482; in a large renovated old building on one of the quieter shopping streets. Price is high because of the location.

★★ **Suisse,** Via Gregoriana 56, 00187, ✆ 678 3649, is a fine old pensione, with large rooms clean enough to satisfy even the Swiss. Ask for a room in the back.

★★ **Doge,** Via Due Macelli 106, 00187, ✆ 678 0038, fax 679 1633. Pretty two-star rooms on a noisy street, a short stroll from the Spanish Steps.

cheap

★★ **Forte,** Via Margutta 61, 00187, ✆ 320 7625. A dull little place well run by its British proprietor.

★ **Fiorella,** Via del Babuino 196, 00187, ✆ 361 0597. A friendly place with 8 simple but well-kept, bathless rooms, whose green tiled rooms and orange candlewick bedspreads have remained unchanged in over a decade. Prime location just below Piazza del Popolo. Often full, so book early.

Near St Peter's and Prati

The area around Vatican City is one of the dullest in Rome, but genteel and with few hassles—a good place to sleep but not to play, though Trastevere is a bus 23 ride away, and Piazza del Popolo is just across the Tiber. Off the main streets noise is usually not a problem.

luxury

★★★★ **Atlante Star,** Via Vitelleschi 34, 00193, ✆ 687 9558, fax 687 2300. Modern, cramped rooms with colour TV, and a beautiful roof garden restaurant from which the stunning views almost compensate for the less-than-stunning food and service. Business centre.

moderate

★★★ **Columbus,** Via della Conciliazione 33, 00193, ✆ 686 5435, fax 686 4874, is a somewhat staid but reliable place in the Renaissance Palazzo

Penitenzieri, and a favourite of visiting cardinals; a few frescoes and a courtyard survive from the good old days. Handicapped access.

★★★ **Hotel S. Anna,** Borgo Pio 133, 00193, © 654 1602 fax 6830 8717. A quiet, smartly refurbished hotel with well-designed rooms and a pretty garden courtyard at the back.

inexpensive

★★ **Prati,** Via Crescenzio 87, 00193, © 687 5357. Pleasant, reasonably priced rooms.

★★ **Adriatic,** Via G. Vitelleschi 25, 00193, © 6880 6386. A clean, simple pensione in the Borgo, but no bargain.

★ **Alimandi,** Via Tunisi 8, 00192, © 679 9343. Next to the Vatican Museums entrance, in atmosphere a cut above its class, though the most winning feature is a large roof garden. Popular with young backpackers.

cheap

★ **Forti's Guest House,** Via Cosseria 2, 00192, © 321 2256. A friendly, popular, and tranquil place to sleep in Prati, well-run by its British owner. Not far from the Metropolitana Lepanto Station.

★ **La Rovere,** Vicolo Sant'Onofrio 5, 00165, © 654 0739. A bit hard to find: cross Ponte Aosta from Via Giulia and go 50 yards to the left to the petrol station and walk up the alley to a nearly traffic-free lane. Very quiet and well run; breakfast available and good hot showers (no private baths).

Near Termini and S. Maria Maggiore

In the 1890s, when this was the newest and choicest district in Rome, the streets around the station spawned hundreds of hotels, some quite elegant. Today the majority of the city's accommodation is still here. Unfortunately, it has gone the way of all such 19th-century toadstool neighbourhoods: overbuilt, dingy, noisy, down at heel and full of petty crooks, not at all the place to savour the real Rome. It's also inconvenient for most of the sights. But there's a wide choice of really cheap hotels, ranging from the respectable, family-run 6 or 7 rooms upstairs, often quite cosy and friendly, to bizarre dives with exposed plumbing run by Sudanese and Sri Lankans for the benefit of visiting countrymen.

At a pinch, as a last resort, this area will do. But it isn't conducive to an enjoyable vacation. If you're looking for the tolerable and cheap, a general rule is to keep to the side streets, like Via Principe Amedeo; the east side of Termini is nicer, though there are fewer choices.

★★★★★ **Le Grand Hotel,** Via Vittorio Orlando 3, 00185, ✆ 4709, fax 474 7307. A sumptuous old hotel in a dreary location just off Piazza della Repubblica. Magnificent decor in the public rooms though they should jettison the lurid green tiles which grace some of the bathrooms.

luxury

★★★★ **Massimo D'Azeglio,** Via Cavour 18, 00184, ✆ 488 0646, fax 482 7341. A grand hotel vintage 1875 that has done its best to ignore the tempora and mores of its surroundings. Air conditioning, TV, and telephones are some of the few concessions to modernity.

moderate

★★★ **Britannia,** Via Napoli 64, 00184, ✆ 488 3153, fax 488 2343. Not too inconvenient, small and up-to-date, with TV, frigo bar, optional air conditioning.

★★★ **Villa delle Rose,** Via Vicenza 5, 00185, ✆ 445 1788, fax 445 1639. Surely the most restful place to stay near Termini, in a former villa, offering 29 well-kept rooms, and a fine little garden.

★★★ **Canada**, Via Vicenza 58, 00185, ✆ 445 7770 fax 445 0749. A pleasant hotel often used by British tour operators with comfortable, thoughtfully designed rooms (radio speakers in the bathrooms!).

inexpensive

★★ **Rimini,** Via Marghera 17, 00185, ✆ 491 2371. Only a hop from the station, but the clean, comfortable rooms are high enough above the street level to miss most of the noise.

★ **Elide,** Via Firenze 50, 00184, ✆ 488 3977, small, friendly, family-run place in fairly quiet street off Piazza della Repubblica, a few frescoes from the old days.

cheap

★ **Tony,** Via Principe Amedeo 79-d, 00185, ✆ 736 994. One of the nicer of the budget places around Termini.

★ **Gexim,** Via Palestro 34, 00185, ✆ 446 0211. A prettily decorated, well-run pensione in a dire-looking palazzo scrawled with graffiti, where you're welcomed by a poster of Albert Einstein.

★ **Restivo,** Via Palestro 55, 00185, ✆ 446 2172. Immaculate pensione run by a sweet old lady, whose hall is cluttered with gifts from affectionate ex clients. If it's full there are other pensione in the same palazzo: **Mari** (✆ 446 2137) and **Cervia** (491 057).

The 'American Ghetto', the vortex of Tourist Rome, remains a choice area for hotels, though lacking the glamour of the '50s. Nowadays the marble-frosted façades of the 1900s conceal packs of well-heeled package tourists and businessmen on expense accounts.

extra luxury

***** **Bernini Bristol,** Piazza Barberini 23, 00187, © 488 3051, fax 482 4266. A luxurious hotel in an ugly brick building at the bottom of Via Veneto; may win first prize in the most tons of marble category. Ask for a room on the upper floor for the fine views over the city, or lounge around in the roof garden.

***** **Excelsior,** Via Veneto 125, 00187, © 4708, fax 482 6205. The hotel with Via Veneto's landmark tower opened its doors in 1911, setting a standard in hotel architecture that Rome has yet to achieve again. Recently bought by CIGA and totally renovated, the reception areas have thicker carpets, bigger chandeliers, and more gilded plaster than any other in Italy. There are saunas, boutiques, a famous bar, and everything else, with as much personal attention as you could desire.

**** **Flora**, Via Veneto 191, 00187, © 489 929, fax 482 0359. Just a step from Villa Borghese, this 1900s confection with its slightly faded elegance and magnificent rooms is a favourite of romantics in Rome.

luxury

***** **Ambasciatori Palace,** Via Veneto 70, 00187, © 47 493, fax 474 3601. A lovely palace from the Roaring '20s, complete with sporty frescoes of Italian Gatsbys. All the luxuries you could ask for.

expensive

*** **La Residenza,** Via Emilia 22, 00187, © 488 0789, fax 485 721. A pleasant base, just off Via Veneto, with beautifully appointed rooms in an old town house and some luxuries more common in the most expensive hotels, including air conditioning.

moderate

*** **Alexandra,** Via Veneto 18, 00187, © 488 1943, fax 487 1804. A fine, old-fashioned moderate-sized hotel; air conditioning optional.

Trastevere

* **Carmel,** Via Goffredo Mameli 11, 00153, © 580 9921. One of the few places to sleep in Trastevere—only 6 rooms in a quiet street.

★ **Esty**, Viale Trastevere 108, 00153, ✆ 588 1201. Near the river. Modern and comfortable rooms; L45,000 (without bath).

Coppodé

cheap

★ **La Panoramica**, Via Arno 33, 00198, ✆ 855 3859, a block east of Viale Regina Margherita. An outlandish location, perhaps, but a fine Art Nouveau building in the middle of the charming Coppodé Quarter. Clean and quiet.

Alternative Accommodation: Students, Pilgrims, Campers

You can save money in Rome but at a cost—nearly every hostel or religious institution locks its doors before midnight. Some are so hard to get to that a fleabag by Termini Station looks good in comparison. And do book early, especially if you come in spring and summer.

Students

For the first two, reserve through the Associazione Italiana Alberghi per la Gioventù (AIG), Via Cavour 44, 00194, ✆ 487 1152.

Ostello del Foro Italico, Rome's youth hostel (IYHF cards required), is inconveniently out in one of Mussolini's dreamlands at Viale delle Olimpiadi 61, ✆ 323 6279. From Termini take bus 492 to Piazza del Risorgimento, and then bus 32 to Foro Italico. Low-grade hospital atmosphere, and stays of no more than three consecutive nights, plastic breakfast, and an early curfew for L18,000 a night.

Residenza Universitaria—Casa dello Studente. In the summer students can stay in Rome's University dormitories, which are a bit more civilized than the youth hostel.

Sandy, Via Cavour 136, 00184, ✆ 483 121 and **Ottaviano**, Via Ottaviano 6, 00192, ✆ 383 956.Two laid-back pensione run by the same family offering some of the cheapest dorm beds in the centre. L20,000.

Salvation Army, Via degli Apuli 39/41, ✆ 446 5236. North of Termini's tracks, off Viale dello Scalo S. Lorenzo. L27,000 for a single.

YWCA (women only), Via C. Balbo 4, ✆ 488 0460 (within walking distance of Termini, off Via Torino, near S. Maria Maggiore). Pleasant staff and a quiet location with a street market outside. L23,000 per person for bed and breakfast in a triple or quad, L29,000 in a double, L35,000 in a single. Book at least 2 weeks in advance.

Religious Institutions

Early to bed, early to rise—and you may have to supply your own soap and towel. Many institutes besides those listed below have places only in the summer, when their students are gone. Ask your local priest or a friend in Orders if they know of any hospitality in Rome (and the English College, near Campo de' Fiori, has a pool).

Protezione della Giovane, Via Urbana 158, ✆ 461 489. Religious foundation set up to protect young women—hence the 9.30pm curfew (extended to a daring 10 pm in summer). For women under 25 only.

Congregazione Suore dello Spirito Santo, Via Pineta Sacchetti 227, 00168 (on the far side on Monte Mario, bus 994), ✆ 305 3101. A relaxing place, but a bit distant. From L25,000 per person. No meals.

Istituto Madri Pie, Via A. De Gasperi 4, 00165 (just south of St Peter's) ✆ 631 967. No, the Pious Mothers do not supply pies, but beds, and a little garden to sit in. Meals available. From L35,000 per person.

Istituto S. Tommaso di Villanova, Viale Romania 7, 00197 (by Villa Ada, bus 4) ✆ 870 274. Rated as a one star hotel—L32,000 single, L42,000 double. Meals available.

Pensionato Concezioniste di Lourdes, Via Sistina 113, ✆ 474 5324. Twenty four single and double rooms for women within a stone's throw of the Spanish Steps. Not particularly cheap though, at L45,000 a night, and there's a 10.30pm curfew.

Suore Pie Operaie, Via di Torre Argentina 76, 00186, ✆ 686 1254. Beds for women for L16,000 per night in five double and triple rooms, a couple of minutes walk from the Pantheon. 10.30pm curfew.

Asunzione, Viale Romania 32, 00197, ✆ 844 4196. Good food and a gorgeous garden—though it's due to start operating on a commercial basis, so prices could be quite high.

Campsites

Capitol, open all year, at Via di Castelfusano 45, in Ostia Antica, ✆ 565 0621. Near the ruins and the Ostia Lido-Rome station. Swimming pool and tennis courts. L8500 per person, L7500 per tent.

Flaminio, open all year, Via Flaminia Nuova km 8.2, ✆ 333 2635. The closest and perhaps the best—buses 202, 203, 204, 205 link it to Piazzale Flaminio (Metro A). L9000 per person, L7800 per tent.

Nomentano (open Mar–Oct), Via della Cesarina 11, © 610 0296. At the corner of Via Nomentana (bus 36 from Termini to Piazza Sempione, then bus 337). L7500 per person, L6000 per tent.

Roma Camping, open all year, Via Aurelia km 8, © 662 3018. (Bus 46 from Piazza Venezia to Piazza dei Giureconsulti, then bus 246). L11,400 per person, L5200 per tent.

Residential Hotels

There are at least a score of these self-catering flatlets but nearly all are out in the suburbs or EUR, and who wants to commute in traffic-ridden Rome? The following are nearest the centre:

Aldovrandi, Via Aldovrandi 15, 00197, © 322 1430. One of the more comfortable, conveniently located residences, just north of Villa Borghese. Air conditioning, TV, telephone, parking, and a swimming pool. 1/2/3 room flats; minimum stay a fortnight. L3–5,000,000 per fortnight and L5–8,500,000 per month.

Aurelia Antica, Via Aurelia Antica 425, 00165 (near Villa Doria Pamphili), © 637 9021. A bit out of the way but quiet and good value: 1/2/3 room flats, maid service, air conditioning, minimum stay one week, L850,000–1,200,000 per week.

In Trastevere, Vicolo Moroni 36, 00153 (north of S. Maria in Trastevere) © 582 1768. TV and telephone, heating but no air conditioning. Minimum one week: 2 beds L770,000, 3 beds L910,000.

Palazzo al Velabro, Via del Velabro 16, 00186; © 679 285; 1/2/3 room furnished flats centrally located near the Capitoline Hill lets for one week or more, with daily maid service, air conditioning, colour TV, garage. Minimum stay one week—L1,220,000–2,213,000.

Ripa, Via Orti di Trastevere 1, 00153, © 58 611, has a garage, handicapped access, bar, TV, telephone in 1/2 room flats with 2/3 beds. Minimum one week, L420,000–1,700,000.

Di Ripetta, Via di Ripetta 231, 00186, © 672 141. Very conveniently located on the Tiber, near the Spanish Steps, with a garage, air conditioning, and TV. 1/2/3 rooms; minimum one week, L1,650,000–2,550,000.

Pantheon di sera

Finding Out What's On 368
Classical Music, Theatre, Opera & Ballet 369

Entertainment and Nightlife

Film 370
Cafés and Bars 370
Ex-pat Pubs 371
Clubs and Discos 372
Live Music 373
Towards Dawn 374
Sex 374

Although Rome's arts and club scenes are hardly among the most dynamic in Europe, it is nevertheless a great city to be in at night. For a start, it's beautiful. Façades and fountains are softly illuminated, cobbles gleam, and through the open shutters of grand palazzi there are glimpses of sumptuously frescoed and stuccoed ceilings. Perhaps the loveliness of their city has made most Romans complacent: if they go out at all at night, they're usually content to simply wander the *centro storico*, pausing perhaps to buy an ice cream or to sit on a café terrace sipping a tisane (Romans are modest boozers).

Which is not to say the city is dull at night. You just have to know where to go to find the action. There are wine bars where you can hob-nob with the yuppies and intellectuals; smart bars which act as a backdrop for the preening and posturing of the designer set; trendy bars where the city's young hedonists congregate before moving on to a club; and, liveliest of all, the hangouts of Rome's vaguely alternative crowd, an eclectic bunch of young ex-pats, bikers, ageing hippies and cultural gurus: the only people in Rome to take alcohol seriously.

Compared with London, Paris and New York, the city's cultural offerings are pretty limited and provincial. Neither its orchestras nor opera company are of international standard, it rarely attracts major international artists, and there's little sign of innovation in either theatre or ballet. The same goes for rock and pop: home-grown fare is pretty dire and visits by major US and UK bands are rare. There is, however, plenty of jazz, and enough Latin-American music for you to salsa every night.

Finding Out What's On

The best source of What's On is *Trova Roma*, a weekly listings supplement which comes free with *La Repubblica* on Thursdays, though obviously it's in Italian. If your Italian is hopeless, the tourist board produces a couple of free multilingual monthly listings magazines—*Un Ospite a Roma* and *Carnet di Roma*—but these are far from comprehensive, concentrating largely on theatre, opera and classical music.

Trova Roma will let you know what's going on each night in the city's clubs and discos, but it's also worth calling in at bars like *La Vetrina* and *Il Batello Ubriaco* where you can usually pick up fliers which give discounted entrance into certain establishments, or, if you're lucky, meet folk who'll get you in free.

Classical Music, Theatre, Opera and Ballet

Since the demise of Rome's communist council *Estate Romana* has lost impetus, though thanks to a determined group of former councillors and culture lovers, there are usually at least some summer events worth catching. Ironically, Rome's other major summer draw was initiated by Mussolini – opera, staged in the Baths of Caracalla. There are also frequent concert performances in picturesque locations, some of them in palazzi which are otherwise closed to the public.

Rome is not a good ballet city, though it's worth keeping an eye out for performances by visiting companies, and though there are scores of theatres for Italian speakers, there's little on offer if you only speak English, except for productions by ex-pat amateurs and performances at the **American Theater Co of Rome,** Via Balilla 13, ✆ 732 822.

There are no language barriers when it comes to music, and in Rome there's usually plenty. The **Teatro dell'Opera** is ranked among Italy's top five, and performs from Nov–May in the theatre in Piazza B. Gigli, off Via del Viminale, ✆ 481 601, ticket office ✆ 488 1755; tickets on sale two days before each performance. In July and August the Opera takes on Cecil B. De Millesque proportions in the Baths of Caracalla, where *Aïda,* complete with real horses and chariots, is a perennial favourite. Tickets are reasonable (from L25,000) and on sale at the Teatro dell'Opera box office.

For symphonic music, there's Rome's celebrated **Accademia Nazionale di Santa Cecilia,** with regular orchestral performances in the auditorium in Via della Conciliazione 4, ✆ 6880 1044; smaller recitals are usually performed at the Accademia's headquarters in Via dei Greci; box office at Via Vittoria 6, ✆ 678 0742 near the Spanish Steps. The **Accademia Filarmonica** performs in the Teatro Olimpico, Piazza Gentile da Fabriano, ✆ 323 4890; the **Rai Orchestra** presents a series of Saturday evening concerts in the Auditorio del Foro Italico, Piazza Lauro de Bosis, ✆ 3686 6625; the **Concerti Italcable** is a series of concerts held between November and April at the Teatro Sistina, Via Sistina 129. For information phone Italcable, ✆ 4770 4664. Medieval, Baroque, chamber and choral music are frequently to be heard at the **Oratorio del Gonfalone,** Via del Gonfalone 32, ✆ 687 5952. There are free classical music concerts in winter sponsored by ARCUM (✆ 721 6558) in the Sala Baldini in Piazza Campitella, ✆ 759 6361. Other frequent concert venues are Castel Sant'Angelo, the Palazzo della Cancelleria, St Paul's within the Walls, and the Aula Magna at the Università La Sapienza. Don't miss an opportunity to hear the Sistine Chapel Choir, one of Italy's finest.

Film

Your chances of taking in a good film are rather slim. All films in Italy are dubbed, and the only English-language cinema is **Pasquino,** Vicolo del Piede near Piazza S. Maria in Trastevere (© 580 3622) which presents a different English-language film, usually a recent second-run, every few days. Cinema clubs are easy to join for a small fee at the door and usually show in the original language. Three to try are **Azzuro Scipioni,** Via degli Scipioni 82, © 370 1094; **Grauco Film Ricerca,** Via Perugia 34, © 782 2311 and **Il Labirinto,** Via P. Magno, © 321 6283. In the dog days of summer the colossal 'bread and circus' marathon outdoor film showings can be a lot of fun, even if in Italian.

Cafés and Bars

Barflies can drink until 1am on some of the loveliest piazzas in Rome, flit to a trendy little bar or late-night drinking den, and see the dawn in at one of Piazza Venezia's raffish all-nighters, the resort of carabinieri, hippies, buskers, whores and Eastern European pimps.

Bevitoria, Piazza Navona 72. *Open 7 pm–1 am. Closed Sun.* The most conducive, and least touristy of Piazza Navona's watering holes, the Bevitoria is a tiny beamed wine bar with tables inside and out, and cellars in the substructures of Domitian's stadium (the owner will show you them when trade is slack). A good range of wine as well as doses of hot mulled wine in cold weather, and a sophisticated range of miniature sandwiches.

Vineria, Campo de' Fiori 15. *Summer 9.30 am–2 pm & always 6pm–around midnight. Closed Sun.* A peaceful place for a sandwich and glass of wine on summer lunchtimes, the Vineria is anything but quiet in the evenings, when it, the pavement outside, and every Vespa seat and car bonnet within a radius of three metres are packed with an animated crowd of bikers, ageing hippies, intellectuals and the more alternative ex-pats. A good place to meet people.

Il Piccolo, Via del Governo Vecchio 74/5. *Evenings only. Closed Sun.* A little wine bar close to Piazza Navona, which attracts an arty-intellectual crowd. Get there early if you want a table — inside or out.

Goldfinch, Piazza Pollarola 31. *Open from around 10pm. Closed Sun.* Demi-mondeish bar to which the more hardened Vineria drinkers stagger after midnight to join a motley crowd of local artisans, gays, ageing transvestites and other Campo de' Fiori oddballs.

La Vetrina, Via della Vetrina 20. *Open 10.30 pm–2 am* (though there are sometimes early evening events with cut-price drinks). *Closed Wed.* Revamps itself several times a year — so look out for invites to the inaugurations. Popular with the clubbing set, so a good place to pick up fliers offering discounted entrance to clubs, and to check out the latest extremes in dance floor fashion.

Il Batello Ubriaco, Via dei Leutari 34. *Open 10.30 pm–2 am. Closed Tue.* Disco bar near Piazza Navona, where you can pick up fliers for clubs and get into the bopping mood on a dance floor designed—with its seaweed and starfish painted walls and ultra-violet lighting—to look like it's underwater. Different music every night—ranging from funk and reggae to Industrial, Indie and Grunge.

Il Cantiniere di San Dorotea, Via di S Dorotea 9. *Open 5pm– 2am. Closed Tue.* Sophisticated wine bar in Trastevere, with a good selection of wines from around the world (which is unusual in patriotic Italy) along with bistro-type food, and an owner who can tell you everything you ever wanted to know about oenology but were afraid to ask.

Il Simposio di Piero Costantini, Piazza Cavour 16. *Open 11 am–3 pm & 7 pm–midnight. Closed all day Sunday and Monday morning.* You would never believe, stepping into this elegant shrine to wine, gracefully arboured with wrought-iron vines, that not long ago it was a pharmacy. A delightful place to spend a smart civilized evening.

Trasté, Via della Lungaretta 76. *Open 5.30pm–midnight. Closed Mon.* A designer-tea room in Trastevere for those who would rather end their evenings sober—although they do serve alcohol, this is really NOT a place in which getting legless is acceptable. Trendy young crowd engaged in earnest conversations, board games and reading magazines.

Bar della Pace, Via della Pace 5. *Open 10.30 am–approx 3 am. Closed Mon.* The *fin-de-siècle* interior, ivy-screened façade and terrace tables placed for views of Santa Maria della Pace, could make this the most delightful bar in Rome. Sadly, anyone lacking a famous face or designer wardrobe can expect frosty service. Polish your repertory of withering looks and go for a mid-afternoon cappuccino or late night drink, though the prices may give you a sleepless night.

Ciampini al Café du Jardin, Viale Trinità dei Monti. *Open 8.30 am–1 am. Closed Tue.* A summer-only bar canopied with trellises outside the Villa Medici. Lovely views if you peep through the creepers, and very romantic.

Castellino, Piazza Venezia. *Open 24 hours daily.* Raffish bar with some seriously dodgy denizens, but the only place in the centre where you can drink (and buy cigarettes) all night.

Ex-pat Pubs

Since the 18th century, when the Grand Tourists hung out in the (now sadly dire) Caffé Greco, Rome's ex-patriates have had their own watering holes, where they can drink anglo-saxon style without shocking the locals. All are lively, most attract a fairly young crowd, and in all of them you should have no problem meeting people.

The Victoria, Via di Gesù e Maria 18. The most anglo-saxon of Rome's ex-pat pubs, as you'll realize when you step in and have to duck immediately to avoid a flying dart (the board's right by the door).

Fiddler's Elbow, Via dell'Olmata 43. Irish pub which is nevertheless popular with the Romans. Young and lively, though the presence of modestly-drinking Italians makes it a little more subdued than Druid's Den.

Druid's Den, Via San Martino ai Monti 28. Animated—occasionally rowdy—Irish pub, popular with the pint-swillers from the FAO. Atmosphere resembles that of a students' union bar.

Clubs and Discos

Rome's discos and clubs hardly rank among the most exciting in Europe, ranging from the exclusive, long-established haunts of the glitterati (where you're unlikely to get in unless you sparkle with money and fame too), through trendy discos where fashion victims bop to not-quite-the-latest House beats, to scruffy alternative venues where you don't need to worry if your clothes are crumpled or your hair unwashed. Rome's clubs are expensive — you can pay L30,000 to L50,000 even in places like Uonna — with entrance prices reflecting the fact that Romans drink modestly: the owners can't count on profitable bar sales, even when the prices are outrageously inflated (as they often are). The main clubbing nights are Thursday, Friday and Saturday, and during the rest of the week entrance is usually cheaper. You'll also find lots of theme nights and special events (like fashion shows) laid on in an effort to attract the crowds.

Uonna, Via Cassia 871, ✆ 3031 1070. Miles out of the centre, so impossible to reach unless you have wheels. Rock, reggae, rap, and Underground (usually far closer to the mainstream surface than anything meriting the same title outside Italy) and a young crowd.

Black Out, Via Saturnia 18, ✆ 756 6791. A must on Friday nights for anyone into Indie, Grunge, New Wave and Punk. It's near Porta Latina, so is fairly easy to get to.

L'Argonauta, Lungotevere degli Artigiani s/n, ✆ 556 5440 Laid back club on a boat moored just beyond the Ponte Testaccio (Trastevere side) with a disco inside and bar on deck, attracting a vaguely alternative, mixed-age crowd and playing a fairly wide range of mainstream music. Good fun, though you'll have to queue to get in.

Piper 90, Via Tagliamento 9, ✆ 855 5398. The Piper has survived two decades by revamping itself every season and laying on theme nights, fashion shows and gigs almost every night. A little passé now, with an enthusiastic pick-up scene.

Alien, Via Velletri 13, ✆ 841 2212. Very hip (for Rome). House music, catwalk style dress, and raised platforms for the show-offs to dance on.

Frankie Go, Via Schiapperelli 29, ✆ 322 1252. A temple to House for Parioli's rich young narcissists.

Soul II Soul, Via dei Fienaroli 30B, ✆ 581 3249. A small club in Trastevere playing black music: from soul to Zairois and dance to reggae.

Jackie O'. Via Boncampagni 11, ✆ 488 5457 A Via Veneto classic which peaked during the *dolce vita* years, continued to attract the flash set during the Seventies and Eighties and has just re-furbished and re-opened, to much press hype. Worth going to if you're young, beautiful and intend to be a star, or if you're sufficiently rich and famous to attract the wannabes. If you're neither of these you probably won't get in anyway.

Live Music

There are any number of live music venues, most of them given over to jazz and Latin American music, virtually all of them unpretentious places where the emphasis is on having a good time rather than cutting a *bella figura*. Most are closed on Sundays, and the more interesting concerts tend to be towards the weekend—check with *Trova Roma* before setting out.

Because of Italian licensing laws virtually all the live music venues are private clubs, which means you have to become a member in order to attend even a single concert. Membership is usually in the order of L15-20,000 and lasts for a year, and though members still have to pay for the more prestigious concerts, there will usually be some free events as well. Very occasionally a club may be persuaded to offer you a discount if you tell them you're only passing through the city. *Enjoy Rome*, Via Varese 39, are attempting to do deals with clubs on behalf of short-term visitors: it's worth contacting them to see if they've succeeded.

The chances of your visit coinciding with a major rock or pop concert are slimmer — many international groups bypass Rome in favour of the trendier northern cities. When they do come, the major venues are **PalEUR** (the Palazzo dello Sport in EUR); **Stadio Flaminio** (at Foro Italico) and Tendastrisce on Via Cristoforo Colombo. Ticket prices are on a par with those in Britain, audiences tend to be rather more subdued. If lesser known, alternative bands come to Rome, they usually play either at the **Circolo degli Artisti,** a former milk-distribution centre on Via Lamarmora near Termini, or **Forte Prenestino** a squatted anarchist centre out on Via Delpino.

Big Mama, Vicolo San Francesco a Ripa 18, ✆ 581 2551. Hot crowded jazz/blues venue in Trastevere. A few 'names', more often local bands playing covers.

Saint Louis Music City, Via del Cardello 13a, ✆ 474 5076. Large complex decked out with US and UK kitsch, with a bar and fast food restaurant. Live jazz/swing nightly (except Sun) and discos after gigs on Fri and Sat.

Caffé Latino, Via del Monte Testaccio 96, ✆ 574 4020. Jazz, soul and salsa pumped out in a small, sweaty room. Go early on Saturdays if you want to get in.

Classico, Vicolo Libetta 7, ℂ 574 4955. Relatively spacious venue showcasing a wide range of local bands.

Alpheus, Via del Commercio 36, ℂ 574 7826. Purpose-built complex, usually with three events happening simultanously in its three halls. Some good jazz concerts.

Caffé Caruso, Via di Monte Testaccio 36, no tel. Latin-American music in one of the caves hollowed into the side of Monte Testaccio.

Club Picasso, Via di Monte Testaccio 63, ℂ 574 2975. Another Testaccio cellar, with live Indie, Funk, Blues, rock and occasionally jazz bands every night.

Music Inn, Largo dei Fiorentini 3, ℂ 654 4934. Serious jazz club, with gigs from Thursday to Sunday.

Alexanderplatz, Via Ostia 9, ℂ 359 9398. Well-established jazz and blues club.

Folkstudio, Via Frangipani 42, ℂ 487 1063. Acoustic, folk, blues, and occasionally avant garde classical music.

Clarabella, Piazza San Cosimato 39. Cute bar in Trastevere where you can play board games and drink cocktails before the Brazilian band begins.

Yes Brazil, Via San Francesco a Ripa 103, ℂ 581 6267. Very popular bar (which could have something to do with the fact that entrance is free) with live Brazilian music from 10 pm.

Towards Dawn

One favourite late night activity is to make the hot *cornetti* circuit, reminiscent of the sweet-tooth delirium that supports 24-hour doughnut shops in American suburbs. Join in the fun at Bar Dante, Via del Corso 259, Quelli della Notte, Via Leone IV 48, or the Forno, a bakery at Vicolo delle Cinque 40; brush sleeves with Rome's underworld at Castellini on Piazza Venezia; or join the transvestites eating freshly-baked pizza at Pizzalandia, Piazza Risorgimento 46A.

Sex

Sex is much more subdued than in most capital cities, but just as tawdry. You can pick up a Brazilian transvestite (very much in fashion, like all things Brazilian) in the shadows of the pyramid at Piazzale Ostiense, or less exotic hookers, keeping warm at roadside braziers, on the Via Appia, beyond the Ring Road. Via Veneto is still a haunt for elegant girls and boys for tourists and businessmen; as a general rule, the further out of the centre you go, the lower the price. Traffic can be dangerous at night—too many Romans get their kicks by smoking, snorting or shooting up and driving around in their cars.

Shopping Hours   376
Sizes   377
Weights and Measures   378
Antiques   378
Books   379
Children   380
Department Stores   380
Food   381
For the Home   382

Shopping

Music   383
Paper, Crafts, Stationery   383
Second-hand and Alternative Clothes   383
Shoes, Gloves & Leather Accessories   383
Unusual and Off Beat   384
Wines/Spirits/Oils   384

'City where all is sold!' sneered Jugurtha, the North African rebel, who found the Romans in the imperial age ready to sell the catapult to flatten themselves. Modern Rome will still sell you just about anything if you pay enough for it, though it is not Italy's most thrilling shopping city. There are few bargains—most Romans buy their clothes and household goods at the markets or department stores, and these are more like Marks and Spencers than Harrods or Liberty's. Nor is it easy to find portable, locally made things: a few high-fashion designers (Milan is the capital of off-the-rack designer fashions, but Rome maintains its *haute couture*, where garments are individually tailored for the one per cent of the population that can afford it), Castelli Romani wine, Piranesi prints, and the odd bit of Baroque bric-à-brac.

Via Condotti, leading straight into the Spanish Steps, is Rome's most famous shopping street, though the whole area between Piazza di Spagna and the Corso (once known as the 'English Ghetto' for its population of fleeceable milords) is full of Rome's fanciest boutiques and shops. Nearly all of Italy's big name designers have outlets here, many so plush that their customers feel obliged to put on the dog just to go in and buy more clothes. Some of the prices suggest that the fleecing has merely gone up-scale. Other areas to try: **Via Cola di Rienzo** for less expensive clothes; **Piazza Navona,** the **Pantheon** and **Campo de' Fiori** for the trendy and off-beat, including a lot of overpriced used clothes that seem to fascinate the French; for monkish, priestly, and nunnish fashions, monstrances or reliquaries (relics are Rome's most traditional souvenir, after all) try **Via dei Cestari**, north of Corso Vittorio Emanuele; for souvenir kitsch, both Termini Station and the streets around the Vatican both offer John XXIII barometers, kooky scarves, and Colosseum ashtrays.

Shopping Hours

Shopping hours are usually from 9 am (or 10 am for high fashion) to 1 or 1.30 pm, and then from 4–7 pm (winter) or 5–8 pm (summer), though some shops stay open all day. Most shops, except for grocer's, are closed Monday morning as well; all close on Sunday, and many close on Saturday afternoons. Food shops usually close on Thursday afternoons. Like many Italians, Romans prefer to do their shopping in the late afternoon and early evening, so you'll find the shops much less crowded in the morning.

Rome's most famous market, at **Porta Portese**—happens every Sunday morning from the crack of dawn until lunch time. The usual contessa's attic junk (chandeliers, Mussolini memorabilia, and gilded stuccoes) has of late been swamped with car parts, plastic buckets, pirated cassettes, and smuggled lighters but with luck and persistance you can still find classic retro clothes and even the occasional designer item. After 10 am it gets very crowded, so watch out for the usual pickpockets. Less intense is the morning new and used clothes market of **Via Sannio**, just outside the gate from Piazza S. Giovanni in Laterano (daily except Sunday) another good hunting-ground for designer cast-offs. There's a print market in **Piazza Fontanella Borghese** (daily except Sunday), and on Tuesday mornings from 10.30–1 you can visit the **Mercato de' fiori**, Rome's wholesale plant and flower market in Via Trionfale. The most colourful food market happens daily except Sunday in **Campo de' Fiori** until lunchtime. There are also good food markets on Piazza Vittorio Emanuele II, Piazza Testaccio and Piazza S.Cosimato.

Italian clothes are lovely, but if you have a large-boned Anglo build, you may find it hard to find a good fit, especially in trousers or skirts; shoes are often narrower than the sizes at home.

Sizes

Women's Shirts/Dresses					Sweaters				Women's Shoes					
UK	10	12	14	16	18	10	12	14	16	3	4	5	6	7	8
US	8	10	12	14	16	8	10	12	14	4	5	6	7	8	9
It	40	42	44	46	48	46	48	50	52	36	37	38	39	40	41

Men's Shirts

UK/US	14	14½	15	15½	16	16½	17	17½
Italy	36	37	38	39	40	41	42	43

Men's Suits

UK/US	36	38	40	42	44	46
Italy	46	48	50	52	54	56

Men's Shoes

UK	2	3	4	5	6	7	8	9	10	11	12
US	5	6	7	7½	8	9	10	10½	11	12	13
It	34	36	37	38	39	40	41	42	43	44	45

Weights and Measures

1 kilogramme (1000g) — 2.2lb

1 etto (100g)— ¼ lb (approx)

1 litre—1.76 pints

1 metre—39.37 inches

1 kilometre—0.621 miles

1 lb—0.45kg

1 pint—0.568 litres

1 quart—1.136 litres

1 Imperial gallon—4.546 litres

1 US gallon—3.785 litres

1 foot—0.3048 metres

1 mile—0.609 kilometres

Antiques

Look in the shops in and along **Via del Babuino** for the most luxurious furniture and paintings, *objets d'art* and Baroque Madonnas and crucifixions in search of a new home. On nearby Via Margutta, Via dei Banchi Nuovi, and Via delle Carrozze, look for 20th-century 'antiques' and bric-à-brac. **Via dei Coronari** is more fun, and a notch below Via del Babuino in prices and quality, perhaps, but the shopkeepers here try to make up for it by rolling out the red carpet, lighting torches and lining the street with kumquat bushes for a twice-yearly antiques festival in mid-May and mid-October. Some of the places to look out for: **Moretti,** at no. 95, with beautiful antique scientific and astronomical instruments; **Bottegantica,** Via di San Simone 70 (a dead-end alley just off Coronari) with antique majolica, and **Marmi Line**, at Via dei Coronari 113, with inlaid marble tables and 'Roman' busts. Most of the antique shops, however, tend to the Baroque sensibility (and most of that is 18th and 19th century stuff). For some exceptions: **Fabrizio Lombardi,** Via dei Coronari 31, for kitschy collectables; **L'Art Nouveau** at no. 221, offering just what its name implies, and more of the same at no. 8; the proprietors of both these places have a very good eye for the most artistic creations of the Belle Epoque and beyond.

Via Margutta is Rome's traditional art lane, and in spring and autumn sponsors outdoor exhibits of some of the most blatantly commercial art you're likely to encounter outside Woolworths. Prints, art books, and old postcards are sold daily except Sunday at markets in Piazza Borghese and Largo dei Lombardi, both on the west side of the Corso. It is a lament of young artists in Rome that Romans don't buy art like the foreigners. If you do find something you like too large to carry home, contact Propileo, Via Cavalese 31, © 305 2530, a specialist in transporting works of art.

Banchi Nuovi, Via dei Banchi Nuovi 37, eclectic, with often interesting shows.

Casali, Piazza Rotonda 81A, for old prints (generally inexpensive) of Rome's favourite subject: Rome.

Codognotto, Via Pianellari 15, fun, not too serious wood sculptures, some fascinating (but expensive).

Ferranti, Via Tor' Millina 26, for a long time this was Rome's best abstract art gallery; standards have dropped of late, but it's still worth a look.

L'Image Poster Art Gallery, Via di Ripetta 254 and Via della Scrofa 67, with lots of choice for lots of lire.

Sala 1, Piazza di Porta S. Giovanni 10, a gallery of fairly highbrow, cultural emphasis.

Sprovieri, Piazza del Popolo 3 (tucked into an alley next to *Rosati*) for famous artists.

Co Design, Via dei Coronari 52, almost inevitably interesting design exhibitions.

Books

Anglo-American Book Co, Via della Vite 57, run by a dour bibliophile, is small but densely packed with good books in English, priced fairly. The best place in Rome to look for anything unusual.

Economy Book Center, Via Torino 136, American-run, wide selection and lots of secondhand paperbacks.

Libri Herder, Piazza Montecitorio, good and scholarly, mostly German but also English, Italian, and many children's books.

Lion Bookshop, Via del Babuino 181, boasts Rome's largest selection of books in English.

Open Door Bookshop, Via della Lungaretta 25, cosy shop selling new and second hand English books in Trastevere.

Rizzoli, in the Galleria Colonna, Largo Chigi 15, is Italy's largest book shop—a good place to look for art books, maps, etc.

Libreria San Silvestro, Piazza S.Silvestro 27, half price art books, old jazz tapes.

Libreria del Viaggiatore, Via del Pellegrino 78, travel books in Italian and English—including this one.

Corner Bookshop, Via del Moro 48, welcoming English bookshop in the heart of Trastevere.

Louise MacDermott, Via dei Giubbonari 30, ✆ 654 5285. Louise MacDermott is a dealer specializing in books in English about Italy. Phone for an appointment to browse through the book-lined rooms of her apartment.

La Grotta del Libro, Via del Pellegrino 169, discount and remaindered Italian books.

Children

Città del Sole, on Via della Scrofa at Largo Toniolo (also next to the Chiesa Nuova), is a small chain, and nothing less than the most charming and innovative toy shops in all Italy; everything clever and creative from L3000 to L300,000.

Lettini, Piazza Navona, features the largest and most aristocratic stuffed animals and dolls in Rome—prices to match.

Regali, Via del Lavatore 87, near Trevi Fountain; charming wooden toys, including giant Pinocchios. Nearby is **Sweet Sweet Italy**, with old-fashioned loose candy—the most colourful shop in Rome.

Tablò, Via della Croce 84 and Piazza di Spagna 96, sells smart (and quite expensive) clothes for children.

Maskara, Via della Scala 66, bizarre and beautiful masks.

Il Palloncino Rosso, Via dei Pettinari 49, clothes for mini fashion victims.

Department Stores

Except for La Rinascente, these are all comparable to Woolworth's, offering reasonable prices for the kind of reasonable clothes most people wear.

COIN, Piazzale Appio, near the Lateran, with the most up-to-date merchandise, good value for clothes and kitchen gear.

La Rinascente, Piazza Colonna and Piazza Fiume, six rather old-fashioned floors.

Standa, Via del Corso 148, Viale Trastevere 60 and Via Cola di Rienzo 173, very popular and economical. The Trastevere branch has a supermarket.

UPIM, Via del Tritone 172 and Piazza S. Maria Maggiore, among others—Italy's Woolworth's.

Designer Fashions

Armani, Via del Babuino 102, Roman outlet of the celebrated Milanese designer; his Emporio (Via del Babuino 140) features younger, more casual styles (though the quality leaves much to be desired).

Battistoni, Via Condotti 57 and 61, in the second courtyard of the Palazzo Caffarelli, a luxurious boutique, long Rome's most fashionable tailor, offering made-to-order shirts and suits; also cashmere sweaters, blazers, and coats with an English touch.

Fendi, Roman-designed furs, fashions, bags, shoes and accessories occupy much of Via Borgognona: nos. 8, 10, 12, and 39.

Givenchy, Via Borgognona 21, very stylish French fashions at French prices.

Krizia, Piazza di Spagna 77, another Milanese offering trendy, flattering clothes for women.

Missoni, Via Babuino 96, colourful dresses and knits; for men, Missoni Uomo at Piazza di Spagna 78.

Saint Laurent Rive Gauche, Via Bocca di Leone 35, a boutique run by French fashion's biggest money maker.

Sorelle Fontana, Salita di San Sebstianello, just off Piazza di Spagna, have been dressing women in smart fashions *all'italiana* since the 1930s.

Testa, Via Frattina 104, fine, elegant Italian tailoring for younger men.

Troncarelli, Via della Cuccugna 15, near Piazza Navona. A small shop specializing in Borsalino hats for men and women.

Ungaro, Via Bocca di Leone 24, sensual feminine attire from Paris.

Valentino, Via Bocca di Leone 16, utterly insane, but always worth a look. Men's fashions may be had at Via Mario de' Fiori 22.

Versace, Via Bocca di Leone 26, one of Italy's more daring international designers.

Il Discount dell'Alta Moda, Via Gesù e Maria 16a, discounted designer fashion—though you'll still need your credit card.

Galassia, Via Frattina 21, collections by hip designers: Gaultier, Comme des Garçons, Ozbek et al.

Food

Confetteria Moriondo e Garaglio, Via della Pilotta 2 (no sign, but in the arch). Rome's finest, fresh, homemade chocolates.

Dolci e Doni, Via delle Carrozze 85 A/B, for homemade marzipan fruits (a Sicilian speciality) and much more.

La Corte, Via della Gatta 1, for lovely smoked fish.

Le Sette Spighe, Via Crescenzio 89, for a look at Italian health foods.

Tazza d'Oro, Via degli Orfani 84, where you can buy special bags of the city's best coffee, the 'Aroma di Roma'.

Pasticceria Valzani, Via del Moro 37b, the oldest cake shop in Rome.

Antico Caffè del Brasile, Via dei Serpenti 21, where the Pope gets his coffee: ask for the 'miscela del Papa'.

For the Home

Art'e', Piazza Rondanini, Rome's headquarters for the height of high-tech gim-cracks, creative kitsch, and Art Deco folly (clocks, kitchen décor, etc.). A great sense of design and a sense of humour (in Italy, would you really expect to see the Andrews Sisters appearing as kitchen canisters?).

Ceramica de Simona, Via Margutta 47, colourful, fun, modern ceramics.

Cesari, Via del Babuino 16, offers Rome's elegant interior design and furniture fabrics.

Pakistan Emporium, Piazza Vittorio Emanuele, near Via Mamiani. Rugs, clothes, brass, etc.

Studio Punto Tre, Via Giulia 145, housewares, wood-inlay tables, artisan fabrics and ceramics.

Trompe l'oeil, Via dei Coronari 107. Just moved into a palazzo? This is the place to come if you want the walls decorating with trompe l'oeil gardens.

Apollodoro, Piazza Mignanelli 17. A shop designed by Paolo Portoghesi selling and exhibiting objects designed by himself, Giò Ponti, Robert Venturi and Michael Graves.

Cassina, Via del Babuino 100. Re-editions of 20th-century classics by Wright, Le Corbusier, Mackintosh etc.

Jewellery

Bulgari, Via Condotti 11, the king of jewellers in the street's most palatial shop that in a previous incarnation was the trattoria where Severn bought the languishing Keats' daily take-away.

Ceccone, Via del Pellegrino 95, for interesting creations in gold with an archaeological bent.

Gemgioielli, Piazza del Quiriti 10, delicate, refined, original designs.

Manasse, Via di Campo Marzio 44, antique jewellery, icons, silver, etc.

Massoni, Largo Goldoni 48, near Via Condotti, a long established family firm much frequented by film stars.

Ourouboros, Via Sant'Eustachio. Exceptional handmade jewellery, often following unique designs.

Via del Coronari 193. Nameless jewellers selling unusual creations incorporating stained glass, metal reliefs and gems.

Music

Ricordi, Rome's finest selection of records and tapes, at four addresses: Via C. Battisti 120; Piazza dell'Indipendenza 24–26; Via del Corso 506; and Viale Giulio Cesare 88.

Disfunzioni Musicali, Via degli Etruschi 4-14. The hippest record shop in town, selling and exchanging new and second discs, CDs and cassetes. Good selection of US alternative bands.

Makumba Center, Via del Vantaggio 28, African and Afro-Caribbean music.

Paper, Crafts, Stationery

Lunadicarta, Vicolo dell'Atleta 10–11, imaginative designs in paper.

Pineider, Via della Scrofa 7/A and Via Due Macelli 68, for paper and art supplies.

Stilo Fetti, Via degli Orfani 82, devoted to antique and modern fountain pens; will also repair your old favourite.

Vertecchi, Via della Croce 70a, in a palace with two telamones sculpted by Bernini's dad Pietro, is Rome's best fine art, hobby, and crafts shop; the branch at no. 38 specializes in papers.

Second-hand and Alternative Clothes

Moon, Via del Governo Vecchio 89a. Vintage classics—a miniature fashion museum, in fact.

Sempreverde, Via del Governo Vecchio 26. Trendy period clothes—the stock is completely changed every month or so.

Cantieri del Nord, Via del Corso 187. The only place in Rome selling PVC shorts and plastic platforms.

Shoes, Gloves, and Leather Accessories

Barrilà, Via Condotti 29, for high fashion shoes.

Beltrami, Via Condotti 19, glamorous shoes for the Hollywood-minded.

Ferragamo, Via Condotti 66 and 73, has beautiful and expensive Florentine shoes for men and women.

Gucci, Via Condotti 18 (also a shop in Via Borgognona). Shoes, purses, suitcases, ties, etc. that need no introduction.

Salato, Raphael, Piazza di Spagna 456 and Via Veneto 104. Rome's modern Raphael puts his masterpieces on your feet instead of the wall, and gets more money for them, too.

Trussardi, Via Bocca di Leone 27, accessories in leather.

Unusual and Off Beat

Ai Monasteri, at the northern end of Corso del Rinascimento. Monastic products from around Italy—choose among Trappist rosé and Franciscan *amaro* from Umbria, along with holy chocolates and remedies to keep your hair in your head.

Curiosità Magia, Via in Aquiro, off Piazza Monecitorio. Antique magic tricks, crystal balls, silly tricks and a thousand surprises.

Imbalsamatore on Via di Sant'Agostino 5, off Corso Rinascimento. Stuffed birds, mounted butterflies, or insects in amber. There's also a selection of pretty geodes and other wonders of the mineral world. **Magic Art**, Via de' Lucchesi, near Trevi Fountain, a suitably mysterious looking shop, with handmade talismans for every purpose, esoteric prints and a mystic owner.

Apistica Romana, Via Ulpiano 55 (off Piazza Cavour), the complete bee shop, with honeys from all over Italy and bee-keeping gear.

De Ritis, Via de'Cestari 1. The latest ecclesiastical fashions, along with Madonnas, crucifixes, monstrances and chalices.

Wines and Booze

Enoteca Buccone, Via di Ripetta 19, a drinker's heaven; 20-year-old bottles of Scotch under an inch of dust.

Enoteca Constantini, Piazza Cavour 16, a wide selection, good for special gifts.

Enoteca Roffi Isabelli, Via della Croce 76, a lovely shop with wines and glamorous olive oils.

La Grapperia, Via della Lupa 17, with over 400 different kinds of grappa. Tastings too!

La Taste, Via dei Bergamaschi, off Piazza di Pietra, ultra-cute wine, herb liqueurs, cosmetics, and love potions, all from France.

Boating	386
Bowling	387
Football	387
Golf	387
Racing	388
Riding	388

Sports/Activities/Children

Swimming	388
Tennis	389
Children's Rome	389

Bad luck those of you wanting to work off the excess pasta: participating in sports is virtually impossible in Rome without paying a hefty fee to become a member of a club. You can, of course, jog or cycle (see p.10 for where to hire bikes) most pleasantly in one of the parks, and swim gratis on some beaches and at Lake Bracciano. The **Lega per L'Ambiente**, Via Salaria 280, © 884 1552 and **Amici della Terra**, Via del Sudario 35, © 687 5308 organize hikes, treks, bike and cross-country skiing excursions outside Rome.

The city is not exactly brilliant for spectator sports, though there are international horse and tennis championships, and, of course, two good football teams, Lazio and Roma.

The main sports complexes are: **Foro Italico**, Viale dei Gladiatori, © 396 4661, built by Mussolini, reserved for football, swimming competitions and water polo, and host to the prestigious **international tennis championships** in May. **Flaminio**, just across the bridge from Foro Italico, has another Palazzetto dello Sport, at Piazza Apollodoro 10, © 396 2272, for tennis, basketball, skating, gymnastics etc. and the **Stadio Flaminio** on Viale Pilsudski, © 323 6539, is also used for football and big events.

EUR has the **Palazzo dello Sport** at Viale del Umanismo, © 592 5107, for basketball, boxing, indoor tennis, and rock concerts; also an Olympic velodrome, field hockey ground, and a pool. You can also watch competions and championships at two private sports complexes, the **Complesso Sportivo Tre Fontane**, Via delle Tre Fontane 1, © 592 6386, in EUR, with running tracks and a covered gym, and, up beyond Villa Ada, the **Acqua Acetosa**, Via dei Campi Sportivi 48, © 807 9248, with fields for rugby, polo, football, etc.

Boating

There are many places in and around Rome where you can charter a boat to sail down the coast. For a list contact the **Comitato Regionale**, Via G G Belli 27, © 321 2992, fax 321 0371. You can also get information by dropping in at **Mal de Mare**, Vicolo del Cinque 46, © 580 9668, a bar in Trastevere which organizes cruises and sailing courses and charters boats. If you're out at Ciampino, you can charter a boat from **Aquarius**, Via del Casale Santarelli 41, Ciampino, © 7584 7352, for a sail down the coast. Lake Bracciano is the main boating lake near Rome, with sailing dinghies for hire in most of its villages, and at many of the lakeside restaurants.

Rowing down the Tiber is a popular Roman sport, but the rowing clubs are very expensive and, on the whole, have long waiting lists. As the clubs won't accept short-term members, it's not worth approaching them unless you're living in Rome. If you are, contact the **Federazione Italiana Canottaggio** at Viale Tiziano 70, ✆ 7984 352, the **Comitato Regionale** (see above) or the **Circolo Canottieri Tevere Remo**, Lungotevere in Augusta 28, ✆ 361 0300. For **canoeing**, get in touch with **Federazione Italiana Canoa–Kayak**, Via G G Belli 27, ✆ 321 4917.

Bowling

Bowling Brunswick, Lungotevere Acqua Acetosa, ✆ 396 6696. There's a new mini-golf course, too.

Bowling Roma, Viale Regina Margherita 181, ✆ 861 184.

Football

Rome has two football teams, Lazio and Roma. The former recently signed Paul Gascoigne, who has generated more excitement by belching on TV (for which he was fined) than scoring goals. Both teams play at the Stadio Olimpico. Matches happen twice a week (Wednesdays at 8 pm and Sundays at 3 pm) from September to May during the Italian league competition, the Campionato Italiano. Ticket prices range from L15,000 to L150,000.

Golf

Golf in Rome is a rich man's sport. During the week a round can cost from L60–100,000. In addition, most clubs will only allow you to play if you're accompanied by a member. If you prefer to watch, the national championships take place in October and the **Roma Masters** in April. For information contact **Federazione Italiana Golf**, Via Flamina 388, ✆ 323 1825.

Castelgandolfo Country Club, Via di Santo Spirito 13, on the Nettunense, after Castelluccia, ✆ 931 3084. Newest, most exclusive, and most challenging course in Rome, designed by Robert Trent Jones in a volcanic basin, with an 18th-century Chigi villa beautifully converted into a club house. Visiting golfers may play up to 8 rounds a year, green fees L80,000.

Circolo Golf Roma, Via di Acqua Santa, ✆ 783 407. L60,000; weekends L80,000.

Golf Club Olgiata, Largo dell'Olgiata 15, ✆ 378 9141. 18 holes; 12 miles. L50,000, weekends L100,000. Closed Mon. Sheraton Golf, Parco dei Medici, Magliana, ✆ 655 6258. The only club inside the main ring-road. Currently being enlarged to 27 holes. L80,000. Closed Tues.

Racing

The time for horse-lovers to visit Rome is May, when the International Horse Show takes place on the Piazza di Siena in the Villa Borghese Park. Events include cavalry charging as well as jumping etc.

Ippodromo di Tor di Valle, Via del Mare, km 9, ℂ 592 4205. Derby in October.

Le Capannelle, Via Appia Nuova, km 12, ℂ 718 3143, is Rome's most famous course, for racing and show jumping.

Cinodromo a Ponte Marconi, Via della Vasca Navale 6, ℂ 556 6258 for dog races.

Riding

There are loads of riding clubs, but none accept short-term members. One of the nearest stables (*maneggio*) is the Circolo Ippico Fiano Romano, between Via Tiberina and Capena; L15 000 per hour, ℂ (0765) 455 019; also try the Circolo Ippico Tor di Quinto, Via Casale Tor di Quinto 6, ℂ 394 873. Contact the Associazione Nazionale Turismo Equestre, Via Monte Santo 68, ℂ 392 3428, or the Federazione Italiana Sport Equestre, Viale Tiziano 70, ℂ 3685 8116 for information on any other possiblities.

Swimming

The best chance of a swim is to go to the coast—the further away from the mouth of the Tiber the better—or up to Lake Bracciano. As you can probably guess by now, Rome's so-called public pools are actually open to members only.   In summer, however, a couple of hotels with pools open them to the public on a daily rate, and there's a pleasant outdoor pool up at EUR. If you're living in Rome and want to join a swimming centre, contact the **Ufficio Sport e Turismo,** Comune di Roma, Via Capitan Bavastro 94, ℂ 5790 2214 for a list of pools. Expect to pay L30,000 membership PLUS L40,000 per month and to have to present a medical certificate.

Piscina delle Rose, Viale America 20, ℂ 592 6717. Open 9 am–9.30 pm (closes at 7 pm at weekends) from June to September.

La Margherita, Via Monti Tiburtini 511, ℂ 451 0552. Open to members only from 10 am–1 pm on Sundays. L10,000.

Hilton, Via Cadlolo 101,   3151. L35–45,000.

Shangri-La, Viale Algeria 141, ℂ 591 6441, L15,000.

Tennis

The International Tennis Championships are held at the Foro Italico in May. Those who prefer to serve themselves can get a list of tennis clubs from the Federazione Italiana Tennis, Viale dei Gladiatori 31, ℂ 321 9041.

Reservations are essential to get a court.

Belle Arti, Via Flaminia 158, ℂ 322 6529. One million lire for yearly membership plus L128,000 per month.

Circolo Stampa, Piazza Mancini 19, ℂ 323 2452. One of the few places where non–members can pay by the hour. Single court for L15,000 and double court for L20,000.

Oasis di Pace, Via Eugenii 2, ℂ 718 4551. Again, no membership and similar prices.

Centro Sportivo Italiano, Lungotevere Flaminio 55, ℂ 361 0096. Membership required, but exceptions made for tourists. Similar rates to the Circolo Stampa.

Children's Rome

Most children love Rome and most Romans love children. The trouble is that the little monkeys never want to see what you want to see, and if you aren't careful your holiday will become a sordid journey into ice cream and pizza blackmail. If your offspring have arrived at the age of reason, a good strategy for a happy holiday is to lay your cards on the table from the beginning—ask them what they'd like to do, and tell them what you want to do, and split the days accordingly (though somehow it always works out better if the adults do their bit first).

You can make Rome come alive for your children with a little homework: read your Livy before a trip to the Forum, so you can recite inspiring tales of noble Romans in the very spot where they took place. A good read for the kids is *Asterix the Gladiator*, which takes place in the Rome of Julius Cæsar, with fine scenes of Roman baths, apartment houses, and the Circus Maximus (although whether or not Rome had Gaulish restaurants is debatable). Most children love the models in the Museum of Roman Civilization in EUR, the Colosseum, Castel Sant'Angelo with its dungeons, a trip to the catacombs, the Trevi Fountain, the Villa d'Este at Tivoli, the Monster Park at Bomarzo, and racing up to the top of St Peter's dome (but poor parents!). Besides these, there is the more obvious kid's stuff—the zoo in Villa Borghese (where you can also hire a bicycle or a rowboat to paddle about in the lakelet); LUNEUR park, which has a certain old fashioned charm, though its carnival attractions are not a bargain; and the frowzy Wax Museum, for a laugh.

If money's no object, there are horse and carriage rides around the historic centre, and hopefully the boat rides down the Tiber will set up again soon (see Ostia Antica).

Rome is not particularly well-off for children's theatre, though it is always worth scanning the pages of *Trova Roma*. There is, however, a puppet show up on the Janiculum park, at Piazza Garibaldi, with outdoor shows in the afternoon. If your kids speak Italian, they may like **Teatro In**, Via degli Amatriciani (near Piazza Navona), which sometimes does Shakespeare. Have your child's portrait (or caricature) drawn in Piazza Navona, or keep them occupied by letting them sit in cafés with crayons and paper. Villa Celimontana, Villa Ada, and the Euro-sculpture park by Porta Ardeatina have large playgrounds. For toy shops, clothes, etc. see Shopping: Children.

Registration and Residency	392
Finding a Flat	392
Finding a Job	394
Finding a School	394
Useful Addresses	395

Living and Working in Rome

'Rome is a world,' wrote Goethe, 'and it would take years to become a true citizen of it. How lucky those travellers are who take one look and leave.' Nevertheless, an estimated 50,000 English-speaking foreigners do live in Rome, so if work, study, or caprice conspire to move you to become a resident you certainly won't be alone. The secret is not going crazy the first two months getting your papers in order. Many ex-pats, keen to preserve their sanity, don't bother. If you prefer to be legal, here's the procedure.

Regististration and Residency

If you are planning to stay in Italy long term without working, you should register with the police within eight days of arrival and apply for a *permesso di soggiorno* from the Ufficio Stranieri at the Questura Centrale on Via Genova. As they are open only in the mornings, like all state offices, you should aim to get there early. The *permesso* lasts for three months, after which time you will need to renew it. If you can prove you have enough money to live on, permission is usually granted, though racist policemen may give non-whites a harder time. Insidious as this is, you should do all you can to appear calm and remain polite.

Anyone who wishes to be registered as a resident should apply to the Anagrafe (registry office) at Via Luigi Petroselli 50. If you are in Italy for work, your employer should help you with the red-tape, though many small businessmen will only take unregistered foreigners (that way they don't have to declare them and pay tax).

Students

Students attending courses at Italian universities or private colleges must obtain a declaration from the Italian Consulate in their home countries before their departure, certifying their 'acceptability'. If you want to study in Rome, especially to do postgraduate work, ask your embassy about scholarships offered by the Italian Ministry of Foreign Affairs (many are never used for lack of requests); or write directly to the Ministry of Foreign Affairs, Direzione Generale per la Cooperazione Culturale Scientifica e Tecnica, Piazzale della Farnesina 1, Roma.

Finding a Flat

Renting

Once you've become a resident, you may suddenly discover it is rather difficult to find a flat to rent. Over half the flats you'll see advertised in the *centro storico* state that tenants have to be non-residents: this does not indicate an unusually high incidence of philoxenic landlords: simply that non-residents are not covered by the same legislation as residents and are less likely to become sitting tenants. As far as you're concerned it's not an insurmountable problem. Just lie.

One important piece of advice if you come looking for a place to stay is to bring lots and lots of money. Rents are very high in Rome (at the time of writing studio and one bedroom flats in the centre go for at least L1,300,000 per month). If you want to fix up accommodation before you go, contact **International Property Services**, Via del Babuino 79, *©* 36 00 00 18. Alternatively look for a flat (or place an ad yourself) in *Metropolitan, Wanted in Rome* (Via dei Delfini 17, *©* 679 0190) available at English bookshops and *Porta Portese* (free, *©* 770 041) from the news-stands, which is full of classifieds; also the Thursday and Sunday editions of *La Repubblica* and *Il Messaggero*; or on the notice boards (which often have flats to share or a single room in a house) at All Saints' Church or the Lion Bookshop, both in Via del Babuino; or upstairs at Centro Susanna, Via XX Settembre 14; or the American Academy, near Porta S. Pancrazio at Via Angelo Masina 5; or outside the PDS centre on Via dei Giubbonari. Most landlords insist on a deposit of two, and sometimes three, months' rent in advance, and it can be the devil to get it back when you leave, even if you give the required three months' notice. If you find a flat through an estate agent their commission is usually 10 per cent of a year's rent. Rental leases are signed through a *commercialista* who represents both you and the landlord and is paid to know all the complicated legal niceties (landlords often have their lawyers along, so you may want to have one, too, in case they try to pull a fast one because you're a foreigner). The lease (usually for one year) may very well specify that you are **not** to become a resident.

Buying

Of course this isn't a problem if you want to buy your own flat or palazzo (current prices are around L3,000,000 a square metre in the centre). When you contact one of Rome's estate agencies (Gabetti is the largest) they will want to know right out how much you are prepared to spend and the neighbourhoods you prefer (if you have school-age children who will be attending one of Rome's several English or American international schools, life will be much easier for your child if you live nearby). Once you find a place you like, make an offer, and if the seller accepts it, you'll be expected to pay 10–15 per cent on signing an agreement called the *compromesso*, which penalizes either you or the seller if either party backs out. The paperwork is handled by a *notaio*, who works for you and the seller, though many people also hire a *commercialista* to look after their affairs. A payment schedule is worked out; Italian mortgages are usually for 50 per cent of the selling price, payable over a 10-year period. Foreigners pay 10 per cent more than Italians, but never have to pay rates. Always transfer payment from home through a bank, taking care to save certificates of the transactions so you can take the money out of Italy when you sell. *Living in Italy*, published by Robert Hale, London 1987, and your Italian consulate are good sources for all the details.

Finding a Job

Finding a job in Rome can be hard. EC residents may register at the nearest *Ufficio di Collocamento* (Manpower Office). Teaching English is the most obvious; qualifications or some experience, while not always essential, may make the difference. *Wanted in Rome, Metropolitan*, and the Roman papers are a good place to look for openings, but it never hurts to show up at a language school and ask for an interview. Some secondary schools take on mother tongue assistant teachers for their language classes.

English-speaking au pairs are also in demand: try the papers or place an ad on the PDS noticeboard on Via dei Giubbonari. The large community of artists and art students means there's always a demand for life models: again, place an ad in *Metropolitan* or *Wanted in Rome* or contact one of the schools directly. If you prefer to work with your clothes on, there are often jobs for skilled secretaries and professionals at FAO, the UN Food and Agriculture Organization.

Secretarial and catering jobs are also available but your chances are slim with only English. As international as Rome is, you'll miss nearly all the fun (and the good jobs) without Italian. If you're still learning, a copy of the annual *English Yellow Pages* (available in most bookshops) may come in handy.

Finding a School

Finding the proper school for your children in Rome can be difficult—there are some 20 international schools, listed in the Rome International Schools Booklet— a good place to start your search, and available at all the schools and at English bookshops. The British Council, Via delle Quattro Fontane 20, 00187 Roma, also has information about schools. Some schools offer programmes to integrate children into the Italian system, if you mean to live in Italy for more than three years; others prepare students for exams and university in Britain, the USA, or Italy. Italian state schools offer a good, rounded education, free to all children living in Italy (after you get all the proper documents translated into Italian and stamped, that is), and sending a young child to a *scuola elementare* or *asilo* (nursery school, run by the *comune* or nuns) will have him or her fluent in Italian in a matter of months. Foreign children adapt amazingly fast because teachers and their peers are irresistibly *simpatico* and helpful.

Alcoholism: just in case you go over the edge. Rome's English language Alcoholics Anonymous (℗ 678 0320) meet at S. Silvestro, St Andrew's, and St Paul's Within the Walls.

Amnesty International: Viale Mazzini 146, ℗ 3751 5403.

Animals: Dog World, Via Zucchelli 22, ℗ 482 7325, will babysit Fido while you're gone. Or look at the small ads in *Metropolitan* and the notice board outside the PDS office on Via Giubbonari.

Auction Houses *Aste* in Italian, can be a good place to pick up furniture. The fortnightly *Bolletino* available in all kiosks, lists items available in legal auctions. Try the Istituto Vendite Giudiziarie, Via Cava Aurelia 96, ℗ 3936 6674 or regular auctions at Monte di Pietà (*see* Pawn Shops). The State Railway auctions unwanted freight in the underpassage of Via Cappellini, ℗ 4730/6908. Art auctions are held around the Spanish Steps in the galleries; Sotheby's is at Piazza di Spagna 90, ℗ 678 1798; Christie's at Piazza Navona 114, ℗ 686 4032.

Baby Sitting Agencies: Arci Donna Roma, ℗ 325 0921. Or look at the ads in *Wanted in Rome*, *Metropolitan*, and on PDS's Via Giubbonari noticeboard.

Bridge Club: Romans, like all Italians, are mean card players. If you are too, meet them and your countrymen by joining Il Clubino, Via C. Lineo 1/A, ℗ 321 6972 (also gin rummy, backgammon, canasta, and mah-jong).

Cars: you have to be a resident to buy one second-hand; non-residents are only allowed to purchase a new car on condition it leaves the country in five days. The law says residents have to change their driving licences and number plates over to Italian ones within a year. Non-residents are only allowed to keep a foreign car in Italy for six months. You may want to lease a *macchina*: try AVIS, Via Tiburtina 1231/A, ℗ 41 99 41, or Eurodollar, ℗ 228 1111.

Christmas: recreating an Anglo-Saxon Christmas can become an obsession. Roman families indulge in tortellini, turkey and a hundred other delicacies, then go out to look at the Christmas cribs (on the Spanish Steps, in S. Maria del Popolo, at the Gesù and S. Ignazio, at S. Marcello in Piazza di San Marcello and in SS. Cosmo e Damiano near the Forum). If the children miss some of the home touches, The Lion Bookshop, Via del Babuino 181, and Economy Book Store, Via Torino 136, stock advent calendars and Christmas crackers; Babington's Tea Rooms offer home-made vintage plum puddings (a 3-year-old 1 lb pudding for an arm and a leg, ℗ 678 6027 to reserve). Midnight Christmas Eve services with English carols at Anglican All Saints', Via del Babuino 153; or Catholic San Silvestro's, Piazza S. Silvestro. To get into St Peter's for midnight mass on Christmas Eve or Christmas Day Mass at 10.15 am requires a ticket procured a few days in advance between 9 and 1 from the Prefectura at the Bronze Door of the basilica. Most Italian Christmas trees come with the roots attached, and are picked up by environmental groups in January.

Cleaners: all the laundrettes (*tintorie*) we could find in Rome insisted that you leave your wash with the staff to do (let us know if you find a self-op!). This naturally works out very expensive. Wash by hand or make friends with someone who has a washing machine.

Environmental Rome: Rome and Italy need all the help they can get, and there is a score of organizations in the city devoted to defending nature and its creatures. Three familiar ones are Greenpeace: Viale Manlio Gelsomini 28, 00153, Friends of the Earth (*Amici della terra*), Via del Sudario 35, © 686 8289, and the World Wildlife Fund: Via Salaria 221, © 859 100. Lega per l'Ambiente, Via Salaria 280, © 884 1552 or 841 3594 is locally very active, and sponsors ecological bike trips (Pedale Verde) in and around Rome.

Health Foods: L'Albero del Pane on Via Sant Maria del Pianto (in the ghetto) is Rome's macrobiotic centre, with its own newspaper, courses, etc. as well as food. It also has an organic fruit and veg shop on Via de'Baullari, just off Campo de' Fiori. The Centro Macrobiotico Italiana, Via della Vite 14, has natural foods and cosmetics, as well as a good restaurant. Le 7 Spighe, Via Crescenzio 76, is a cultural centre as well as a restaurant. Il Canestro, Via Luca della Robbia 47 is a good place for organically grown vegetables, etc.

Home Deliveries: you can have a Chinese meal delivered by Mille Una Cena, © 323 1388, which also does pizza, Italian and Arabic food. Phone an hour in advance for Chinese or pizza, and ninety minutes ahead for Arabic or Italian.

Horseradish: after a few months in Rome finding horseradish, not to mention Marmite, peanut butter, Kelloggs, hot Madras curry, and nachos can become an obsession. Romans may be almost immune to foreign cuisines, but you can find all of the above, and lots, lots more at Castroni, Via Cola di Rienzo 196, © 687 4383, the grocery shop at the top of Via Natale del Grande in Trastevere, and at Ruggieri on Campo de' Fiori.

Pawn Shop: this is the Monte di Pietà, run by a major bank. In Rome it is at Piazza del Monte di Pietà 33, © 67 071. Romans use it to store their valuables while on holiday, and you may want to as well once you've seen the statistics of burglaries. Uncollected items are regularly auctioned off in the mornings.

Plumbers: 24-hour emergency service: Artigiana A Mazzoli, © 756 983 or 5820 5924. Or look in the Yellow Pages under Idraulici.

Radio: you can get the BBC's schedule of broadcasts to Rome by writing to Auntie at Piazza Collegio Romano 1a, © 678 9916, though you can nearly always find the BBC if you fiddle with the dial long enough). Vatican Radio broadcasts news in Italian, French and English at 8am and noon from Mon–Sat. (526AM/93.3/105 FM). The US Armed Forces comes in after sunset at 1107 AM, with major league baseball games nightly during the season beginning around 2 am local time (but that's about all it's good for).

Turkish baths: Via Poli, around the corner from the Trevi fountain. Very expensive.

Ostia Antica   398
Etruscan Towns   407
North to Lake Bracciano   410
The Monster Park of Bomarzo   412
Viterbo   413
Lake Vico and Caprarola   416
Tivoli   417
Up the Aniene Valley to Subiaco   420

Day Trips from Rome

Zagarolo and Palestrina   422
Castelli Romani   425
Pontine Marshes, Anzio and Nettuno   432

'... I am convinced that no inhabited site among the peoples of old was as badly placed as Rome,' wrote Goethe in 1768. 'In the end, when they had swallowed up everything, in order to live and enjoy life, the Romans had to move out again and build their country villas on the sites of the cities they had destroyed.' They are still doing it. A *scampagnata*, the Romans call it—an escape into the countryside, the celebrated Campagna Romana, beloved of landcape artists in the 18th and 19th centuries. Since Goethe's day it has become an urban-suburban-rural grab-bag, blasted by the curse of car lots and uncontrolled speculation, though some corners have managed to keep a modicum of pristine delight. When Rome begins to wear you down, such places are worth seeking out. Some suggestions: the countryside and gardens around Tivoli and the Castelli Romani, being perhaps the most easily accessible; Lake Nemi and the botanical paradise of Ninfa the most enchanting; Viterbo the most medieval; Cervéteri and Tarquinia the most Etruscan; the Monster Park of Bomarzo the most bizarre. But there are times when it's best not to do as the Romans do, especially at weekends, when planning a jaunt into the country—unless conga-lines of cars inching along the *autostrade* is your cup of tea.

The day trips proceed clockwise from Ostia Antica. Most will occupy the better part of a day, though with a car you can combine two, like Caprarola and the Bomarzo Monster Park or Palestrina and Subiaco.

Down the Tiber: Ostia Antica

After Pompeii and Herculaneum, **Ostia Antica** is the best preserved Roman town in Italy, a fascinating lesson on everyday life in ancient Rome itself. Set amid parasol pines and wild flowers, it is as lovely as it is interesting, its brick walls festooned with garlands of ivy, its ruined temples home to scores of sunning lizards and tiny blue butterflies.

Getting Around

Ostia Antica is very easy to reach; overland Metropolitana trains depart every 30 minutes from **Ⓜ** Magliana on Line B. It takes 30 minutes, and the excavations are only a five-minute walk away. Alternatively, from Porta San Paolo drive out 23 km along Via del Mare, which runs parallel to the ancient Via Ostiense. It's also worth finding out whether the boat trips down the Tiber to Ostia Antica have started up again. At the time of writing they had been suspended indefinitely. Contact **Tourvisa**, Via Palestro 70, Ⓒ 446 3481.

Buy picnic supplies in the village of Ostia (see below); the other alternative is the unashamedly touristy **Allo Sbarco di Enea** © 565 0034 (*closed Mon*) with a Ben Hur chariot in the yard, located between the excavations and the station; dining under the trellis in summer. Average food; L60,000. In Lido di Ostia there are plenty of pizzerias and fish restaurants, though don't expect to find any bargains.

According to legend, Ostia was founded in the 6th century BC by the fourth king of Rome, Ancus Martius, although archaeological evidence prefers a 4th century date. Its name derives from *Ostium*, or river mouth, for it was here 'that the waters of the Mediterranean mingled with the Tiber', as the Romans used to joke. Originally built as a walled *castrum*—perhaps the prototype for all subsequent 'camps' that in the next four centuries would stretch from Britain to the Near East—Ostia both guarded the main entrance to Rome and produced salt from the surrounding marshes. Rome's growing sea trade soon made it a thriving port; the First Punic War made it of necessity a naval base as well. Its major setback came from its own mother's hands, when the Romans under Marius sacked it; Sulla immediately rebuilt it, with the wall that still bears his name (the Cinta Sillana).

By the 1st century AD, the port of Ostia could no longer handle Rome's insatiable demand for more and more goods, and Claudius began a new port at Portus. But still Ostia grew. After Rome's great fire of 64 AD, Nero sent tons of debris down the Tiber to reclaim the surrounding swamplands. Hadrian poured money into the town, rebuilding it as a 2nd-century garden suburb for middle and working class families. Although many businesses had relocated to Portus, Ostia's warehouses, *horreae*, had the task of managing Rome's enormous dole, the *Annona*.

Ostia's worst enemy proved to be Constantine, who conferred all of its ancient rights as a city to Portus, perhaps because the residents had little use for his new religion—18 mithraeums have been uncovered so far, in contrast to only a handful of Christian buildings. Still, the city survived as a residential backwater; new, more splendid *domus*-style homes were built, until the 5th century brought total decadence, and even worse, malaria. Ostia was neglected, looted, and covered with sand; the silt of the Tiber moved the coastline a few miles west, and in 1575 a flood altered the course of the Tiber.

The **excavations of Ostia** (*open from 9 to one hour before sunset, L8000*), begun in the 19th century, have so far uncovered two thirds of the city. Earlier shovels and chisels were at work along the **Via delle Tombe**, at the entrance to the site; fortune hunters have left only a few columbaria and sarcophagi undamaged. The road from Rome, **Via Ostiense**, its flagstones deeply grooved by ancient cart wheels, leads up to the Republican-era **Porta Romana**, Ostia's main gate. Emperor Domitian added two winged Minerva Victories to flank the gate, one of which survives in the **Piazza della Vittoria**, a weird creature that would not look out of place in the science-fiction palace of Ming the Merciless.

Once through the gate, Via Ostiense becomes the main street, the **Decumanus Maximus**; on the right it passes a series of **Horrea**, or warehouses, one of which was converted in the 1st century AD by the ancient equivalent of the bus drivers' union into a bath complex, known as the **Baths of the Cisiarii**; a mosaic in the frigidarium shows the guild members at work, carting passengers about in wagons. The fancier **Baths of Neptune**, still on the right side of the Decumanus, were built by Hadrian and decorated with elaborate mosaics of frolicking sea gods and a palaestra for gymnastics. Just before the baths, Via dei Vigili leads back to a fine *Mosaic of the Winds*; on the left Hadrian built the **Police and Firemen's Barracks** marked by a curious, steeply inclined ramp (an early version of a firemen's pole?). The mosaic in the centre, of men leading a bull to sacrifice, was part of the barracks' shrine to the deified emperors, or *Augusteum*. On the narrow lane behind the barracks is a well-preserved row of *insulae*, with their shops on the ground floor and stairs leading up to the flats (the average *insulae* at Ostia had four floors). The shop at the end of the lane, facing the Decumanus, was the **Tavern of Fortunatus**, with a mosaic advertisement from the halcyon days before Madison Avenue: 'Fortunatus says: if you're thirsty, drink a bowl of wine.'

Beyond stands the much-restored **Theatre**, built by Agrippa, who included shops in the arcades under the seats, one now selling souvenirs, another is a bar, and a third the WC. Three marble masks, once part of the stage decoration, have been set up on tufa columns. In front of the theatre is the fascinating **Forum of the Corporations**, a quadrangle where 61 of Ostia's various maritime concerns had their offices around a quadrangle. The temple in the centre was dedicated either to Ceres or 'Annona Augusta', the Divinity of Imperial Provisions, to which each firm was devoted, heart and soul. Black and white mosaics indicate the special business of each (most depict cargo ships; those with elephants and reindeer dealt in land transport), its trademark, and the nationality of its merchants and fitters. Ponder them, and as Jérôme Carcopino wrote, 'And suddenly you see the throngs of people, strangers to each other, born in far distant lands, rowing to meet each other here in answer to the needs of Rome, and you feel that there gravitates for-ever round this unforgettable enclosure not only the mass of goods which Rome appropriated for herself in every corner of the earth, but the cortège of docile nations whom she had consecrated to her service'. Or picture Rome as a queen termite, too bloated to move, with scores of tiny servants whose sole job is to bring food to drop in her insatiable maw.

Next to the Forum is the **House of Apuleius**, a *domus* with a peristyle, like the houses of Pompeii; adjacent, along the Decumanus, is the well-preserved **Mithraeum of the Seven Spheres**, named for the seven semicircles shown on the mosaic floor, symbolizing the seven stages of initiation and/or the seven planets. Its neighbour, the **Great Horrea**, the largest warehouse in Ostia, has a porticoed court surrounded by some 60 small rooms for storing corn. Across the Decumanus, the **Seat of the Augustales** was the headquarters of the priests in charge of the official emperor-worship.

Via dei Molini and Via Semita dei Cippi mark the eastern limits of the original *castrum*. Via dei Molini is named for the **Apartment of the Millstones** (still containing mills and olive presses). The adjacent **Casa di Diana**, one of more posh *insulae*, was originally four storeys, with taverns and shops on the ground floor and spacious flats above, with its own latrine, balconies, cistern and pool in the court, and its own private mithraeum. Across Via di Diana, don't miss the **Thermopolium**, or snack bar, which wouldn't look out of place in Rome today with its shiny marble bar and shelf to display the various snacks, these illustrated by a surviving fresco; it has a small wine cellar, vessels set in the floor for storing oil, and an area for sitting outside in good weather, complete with a little fountain. Next to the Casa di Diana, the **Casa dei Dipinti**, was equally large, and the most luxurious *insula* ever found, once entirely covered on the outside with festoons and paintings; through the gate you can see a colourfully frescoed room. Climb the stairs to the top floor for a view of the excavations.

Just to the north, a converted 15th-century salt deposit now contains the **Museo Ostiense** (*daily 9 am–1 pm*). Among the most interesting items are the bas-reliefs in the first room, portraying daily life in ancient Ostia (including a birth scene) and beyond, a 1st-century BC round relief of the twelve gods, statues of Mithras stabbing the bull, Trajan in a cuirass (looking very uncomfortable with a slice of his abdomen missing), also Perseus with Medusa's head, Julia Domna (Septimius Severus' wife), dressed as Ceres; the headless but very virile *Hero in Repose*; Maxentius as Pontifex Maximus; a beautifully carved sarcophagus of a boy from Pontus' necropolis at Isola Sacra, and what is believed to be a portrait of Christ, a beautiful polychrome *opus sectile* pavement. Strangest of all are the marble footprints, facing in opposite directions. Found in the temple of the war goddess Bellona, they were probably a soldier's votive offering of thanks for returning safely from war.

From the museum, Via Tecta leads past the **Piccolo Mercato**, an amazingly well-preserved grain warehouse, and continues into the **Forum**, with its two temples facing each other across the square: nearest, with the broad stairway, is the **Capitolium**, a temple dedicated to the Etruscan/Roman trinity of Jupiter, Juno,

Ostia Antica

200 m
200 yds

Tiber River

N

1
2
3
4
56
5
6
7
8
11
13 15
12
14
16
18
9 10
54
38
39
36
37
33
58
34
57
35
41
42
43
47
46
28
59
30
44
29
45 48
31
32

VIA DELLE FOCE
VIA DEGLI AURIGHI
DECUMANUS MAXIMUS
VIA DELLA FORNACE
VIA DELLE CORPORAZIONI
VIA DEI VIGILI
Forum
CARDO MAXIMUS
VIA DELLA SEMITA DEI CIPPI

Ancient
Coastline

VIA DEL ROMAGNOLI

To Ostia Lido

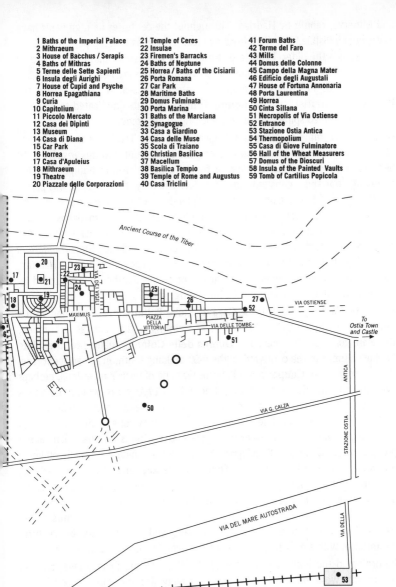

1 Baths of the Imperial Palace
2 Mithraeum
3 House of Bacchus / Serapis
4 Baths of Mithras
5 Terme delle Sette Sapienti
6 Insula degli Aurighi
7 House of Cupid and Psyche
8 Horrea Epagathiana
9 Curia
10 Capitolium
11 Piccolo Mercato
12 Casa dei Dipinti
13 Museum
14 Casa di Diana
15 Car Park
16 Horrea
17 Casa d'Apuleius
18 Mithraeum
19 Theatre
20 Piazzale delle Corporazioni

21 Temple of Ceres
22 Insulae
23 Firemen's Barracks
24 Baths of Neptune
25 Horrea / Baths of the Cisiarii
26 Porta Romana
27 Car Park
28 Maritime Baths
29 Domus Fulminata
30 Porta Marina
31 Baths of the Marciana
32 Synagogue
33 Casa a Giardino
34 Casa delle Muse
35 Scola di Traiano
36 Christian Basilica
37 Macellum
38 Basilica Tempio
39 Temple of Rome and Augustus
40 Casa Triclini

41 Forum Baths
42 Terme del Faro
43 Mills
44 Domus delle Colonne
45 Campo della Magna Mater
46 Edificio degli Augustali
47 House of Fortuna Annonaria
48 Porta Laurentina
49 Horrea
50 Cinta Sillana
51 Necropolis of Via Ostiense
52 Entrance
53 Stazione Ostia Antica
54 Thermopolium
55 Casa di Giove Fulminatore
56 Hall of the Wheat Measurers
57 Domus of the Dioscuri
58 Insula of the Painted Vaults
59 Tomb of Cartilius Popicola

and Minerva, rebuilt by Hadrian. Throughout the centuries its high walls have always been visible, and were used by local farmers as a sheep pen. Across the Forum stands the older **Temple of Rome and Augustus**; marble fragments of both temples that escaped the busy medieval lime kilns lay near each. Much less has survived of the other Forum buildings, the **Curia**, seat of Ostia's Senate, the **Basilica** (the courts), and the **Round Temple**, probably dedicated to emperor worship; its ruined spiral staircase once led up to the dome.

Next to the Temple of Rome and Augustus the **Casa Triclini** is named for the dining couches found in the rooms along the right; built into this *insula*'s right hand corner is the public lavatory, or **forica**, a 20-holer once equipped with a revolving door and a constant flow of water. The only thing lacking was paper; the Romans used swabs on the end of sticks (hence the expression 'to get the wrong end of the stick'). Across from the loo were the **Forum Baths**, Ostia's largest (2nd century AD, but remodelled many times). You can make out the furnaces used for heating the steam baths and *caldarium*, and the ornate *frigidarium* for cooling off. Just to the south is another bath complex contributed by Hadrian, the **Terme del Faro**, named for its mosaic of Ostia's lighthouse surrounded by sea creatures; it also has a fresco of a bull-riding nereid.

Across the Cardo Maximus is the **Casa di Giove Fulminatore**, decorated with a relief of a foot-long phallus, like an arrow pointing to the door (as at Pompeii, these are good luck charms). The **Domus delle Colonne**, named for the white marble columns in the courtyard, is the next building south; in the adjacent lane, the 3rd-century AD **Caupona del Pavone** was one of Ostia's nicer inns, perhaps even the one mentioned by St Augustine in his *Confessions*, where he had his famous conversation with his mother St Monica before their departure for Africa—though as Monica fell ill and died before they set sail, the inn may not have been so nice after all. Near the **Porta Laurentina** is the triangular sacred precinct of the **Campo della Magna Mater**, most of which was strictly off-limits for women. Against the gate is the **Temple of Bellona** and its college of adepts, the **Schola of the Hastiferii**; here, too, flanked by two telemones of Pan, is the **Sanctuary of Attis**, part of the **Temple of Cybele**, the Great Mother. A slight detour from the gate up Via Semita dei Cippi will take you to the **Domus of the Vestibule**, with a fine polychrome mosaic, and the **Domus of Fortuna Annonaria**, with a mosaic of the she-wolf, a nymphaeum, and a one-hole *forica*.

Returning to the Forum, walk beyond the Curia to Via Epagathiana, a street marking the western limits of the *castrum*—a puny place compared to Ostia's later size. On the right is **Horrea Epagathiana**, a private warehouse, with the two owners' names still inscribed over the door and a large swastika in the floor mosaic (one of the most ancient sun symbols, though once its religious meaning was forgotten, it became a lucky charm if the arms bent to the right, and bad luck if they went to the left). Across the lane stands the **House of Cupid and Psyche**, an attractive 4th-century domus named for the statue group discovered within; it has a lavish *opus sectile* pavement, and is believed to have been owned by a wealthy merchant who preferred Ostia in its decline to dense and noisy Portus. The adjacent **Baths of Buticosus** is named for a bath attendant whose portrait in mosaic was discovered here, along with another rollicking mosaic of sea monsters.

South of here the Decumanus Maximus forks; the branch called Via della Foce continues towards the Tiber. On the right are the **Baths of Mithras**, this one especially good for exploring its subterranean plumbing if it's not flooded by ground water; note the marks left by the water wheel, which filled the lead pipes running into the boiler. Next door is the **Hall of the Wheat Measurers**, with a fine mosaic illustrating their tasks.

Heading back along Via delle Foce, note the high-walled group of buildings on the right, nearly all built by Hadrian in what may have been a kind of ancient self-sufficient estate complex, with condominiums, baths, a mithraeum, and shops. First on the right is the **House of Bacchus** and the **House of Serapis**, a pair of *insulae* with one of Ostia's finest mosaics, of Bacchus and Ariadne; next are Hadrian's **Baths of Trinacria**, with more fine mosaics and plumbing fixtures underground. Then come the **Baths of the Sette Sapienti**, or Seven Sages, though here you'd call them the seven wise guys: each is frescoed with a caption with advice on how to wash your rude parts. Don't miss the beautiful mosaic of a hunting scene in the circular hall. Adjacent to the baths is the **Insulae Aurigi**, or House of the Charioteers, named for its fresco of two jockeys; its high, upper level of arches gives a fair idea of what the insulae looked like.

The last section of Ostia lies along the extension of the Decumanus Maximus to the Porta Marina. Head back to the fork; wedged between the two streets is a presumed **Christian Basilica**, while across the Decumanus is the **Macellum**, or meat market, complete with mosaics and marble counters and basins that once held live fish. The **Schola di Traiano**, headquarters of a corporation (of shipbuilders?), was a monumental complex with a long niched pool, named for the statue of Trajan discovered on the site. Further down and across the Decumanus stands the **Insula of the Painted Vaults** (usually closed, but you could try asking for access at the museum), an apartment house built by Hadrian and later converted into a *lupanare*, or bordello, as the traces of fresco and graffiti bear witness. Evidence suggests that the ancient sex business was fairly specialized; a mosaic nearby that the tour groups never get to see depicts the services offered by male dwarfs. This is right next to Ostia's high rent district, another complex of *insulae* built by Hadrian, luxurious and most innovative in style, the perfect home for an upper crust Roman. First, there's the **Casa delle Muse**, with a restored roof and wall paintings of Apollo and the Muses (though again only visible through a gate); the **Casa dei Giardini**, the Garden Homes, which looked onto their private garden like a Bloomsbury square; and the **Domus of the Dioscuri**, embellished with beautiful polychrome mosaics of the 4th century.

The Decumanus leaves Ostia by the **Marine Gate**, which by the time of Hadrian had been built over by citizens who felt no threat from a sea they called their own. One of the old towers was converted into an inn, the **Caupona of Alexander Helix** whose name may be read on the floor mosaic; other mosaics in the tavern show Egyptian contortionist-dancers, Venus, and two wrestlers. Beyond the gate, towards the ancient beach, stood funerary monuments, including the imposing travertine **Monument of C. Cartilius Poplicola**, along with some seaside villas and the **Baths of Marciana**, with mosaics of athletes warming up in the dressing room. Four tall columns with composite capitals are all that remains of the **Synagogue** (1st century AD), which stood right on the beach; some of the mosaic floor remains, as well as the apse that once held the ark of the Torah, and an adjacent oven probably used to bake unleavened bread.

From the excavations it's a 10-minute walk to the sleepy hamlet of **Ostia**, founded in 831 as 'Gregopolis' by Pope Gregory IV, to defend Rome after the Saracens captured Sicily. Pope Julius II, while he was still Ostia's cardinal, built the huge brick **Castello** (*currently closed for restoration*), Ostia's 1483 landmark sample of Renaissance fortifications. It frightened the Turks and would-be marauders up the Tiber until the river itself moved; now it holds a humble historical collection. Within the walls of Ostia are Renaissance-era attached houses built for workers in the papal salt pans, and the small Renaissance church of **Sant'Aurea**, built over the 5th-century basilica of Ostia's first martyr. Ask if the **Episcopio**, or bishop's palace is open, to see the unusual decorations by Baldassare Peruzzi in 1511–13, recently discovered under layers of whitewash. Julius at the time was trying to kick the French out of Italy, and the 15 grisaille frescoes, adaptations of scenes from Trajan's Column, painted to look like reliefs, are pure Renaissance flattery, comparing wars of the Pope to conquests of the Emperor.

Remains of **Portus**, Emperor Claudius' new port, were found during the construction of Fiumicino Airport. In ancient times its most spectacular feature was its lighthouse, the **Pharos of Portus**, built on an artificial island, created by sinking the massive ship that transported the Vatican obelisk from Egypt. Trajan later added a canal linking the port to the Tiber, creating an island known as the **Isola Sacra** (*the site is closed to the public, but fans of Claudius, wishing to pay homage to their stammering hero, should follow the sign to Fiumicino on SS 296 across the Tiber*).

Isola Sacra was the necropolis of ancient Portus until the 4th century, discovered excellently preserved under layers of sand. The inhabitants of Portus, unlike many

Romans, had to work for a living and couldn't afford big fancy monuments. Instead the dead were laid out in simple barrel-vaulted tombs or 'trunk tombs' shaped like 19th-century travelling trunks, or had their ashes deposited in columbaria. Many opted for fine terracotta, stucco, or mosaic decoration, often depicting the deceased's trade; one Egyptophile lies under a baby brick pyramid.

Of **Porto** itself, only a small village remains, though there are plans to excavate the ancient ports of Claudius and Trajan. The latter's hexagonal docks have survived as a little inland lake, **Lago Traiano**, on Via Portuensis; you may see it when flying into Fiumicino airport. The **Museo delle Navi Romane** near the airport (*open 9–1, Tues and Thurs also 2–5, closed Mon, L2000*) contains seven ships uncovered during the construction of the airport in 1961.

From the seaside town of **Fiumicino**, take bus 020 north to the relatively benign pine shaded beach of **Fregene**, or bus 02 back past Ostia Antica to Rome's own beach, the nightmarish **Lido di Ostia**. A monument at Idroscalo, near the mouth of the Tiber, marks the spot where film director Pier Paolo Pasolini was murdered in 1975; if you swim here the pollution will kill you, too. Better, less crowded beaches are further south, in the pine forests of **Castel Fusano** and beyond.

Etruscan Towns: Cervéteri, Civitavecchia, Tarquinia, Tuscania

It is hard to believe, but this empty quarter of northern Lazio, often used by Cinecittà for its spaghetti western sets, was the richest and most heavily populated part of ancient Etruria, including the only two sites worth visiting for those not enchanted with archaeology: the museums and necropoli at Cervéteri and Tarquinia. Of the cities themselves, little remains. Living Etruscans preferred ephemeral homes and temples of wood and clay, but when it came to the afterlife they built for eternity. Their cities of the dead, of tombs made of stone and carved in the rock, contained reproductions of their luxuries and favourite things, 'a pleasant continuance of life, with jewels and wine and flutes playing for the dance,' as D. H. Lawrence wrote.

Getting Around

ACOTRAL buses from Via Lepanto (Metro A) go to Cervéteri (46 km), Tarquinia (96 km), and Tuscania (130 km); both towns may also be reached by train from Termini, and then by catching a bus from the local station. By car, take Via Aurelia (SS 1).

Lunch

Near Cervéteri at Ceri you can eat well and cheaply at **Sora Lella**, in Piazza Alessandrina 1 (actually Ceri is so small it's hard to miss); *closed Wed and in Sept.* Alternatively, the Etruscans certainly won't mind if you bring a picnic.

Cervéteri

Locally famous for its artichokes, **Cervéteri** is named for the abandoned medieval citadel of *Caere Vetere* ('Old Caere') in memory of Caere, the Etruscans' richest city. Caere also had the closest cultural ties to Greece; according to Herodotus, it was the only non-Greek city with a sanctuary at Delphi. It had three seaports (for a population of 25,000) and mined the Tolfa mountains for the metals it exchanged for Attic vases and other luxury goods. Decline began when the Greek cities in southern Italy defeated the Etruscan fleet in 474 BC, ending their naval supremacy. Caere then turned to agriculture and became a close ally of Rome. A falling out came in the 3rd century BC, when Caere rebelled and was put in its place, minus the rights of full Roman citizenship. In the early Middle Ages the city was abandoned, then had a brief renaissance in the 13th century; the Orsini later added a small castle in the piazza, which now serves as the **Museo Nazionale di Cervéteri** (*open 9–2, closed Mon, L8000 which includes entrance to the necropolis*) with a well-arranged display of tomb finds from the 8th–1st centuries BC, including a magnificent collection of Greek and Greek-style vases.

It's a 2 km drive or walk up from here to the round tufa mound of the **Banditaccia Necropolis** (*turn right from the piazza, and then right again on the narrow branch lane; open daily except Mon, 9–one hour before sunset, same ticket at museum*). This is only one of Cervéteri's four cemeteries (which cover three times the area as the city for the living!), but it's the most interesting, in a park setting of cypresses and parasol pines. The tombs were laid out in the form of a town, with streets and squares, an Etruscan Model Tumulus Show where you can see every style available, from the early grave trenches carved in the tufa to 'cube' tombs resembling houses, to the round mounds with hypogeums carved into the rock below—heavy stone domes, set low to the ground that look more like defence bunkers than tombs. The largest measure over 40 m in diameter, and in them you can see the forerunners of the Mausoleums of Augustus and Hadrian. The tombs of men are marked at the entrance with a phallic symbol, while women get a little house.

Not all of the tombs are lit; the site is quite large, and you may want to buy the map on sale at the entrance to find your way. For serious exploration, ask a guide to unlock and light the more distant tombs for you, though in winter and early spring these may well be flooded. Don't miss the **Tomb of the Capitals** near the entrance, carved from tufa to resemble Etruscan houses, or the **Tomb of the Shields and Chairs**, with unusual military decoration; another, even stranger, the **Tomb of the Stuccoes** is covered with painted stone reliefs of cooking utensils and other household objects.

Civitavecchia and Tarquinia

Between Cervéteri and Tarquinia, you'll pass the not-so-old-looking city of **Civitavecchia**, a port for Rome and the gateway for ferries to Sardinia. The big fortress overlooking the harbour was designed by Michelangelo for the popes, but there's little else to detain you. Further up the coast, **Tarquinia** is a large, modern town of interest in its own right, with a 12th-century Cosmatesque church and a Roman aqueduct, rebuilt in the Middle Ages and still in use. In the 15th-century Palazzo Vitelleschi, many of the finest discoveries from the Etruscan city and its necropolis have been assembled for the **Museo Nazionale Tarquinia** (*9–2, closed Mon, L8000. Stays open later in summer: © 0766 856036 for details*).

The stars of the collection are the famous **Winged Horses** from the 'Altar of the Queen' temple on the acropolis; beautiful beasts, but made of clay like most Etruscan temple decorations, which explains why so few have survived. Well-carved sarcophagi are present in abundance, and there is a collection of Greek vases by some of the greatest 6th–5th century Attic painters. The Etruscans were talented at ceramics, too, as seen by the fine samples of *bucchero* ware, black pottery incised or painted with puzzling Etruscan images. Some of the paintings from the tombs have been relocated here for their protection, including scenes of chariot-riding and athletics—almost any subject is likely to turn up on Etruscan tomb walls; the **Tomb of the Triclinium** with its dancers is one of the most beautiful.

There isn't enough staff to keep open the hundreds of tombs at Tarquinia's **necropolis** (same ticket and hours as museum), all that remains standing of the city of 100,000 strong that dominated southern Etruria for centuries and enforced on Rome its early dynasty of Etruscan kings *(open daily except Mon, 9–7; the tombs are a 15-minute walk from the museum)*. The few you can see on any given day, however, rank among the finest examples of Etruscan painting. Tombs like that of the 'Augurs' and the 'Lionesses' with their beautiful 'Ionic' style paintings, seem remarkably close to the art of ancient Crete. These began to appear in the 6th century BC, and only in the tombs of the richest Etruscans; more typical of the rest is the 'Tomb of the Warrior', carved simply out of the tufa and hung with arms and trophies. The 'Tomb of the Leopards' is decorated with fascinating scenes of an Etruscan feast.

Tuscania

Northeast of Tarquinia, **Tuscania** stands alone in one of the emptiest, eeriest corners of Italy, a region of low green hills where you will find Etruscan ruins, old castles, and religious shrines but no people. Tuscania was a leading Etruscan city after the 4th century BC, and regained its importance for a short while in the early Middle Ages. Today the city is still recovering from a bad earthquake in 1971.

Etruscan sarcophagi from several nearby necropolises are on display in the **Museo Archeologico** in the former S. Maria del Riposo (*daily except Mon, summer 9–1.30 and 2.30–6, winter 9–1.30 and 2–5, free,© 0761 436209*);best among them are the complacent bonvivants of the Curunas family reclining lazily on their urns, and a mysterious Etruscan rebus from the 6th-century BC 'tomb of the Dado' in Pescheria.

But enough of Etruscans: Tuscania is most worth a stop for its two unique churches east of town. **San Pietro** and **Santa Maria Maggiore** were both begun in the 700s, with additions in the 11th and 12th centuries. Besides their carved altars, pulpits, and bits of painting from the 8th–14th centuries, both churches' best features are their unusual sculpted façades—San Pietro's especially, with colourful Cosmati work, fragments of ancient sculpture, and outlandish carved grotesques. Perhaps some of the churches in Rome looked like this before their Renaissance and Baroque rebuilding.

North to Lake Bracciano

This route includes the ruins of Veio, or *Veii*, which from the 8th–6th centuries BC was the largest city in the Etruscan Federation and Rome's most bitter rival. From Veio it continues to Lake Bracciano, a favourite weekend resort of the Romans, who often use its storybook castle for film sets.

Getting There

ATAC bus 201 from Piazza Mancini (across the Tiber from the Foro Italico) will take you to La Giustiniana, where you can pick up bus 032 to Isola Farnese and Veio; ACOTRAL bus from Via Lepanto (Metro A) or train from Termini for Lake Bracciano. If you're driving to Veio, take Via Cassia (N 2) to La Storta; after another km you'll see a sign for Isola Farnese and the excavation. From here, Via Braccianese Claudia continues to the lake.

Lunch

There are innumerable places to eat along Bracciano's shores, but all seem designed to exploit the massive weekend exodus of Romans. Pay above the odds for an average meal, or buy picnics in Bracciano or Anguillara Sabazia.

Veii

The sparse, scattered remains of ancient **Veii**, once enclosed in walls 11 km around, make it the most difficult Etruscan site to visit, with more of the country ramble to it than archaeological thrill. Compensating for the meagre ruins, however, is Veii's striking position, on a sheer tufa plateau over a moat formed by two streams. But these natural defences were not enough for the ancient Veians; they wanted a port, and managed to muscle in a fortified trading post on the Tiber—defying the claims of both Cervéteri and the Latins of Alba Longa. In 753 BC the Latins, under the leadership of Romulus, united with Cerveteri to oust Veii from its Tiber port, founding in its place *Rumon*, which as any Etruscan will tell you really means 'city on the river'.

Veii, minus a port and the precious salt pans of Ostia, held a mighty grudge against the new town of Rome. When Rome's Fabii clan took it upon themselves to patrol and harass Veii, the Veians ambushed and massacred all but one (475 BC). Some 25 years later, neither city could tolerate the other, and a fight to the finish became inevitable; of all Rome's wars, this was the most crucial, for its very existence was at stake. Veii called upon its fellow Etruscan cities for aid (none came) and the Romans under M. Furius Camillus began a siege that ended only when the Romans unblocked one of Veii's marvellous irrigation tunnels leading under the walls. Veii was thus surprised, captured and thoroughly destroyed; its chief deity, Juno, was carted off to a new temple on the Aventine. Julius Cæsar and Augustus tried to plant a colony on the site, but it never prospered.

The excavations of **Veio** *are open daily except Mon, 9 am–1 pm and 4–7 pm; L8000.* Among the remains to be seen are the Temple of Apollo (where the Villa Giulia's beautiful Apollo of Veio was found), cisterns, a tunnel in the rock (where Camillus led the Romans?), and best of all, the 7th-century BC **Tomba Campana**, containing some of the oldest Etruscan paintings ever discovered, of strange Etruscan animals, and Mercury escorting the dead to the underworld. Further up the path is the **Ponte Sodo**, an Etruscan bridge and a lovely spot for a picnic.

Lake Bracciano

Seven km from Veii towards Lake Bracciano are the picturesque ruins of the **Castle of Galéria** with the pretty little hamlet of **Santa Maria di Galéria** below. Another 16 km will bring you to the shores of **Lake Bracciano**. This broad sheet of water, sloshing about in the round volcanic crater of Mt Sabatini, is best known for its eels, whose babies sometimes get sucked in to the fountains in St Peter's Square and clog the pipes. From June–Sept you can take boat tours from the town of **Bracciano**, but the best view of it is from the ramparts of the grim, five-towered **Castello degli Orsini**, stronghold of the bearish clan from 1470 to 1696, when they ceded castle and town of Bracciano to the Odescalchi (*open daily except Mon 10–12 and 3–6, guided tours only, L6000*).

Although the Orsini were usually supporters of the papacy against their nemesis, the Colonna, they knew the Roman pot could boil over at any time, and built this castle as a private bunker close to Rome—not exactly in the style of the day, but when did the Orsini ever care to be progressive? It served them in good stead, fending off the attack of the entire papal army of Alexander VI, when the Orsini were caught fraternizing with the French invader, Charles VIII. Frescoes and painted ceilings by Antoniazzo Romano in the 1490s, later frescoes by the two Zuccari, busts of the Orsini by Bernini, and suits of armour are the artistic highlights within. *If you like the castle, you can rent it for a memorable party; © 679 2154 or 902 4003.*

During World War I, Lake Bracciano was Italy's dirigible and seaplane testing area. Two old hangars in **Vigna di Valle**, 6 km east of Bracciano, were converted in the 1970s to hold the **Historical Museum of the Italian Air Force** (*daily except Mon, 9–4, free*). Exhibits include a model of Leonardo da Vinci's wing flapping machine, fighter planes, racing planes, sea planes, planes that went to the North Pole and the plane that D'Annunzio flew over Vienna in 1918. Most curious of all is a hot air balloon launched from Paris in 1804 in honour of Napoleon's coronation, bearing instead of a basket a large glass replica of the little emperor's crown. Considering Napoleon's later watery problems, from his island exiles to Waterloo and Wellington, it was no small omen that the glass crown fell into Lake Bracciano before reaching Rome.

A scenic road (especially between Bracciano and Trevignano on the north shore) encircles the lake. Only ruins remain of the Orsini castle in pretty **Trevignano Romano**; make the walk up to see the church of the **Assunta**, for its views over the lake and beautiful fresco of the Assumption by the school of Raphael.

The Monster Park of Bomarzo

Bomarzo is one of the most woebegone little comunes in this part of Italy, a setting that adds to the uncanny charm of its late Renaissance Parco dei Mostri, located just below the town. So does the habit of the present owners of running it like an Alabama roadside attraction, complete with tame deer for the children to pet, an albino peacock, miniature goats, and plenty of souvenirs.

Getting Around /Lunch

Bomarzo may be reached by train from Termini or by ACOTRAL bus from Via Lepanto (Metro A); it combines well with a trip to Viterbo, or Lake Vico and Caprarola if you have a car. For lunch, make use of the picnic tables and bar at the Monster Park; or try one of Bomarzo's humdrum tratts.

The Monster Park is open daily 8.30 am–5 pm in winter and 8.30 am–7.30 pm in summer, adm L10,000, children under 8 L8000, © 0761 924029. Curiously, a few of the same sculptors who worked on St Peter's in Rome made this shabby little nightmare, hidden away in the Lazio hills. Somehow the two works seem related, opposite sides of the coin that may help in explaining the tragic, neurotic atmosphere of late 16th-century Italy. One of the Orsini commissioned this collection of huge, strange sculptures; he called it his *Sacro Bosco*—Sacred Wood—and in its present state it's impossible to tell whether it was the complex allegory it pretends to be, or just a joke.

Near the entrance stands the impressive though dilapidated **Tempietto**, a domed temple of uncertain purpose attributed to Vignola. From here, wander the ill-kept grounds, encountering at every turn colossal monuments and eroded, illegible inscriptions: there's a screaming face, with a mouth big enough to hold several people, a dining table and benches, beneath a warning that reads 'every thought flees'; a life-sized elephant, perhaps one of Hannibal's, crushing a terrified Roman soldier in its trunk; a giant wrestler, in the act of ripping a defeated opponent in two from the legs up; and a leaning tower, just for fun. Under every glade decayed Madonnas, mermaids, sphinxes, nymphs, and harpies wait to spook you. All are done in a distorted, almost primitive style. It would be almost too easy to read too much into these images; a cry of pain from the degraded, humiliated Italy of the 1560s, half-pretending madness as the only way to be safe from the Spanish and the Inquisition—or perhaps merely a symbol for the loss of mental balance that followed too many centuries of high culture and over-stimulation. Whatever, the Monster Park will make you feel like an archaeologist, discovering some peculiar lost civilization. Perhaps the Italians understand it too well; it may be the only important monument of the 16th century that neither the government nor anyone else is interested in preserving.

Viterbo

Viterbo ought to be visited. It has the kind of medieval spirit that the popes baroqued over in Rome; and where else can you drink in a café on Death Square, or stroll over to the Piazza of the Fallen to pay your respects to Our Lady of the Plague? Surrounded by grey, forbidding walls and ghastly modern districts, Viterbo is actually a living medieval town inside, with well-preserved 13th-century streets brightened with flowers and fountains. The population seems evenly divided between teenagers on scooters and blasé young soldiers from Italy's biggest army base.

Getting Around/Lunch

Viterbo can be reached by the excruciatingly poky Ferrovie Roma-Nord, from the Piazzale Flaminia station; or by ACOTRAL buses from Saxa Rubra. Go between Thursday and Sunday for a chance to lunch at **Richiastro**, Via della Marrocca 18 (next to the Palazzo Mazzatosta) for its excellently prepared traditional dishes, which have little to do with Rome's.

Like the rest of Lazio, Viterbo has seen more than its share of troubles, most of them traceable to the proximity of Rome. But that same geographical fact also gave the town its greatest period of glory. For much of the 13th century, Viterbo, and not Rome, was the seat of the popes. In this most confusing period of Italian history, over a dozen popes were crowned, died, or at least spent some time here, in short stays on their way to or from France, Tivoli—and sometimes even Rome. In 1309, when the 'Babylonian Captivity' began, Viterbo could only decline, and when the popes returned from Avignon, the city that once was Rome's strongest rival found itself a mere provincial town in the Papal States.

In Viterbo's centre, two not-so-fierce lions, the city's ancient symbols, gaze out over the 13th-century **Palazzo del Podestà** with its clock tower, and the **Palazzo Comunale** of the 1460s, the typical pair of buildings representing the often conflicting imperial and local powers. The politicians won't mind if you look around the Palazzo Comunale and its fine Renaissance courtyard; if you ask, they'll let you see the Council Chamber, the **Sala Regia**, done in fanciful Mannerist frescoes on the history of Viterbo from Etruscan times. Across the square, the Roman sarcophagus built into the façade of **Sant'Angelo** contains the body of a medieval lady of incomparable virtue named Galiena; accounts of her fatal charm and sad demise vary from one Viterban to another.

From here, Via Ascenzi leads under the arch to the Piazza dei Caduti and the **Madonna delle Peste**, an octagonal Renaissance church next to the tourist office. Beyond, at the walls, stands the **Rocca** built by Cardinal Albornoz in 1354 to keep watch on the Viterbans when the pope returned to Rome. This squat palace-fortress has been restored to hold the small collection of the **Museo Archeologico** *(open 9 am–2 pm, closed Mon, L4000. May begin to open afternoons in summer, phone the EPT in Viterbo, © 0761 234 795 for details)*. Two of Viterbo's 13th-century popes are buried in the 13th-century **San Francesco** church, near Porta Murata at the northern end of the walls. Nearby, off Piazza Verdi, stands the late 19th-century church of **Santa Rosa**.

Santa Rosa enshrines the considerable remains of Viterbo's 13th-century patroness, too holy to decompose and usually on display for all to see. Rosa's preaching helped the Viterbans defeat a siege by the heretical Emperor Frederick II in 1243, and to commemorate her, each year on 3 Sept the local men carry a 30 m wooden steeple called the *macchina* through the streets, surmounted by an image of the saint. Local artists create a new *macchina* every four years; the best are works of art.

East of Piazza del Plebiscito, Via Cavour takes you to the **Casa Poscia**, an interesting 13th-century house on a stairway to the left, and then to the **Fontana Grande**, the best of Viterbo's many fountains. Via Garibaldi leads east to the

Roman Gate and **San Sisto**, a church in parts as old as the 800s, with an altar made of sculptural fragments. Outside the walls and across Viale Capocci, the 13th-century **Santa Maria della Verità** suffered terrible vandalism at the hands of the 18th-century redecorators. The frills and plaster frosting are gone now, but only a few bits survived of the Renaissance frescoes by Melozzo da Forli. The Cappella Mazzatosta, behind an iron grille, has good frescoes of the *Marriage of the Virgin* by a local Renaissance artist named Lorenzo of Viterbo. In the adjacent cloister, a fine work from the 1300s, Viterbo keeps its **Museo Civico** with a small archaeological section and a picture gallery, though this may still be closed for restoration.

From Piazza del Plebiscito, Via S. Lorenzo leads into the heart of Viterbo's oldest quarter. Three blocks down and off to the left, **Santa Maria Nuova** is the best-preserved of the city's medieval churches. On the façade there is an ancient image of Jupiter set into the portal and a small outdoor pulpit where St Thomas Aquinas once preached. On the other side of Via S. Lorenzo, Viterbo's old market square faces the **Gesù Church** (11th century), a medieval tower-fortress, one of several left in the city, and a palazzo that long ago was the town hall. To the south, trailing down from the aforementioned **Piazza di Morte**—ironically one of the lovelier squares in Viterbo—the **San Pellegrino** quarter hangs its web of alleys, arches, and stairs along Via S. Pellegrino with a romantic and thoroughly medieval air, though in fact few of the buildings are quite that old.

In the opposite direction from San Pellegrino, a bridge on Roman and Etruscan foundations called the **Ponte del Duomo** carries over to Piazza San Lorenzo and the **Papal Palace**, begun in the 1260s by Alexander IV. Moving the papacy to Viterbo (then pop. 60,000) from Rome (then pop. 18,000, of mostly bullies and layabouts) seemed like a good idea at the time, and this squarish, battlemented palace, very much in the style of a medieval city hall, is a finer building than the pope's present address in Rome, though admittedly much smaller. On its handsome open Gothic loggia, you will see in the decoration lions (for Viterbo) interspersed with the striped coat-of-arms of the French pope Clement V, who completed the building.

But fate conspired against the move from the start: Alexander IV died 17 days after settling into the palace. Five popes were afterwards elected in conclaves held in the Great Hall, among them, Urban IV, who was chased out by the Imperial army of Manfred, and then Clement IV, who died two weeks after his coronation. In selecting his successor, arguments between the French and Italian factions led to a two-year deadlock among the cardinals. The exasperated Viterbans tried to speed up the conclave, first by locking the cardinals in the palace, and then by tearing off the roof; somehow, according to the story, the churchmen got around this by making tents in the Great Hall. Finally the people decided to starve them out, and before long the Church was blessed with the rather undistinguished compromise of Gregory X. He had the roof fixed, but maybe skimped on the materials, for the whole thing came down six years later on the head of his successor, John XXI, who was quickly entombed next door in the plain Romanesque **Cathedral**. That was the last straw; the cardinals high-tailed it back to Rome before Viterbo ruined the Church altogether.

East of Viterbo, the road for Orte enters the old suburb of La Quercia, passing in front of a landmark of Renaissance architecture: **Santa Maria della Quercia**, built in the late 1470s. Its distinctive 1509 façade has a carved oak tree (*quercia*), lions, and lunettes by Andrea della Robbia over the doors. Inside, the beautiful marble tabernacle contains a miracle-working painting of the Virgin, and there is also a fine Gothic cloister. Ask someone to let you into the **Museo degli Ex-Voto**, a collection of some 200 devotional plaques brought to this shrine over the centuries, painted with endearing scenes of miracles attributed to the Madonna.

Six km further east is **Bagnaia**, an old hill village expanded by wealthy Viterban bishops into a residential town. In the 1570s they commissioned Vignola to create the **Villa Lante** (*open daily Jan, Feb, Nov, Dec 9 am–4 pm; Mar and Oct 9 am–5.50 pm; April and Sept 9 am–6.30 pm; May to Aug 9 am–7.30 pm. Guided tours of the garden every half hour; L4000*). Besides the two villas, now shuttered and decayed, there is one of the most striking of all Italian Renaissance gardens, geometrically arranged and full of groves and statuary; water from the fountains cascades down decorative stairs and terraces—an impressive sight, especially when they feel up to turning it on.

This road continues through the beech forests of the Cimino hills, meeting the town of **Soriano nel Cimino**, with a medieval castle and an extinct volcano, Mt Cimino, for a neighbour. South of Viterbo, towards Lake Vico, is the lovely town of **San Martino al Cimino**, built around a fine 13th-century Cistercian abbey, in the French Gothic style; the town itself is an unusual example of Baroque planning, full of trees and half-surrounded by a single curving lane of terraced houses.

Lake Vico and Caprarola

This route takes in one of Lazio's most charming lakes and one of the most majestic Renaissance spreads in Italy—a model for the US Defense Department— built by the incorrigibly insatiable Farnese.

Getting There/Lunch

ACOTRAL buses from Saxa Rubra. There are tables and shady spots for a picnic around the lake.

The smallest and perhaps loveliest of the lakes north of Rome, **Lake Vico** is ringed by rugged hills; parts of the shore are unspoiled marshes, a favourite stop for migratory birds, now protected as a wildlife preserve. At the northern edge, this ancient crater has a younger volcano (also extinct) poking up inside it: **Monte Venere**. Pristine and unpolluted, it is one of the best swimming holes in Lazio. You can combine a dip with a visit to one of Italy's most arrogantly ambitious late Renaissance palaces, the **Villa Farnese in Caprarola**, located just over the hill (*open daily Jan, Feb, Nov, Dec 9 am–4 pm; Mar 9 am–5 pm; April, May and Sept 9 am–6 pm; June, July and Aug 9 am–7 pm; Oct 9 am–5.30 pm; L4000*).

When Alessandro Farnese, member of an obscure noble family of Lazio, set his sister Giulia up as mistress of Pope Alexander VI, his fortune was made; Alessandro later became Paul III, a great pope who called the Council of Trent, rebuilt Rome, and kept Michelangelo busy—but also a rotten pope, who oppressed his people, refounded the Inquisition, and became the most successful grafter in papal history. Before long the Farnese family ruled Parma, Piacenza, and most of northern Lazio. With the fantastic wealth Alessandro accumulated, his grandson, also named Alessandro, built this family headquarters; Vignola, the family architect, turned the entire town of Caprarola into a setting for the palace, ploughing a new avenue through the centre as an axis that led to a grand stairway, then a set of gardens (now disappeared), then another stairway up to the huge pentagonal villa, built over the massive foundations of an earlier, uncompleted fortress. The villa today is empty; the Farnese lost everything in later papal intrigues, and someone, sometime, had to sell the furniture.

Nevertheless, it is still an impressive if not very cosy home; some of the highlights of the tour include Vignola's elegant central courtyard, a room with uncanny acoustical tricks that the guides love to demonstrate, a room frescoed with the *Labours of Hercules*, another with a wonderful ceiling painted with figures of the constellations, and Vignola's incredible **spiral staircase** of stone columns and neo-classical frescoes. The best part, however, is behind the extensive park of azaleas and rhododendrons: a 'Secret Garden' populated with grotesques and fantastical *telemones* that recall the Monster Park (there's a connection; one of the Orsinis of Bomarzo was Alessandro Farnese's secretary), and finally, a delightful summer house called the **Little Palace of Pleasure**.

Tivoli

The most popular day trip from Rome, Tivoli offers both natural beauty and some of the more unbridled efforts of the human imagination—the unique gardens of the Villa d'Este, the ruins of Hadrian's country retreat, the size of a small city, and the plunging artificial waterfall of the Villa Gregoriana.

Tivoli (31 km) is easiest reached by ACOTRAL buses, departing every 15 min from the bus station at Ⓜ Rebibbia on Metro Line B. By car, take the Via Tiburtina.

Lunch

Hadrian's Villa is a great place for a picnic lunch, and Tivoli has no lack of restaurants: the admittedly touristy **Sibilla**, next to the 'Temple of the Sibyl' on Via della Sibilla is fun, and serves good grilled trout; or try **Del Falcone**, on medieval Via del Trevi 34, with good food and pizza but no view. Both closed Monday.

Ancient *Tibur*, set in a cliff with a beautiful view over the Roman *campagna*, became a sort of garden retreat for the Senatorial class in the early days of the empire. But a town with a view is also usually easily defensible, and by the early Middle Ages, despite all the dirty work of Goths and Huns, Tibur had changed its name to Tivoli and managed a successful transition from posh resort to gutsy, independent hill town. Once, in its struggles with Rome, it even defeated its bossy neighbour and captured a pope. But pachydermic Rome never forgets a grudge, and in the 1460s Pope Pius II built a castle, the **Rocca Pia**, at the town's door to keep Tivoli in line. Wealth returned in the late Renaissance in the form of money-bags cardinals; one in particular, Ippolito d'Este, son of Lucrezia Borgia and Duke Ercole I of Ferrara, created in 1550 perhaps the most fantastically worldly villa and gardens Italy had seen since antiquity, the **Villa d'Este** (*open 9–one hour before sunset; from May–early Oct the gardens are usually illuminated nightly except Mon from 9–12 pm (contact the EPT in Rome for details); adm L5000*).

The musty villa itself, designed by Pirro Ligorio and heavily coated with Mannerist frescoes, was rented by Franz Liszt from 1865 until his death in 1886 (and the inspiration for his *Fountains of the Villa d'Este*). But the residence is entirely upstaged by the gardens, set on a descending series of terraces. Among the palms and cypresses water shoots and cascades from an incredible hydraulic fantasyland, weaving intricate patterns of water: the *Fountain of Glass* by Bernini, the stuccoed *Grotto of Diana*, the *Fountain of Dragons*, the *Fountain of the Owl and Birds*, a favourite water trick that no longer warbles or moves; nor has the cardinal's *Water Organ* worked for donkey's years. One of the most curious features is *Little Rome*, a pint-sized replica of the Tiber Island in Rome, with models of ancient buildings.

Tivoli has an interesting Romanesque church with early medieval frescoes, **San Silvestro**, located on steep and narrow Via del Colle (just north of the Villa d'Este); at the bottom, just beyond the gate are the remains of the vast **Sanctuary**

of Hercules (2nd century BC), once the office of the Sibyl of Tivoli. Like Cumae near Naples, Tibur had a college of Sibyls (pictured so memorably on the Sistine Chapel ceiling and elsewhere, for the sake of the story that they prophesied the birth of Christ). The presence of these oracular ladies, cousins to the oracle at Delphi, show the influence of Greek thought and religion in Latium from the earliest times. The stiff climb up Via del Colle leads eventually to Tivoli's gaudy 17th-century **Cathedral** at the corner of Via del Duomo, containing a moving, 13th-century wooden sculpture of the *Deposition*.

From here, Via del Colle becomes Via Valerio and crosses the Aniene on its way to the nearly vertical gardens of the **Villa Gregoriana** (*open 9 until one hour before sunset, L2500*). The gardens were named in honour of Pope Gregory XVI, who in 1831 put an end to the regular flooding of the Aniene with the construction of a vast double tunnel through Mt Catillo. The river then emerges with dramatic flair high up in a natural chasm, forming a 120 m pluming mist of rainbows called the **Grande Cascata**. Shady paths wind down past various viewpoints over the waterfall; if you can trick yourself into forgetting about the awful climb back up, descend past the rather scanty remains of a Roman villa to the artificial **Cascata Bernini** and the limestone cavern called the **Grotta della Sirena**, where the waters are squeezed into an abyss. From the bottom a path leads up the other lip of the chasm, the acropolis of *Tibur*, where stand two remarkably well-preserved Roman temples, the famous circular **Temple of Vesta** and the rectangular **Temple of the Sibyl** as fancy has named them (if you don't care to climb, they can also be reached from above, on Via della Sibilla). Both temples date from the Republican era; the Temple of Vesta, in particular, with its beautiful frieze and Corinthian columns was a favourite of romantic tourists, and has been reproduced in many a Hyperborean's park.

Along the Via Tiburtina towards Rome are the strange, sheer-sided travertine quarries that have helped Tivoli make a living since ancient times. Almost all of Rome is built of it; one solemn grey variety went into the Colosseum, the city gates, and most of the other ruins. The other, streaked with beige and black, is the material Mussolini used for scores of railway stations all over Italy. Nowadays demand is still great, and Tivoli ships travertine all over the world.

Just outside Tivoli, signs direct you to the quiet residential neighbourhood that has grown up around **Hadrian's Villa** (*Villa Adriana*), an 180-acre spread that was nothing less than one man's personal World's Fair and the largest villa ever built in the entire Roman Empire; the Villa d'Este is a mere anthill in comparison (*the ACOTRAL bus from Rome leaves you a 20-min walk away at the Bivio Villa Adriana; local buses from Tivoli will take you much nearer the entrance; open daily 9–one hour before sunset, adm L8000.*)

To get some idea of the scale on which a 2nd-century AD emperor could build, stop first at the room-sized model of the villa near the entrance. Made entirely of marble and travertine, and about the same size as the monumental centre of Rome—the Imperial Fora included—Hadrian's dream 'house' clearly shows the excess that even the most intelligent and useful of emperors was capable of. Archaeologists have found features that would surprise even a Californian—a heated beach with steam pipes under the sand, and a network of subterranean service passages for horses and carts (a private Underground!). Other emperors used the villa until Constantine, unable to create anything as fine, plundered it to embellish Constantinople; invaders, builders, and lime burners gnawed at it until Pope Alexander VI began the first excavations. Yet despite the depredations many of the finest Roman statues in Europe's museums were discovered here.

Hadrian fancied himself as an architect, contributing to the Pantheon, the Temple of Venus and Rome, and the urban redevelopment of Ostia Antica; but unlike most dilettantes, he had the resources of the Roman empire at its peak at his disposal. Hadrian especially wanted to remember famous buildings he had seen on his travels, and helped design reproductions: the **Stoa Poikile** of Athens, near the entrance, a rectangular peristyle with a massive fish pond in the centre; the **Canopus**, or Temple of Serapis near Alexandria, complete with a canal reproducing the Nile and decorated with Egyptian statues (now mostly restored; a nearby **Museum** contains finds from the most recent excavations); the **Platonic Academy** in an ancient olive grove, with an Odeion, a round Temple of Apollo, and beyond this, the entrance to an underground rectilinear hell, or **Hades**. Baths, libraries, an imperial palace, nymphaeums, temples, Praetorian barracks, and a reproduction of the Valle di Tempe with a Greek theatre are among the other buildings discovered in the ongoing excavations. But the most charming corner of the complex is the so-called **Naval Theatre**, actually a little circular palace on an island in an artificial lagoon, attainable only by a retractable bridge on rollers; it may have been Hadrian's private retreat, where he could escape the cares of empire to write poetry and paint.

Up the Aniene Valley to Subiaco

The scenery on this trip is especially pretty, varied and wooded and dotted with unspoiled hill towns. It ends at the ancient monasteries of Subiaco, where St Benedict became the father of Christian monasticism.

Getting There/Lunch

Although the Aniene valley is easiest reached by car, ACOTRAL buses from Ⓜ Rebibbia (metro line B) go to Vicovaro, Licenza, Antícoli Corrado, and Subiaco as well. The quiet groves and fields along the route beg for a picnic, your best option for lunch.

One of the first tempting stops in the valley is **Vicovaro** (46 km east of Rome), noted for its little octagonal Renaissance **Tempietto di San Giacomo** (1450), a work by two Dalmatian architects, Domenico da Capodistria and Giovanni Dalmata, who designed the charming porch. Just beyond Vicovaro, a road turns left up a lovely valley towards Licenza for **Horace's Sabine farm** (always open; tip the custodian. Bus riders should ask the driver to stop at the unpaved lane leading to the *Villa d'Orazio*).

No farm has ever enjoyed as many poetic musings as the country estate Maecenas gave to Horace in 33 BC, which was all the poet asked for in the world: 'a portion of land, not so big, a garden and near the house a spring of never-failing water, and a little wood beyond. The gods have done more and better. It is well. I ask no more.' The spring still flows; the lovely mosaics, pavements, garden swimming pool, and some of the lead pipes and the pretty surroundings survive to complete Horace's picture of an idyllic retreat. The custodian of the site has a roomful of small finds from the excavations; the more interesting items are in the little Antiquarium *(open 9–4)* 8 km up the road in the castle of **Licenza**, one of Lazio's handsomest hilltowns.

Most of the hilltowns in the Aniene valley have escaped the worst of modern tourism, like lovely **Antícoli Corrado** on its steep cliff, famous for producing the most beautiful artists' models in Rome. The town has had an art colony of its own for almost two hundred years, whose works fill the town museum. Recently discovered frescoes by their predecessors in the 1100s may be seen in the well-preserved church of **San Pietro**, in the piazza with a fountain of Noah's Ark. Another striking town, **Saracinesco**, was founded on a crag by Saracen raiders in the 9th century; the present townspeople are their direct descendants.

Few towns, however, can claim as glorious a past as **Subiaco**, 74 km from Rome at the head of the Aniene valley, where in the troubled late 5th century St Benedict retired here, wrote his *Rule* and set Christian monasticism on its way. All through the dark centuries his monasteries provided a haven for learning and piety, and retained so much standing in the 1460s that the first printing press in Italy was brought here by two monks from Germany.

Originally Subiaco had 12 monasteries; those not destroyed by the Lombards fell to earthquakes and the worldly ambition of the monks. Today there are but two, 2.5 km above town, reached by road or footpath, both passing by way of the dismal remains of Nero's once grand Sublaqueum villa and his dried-out artificial lake. The first monastery, the **Convento di Santa Scholastica** (Benedict's twin sister) is shown daily *(9–12.30 and 4–7; free, closed during Sun mass, 10–11.30)*. A feudal abbey in the Middle Ages, and later ruled by princely abbots of Rome's noblest families, S. Scholastica remains a holy bulwark of the faith, guarded by a stout Romanesque campanile. It has three cloisters, the first that you come to built in 1580, incorporating columns from Nero's villa; the second, an early Gothic cloister of 1052; the third, beautifully decorated in the 13th-century by the Cosmatis. The library contains the first two books printed in Italy. Apparently the Germans and their newfangled contraption upset the monastery's scribes, and after printing these two tomes they went off in a huff to Rome.

Further up is the **Convento di San Benedetto**, or Sacro Speco, named for the cavern to which St Benedict retired as a hermit and attracted his first disciples *(open daily 9–12.30 and 3–6; free)*. Partly natural, and partly built into the mountain side, the monastery includes an a 14th-century **Upper Church** with fine Sienese frescoes and a 13th-century **Lower Church**, built on several levels to incorporate the St Benedict's Holy Grotto, now lined with marble from Nero's villa. The frescoes illustrating the saint's life are by a Master Consulus, a 13th-century painter. In 1210, an anonymous monk painted the *Portrait of St Francis* upstairs in the Chapel of St Gregory, believed to be the first live portrait done in Italy since Roman times. Don't miss the 15th-century frescoes of deathly Death along the Scala Santa, leading to the Shepherd's Grotto, this containing a rare fresco from the 700s. From here you can see what was an ancient bramble where Benedict had lain to mortify his flesh, but which turned into a rose tree at the gentler touch of St Francis.

Nearby, at the bottom of the gorge of the Aniene, there's a beautiful little lake with a waterfall; it may have been one of the three mentioned by Tacitus in connection with Nero's villa. Just outside Subiaco town, the church of **San Francesco** contains frescoes attributed to Pinturicchio, Sodoma, and Sebastiano del Piombo, and on the altar a triptych undoubtedly by Antoniazzo Romano, who knew enough to sign his work.

Zagarolo and Palestrina

Zagarolo is an attractive, wine-producing town; Palestrina, like Tivoli, was an ancient rival of Rome, and preserves fascinating remains of the ancient Temple of Fortune, mother of the gods; Agnani, further afield and seldom visited by tourists, retains the memory of an historic slap.

Getting There

ACOTRAL buses from Ⓜ Anagnina (metro line A) to both towns. Take the bus so you can doze through the gruesome eastern suburbs that go on endlessly along Via Casilina.

Lunch

In Palestrina lunch can be anything from a slice of pizza or a picnic in the city park, to a plate of homemade fettuccine at the **Stella**, an old favourite (Piazza della Liberazione 3, L30,000). One advantage to driving, however, is that you can detour south 9 km to Làbico for lunch in one of Lazio's top restaurants: the **Vecchia Osteria**, Via Casilina km 38.3, where regional specialities become sublime (*reserve:* © *951 0032, L80,000; closed Sun eve and Mon*).

Zaragola

The beginning of this excursion couldn't be less auspicious. Lost in the sprawl as you leave Rome is the tomb of St Helena, mother of Constantine, called the **Tor Pignattara**, built in 330, and further on, the dried-up site of **Lake Regillus**, near Pantano Borghese, where Castor and Pollux helped the Romans defeat the Latins in 496 BC (see the Roman Forum). Beyond these forlorn memories of the past, the scenery perks up with woodlands and vineyards around **Zagarolo**, a half medieval, half Baroque town of churches, theatrical squares and palaces, and a thoroughly strange gate, the **Porta di S. Martino**, decorated with reliefs of armour in curling ribbons. The 13th–18th-century **Palazzo Rospigliosi** has frescoes by the Zuccari and period furnishings (*open for tours on request;* © *475 4344*).

Palestrina

Another 5 km leads up to **Palestrina**, ancient *Praeneste*, the birthplace of the composer Giovanni Pierluigi da Palestrina (1524–94) who invented the polyphonic mass in the nick of time, just when the Council of Trent was about to ban church music altogether, with its melodies straight from popular love songs and the tavern. But Praeneste was on the map long before there was such a thing as a church. One of the oldest Latin towns, traditionally founded by Telegonus, son of Odysseus and Circe, it predates Rome and long battled the upstart on the Tiber before making an alliance, rebelling, submitting, etc. But it had something even Rome couldn't match—the greatest Hellenistic temple in Italy, dedicated to Fortune, the mother of gods: the **Sanctuary of Fortuna Primigenia**. When Palestrina was bombed in the war, it revealed that the sanctuary was as large as the entire modern town. Like many ancient temples, it was built into the side of a hill, neatly combining nature with architecture—though here on a scale previously unheard of. No one is sure when it was built, but in 80 BC it was partially burned during the Social Wars, and rebuilt by Sulla; it was revolutionary in its use of the Roman's special, high-silica concrete that would later top the Pantheon and vault a hundred baths.

Remains of the ancient sanctuary stretch from the bottom to the top of Palestrina in a series of wide, artificial terraces. Along Via degli Arcioni, you can see the first level of arches that supported the town core; from the ACOTRAL bus stop, near the top of Via degli Arconi, a road curves up to the 17th-century **Porta del Sole** and the remains of *Praeneste*'s cyclopean polygonal walls. Continue up to Via Anicia and turn left for Piazza Regina Margherita, on the terrace of the ancient Forum. Like squares in Rome, it has a certain spontaneous cubism, embellished with a pizza shop, a statue of Giovanni Pierluigi, a section of the ancient road and steps, and the unique, brick collage façade of the **Cathedral**, built in the 5th century on the foundations of an ancient temple, perhaps dedicated to Jupiter. The nave is lined with a frieze of portraits of Palestrina's cardinals; in the left aisle is a copy of the *Palestrina Pietà*, sometimes attributed to Michelangelo (the original was carted off to Florence).

Adjacent to the cathedral are Corinthian columns embedded like fossils in the side of the former Seminary. This was built around *Praeneste*'s sacred area and at the time of writing is closed to the public (though you can try asking at the tourist office in Piazza S. Maria degli Angeli). Within is the so-called **Apsidal Hall** (perhaps a temple of Isis) where the famous Barberini mosaic was discovered (see below); the **Aerarium**, or treasury, containing the remains of an obelisk, busts, and votive offerings; and the **Antro delle Sorti**, formerly believed to be the home of the oracle, and now thought to be the temple of Serapis, decorated with a beautiful mosaic of Alexandria.

Above rise the great steps of terraces leading to the main sanctuary of Fortune. To get there, continue up the steep streets and stairways to the top of Palestrina—if you're driving, begin with Via delle Monache from Piazza S. Maria degli Angeli and zigzag up to Piazza della Cortina. This, the highest terrace, was once the courtyard of the sanctuary's theatre; the cavea of seats was restored in 1640 to form the steps of the Palazzo Colonna-Barberini, built around the highest temple in the sanctuary. It now houses the **Museo Nazionale Archeologico Prenestino** (*open daily 9–3.30—later in summer, tel 953 8100 for details—L6000, which includes access to the excavations.*)

The museum contains a model of the sanctuary, a fine bas-relief of a triumph with a slave whispering in the *triumphator*'s ear, pine cone-shaped tombstones, eroded busts, the *cistae*, or bronze vanity cases with etched pictures (a local speciality) and most splendiferous of all, on the top floor, the exquisite **Barberini mosaic of the Nile**, a brilliantly coloured Hellenistic masterpiece of the 2nd century BC, showing the Nile in flood, with all of Egypt's flora and fauna on islands in the stream, a lovers' banquet, a religious procession, the Canopus of Alexandria, obelisks, a towered city, etc.

Opposite the museum is the excavated area of the sanctuary; from the large rectangular courtyard steps descend to a colonnaded terrace, and then down again to the **Terrazza degli Emicicli**, or hemicycles, lined with Doric columns high up on a huge wall and the famous oracle of Fortune in the centre. This was the heart of the sanctuary, where the Sibyl of Palestrina responded to queries with *sorti*, or small wooden lots with letters carved in them, some of which were discovered in a well. From here there is a splendid view reaching to the sea, and it is said that in ancient times—until the temple was disbanded in the 4th century—that two fires would be lit every night from here as beacons for sailors.

To the left of the museum is the pretty little church of **Santa Rosalia** (1660), and beyond it, on the road up to Palestrina's citadel, the ruined **Castel S. Pietro** (3.5 km), once the property of the Colonna. Pietro da Cortona made the altarpiece in its little church, but the magnificent view steals the show.

East of Palestrina and the Castelli Romani, towards Frosinone, is the humble corner of Lazio known as the **Ciociaria**, after the *ciocie*, or bark sandals, worn by the countrymen not so long ago when this was one of the backwaters of Italy. As they were the first outsiders to come to the new capital of Italy seeking work, Romans tend to call all new arrivals *Ciociari*—and rarely in a flattering vein.

From Palestrina Via Casilina leads out to **Anagni**, which as small as it is, held centre stage in European politics on several occasions during the Middle Ages. Four 14th-century popes were born here, and several others made it their summer home. Greatest among them was Boniface VIII, a nasty intriguer who had the poor timing to loudly proclaim the temporal supremacy of the popes long before anyone took the idea seriously. Captured in Anagni by the Colonna family and the King of France, Boniface received a resounding slap across the face from Sciarra Colonna—the famous 'slap of Anagni', putting a temporary end to papal dreams of world domination. Parts of Boniface's palace may still be seen, along with the stout and squarish **Cathedral**, one of the finest in central Italy, sharing a little of the genius of Tuscan and Apulian churches of the same period. Outside, it is 11th-century Romanesque; a rebuilding in the 1300s left it tentatively Gothic within. There is a Cosmatesque pavement and a wonderful 13th-century stone baldachin over the altar. Be sure to see the crypt, with blue and gold Byzantine frescoes from the 1200s that are among the best of their kind in Italy. Take time for a walk around Anagni, a medieval time-capsule with its walls, towers, and palaces like the **Casa Barnekow** that have changed little in 600 years.

Castelli Romani

'Extinction' may be one of the dirtiest words of the 20th century, but with volcanoes it usually translates into lovely scenery, romantic lakes, and fertile soil for vines. Such are the charms of the Alban Hills, the ruins of a horseshoe-shaped crater 60 km round just south of Rome. But Rome was still a twinkle in Mars' eye when the ancient Latins found these hills a convivial place to settle, and their villages, the foundations of the small towns called the Castelli Romani, grew to become some of the strongest members of the Latin League. Since being pounded into submission 2200 years ago, their role has been reduced to that of providing the capital with wine, flowers, and a pleasant place to spend summer weekends. Heavy bombing in 1944 during the battle for Rome wrecked many fine old churches, villas, and artworks in the Castelli, and though the damage has been repaired, much is new; some of the nearer Castelli are becoming strangled in Rome's suburban tentacles. Still, the countryside, especially around Lake Nemi, is beautiful. Another attraction are the numerous old-fashioned wine cellars; so old that one in Marino, along the lake road, was formerly used as an underground Mithraeum, and has a fine fresco of the god inside.

The ruins and gardens of Ninfa, one of the most enchanting places near Rome, can only be seen by booking ahead on weekends (see below).

Getting There

All the Castelli and Cori can be reached by ACOTRAL bus, from the depot at the Anagnina Metropolitana A station; there's also a little train to Frascati departing from Termini station. While connections between the towns are frequent, the links are not always convenient; with a car you can easily see the highlights in a day.

Lunch

There is no lack of places to eat and drink: aim for **La Nuova Tavernetta**, high up in Rocca Priora (Via Roma 37, with beautiful pasta and beautiful views; *open daily* L60–80,000); or **La Torre** in Marino (Via M. Montecchi, tasty home cooking; *closed Mon*, L45,000). **Al Fico Nuovo**, one of a score of eateries in Grottaferrata, is owned by Claudio Ciocca, whose face you may recognize from a score of Fellini films; good fish and other dishes from other corners of Italy (outdoors in summer, Via Anagnina 86, *closed Wed*, L40,000). Or near Lake Nemi, in Genzano di Roma, **Il Castagnone**, Via Nemorense 13, in a pretty setting, well known for its many tasty, and many varied pasta dishes (L60,000, *open daily*).

Frascati

Frascati, the nearest of the Castelli (21 km, on Via Tuscolana) and one of the most visited, was a medieval replacement for the ancient Etruscan and Latin city of Tusculum, which whipped the Romans in 1167, and was destroyed in a vendetta in 1191. Ancient Tusculum was famous for its magnificent villas, most famously Cicero's, and Frascati inherited the tradition on its refreshing hillside.

Unfortunately Field Marshal Kesselring made it his headquarters, and 80 per cent of the town was destroyed in the bombing to squeeze him out. Still famous for its white wine, Frascati is mostly visited for its two parks: the magnificent 17th-century **Villa Aldobrandini**, also known for its views over Rome (*open 9–1, closed Mon. Free tickets from the tourist office in the main square, Piazza G. Marconi, open Mon–Fri 9–1 and 3.30–6.40, Sat 9–1, closed Sun*), and the shady **Villa-Torlonia**, once part of a 16th-century estate, notable for its grand derelict fountain by Carlo Maderno called the Theatre of Waters. In the centre of Frascati, Piazza San Pietro has a pretty fountain and cathedral much-restored after the bombing; and beyond the fountain, the church of the **Gesù** designed by Pietro da Cortona, decorated with frescoed 'perspectives' by Antonio Colli.

Tusculum, Frascati's predecessor and fief of Senatrix Theodora, whose family ran Rome for two centuries, lies 5 km east, on a minor road from Villa Aldobrandini. Its brutal 1197 sack by the Romans was the medieval equivalent of a saturation bombing, but you can still pick out the ruins of the 'Villa of Cicero' and have a picnic in the well-preserved theatre. Climb up to the former citadel (760 m) for one of the finest views over the Alban Hills.

Grottaferrata and Marino

Grottaferrata, another Castelli town only 3 km south of Frascati, was built around an 11th-century abbey, the well-fortified Basilian **Abbazia di Grottaferrata**, founded by SS. Nilus and Bartholomew and still home to a congregation of Greek Catholic monks (*open daily except Mon, 8.30–12 and 4.30–6; free, and shown by a monk; offering*). The monastery's museum contains some beautiful classical sculpture, as well as frescoes, vestments, and icons, all with a Greek touch. The abbey church of **Santa Maria**, consecrated in 1025, has a colourful 12th-century campanile and a wonderfully carved marble portal of the same period, topped by a Byzantine mosaic. In the **Chapel of St Nilus**, Domenichino painted what fans claim are his best frescoes, on the lives of the abbey's founders.

Another 6 km will take you to **Marino**, like Frascati a famous wine town that suffered seriously during the war. Marino's topers are devoted to the local stuff; on any sleepy afternoon the old-fashioned wine shops will be the only establishments open. The liveliest time to visit is the first Sunday in October, when the town's fountains flow with last year's vintage in its merry *Sagra dell'Uva*. One of these, the **Fountain of the Four Moors** in Piazza Lepanto, commemorates the many natives who fought in the Battle of Lepanto—a Turkish shield taken as a trophy still hangs in the church of San Barnaba.

Lake Albano and Monte Cavo

From Marino you can continue along the panoramic **Via dei Laghi** (SS 217) which overlooks the elliptical **Lake Albano**. Romans, whose taste for vicarious battles followed them even on holiday, used to come to watch mock sea fights from their lakeside villas; now they prefer trout fishing. Beyond the lake there's a turn-off for **Rocca di Papa**, a dramatically sited town, with a picturesque medieval citadel named the *Quartiere dei Bavaresi* after the Bavarian troops of Emperor Ludwig stationed here in the 1320s. A private toll road leads up from Rocca di Papa to the second highest of the Alban Hills, **Monte Cavo** (948 m; or you can walk up from town).

Monte Cavo, the ancient *Mons Albanus*, was the sacred mountain of the Latin tribes. Aeneas' son Anchises founded Alba Longa, their most ancient city and political centre nearby at Castel Gandolfo (see below), while at the summit was the sanctuary of Latian Jupiter, the cult centre of all Latium. Sir James Frazer writes how one of the ancient kings of Alba Longa considered himself the equal of Jupiter, inventing machines that mimicked thunder and lightning, banging and sparking enough to drown out the real storm. Jupiter did not take kindly to the competition and blasted the impudent king with a tremendous thunderbolt, followed by a cloudburst that drowned his very palace under the waters of Lake Albano, traces of which, legend says, are visible when the water is low.

Despite this setback, Mons Albanus remained the political and religious centre of the Latin League until the Romans *did* steal Jupiter's thunder by building him a superior temple on the Capitol. But the importance of his first sanctuary was never forgotten, and it became the practice for any conquering hero whose victories weren't momentous enough for the Forum to be given a second-class triumph here, along Mt Cavo's Via Triumphalis. The footpath from the upper reaches of Rocca di Papa follows its route beyond the **Campi d'Annibale**, the hollow of an ancient crater, where Hannibal and his elephants are said to have camped, to the top where there are fabulous views in all directions. No trace of the temple of Jupiter Latiaris has ever been discovered here; as god of sky, thunder, and oaks he was apparently worshipped outdoors in a sacred grove. Tarquin the Proud built a wall to define the sacred precinct, and when Cardinal Henry, Duke of York, built a Passionist monastery here (since converted into a hotel) he reused some of its blocks. Where the ancient pagans and not so ancient Passionist fathers worshipped, there is now a television transmitter.

Lake Nemi

Next along the Via dei Laghi is **Nemi**, a picturesque little village wrapped around its 9th-century castle, famous for its June strawberry festival. From here (or from **Genzano**; see below), you can go down to the magical 'Mirror of Diana', the round, deep, blue **Lake Nemi**, its still waters encompassed by dripping forests and plastic-coated strawberry farms. As it descends, the road passes the meagre ruins of the **Temple of Diana Nemorensis**, the celebrated sanctuary of Diana of the woodlands, in whose forest, known as the grove of Aricia, were held the barbaric rites that inspired Sir James Frazer's monumental *The Golden Bough*, the foundation of modern anthropology. Within this sanctuary grew an oak forest, guarded by a priest known as King of the Wood, a former runaway slave who had become Diana's priest by plucking a sprig of mistletoe from the trees, which gave him the right to fight and slay the former king. And so, even into the days of Hadrian, the next king would be made by slaying the former. Ancient authorities linked the mistletoe to the golden bough plucked by Aeneas before his descent into the underworld.

Caligula took a special interest in the cult, so much so that when he tired of one king he purposefully set a runaway slave to kill him. He had two magnificent ships constructed to ferry visitors across the lake to the temple (and entertain with his notorious perversities on the way). These ships were sunk during the time of Claudius, and although they were discovered in 1446 by Leon Battista Alberti, they remained in a remarkable state of preservation at the bottom of the lake until 1932, when Mussolini had them brought up. It's a shame that they didn't stay there a little longer, for as a last act of gratuitous chagrin the retreating Germans set fire to the lakeshore **Nemi Museum of Roman Ships** (*daily 9–12, L2000*) and burnt them to cinders. The museum has since been reconstructed, with bronze figurines and bits salvaged from the fire, and models one fifth the size of the originals; ask in the village if it's been reopened.

Across Lake Nemi from Nemi is the larger town of **Genzano di Roma**, overlooking the Via Appia; it is best known for the *Infiorata* on the Sunday after Corpus Domini, when the streets are covered with patterns made from over 8,000 lbs of flower petals.

Viaducts Up the Via Appia

From here the Via Appia crosses a series of viaducts on it way to Rome, passing by way of **Aríccia**, a pretty village immersed in trees, with summer villas. It boasts several minor works by Bernini, who was employed by the Chigi to beautify the village, beginning with the unexciting **S. Maria di Galloro** on the edge of the town. Within Aríccia, he restored the medievalesque **Palazzo Chigi**, set in a gorgeous park, while his round, domed **Santa Maria dell'Assunzione** resembles the nipple of a baby's bottle with porticoes and two bell towers.

The biggest viaduct of all, the three-tiered Ponte di Aríccia, passes on the left the striking truncated cones of the so-called **Tomb of the Horatii and Curiatii**, built in the Etruscan style. Roman legend has it that three Roman Horatii and three

Latin Curatii fought in single combat to end the war between Alba Longa (see above) and Rome during the reign of Tullus Hostilius; but Alba Longa's tyrant proved deceitful, resulting in its total destruction by the Romans.

Alba Longa's name lingers, however, in **Albano Laziale**, the next important town up the Via Appia. But spoilsport historians insist it wasn't founded until Septimius Severus created a large permanent camp for the 2nd Legion here, called *Castra Albano*, ostensibly to defend the Via Appia but perhaps more to impress travellers and get the troops out of Rome. The modern town, shaped like a wedge on the slope of Monte Cavo's crater, just about fills the space of the legion's huge camp. Along the main Corso Matteotti, the church of **San Pietro** was built over the camp's baths in the 6th century and has a fine Romanesque campanile. On the next street up, Via Don Minzoni, you can see the mighty ruins of the **Porta Praetoria**, the camp's principal gate, rediscovered after a bomb fell on the surrounding buildings. Via Saffi continues up, past **S. Maria della Rotonda** (on the left), an unusual circular medieval church built over a nymphaeum of Domitian; inside there's a pulpit of Cosmati work on an ancient column. At Via Saffi 100 is a perfectly preserved underground reservoir, or **Cisternone**, carved into the living rock to supply the troops, and still used today to hold Albano's water. Ruins of the **Amphitheatre** lie behind the church in genteelly dilapidated Piazza San Paolo. From the very top of the hill, you can see Lake Albano shimmering far below.

Castel Gandolfo

The prettiest route from Albano to **Castel Gandolfo** is the upper of Urban VIII's two roads, called the **Galleria di Sopra**, or upper tunnel, for its roof of interwoven ilex branches—the lower 'tunnel', the **Galleria di Sotto** is the busy main road. The Upper Road begins above Albano's Piazza San Paolo and follows the rim of Mt Cavo's crater, with views of the lake and the surrounding country. Castel Gandolfo itself is a happy little village, perched 1400 ft above Lake Albano, and famous as the Vatican enclave where the pope spends the dog days of summer. The discovery of an Iron Age necropolis used from the 9th–7th centuries BC strengthens Castel Gandolfo's claim that it was the site of Alba Longa. Interestingly, the graves were found coated with a thin layer of lava, supporting the old, discredited legend that volcanic eruptions forced the early inhabitants down from these hills to Rome. Finds from the cemetery are in EUR's Museo Preistorico.

Castel Gandolfo is named for the Gandolfi family of Genoa, who built a castle here in the 12th century. The **Papal Palace** was constructed on its ruins by Carlo Maderno in 1624, and was much remodelled by Pius IX. To attend the Pope's general audience on Wednesdays at 11 am you need tickets from the Vatican (see Vatican info, p. 24), though on Sundays at noon John Paul II appears to give a homily to the crowd in the palace courtyard. The other thing to do in Castel Gandolfo is walk down the track below the rail station to the cave entrance of the **Emissarium,** a tunnel nearly 1½ km long, carved in the living rock by the Romans in 397 BC. At the time the war with Veii seemed endless, and they asked an oracle what it took to win. 'Drain the lake,' came the reply, and so they did in their literal Roman way. They did the job well; the Emissarium is still used to control the level of the lake.

Velletri and Ninfa

If you really want to escape Rome and its bedroom townlets, continue south instead of north along the Via Appia from Genzano to **Velletri**, an ancient Volscian town that has grown to become the largest of the Castelli (*40 km from Rome, the last ACOTRAL stop*). Although bombed to smithereens in the war, its landmark **Torre del Trivio**, a leaning 45 m needle-like campanile from 1353, has been restored. The communal museum contains a collection of Volscian sarcophagi, while the crazy quilt of a **Cathedral**, built over a Roman basilica, has artworks from the Cosmati to the hapless 1950s, with nearly every style in between. Under the portico is the entrance to a small **museum**, with Madonnas by Gentile da Fabriano and Antoniazzo Romano and a fairy tale Byzantine reliquary from the 12th century.

With a car you can press on further, into the Monte Lepini and some charming old hill towns well off the beaten track. **Cori**, like Rome and so many other Latin towns, likes to trace its founding to Trojan refugees. It may well be 3000 years old; that, at least, is the date archaeologists assign to its 'cyclopean' walls, built of huge, neatly fitted polygonal chunks of rock, still visible in many places. There are also many Roman ruins, including an intact bridge and the **Temple of Hercules** (really a temple of Jupiter), a small Doric building complete except for its roof.

Three interesting towns beginning with 'N' lie 10 km further south, especially **Ninfa**, a 'Medieval Pompeii' abandoned in the 17th century because of malaria. A great many of the buildings survive in an exceptionally romantic setting of small streams and lakes, overgrown with wildflowers and trees that now form part of the **Caetani Botanical Gardens** (*open 9–12 and 2.30–6 on the first Sat and Sun of each month, from April to Oct; adm L6000; make reservations through the Amministrazione Caetani, Via delle Botteghe Oscure 32, Rome, © 689 6522 after 7 pm*). **Norma,** built on the edges of a steep, curving cliff, seems almost like a city hanging in the air. Nearby are more cyclopean walls around the ruins of **Norba**, once capital of Rome's bitter enemies, the Volscians. It was besieged and destroyed by the legions in the Social Wars in 89 BC, never to be rebuilt.

> *... nowhere else has the creative power of Fascism left a deeper mark. The immense works can be summed up in the lapidary phrase of Il Duce: 'You redeem the land, you found some cities.'*
>
> *– From a 1939 Italian guidebook*

From the Castelli Romani, the Via Appia continues south into a region you wouldn't have travelled 60 years ago, when the broad plain of the **Pontine Marshes**, or Agro Pontino, was the biggest no man's land in Italy, wracked by malaria and healthy only for the water buffalo. Julius Cæsar was the first to plan its drainage, but the design died with him. Augustus later dug a ditch along the Via Appia to reclaim the swamps, and canal barges helped to make the soles on many a traveller's caligae last a bit longer. In the Dark Ages the canals became blocked up when no one had the money to keep them cleared. Once again, during the 13th century, some of the marshes were drained, but a few centuries of papal rule had the area back to its pristine emptiness when Mussolini decided to make it one of the showpieces of his regime. Today, except for the small corner preserved as a park and wildlife refuge, the Pontine Marshes no longer exist, and brand-new towns like Aprília, Pomezia, Pontinia, and Sabaudia sit amidst miles of prosperous farms as curious monuments to the brighter side of fascism.

Getting There

This area is served by hourly ACOTRAL buses departing the Metro B station EUR Fermi; the trip takes a bit more than an hour; trains from Termini make the trip to Anzio and Nettuno in the same time.

Lunch

One reason to go is to eat fish: in Anzio try either **All'Antica Darsena** (L65,000, *closed Mon*) or **Da Alceste** (L75,000, *closed Wed*), both in Piazza Sant'Antonio, and both offering tasty fresh seafood. In Nettuno, you'll find the same speciality, at **Gambero Secondo**, Via della Liberazione 50 (L50,000, *closed Mon*).

Along N 148, **Pomezia** is just east of the site of ancient **Lavinium**, which readers of Virgil will recognize as the town founded by Aeneas and named for Lavinia, daughter of the local king Latinus who becomes the hero's wife at the end of the *Aeneid*. It was the custom of elected officials in Rome to make a sacrifice in Lavinium. Beyond that, nothing was known until the 1950s, when archaeologists studying aerial photos taken during the war noticed that the flora growing near the village of Prática di Mare had a different shade from its surroundings, a telltale sign of ancient ruins. Excavations over the past 30 years have revealed a row of

13 stone altars from the 6th–4th centuries BC and an even earlier, monumental tomb that may have been worshipped as Aeneas'. In 1977 some 100 life-size terracotta votive statues from the 5th–4th centuries BC were discovered under the wall of a temple of Minerva, apparently deposited in a pit in the 2nd century BC when a new temple was constructed. Many of the statues are of children carrying toys and pets, believed to have been left with the goddess while the real child passed to adulthood. Others are of Minerva, and one that has especially interested scholars, a 4th-century BC terracotta copy of the wooden Palladium, the statue of Athena that Aeneas was said to bring from Troy. This ended up as one of the Vestal Virgins' holiest of holies; its discovery in Lavinium suggests not only an early link between Greek and Latin cultures, but a mythic tradition much older than Virgil.

Between Pomezia and Aprília, is **Ardea**, the capital of King Turnus, Aeneas' rival for the hand of Lavinia. It is also a pilgrimage destination for admirers of one of Italy's best contemporary sculptors, Giacomo Manzù, who lives in a villa in town; the **Raccoltà Amici di Manzù** © 913 5022 (a branch of the National Museum of Modern Art) in the village displays over 400 works, including portraits of the sculptor's friend Pope John XXIII, his Swedish wife Inge, and his children, as well as sketches and jewellery (*open daily 9 am–7 pm, free*).

If you drive along the coast you'll find many boring beaches, and **Anzio**, the Antium of the ancient Volscians. Antium was one of the more uppity cities from Rome's point of view—here Coriolanus took refuge when banished from Rome in 491 BC; shortly after Antium was captured, then rebelled again, and in 338 BC was recaptured and humiliated by having all of its ships stripped of their beaks, or rostra, which were carted off to became the rostrums of the Roman Forum. Caligula and Nero are believed to have been born here, and the latter built a large seaside villa, traces of which may still be seen at the promontory of Arco Muto (where the Apollo Belvedere was discovered in 1510).

After that the town then fell out of history until January 1944, when British, American, and Polish troops found its beaches an ideal spot for a landing; that bloody but successful end run forced the Germans to abandon their Gustav Line and opened the way for the liberation of Rome. Not surprisingly, much of Anzio had to be rebuilt after the war, and British and Polish military cemeteries stretch from Anzio up to an ominiously named crossroads called Campo di Carne (Field of Flesh). The largest American military cemetery in Italy is near **Nettuno**, with 7862 graves near the beach head. A nearly solid 3 km of beach umbrellas and pizzerias link Anzio to Nettuno, though above the beacharama Nettuno has retained its moated **Castello**, built for Alexander VI, and a pretty medieval quarter, the **Borgo**. Anzio does it one better with summer hydrofoils to the beautiful crescent island of **Ponza**, Lazio's Capri, offering the possibility of a long day trip from Rome.

Acroterion: decorative elements along the roofline of a temple.

Aedicule: a decorative niche, often a free-standing structure dedicated to a god—the ancestors of modern Rome's street-corner shrines.

Ambo: a pulpit; in medieval churches they usually come in pairs (ambones). Rome's are often elaborately decorated by the artists of the Cosmati school.

Amoretti: cupids or cherubs—used heavily as decoration in Baroque period.

Amphitheatre: elliptical, open theatre, used for gladiatorial shows, *naumachiae* and animal slaughters. Long before the Colosseum, Rome invented the form with two wooden theatres, side by side, that could be rolled together for big spectacles.

Annona: ancient Rome's public grain distribution—the dole (the food shop in the Vatican is still called the *Annona*).

Atrium: entrance court of an ancient Roman house or early church.

Baldacchino: baldachin, a columned stone canopy over an altar.

Basilica: a rectangular building, usually divided into three aisles by rows of columns. In ancient Rome, this was the common form for law courts and other public buildings, and Roman Christians adopted it for their early churches.

Bucchero ware: a type of delicate black pottery, often with incised decoration; a favourite of the Etruscans.

Caldarium: the hot room of a Roman bath.

Campanile: a bell tower.

Cartoon: the preliminary sketch for a fresco or tapestry.

Cavea: the semicircle of seats in an ancient theatre.

Caryatid: a supporting column or pilaster carved into the draped figure of a woman (male ones are called *atlantes* or *telamones*).

Chiaroscuro: the arrangement or treatment of light and dark areas in a painting.

Glossary

Chthonic: referring to the underworld deities of classical religion.

Ciborium: a tabernacle; a construction on or behind an altar containing the sacramental host.

Clivus: Latin word for a street or alley on the slope of a hill.

Columbarium: a tomb, often underground, with niches in the walls for the dead.

Comune: any Italian unit of local Government, from the Comune di Roma down to the smallest village.

Confessio: a crypt beneath the high altar of a church, often containing relics of a saint.

Confraternity: a religious lay brotherhood, serving some specific charitable work.

Contrapposto: the dramatic, but rather unnatural twist in a statue, especially in a Mannerist or Baroque work, derived from ancient art.

Corbel: a stone or timber support projecting from a wall.

Cryptoporticus: any vaulted or colonnaded underground room or passage.

Cupola: a dome or rounded vault forming a roof or a ceiling.

Cyclopean Walls: fortifications built of enormous, irregular, polygonal blocks, without mortar, as in the pre-Roman cities of Latium.

Diaconicon: deaconry; one of the public welfare and supply centres, associated with various churches, set up by Pope Gregory the Great in the 590s.

Exedra: (It. *esedra*) a semicircular recess.

Ex-voto: an offering (a terracotta figurine, painting, medallion, silver bauble or whatever) made in thanksgiving to a god or Christian saint; the practice has always been present in Italy.

Frigidarium: cold room of a Roman bath.

Graffito: originally, incised decoration on buildings, walls, etc; only lately has the word come to mean casually-scribbled messages in public places.

Greek cross: in the floor plans of churches, a cross with equal arms. the more familiar plan, with one arm extended to form a nave, is called a *Latin cross*.

Grotesque: ancient decoration with carved or painted fanciful faces or forms, used by the Etruscans and Romans, and back in fashion during the Renaissance.

Horrea: a workshop or warehouse.

Insula: an ancient Roman multi-storey block of flats.

Intarsia: a mosaic or inlay work in wood or stone.

Loggia: an open-sided gallery or arcade.

Lunette: semicircular space on a wall, above a door or under vaulting, either filled by a window or by a mural painting.

Matroneum: the elevated women's gallery around the nave of a church. Segregating women at mass was a Byzantine practice that spread to Rome in the 6th and 7th centuries.

Meta: the turning posts at either end of a stadium or circus, often marked by an obelisk or other monument. Meta also meant a pyramidal tomb, like the one at Porta S. Paolo.

Mithraeum: temple of the god Mithras (see S. Clemente).

Narthex: the enclosed porch of a church.

Naumachia: a mock naval battle, like those staged in the Colosseum.

Nimbus: a halo; in some early Christian art, a square one denotes that the character portrayed was still living.

Nymphaeum: originally a temple of the nymphs, later, any decorative pavilion, well house or fountain, often with statues of nymphs or marine deities (an ancient Roman returning today would think the Trevi fountain some outlandish sort of nymphaeum).

Opus reticulatum: masonry with diamond-shaped blocks.

Opus sectile: stone inlay or tiling of coloured marble (ancient Roman *intarsia*).

Orders: architectural systems of proportion, based on the widths of a building's columns, ranging from the squat, plain Doric to the slender Ionic and the Romans' favourite, the even more delicate Corinthian. Codified by the classical writer Vitruvius, and rediscovered in the Renaissance.

Palazzo: not just a palace, but any large, important building (the word comes from Rome's *Palatium*).

Pendentives: four curved, triangular pieces, springing from four piers, that help support a dome or cupola.

Peristyle: a court surrounded by colonnades.

Pietra Dura: rich inlay work (in tables, etc.) using semi- precious stones.

Piscina: an artificial tank or reservoir used as a swimming pool or fishpond by the Romans; in a church, a basin set into the wall and used for washing communion vessels.

Pomerium: the sacred boundary of the ancient *urbs*, not necessarily corresponding to the walls. Within it, it was unlawful to bear arms or bury the dead.

Predella: smaller paintings on the panel below the main subject of a painted altarpiece, or the step or platform on which an altar is placed.

Presepio: a Christmas crib.

Putti: (or *Amoretti*) flocks of painted or plaster cupids or cherubs with rosy cheeks and bums, derived from ancient decoration, that infested much of Italy in the Baroque era.

Pulvin: a stone, often trapezoidal, that replaces or supports a capital. Seen in many of Rome's medieval cloisters.

Quadriga: chariot pulled by four horses (*biga*, two horses, *triga*, three).

Quattrocento: the 1400s, or 15th century, in the Italian way of referring to centuries (*trecento, quattrocento, cinquecento, seicento, settecento*, etc.).

Saepta: an open space for voting; often surrounded by columned porticos, like the Saepta Julia in the Campus Martius.

Sedia gestatoria: the litter used to carry a pope over the heads of the crowd, accompanied by lackeys with peacock-feather fans; John Paul II prefers his jeep.

Sinopia: the preliminary sketch for a fresco.

Spina: the centre wall of a circus track, lined with monuments.

Stele: a vertical funeral stone.

Telamon(es): a male figure used like a caryatid as a supporting column or pilaster.

Tenebroso: the contrast of darkness and illuminated subjects used with such effect by Caravaggio and his followers.

Tessera: one of the stone or glass cubes, or enamelled chips, used in mosaics.

Thermae: a bathhouse.

Titular cardinal: since early times, each cardinal, whether he resides in Rome or not, is the titular head of a Roman parish church, claiming the title and usually the honours belonging to the office, but without the associated duties.

Transenna: stone or metal screen separating the altar from the rest of an early church.

Triclinium: the main hall of a wealthy Roman's house, used for dining and entertaining. Also the three-seater couches on which they dined.

Triumphal arch: in churches, this means the arch in front of the apse, over the high altar. Often decorated with mosaics.

Trompe l'oeil: art that uses perspective effects to deceive the eye—for example, to create the illusion of depth on a flat surface, or to make columns and arches painted on a wall seem real.

Vicus: a modern *vico* is an alley, but in ancient times a *vicus* was the principal street of a quarter.

The fathers of modern Italian were Dante, Manzoni, and television. Each did its part in creating a national language from an infinity of regional and local dialects; the Florentine Dante, the first to write in the vernacular, did much to put the Tuscan dialect in the foreground of Italian literature. Manzoni's revolutionary novel, I promessi sposi, heightened national consciousness by using an everyday language all could understand in the 19th century. Television in the last few decades is performing an even more spectacular linguistic unification; although the majority of Italians still speak a dialect at home, school, and work, their TV idols insist on proper Italian.

Perhaps because they are so busy learning their own beautiful but grammatically complex language, Italians are not especially apt at learning others. English lessons, however, have been the rage for years, and at most hotels and restaurants there will be someone who speaks some English. In small towns and out-of-the-way places, finding an Anglophone may prove more difficult. The words and phrases below should help you out in most situations, but the ideal way to come to Italy is with some Italian under your belt; your visit will be richer, and you're much more likely to make some Italian friends

Italian words are pronounced phonetically. Every vowel and consonant is sounded. Consonants are the same as in English, except the c which, when followed by an 'e' or 'i', is pronounced like the English 'ch' (cinque thus becomes cheenquay). Italian g is also soft before 'i' or 'e' as in gira, or jee-ra. H is never sounded; z is pronounced like 'ts'. The consonants sc before the vowels 'i' or 'e' become like the English 'sh' as in sci, pronounced shee; ch is pronouced like a 'k' as in Chianti, kee-an-tee; gn as 'ny' in English (bagno, pronounced ban-yo); while gli is pronounced like the middle of the word million (Castiglione, pronounced Ca-stee-lyon-ay).

Vowel pronunciation is: a as in English father; e when unstressed is pronounced like 'a' in fate as in mele, when stressed can be the same or like the 'e' in pet (bello); i is like the i in machine; o like 'e', has two sounds, 'o' as in hope when unstressed (tacchino), and usually 'o' as in rock when stressed (morte); u is pronounced like the 'u' in June.

The accent usually (but not always!) falls on the penultimate syllable. In Rome the informal way of addressing someone as you, tu, is widely used; the more formal lei or voi is commonly used in provincial districts.

Language

Useful words and phrases

yes/no/maybe	si/no/forse
I don't know	Non lo so
I don't understand (Italian).	Non capisco (l'italiano).
Does someone here speak English?	C'è qualcuno qui che parli inglese?
Speak slowly	Parla lentamente
Could you assist me?	Mi potrebbe aiutare?
Help!	Aiuto!
Please	Per favore
Thank you (very much)	(Molte) grazie
You're welcome	Prego
It doesn't matter	Non importa
All right	Va bene
Excuse me	Scusi
Be careful!	Attenzione!
Nothing	Niente
It is urgent!	È urgente!
How are you?	Come sta?
Well, and you?	Bene, e lei?
What is your name?	Come si chiama?
Hello	Salve or ciao (both informal)
Good morning	Buongiorno (formal hello)
Good afternoon, evening	Buona sera (also formal hello)
Good night	Buona notte
Goodbye	Arrivederla (formal), arrivederci, ciao (informal)
What do you call this in Italian?	Come si chiama questo in italiano?
What?	Che?
Who?	Chi?
Where?	Dove?
When?	Quando?
Why?	Perchè?
How?	Come?
How much?	Quanto?
I am lost	Mi sono perso/a
I am hungry	Ho fame
I am thirsty	Ho sete
I am sorry	Mi dispiace
I am tired	Sono stanco/a
I am sleepy	Ho sonno
I am ill	Mi sento male
Leave me alone	Lasciami in pace
good	buono/bravo
bad	male/cattivo
It's all the same	Fa lo stesso
slow	piano
fast	rapido
big	grande
small	piccolo/a
hot	caldo/a
cold	freddo/a
up	su
down	giú
here	qui
there	lí

Shopping, service, sightseeing

I would like	Vorrei
Where is/are	Dov'é/Dove sono
How much is it?	Quanto viene questo?
open	aperto
closed	chiuso
cheap/expensive	a buon prezzo/caro
bank	banca
beach	spiaggia
bed	letto
church	chiesa
entrance	entrata
exit	uscita
hospital	ospedale
money	soldi
museum	museo
newspaper (foreign)	giornale (straniero)
pharmacy	farmacia
police station	commissariato
policeman	poliziotto
post office	ufficio postale
sea	mare
shop	negozio
telephone	telefono
tobacco shop	tabaccaio
WC	toilette/bagno
men	Signori/Uomini
women	Signore/Donne

Time

What time is it?	Che ore sono?
month	mese
week	settimana
day	giorno
morning	mattina
afternoon	pomeriggio
evening	sera
today	oggi
yesterday	ieri
tomorrow	domani
soon	presto
later	dopo, più tardi
It is too early	È troppo presto
It is too late	È troppo tardi

Days

Monday	lunedi
Tuesday	martedi
Wednesday	mercoledi
Thursday	giovedi
Friday	venerdi
Saturday	sabato
Sunday	domenica

Numbers

one	uno/una
two	due
three	tre
four	quattro
five	cinque

six	sei
seven	sette
eight	otto
nine	nove
ten	dieci
eleven	undici
twelve	dodici
thirteen	tredici
fourteen	quattordici
fifteen	quindici
sixteen	seidici
seventeen	diciassette
eighteen	diciotto
nineteen	diciannove
twenty	venti
twenty-one	ventuno
twenty-two	ventidue
thirty	trenta
thirty-one	trentuno
forty	quaranta
fifty	cinquanta
sixty	sessanta
seventy	settanta
eighty	ottanta
ninety	novanta
hundred	cento
one hundred and one	cento uno
two hundred	duecento
thousand	mille
two thousand	duemila
million	milione
billion	miliardo

Transport

airport	aeroporto
bus stop	fermata
bus/coach	auto/pulmino
railway station	stazione ferroviaria
train	treno
track/platform	binario
port	porto
port station	stazione marittima
ship	nave
automobile	macchina
taxi	tassì
ticket	biglietto
customs	dogana
seat (reserved)	posto (prenotato)

Travel Directions

I want to go to	Desidero andare a
How can I get to?	Come posso andare a?
Do you stop at?	Ferma a?
Where is?	Dov'è?
How far is it to?	Quanto siamo lontani da?
When does the leave?	A che ora parte ?
What is the name of this station?	Come si chiama questa stazione?
When does the next leave?	Quando parte il prossimo?
From where does it leave?	Da dove parte?
How long does the trip take?	Quant'è lungo il viaggio?

How much is the fare?	Quant'è il biglietto?
Good trip!	Buon viaggio!
near	vicino
far	lontano
left	sinistra
right	destra
straight ahead	sempre dritto
forward	avanti
backward	indietro
north	nord/settentrionale
south	sud/mezzogiorno
east	est/oriente
west	ovest/occidente
around the corner	dietro l'angolo
crossroads	bivio
street/road	strada
square	piazza

Driving

car hire	noleggio macchina
motorbike/scooter	motocicletta/Vespa
bicycle	bicicletta
petrol/diesel	benzina/gasolio
garage	garage
This doesn't work	Questo non funziona
mechanic	meccanico
map/town plan	carta/piantina
Where is the road to?	Dov'è la strada per?
breakdown	guasto or panne
driver's licence	patente di guida
driver	guidatore
speed	velocità
danger	pericolo
parking	parcheggio
no parking	sosta vietata
narrow	stretto
bridge	ponte
toll	pedaggio
slow down	rallentare

Italian menu vocabulary

Antipasti
These before-meal treats can include almost anything; among the most common are:

Antipasto misto	mixed antipasto
Bruschetta	toast with garlic or tomatoes
Carciofi (sott'olio)	artichokes (in oil)
Crostini	liver paté on toast
Frutti di mare	seafood
Funghi (trifolati)	mushrooms (with anchovies, garlic, and lemon)
Gamberi al fagiolino	shrimp with white beans
Mozzarella (in carrozza)	buffalo cheese (fried with bread in batter)
Olive	olives
Prosciutto (con melone)	raw ham (with melon)
Salame	cured pork
Salsicce	dry sausage

Minestre e Pasta

These dishes are the principal typical, first courses (*primo*) served throughout Italy.

Agnolotti	filled pasta half circles
Cacciucco	spiced fish soup
Cannelloni	meat and cheese rolled in pasta tubes
Cappelletti	small ravioli, often in broth
Crespelle	crepes
Fettuccine	long strips of pasta
Frittata	omelette
Gnocchi	potato dumplings
Lasagne	sheets of pasta baked with meat and cheese sauce
Minestre di verdura	thick vegetable soup
Minestrone	soup with meat, vegetables, and pasta
Orecchiette	ear-shaped pasta, usually served with turnip greens
Panzerotti	ravioli filled with mozzarella, anchovies, and egg
Pappardelle alla lepre	pasta with hare sauce
Pasta e fagioli	soup with beans, bacon, and tomatoes
Pastina in brodo	tiny pasta in broth
Penne all'arrabbiata	quill-shaped pasta in hot spicy sauce
Polenta	cake or pudding of corn semolina, prepared with meat or tomato sauce
Risotto (alla Milanese)	Italian rice (with saffron and wine)
Spaghetti all'Amatriciana	with spicy sauce of salt pork, tomatoes, onions, and hot pepper
Spaghetti alla Bolognese	with ground meat, ham, mushrooms, etc.
Spaghetti alla carbonara	with bacon, eggs, and black pepper
Spaghetti al pomodoro	with tomato sauce
Spaghetti al sugo/ragu	with meat sauce
Spaghetti alle vongole	with clam sauce
Stracciatella broth	with eggs and cheese
Tagliatelle	flat egg noodles
Tortellini al pomodoro/panna/in brodo	pasta caps filled with meat and cheese, served with tomato sauce, cream, or in broth
Vermicelli	very thin spaghetti

Secondo

Carne

Second courses

Meat

Abbacchio	milk-fed lamb
Agnello	lamb
Animelle	sweetbreads
Anatra	duck
Arista	pork loin
Arrosto misto	mixed roast meats
Bistecca alla fiorentina	Florentine beef steak
Bocconcini	veal mixed with ham and cheese and fried
Bollito misto	stew of boiled meats
Braciola	pork chop
Brasato di manzo	braised meat with vegetables
Bresaola	dried raw meat similar to ham
Capretto	kid
Capriolo	roe deer
Carne di castrato/suino	mutton/pork
Carpaccio	thin slices of raw beef in piquant sauce
Casoeula	winter stew with pork and cabbage
Cervello (al burro nero)	brains (in black butter sauce)
Cervo	venison
Cinghiale	boar

Coniglio	rabbit
Cotoletta (alla Milanese/alla Bolognese)	veal cutlet (fried in breadcrumbs/with ham and cheese)
Fagiano	pheasant
Faraona (alla creta)	guinea fowl (in earthenware pot)
Fegato alla veneziana	liver and onions
Involtini	rolled slices of veal with filling
Lepre (in salmì)	hare (marinated in wine)
Lombo di maiale	pork loin
Lumache	snails
Maiale (al latte)	pork (cooked in milk)
Manzo beef	
Osso buco	braised veal knuckle with herbs
Pancetta	bacon
Perdice	partridge
Petto di pollo (alla fiorentina/bolognese/ sorpresa)	boned chicken breast (fried in butter/with ham and cheese/stuffed and deep fried)
Piccione	pigeon
Pizzaiola	beef steak with tomato and oregano sauce
Pollo (alla cacciatora/alla diavola/alla Marengo)	chicken (with tomatoes and mushrooms cooked in wine/grilled/ fried with tomatoes, garlic and wine)
Polpette	meatballs
Quaglie	quails
Rane	frogs
Rognoni	kidneys
Saltimbocca	veal scallop with prosciutto and sage, cooked in wine and butter
Scaloppine	thin slices of veal sautéed in butter
Spezzatino	pieces of beef or veal, usually stewed
Spiedino	meat on a skewer or stick
Stufato	beef braised in white wine with vegetables
Tacchino	turkey
Trippa	tripe
Uccelletti	small birds on a skewer
Vitello	veal

Pesce / Fish

Acciughe or Alici	anchovies
Anguilla	eel
Aragosta	lobster
Aringa	herring
Baccalà	dried cod
Bonito	small tuna
Branzino	sea bass
Calamari	squid
Cappe sante	scallops
Cefalo	grey mullet
Coda di rospo	angler fish
Cozze	mussels
Datteri di mare	razor (or date) mussels
Dentice	dentex
Dorato	gilt head
Fritto misto	mixed fish fry, with squid and shrimp
Gamberetti	shrimps
Gamberi (di fiume)	prawns (crayfish)
Granchio	crab
Insalata di mare	seafood salad
Lampreda	lamprey
Merluzzo	cod
Nasello	hake
Orata	bream

Ostriche	oysters
Pesce spada	swordfish
Polipi	octopus
Pesce azzuro	various types of small fish
Pesce San Pietro	John Dory
Rombo	turbot
Sarde	sardines
Seppie	cuttlefish
Sgombro	mackerel
Sogliola	sole
Squadro	monkfish
Tonno	tuna
Triglia	red mullet (rouget)
Trota	trout
Trota salmonata	salmon trout
Vongole	small clams
Zuppa di pesce	mixed fish in sauce or stew

Contorni / Side Dishes, Vegetables

Asparagi (alla fiorentina)	asparagus (with fried eggs)
Broccoli (calabrese, romana)	broccoli (green, spiral)
Carciofi (alla giudia)	artichokes (deep fried)
Cardi	cardoons, thistles
Carote	carrots
Cavolfiore	cauliflower
Cavolo	cabbage
Ceci	chickpeas
Cetriolo	cucumber
Cipolla	onion
Fagioli	white beans
Fagiolini	French (green) beans
Fave	fava beans
Finocchio	fennel
Funghi (porcini)	mushroom (boletus)
Insalata (mista, verde)	salad (mixed, green)
Lattuga	lettuce
Lenticchie	lentils
Melanzana (al forno)	aubergine/eggplant (filled and baked)
Mirtilli	bilberries
Patate (fritte)	potatoes (fried)
Peperoni	sweet peppers
Peperonata	stewed peppers, onions, etc. similar to ratatouille
Piselli (al prosciutto)	peas (with ham)
Pomodoro	tomatoes
Porri	leeks
Radicchio	red chicory
Radice	radishes
Rapa	turnip
Sedano	celery
Spinaci	spinach
Verdure	greens
Zucca	pumpkin
Zucchine	courgettes (zucchini)

Formaggio / Cheese

Bel Paese	a soft white cow's cheese
Cacio/Caciocavallo	pale yellow, often sharp cheese
Fontina	rich cow's milk cheese
Groviera	mild cheese

Gorgonzola	soft blue cheese
Parmigiano	Parmesan cheese
Pecorino	sharp sheep's cheese
Provolone	sharp, tangy cheese; dolce is more mild
Stracchino	soft white cheese
Frutta	(Fruit, nuts)
Albicocche	apricot
Ananas	pineapple
Arance	oranges
Banane	banana
Cachi	persimmon
Ciliegie	cherries
Cocomero	watermelon
Composta di frutta	stewed fruit
Dattero	date
Fichi	figs
Fragole (con panna)	strawberries (with cream)
Frutta di stagione	fruit in season
Lamponi	raspberries
Macedonia di frutta	fruit salad
Mandarino	tangerine
Melagrana	pomegranite
Mele	apples
Melone	melon
More	blackberries
Nespola	medlar fruit
Pera	pear
Pesca	peach
Pesca noce	tangerine
Pompelmo	grapefruit
Prugne/susina	plum
Uva	grapes

Dolci / Desserts

Amaretti	macaroons
Cannoli	crisp pastry tube filled with ricotta, cream or chocolate
Coppa gelato	assorted ice cream
Creme caramel	caramel topped custard
Crostata	fruit flan
Gelato (produzione propria)	ice cream (homemade)
Granita	flavoured ice, usually lemon or coffee
Monte Bianco	chestnut pudding with whipped cream
Panettone	sponge cake with candied fruit and raisins
Panforte	dense cake of chocolate, almonds, and preserved fruit
Saint Honoré	meringue cake
Semifreddo	refrigerated cake
Sorbetto	sherbet
Spumone	a soft ice cream
Tiramisù	cream, coffee, and chocolate dessert
Torrone	nougat
Torta	tart
Torta millefoglie	layered custard tart
Zabaglione	whipped eggs and Marsala wine, served hot
Zuppa inglese	trifle

Bevande / Beverage

Acqua minerale con/senza gas	mineral water with/without fizz
Aranciata	orange soda
Birra (alla spina)	beer (draught)
Caffè (freddo)	coffee (iced)

Cioccolato (con panna)	chocolate (with cream)
Gassosa	lemon-flavoured soda
Latte	milk
Limonata	lemon soda
Succo di frutta	fruit juice
Tè	tea
Vino (rosso, bianco, rosato)	wine (red, white, rosé

Cooking terms, miscellaneous

Aceto (balsamico)	vinegar (balsam)
Affumicato	smoked
Aglio	garlic
Alla brace	braised
Bicchiere	glass
Burro	butter
Caccia	game
Conto	bill
Costoletta/Cotoletta	chop
Coltello	knife
Cotto adagio	braised
Cucchaio	spoon
Filetto	fillet
Forchetta	fork
Forno	oven
Fritto	fried
Ghiaccio	ice
Griglia	grill
Limone	lemon
Magro	lean meat/or pasta without meat
Mandorle	almonds
Marmellata	jam
Menta	mint
Miele	honey
Mostarda	candied mustard sauce
Nocciole	hazelnut
Noce	walnut
Olio	oil
Pane (tostato)	bread (toasted)
Panini	sandwiches
Panna	fresh cream
Pepe	pepper
Peperoncini	hot chili peppers
Piatto	plate
Pinoli	pine nuts
Prezzemolo	parsley
Ripieno	stuffed
Rosmarino	rosemary
Sale	salt
Salmì	wine marinade
Salsa	sauce
Salvia	sage
Senape	mustard
Tartufi	truffles
Tazza	cup
Tavola	table
Tovagliolo	napkin
Tramezzini	finger sandwiches
Umido	cooked in sauce
Uovo	egg
Zucchero	sugar

Bloch, Raymond, *The Etruscans and The Origins of Rome* (Thames and Hudson, 1958, 1960). Light cast on mysterious subjects.

Chandlery, P.J., *Pilgrim Walks in Rome* (Manresa Press, 1908). The Jesuit mystery tour of all the relics and shrines.

Carcopino, *Jérôme, Daily Life in Ancient Rome* (Penguin, 1981). A thorough and lively account of Rome at the height of empire—guaranteed to evoke empathy from modern city dwellers.

Crawford, Frances Marion, *Ave Roma Immortalis* (Macmillan, 1902). A passionate, often royally purple conjuration of Rome's most evocative ghosts.

Gibbon, Edward, *The History of the Decline and Fall of the Roman Empire* (Penguin Abridged ed., though for the famous footnotes get the unabridged volumes). Virile barbarians and Romans slowly losing the knack—or was it really the lead in their water?

l'edicola

Further Reading

Goethe, *Italian Journey* (Penguin 1962, trans. by W.H. Auden and Elizabeth Mayer). Goethe spent most of his time in Rome—a unique view of the ex-pat and artsy set of 1768.

Grant, Michael, *History of Rome* (Faber and Faber 1979). A good modern account of events up to the fall of Rome.

Hamilton, Edith, *The Roman Way* (Norton, 1984). A charming look at the ancient Romans through the eyes of their own writers.

Hare, Augustus, and St. Clair Baddeley, *Walks in Rome* (George Allen 1903).

Henig, Martin, (ed.), *A Handbook of Roman Art* (Phaidon, 1983). A beautifully illustrated survey of the visual arts produced by Rome and its empire.

Hibbert, Christopher, *Rome: The Biography of a City* (Penguin 1987). An anecdotal survey from legendary times up to Mussolini.

Lees-Milne, James, *Roman Mornings,* (Collins 1956). A rather precious, detailed analysis of eight buildings in Rome.

Livy, *The Early History of Rome* (Penguin, 1960).

Llewellyn, Peter, *Rome in the Dark Ages* (Faber and Faber, 1971). In which Rome's most obscure centuries prove to be full of surprises, and not so dark after all.

Mitchell, Bonner, *Rome in the High Renaissance* (University of Oklahoma, 1973). A brief account of Rome in the times of Leo X.

Morton, H.V., *A Traveller in Rome* (Methuen, 1957). Highly readable personal view of the city; one of the classics.

Ogilvie, R.M., *Early Rome and the Etruscans* (Fontana 1976). On the birthpangs of Rome, 600 bc–390 bc.

Revel, Jean-François, *As For Italy* (Weidenfeld and Nicolson, 1959). Devastating critique of modern Italy, with a special slap for Rome, including a day in the life of a spoiled bourgeois princess.

Scherer, Margaret, *Marvels of Ancient Rome* (Phaidon, 1955). A look at the ruins, and how people since ancient times have looked at them; excellent photographs.

Suetonius, Gaius, *The Twelve Cæsars* (Penguin, 1957, trans. by Robert Graves). The sourcebook of scandal in the original Cæsar's Palace.

Vasari, Giorgio, *Lives of the Artists* (Penguin, 1985). Source book for tales of Michelangelo and his Renaissance rivals.

Wittkower, Rudolf, *Art and Architecture in Italy 1600–1750* (Penguin, 1982). Fun to read; a scholarly critic makes the Baroque understandable—and at times, almost lovable.

Yallop, David, *In God's Name* (Jonathan Cape, 1984). A harrowing account of Vatican intrigue and death of John Paul I.

Young, Norwood, *The Story of Rome* (J.M. Dent, 1901). Volume in the excellent Medieval Towns series.

Abbazia di Grottaferrata 426–7
Abbazia delle Tre Fontane 255, 335
Accademia di San Luca 190
Accademia dei Lincei 281
accommodation
hotels 353–64, other 364–6
longer residence 392–94
Achilleus, Saint 266
Acilii family 328
Acqua Claudia 143, 144, 243
Acqua Felice 224
Acqua Paola 283
Acqua Vergine 189, 195, 197, 210
Adrian I, Pope 59, 98
Adrian IV, Pope 60, 300
African Museum 212
Agapetus I, Pope 145
Agnes, Saint 160, 329
Agrippa, Cornelius 152, 168, 400
Agrippina (wife of Claudius) 142
air, arriving by 6–7
Air Force Museum 412
Alaric the Goth 58, 116, 118, 123
Alba Longa 50, 427, 429, 430
Albano, Lake 427
Albano Laziale 429
Alberic see John XI
Alberti, Leon Battista 82, 83, 428
Albornoz, Cardinal 414
Alexander IV, Pope: begins palace at Viterbo 415
Alexander VI, Pope 42, 62, 73
Bernini's elephant 151
Borgia Apartment 318–19
and Bregno 202
builds castello at Nettuno 433
builds S. Rocco 199
and Castel S. Angelo 306
excavates Hadrians' Villa 422
gift of gold 359
Orsini against 411
rebuilds Porta Settimiana 280
tomb 173
Alexander VII, Pope 158, 202, 203
Bernini's monument in St. Peter's 288
Alexander Severus 146

Alfonso XIII, King 172
Alfred, King 303
Algardi, Alessandro 78, 83, 95, 184, 214
monument of Leo XI in St. Peter's 288
park of V. Doria Pamphili 335
St. Leo relief in St. Peter's 288
Altar of the Nation (Vittoriano) 40, 64, 83, 84, 90
Altar to the Unknown God 130
Alunno see Niccolo
Ambrose, Saint 118
American church 223
American war cemetery 433
Ammannati, Bartolommeo 196, 198, 210, 283
Amulius 50
Anacletus II, Pope 60
Anagni 425
'slap of Anagni' 425
Ancus Martius 399
Andrea del Castagno 315
Andrea del Sarto 174, 214, 220
Angelico, Fra 151, 220, 318, 322
Anicii family 275
Aniene valley 420–2
Annia Regilla 264
Annona (e) 99, 399
Anterus, Pope 265
Antichi, Prospero 224
Anticoli Corrado 421
Antinous (favourite of Hadrian) 208, 311
antiques, buying 378–9
Antium (now Anzio) 432–33
Antonello da Messina 214
Antoninus Pius, Emperor 57, 188
Antonio da Viterbo 318
Anzio 432–33
Apollo Belvedere 312, 432
Apollodorus of Damascus 69, 110, 139, 152, 231
Apollonius of Athens 313
Appian Way see Via Appia Antica
Appius Claudius 260
Aqua see Acqua
Ara Pacis 70, 199
Arch of Augustus 121
Arch of Constantine 70, 130

Arch of Dolabella 143
Arch of Drusus 263
Arch of Gallienus 236
Arch of Janus 98
Arch of Marcus Aurelius 95
Arch of Septimius Severus 118
Arch of Titus 123
Arch of the Tolomei 275
Archiginnasio Romano 154
Arcus Argentarium 97
Ardea 432
Aretino, Pietro 321
Arezzo, Margaritone d' 322
Argentina theatre 167–8
Argiletum 117
Ariccia 429
Arnold of Brescia 60, 300
Arnolfo di Cambio 73
baldacchini 256, 276
tombs 92, 240
other works 95, 140, 235
Arp, Jan 210
Arpino, Cavaliere d' 76, 190, 296
art and architecture 67–80
Etruscan 68, see also Etruscans
ancient Rome 68–71
early Christian and medieval 71–3
Renaissance 73–5
Counter-Reformation era 75–7 Baroque 77–9
post-Baroque to present 79–80
glossary of terms 434–7
art, buying 378–9
Asylum 93
Attila the Hun 58, 288
auction houses 395
Auditorium of Maecenas 237
Augustine, Saint 118, 406
Augustus, Emperor: aqueduct 189
Ara Pacis 70, 199
birthday sundial 187
brings back obelisk of Ramses II 201
building works 101, 119, 121, 129, 249
drains Pontine Marshes 431
erects Golden Milestone 118
fear of lightning 31
home on Palatine 126, 128, 249

Index

Italic numbers indicate maps; bold numbers indicate main reference; churches are grouped together under 'C'.

mausoleum 199, 235
and Praetorian Guard 332
reign 56
uses sculpture as propaganda
70
Aula of Isis 129
Aurelian, Emperor 32, 110,
188, *see also* Aurelian
Walls
Aurelian Walls 57, 63, 253,
304, 332
gates 203, 252, 263, 280,
329
Muro Torto section 208
Museum of the Walls 263
Aventine hill 248–9
'Aventine Secession' 54, 248

baby-sitting agencies 395
Babylonian Captivity 73, 151,
414
Baciccio (Gian Battista Gaulli)
166
Bacon, Francis 319
Bagnaia 416
Baker's Tomb 243
Balla, Giacomo 209
ballet 369
banks 21–2
Baptistry of St. John 241
Barberini family 221–23
Cardinal Antonio 223
see also Urban VIII
Barberini mosaic of the Nile
(Palestrina) 424
Barbo, Cardinal *see* Paul II
Barracco, Giovanni 170
Bartolommeo di Giovanni 181
Barzini, Luigi (quoted) 77
basilicas 69
Basilica Aemilia 117
Basilica Julia 119
Basilica of Maxentius 69, 95,
233
Basilica of Porta Maggiore 243
Basilica Ulpia 110
Basilicas, Christian *see*
churches
Bastione del Sangallo 263
baths 69
Baths of Agrippa 152: *see also*
Pantheon
Baths of Caracalla 69, 146, 154
241, 323
Baths of Diocletian 69, 224,
225
Baths of Severus 130
Baths of Trajan 139, 231
Bazzani, Cesare 40
Bazzi, Giovanni Anton *see*
Sodoma

beaches 407, 433
Beardsley, Aubrey 210
Beccafumi, Domenico 184,
185, 220
Belisarius 252, 263, 304
Belli, Giacchino 36, 27
Bellini, Giovanni 96, 184, 214,
323
Benedict IX, Pope 42
Benedict XIV, Pope 133
Benedict, Saint 275, 421, 422
Benevenuto, Disertori 210
Bernard, Saint 335
Bernini, Gianlorenzo 62, **77–8**
baldacchino in St. Peter's
296
'Breezy Maniacs' 197, 307
busts 184, 214, 232, 411
campaniles on St. Peter's 292
Chigi chapel 205
churches 204, 218–9, 223,
243
ciborium in St. Peter's 295
Ecstasy of St. Teresa 223–4
floor of St. Peter's portico
293
fountains 160–61, 167,
221–22, 328, 418
interior of St. Peter's 293
monuments 295, 297, 298
palazzi 182, 186, 218, 220
and Pantheon 153–4
rivalry with Borromini 160
Sala Ducale 321
statues 78, 95, 266, 277,
293, 296
St. Peter's Square 289–90
Tribune in St. Peter's 297
works at Ariccia 429
other works 83, 96, 151,
197, 198, 213
Bernini, Pietro 195, 214
Bersaglieri museum and
monument 329
Bessarione, Cardinal 182, 261
Biagio da Cesena 321
Biblioteca Nazionale 332
Bicci di Lorenzo 83
bicycles, hiring 10, 204
Blake, William 210
Bloemen, Giovanni van 190
boating 386–7
Bocca della Verità 98
Boccioni, Umberto 209
Bomarzo Monster Park 412–13
Bonaparte family: Letizia
(Napoleon's mother) 84,
280
Pauline 157, 168, 196, 213,
329 *see also* Napoleon
Bontigli, Benedetto 315

Boni, Giacomo 127
Boniface IV, Pope 119
Boniface VIII, Pope 42, 60,
240, 425
Boniface IX, Pope: tomb 240
Bonny Prince Charlie *see*
Stuart, Charles
bookshops 379–80
Borghese family 212–13
Camillo (Napoleon's brother-
in-law) 207, 208, 213
Camillo (Pope) *see* Paul V
Marcantonio 207, 213
Scipio(ne) 207, 212, 213,
266, 331
Borgia family 230, 318
Cesare 113, 230, 318
Duke of Gandia 318
Lucrezia 318
see also Alexander VI
Borgo 289, 303, 317
Borromini, Francesco **77**
facade of Coll. di Propaganda
Fide 197
grille in St. Peter's 295
palazzi 159, 175, 220
Philippine Oratory 171
rivalry with Bernini 160
S. Carlino 219–20
other churches 155, 159,
197, 238, 262, 282
Botanical Gardens 281
Botticelli, Sandro 73, 182, 321
Boucher, François 221
bowling 387
Bracciano, lake and town
411–12
Bramante, Donato 61, **73–4**
cloister at S. M. della Pace
158
design for St. Peter's 123,
198, 292
rivalry with Michelangelo 319
Tribune in S.M. del Popolo
202
Vatican galleries 311
Villa Giulia 171
other works 170, 262, 315,
322
death 292
Braque, Georges 209
Braschi, Gianangelo *see* Pius VI
Breakspear, Nicholas *see*
Adrian IV
Bregno, Andrea 182, 202, 303
screen in Sistine Chapel 321
Breughel family 184, 185, 280
bridges *see* Pons, Ponte
Brill, Paul 321
British Military Cemetery 254
Broglio, Mario 210

Bronzino, Agnolo 181, 220
Browning, Elizabeth Barrett
    196, 198
Browning, Robert 198
Bruno, Giordano 176, 304
Brutus, Lucius Junius 51
Burchfield, Charles 319
Burne-Jones, Sir Edward 210
bus and tram travel 8–9
    to other towns 9–10
Byron, George Gordon, 6th.
    Baron: lodgings 195
    monument and bust 214
    wax of 180
    on city of Rome 195
    on Colosseum 133
    on col. of Phocas 119
    on Keats 195
    on Scipio tomb 262

Cacus 128
Caelian hill 136, 144, 145
Caelius (astronomer-
    geographer) 174
Caesar, Julius 56
    his Forum 112
    loots Temple of Saturn 119
    plans to drain Pontine
        Marshes 431
    site of murder 176
    theatre 100
    urban planning and building
        works 40, 110, 112, 118,
        119
    death 121
Caetani family 101, 261, 268,
    see also Boniface VIII
Cagliostro, Count of 306
Calciografia Nazionale 189
Caldarini, Guglielmo 39
calendar of annual events
    14–16
Caligula, Emperor 57, 126,
    241, 428, 432
Calixtus, Saint 264
Camerino, Iacopo da 240
Campo de' Fiori 176
campsites 365–6
Campus Martius 148, 164,
    168–9, 187
Campus Sceleratus 332
Canaletto, Antonio 221
Canova, Antonio 80, 261
    arranges Chiaramonti Gallery
        311
    Perseus 313
    sculpture of Pauline
        Bonaparte 213
    works in St. Peter's 297,
        298, 300
    other works 157,182, 268

Canuti, Domenico Maria 111
Capitoline hill 89–97
Capitoline Museums 85, 86,
    94–6
Capodistria, Domenico da 420
Caprarola 417
Capuchin Cemetery 223
car hire and travel 11–12
Caracalla, Emperor 118, 182,
    see also Baths
Carafa, Giovanni see Paul IV
Caravaggio, Michelangelo
    Merisi da 77, 203
    three works on S. Matthew
        156
    Deposition 233
    S. Cecilia 175
    other works 96, 156, 184,
        214, 221, 280–1
Carnival 38–9
Carrà, Carlo 209
Carracci, Annibale 76, 173,
    203, 284
carrozze 11
cars, buying 395
Casa di Burcardo 168
Casa del Cardinale Bessarione
    261
Casa dei Cavalieri di Rodi 111
Casa Crivelli 171
Casa Madre dei Mutilati 307
Casa dei Mattei 275
Casale Rotondo 269
Casino dell'Aurora 331
Casorati, Felice 210
Castel Gandolfo: village and
    papal palace 429–30
Castel Sant'Angelo 303–7
Castelli Romani 425–31
Castor and Pollux (Dioscuri)
    92, 120,217
catacombs 260 260–61, 263,
    264
    Jewish 258
    Priscilla 328
    S. Agnese fuori le Mura
        329–30
    S. Cyriaca 244
    S. Domitilla 266
    S. Pancrazio 336
    S. Sebastiano 266
    St. Calixtus 264, 264–5
Catherine of Siena, Saint 151
cats 30
Catullus 40,126, 175
Cavallini, Pietro 73
    frescoes 97, 241, 276
    mosaic 278
    school of 274
    tomb painting 92
Cecilia, Saint 265, 276

Cecilia Metella, tomb of 268
Celestine V, Pope 42
Cellini, Benvenuto 133, 157,
    299, 304
Cenci, Beatrice 221, 304
Cerquozzi, Michelangelo 79,
    175
Cervéteri 37–1
Cestius, Gaius 253
Cézanne, Paul 209
Chagall, Marc 319
Charlemagne 59, 238, 299
Charles Stuart see Stuart
Charles V, Emperor 155, 171
Chigi family 203, 281, 429
    Agostino 203, 281
    see also Alexander VII
children, gifts for 380
children, Rome for 389–90
Chini, Galileo 209
Chirico, Giorgio de 209
Christina, Queen of Sweden
    196, 202, 210, 280
    monument 295
    tomb 300
Christmas services 295
church services in English 25
churches: All Saints 201
    Anagni Cathedral 425
    Assunta (Trevignano) 412
    Chiesa Nuova (S. Maria in
        Vallicella) 170
    Domine Quo Vadis? 263
    Gesù 76, 165–6
    Gesù (Frascati) 426
    Gesù (Viterbo) 415
    Gesù e Maria 204
    Palestrina Cathedral 423
    S. Adriano 117
    S. Agnese in Agone 159
    S. Agnese fuori le Mura 72,
        329–30
    S. Agostino 156
    S. Alessio 250
    S. Andrea delle Fratte 197
    S. Andrea al Quirinale 218
    S. Andrea della Valle 76, 168
    S. Anselmo 251
    S. Antonio dei Portoghesi
        156
    SS. Apostoli 182
    S. Aurea (Ostia) 406
    S. Bartolomeo 103–4
    S. Benedetto 275
    S. Bernardo 223
    S. Biagio 90
    S. Bibiana 243
    S. Carlino 219–20
    S. Carlo in Corso 198
    S. Caterina dei Funari 167
    S. Cecilia 276–7

churches (cont'd)
S. Cesareo 261
S. Clemente 139–41
S. Cosimato 277
SS. Cosma e Damiano 72, 134
S. Costanza 72, 330
S. Crisogono 274
S. Croce in Gerusalemme 242
SS. Domenico e Sisto 111
S. Eligio degli Orefici 172
S. Eustachio 154
S. Francesca Romana (S. Maria Nova) 123, 130,**133–4**
S. Francesco a Ripa 277
S. Francesco (Subiaco) 422
S. Francesco (Viterbo) 414
S. Giacomo degli Incurabili 204
S. Giorgio in Velabro 97
S. Giovanni Decollato 98
S. Giovanni dei Fiorentini 171
S. Giovanni in Oleo 262
SS. Giovanni e Paolo 144
S. Giovanni a Porta Latina 261
S. Girolamo degli Schiavoni 199
S. Giuseppe dei Falegnami 112
S. Gregorio 103
S. Gregorio Magno 145
S. Ignazio 185
S. Ivo 155
St. John Lateran (S. Giovanni in Laterano) 237–40 (*239*)
S. Lorenzo fuori le Mura 72, 244
S. Lorenzo in Lucina 198
S. Lorenzo in Miranda 116
S. Lorenzo in Panisperna 331
SS. Luca e Martina 112–12
S. Luigi dei Francesi 155–6
S. Marco 83
S. Maria degli Angeli 224
S. Maria dell'Anima 157–8
S. Maria Antiqua 121, 123
S. Maria d'Aracoeli 91–2
S. Maria dell'Assunzione (Ariccia) 429
S. Maria in Campitelli 101
S. Maria della Concezione 223
S. Maria della Consolazione 97
S. Maria in Cosmedin 72, **98–9**
S. Maria in Domnica 72

churches (cont'd)
S. Maria di Galloro (Ariccia) 429
S. Maria (Grottaferrata) 427
S. Maria di Loreto 109
S. Maria Maggiore 72, 233–6 (*234*)
S. Maria Maggiore (Tuscania) 410
S. Maria ad Martyres *see* Pantheon
S. Maria dei Miracoli 202
S. Maria di Monserrato 172
S. Maria in Montesanto 202
S. Maria Nuova (Viterbo) 415
S. Maria dell'Orazione e della Morte 172
S. Maria dell'Orto 277
S. Maria della Pace 158
S. Maria del Popolo 202–3
S. Maria del Priorato 251
S. Maria della Quercia (Viterbo) 416
S. Maria della Rotonda (Albano Laziale) 429
S. Maria della Scala 280
S. Maria Scala Coeli 335
S. Maria dei Sette Dolori 282
S. Maria sopra Minerva 73, 151–2
S. Maria in Trastevere 278–9
S. Maria in Vallicella (Chiesa Nuova) 170
S. Maria della Verità (Viterbo) 414–5
S. Maria in Via Lata 183
S. Maria della Vittoria 223–4
S. Martino ai Monti 231
S. Nicola in Carcere 100
SS. Nome di Maria 109
S. Omobono 100
S. Onofrio 284
S. Pancrazio 336
S. Pantaleo 169
S. Paolo alle Tre Fontane 335
St. Paul's Outside the Wall (S. Paolo fuori le Mura) 255
S. Pietro (Albano Laziale) 429
S. Pietro (Anticoli Corrado) 421
S. Pietro in Montorio 282
SS. Pietro e Paolo 334
S. Pietro (Tuscania) 410
S. Pietro in Vincoli 330–1
S. Prassede 72, 232
S. Prisca 251–2
S. Pudenziana 72, 235–6
SS. Quattro Coronati 141–2
S. Rocco 199

churches (cont'd)
S. Rosa (Viterbo) 414
S. Rosalia (Palestrina) 424
S. Saba 252
S. Sabina 72, 249–50
S. Salvatore in Lauro 161
S. Sebastiano 266
S. Silvestro 188
S. Silvestro (Tivoli) 418
S. Sisto (Viterbo) 414
S. Spirito in Sassia 303
S. Stefano Rotondo 143
S. Susanna 223
S. Teodoro 97
S. Tommaso in Formis 143
S. Urbano 267
SS. Vincenzo ed Anastasio 189, 335
S. Vitale 331
Sacro Cuore del Suffragio 307
Tivoli Cathedral 418
Trinità dei Monti 196
Velletri Cathedral 430
see also Convento
Cicero 56, 126, 426
Cincinnatus 51
Cinecittà 33, 64, 330–31
Ciociaria 424
Circus of Maxentius 267
Circus Maximus 248–9
Città Universitaria 331–2
Civitavecchia 409
Claudian Aqueduct *see* Acqua Claudia
Claudius, Emperor 142, 243, 399
Clement I, Pope and Saint 139, 140
Clement IV, Pope 415
Clement V, Pope 60, 415
Clement VII, Pope: lack of artistic masterpieces 74
roads 201
and Sack of Rome (1527) 62, 304, 306
tomb 151
Villa Madama 326
Clement XII, Pope 188
climate 16–17
Clivo di Scauro 144
Cloaca Maxima 40, 112, 116
clothes: buying 380–81, 383–4
Colle Oppio 138, 139
Collegio di Propaganda Fide 197
Collegio Romano 183
Colli, Antonio 426
Colonna family 60, 169, 180–2, 199, 425
Marcantonio 78, 163
Sciarra and 'slap of Anagni' 425, *see also* Martin V

Colonna, M. (artist) 174
Colosseum 57, 69, **131–3**
    allowed to decay 106
    origin of name 138
Colossus of Nero 131, 138
Columbarium of Pomponius
    Hylas 263
Column of the Immaculata 197
Column of Phocas 119
Comitium 117
Commodus, Emperor 187, 269
Compagnia della Buona Morte
    172
concessionary fares, entrance
    fees etc. 26
Consorti, Vico 293
Constans II, Emperor 126, 133,
    153
Constantia (Constantine's
    daughter) 330
Constantine, Emperor 58, 71
    admires Trajan's Forum 110
    Arch 130
    Baptistry of St. John 241
    completes Basilica of
        Maxentius 123
    Donation of 142
    first church 237
    neglects Ostia 399
    old St. Peter's 291–2, 296,
        301
    other churches 244, 330
    plunders Hadrian's Villa 419
    shrine to St. Paul 255
    vision of Cross 130, 327
Conitantius II, Emperor 241
consulates 17–18
Consulus, Master 422
Conte see Jacopino
Convento dei Cappuccini 222
Convento di S. Benedetto
    (Subiaco) 421–2
Convento di S. Scholastica
    (Subiaco) 421
Coppedé Quarter 330–31
Cori 430
Coriolanus 432
Cornacchini, Augusto 293
cornetti, hot 374
Corot, Jean B.C. 210
Correggio, Antonio 184, 214
Corsini family 280
Corso (Via del) 178, 201
Corso Vittorio Emanuele 164
Cortona see Pietro da Cortona
Corviale 40
Cosmas, Saint 134
Cosmati family 72, 92, 99,
    241, 421, 430
    Giovanni 152, 235
    Master Jacopo 252

Council of Trent 75
Counter-Reformation, art of
    75–7
courses for visitors 26
Crassus 56, 268
Credi, Lorenzo di 190
credit cards 22–3
Crescenzi family 60, 100, 155
crime 18–19
Crivelli, Carlo 322
Crocetti Venanzio 293
Cyptoporticus, Nero's 127
Curia 117
Curiatii 269, 429
Curtius, Marcus 120
customs formalities 8
Cybele, cult of 32, 127–8
Cyril, Saint 140

Daddi, Bernardo 322
daily life in ancient Rome 43–8
Dalmata, Giovanni 300, 321,
    420
Damasus, Pope 265
Damian, Saint 134
Daniele da Volterra 196, 238,
    321
D'Annunzio, Gabriele 283
Danti, Ignazio 315
David, Jacques Louis 157
De Gasperi, Alcide 244
De Rossi, Giambattista 261
De Sica, Vittorio 64
Degas, Edgar 210
Delacroix, Eugène 210
department stores 380
Diana Nemorensis, cult of 428
Diocletian, Emperor 117, 224,
    266
Dionysius of Halicarnassus 89
Dionysius, Pope 265
Dioscuri (Castor and Pollux)
    92, 120,217
disabled, facilities for 12
Dolabella 143
Dolci, Carlo 281
'Doll's House' 171
Domenichino 77, 168, 323,
    427
domes 30–31
Domitian, Emperor: aqueduct
    130
    buildings on Palatine 129–30
    stadium 158, 168
    other building works 96,
        126, 400, 429
    and cult of Isis 154, 160
    roads 167
Domitilla, Saint 266
Domus Augustana 129

Domus Aurea 39, 69, 127,
    138–9, 142, 231
    Cryptoporticus 129
    inspires Raphael 318
    statue of Nero (Colossus)
        131, 138
Domus Flavia 129
Donatello 73, 91, 299
Donation of Constantine 142
Donghi, Antonio 210
Doria Pamphili Gallery and
    Palace 183–4
Dossi, Dosso 214, 306
Duca, Giacomo del 109
Duccio, Agostino di 151
Duchamp, Marcel 209
Dughet, Gaspard 181, 231
Duquesnoy François 78, 109,
    175, 184, 297

Education Ministry 277
Elagabalus 129
Embriago (designer of Water
    Clock) 208
emergencies: medical 20–21
emergency telephone number
    19
English church 201
entertainment & nightlife
    367–72
Ernst, Max 210
Este, Ippolito d' 418
Ethelwolf, King 303
Etruscan Museum 210–11
Etruscan towns 50–54
Etruscans 50–54
    art 68, 70, 211
    art museums **210–11**, 280,
        314–15, 409
Eudoxia, Empress 230
Eugenius IV, Pope 261, 293
EUR 333–5
Eurysaces the baker 243
Eutychianus, Pope 265
Ex-Mattatoio 254

Fabian, Pope 265
Farnese family 281, 417
    Alessandro (grandson of Paul
        III) 127, 165, 417
    Alessandro (Pope) see Paul III
    Giulia 173, 297
    Villa in Caprarola 417, see
        also Palazzo Farnese
Farnesian Gardens see Orti
    Farnesiani
Fatebenefratelli hospital 103
Fattori, Giovanni 210
Fausta (wife of Constantine)
    237
Feininger, Lyonel 319

Felix I, Pope 43, 265
Fellini, Federico 40, 208, 222, 333
  quoted 33, 64
Ferrazzi, Ferruccio 209
festivals *see* calendar of events
Filarete, Antonio 293
films, English-language 370
films and film industry 33–4, 64, 222, 332–3
  Sartorio film 186
Finance Ministry 64, 328
folk clubs 373–4
Folklore Museum 279–80
Fonseca, Gabriele 198
Fontana, Carlo 79
  font cover in St.Peter's 298
  fountain 278
  interior of SS. Apostoli 182
  pietra dura in S. M. del Popolo 202
  portico of S. Crisogono 274
  portico of S. M. in Trastevere 278
  two domed churches 202
Fontana, Domenico 76
  chapel for Sixtus V 233
  façade of St. John Lateran 240
  façade of Trinità dei Monti 196
  moves Vatican obelisk 190–91
  obelisk of Ramses II 201
  rebuilds Lateran palace 241, Salone Sistina 322
food and drink 337–52
  buying 381, 384
  health food shops 396
football 387
Foreign Ministry 327
Formosus, Pope 238
Foro Italico (Foro Mussolini) 40, 326–7
Forum 69
  Antiquarium 123
  of Augustus 111
  Boarium 98
  of Caesar 112
  Holitarium 100
  of Nerva 112
  Piscarium 101
  Roman 113–123 (*114–5*)
  allowed to decay 106
  of Trajan 69, **110–11**, 182
  of Vespasian 111
Fosse Ardeatine massacre **265**, 282
fountains: Acqua Acetosa 328
  Acqua Felice 224
  Acqua Paola 77

fountains (cont'd)
  Api 222
  Barcaccia 195
  Il Facchino 183
  at Marino 427
  Mascherone 172
  Noah's Ark (Anticoli Corrado) 421
  P. Farnese 172
  P. Firdusi 209
  P. Pietro d'Illiria 249
  P. di S. Maria in Trastevere (Fontana) 278
  P.Vittorio Emanuele (ruined) 236
  Paola 283
  Piazza Navona (Bernini) 160
  Quattro Fontane 220
  Silenus ('Baboon') 201
  St.Peter's Square 290
  Tartarughe 167
  Theatre of Waters (Frascati) 426
  Trevi 188–9
  Tritone 221
  Villa d'Este (Bernini) 418
  in Viterbo 414
  Water Clock 208
Fragonard, Jean Honoré 221
Francis, Saint 277, 422
Frangipane 184
Frangipane Tower 156
Franzoni, Francesco Antonio 313, 314
Frascati 426–7
Frazer, Sir James 428, 429
French church 196
Fuga, Fernando 79, 172, 218, 233, 241

Gaddi, Taddeo 306
Gagliardi 156
Galen (2nd. cent. doctor) 103
Galilei, Alessandro 238
Galileo Galilei 151, 196, 281
Galla Placidia 255
Galleria Borghese 212–13
Galleria Colonna 180–82, 187
Galleria Doria Pamphili 183–5
Galleria Nazionale d'Arte Antica 220–21, 280
Galleria Nazionale d'Arte Moderna 209–10
  building 40
  Manzù collection at Ardea 433
Galleria Pallavicini 331
Galleria Sciarra 190
Galoppatoio 208
Gandolfi family 430
Garibaldi, Anita 284

Garibaldi, Giuseppe 63, 156, 282, 284
Garofalo (Benvenuto Tisi) 221
Gastaldi, Cardinal 202
Gaulli, G.B. 79
Gelasius I, Pope 261
Genseric the Vandal 58
Gentile da Fabriano 96, 322, 431
Gentileschi, Artemisia 175
Gentileschi, Orazio 174–5
Genzano di Roma 429
Gerard, Baron François 157
Gerbert *see* Sylvester II
Géricault, Théodore 210
Gerrnan cemetery 302
German church 157
German occupation (World War II) 64
Geta, Emperor 118
Gherardi, Antonio 279
Ghirlandaio, Domenico 73, 321
Giordano, Luca 184, 281
Giorgetti, Antonio 266
Giorgione 83
Giotto 73, 240, 293, 322
Giovanni da Modena 83
Giovanni da San Giovanni 142
Giovanni da Udine 138, 317, 319
Giovanni di Paolo 184
Giovanni of Rome 322
Giovannipoli 255
Giuliano da Maiano 83
Giulio Romano 75
  builds Villa Madama 326
  finishes Raphael's last painting 323
  frescoes 158, 196, 306
  paintings in V. Farnesina 282
  and Raphael's Stanze 317
Goethe: quoted 288, 392, 398
  son's grave 254
Goethe Museum 204
Golden Milestone 118
golf 387–8
Goya, Francisco 210
Gozzoli, Benozzo 92
Gracchi, the (Tiberius and Gaius Gracchus) 55, 90
graffiti 36–7
Gramsci, Antonio 254
Grassi, Padre Orazio 185
Gratian, Emperor 117
Greco, Domenikos (El Greco) 221
Greco, Emilio 298
Greek influences 50, 68, 70, 71, 72, 98, 248
Gregorian chant, where to hear 246, 251

Gregorini, Domenico 242
Gregory the Great, Pope 59,
  99, 145
  and salvation of Trajan 109
  vision of St. Michael 304
Gregory III, Pope 152
Gregory IV, Pope 83, 406
Gregory VII, Pope 60
Gregory X, Pope: election 416
Gregory XI, Pope 61, 151
  monument in S. Francesca
    Romana 134
Gregory XIII, Pope 170, 315
Gregory XVI, Pope 311, 314,
  323, 419
Grottaferrata 427
Grotto of Egeria 267
Guardi 221
Guercino 76
  Burial of St. Petronilla 95, 297
  Et in Arcadia Ego 221, 281
  Venus 190
  other works 83,182, 184
Guidetti, Guidetto 167
Guiscard, Robert 60
gypsies 18, 236

Hadrian, Emperor 57, 110
  and Antinous 206
  designs Castel S. Angelo
    304,307
  memorials to Trajan 109
  Pantheon 152–4
  repaves Appian Way 260
  Temple of 186
  Temple of Venus and Rome
    (attrib.) 130
  villa at Tivoli 311, 313,
    419–20
  work at Ostia 400, 404, 405,
Hadrian I, Pope 72
Hadrian VI, Pope 158
Hadrian's Mausoleum *see*
  Castel Sant' Angelo
Hadrian's Villa (Tivoli) 311,
  313, **419–20**
Hannibal 428
Helena, Saint (mother of
  Constantine) 241
Henry, Duke of York, Cardinal
  298, 300, 428
Herodes Atticus 264, 267
Hildebrand, Pope 235
history of Rome **49–66**
  early 50–55
  Caesar to Augustus 56
  decline of the empire 58
  Gothic rule 58
  papacy moved to Avignon 60
  papacy restored 61
  Renaissance 61–2

end of papal rule 62–4
  Italian independence 63
  twentieth century 63–6
Hogarth, William 210
Holbein, Hans, the Younger 221
Honorius I, Pope 130, 263,
  329, 335
Honorius III, Pope 244, 250, 335
Honorius (son of Theodosius)
  255
Horace 57, 116, 421
  Sabine farm 421
Horatii 269, 429
hotels 352–64
Houdon, Jean-Antoine 80
House of Augustus **128**, 249
House of the Crescenzi 100
House of the Griffins 129
House of Laurentius Manlius
  102
House of Livia 128
House of SS. John and Paul
  144
House of the Vestals 122

Ignatius Loyola, Saint 166,
  185, 256
Ilarius Fuscus, tomb of 269
Ina of Wessex, King 303
Innocent III, Pope 60, 240, 303
Innocent VIII, Pope:
  Pollaiuolo's monument 298
Innocent X, Pope 43,159,160,
  183, 184, 238
  Velazquez portrait 184
insula: best surviving example
  90–91
Invincible Sun, cult of 32, 188
Isis, cult of 32,154

Jacopino del Conte 96, 221
Janiculum hill 282–4
jazz clubs 373–4
'Jesuit style' 166
jewellery: buying 382
Jewish catacombs 258
Jewish Ghetto 102–3
Jewish Synagogue 103
jobs *see* working in Rome
John VIII, Pope 255
John XI, Pope (Alberic) 59–60,
  251
John XII, Pope 42
John XXI, Pope: death 416
John XXIII, Pope 293, 298,
  300, 302, 433
John Paul I, Pope 300, 320
John Paul II, Pope 103, 291,
  302, 430
John, Saint 262
John, Saint (4th century) 144

John the Divine, Saint: on
  Rome 35–6
Julian the Apostate 117, 119
Julius I, Pope 278
Julius II, Pope 61, 73
  acquisitions 138, 313
  and Bramante 202, 292, 311
  Castello at Ostia 406
  destroys Il Sodoma frescoes
    282
  and Michelangelo 74, 230,
    319–22
  and Raphael's Stanze 315–18
  other works 161, 171, 182
Julius III,Pope 210
Juno Moneta, temple of 91
Justin II, Pope 299
Justinian, Emperor 58
Juvarra, Filippo 197
Juvenal 57, 248

Kandinsky, Wassily 210
Kauffmann, Angelica 80, 190,
  197
Keats, John 195–6, 253
Keats-Shelley Memorial House
  195–6
Kesselring, Fieldmarshal 427
Keyser, Thomas de 184
Klee, Paul 210
Klimt, Gustav 209
Kokoschka, Oskar 319

Lackovic, Ivan 319
Lacus Curtius 120
L'Alunno *see* Niccolò
Landini, Taddeo 167
Lanfranco, Giovanni 168, 297
language: Etruscan legacy 54
  Roman legacy 41
  useful vocabulary **438–47**
Laocoön statue 138, 313
Lapis Niger 118
Largo Argentina temples 167
Lateran museum 240
Lateran palace 241
laundry 396
lavatories 27–8
Lavinia 432
Lavinium 432
Lawrence, Saint 198, 244, 331
Lega, Silvestro 210
Lemoyne, Jean Baptiste 198
Leo I, Pope (Leo the Great) 58,
  298
Leo III, Pope 59, 72
Leo IV, Pope 289, 298
Leo X, Pope 42, 62, 74, 155
  begins S. Giovanni dei
    Fiorentini 171
  and Borgia Apartment 319

builds Via di Ripetta 201
  and Castel S. Angelo 305
  and Piazza Navicella 143
  and Raphael's Stanze 318
  tomb 15
Leo XI, Pope: monument in
  St. Peter's 298
Leo XII, Pope 133
Leonardo da Vinci 323
Leopold II 182
Lepidus, Marcus Aemilius 116
Liberius, Pope 233
Library of Agapetus 144–5
Library, National 332
Licenza 421
Ligorio, Pirro 75, 98, 302, 418
Lippi, Filippino 152
Lippi, Fra Filippo 185, 220, 322
Liszt, Franz 418
living and working in Rome
  391–4
Livy 51, 120
Longhi, Martino 78, 97, 189,
  199
Lorenzetti, Pietro 322
Lorenzetto (Lorenzo Lotti) 203
Lorenzo of Viterbo 415
Lorraine, Claude 184
lost property 19
Lotto, Lorenzo 96, 185, 214,
  306, 315
Lucius, Pope 265
Lucretia 51
Lucullus 207
Ludus Magnus 139
LUNEUR Park 334–5
Lupercal 128
Luther, Martin 241
Lysippus: Apoxyomenos 312

Macaulay, Thomas Babington,
  1st. Baron (quoted) 120
Macbeth: visits Rome 303
Maccabees, the seven 231
Macchiaioli 210
Madama Lucrezia (talking
  statue) 36, 83
Maderno, Carlo 76
  builds Castel Gandolfo 430
  façade of S. Susanna 76, 223
  fountains 290, 427
  Palazzo Barberini 220
  St. Peter's 76, 292, 296
  other churches 168, 204, 256
Maderno, Stefano 276
  statue of St. Cecilia 265
Maecenas 421
  gardens and Auditorium
  236–7
Magic Door 236

Maiano see Giuliano da
  Maiano
Maidalchini, Olimpia 183, 184
Malta, Knights of 251
Mamertine Prison 112
Mancini, Maria 181
Manet, Edouard 210
Manzù, Giacomo 244, 293,
  433
Marble Stadium 40, 327
Marcellus 100
Marcillat, Guillaume de 203
Marcus Aurelius, Emperor 57,
  110
  Arch 95
  column 70, 187
  statue 93
Marcus Servilius: tomb of 268
Marforio (talking statue) 36, 94
Margaret of Parma 155
Marino 427
Marius, Gaius 55
Mark Antony 119, 121, 126
Mark, Pope 83
markets (present-day) 377
Marozia 59
Martin V, Pope (Oddone
  Colonna) 61, 181, 240
Martini, Simone 322
Masaccio 140
Masolino 73, 140
Mastelletta, Il 221
Matisse, Henri 318
Mattei, Ciriaco 144
Mattei family 253–4
Mausoleum of Augustus 199
  obelisk from 235
Mausoleum of the Fosse
  Ardeatine 265
Mausoleum of Lucilius Peto 330
Maxentius, Emperor 123, 268,
  327
Mazarin, Cardinal 189, 331
Mazzini, Giuseppe 63, 218
Mazzolino, Ludovico 184
Mazzoni, Giulio 174
medical problems 20–21
Medici family 143, 155
  Lorenzo 42, 155
  see also Clement VII, Leo X
Melozzo da Forlì 73
  mosaic vault in S. Croce 242
  other works 83, 154, 218,
  322, 415
Memling, Hans 185
Messalina 207
Messina see Antonello da
  Messina
Meta Sudans 131
Methodius, Saint 140
Metropolitana 10

Metsys, Quentin 221
Michelangelo Buonarroti 73,
  74–5, 84
  Carthusian cloisters 224
  harbour at Civitavecchia 409
  last frescoes 321
  Last Judgement 75, 320
  Moses 230
  Palazzo Farnese 173
  Pietà 295
  redesigns Capitol 93
  Sistine Chapel 319–22
  sources of inspiration 123, 313
  St.Peter's 292, 295
  tomb of Julius II 230
  other works 151, 173, 182,
  210, 226, 289, 305, 329,
  424
Millet, Jean François 210
Milvian Bridge 327
Minguzzi, Luciano 293
Ministry of Justice 39
Mino da Fiesole 152, 202,
  276, 299, 321
Mirabilia Urbis Romae (12th-
  cent chronicle) 89
Miró, Joan 210
Mitelli, A. 174
Mithraism 141, 251–2
Model Prison 172
Modena see Giovanni da
  Modena
Modigliani, Amedeo 209
Mola, Pier Francesco 79, 181,
  281
Momo, Giuseppe 311
Monaco, Lorenzo 322
Mondrian, Piet 209
Monet, Claude 210
Monica, Saint 404
'Monkey Tower' 156
Mons Albanus (Monte Cavo)
  428
Montagna, Bartolommeo 306
Monte Cavo (Mons Albanus)
  428
Monte Gianicolo
  (Janiculum hill) 282–4
Monte Mario 326
Monte Testaccio 254
Montelupo see Raffaello
Monument to the Fallen 283
Moore,Jacob 207
Moro, Aldo 64, 166
Morris, William 210
mosaics 71
Mosque 328
Mulhooly, Father Joseph 139
Munch, Edvard 210, 319
Murillo 280
Muro Torto 208

Museo dell'Alto Medioevo 334
Museo delle Arti e delle
  Tradizioni Popolari 334
Museo Barracco 170
Museo Civico di Zoologia 212
Museo della Civiltà Romana
  334
Museo delle Mura 263
Museo Napoleonico 157
Museo Nazionale Etrusco
  210–11
Museo Nazionale Orientale
  237
Museo Nazionale Romano 225
Museo del Palazzo Venezia
  82–3
Museo Preistorico Etnografico
  334
Museo di Roma 169
Museo Torlonia 280
Museo della Via Ostiense 253
Museum of Criminology 172
Museum, Goethe 204
Museum of the Grenadiers of
  Sardinia 242
Museum of the Infantry 242
Museum of Instruments 242–3
museum, Jewish 103
Museum of Marine Flags 84
Museum of Purgatory 307
Museum of the Risorgimento
  284
Museum of Sculpture
  (open-air) 92–3
museums: see also Museo and
  Capitoline Museums,
  Vatican Museums, Galleries
museums outside Rome
  Air Force M. 412
  Cerveteri 408
  m. of Roman Ships at Nemi
    429
  Ostia 407
  Palestrina 424
  Tarquinia 409
  Tuscania 410
  Velletri 431
  Viterbo 414, 415
music 373–4
  buying records and tapes 383
Mussolini, Benedetto (Il Duce)
  82, 83
  Ara Pacis and Augustus'
    Mausoleum 199–200
  archaeological works 101,199,
    429
  and art 80
  Cinecittà 332
  EUR 333–5
  Olympics complex 326
  residence 329

roads 90, 111,145
  other references and
    anecdotes 134, 146, 165,
    186, 226, 432

Napoleon 63, 84, 157, 202
  replica crown 412
Napoleon III 63, 280
Narses 182, 263
Nemi, Lake and town 428
Nereus, Saint 266
Neri di Bicci 220
Nero, Emperor 57
  birthplace 433
  buildings on Palatine 126,
    130
  burial place 202
  and Ostia 399
  villa at Subiaco 421, 422
  see also Domus Aurea
Nero's Golden House see
  Domus Aurea
Nervi, Pier Luigi 327, 334
Netscher, Caspar 182
Nettuno 433
Niccolò Alunno 181, 220
Niccolò of Rome 322
Niceron, Jean François 221
Nicholas V, Pope 61, 300, 315,
  322
  plans new St. Peter's 292
Ninfa 426, 431
Nittis, Giuseppe de 210
Norba 431
Norma 431
Novelli, Pietro 83
Numa Pompilius 51, 267
Numitor 50

obelisks: from Antinous' tomb
  208
  Bernini's elephant 151
  on Fountain of Rivers 160
  Mussolini's in Foro Italico
    326
  O. of Axum 146
  in P. Navona 160
  P. della Rotonda 154
  at Pal. Montecitorio 186
  Pharaoh Ramses II 201
  Piazza dell'Esquilino 235
  on Quirinale 217
  tallest in world 240
  at Trinità dei Monti 196
  Vatican Obelisk 290, 302
Octavian see Augustus
Oderisi, Pietro 73
Odoacer the Goth 58, 126
O'Donnell, Roderick 283
Old Pretender see Stuart,
  James

Olympic Village 327
O'Neill, Hugh 283
opera 369
Oratory of the Forty Martyrs
  121
Orsini family 60, 417
  and Colonnas 180, 181, 412
  monster sculptures 413
  property outside Rome 408,
    411
  property in Rome 101, 155,
    161
Orti Farnesiani 127
Osino, Bruno da 210
Ospedale Fatebenefratelli 103
Ospedale San Gallicano 274
Ospedale di Santo Spirito in
  Sassia 303
Ostia Antica 398–407, (402–3)
  ancient Synagogue 406
  baths 400, 405
  Decumanus Maximus 400–7
  forum 401
  Forum of the Corporations
    400
  Great Horrea 401
  museum 401
  theatre 400
Ostia hamlet 406
Ovid 249

Paedagogium 130
Palace of Tiberius 97
Palatine Antiquarium 130
Palatine hill 123–27, (124–5)
  allowed to decay 106
Palazzetto Venezia 83
Palazzetto Zuccari 196–7
Palazzina Borghese 212
Palazzo Anguillara 274
Palazzo Barberini 220
Palazzo Bonaparte 84
Palazzo Borghese 198
Palazzo Braschi 169
Palazzo della Cancelleria 170
Palazzo Cenci 102
Palazzo Chigi 187
Palazzo Chigi (Ariccia) 429
Palazzo della Civiltà del Lavoro
  334
Palazzo Colonna 180–2
Palazzo dei Conservatori see
  Capitoline Museums
Palazzo della Consulta 218
Palazzo dei Convertendi 302–3
Palazzo Corsini 280–1
Palazzo Doria Pamphili 183–5
Palazzo dell'Esposizione 331
Palazzo Farnese 172
Palazzo di Giustizia 307
Palazzo Madama 155

Palazzo Massimo alle Colonne 169
Palazzo Montecitorio 186
Palazzo Muti 182
Palazzo Nuovo see Capitoline Museums
Palazzo Odescalchi 182
Palazzo Pamphili 159
Palazzo dei Penitenzieri 303
Palazzo del Quirinale 218
Palazzo Rospigliosi 331
Palazzo Rospigliosi (Zagarolo) 423
Palazzo Ruspoli 198
Palazzo del Sant'Uffizio 302
Palazzo di Sapienza 155
Palazzo Spada 174
Palazzo di Spagna 197
Palazzo dello Sport 334
Palazzo Taverna 161
Palazzo Torlonia 303
Palazzo Venezia 83, 165
Palazzo Viminale 331
Palazzo Wedekind 187
Palestrina, Giovanni Pierluigi da 423
Palestrina (town) 423–5
Palma Vecchio 96
Pamphili family 183, 335, see also Innocent X
Pancrazio, Saint (St. Pancras) 336
Pannini, Giovanni Paolo 221
Pantaleo, Saint 169
Pantheon **152–4**, 196
papal audiences 24
  at Castel Gandolfo 430
Parco Savello 449
Parioli 327–8
Parmigianino, Francesco 184
Paschal I, Pope 72
  builds S. Cecilia 276
  builds S. Prassede 232
  work on other churches 142–3
  moves body of St. Cecilia 265
Paschal II, Pope 141, 202
Pasolini, Pier Paolo 407
pasquinades see talking statues
Pasquino (talking statue) 36–7
Passalacqua, Pietro 242
Paul II, Pope 73, 82, 83, 299
Paul III, Pope (Alessandro Farnese) 62, 172–3, 417
  and Castel S. Angelo 306
  and Michelangelo 75, 292, 321
  monument in St. Peter's 297
Paul IV, Pope 42–3, 152

Paul V, Pope (Camillo Borghese) 212, 235, 283, 292
  destroys S. Agnese mosaics 330
  and Palazzo Borghese 198
Paul VI, Pope 223, 300, 318
Paul, Saint 251, 255, 266
  and Simon Magus 134
Paul, Saint (4th century) 144
pawn shop 296
Pelagius II, Pope 244
Penni, Francesco 323
Perugino 73
  and Raphael's Stanze 315
  work in Sistine Chapel 74, 321
  other works 151, 214, 220, 322
Peruzzi, Baldassare 75
  as architect for St. Peter's 292
  bishop's palace at Osda 406
  Casino of Pius IV 302
  Pal. Massimo alle Colonne 169
  and Raphael's Stanze 315
  tomb of Hadrian VI 158
  Villa Farnesina 282
  other works 101, 158, 172, 283
  his tomb 154
Peter, Saint: adopted daughter 266
  bones discovered 301
  chains 230
  chair 297
  funerary banquets for 267
  imprisonment 112
  and Prassede and Pudenziana 232, 235–6
  'Quo Vadis, Domine?' 263
  and Simon Magus 134
  venerated statue in St. Peter's 296
Peter's Pence 303
Petronilla, Saint 266
pharmacies 20–21
pharmacy, 18th century 280
Philip Neri, Saint 170
Philippine Oratory 171
Phocas (Byzantine Emperor) 119, 126
Piacentini, Marcello 331, 334
Piazza Augusto Imperatore 199
Piazza Bocca della Verità 98
Piazza del Campidoglio 92
Pi dei Cavalieri di Malta 250
Piazza dei Cinquecento 226
Piazza Giacchino Belli 274
Piazza dell'Indipendenza 332
Piazza dei Mercanti 275

Piazza Navicella 142
Piazza Navona 158–9
Piazza in Piscinula 275
Piazza del Popolo 201–02
Piazza della Repubblica 224
Piazza della Rotonda 154
Piazza di S. Maria Maggiore 233
Piazza di S. Maria in Trastevere 277–8
Piazza San Pietro 289–91
Piazza di San Silvestro 188
Piazza di Sant'Ignazio 185
Piazza di Siena 214
Piazza di Spagna 194–6
Piazza Venezia 83
Piazza Vittorio Emanuele 236
Picasso, Pablo 319
Piccola Farnesina 169–70
Piccolomini family 168
pickpockets and other thieves 18–19, 113
Pierleoni family 101, see also Anacletus II
Piero della Francesca 315
Piero di Cosimo 214, 220
Pietà, Michelangelo's 295
Pietro da Cortona 77
  altar at Palestrina 425
  dome of S. Carlo 198
  frescoes 79, 159, 170, 218, 244
  Gesù church at Frascati 427
  Rape of the Sabines 96
  S. Maria in Via Lata 183
  S. M. della Pace 158
  SS. Luca e Martina 112–13
  Trevi fountain 188
  Triumph of Divine Providence 221
Pietro d'Illiria 249
Pincio hill 195, 207–08
Pinturicchio, Bernardino 73, 91, 202–03,318,422
Piombo, Sebastiano del see Sebastiano
Piranesi, Giambattista 80, 189, 250, 251
Pisanello, Antonio 83
Pisis, Filippo de 210
Pius II, Pope 73, 168, 418
Pius III, Pope: tomb 168
Pius IV, Pope 302, 321, 329
Pius V, Pope 196
Pius VI, Pope 169, 217, 300, 313
Pius VII, Pope 84, 298, 311
Pius IX, Pope 63, 197, 244, 329, 430
Pius X, Pope 291, 298
Pius XI, Pope 324

Pius XII, Pope 301
plaques 37
Plautinius Lateranus 237
Police Station, world's oldest
    275
Policlinico hospital 332
Pollaiuolo, Antonio 95, 298
Pomezia 433
Pompey the Great 56
    theatre 100, 174, **175–6**
Pomponius Hylas 263
Pons Aemilius 100
Pons Cestius 104
Pons Fabricius 103
Ponte di Ariccia viaduct 429
Ponte Milvio (Ponte Mollo) 327
Ponte Nomentana 330
Ponte Rotto (Pons Aemilius)
    100
Ponte Sant'Angelo 307
Pontianus, Pope 265
Pontifex Maximus, office of 121
Pontine Marshes 432
Pontormo, Jacopo 174
Ponza (island) 433
Ponzio, Flaminio 77, 212, 266
popes 42–3, 62–4 and see
    under names of popes
Porta Asinara 241
Porta, Giacomo della **76**
    chapel in St.Peter's 297
    dome of St. Peter's 292
    designs S. Andrea della Valle
        168
    exterior of S. Ivo 155
    exterior of S. Luigi dei
        Francesi 155
    façade of Gesù 165
    other churches 100, 171,
        261, 335
    fountains 167, 201
Porta, Guglielmo della 297
Porta Maggiore 243
Porta Magica 236
Porta Pia 329
Porta Pinciana 214
Porta del Popolo 202
Porta di S. Giovanni 242
Porta S. Pancrazio 284
Porta S. Paolo 255
Porta S. Sebastiano 263
Porta Settimiana 280
Porta Portese market 277, 377
Portico of the Dei Consentes
    119
Portico Egiziano 208
Portico of Octavia 37, 101
Portus (now Porto) 399, 407
postal services 24
    main Post Office 188

Poussin, Nicolas 198, 201,
    221, 323
Pozzo, Andrea 79, 185
Praeneste see Palestrina
Praetorian Barracks 332
Prassede, Saint 232, 236
Praxiteles 94, 313
Preti, Mattia 281
Priory of the Sovereign Order
    of Malta 251
Protestant Cemetery 253
public holidays 23
pubs 371–2
Pudenziana, Saint 232, 235
Punic Wars 55
Pyramid of Gaius Cestius 253

Quintilius, Condianus 269
Quintilius, Maximus 269
Quirinale hill 217

racing 388
Raffaello da Montelupo 305
Raggi, Antonio 219
Raguzzini, Filipp(in)o 79, 185,
    274
Rahere (Henry II's jester) 335
Rainaldi, Carlo 78
    casino in Orti Farnesiani 127
    S. Maria in Campitelli 101
    other churches 168, 202
    unrealized plan for S. Agnese
        in Agone 159
Rainaldi, Girolamo 159
Raphael (Raffaello Sanzio) **74**,
    138
    builds Villa Madama 326
    Chigi chapel 203
    Deposition 214
    designs S. Eligio 172
    homes 161, 171, 303
    Loggie in Vatican 317–18
    paintings, Galatea 281
    Isaiah 156
    La Fornarina 220
    Lady and the Unicorn 214
    last p. 323
    School of Athens 316
    other churches 158,184, 190, 323
    replaces Bramante on
        St. Peter's 292
    Stanze 315–18
    tomb 154
    death 220, 303
rats 41, 222
Regia 121
Regina Coeli Prison 282
registering with police 8, 392
Regolini-Galassi tomb 314
religion in early Rome 31–3

religious institutions, accom-
    modation in 365
religious matters 24–6
    events 14–16
Remus see Romulus and
    Remus
Reni, Guido 77
    Crucifixion in S. Lorenzo in
        Lucina 198
    fresco in S. Gregono Magno
        145
    frescoes in Casino
        dell' Aurora 331
    Portrait of a Girl 221
    other works 170, 181, 281
Renoir, Pierre Auguste 210
residence permits 392
restaurants and cafés **342–52**
    see also beginning of each
    walk
Reynolds, Sir Joshua 197
Rhea Sylvia 50
Rhodes, Knights of 111
Riario, Cardinal Raffaele 170
Ricci, Sebastiano 181
riding 388
Rienzo, Cola di 61, 90, 241
Ristoro, Fra 151
Robbia, Andrea della 416
Rocca di Papa 428
rock music 373–4
Rodin, Auguste 210
Roma, Goddess 32, 93
Roma Quadrata 128
Romano, Antoniazzo 242, 284,
    412, 422, 431
Romano, Giulio see Giulio
Romulus and Remus 50–51,
    97, **126**, 248
    bronze Wolf 95
    Romulus 93, 411
    see also Lupercal
Romulus (son of Maxentius),
    tomb of 268
Rosa, Saint 414
Rosa, Salvator 79, 96, 190, 281
Rosellini, Roberto 332
Rossetti, Dante Gabriele 210
Rossi, Giovanni Battista see
    De Rossi
Rossini, Gioacchino 168
Rosso Fiorentino (G. B. Rosso) 75
Rosso, Medardo 210
Rostra, Imperial 118, 119, 240
Rostra, Republican 117, 433
Rovere, Giuliano della see
    Julius II
Rubens, Peter Paul 96, 170,
    181, 201, 280
Rusconi, Camillo 295

Sabina, Saint 250
Sacchi, Andrea 79, 221
Sacconi, Giuseppe 84
Sack of Rome (390 BC) 51, 54, 91, 102
Sack of Rome (1527) 50, 75, 117
Sacred Way see Via Sacra
Sacro Bosco 267
Saepta 152
Salita di S. Francesco di Paola 229
Salustri, Carlo (Trilussa) 279
Salvi, G.B. see Sassoferrato
Salvi, Nicola 79, 189
Salviati, Francesco 75, 98, 181, 203
San Martino al Cimino 416
Sancta Sanctorum 241
Sanctis, Francesco de 79, 195
Sandby, Paul 279
Sangallo, Antonio da, the Younger 75
as architect for St. Peter's 292
Bastione 263
his house 171
Loggia in Castel S. Angelo 306
Piccola Farnesina 169
other works 109, 158, 171, 172, 303
Sangallo, Giuliano da 157, 173, 233
Sanpietrini 279, 300
Sansovino, Andrea 91, 156, 203
Sansovino, Jacopo 83, 171, 242
Santi, Giovanni (Raphael's father) 322
Santo Bambino icon 92
Saracinesco 421
Sarto, Andrea del see Andrea
Sartorio, Giulio Aristide 80, 186, 190, 210
Sassoferrato (G. B. Salvi) 250
Saturnalia 119
Scala Santa 241
Scalae Caci 128
Scanderbeg 252
Schola Anglorum 303
Scholastica, Saint 421
schools 394
Schwitters, Kurt 209
Scipio family 262
tomb 263, 312
scooters, hiring 11
sculpture 70, 78
Sebastian, Saint 266
Sebastiano del Piombo 185, 203, 281, 283, 422
self-catering flatlets 366
Seneca, tomb of 268–9

senior citizens, concessions for 26
Sepolcro degli Scipioni 262, 312
Septimius Severus 98, 118, 145, 430
Septizonium 145, 233
Serena, (wife of Stilicho) 128
Servian Wall 226, 236
Servius Tullius 51, 230, 251
Sette Sale 231
Severn, Joseph 195, 253
sex 374
Shell Museum 212
Shelley, Percy Bysshe 102, 195
grave 253
shopping 375–84
opening hours 376–7
sizes 377
unusual shops 384
Sibyls and Sibylline Books 31, 103, 129, 419, 425
prophecies 91, 120, 127
Sienkiewicz, Henryk 198
Signorelli, Luca 306, 315
Signorini, Telemaco 210
Simon Magus 134
Simonetti, Michelangelo 314
Siqueiros, David Alfaro 319
Sistine Chapel 319–22
Sisto, Fra 151
Sixtus II, Pope 265
Sixtus III, Pope 235
Sixtus IV, Pope 202, 230, 299, 300, 319
Sixtus V, Pope: chapel in S. M. Maggiore 235
and removal of Vatican Obelisk 299
removes Septizonium ruins 145
urban planning and obelisks 76, 201, 220
other works 224, 241, 322
sizes 377
slaughter house, old 254
Slodtz, Michelangelo 298
Smaragdus 119
Sobieska, Clementina 182, 298
Sodoma, Il (Giovanni Antonio Bazzi) 220, 282, 315, 422
Soria, Giovan Battista 145, 223, 274
Soriano nel Cimino 416
Spada, Cardinal Bernardino 174
Spagnoletto, Lo 184
Spanish Church 172, 282
Spanish Steps 192, 196
Spartacus 55, 260
Spellman, Cardinal Francis 144

Spenser, Edmund: on Rome 106
sports and activities 385–90
Starnina, Gherardo 83
Stephen I, Pope 265
Stephen VII, Pope 42, 238
Stilicho (Vandal general) 97
stone: types used in building 34–5, 69, 419, 423
Story, William 254
St. Peter's Basilica 39, **291–302** (294)
Ancient Necropolis 301–02
dome 296–7, **300–01**
doors and porticoes 293
grottoes 299
High Altar 296
Navicella mosaic 297
old church and construction of the new 291–2
Treasury 298–9
Trophy of Gaius 301
view from Priory 251
St. Peter's Square 289–91
Strozzi, Maddalena 214
Stuart, Charles (Bonnie Prince Charlie, The Young Pretender) 11, 182, 298, 300, 326
Stuart, Henry see Henry Duke of York
Stuart, James (The Old Pretender) 182, 298, 300, 326
students: accommodation 364–5
concessions for 26
studying in Italy 392
Subiaco 421–2
Subura, daily life in 43–8
Suetonius 57
Sulla 56, 399, 423
swimming 388–9
Swiss Guards 289
slaughtered in 1527 304
Sylvester I, Pope and Saint 142, 231
Sylvester II, Pope 240, 242
Symmachus (orator) 117–18
Symmachus, Pope 329
Symonds, J. Addington 254

Tabularium 93
talking statues 36–7, 173
Madama Lucrezia 83, 160
Marforio 94
Pasquino 161
Tannhauser 303
Tarpeian Rock 97
Tarquinia 409

Tarquins 41, **51–4**, 68
  T. Priscus 51
  T. Sextus 51
  T. Superbus (the Proud) 31,
    51, 96, 249, 428
taxis 6, 9
Teatro Argentina 167–8
Teatro d'Opera 331
telephones 27
Tempietto, Bramante's 74,
  282, **283**
  Bernini's miniature 295
Temple of Aesculapius 209
Temple of Alatri 211
Temple of Antoninus Pius
  Faustina 116
Temple of Apollo 101, 129
Temple of Castor 120
Temple of Claudius 142
Temple of Concord 119
Temple of Cybele 127
Temple of the Deus Rediculus
  264
Temple of Divine Vespasian 119
Temple of Fortuna 99
Temple of Hadrian 186
Temple of Isis 154, 160
Temple of Janus 117
Temple of Julius Caesar 121
Temple of Jupiter 96–7
Temple of Mars Ultor
  (Avenging Mars) 111
Temple of Minerva 152
Temple of Minerva Medica
  243
Temple of Romulus 123
Temple of Saturn 119
Temple of Serapis 182
Temple of Trajan 109–10
Temple of Veiovis 93
Temple of Venus and Rome
  130, 134
Temple of Vesta 99, 121
Temples, Republican-era 167
tennis 389
Tennyson Alfred, Lord 197
Teresa, Saint 223–4
Termini Station 226, 228
Testaccio *see* Monte Testaccio
Thackeray, William Makepeace
  197
theatre in ancient Rome 69,
  175–6
  t. of Balbus 166
  t. of Marcellus 100
  t. of Pompey 100, 174,
    175–6
theatre, present-day 369
Theodora, Empress 59, 427
Theodora (mother of Paschal I)
  232

Theodoric the Goth 58, 117,
  126, 130, 145
Theodosius, Emperor 255
Thomas Aquinas, Saint 415
Thorvaldsen, Bertel 80, 157,
  214, 298
Tibaldi Pellegrino 306
Tiber Island 103
Tiberius, Emperor 57, 119
  palace on Palatine 97, 127
Tintoretto, Jacopo 96, 221
Titian (Tiziano Vecelli):
  Madonna dei Frari 323
  Portrait of Doge Niccolò 323
  Sacred and Profane Love 214
  other works 174, 184, 190,
    221
Titus Emperor 123, 132, 138
Tivoli 417–20
toilets 27–8
Tolomei family 275
Torlonia family 330
Torre de' Conti 111
Torre del Grillo 111
Torre delle Milizie 111
Torre Papita 167
Torrigiano, Pietro 299
Torriti Iacopo 73, 233, 240
Totila, King of the Goths 36,
  58, 189
Toulouse-Lautrec, Henri 210
tourist information offices 28
Toy Fair 159
train: arriving by 7
  travel concessions 26
Trajan, Emperor 112, 138, 407
  Column 109, 334
  Forum 69, **110–11**, 164
  Market 110
  Temple 109–10
  death 109
Trastevere 271–284
Treaty of Rome 93
Trevi fountain 188–9
Trevignano Romano 412
Tribune (Fuga) 241
Triclinium, Domitian's 129
Trident (3 roads) 201
Trilussa (Carlo Salustri) 280
Trophies of Marius 236
Trophy of Gaius 301
Tullianum 112
Tullius Hostilius 51, 430
Turner, Joseph Mallord
  William 197
Tuscania 409–10
Tusculum 427
Twelve Tables 54, 248

Udine Giovanni da *see*
  Giovanni

Umberto I, King, tomb of 154
Umbilicus Romae 118
UN Food & Agriculture
  Organization 146
Underground *see*
  Metropolitana
University 331–2
University (old papal) 154
Urban I, Pope 267, 269
Urban IV, Pope: election 415
Urban VI, Pope 43
Urban VIII, Pope: Bernini's
  monument 297
  consecrates new St. Peter's
    292
  loots Pantheon bronze for
    Bernini's baldacchino 37,
    296
  Pal. Barberini 220, 221
  roads to Castel Gandolfo 430
Utrillo, Maurice 210

Vaga, Perin del 75, 196, 306,
  316, 319
Valadier, Giuseppe 80, 182,
  199, 202, 208
Valerian, Emperor 265, 266
Valvassori, Gabriele 183
Van Dyck 96
Van Gogh Vincent 210
Vanvitelli, Luigi *see* Wittel
Vasanzio, Giovanni (Jan van
  Zanten) 212, 266
Vasari, Giorgio 98, 210, 283
Vassalletto, Pietro 72, 240
Vatican Citv 288–9, 302–3
  see also Castel St. Angelo, St.
    Peter's, Vatican Museums
Vatican Museums **309–324**,
  (*308*)
  Borgia Apartment 318–19
  Braccio Nuovo 312
  Bramante galleries 311
  Chapel of Nicholas V 318
  Chapel of Urban VIII 318
  Chiaramonti Sculpture
    Gallery 311–12
  Court of the Belvedere 312
  Egyptian Museum 311
  Gallery of the Candelabra
    315
  Gallery of Maps 315
  Gallery of Modern Religious
    Art 318
  Gallery of Pius V 315
  Gallery of the Tapestries 315
  Gallery of Urban VIII 322
  Gregorian Etruscan Museum
    314–15
  Hall of the Immaculate
    Conception 315

Vatican Museums (cont'd)
 Library Gallery 321
 Museo Gregorio Profano 323
 Museo Missionario
  Etnologico 324
 Museo Pio Cristiano 323,
  Museo Pio-Clementino 312
 Pinacoteca 322–3
 Regolini-Galassi tomb 314
 Sala della Biga 314
 Sala Ducale 321
 Sala dei Palafrenieri 318
 Sala Paolina 321
 Salone Sistina 322
 Sobieski Room 315
 Stanze of Raphael 315–18
 see also Sistine Chapel
Vecenaj, Ivan 319
Veii (now Veio) 54, 411
Velabrum, the 97
Velazquez, Diego 96, 184
Velletri 431
Venus Cloacina, Shrine of
 116–17
Veronese, Paolo 96
Verrocchio, Andrea del 152
Verschaffelt, van 305
Vespasian, Emperor 119, 123,
 132, 138
Vestal Virgins 50, **122**, 128,
 132, 332
Via Appia Antica **257–70**
 catacombs and tombs 262–3,
  264–7, 268–9
 construction 261
 museum 263
Via Appia Nuova 261
Via del Babuino 201
Via delle Botteghe Oscure 166
Via dei Cestari 150
Via della Conciliazione 302
Via Condotti 197
Via dei Coronari 161
Via del Corso 178, 201
Via dei Fori Imperiali 112
Via della Gatta 150
Via del Gesù 150
Via dei Giubbonari 175
Via Giulia 171–2
Via Lata see Corso
Via Margutta 201
Via Nazionale 331
Via Nomentana 329, 330
Via dell'Orso 156
Via Ostiense 253, 399
Via del Portico d'Ottavia
 102
Via di Ripetta 201
Via Sacra 106, **116**, 122
Via Salaria 330

Via della Tribuna di Tor de'
 Specchi 90
Via del Tritone 187
Via Veneto 22
Vico, Lake 417
Vicovaro 421
Victor Emmanuel Monument
 see Altar of the Nation
Vignola, Giacomo da 75
 Gesù interior 165
 Orti Farnesiani 127
 Pal. Borghese 198
 S. Maria dell'Orto 277
 Villa Farnese (Caprarola) 417
 Villa Giulia 210
 other works 413, 416
Vignola, La (pavilion) 145
Villa Ada 328
Villa Aldobrandini (Frascati) 427
Villa Borghese gardens 206
Villa Celimontana 143
Villa Doria Pamphili 335–6
Villa d'Este (Tivoli) 418
Villa Farnese in Caprarola 417
Villa Farnesina 281–2
Villa Giulia 210–12
 Museum 68
Villa Gregoriana gardens
 (Tivoli) 419
Villa Madama 326
Villa Medici 196
Villa of the Quintilii 269
Villa Stuart 326
Villa Torlonia 330
Villa Torlonia (Frascati) 427
Villa Torlonia (Mussolini's) 329

Viminale hill 331
Virgil 50, 90
Virginia (Roman heroine) 117
Visconti, Luigi 64
Viterbo 413–16
 papal elections at 415
Vitruvius 283
Vittoriano see Altar of the
 Nation
Vittorio Emanuele II, King:
 tomb 154
Volterra see Daniele
Vulca (Etruscan sculptor) 211
Vulcanal 118

Water Clock 208
Wax Museum 180
weddings 93
weights and measures 378
Whistler, James 210
Winckelmann, Johan 80
wine 340
 buying 384
wine bars 370–71
Wittel, Gaspare van (Vanvitelli)
 190, 221, 224
working in Rome 391–96

Zagarolo 422, 423
Zanardelli, Giuseppe 84
Zephyrinus, Pope 265
Zoo 212
Zuccaro(i) Federico 76, 167,
 197, 412, 423
Zuccaro(i), Taddeo 76, 97,
 250, 412, 423

Answers to Dome Quiz

1. Sant'Ivo alla Sapienza
2. S. Maria del Popolo
3. S. Luigi dei Francesi
4. SS. Nome di Maria
5. S. Carlo alle Quattro Fontane
6. S. Maria in Campitelli

It's only too easy to be overwhelmed by Rome, and, especially if time is short, to be at a loss over what you should see or do first. Unless you're a true aficionado of antiquity, connoisseur of churches or Baroque buff, don't make the mistake of simply rushing to visit the 'important' sites. Remember that Romans are skilled in the art of 'far niente' (doing nothing). Take a leaf from their book—some of the greatest pleasures in Rome are simply to be had strolling the streets of the *centro storico* and Trastevere (Walks IV, V, VII and XIII), dawdling in cafés, poking your nose into the workshops of antique restorers, and, above all, watching people.

- Piazza Navona (if you can afford it, from the terraces of Tre Scalini or Caffè Colombia)
- Campo de' Fiori market
- Pantheon
- Sant' Ignazio
- Santa Maria sopra Minerva
- Trevi fountain
- Santa Maria del Popolo
- Galleria Borghese
- Colosseum
- San Clemente
- Santa Maria in Trastevere
- Piazza di Spagna
- Designer window shopping on Via Condotti
- Valentino's window display on Via Bocca di Leone
- Antique window shopping on Via Condotti
- Piazza Farnese at night—when the lights are on in the Palazzo and you can glimpse its sumptuous frescoes
- Sunsets: in the Pincio Gardens, on the Janiculum and from a café table on Piazza Navona or Campo de' Fiori
- Neopolitan pastries at Bella Napoli
- Custard *cornetti* from Pasticceria Farnese
- Pizza sandwiches from Via Governo Vecchio 28
- *Granita di caffè* at Tazza d'Oro
- Mulled wine at the Bevitoria Navona
- Il Piccolo Wine Bar
- A *caprese* salad at Cernaio
- Pasta with artichokes and ricotta, followed by homemade *tiramisù* at Edy's
- More artichokes at a Roman-Jewish dinner al fresco by the Portico d'Ottavia at Giggetto
- *Penne primavera* at Il Generale
- An ice cream survey: check out Giolitti, Gelateria della Palma, Alberto Pica and the nameless *gelateria* on Campo de' Fiori
- An evening stroll in Trastevere
- Picnics in the Villa Borghese Park, on the Palatine
- Bopping on a barge—at L'Argonauto
- Porta Portese Sunday morning fleamarket

Rome Highlights